From Age to Age

From Age to Age

The Unfolding of Biblical Eschatology

KEITH A. MATHISON

P&R PUBLISHING
P.O. BOX 817 • PHILLIPSBURG • NEW JERSEY 08865-0817

Page design and typesetting by Lakeside Design Plus

Printed in the United States of America

Library of Congress Cataloging-in-Publication Data

Mathison, Keith A., 1967–
From age to age : the unfolding of biblical eschatology / Keith A. Mathison.
p. cm.
Includes bibliographical references and indexes.
ISBN 978-0-87552-745-1 (cloth)
1. Eschatology—Biblical teaching. 2. Bible—Criticism, interpretation, etc.
I. Title.
BS680.E8M38 2009
236—dc22

2008048668

to

Dr. R.C. Sproul

Contents

Preface

This is the fifth book I've written with my two index fingers and right thumb. I do take some comfort in the fact that J. R. R. Tolkien typed the successive drafts of his great book *The Lord of the Rings* with only two fingers, but there were times during the composition of my work when I sorely wished I had learned to type. In spite of its slow progress, however, the writing of this book has been a blessing. Every time we prayerfully dig into the Word of God, we are instructed, encouraged, and exhorted, and my own study has been no exception.

Several friends have asked why I have chosen to write another book on the subject of eschatology. This is a fair question that deserves a reasonable response. In the first place, my interest in biblical eschatology began not long after I became a Christian, and it has continued to this day. This book is, first and foremost, the result of this personal interest. The ongoing controversies concerning eschatology are another reason for the writing of this book. When the church has been arguing about a subject for as long as it has been arguing about the subject of eschatology, it can never hurt to go back to the Word of God and see if any fresh insight can be found.

The process of writing this book, although an encouragement and blessing, has not been without challenges. The pathway has included unexpected detours as well as wrong turns and dead ends. I have been forced many times to rethink previous conclusions. Sometimes such rethinking has resulted in the confirming of my convictions. At other times, further reflection has led to the discovery of mistakes in need of correction.

I am encouraged by the words of Augustine, who wrote, "I freely confess, accordingly, that I endeavor to be one of those who write because they have made some progress, and who, by means of writing, make further progress." Augustine went on to explain how he dealt with errors found in his earlier works (NPNF, 1:490).

I certainly do not consider this book to be the last word on the "last things," or even *my* last word on the last things. It is merely my attempt to contribute to the ongoing theological conversation. It is my sincere hope and prayer that it will be of help to other students of Scripture.

There are a number of people whose help has been invaluable and without whom I could not have finished this project. I would like to thank first of all a man who is my pastor and my mentor, Dr. R. C. Sproul. His ministry and his example have been a great encouragement and great example to me for many years now, and he has continually encouraged my research and writing. His admonition to teach what the Bible teaches and not what we might want it to teach is one we would all do well to heed. It is for these reasons that I gratefully dedicate this book to him.

There are several others to whom thanks are due. First, I thank Allan Fisher for asking me to begin this daunting project. I'm not sure I would have taken the first step had it not been for his encouragement. I also thank my colleague Chris Donato, who read large portions of the manuscript and who offered many helpful suggestions. Another colleague, Kevin Struyk, saved me countless hours by picking up numerous books and articles at the local seminary. And once again, I owe special thanks to Grace Mullen at the library of Westminster Theological Seminary. I have lost count of the number of bibliographical references she has helped me track down and verify and the number of articles she has located that I could not find anywhere else. I also thank my parents for their encouragement throughout the long process of writing this book. Finally, I thank my wife Tricia and my children Sarah and Joseph for bringing so much joy to my life.

A brief word about translation and transliteration is necessary. Unless otherwise noted, I have used the English Standard Version of the Bible throughout this work—with one important exception. Where the ESV translates the Hebrew divine name (*YHWH*) as "Lord," I translate it consistently as "Yahweh." Most English versions follow the same practice as the ESV, translating the divine name as "Lord."[1] I agree with Michael Williams, however, that to translate it in this way obscures the fact that it is God's revealed name, "not a title or an office."[2] For the apocryphal books, I have used the New Revised Standard Version. With the exception of occasional instances in quotations from the works of other authors, I have transliterated all Hebrew and Greek words in the body of the text. In the footnotes, I have sometimes provided the Hebrew or Greek text in addition to the transliteration.[3]

1. Very few English versions translate the divine name as a name. The Darby Bible (1884/1890) and the American Standard Version (1901) translate the divine name as "Jehovah." The New Jerusalem Bible translates the divine name as "Yahweh."

2. Williams 2005, 28.

3. For Hebrew transliteration, I have used the general purpose style outlined in the *SBL Handbook of Style* (§5.1.2).

Abbreviations

General

A.D.	anno Domini
B.C.	before Christ
DSS	Dead Sea Scrolls
Gk.	Greek
Heb.	Hebrew
LXX	Septuagint

Bible

Old Testament

Gen.	Genesis
Ex.	Exodus
Lev.	Leviticus
Num.	Numbers
Deut.	Deuteronomy
Josh.	Joshua
Judg.	Judges
Ruth	Ruth
1 Sam.	1 Samuel
2 Sam.	2 Samuel
1 Kings	1 Kings
2 Kings	2 Kings
1 Chron.	1 Chronicles
2 Chron.	2 Chronicles

Ezra	Ezra
Neh.	Nehemiah
Esth.	Esther
Job	Job
Ps./Pss.	Psalms
Prov.	Proverbs
Eccl.	Ecclesiastes
Song	Song of Solomon
Isa.	Isaiah
Jer.	Jeremiah
Lam.	Lamentations
Ezek.	Ezekiel
Dan.	Daniel
Hos.	Hosea
Joel	Joel
Amos	Amos
Obad.	Obadiah
Jonah	Jonah
Mic.	Micah
Nah.	Nahum
Hab.	Habakkuk
Zeph.	Zephaniah
Hag.	Haggai
Zech.	Zechariah
Mal.	Malachi

New Testament

Matt.	Matthew
Mark	Mark
Luke	Luke
John	John
Acts	Acts
Rom.	Romans
1 Cor.	1 Corinthians
2 Cor.	2 Corinthians
Gal.	Galatians
Eph.	Ephesians
Phil.	Philippians

Col.	Colossians
1 Thess.	1 Thessalonians
2 Thess.	2 Thessalonians
1 Tim.	1 Timothy
2 Tim.	2 Timothy
Titus	Titus
Philem.	Philemon
Heb.	Hebrews
James	James
1 Peter	1 Peter
2 Peter	2 Peter
1 John	1 John
2 John	2 John
3 John	3 John
Jude	Jude
Rev.	Revelation

Scripture Versions

ASV	American Standard Version
ESV	English Standard Version
KJV	King James Version
NAB	New American Bible
NASB	New American Standard Bible
NEB	New English Bible
NIV	New International Version
NJB	New Jerusalem Bible
NKJV	New King James Version
RSV	Revised Standard Version

Josephus

Ant.	*Antiquities of the Jews*
J.W.	*Jewish War*
Life	*The Life of Flavius Josephus*

Secondary Sources

Journals, Periodicals, Major Reference Works, and Series

AB	Anchor Bible
ABD	D. N. Freedman (ed.), *Anchor Bible Dictionary*

ACNT	Augsburg Commentaries on the New Testament
AnBib	Analecta biblica
ANET	J. B. Pritchard (ed.), *Ancient Near Eastern Texts*
AOTC	Apollos Old Testament Commentary
APOT	R. H. Charles (ed.), *Apocrypha and Pseudepigrapha of the Old Testament*
AUSS	*Andrews University Seminary Studies*
AUMSR	Andrews University Monograph Studies in Religion
AUSDDS	Andrews University Seminary Doctoral Dissertation Series
BCOTWP	Baker Commentary on the Old Testament Wisdom and Psalms
BDAG	F. W. Danker (rev. and ed.), *Greek-English Lexicon of the New Testament*
BDB	F. Brown, S. R. Driver, and C. A. Briggs, *Hebrew and English Lexicon of the Old Testament*
BDF	F. Blass, A. Debrunner, and R. W. Funk, *A Greek Grammar of the New Testament*
BECNT	Baker Exegetical Commentary on the New Testament
Bib	*Biblica*
BIS	Biblical Interpretation Series
BLS	Bible and Literature Series
BNTC	Black's New Testament Commentaries
BSac	*Bibliotheca Sacra*
BSC	Bible Student's Commentary
BST	The Bible Speaks Today
BTB	*Biblical Theology Bulletin*
BZAW	Beihefte zur *ZAW*
CBQ	*Catholic Biblical Quarterly*
CC	Continental Commentary
CCom	Communicator's Commentary
CGTC	Cambridge Greek Testament Commentary
DBI	L. Ryken et al. (eds.), *Dictionary of Biblical Imagery*
DSB	The Daily Study Bible
DTIB	Kevin J. Vanhoozer (ed.), *Dictionary for Theological Interpretation of the Bible*
EBC	Expositor's Bible Commentary

ECC	Eerdmans Critical Commentary
EDT	W. A. Elwell (ed.), *Evangelical Dictionary of Theology*
EvQ	*Evangelical Quarterly*
ExpTim	*Expository Times*
FOTL	The Forms of Old Testament Literature
GKC	*Gesenius' Hebrew Grammar*, ed. E. Kautzsch, trans. A. E. Cowley
GNS	Good News Studies
HALOT	W. Baumgartner et al., *Hebrew and Aramaic Lexicon of the Old Testament*
HNTC	Harper's New Testament Commentaries
HSM	Harvard Semitic Monographs
IBHS	Bruce K. Waltke and M. O'Connor, *An Introduction to Biblical Hebrew Syntax*
ICC	International Critical Commentary
IDB	G. A. Buttrick (ed.), *Interpreter's Dictionary of the Bible*
ILPT	International Library of Philosophy and Theology
Int	*Interpretation*
IRT	Issues in Religion and Theology
ISBE	G. W. Bromiley (ed.), *International Standard Bible Encyclopedia*, rev.
ISFCJ	International Studies in Formative Christianity and Judaism
IVPNTC	The IVP New Testament Commentary
JAOS	*Journal of the American Oriental Society*
JBL	*Journal of Biblical Literature*
JETS	*Journal of the Evangelical Theological Society*
JNES	*Journal of Near Eastern Studies*
Joüon	Paul Joüon, *A Grammar of Biblical Hebrew*, trans. T. Muraoka
JSNT	*Journal for the Study of the New Testament*
JSNTSup	JSNT Supplement Series
JSOT	*Journal for the Study of the Old Testament*
JSOTSup	JSOT Supplement Series
JSP	*Journal for the Study of the Pseudepigrapha*
JSPSup	JSP Supplement Series
JTS	*Journal of Theological Studies*

LCC	Library of Christian Classics
LCL	Loeb Classical Library
LEC	Library of Early Christianity
MLBS	Mercer Library of Biblical Studies
MPS	The Master's Perspective Series
NAC	New American Commentary
NCB	New Century Bible
NCBC	New Cambridge Bible Commentary
NIBC	New International Biblical Commentary
NICNT	New International Commentary on the New Testament
NICOT	New International Commentary on the Old Testament
NIDNTT	Colin Brown (ed.), *New International Dictionary of New Testament Theology*
NIDOTTE	W. A. VanGemeren (ed.), *New International Dictionary of Old Testament Theology and Exegesis*
NIGTC	New International Greek Testament Commentary
NIVAC	NIV Application Commentary
NovT	*Novum Testamentum*
NovTSup	Novum Testamentum, Supplements
NPNF	Nicene and Post-Nicene Fathers
NSBT	New Studies in Biblical Theology
NTC	New Testament Commentary
NTM	New Testament Monographs
NTP	New Testament Profiles
NTS	*New Testament Studies*
NTTS	New Testament Tools and Studies
OBS	The Oxford Bible Series
OTL	Old Testament Library
PNTC	Pillar New Testament Commentary
PTMS	Princeton Theological Monograph Series
SacPag	Sacra Pagina
SBET	*Scottish Bulletin of Evangelical Theology*
SBL	Society of Biblical Literature
SBLDS	SBL Dissertation Series
SBLMS	SBL Monograph Series
SBT	Studies in Biblical Theology
SBTS	Sources for Biblical and Theological Study

SHS	The Scripture and Hermeneutics Series
SJT	*Scottish Journal of Theology*
SNTSMS	Society for New Testament Studies Monograph Series
SubBi	Subsidia biblica
TCGNT	B. M. Metzger, *A Textual Commentary on the Greek New Testament*
TDNT	G. Kittel and G. Friedrich (eds.), *Theological Dictionary of the New Testament*
TDOT	G. J. Botterweck et al. (eds.), *Theological Dictionary of the Old Testament*
Them	*Themelios*
TLOT	E. Jenni and C. Westermann (eds.), *Theological Lexicon of the Old Testament*
TNTC	Tyndale New Testament Commentaries
TOTC	Tyndale Old Testament Commentaries
TrinJ	*Trinity Journal*
TWOT	G. Archer et al. (eds.), *Theological Wordbook of the Old Testament*
TynBul	*Tyndale Bulletin*
VT	*Vetus Testamentum*
VTSup	Vetus Testamentum Supplements
WBC	Word Biblical Commentary
WCS	Welwyn Commentary Series
WEC	Wycliffe Exegetical Commentary
WPC	Westminster Pelican Commentaries
WTJ	*Westminster Theological Journal*
WUNT	Wissenschaftliche Untersuchungen zum Neuen Testament
ZAW	*Zeitschrift für die alttestamentliche Wissenschaft*

Introduction

At various times in her history, different doctrines have been at the center of the church's attention. In the first few centuries after the death and resurrection of Christ, for example, the church struggled mightily to formulate accurately the biblical teaching concerning the Trinity and the person of Christ. The fruit of this struggle is found in the writings of numerous church fathers and in the Nicene Creed and the Definition of Chalcedon. Many centuries later, during the Reformation, soteriology and ecclesiology became the central focus of much of the church's attention. Debates surrounding those doctrines continue to this day. Eschatology, on the other hand, while not ignored in earlier centuries, truly moved to the forefront of the church's attention in the nineteenth and twentieth centuries. From the emergence of popular dispensationalism in the late nineteenth century to the influential writings of Albert Schweitzer, C. H. Dodd, Jürgen Moltmann, and others in the twentieth century, it is clear that eschatology has risen to a place of prominence in biblical, theological, and historical studies.

Defining Eschatology

What do we mean when we speak of "eschatology"? The English word is based on a combination of two Greek words: *eschatos* ("last") and *logos* ("word"). Traditionally, eschatology has been defined as the "doctrine of the last things" in relation to both the individual (e.g., death and the intermediate state) and cosmic history (e.g., the return of Christ, the general resurrection, the final judgment, heaven, and hell).[1] Because of this definition, most studies of eschatology have limited themselves to a discussion of events that have yet to occur—events at the end of the individual's life or events at the end of history.[2]

Eschatology in a broader sense, however, concerns what Scripture teaches about God's purposes in Christ for history. As such, eschatology does include a study of the consummation of God's purposes at the end of history, but it also includes a study of the stages in the unfolding of those purposes.[3] This understanding of eschatology affects the content of this volume in a number of ways. If, for example, the first coming of Christ inaugurated "the last days," then a study of biblical eschatology must include a study of Christ's first advent as well as his second. It must also include a study of God's preparation in history for the eschatological first advent of Christ. In other words, eschatology must involve a redemptive-historical study of the entire Bible. This book is written with this broader understanding of eschatology in mind.

Biblical Theology

The subtitle of this book is *The Unfolding of Biblical Eschatology*. The subtitle indicates something about the basic approach I have taken to the subject under consideration. The inspiration for this approach lies in the works of Reformed biblical theologians such as Geerhardus Vos and Herman Ridderbos, as well as others such as William Dumbrell.[4] Following their lead, I have approached the subject of eschatology from the perspective of biblical theology. There are many outstanding works that approach the subject from the perspective of systematic theology, but this book is not one of them.[5] It is important to note that biblical theology should not be understood as a substitute for systematic theology. Both are necessary.

1. Hoekema 1979, 1.
2. E.g., Hendriksen 1959; Helm 1989.
3. Smalley 1998, 265.
4. See Vos 1948, 1991; Ridderbos 1962; Dumbrell 1985, 1994.
5. E.g., Hoekema 1979; Venema 2000. Those works that approach the subject from the perspective of systematic theology are organized topically. Each section or chapter will summarize everything the Bible has to say on any given eschatological topic. There will, therefore, be sections or chapters on topics such as death, the second coming, the millennium, and the final judgment.

Biblical theology is simply a different, and complementary, approach to the same biblical teaching.

But what exactly is "biblical theology"? Many trace the origins of biblical theology to the inaugural lecture of the theologian Johann Gabler in 1787, in which he distinguished biblical theology from systematic theology.[6] Gabler, however, was deeply committed to a rationalistic approach to the Bible, so his understanding of "biblical theology" necessarily differs from the understanding of those who accept Scripture as the inspired Word of God. Some identify "biblical theology" with the so-called biblical theology movement of the mid-twentieth century. This movement, however, was strongly influenced by neoorthodoxy and accepted the methodology of higher criticism. It ultimately collapsed under the criticisms of Langdon Gilkey and James Barr.

Setting aside these inadequate versions of "biblical theology," how should we understand it? The Reformed theologian Geerhardus Vos provides a helpful introductory definition. "Biblical Theology," he writes, "is that branch of Exegetical Theology which deals with the process of the self-revelation of God deposited in the Bible."[7] A helpful expanded definition is provided by Paul Williamson:

> Biblical theology is arguably best thought of as a holistic enterprise tracing unfolding theological trajectories throughout Scripture and exploring no biblical concept, theme or book in isolation from the whole. Rather, each concept, theme or book is considered ultimately in terms of how it contributes and advances the Bible's meta-narrative, typically understood in terms of a salvation history that progresses towards and culminates in Jesus Christ.[8]

When we view biblical theology from this perspective, it could be argued that this approach had its true precursors in the work of the early Reformed covenant theologians, particularly men such as Johannes Coc-ceius (1603–69).[9]

Many attempts at biblical theology have failed because of an exclusive focus on the human authors of Scripture. Particular books and/or authors

6. See *DTIB*, 84.

7. Vos 1948, 5. For a fuller explanation of the idea of biblical theology by the same author, see Vos 2001, 3–24.

8. Williamson 2007, 17.

9. See Golding 2004, 14–16.

are studied in isolation from the larger biblical context. The Bible is a collection of sixty-six books written by various authors over a vast period of time, but it is also a single book inspired by God.[10] Charles Scobie explains the significance of this fact for our approach to biblical theology:

> This means that the individual books and authors are to be studied not only in their original historical contexts, but also in the context of canonical Scripture as a whole. This does affect the way books are interpreted; the canonical Bible is more than the sum of the sixty-six books that it contains. The OT is read in light of the NT, and vice versa.[11]

In other words, a biblical theology that takes seriously the divine inspiration of Scripture will be a "whole-Bible biblical theology."[12]

The fact that there is one ultimate author of the whole Bible also means that it is not futile to seek an underlying unity among the sixty-six books. Numerous biblical theologians have despaired of finding any unifying principle for the Old Testament alone, much less the entire Bible. Gerhard Hasel, for example, says, "It has been demonstrated that any attempt to elaborate an OT theology on the basis of a center, key concept, or focal point inevitably falls short of being a theology of the entire OT, because no such principle of unity has as yet emerged that gives full account of all the material in the Bible."[13] This conclusion stems not only from a failure to take into account the Bible's one ultimate author, but also from a failure, ironically, to consider how the different types of books in Scripture are related.

If we look carefully at the content of the biblical books, we notice that some of them present an ongoing redemptive-historical narrative. The Pentateuch and the historical books, for example, provide a historical account that proceeds from creation to the restoration of Israel from exile. In the New Testament, the Gospels and Acts function in the same way. These books, which outline redemptive history, form the narrative backbone or framework of the Bible. Other books assume that framework as their context.[14] Most of the Old Testament prophets, for example, wrote their books during the

10. Waltke 2007, 10.
11. Scobie 2003, 74–75.
12. Hafeman and House 2007, 15.
13. Hasel 1982, 93.
14. Ciampa 2007, 255.

history narrated in 2 Kings. The apostle Paul wrote most of his epistles during the history narrated in the book of Acts. All of the biblical books that are not historical narrative were written during the times described in that narrative. Many of them interpret the events that are described in that narrative. It is in this historical narrative, this backbone of the Bible, that we see a unifying principle in the history of the outworking of God's plan to establish his kingdom. This plan involves his covenants with man and his work of redemption, and it culminates in the person and work of Jesus Christ.

Hermeneutical Considerations

Before proceeding further, it is necessary to deal briefly with some basic hermeneutical issues. The term "hermeneutics" is used to refer to "the study of those principles that should guide our work of interpretation."[15] Hermeneutics has been considered an important issue throughout the history of the church, but it is hardly an exaggeration to say that it is *the* issue in much of the Western church and culture today.[16] Contemporary hermeneutical discussions are often quite sophisticated and complex, and to enter into this larger discussion in detail would require a separate volume of considerable size.[17] However, while a detailed explanation of these issues is beyond the scope of this book, it is necessary at this point to explain briefly some of the factors that influence my interpretation of Scripture.

The Reformed Tradition and Scripture

In the first place, I acknowledge without apology that I approach the interpretation of Scripture as a Christian believer who stands within the Reformed tradition. The word "Reformed" is typically used to distinguish the Calvinistic branch of the sixteenth-century Protestant Reformation from the Lutheran and Anabaptist branches.[18] The doctrines of the Reformed Protestant churches were most clearly expressed in confessions and catechisms such as the Gallican Confession (1559), the Scots Confession

15. Silva 1996b, 15.

16. See Lundin 1993.

17. For an introduction to some of the many issues involved, see Thiselton 1980; Cotterell and Turner 1989; Thiselton 1992; Silva 1996b; Vanhoozer 1998; Lundin, Walhout, and Thiselton 1999; Osborne 2006.

18. See *EDT*, 921.

(1560), the Belgic Confession (1561), the Heidelberg Catechism (1563), the Second Helvetic Confession (1564), and the Westminster Confession of Faith (1647).[19] Some of the most important theologians in the history of the Reformed tradition are John Calvin, Francis Turretin, John Owen, Jonathan Edwards, Charles Hodge, Benjamin B. Warfield, Herman Bavinck, and Louis Berkhof.

It is important for the readers of this book to understand that I stand within this Reformed confessional tradition. Every reader of this book stands within his or her own basic theological (or atheological) tradition, be it Reformed, Lutheran, dispensationalist, or something else. These traditions profoundly influence and shape our basic worldview and assumptions, which then affect the way in which we approach theological and biblical questions. In fact, they often dictate the very questions that we ask. In describing myself as a Reformed Christian, I am simply informing the reader as well as consciously reminding myself of the theological tradition within which I stand as I proceed to examine this topic.

Philosophy and Scripture

Even a cursory reading of the history of Christian hermeneutics and theology will quickly reveal the effects philosophical presuppositions have had on biblical interpretation and theological reflection. From the neo-Platonism of certain early church fathers to the nominalism of many late medieval scholastics, from the neo-Kantianism and existentialism of Rudolf Bultmann to the deconstructionism of John Dominic Crossan, philosophical presuppositions are unavoidable. Those who believe they do not have any philosophical presuppositions when they approach Scripture are simply unconscious of them and more easily misled by them.

Those of us who were born in the West in the twentieth century have been raised in a culture whose very way of seeing the world has been shaped by numerous philosophical strands of thought.[20] We simply cannot change the fact that we live after Descartes and Hume, after Kant and Hegel, after Marx and Nietzsche, and after Rorty and Derrida. The intellectual world in which we live has been affected in various ways, not only by rationalism

19. See Cochrane 2003.

20. Of course, various philosophical strands of thought have also influenced those born in the East.

and empiricism, but also by pragmatism, naturalism, existentialism, and relativism. We live in an era in which the confident arrogance of modernism is gradually giving way to the skeptical arrogance of postmodernism. These various philosophies affect the way we think about God, man, language, revelation, history, science, ethics, politics, and more. Although we cannot pretend that these various strands of thought have not been part of the very intellectual air we breathe, we can make every effort to become self-consciously aware of the ways in which they influence and affect us. Only then are we able to detect these influences in our own thinking and critically examine them.

Certain philosophical strains of thought that arose during the Enlightenment resulted in a fierce antisupernaturalism that entailed the rejection of the possibility of special revelation. The Bible began to be seen as a merely human book whose teachings should be measured against the ultimate standard of autonomous human reason. The traditional Christian view of revelation, sometimes referred to as the *propositional* view, was then rejected.[21] In contrast with the modernist view, I affirm that the traditional view of revelation is defensible, and I affirm that God has in fact revealed himself and his will in the Bible.[22] I approach Scripture, therefore, as the inspired, infallible, and inerrant Word of the living God.

Because of the nature of scriptural revelation, a word must be said about language. The literature that exists on issues related to this topic is enormous, and it is not possible in this brief space to list every relevant issue, much less discuss all of them. It is necessary, however, to mention a few basic issues relevant to the purpose of this section. In the early twentieth century, two of the most significant challenges to the traditional Christian understanding of language were those set forth by logical positivists on the one hand and neoorthodox theologians on the other. Logical positivists attempted to make the case that all religious language is cognitively meaningless because it claims to speak of things that are not empirically verifiable.[23] Neoorthodox theologians raised different questions about the adequacy of human language because of their belief that revelation is essentially a

21. This traditional view is often caricatured as the belief that *all* revelation is propositional or that everything in Scripture is a proposition. For a response to this caricature, see Nash 1982, 44–45.

22. A thorough defense of this basic presupposition is beyond the scope of the present volume. For a defense of the traditional view of revelation, see Nash 1982, 43–54; see also Jensen 2002.

23. E.g., Ayer 1952.

nonpropositional personal encounter with God.[24] These challenges to the traditional Christian understanding of language are not at the forefront of the debate today. Logical positivism and the verification principle upon which it rests have repeatedly been shown to be self-referentially incoherent.[25] The neoorthodox doctrine of revelation and its claims about the inadequacy of human language, while still popular in many circles, have also been shown to be seriously flawed.[26]

In the late twentieth century and early twenty-first century, deconstructionists such as Jacques Derrida and neopragmatists such as Richard Rorty are presenting the most serious philosophical challenges to a Christian understanding of language. Both Derrida and Rorty reject the idea that we can know whether our language refers to any kind of extralinguistic reality. Derrida rejects what he refers to as logocentrism, "the belief that there is some stable point *outside* language—reason, revelation, Platonic Ideas—from which one can ensure that one's words, as well as the whole system of distinctions that order our experience, correspond to the world."[27]

The neopragmatic philosophy of Richard Rorty has been applied to literary criticism most effectively by Stanley Fish, who argues that meaning is not found in a text or in the intention of an author. Instead, readers produce meaning in the act of reading.[28] The views expressed by each of these authors are much more complex and nuanced than can be explained in this short space. Suffice it to say that the philosophies of Derrida, Rorty, and their disciples are incoherent. Despite objections to the contrary, their views inevitably result in a linguistic nihilism that renders pointless both writing and reading.[29] Their views are incompatible with a Christian understanding of revelation.

History and Scripture

Questions related to history and biblical interpretation are numerous and important.[30] One of the most obvious of these questions concerns the historicity of the events recorded in Scripture. Until the seventeenth and

24. E.g., Brunner 1946.
25. See Evans 1982, 141–44.
26. See Jensen 2002; Nash 1982, 35–41; Packer 1980.
27. Vanhoozer 1998, 53.
28. See Fish 1980.
29. For an informed critique of both views, see Vanhoozer 1998.
30. See Bartholomew et al. 2003.

eighteenth centuries, most within the church simply assumed that the events described in Scripture were historically accurate. The first rumblings of real discontent with the traditional view began to be felt with the rise of philosophical rationalism in the writings of Descartes, Spinoza, and Leibniz, and with the rise of skeptical empiricism, particularly in the work of David Hume. Among those who attempted to formulate a rationalist religion in response to these philosophical movements were the English deists.[31]

The deists insisted "that the supernatural cannot be admitted as a factor in history."[32] This fundamental assumption affected many influential scholars. The work of Hermann Reimarus, for example, which was posthumously published by Gotthold Lessing, expressed grave doubts about the historical value of Scripture. The philosophical writings of Immanuel Kant raised doubts about whether it is even humanly possible to discover history as it actually was. His writings contributed to the growing historical skepticism of the age. The influence of Kant's thought upon biblical studies continued to be felt well into the twentieth century.[33] It continues to be felt even today.

In 1835, David Friedrich Strauss's *Life of Jesus* was published and proved to be a hugely controversial book that changed the face of biblical scholarship.[34] Strauss argued that biblical accounts of the supernatural were instances of "mythical" language.[35] His work caused no small controversy both in Germany and England and profoundly influenced numerous scholars in subsequent generations. Rudolf Bultmann, for example, is well known for his twentieth-century project of demythologization.[36] Since Strauss's time, it has become commonplace in critical biblical scholarship to deny the historical nature of much, if not all, of the biblical record. The most well known contemporary example of this tendency is found in the work of the Jesus Seminar.[37]

The historical claims of these skeptical critical scholars are based upon faulty philosophical assumptions, and they are also based upon a failure

31. Brown 1990, 202–7.

32. Brown 1990, 212.

33. See Thiselton (1980, 205–17) for a discussion of the Kantian influence on the work of Rudolf Bultmann.

34. Strauss 1972.

35. See Neill and Wright 1988, 13–20.

36. Bultmann 1961.

37. See Funk and Hoover 1993; Funk 1998.

to deal with the actual evidence. Numerous scholars have addressed the problematic philosophical assumptions of the critics.[38] The actual positive evidence confirming the historical accuracy of Scripture has also been dealt with in numerous works.[39] The "assured results" of skeptical biblical criticism have been demonstrated time and again to be anything but assured.

Exegesis of Scripture

As a Reformed Christian I confess that Scripture, as the inspired and inerrant Word of God, is our sole source of written divine revelation. The fact that Scripture is inspired, however, does not mean that it is written in some mysterious and esoteric heavenly language. It is not an ahistorical document that fell from the sky. The human authors of Scripture were real men who wrote in real human languages (Hebrew, Aramaic, and Greek) within real historical contexts. What this means is that the proper interpretation of Scripture requires some understanding of the nature of human language in general, the languages of Scripture in particular, and the broader historical context within which the various books were written and received.[40] In other words, it requires an understanding of both text and context.

Human beings are created in the image of God, and as such have been given the gift of language in order to communicate with their Creator and with one another. John Searle rightly observes that to speak a language—any language—is to engage "in a (highly complex) rule-governed form of behavior."[41] When those rules are mastered and when language is functioning properly, human beings are able to understand and to be understood. In other words, they are able to communicate through the spoken word and through written texts.

In order to understand any text, one of the first steps that must be taken is to determine its genre.[42] Since language is governed by certain rules, and since many of those rules depend on genre, it is important to understand

38. See, for example, Provan, Long, and Longman 2003, 37, 43–49; Coady 1992; see also Plantinga 2003. For a specific critique of the faulty methods and assumptions of the Jesus Seminar, see Wilkins and Moreland 1996; Wright 1999b.

39. E.g., Kitchen 2003; Bruce 1981; Blomberg 1987; Evans 1996.

40. For helpful introductions to Old and New Testament exegesis, see Stuart 2001; Bock and Fanning 2006; see also Carson 1996.

41. Searle 1969, 12.

42. As Hirsch (1967, 76) explains, "All understanding of verbal meaning is necessarily genre-bound."

what kind of communicative act is taking place in a given text.[43] The importance of understanding the genre of a particular communicative act may be illustrated by reference to the *War of the Worlds* panic in 1938. When Orson Welles began reading a dramatic adaptation of H. G. Wells's story over the radio, many listeners mistook one genre (drama) for another (a factual news report) and thus believed that Martians were invading the earth. Those who panicked that night understood the meaning of the individual words and sentences. They understood the grammar and syntax. But that was not sufficient. Because they failed to recognize the correct genre, they completely misinterpreted what they were hearing. The same kinds of problems can occur when the text of Scripture is being interpreted. If poetry is interpreted as historical narrative, for example, or if historical narrative is interpreted as parable, misunderstanding is inevitable.

In order to determine the genre of a text, both the text itself and certain contextual factors must be taken into consideration. Kevin Vanhoozer helpfully defines context as "the various factors one has to take into consideration together with the text in order to understand the author's intention."[44] The context can help us to determine, for example, whether a particular biblical author is speaking literally or figuratively. If the context indicates that the author is writing poetry, there is a strong likelihood that figurative language will be used.

Canonical and historical contexts are also important in the task of exegesis. If the Bible as a whole is understood to be a complete and unified text communicated by God, then the various books of the Bible cannot be fully understood as merely self-contained individual texts. They must be understood within the context of the whole Bible. Individual texts must also be interpreted within their historical context. As an example, it is important to know whether a particular Old Testament prophecy was written before, during, or after the exile.

The building blocks of larger texts are words and sentences. An understanding of both the smaller building blocks and the larger contexts is necessary for proper interpretation. In fact, to understand one requires an understanding of the other. As Anthony Thiselton explains, "understanding a whole stretch of language or literature depends on an

43. Questions of genre are closely related to the kinds of issues discussed in various works on speech-act theory (e.g., Austin 1962; Searle 1969, 1979).

44. Vanhoozer 1998, 250.

understanding of its component parts, while an understanding of these smaller units depends, in turn, on an understanding of the total import of the whole."[45] The interpreter, then, must continually move from one to the other.

The purpose and role of individual words in the actual use of language have often been misunderstood with negative exegetical results.[46] It is important to observe, for example, that the basic unit of linguistic meaning is the text as a whole taken in its broader context. The basic unit of meaning is not the individual word taken in isolation.[47] Most individual words are polysemous, that is, they have a range of possible meanings.[48] Which of those possible meanings is the specific meaning of a word is determined by the use of that word in a particular sentence.[49] It must also be remembered, however, that the meaning of an individual sentence is also determined by its context.[50] In short, proper exegesis requires a careful examination of the details (e.g., vocabulary, grammatical and syntactical issues) as well as the larger picture (e.g., genre, historical context).

Two final issues that must be addressed concern the necessity of faith for proper interpretation and the illuminating work of the Holy Spirit. According to some authors, such as Moisés Silva, "a right relationship with [the] divine author is the most fundamental prerequisite for proper biblical interpretation."[51] This statement is supported by biblical passages such as 2 Corinthians 3:14–16 and 4:4, which seem to presuppose the necessity of faith for proper understanding.

45. Thiselton 1980, 104.

46. See Carson 1996, 27–64.

47. Vanhoozer 1998, 310–11.

48. A cursory glance at the entries in any substantive dictionary will reveal the truth of this statement. The English word "round," for example, has some seventy distinct possible meanings listed in the *Oxford English Dictionary*.

49. The meaning of the word "board," for example, depends on whether we are speaking of the materials found in a carpenter's shop, a company's group of managing directors, or the act of getting on a bus, train, ship, or airplane.

50. The sentence "I saw her duck" can mean either "I saw her duck her head," or it can mean "I saw a duck that belongs to her." The context will determine the precise meaning. The meaning of the sentence "Students hate annoying professors" depends on whether the word "annoying" is being used as a verb or an adjective. Only the context will reveal the intended meaning. The potential ambiguity of sentences has often been used to humorous effect. Many are familiar with Groucho Marx's one-liner: "I once shot an elephant in my pajamas." The ambiguity is revealed in the punch line: "How he got in my pajamas, I'll never know."

51. Silva 1996b, 15.

Because Scripture is to be interpreted in and by the community of faith, faith is a necessary prerequisite for a full and proper interpretation of Scripture as a whole. However, this does not mean that an unbeliever is unable to understand anything in Scripture. Both the believer and the unbeliever can understand the basic propositional content of a given biblical text. They are both able to use the available linguistic tools to gain an understanding of Hebrew and Greek vocabulary, grammar, and syntax. They are both able to study the historical context and determine the genre of a text. However, to use a term coined by the speech-act theorists, the text has a different "illocutionary effect" on the believer than it has on the unbeliever.

Here an illustration may prove helpful. Imagine that you move into an old home and find a dusty box of letters in the attic. In the box, you find a love letter written by a Mr. Jones to a Mrs. Jones in 1858. You can read the letter and understand the propositional content in the same way that Mrs. Jones was able to understand the propositional content in 1858. But the force and effect of the letter are different for you because it was not directly addressed to you. Something similar occurs when an unbeliever interprets Scripture. The unbeliever can understand the propositional content, but the unbeliever does not believe that God is the author of the text, and he certainly does not believe that the text is directed in any way to him.[52]

The illuminating work of the Holy Spirit is also necessary for full and proper interpretation of Scripture. The Spirit was sent to teach the church (John 14:26) and to guide the church into all truth (John 16:13). The Spirit is given in order that believers might know and understand (1 Cor. 2:12). As the one who inspired the Scriptures, the Spirit is also the one who reveals its full meaning to the people of God. The illumination of the Spirit should not, however, be understood as an alternative to careful exegetical study. We should not expect the Spirit to reward intellectual laziness by providing grammatical, syntactical, and contextual information that we have failed to learn. Because the illuminating work of the Spirit is both necessary and mysterious, those who would interpret the Word of God rightly must be in prayerful communion with God.

52. Thiselton 1992, 598.

Structure and Approach

The contents of this book follow a generally canonical order, with two exceptions. First, in the chapters dealing with the Old Testament prophetic books, the individual books are dealt with in chronological order. This allows us to see the messages of the various prophets within the broader narrative context of redemptive history, as both Israel and Judah spiraled down toward exile. Second, in the chapters dealing with the Pauline Epistles, the individual epistles are also dealt with in chronological order. Again, this allows us to see the epistles more clearly against their narrative background in the book of Acts.

The approach I have taken throughout the book can be described as a "narrative method," a method that traces "the theological development of the ideas in a book."[53] Grant Osborne explains well the strengths and weaknesses of such an approach: "This [method] has enormous value in helping students see how themes emerged and intertwined in the development of the book, but it can often degenerate into a glorified survey of the contents of the book."[54] In one sense, this is a weakness. However, when examining a theme, such as eschatology, it can be beneficial to survey the contents of the biblical books, emphasizing where and how each book develops this theme. A survey in which the unified message of Scripture is emphasized can also be helpful in countering the widespread assumption that the Bible is merely a collection of disparate writings.

I have attempted to alleviate the potential problem to some degree by adapting the approach somewhat. If we compare the content of Scripture to a pathway through a large forest, the bulk of each chapter consists of a more or less detailed look at the trees on a particular section of the path. Throughout the bulk of each chapter, we are using a zoom lens, as it were, looking at the specific eschatological themes as they are developed in the individual books. At the end of each chapter, however, we pull back with a wide-angle lens to get a broader perspective of where we are in terms of the big picture of the biblical narrative. The reader will gain the most benefit from this approach if he or she prayerfully reads the relevant section of Scripture prior to our discussion of it.

53. Osborne 2006, 369.
54. Osborne 2006, 369.

PART 1

THE OLD TESTAMENT

1

The Pentateuch (1)

Genesis

Most people, when reading a book, do not begin with the final chapter. In fact, the contents of a book's final chapter will usually make little sense if the reader does not know what has preceded it. Many Christians, however, in their desire to understand what the Bible teaches about the last days, begin by turning to the book of Revelation. The book of Revelation is certainly important for an understanding of the outworking of God's redemptive work in history, but the book of Revelation is, so to speak, the final chapter. In order to understand biblical eschatology, we must understand the entire Bible. It is true that biblical eschatology focuses on the end of redemptive history, but the end of that history can only be understood within the context of the whole of that history. The redemptive events described in the New Testament are the fulfillment of the promises found in the Old Testament. These ancient promises go back to the very beginning, to the five books of Moses.

The Pentateuch in Context

Christians and others have used the term "Pentateuch" since at least the third century to refer to the first five books of the Bible. In Jewish tradition, however, these books are usually referred to as the Torah and are the first section of the Tanakh, the Hebrew Bible.[1] The overarching genre of the Pentateuch is historical narrative, but it also contains other genres such as law and poetry. The historical narrative of the Pentateuch, like that of the other historical books of the Old Testament, may best be described as theological history. In other words, the Pentateuch is a historical account written for a specific purpose, namely to reveal the nature of Israel's God.[2]

The books of the Pentateuch themselves nowhere indicate the name of their author, but the New Testament and Jewish tradition both attribute authorship to Moses (Matt. 19:7; 22:24; Mark 7:10; 12:26; John 1:17; 5:46; 7:23).[3] In the nineteenth century, this traditional understanding of the authorship of the Pentateuch was challenged with the rise of the documentary hypothesis. According to this hypothesis, the Pentateuch is composed of four distinct sources: the Yahwistic source (J), the Elohistic source (E), Deuteronomy (D), and the Priestly source (P). These sources were gradually combined and edited, eventually resulting in the final form of the Pentateuch in approximately the fifth century B.C. It is well beyond the scope of this work to provide a critique of the documentary hypothesis.[4] Suffice it to say, however, that while more conservative scholars have always rejected the hypothesis, critical scholars are now reevaluating it as well. The literary unity of the Pentateuch is now much more widely acknowledged.[5]

Among those who accept not only literary unity but also Mosaic authorship for the Pentateuch, there is a general consensus regarding its original audience and the historical occasion for its writing. These five books were written and originally addressed to the people of Israel during that time in their history following the exodus from Egypt when they were on the

1. Alexander 2002, 3.

2. Dillard and Longman 1994, 64.

3. Both Jewish and Christian scholars have also acknowledged that some later minor editing occurred.

4. For a traditional conservative Christian critique of the documentary hypothesis see Allis 1949; see also Harrison 1969, 1–82. For a helpful Jewish critique, see Cassuto 1961. For more recent studies see Kikawada and Quinn 1985; Wenham 1988; Garrett 1991; and Whybray 1994.

5. Reevaluation of the documentary hypothesis by critical scholars, however, has not led to their acceptance of Mosaic authorship.

plains of Moab, east of the Jordan River preparing to enter the Promised Land.[6] Moses, their leader since the exodus from Egypt, would not be entering the land with them (Num. 20:12). But because he knew what his people needed, he composed the Pentateuch. Within these five books, Moses explains to the people of Israel who they are, why God brought them out of Egypt, and what God expected of them in terms of his covenant with them. The Pentateuch, then, was originally addressed to a specific people (Israel) within a specific historical context (the eve of their conquest of Canaan).

For the sake of convenience, it is helpful to deal with each of the five books of Moses as separate documents. It should be noted, however, that the five books of the Pentateuch are in actuality a unified literary entity. As T. D. Alexander observes, the later books of the Pentateuch presuppose knowledge of the earlier books, while the earlier books are incomplete without the later ones.[7] In addition, the Pentateuch as a whole has a distinct thematic connection with the books of Joshua to 2 Kings. As we look at the individual books and the smaller sections within each of these books, this larger literary context must always be kept in mind.

Genesis

The book of Genesis may be divided into two major sections: the primeval history (1:1–11:26) and the patriarchal history (11:27–50:26). Within this broad outline there exists a distinctive literary structure. Following a brief prologue (1:1–2:3), the book is divided into ten sections of varying length that are indicated and introduced by variations of the phrase "These are the generations [*toledot*] of . . ." (2:4; 5:1; 6:9; 10:1; 11:10; 11:27; 25:12; 25:19; 36:1; 37:2). Some of the *toledot* headings introduce extended historical narratives, while others introduce genealogies.

The Primeval History (Gen. 1:1–11:26)

Of the fifty chapters of Genesis, the first eleven narrate what is often referred to as the primeval history. These chapters recount history from creation to the time of Abram's call. The amount of space the author devotes to the primeval history (eleven chapters) compared to the amount of space

6. Sailhamer 1992, 5–6.

7. Alexander 2002, xv n. 3.

he devotes to the patriarchal history (thirty-nine chapters) indicates that the primeval history is essentially introductory and preparatory. The patriarchal narratives are the author's primary interest. The first eleven chapters of Genesis place the patriarchs into a broader creational context. They reveal, as Gordon Wenham observes, that the "God who called Abraham was no local divinity but the creator of the whole universe."[8] Genesis 1–11, then, provides the historical and theological background to Abram's call and ultimately to the birth of Israel. These chapters reveal the hopeless situation of fallen man without the gracious intervention of God, and they set the stage for the revelation of God's covenantal promises to Abraham, Isaac, and Jacob. These promises are the means by which God will begin to fulfill his original purposes for all of creation.[9]

When read in its ancient Near Eastern context, it also becomes evident that the primeval history of Genesis 1–11 presents its readers with a worldview that is dramatically different from that of the surrounding cultures.[10] It directly challenges the contemporary pagan views of deity, the universe, and the nature and purpose of mankind. Israel had only recently been redeemed from the idolatrous environment of Egypt and was soon to come into contact with the equally idolatrous environment of Canaan. The primeval history reveals to Israel the truth about God, creation, and sin that the people would have to understand in order to counter and resist the false pagan worldviews surrounding them on every side.

The Creator and His Creation

An examination of the structure of Genesis indicates that the creation account in Genesis 1:1–2:3 functions as a prologue or introduction to the book as a whole. In this prologue, the people of Israel learn that their God, the God who brought them out of Egypt, is not merely some local tribal deity. He is not like the false gods of the surrounding nations. Instead, he is the Creator of the universe and the only true God. He is the sovereign King over all. This passage beautifully describes God's creation of all things followed by his rest from his labors.

8. Wenham 1987, xxii.
9. Wenham 1987, l; see also Sailhamer 1992, 81.
10. Livingston 1974.

In Genesis 1:1 we read: "In the beginning, God created the heavens and the earth." The temporal clause "In the beginning" points to the fact that the space/time universe in which we live had an absolute beginning.[11] It is not eternal. The subject of this first sentence of Genesis is "God," the one who created the universe. The word translated "God" here is *'elohim*, and it is used some thirty-five times in the prologue alone. This chapter is predominantly about him. God is said to have created "the heavens and the earth." In other words, God created the universe and all that is in it. The universe did not come into being by spontaneous generation. Everything that is owes its existence to God (Neh. 9:6; Rev. 10:6; Col. 1:16).[12] As the Creator, God is also the sovereign King over all that he has made, and all that he has made exists to glorify him (Col. 1:16; Rev. 4:11).[13] He is the Great King, and the creation is intended to be his kingdom.

Genesis 1:2 describes the universe as "without form and void."[14] With the universe in this condition, the Spirit of God hovers over the formless deep. On the first three days of creation God creates light (1:3–5), the sky and seas (1:6–8), and dry land and plants (1:9–13). On the last three days of creation, these separate spheres are filled as God creates the heavenly lights (1:14–19), the birds and fish (1:20–23), and finally the land animals and man (1:26–31).[15] There is a parallel, then, between the creative work of the first three days and the creative work of the last three days. In contrast to those pagan religions and philosophies that believe the physical world to be inherently evil, God repeatedly describes the created material world as "good" (1:4, 10, 12, 18, 21, 25, 31).[16]

On the fourth day, God creates the sun, the moon, and the stars. Aside from the creation of man on the sixth day, more attention is given to this aspect of creation than to any other. The probable reason for such detailed attention is that the sun and the moon were considered to be important gods in ancient Near Eastern thought while the stars were believed to

11. Kelly 1999, 57. For a comprehensive defense of the doctrine of *creatio ex nihilo* or "creation out of nothing," see Copan and Craig 2004.

12. Wenham 1987, 36.

13. This doctrine of sovereign creation will be echoed in later eschatological texts that refer to God's creation of a "new heavens and a new earth" (Isa. 65:17; Rev. 21:1).

14. Heb. תֹהוּ וָבֹהוּ (*tohu wabohu*).

15. For information on the debate over the nature of the days of creation, see Hagopian 2001.

16. Kelly 1999, 87.

impact human lives. In its account of the fourth day of creation, Genesis makes it clear that the sun, moon, and stars are a part of God's creation called into being by his mighty word.[17] They are not gods to be worshiped or consulted.

On the fifth and sixth day, God creates birds, fish, and land animals, each according to its own kind. The climax of the creative work of God, however, is reached with the creation and blessing of man.[18] In Genesis 1:26, God says, "Let us make man in our image, after our likeness."[19] The words *tselem* and *demut*, translated "image" and "likeness" respectively, are generally synonymous in this context.[20] Their use in this verse indicates that man is like God in certain respects, but their use also indicates that there is a distinction between the Creator and the creature. Likeness is not identity. Man is like God in that he is a rational and moral being who is personal and relational. Man is unlike God in that he is, among other things, a finite creature.

Verse 27 reveals that the creation of man in God's image entailed the creation of man and woman. The man and woman are created for union and communion with their Creator as well as with each other. As a consequence of being made in the image of God, man is given dominion over the rest of creation (Gen. 1:28; Ps. 8:6–8). This "dominion mandate" is the first clear hint in Scripture of God's creational purpose. The first man, created in the image of God, exercises a representative kingship role.[21] Man is created in God's image and is given "dominion." He is a "vicegerent," or representative, ruling as king on behalf of God.[22] This text indicates that God's plan is to establish his kingdom on earth.

God is said to have "blessed" the man and the woman he created in his image, commanding them to be fruitful and to multiply (Gen. 1:28). John Sailhamer rightly notes that "at the center of God's purpose in creating

17. Wenham 1987, 21.

18. Wenham 1987, 38; Dempster 2003, 56–57.

19. For an extended discussion of the meaning of "the image of God," see Hoekema 1986, 11–101. See also Calvin, *Institutes*, 1.15, and Berkhof 1939, 202–10.

20. For example, Genesis 1:27 and 9:6 use only the word *tselem* to describe the concept of the image of God, while Genesis 5:1 uses only the word *demut*. Genesis 5:3 uses both words but reverses their order and the order of the prepositions used in 1:26. This seems to indicate that either word, or both, can be used to describe the concept of the image of God.

21. Dumbrell 1984, 34.

22. Wenham 1987, 33.

humankind was his desire to bless them."[23] In order to understand Genesis, it is crucial to recognize the prominence of the theme of blessing throughout the book. Out of the approximately 400 occurrences of the Hebrew root *brk* in the entire Old Testament, 88 (almost one-fourth) are found in Genesis.[24] The word "blessing" is used in several contexts in Scripture, but as Christopher Mitchell observes, when it is used in the context of God blessing man, as in verse 28, it may be defined as "any benefit or utterance which God freely bestows in order to make known to the recipient and to others that he is favorably disposed toward the recipient."[25]

After blessing the man and the woman and giving them their mandate to be fruitful, to fill the earth, and to have dominion, God beholds the work of his hands and declares it to be very good (1:28–31). Following the creation of the heavens and the earth, God then rests on the seventh day (2:1–2). Scripture informs us in this text that God "blessed" the seventh day and "made it holy" (2:3). God blesses and sanctifies the day that represents the consummation of his creative work.[26] We see then that the prologue of Genesis 1:1–2:3 moves from God's creative work to God's blessed rest, the goal of creation.

The Garden and the Fall

Genesis 2:4 introduces the first major section of the book: the "generations [*toledot*] of the heavens and the earth." This section of Genesis (2:4–4:26) explains what happened to God's good creation. Genesis 2:4–7 describes God's creation of the man (*'adam*) from the dust of the ground (*'adamah*). Verses 8–14 then paint a vivid picture of the garden planted in Eden by God, the garden in which he placed the man he had created. The garden is the place of God's unique presence much like the tabernacle and the temple at a later point in Israel's history.[27] In fact, as G. K. Beale

23. Sailhamer 1992, 405.

24. See *NIDOTTE*, 1:757; Mitchell 1987, 185.

25. Mitchell 1987, 165. Mitchell also observes that in the context of man blessing man in the Old Testament, blessing means either "declarations that God has blessed and/or will bless the person to whom the benediction is addressed," or "wishes or prayers for God to bless" (pp. 167–68). When man blesses God, blessing refers to "man's natural response to God's benefaction" (pp. 169–70).

26. There is some indication in the text of Genesis and other passages of Scripture that God's creation Sabbath is eternal (see Collins 2006, 88–93).

27. Waltke 2001, 85. Also see the comments on Exodus 25–31 in chapter 2 for a more detailed discussion of the similarities between the tabernacle and the creation narrative.

observes, "the Garden of Eden was the first archetypal temple in which the first man worshipped God."[28] In the midst of this garden stand the tree of life and the tree of the knowledge of good and evil (2:9). These trees, in particular the latter, become central to the following narrative.

God gives to the man he has created a command, telling him that he may eat of any tree in the garden, but he is forbidden to eat from the tree of the knowledge of good and evil (2:15–17).[29] He is then given a warning: "in the day that you eat of it you shall surely die" (v. 17). God's command is not arbitrary. The purpose of the command is "to raise man for a moment from the influence of his own ethical inclination to the point of a choosing for the sake of personal attachment to God alone."[30] God's command presents Adam with the choice between life and death, between blessing and judgment. If Adam disobeys the command by eating of the tree of the knowledge of good and evil, the result will be death (Gen. 2:17). By means of this command, God puts Adam's obedience to the test. Will he submit to God in faith or will he reject God and assert his own moral autonomy?

What is the nature of this arrangement that God makes with Adam? Is it a covenant? It has been objected that the word "covenant" does not appear in this text, but it is important to note that the presence of a word is not necessary for the presence of a concept.[31] It may also be objected that this arrangement with Adam does not involve any oaths or ceremonial rituals. However, as C. John Collins observes, this objection mistakenly "takes the features of *certain* covenants and makes them normative for *all* covenants."[32] We shall examine the nature of covenants more fully in our

28. Beale 2004, 66. Beale also suggests that because "Adam and Eve were to subdue and rule 'over all the earth,' it is plausible to suggest that they were to extend the geographical boundaries of the garden until Eden covered the whole earth" (pp. 81–82).

29. As Dumbrell (1984, 38) explains, "The phrase 'knowledge of good and evil' is better taken . . . as referring to the exercise of absolute moral autonomy, a prerogative which the Bible reserves to God alone."

30. Vos 1948, 32. See also Robertson 1980, 84.

31. As we shall see, the word "covenant" does not appear in the text that describes the institution of the Davidic covenant either (2 Sam. 7). But that arrangement is elsewhere referred to as a "covenant" (e.g., Ps. 89:3, 28, 34, 39). The same is true in the case of this arrangement between God and Adam. Two other texts (one biblical and one apocryphal) apparently speak of this arrangement as a "covenant." Although there is some disagreement about the interpretation, it is possible that Hosea 6:7 is a reference to this arrangement. The apocryphal book Ecclesiasticus also speaks of this arrangement as a "covenant" (14:17).

32. Collins 2006, 113.

discussion of the covenantal arrangement with Noah in Genesis 6. Suffice it to say at this point that the arrangement between God and Adam may properly be understood as a covenant.[33]

Genesis 2:18–25 details the creation of the woman and her relationship to the man as his helper.[34] Then in Genesis 3:1, a new character enters the narrative. The serpent is an instrument of Satan, the adversary of God.[35] Genesis does not explain the origin of this deceiver or how he came to be God's enemy; it simply explains that he cleverly tempts the woman to eat that which God had forbidden (3:2–5). The entrance of sin into human history is then recorded in a few short words: "So when the woman saw that the tree was good for food, and that it was a delight to the eyes, and that the tree was to be desired to make one wise, she took of its fruit and ate, and she also gave some to her husband who was with her, and he ate" (3:6).[36] By listening to the words of the serpent rather than submitting to the word of God, man allowed Satan to usurp dominion and establish his own kingdom in place of God's.[37]

God's good creation has now been marred by sin. Evil has reared its head, and God's goal of establishing his kingdom on earth has been challenged by a usurper. An important question has now been raised. Has God's good creation been permanently ruined, or can it be redeemed? If it can be redeemed, how will God accomplish this redemption? The answers to these questions are set forth throughout the remainder of Scripture, but a hint is given immediately following Adam's sin.

God's response to Adam's disobedience is swift. After confronting the man and the woman, who both attempt to shift the blame (3:8–13), God pronounces his judgment first to the serpent, then to the woman, and finally to the man (3:14–19). He pronounces a curse on the serpent (3:14), but

33. The Westminster Confession of Faith refers to this covenant as a "covenant of works" (7.2). The Westminster Larger Catechism (Q. 20) and Shorter Catechism (Q. 12) refer to it as a "covenant of life." For a helpful survey of Reformed writings on the covenant with Adam, see Ward 2003.

34. The Hebrew word עֵזֶר (*'ezer*), translated "helper," appears nineteen times in the Old Testament. Sixteen times it is used in reference to God, indicating that the term does not carry connotations of inferiority.

35. Waltke 2001, 90.

36. Dumbrell (1984, 38) explains that by eating the fruit from the tree of the knowledge of good and evil "man was intruding into an area reserved for God alone, and the violation of the command is tantamount to an assertion of equality with God, a snatching at deity."

37. See John 12:31; 14:30; 2 Cor. 4:4, where Satan is designated ruler of the world.

in the process of pronouncing this curse, God makes a promise that gives mankind reason for hope. Man's fall has resulted in the need for divine redemption, a need that God immediately addresses. To the serpent he says, "I will put enmity between you and the woman, and between your offspring and her offspring; he shall bruise your head, and you shall bruise his heel" (3:15). This verse has often been referred to as the *protevangelium*, or the first gospel. It is grace and mercy in the midst of the ultimate tragedy. It is also a forward-looking promise, an eschatological promise.

God's pronouncement hints that humanity will henceforth be divided into two communities: the seed of the woman and the seed of the serpent.[38] God promises that he himself will initiate and perpetuate conflict between them. The verb translated "bruise," as Wenham explains, is iterative. "It implies repeated attacks by both sides to injure the other."[39] The text, therefore, is profoundly eschatological in that it points to "a long struggle between good and evil, with mankind eventually triumphing."[40]

After pronouncing the curse upon the serpent, God turns to the woman and tells her that childbirth will now be accompanied by intense suffering (3:16). She is also told that her "desire" will be for her husband. The similarities between this statement and that in 4:7 indicate that what God means is that the woman will desire to dominate her husband. God's judgment on the man is the lengthiest (3:17–19). Because he has disobeyed God's explicit command, the ground will be cursed, and the growing of food will now be extremely difficult. The land will now bring forth thorns and thistles. God's natural creation has been corrupted because of man's sin, and it now stands in need of redemption (Rom. 8:19–22). Finally, the man is told that he will return to the ground from which he was taken. In other words, he will die.[41]

38. Waltke 2001, 93.

39. Wenham 1987, 80.

40. Wenham 1987, 80. Allusions to this text may be found in the New Testament (Rom. 16:20; Heb. 2:14; Rev. 12:1–17).

41. On the basis of a comparison with 1 Kings 2:36–46, Vos (1948, 38) suggests that this death sentence can be understood as the fulfillment of the threat of Gen. 2:17, if the words "in the day" are understood as a Hebrew idiom meaning "as surely as." Waltke (2001, 87–88) argues that the threat in Gen. 2:17 referred primarily to spiritual death and that physical death was an additional judgment pronounced after man sinned. Whether Vos is correct or not about the Hebrew idiom, it is certain that on the day Adam sinned, spiritual death occurred, and the process of physical death began. See also Collins 2006, 116–19, 160–62; Ward 2003, 113 n. 4.

After graciously providing clothes for the man and the woman (Gen. 3:21), God exiles them from the garden to prevent them from eating of the tree of life and perpetuating their fallen condition forever (3:22–24).[42] By disobeying God, man has cut himself off from the place of God's unique presence and blessing. He has allowed Satan to establish his dominion on earth (John 12:31; 14:30; 2 Cor. 4:4). He has separated himself from the one who is life itself (Ps. 36:9). The restoration of God's kingdom and blessing and the redemption of man will become of primary importance throughout the remainder of the book of Genesis and throughout the entire Bible.[43] These are fundamental elements of biblical eschatology.

These first three chapters of Genesis were of particular significance to Israel on the borders of the Promised Land because Israel shared many similarities with Adam. William Dumbrell explains:

> Significant for biblical eschatology are the several analogies that can be drawn between the man Adam and the nation Israel: Israel was created, as was Adam, outside the divine space to be occupied—Israel outside of Canaan and Adam outside of the garden. Both Israel and Adam were placed in divine space: Israel in Canaan and Adam in Eden. Israel was given, as was Adam, law by which the divine space could be retained.[44]

The question for Israel was simple. Would she obey the law, or would she, like Adam, disobey and be exiled from the land? If Adam proved unfaithful to God in the perfect environment, could Israel hope to keep the law in a land surrounded by idolaters?[45]

The Spread of Sin

Genesis 4–11 tells of the spread of sin throughout the earth, demonstrating man's desperate need of God's redemption.[46] As Geerhardus Vos explains, this era of history clearly shows the consequences of man's sin when left to itself.[47] Genesis 4 concludes the first major section of Genesis (2:4–4:26) by telling the story of the murder of Abel by his brother Cain

42. Dumbrell 1984, 37.
43. Ciampa 2007, 258.
44. Dumbrell 1994, 29.
45. Waltke 2001, 101.
46. Ross 1988, 77–78.
47. Vos 1948, 45.

and Cain's subsequent exile. Genesis 5:1 begins a new section: "the book of the generations [*toledot*] of Adam." The first part of this section (5:1–32) is a genealogy of ten generations from Adam to Noah. The dominant theme throughout this genealogy is death. The words "and he died" are the common refrain, repeated over and over. Because of Adam's sin, the guilt of sin, a corrupted nature, and death have come to all men.

There is, however, reason for hope. When the genealogy reaches Enoch, we do not find the expected words "and he died." Instead, verse 24 says, "Enoch walked with God, and he was not, for God took him." To "walk with God" indicates a special intimacy with God. To say that Enoch was not and that God took him indicates that he somehow suddenly disappeared.[48] Allen Ross comments, "This one exception to the reign of death provides a ray of hope for the human race, as if to say that death was not the final answer."[49]

The second part of "the book of the generations of Adam" is found in Genesis 6:1–8. The key theme of this section is the wickedness of man. Verses 1–4 speak of the "sons of God" taking the daughters of men as their wives and bearing children with them. This notoriously difficult text has been understood in a number of ways: (1) many have understood the "sons of God" to be fallen angels; (2) others have understood them to be lesser gods in the divine pantheon; (3) some have suggested that they are the descendants of Seth; (4) some have argued that they are despotic and tyrannical rulers descended from the wicked Lamech (4:18–24). The best explanation appears to be one that combines elements of (1) and (4). As Ross explains, "Fallen angels left their habitation and indwelt human despots and warriors, the great ones of the earth."[50] If this interpretation is correct, the phrase "sons of God" here refers to demon-possessed human tyrants. God looks down on this widespread wickedness and determines to send a cataclysmic judgment upon man and all of creation (6:5–7). There is, however, grace in the midst of this judgment, as one righteous man, Noah, finds favor in the eyes of the Lord (6:8). He will be saved from the wrath to come.

Genesis 6:9–9:29 is the third section of Genesis: "the generations [*toledot*] of Noah." These chapters describe the flood and God's covenant with

48. Waltke 2001, 115.

49. Ross 1988, 174.

50. Ross 1988, 182; see also Waltke 2001, 117.

Noah. God sees the widespread wickedness of man and determines to send a destructive flood as judgment (6:12–13).[51] God informs Noah of what he intends to do and instructs Noah to build an ark (6:13–17). God then tells Noah, "I will establish my covenant with you . . ." (6:18). This is the first instance in Scripture where the significant term *berit* is used, and it is the first instance where the concept of "covenant" is explicitly mentioned.[52]

Although English versions of the Bible usually translate the word *berit* as "covenant," there is some disagreement among scholars about the precise meaning of the Hebrew word.[53] Part of this difficulty is due to the wide semantic range of the word.[54] In addition to being used to refer to the various covenants between God and man, the word is used to describe things as diverse as marriages (Mal. 2:14), personal bonds of friendship (1 Sam. 18:3), arrangements between a people and their king (2 Sam. 5:3), vows to put away foreign wives (Ezra 10:3), commitments to dethrone and replace a queen (2 Kings 11:4), and more. In addition, we find references to a *berit* being made with stones and beasts (Job 5:23), with one's eyes (Job 31:1), with Leviathan (Job 41:4), with death (Isa. 28:15, 18), and with the day and night (Jer. 33:20, 25).

The diversity of contexts in which the word *berit* is found has made it difficult for lexicographers to find a single concept that is common to all of them, a linguistic common denominator as it were. Etymology has not proven helpful, because there is no agreement on the origin of the word.[55] Many scholars have focused on ancient Near Eastern texts from surrounding nations in an attempt to discover the basic meaning of the biblical

51. In later books of the Bible, the flood becomes a paradigm of God's eschatological judgment (Isa. 8:7–8; Matt. 24:37–39; Luke 17:26–27).

52. Other terms are used for "covenant" in addition to *berit* (e.g., *'amanah*, *hozeh*, and *'edut*), but the absence of any of these words in a given text does not necessarily mean the absence of the concept. As we have already observed, the word for "covenant" is not found in the historical narrative describing the inauguration of the Davidic covenant, but other texts do describe it as a "covenant" indicating that the concept of "covenant" is present even if the word is not. And as we have already seen, the covenant concept is present in the early chapters of Genesis describing the arrangement between God and Adam.

53. See *HALOT*, s.v. בְּרִית; *NIDOTTE*, 1:747–55.

54. As Grant Osborne (2006, 100) explains, "The semantic range of a word is the result of the synchronic study, a list of the ways the word was used in the era when the work was written."

55. In any case, etymology must be used with caution. The meaning of a given word often changes over time, so etymology may not tell us anything about the contemporary meaning of a word. The meaning of a word is determined by its usage in a given context, not necessarily by its origin (see *NIDOTTE*, 1:752).

word.[56] None of these studies, however, has led to complete agreement. The standard lexicons and dictionaries reflect the difficulty in the different basic definitions they provide for *berit.*[57]

In the end, the meaning of the word *berit* must be determined by examining its usage in the Old Testament. In all of the various Old Testament contexts, *berit* seems to be used generally to refer to an arrangement involving two or more parties.[58] The kind of arrangement depends upon the context. It may be either a unilateral commitment[59] or a bilateral agreement[60] (i.e., pact[61] or bond[62]), either of which entails certain obligations.[63] Many of these arrangements are ratified by a solemn oath[64] and/or a ceremonial rite[65] that either confirms an existing relationship or establishes a new one.[66] Some of these

56. George Mendenhall (*IDB*, 1:716–17), for example, has looked at ancient Near Eastern secular covenants and discerned four types: the suzerainty covenant in which a superior binds an inferior to certain obligations; a parity covenant in which both parties are bound by an oath; a Patron covenant in which the superior binds himself to an obligation for the benefit of the inferior; and a promissory covenant in which one party simply guarantees the future performance of some obligation. M. Weinfeld (*TDOT*, 2:270; Weinfeld 1970) distinguishes between suzerain-vassal treaties and royal grant treaties.

57. The word is defined as a "pact" (BDB, 136–37), an "agreement" (*HALOT*, 1:157–58), an "obligation" (*TDOT*, 2:255; *TLOT*, 1:256), a "mutual commitment" (*NIDOTTE*, 1:752), a "solemn promise made binding by an oath" (*IDB*, 1:714), and an "agreement" involving promises made under oath (*ABD*, 1:1179).

58. More specific definitions do not account for all Old Testament uses of the word.

59. See Mendenhall 1955, 5.

60. *HALOT*, 1:157. As Louis Berkhof (1939, 262) explains, "The word *berith* may denote a mutual voluntary agreement (dipleuric), but also a disposition or arrangement imposed by one party on another (monopleuric)."

61. BDB, 136.

62. Robertson 1980, 5.

63. *TLOT*, 1:256–66; McComiskey 1985a, 63. The obligations involved depend on the specific covenant as well as the type of covenant. As we shall see, some covenants closely resemble ancient Near Eastern suzerain-vassal treaties, which contain mutual obligations (Kline 1963). Other covenants closely resemble ancient royal land grants that were given in the form of unilateral promissory oaths, in which the one making the promise unilaterally swears to fulfill certain self-imposed obligations (Weinfeld 1970).

64. Williamson 2007, 39; *TDOT*, 2:256. In some covenants between God and man, God alone makes the oath (e.g., Gen. 15). In other covenants, both God and the human participants in the covenant make oaths (e.g., Ex. 24).

65. *TDOT*, 2:262; Kalluveettil 1982, 11.

66. Kalluveettil 1982, 103. Several scholars understand "relationship" to be part of the basic definition of "covenant" (e.g., Robertson 1980, 5; McComiskey 1985a, 63; Williams 2005, 45). Kline (2000, 5) has argued, on the other hand, that the definition of "covenant" should be distinguished from the relationship that it effects (cf. Hafemann 2007, 26).

arrangements are accompanied by an external sign (e.g., the rainbow in the Noahic covenant, circumcision in the Abrahamic covenant, the Sabbath in the Mosaic covenant).[67] In Scripture, such arrangements are made between God and man (e.g., Noah, Abraham, David) and between human parties (e.g., Jonathan and David in 1 Sam. 18:3). The specific nature of these arrangements, or "covenants," will be examined in the course of our study.

During the flood God graciously preserves a remnant of humanity, Noah and his family, from certain destruction (Gen. 7:23).[68] In the hands of God, the flood becomes an act of re-creation, a watery chaos from which the new world emerges.[69] After the floodwaters subside, Noah worships God, and God promises to never again "strike down every living creature" (8:20–22). He will preserve the earth until the final judgment (2 Peter 2:4–12; 3:4–7).[70] This promise, as Paul Williamson explains, "gives us the assurance that God will sustain the creation order, despite the chaos that continually threatens to engulf it."[71]

God then blesses Noah and his sons (Gen. 9:1–7). His blessing here is almost, but not quite, identical to the original blessing of Adam and Eve at creation (1:28–30). The similarities and differences are noted by Roy Ciampa.

> In chapter 9 Noah becomes a kind of second Adam, and he receives the same command as was given in Genesis 1:28, "Be fruitful and multiply and fill the earth," with the creatures of the air, earth and water once again mentioned. But there is something different. Noah is not told to subdue the earth and have dominion over all those creatures. He is told that they will fear him and that they are now given to him for food. There is a new start, but we have not been brought all the way back to the clean slate of Genesis 1.[72]

In other words, with Noah there is a new start, but Noah is not starting at the same place Adam started. The flood did not permanently solve the problem of sin and death.

67. *TDOT*, 2:263.

68. See Hasel 1974, 135–36. Hasel explains, "The unique event of the total annihilation of the existence of man in the flood actualized the possibility of a continuation of human existence through the salvation of a remnant" (p. 140).

69. Waltke 2001, 127–29.

70. Waltke 2001, 143.

71. Williamson 2007, 67; see also Golding 2004, 149–50.

72. Ciampa 2007, 262.

In Genesis 9:8–17, God formally establishes his covenant with Noah and provides the sign of the rainbow. As William Dumbrell explains, "God's covenant with Noah can be called eschatological in the sense that it reestablishes the divine plan for creation."[73] It demonstrates clearly the connection between creation and redemption.[74] The relationship between the universal creational scope of the covenant and God's redemptive work is significant. Williamson notes, "the universal scope of this covenant implies that the blessing for which humanity had been created and the creation had now been preserved will ultimately encompass not just one people or nation, but rather the whole earth."[75] The kingdom of God and his blessing for mankind will be reestablished on earth.

In Genesis 9:18–29, we find a text that was important to the Israelites on the border of Canaan as they were preparing to go into the Promised Land. The theme of this section is blessing and cursing upon Noah's sons Shem, Ham, and Japheth. Noah, who until this point has been described as righteous, becomes drunk and lies naked in his tent (9:20–21). Ham, the father of Canaan, discovers him there but rather than honor his father by covering him, he tells his brothers. Shem and Japheth then cover their father. When Noah discovers what has been done, he pronounces curses on Canaan and blessings on Shem and Japheth. This is significant because, as Bruce Waltke explains, "The Canaanites succeed the Cainites as the curse-laden descendants of the Serpent."[76] Israel had to understand that in order to receive the land and the blessing, this curse on the Canaanites would have to be carried out.[77]

The fourth section of Genesis, "the generations [*toledot*] of the sons of Noah, Shem, Ham, and Japheth" (10:1–11:9), contains two major parts: the table of nations and the story of the tower of Babel. The table of nations lists seventy nations. Fourteen are descended from Japheth; thirty are descended from Ham; and twenty-six are descended from Shem. The nations descended from Japheth have little interaction with Israel during

73. Dumbrell 1994, 31.

74. Robertson 1980, 110–11. As Dumbrell (1984, 27) explains, since a flood would be an appropriate response to man's wickedness in any age, "mankind has been preserved by grace alone." More specifically, in 1 Peter, the salvation of Noah from the flood is viewed as a type of Christian salvation (1 Peter 3:20–21).

75. Williamson 2007, 68.

76. Waltke 2001, 150.

77. Ross 1988, 218.

her later history. From Ham, however, would come not only the Canaanites but also several of Israel's most significant enemies including Egypt, Philistia, Assyria, and Babylon (10:6–13). The descendants of Shem will eventually include Israel.

After describing the fruitful multiplication of Noah's sons, the text turns to the last great judgment upon mankind during the primeval history—the tower of Babel (11:1–9). The people have decided to build "a city and a tower with its top in the heavens," and they say, "let us make a name for ourselves, lest we be dispersed over the face of the whole earth" (11:4). This project is an affront to God because the tower is an alternative to his kingdom. It is the city/kingdom of man opposed to the city/kingdom of God.[78] God immediately judges this act of pride and arrogance by confusing the language of men and dispersing them (11:5–9). Ross explains the significance: "With this story the common history of all humankind comes to an abrupt end, as the human race is hopelessly scattered across the face of the entire earth."[79]

Genesis 11:10–26 is the fifth section of Genesis: "the generations [*toledot*] of Shem." This genealogy is a transitional text that narrows the focus of Genesis to Abram. Just as there were ten generations between Adam and Noah, there are ten generations between Shem and Abram. The purpose of this section, then, is to trace Abram's ancestry back to Shem.[80] It demonstrates that the call of Abram (Gen. 12:1–3) was not arbitrary. Abram was a man "whose ancestors represented faith in the Lord and to whom the promise of blessing had been extended."[81]

Taken as a whole, Genesis 1–11 provides the necessary context for understanding the patriarchal narratives of chapters 12–50. Gordon Wenham helpfully summarizes the importance of these first chapters of Genesis:

> With 11:26 the scene has finally been set for the patriarchal history to unfold. The opening chapters of Genesis have provided us the fundamental insights for interpreting these chapters properly. Gen 1 revealed the character of God and the nature of the world man finds himself in. Gen 2 and 3 portrayed the relationship between man and woman, and the effects man's disobedience has had on man-woman and divine-human relations. Chap. 5 sketched the

78. Dumbrell 1984, 61.
79. Ross 1988, 242.
80. Ross 1988, 249.
81. Ross 1988, 250.

long years that passed before the crisis of the great flood (chaps. 6–9), which almost destroyed all humanity for its sinfulness. The table of nations (chap. 10) started the process of Israel's geographical and political self-definition with respect to the other nations in the world, but Gen 11:1–9 reminded us that the nations were in confusion and that mankind's proudest achievements were but folly in God's sight and under his judgment.

However, according to 11:10–26, just five generations after Peleg, whose lifetime according to 10:25 saw the confusion of languages at Babel, Abram arrives. As 12:3 will declare, it is through him that all the families of the earth will be blessed. Man is not without hope.[82]

The Patriarchal History (Gen. 11:27–50:26)

The patriarchal history does not technically begin at Genesis 12:1, but at 11:27 with "the generations [*toledot*] of Terah." Unfortunately, modern chapter divisions introduce an unnatural break in the text. Within the patriarchal history there are five sections marked by *toledot* headings, but since two of these are brief genealogies, the patriarchal history may be helpfully divided into three major parts: the story of Abraham (11:27–25:11); the story of Jacob (25:19–35:29), and the story of Joseph (37:2–50:26). Each of these three major parts begins with a revelation from God that sets the stage for what follows (12:1–3; 25:22–23; 37:5–9).[83]

The overarching focus of the patriarchal history is on God's gracious promises of blessing, promises that are given first to Abraham, then to Isaac, and finally to Jacob. The importance of these promises for understanding the remainder of Scripture and biblical eschatology cannot be overstated. They are, as Willem VanGemeren explains, "the very platform of the history of redemption."[84] The centrality of the patriarchal promises and history may be observed in the fact that God himself comes to be known in subsequent biblical history as "the God of Abraham, Isaac, and Jacob" (Ex. 3:6, 15, 16; 4:5; 1 Kings 18:36; 1 Chron. 29:18; 2 Chron. 30:6; Acts 3:13).[85] The very name of God becomes intimately associated with the patriarchs to whom he makes the promises.

82. Wenham 1987, 253–54.
83. Wenham 1994, 168–69.
84. VanGemeren 1988a, 122.
85. Bartholomew and Goheen 2004, 57–58.

Abraham: Promise and Covenant

Genesis 11:27–32 introduces the sixth section of Genesis, the "generations [*toledot*] of Terah" (11:27–25:11). The main body of the narrative is found in 12:1–22:19. Genesis 22:20–25:11 then serves as an epilogue to the entire section.[86] The main body of the narrative begins with the call of Abram (12:1–9) and ends with his supreme test, God's command to sacrifice Isaac (22:1–19). The stories between the call of Abram and his test focus on God's promise of the land (12:10–15:21) and his promise of offspring (chs. 16–21).[87]

The call of Abram in Genesis 12:1–9 is a pivotal point in redemptive history. According to Gordon Wenham, no section of Genesis is more significant than 11:27–12:9.[88] It is, as Bruce Waltke observes, "the thematic center of the Pentateuch."[89] While the first eleven chapters of Genesis focus primarily on the terrible consequences of sin, God's promises to Abram in Genesis 12 focus on the hope of redemption, of restored blessing and reconciliation with God. God is going to deal with the problem of sin and evil, and he is going to establish his kingdom on earth. How he is going to do this begins to be revealed in his promises to Abram.[90] The remaining chapters of Genesis follow the initial stages in the fulfillment of these promises. Thus Genesis 12:1–9 sets the stage for the remainder of Genesis and the remainder of the Bible.[91]

The key section of Genesis 12:1–9 is the explicit call of God to Abram found in verses 1–3:

> Now Yahweh said to Abram, "Go from your country and your kindred and your father's house to the land that I will show you. And I will make of you

86. Ross 1988, 80–81.
87. Ross 1988, 254–55.
88. Wenham 1987, 281.
89. Waltke 2001, 208.
90. Williamson 2007, 77; Dumbrell 1984, 47.
91. Bruce Waltke (2001, 209) elaborates on this important point: "The call of God to Abraham is the sneak preview for the rest of the Bible. It is a story of God bringing salvation to all tribes and nations through this holy nation, administered at first by the Mosaic covenant and then by the Lord Jesus Christ through the new covenant. The elements of Abraham's call are reaffirmed to Abraham (12:7; 15:5–21; 17:4–8; 18:18–19; 22:17–18), to Isaac (26:24), to Jacob (28:13–15; 35:11–12; 46:3), to Judah (49:8–12), to Moses (Ex. 3:6–8; Deut. 34:4), and to the ten tribes of Israel (Deut. 33). They are reaffirmed by Joseph (Gen. 50:24), by Peter to the Jews (Acts 3:25), and by Paul to the Gentiles (Gal. 3:8)."

> a great nation, and I will bless you and make your name great so that you will be a blessing. I will bless those who bless you, and him who dishonors you I will curse, and in you all the families of the earth shall be blessed."

The theme of God's call to Abram is evident in the fivefold repetition of the key terms "bless" or "blessing." Also important is the repetition of the word "you" and "your." Man's sin has resulted in God's curse (Gen. 3:14, 17; 4:11; 5:29; 9:25), but here God promises to form a people for himself and to restore his original purposes of blessing for mankind (Gen. 1:28).[92] Abram is somehow going to be the mediator of this restored blessing.

Within God's call of Abram there are four basic promises: (1) offspring, (2) land, (3) the blessing of Abram himself, and (4) the blessing of the nations through Abram.[93] In verse 1, God commands Abram to leave his home and go to the land that he will show Abram. The promise of land is not explicit in this initial command. It is made explicit only when Abram reaches the land of Canaan. At that point, God promises Abram, "To your offspring I will give this land" (12:7). This promise of land becomes a key theme throughout the remainder of the Old Testament.[94] It is especially prominent in the remainder of the Pentateuch and in the books referred to in the Hebrew canon as the Former Prophets (Joshua, Judges, Samuel, and Kings). In terms of God's kingdom purposes, the land promise indicates that God has not abandoned his plan to establish his kingdom on earth. The land promise would have certainly been important to Israel at the time the Pentateuch was originally composed. As Israel stood on the plains of Moab, they were assured that the land they were about to enter had been promised to Abraham and to his offspring by God himself.

In Genesis 12:2, God promises that he will make of Abram "a great nation." This promise will be fulfilled initially in the birth of the nation of Israel.[95] This promise necessarily implies that Abram will have offspring, but like the promise of land, the promise of offspring is made explicit only when Abram reaches Canaan (12:7). The promise of offspring is also related to God's ultimate kingdom purposes. Just as the land promise provides a realm for God's kingdom in the midst of his creation, the promise of offspring

92. See McComiskey 1985a, 15–58.

93. As VanGemeren (1988a, 108) observes, Abraham (22:17–18), Isaac (26:3–4), and Jacob (28:13–15) each received God's fourfold promise.

94. See Johnston and Walker 2000.

95. Dumbrell 1984, 66–67.

anticipates a people for his kingdom. God then promises to bless Abram and make his name great so that he will be a blessing.[96]

The fourth element of God's promise is that in Abram "all the families of the earth shall be blessed" (12:3). Abraham will be the head of the "one family by whom all of the other families of the earth will be blessed."[97] In fact, the blessing of all the families of the earth is the primary purpose behind God's calling of Abram. His calling and the promises he is given are not ends in themselves. Abram is promised offspring, a land, and personal blessing in order that he might be the mediator of God's blessing to all the families of the earth.[98] As we proceed, the eschatological significance of God's promises to Abram and his determination to bless all the families of the earth will become clearer. As we will see, this blessing will come through the establishment of God's kingdom. From this point forward in Genesis, "the writer's primary concern is to trace the development of God's resolution to bless."[99]

The promise of God is endangered when Abram goes to Egypt during a famine and lies in order to protect himself. As a result of his dishonesty, Sarai is taken into the house of Pharaoh. God, however, will not allow his promises to be thwarted and providentially intervenes (12:10–20). After Abram returns to Canaan, he separates from his nephew Lot (Gen. 13). God then reaffirms the promise of land (13:14–15) and expands the promise of offspring, telling Abram that his offspring will be as numerous as "the dust of the earth" (13:16). In Genesis 14, Abram rescues Lot from warring kings and is then blessed by the mysterious Melchizedek, king of Salem (14:19–20). Melchizedek's name means "king of righteousness," and he is said to be both a king and a priest (14:18). According to Hebrews 7:1–3, he is a type of Jesus the Messiah.[100]

96. Williamson (2007, 78–79) argues that because of the imperative form of the verb the words וֶהְיֵה בְּרָכָה (*weheyeh berakah*) at the end of verse 2 should be translated as a second command, "Be a blessing," rather than as a certain consequence ("so that you will be a blessing"). This is a possible translation, and the ASV does translate the words in this way, but it is not required. In this type of sentence, the imperative verb can express a consequence (See GKC, §110i; Joüon, §116h).

97. *NIDOTTE*, 4:665.

98. Alexander 2002, 85–86. Allusions to this promise are found in prophetic texts such as Isaiah 19:24 and Jeremiah 4:2.

99. Ross 1988, 253.

100. In general, a "type" is a person, institution, or event that prefigures a subsequent greater event.

Genesis 15 marks the formal establishment of the Abrahamic covenant. In Genesis 12, God had made certain promises to Abram, including the promise of offspring. In chapter 15, Abram voices concern, saying to God, "Behold, you have given me no offspring, and a member of my household will be my heir" (v. 3). God then tells Abram, "your very own son shall be your heir," and promises him that his offspring will be as numerous as the stars of heaven (vv. 4–5). Abram has been promised a son. And what is Abram's response to God's promise? He "believed Yahweh, and he counted it to him as righteousness" (v. 6). Abram is a man of faith. He trusts God and believes that what God has promised, he will certainly do. And God counts it to him as righteousness.[101]

In Genesis 15:7, God tells Abram, "I am Yahweh who brought you out from Ur of the Chaldeans to give you this land to possess." This historical prologue to the Abrahamic covenant foreshadows the historical prologue to the Ten Commandments, which reads in part: "I am Yahweh your God, who brought you out of the land of Egypt" (Ex. 20:2). Abram asks God how he is to know that he will possess the land (Gen. 15:8). God's response takes the form of a ceremonial rite. God commands Abram to bring him several animals, which Abram then cuts in half and places on the ground (vv. 9–11). Abram falls into a deep sleep, and God tells him that his offspring will be sojourners in a foreign land and that they will be afflicted for four hundred years before he brings them back to the land of Canaan (vv. 12–16).[102]

In the form of a smoking fire pot and a flaming torch, God proceeds to pass between the pieces of the animals and makes a covenant with Abram (vv. 17–18). The meaning of this practice is not immediately transparent today, but its meaning would have been clear to the original readers. In such a ceremony, the one passing between the pieces of the animals indicated that he was taking a self-maledictory oath upon himself.[103] In other words, God invokes a curse of death upon himself if he fails to fulfill the promises he has made to Abram. This ceremony is a way of saying, in effect, "May I be torn in pieces as these animals have been torn in pieces if I should

101. In this context, the verb *hashab*, which is translated "counted," means to credit to one's account (Lev. 7:18; 17:3–4; Num. 18:27, 30; Ps. 32:2; Prov. 27:14). See *NIDOTTE*, 2:305–6.

102. As Waltke observes, God's promise "reveals his sovereign control over history" (Waltke 2001, 247).

103. Robertson 1980, 130.

break my promise" (see also Jer. 34:18).[104] Abram could receive no greater assurance of God's commitment to his promises.[105]

Having established the covenant in Genesis 15, God confirms or ratifies it in Genesis 17 by changing Abram's name and by instituting circumcision as the seal of the covenant.[106] Wenham observes, "Whereas inaugurating the covenant was entirely the result of divine initiative, confirming it involves a human response."[107] Abram is ninety-nine years old when God appears to him and reaffirms his covenant promises. God gives Abram a command, saying, "walk before me, and be blameless . . . ," indicating that God expects continued faithfulness from Abraham (v. 1). God will later declare that the very reason he chose Abraham was that Abraham might "command his children and his household after him to keep the way of Yahweh by doing righteousness and justice, so that Yahweh may bring to Abraham what he has promised him" (18:19; 22:15–18; 26:5).

God tells Abram that he will be "the father of a multitude of nations" (17:4). This promise may be understood in both a biological and a spiritual sense.[108] Abram is, in fact, the biological father, not only of Israel, but of many nations (Gen. 25:1–4; 25:12–18; 36). However, the Hebrew word *'ab*, translated as "father," does not always refer to a biological father (cf. Gen. 45:8; Judg. 18:19; 1 Sam. 24:11; 2 Kings 6:21; Isa. 22:20–21). Abram is best understood as the "father of a multitude of nations" in the sense that he is for them the mediator of God's blessing. Support for this understanding of Abram's fatherhood is found in Genesis 17 in the instruction given to Abram to give the covenant sign of circumcision both to his physical offspring and to those who are not his physical offspring (vv. 12–13).[109]

Having promised Abram that he would be the father of a multitude of nations, God changes his name to "Abraham" (17:5). His old name,

104. See Robertson 1980, 130.

105. The Abrahamic covenant is in the form of a unilateral promissory oath. As such it closely resembles ancient royal land grants that were given by kings to loyal subjects (Wenham 1987, 333; Weinfeld 1970).

106. Nehemiah 9:7–8 seems to view the events of Genesis 15 and 17 as two elements of a single Abrahamic covenant (Waltke 2001, 263). Nehemiah speaks of the giving of the new name Abraham (Gen. 17) and the promise of land and offspring (Gen. 15) as aspects of the one covenant with Abraham. For the argument that Genesis 15 and 17 present two distinct but related covenants, see Williamson 2007, 89–91.

107. Wenham 1994, 20.

108. Waltke 2001, 260.

109. Alexander 2002, 86–87; Waltke 2001, 260.

"Abram," means "exalted father." His new name is a wordplay on the Hebrew words for "father" (*'ab*) and "crowd" (*hamon*).[110] One can only imagine the reaction of those who knew this elderly and childless man when he informed them of his new name ("father of a multitude"). Yet every time he was addressed as "Abraham," he would be immediately reminded of God's promise to him.[111] God would give him descendants, and they would be as numerous as the stars in the heavens. This he firmly believed.

God's promises to Abraham have been incredible thus far: land, offspring, personal blessing, a source of blessing to the nations (Gen. 12:1–7), descendants as numerous as the dust of the earth or the stars of heaven (13:16; 15:5), a son of his own (15:4). And now, when Abraham is ninety-nine years old, God makes yet another amazing promise. He declares to Abraham, "kings shall come from you" (17:6), indicating again God's purpose to establish his kingdom. The Abrahamic covenant here anticipates the Davidic covenant (2 Sam. 7:5–16; 1 Chron. 17:4–14). Ultimately, kings descended from Abraham will be involved in the fulfillment of the promise of blessing to the nations.[112] Here we begin to see the close interrelationship between covenant and kingdom. The covenants not only serve to administer each successive form of God's kingdom on earth but have as their ultimate goal the full restoration of God's universal kingdom.[113]

The covenant has been made with Abraham, promising him offspring among many other blessings, but in Genesis 17:7, for the first time, God declares that he is not only going to give Abraham offspring, but that he is also going to establish his covenant with Abraham's offspring. By declaring that he will establish his covenant with Abraham's offspring, God gives the covenant a future orientation. As he did in his covenant with Noah, God describes this covenant as "everlasting" (cf. 9:16). The use of this word indicates "that a permanent relationship is envisaged, as durable as life itself."[114] The heart of this covenant is found in verse 8, in God's promise, "I will be their God."

110. Waltke 2001, 259–60.

111. Ross 1988, 332.

112. See also Psalm 72 (esp. vv. 9–11, 17), which clearly associates the blessing of the nations with the rule of an eschatological Davidic king.

113. See Kline 2000, 4; Dumbrell 1984, 42.

114. Wenham 1994, 29.

God gives Abraham the sign of the covenant in Genesis 17:9–14. He commands Abraham to keep his covenant (v. 9), and tells him that the covenant he is to keep is the circumcision of every male (v. 10). Circumcision is to be a "sign of the covenant" between God and Abraham (v. 11).[115] Every male in his household, whether his natural offspring or not, is to be circumcised (vv. 12–13). Those who are not circumcised will be cut off from the people of God because they have broken God's covenant (v. 14). The sign of circumcision, the removal of the foreskin from the male sexual organ, was appropriate to a covenant that ratified the promise of offspring.[116] This outward sign both signified and necessitated a corresponding cleansing of the heart (Lev. 26:41; Deut. 10:16; Jer. 4:4; 9:25–26).[117] Circumcision, then, "symbolized the inner purification necessary for a life of obedience and love to God."[118] It is also important to observe that from the time of its institution, circumcision was not a racial sign but a covenantal sign. It was required to be given to foreigners within Abraham's household. It was, therefore, open to Gentiles (Ex. 12:43–49), and those Gentiles who submitted to the covenant sign became a part of the visible covenant people of God.

Genesis 18–19 recounts the story of the judgment of Sodom and Gomorrah, a judgment that becomes a paradigm for future divine judgments. In Deuteronomy, for example, Moses will use the imagery of Sodom and Gomorrah to describe the curses of the covenant (Deut. 29:23; 32:32). The prophets use this imagery to describe the kind of judgment that will befall Israel's enemies (e.g., Jer. 49:17–18; Zeph. 2:9). The prophets also use this imagery to describe the judgment that will fall upon Israel herself when she forsakes God and embraces wickedness (e.g., Isa. 3:9; Jer. 23:14;

115. It is worth noting that in this text, circumcision is identified by God both as "my covenant" and as "a sign of the covenant." There is a close relationship here between the sign and the thing signified.

116. Ross 1988, 333.

117. The outward sign did not, however, automatically effect the internal change. Otherwise God would not call those who had been circumcised in the flesh to be circumcised in their heart as well. Faith was required. Abraham, for example, experienced circumcision of the heart before he was given the outward sign of that reality. For him it was a seal of his existing faith (Rom. 4:10–12). Isaac, on the other hand, received the outward sign of inward purification when he was only eight days old (Gen. 21:4). The reception of this sign did not automatically confer upon him the inner purification that it signified. Instead, it required Isaac to be circumcised in his heart, to exercise the faith of his father Abraham and to love God.

118. Robertson 1980, 153.

Amos 4:11). Finally, our Lord Jesus Christ uses the imagery of Sodom and Gomorrah to describe his coming judgment (Luke 17:28–30).

When Abraham is one hundred years old, God fulfills his promise to give Abraham and Sarah a son (Gen. 21:1–7). Sarah gives birth to a boy, and Abraham names the child Isaac, which means "he laughs." As Wenham explains, "This is the most visible fulfillment of any of the promises so far and also the most central, for without a son Abraham could never have a multitude of descendants, inherit the land, or be a blessing to all the nations."[119] In Genesis 22, however, a dramatic turn occurs as Abraham's faith in God's promises is put to the ultimate test. Verse 1 of this chapter immediately states that "God tested Abraham." With these words, the reader is given insight into what follows, but this is insight that Abraham himself did not have at that time.

God commands Abraham to take Isaac to Moriah and sacrifice him there (22:2). Abraham faces a conflict here between faith in the promises of God and obedience to a command of God that would seem to require the nullification of those promises. On a more existential level, Abraham faced a conflict between his love for his only son (22:2) and his love for God.[120] Abraham makes the necessary preparations and after a three-day journey, he reaches Moriah. In obedience to God's command, Abraham prepares to sacrifice Isaac, but at the last possible moment God intervenes and stays Abraham's hand. We are not told in Genesis how Abraham reconciled the conflict he faced, but Hebrews 11:17–19 indicates that Abraham believed that if Isaac died, God would raise him from the dead. Abraham has passed the test, and as he lifts his eyes he sees a ram caught in a thicket, which he then offers as a sacrifice to God (22:13). In verses 16–18, God emphatically reaffirms his promises to bless Abraham, to multiply his offspring, and to bless all the nations of the earth.

Genesis 22:20–25:11 serves as an epilogue to the story of Abraham. Here we read of the death of Sarah (23:2) and Abraham's purchase of a burial plot for her in the field of Machpelah in the land of Canaan (23:19). This small piece of land is the first part of Canaan to be owned by Abraham. His purchase is the first step toward the fulfillment of God's promise to give all of the land to Abraham and his offspring. The story of the marriage of Isaac to Rebekah is then told in Genesis 24. And in Genesis 25, we read

119. Wenham 1994, 86–87.

120. Wenham 1994, 113. See also Kierkegaard 1983.

of the death of Abraham. When he was 175 years old, "Abraham breathed his last and died in a good old age, an old man and full of years, and was gathered to his people" (25:8).[121] He did not live to see the fulfillment of all of God's promises, but he died in faith, and those promises remained the framework of God's eschatological plan of redemption.

Jacob: Conflict and Blessing

The story of Abraham is followed by a brief genealogy, "the generations [*toledot*] of Ishmael," in the seventh section of Genesis (25:12–18). The eighth section of Genesis (25:19–35:29) is the second major part of the patriarchal history: the story of Jacob. This story begins with God's revelation to Rebekah, the bride of Isaac, concerning the two children struggling in her womb (25:21–22). God declares to Rebekah, "Two nations are in your womb, and two peoples from within you shall be divided; the one shall be stronger than the other, the older shall serve the younger" (v. 23). Eventually Rebekah gives birth to twin boys. Esau is born first, and his brother Jacob is born second, holding on to Esau's heel (vv. 25–26). Esau grows up to be a skillful hunter, while Jacob is said to be "a quiet man, dwelling in tents" (v. 27). Isaac loves Esau, but Rebekah loves Jacob (v. 28).

Esau displays a rash and foolish attitude early in the narrative when he is persuaded by Jacob to sell him his birthright in exchange for bread and a bowl of stew (25:29–34). Already God's revelation to Rebekah is beginning to be fulfilled. In Genesis 26, God reaffirms to Isaac the promises made to Abraham, promises of a multitude of offspring, of land, of personal blessing, and the promise that in his offspring all the nations of the earth will be blessed (vv. 2–5). In his old age, Isaac prepares to bless Esau, but Rebekah makes plans to ensure that Jacob receives the blessing instead (Gen. 27:1–17). The entire story presupposes the belief of Isaac and Jacob in the efficacy of the patriarchal blessing. As Wenham explains, "Clearly, Genesis sees the deathbed blessing as more than a prayer for the future; it is a prophecy whose fulfillment is certain."[122] After deceiving Isaac in order to receive the blessing (27:18–29), Jacob is forced to flee to his uncle Laban because his brother Esau now intends to kill him (27:41–28:5).

121. The words, "gathered to his people" indicates a belief in the soul's continued life after the death of the body.

122. Wenham 1994, 216.

During his journey from Beersheba toward Haran, Jacob has a dream in which God reveals himself and reaffirms the covenant promises. Jacob renames the place Bethel, which means "the house of God" (28:10–22). Upon reaching the home of his uncle Laban, Jacob encounters Laban's daughter Rachel and agrees to work for seven years in order to marry her. At the end of the seven years, however, Jacob is tricked into marrying Rachel's older sister Leah instead. Although extremely unhappy about the situation, he agrees to work another seven years for Rachel (29:1–30). Genesis 29:31–30:24 narrates the birth of Jacob's first eleven sons and one daughter. The birth of Joseph to Rachel who, like Sarah and Rebekah, has been barren (29:31; cf. 11:30; 25:21), is the turning point of the narrative.[123]

Despite Laban's every effort, Jacob prospers (30:25–43) and is finally commanded by God to leave Laban and return to his home (31:1–3). During his return journey, Jacob has a strange encounter. A man wrestles with him, but Jacob realizes that the man is more than he appears to be for he declares that he will not release the man unless he receives a blessing from him (32:22–26). The man then tells Jacob that his name will no longer be Jacob, but Israel instead, "for you have striven with God and with men, and have prevailed" (v. 28). Jacob's new name Israel means "He strives with God," and it was to become the name of the nation descended from Jacob's sons.

After a surprising reunion with his brother Esau, a reunion that demonstrates to Jacob something of the divine nature of forgiveness (33:1–11), Jacob continues on his journey until he reaches the city of Shechem (v. 18). He is told by God to go to Bethel (35:1), and after arriving there, God reaffirms the covenant promises and confirms that Jacob's name is now Israel (vv. 9–12). Jacob's beloved wife Rachel dies giving birth to Benjamin during their journey from Bethel to Ephrath (vv. 16–20). The story of Jacob then ends with the death of his father Isaac (vv. 28–29). God has reaffirmed his promises to Jacob, but at this point in history they remain largely unfulfilled, forcing us to look toward the future, to Jacob's sons.

Joseph: From Canaan to Egypt

Jacob's story is followed by "the generations [*toledot*] of Esau," the ninth section of Genesis (36:1–37:1). It provides a genealogy of Isaac's older son.

123. Wenham 1994, 170.

The third major part of the patriarchal history, however, begins at 37:2 with the tenth and final section of Genesis: the story of Joseph. This lengthy narrative provides a transitional link between the history of the patriarchs and the exodus of Israel from Egypt. It relates how the tribes of Israel came to be in Egypt and demonstrates God's providential outworking of his plans. The story shows the beginning of the fulfillment of God's promise to make Abraham's offspring as numerous as the stars of heaven, and it shows the beginning of the fulfillment of God's promise to bless all the families of the earth through Abraham's offspring.

Like the first two major parts of the patriarchal history, the story of Joseph begins with a revelation from God, two dreams in which Joseph sees a symbolic representation of his brothers bowing down to him (37:5–11). His brothers, provoked to jealousy by his dreams and by the favoritism shown to Joseph by their father, sell Joseph to Midianite traders who then sell him to the Egyptians (vv. 12–36). Upon arriving in Egypt, Joseph becomes a slave in the house of Potiphar and is so successful that he is put in charge of the entire household (39:1–6). Because of false accusations by Potiphar's wife, however, Joseph is unjustly imprisoned (vv. 7–20), but God remains with him and even in prison he is given responsibility (vv. 21–23).

In prison, Joseph interprets the dreams of two fellow prisoners, Pharaoh's cupbearer and baker, and his interpretations are ultimately proven to be accurate (40:1–23). Two years later, Pharaoh himself begins to have disturbing dreams that no one is able to interpret. His cupbearer, who had since been released from prison, remembers Joseph, who is then brought before Pharaoh in order to see if he will be able to interpret these dreams (41:1–24). Joseph does interpret the dreams, telling Pharaoh that after seven years of great abundance there will be seven years of severe famine. He advises Pharaoh to put someone in charge of gathering and saving food during the seven years of abundance to prepare for the seven years of famine (vv. 25–36). Pharaoh names Joseph to this position of responsibility, and when the famine comes, the people of Egypt and many other nations are saved from starvation because of Joseph's efforts (vv. 37–57). Already God is using Abraham's offspring to bless the families of the earth.

After a number of years, Joseph is reconciled with his brothers and reunited with his father, and the entire family moves to Egypt because of the severity of the famine (42:1–46:34). By the time the family of Jacob enters Egypt they number seventy.[124] Once in Egypt, the family of Jacob settles in the fertile land of Goshen, and they begin to prosper and multiply (47:1–28). As Jacob nears death, he has Joseph swear to him that he will not bury Jacob in Egypt but will return him to the land of promise for burial (vv. 29–31). Jacob understands that Egypt is not his true home (cf. 50:25).

As Jacob draws close to death, he gathers his sons together to pronounce his last words concerning them (Gen. 49). As John Sailhamer notes, this is the first of three places in the Pentateuch where the author inserts a lengthy poetic section at the close of a long narrative (cf. Num. 24; Deut. 32–33). All three poetic sections have certain features in common. Sailhamer explains, "In each of the three segments, the central narrative figure (Jacob, Balaam, Moses) calls an audience together (imperative: Ge 49:1; Nu 24:14; Dt 31:28) and proclaims (cohortative: Ge 49:1; Nu 24:14; Dt 31:28) what will happen (Ge 49:1; Nu 24:14; Dt 31:29) in 'the end of days' (Ge 49:1; Nu 24:14; Dt 31:29)."[125]

Jacob says to his sons at this time, "Gather yourselves together, that I may tell you what shall happen to you in days to come" (Gen. 49:1).[126] The meaning of the phrase "days to come" or "the latter days" (cf. Num. 24:14) must be determined by its context. In general, as Allen Ross explains, it "should be interpreted to mean an undetermined time in the future, early or late (cf. Dan. 2:28–29, 45; Ezek. 38:16; Jer. 23:20)."[127] Jacob speaks to all of his sons, but it is his words to Judah that are most significant for our understanding of biblical eschatology (Gen. 49:8–12). Jacob's words to Judah anticipate the rise of the Davidic king and more.

In Genesis 49:10, Jacob says, "The scepter shall not depart from Judah, nor the ruler's staff from between his feet, until tribute comes to him; and to him shall be the obedience of the peoples." This verse is considered by some to be the first clearly messianic prophecy in the Old Testament.[128] The precise translation of the words "until tribute comes to him" is disputed because of the ambiguity of the Hebrew, but as Wenham notes, "all at least agree that this line is predicting the rise of the Davidic monarchy

124. This is the same number of nations found in the table of nations in Genesis 10.

125. Sailhamer 1992, 36.

126. "In days to come" is a translation of the Hebrew בְּאַחֲרִית הַיָּמִים (*be'aharit hayyamim*).

127. Ross 1988, 700; see also Wenham 1994, 471.

128. E.g., Dumbrell 1994, 37.

and the establishment of the Israelite empire, if not the coming of a greater David."[129] The main point of Jacob's words to Judah is that the scepter, a symbol of kingship, would belong to the tribe of Judah until the coming of the one to whom such royal status truly belongs. In the Old Testament, this prophecy is initially fulfilled by David. In the New Testament, it is fully and finally fulfilled by Jesus Christ, the Son of David and the Lion of the tribe of Judah (Matt. 1:1; Rev. 5:5).

Summary

Genesis is the book of first things, but it is nevertheless essential for an understanding of the last things. Later eschatological texts presuppose a grasp of the many themes and concepts introduced in Genesis. It is in Genesis that we are introduced to the major eschatological themes of kingdom and covenant, blessing and cursing, promise and fulfillment. It is in Genesis that we find the first hints of a coming Messiah who will crush the head of the serpent and redeem his people.

In Genesis, we learn that the entire universe and all that is in it was created *ex nihilo* by God. He is the Great King, the Creator who is sovereign over all, and everything exists for his glory. Genesis also teaches that the original creation was declared by God to be good, and thus the Bible consistently rejects any assumption that the physical material world is inherently evil or corrupt. Its present corruption is a result of the fall.

The first chapters of Genesis teach us that human beings were created in the image of God for union and communion with God. God gave man dominion indicating his creational plan to establish his kingdom on earth. God's desire for man at creation was to bless him and commune with him, and the garden was the place of God's special presence with man. Another theme important to biblical eschatology that is introduced in the creation narratives is that of God's rest. His creative work moved toward the goal of blessed rest.

In the early chapters of Genesis, God also reveals how the good creation came to be in the state we find it in today. Man's disobedience and fall into sin resulted in God's judgment upon man. The introduction of sin into human history led to God's curse and the introduction of death, and man was removed from Eden. Sin and its results are revealed in Genesis to be

129. Wenham 1994, 478. See Ezekiel 21:27 for a similar text.

the problem in man and in the world. In the narrative of the fall, Genesis also introduces the serpent who is a tool of Satan, the archenemy of God. Satan becomes the "ruler" of the world, usurping the dominion God gave to man. But God promises that there will be perpetual conflict between the seed of the serpent and the seed of the woman, and that Satan will ultimately be destroyed. He will not thwart God's purposes. He will be overthrown, and God's kingdom will be established.

The remaining chapters of Genesis explain how sin and death spread and how God's judgment and grace were initially revealed. With the call of Abraham, the book of Genesis introduces God's plan for the restoration of blessing to man. God makes a number of promises to Abraham, promises of land, and offspring, and personal blessing. And all of these promises are given in order to fulfill another promise, namely, that through Abraham and his offspring, God will bless all the families of the earth.

The promise of land is particularly significant in the Pentateuch and in the Former Prophets. The land promise indicates that God has not abandoned his plan to establish his kingdom on earth. The Abrahamic covenant, then, is a statement of God's purposes, that which he will certainly accomplish—the redemption and blessing of man and the establishment of God's kingdom. The remainder of the book of Genesis traces the partial fulfillment of God's promises through the families of Abraham, Isaac, and Jacob. By the end of Genesis, however, Abraham's offspring are found living in Egypt far from the land of promise.

2

The Pentateuch (2)

Exodus to Deuteronomy

Within the book of Genesis, chapters 1–11 serve as a prologue to the patriarchal history of chapters 12–50. Within the Pentateuch as a whole, the book of Genesis serves a similar function. It introduces the irrevocable covenant that God made with Abraham, Isaac, and Jacob. It explains how the sons of Israel came to be in Egypt. It sets the stage, as it were, for the defining moment in Israel's history, the exodus from Egypt and the giving of the law at Mount Sinai. However, whereas the book of Genesis covers thousands of years of history and centers on the stories of a handful of individuals, the remaining four books of the Pentateuch slow down the narrative pace. The events in these books take place within the lifetime of one man, Moses. Genesis revealed God's promises to Abraham. The promise of a son has already been fulfilled. The books of Exodus through Deuteronomy reveal God beginning to fulfill the remaining promises.

Exodus

Because the Pentateuch is a single literary unit, each of its five books must be understood in relation to the others. Peter Enns helpfully suggests that Exodus be read as one of five chapters of a single book, rather than as a separate and isolated book.[1] It is a record of one stage in the larger history of Israel recounted in the Pentateuch. It is a "sequel" to Genesis.[2] The connection between the two books is clear. In Genesis 15:13, God had revealed to Abraham that his descendants would be afflicted in a foreign land for four hundred years. In Genesis 50:24, Joseph had told his brothers in Egypt that God would deliver them and bring them to the land he had promised to Abraham, Isaac, and Jacob (cf. Gen. 46:4). Genesis, then, anticipates Exodus, and Exodus continues the story begun in Genesis.

The book of Exodus does not have the same kind of obvious structural markers found in Genesis, but it may be divided into three major sections. In Exodus 1–18, God redeems Israel from bondage in Egypt. In chapters 19–24, God gives Israel the law at Mount Sinai. In chapters 25–40, God prepares Israel for his holy presence by providing instructions for the tabernacle and for the priesthood. The first eighteen chapters of Exodus, then, are primarily historical narrative. Chapters 19–40, on the other hand, are primarily a record of the laws and instructions that God gave to Israel at Mount Sinai. Throughout the book as a whole, there are a number of significant eschatological themes.

God's Redemption of Israel (Ex. 1–18)

The book of Exodus begins where the book of Genesis ends, with the sons of Israel in Egypt. However, when the book of Exodus begins, Israel has been in Egypt for over four hundred years (Ex. 12:40). They have multiplied greatly, demonstrating that God is already fulfilling his promises to Abraham (Ex. 1:7; Gen. 13:16; 15:5; 22:17). Their great numbers, however, initiate a chain of events leading to the exodus. As the book of Exodus begins, Joseph is long dead, and Egypt is under a new Pharaoh. He sees Israel's great numbers as a threat (Ex. 1:9). Israel is, therefore, forced into slavery in Egypt and suffers greatly. The oppression of Israel does not, however, stop their multiplication (1:12). Because of this, Pharaoh instructs

1. Enns 2000, 40; see also Stuart 2006, 20.

2. Sarna 1996, 5.

the midwives to kill all newborn Israelite males (1:15–16). When this plan too is thwarted, Pharaoh commands the Egyptian people to drown all newborn Hebrew males in the Nile (1:22). Pharaoh has thus set himself against God's people and against God's plan.

Exodus 2 introduces us to Moses. He is born into the tribe of Levi (2:1–2), and from the moment of his birth he is in danger because of the genocidal decrees of Pharaoh. In order to save her infant son, his mother builds a small basket and hides him among the reeds in the river. In a truly ironic twist, he is rescued by the daughter of Pharaoh, and his own biological mother is made his nurse (2:3–10). The daughter of Pharaoh names this Hebrew boy Moses. The book of Exodus does not reveal anything further about Moses' early years. Instead it moves to a point of crisis in Moses' life after he has reached adulthood. One day, he witnesses an Egyptian beating a Hebrew, and he kills the Egyptian (2:11–12). Moses soon discovers that what he has done has become known to the people and to Pharaoh, so he flees from Egypt into the land of Midian where he settles and marries (2:13–22).

Eventually, Pharaoh dies, but the suffering and oppression of the people of Israel continue, and they cry out for rescue (2:23). The response to this cry is crucial for an understanding of the book of Exodus: "God heard their groaning, and God remembered his covenant with Abraham, with Isaac, and with Jacob" (2:24). What this means is that the coming redemption of Israel from Egypt is grounded in the already existing Abrahamic covenant. God had specifically promised the salvation of Israel from Egyptian bondage in his covenant with Abraham (Gen. 15:13–14). Now he is about to fulfill that promise.

Exodus 3:1–4:17 tells the story of the call of Moses. The angel of the Lord appears to Moses in a burning bush at Mount Horeb/Sinai (3:1–2). As one who is both distinguished from God and yet equated with God (v. 4), the angel of the Lord prefigures Jesus Christ (see John 1:1).[3] God reveals himself to Moses as "the God of Abraham, the God of Isaac, and the God of Jacob" (Ex. 3:6). On the basis of Jesus' use of these words in Matthew 22:31–32, R. Alan Cole notes that this text, "early and unselfconscious though it is, is the beginning of the revelation of life after death."[4]

3. For other biblical passages on the angel of the Lord, see, for example, Gen. 16:7, 9, 11; 22:15; 31:11, 13; Num. 22:22–35; Judg. 2:1–5; 6:11–23; Zech. 3:1–6; 12:8.

4. Cole 1973, 27.

The truth about the afterlife, hinted at here, is progressively revealed throughout Scripture.

God tells Moses that he has seen the affliction of his people in Egypt and that he has come down to deliver them and bring them up to Canaan (Ex. 3:7–8). He commissions Moses to go to Pharaoh in order to bring the people out of Egypt (vv. 9–12). Moses then asks what he should tell the people of Israel if they should ask the name of the God who has sent him to them (v. 13). What is God's response? "God said to Moses, 'I AM WHO I AM.' And he said, 'Say this to the people of Israel, "I AM has sent me to you"'" (v. 14).[5] He continues, "Say this to the people of Israel, 'Yahweh, the God of your fathers, the God of Abraham, the God of Isaac, and the God of Jacob, has sent me to you.' This is my name forever, and thus I am to be remembered throughout all generations" (v. 15).[6] The God who is present with Israel is the God who is, and he is the God of their fathers. Despite Moses' protestations, God sends him to Egypt to deliver his people from slavery (3:15–4:17).

Moses returns to Egypt, and he and his brother Aaron declare to the people of Israel that God has seen their affliction and will soon deliver them (4:18–31). He has been instructed to tell Pharaoh to release Israel, God's "firstborn son," and to tell him that if he refuses to let Israel go, God will kill his firstborn son (vv. 22–23).[7] When Moses demands Israel's release, however, Pharaoh refuses and oppresses Israel even more harshly (5:1–19). The Israelites complain bitterly to Moses, initiating a pattern that continues throughout the book of Exodus (5:20–21; 6:9–12; 14:11–12; 15:24; 16; 17:1–7; 32). Despite their complaints, God remains faithful to his promise to deliver Israel (6:1–13), a promise that is grounded in his covenant with Abraham.[8] Pharaoh's refusal to let Israel go, however, initiates a series of plagues that God sends in judgment upon Egypt (chs. 7–12).[9]

The literary structure of Exodus divides the plagues into three groups of three. The tenth and final plague is a climax to the entire series.[10] The first

5. "I AM WHO I AM" (v. 14a) is a translation of the Hebrew אֶהְיֶה אֲשֶׁר אֶהְיֶה (*'ehyeh 'asher 'ehyeh*), while "I AM" (v. 14b) is a translation of the Hebrew אֶהְיֶה (*'ehyeh*).

6. For more on the meaning of the divine name Yahweh, see *NIDOTTE*, 4:1295–1300.

7. Cole 1973, 78; Motyer 2005, 91.

8. McComiskey 1985a, 67.

9. These plagues are more than a judgment upon Egypt, however. They are also a judgment upon Egypt's false gods (Ex. 12:12; Num. 33:4).

10. Enns 2000, 208.

series of judgments involves plagues of blood, frogs, and gnats (7:1–8:19). The second series involves plagues of flies, the death of livestock, and boils (8:20–9:12). The third series involves plagues of hail, locusts, and darkness (9:13–10:29).[11] In several of these plagues, God specifically distinguishes between the people of Israel and the people of Egypt (8:23; 9:4, 26; 10:23). However, despite God's demonstration of his power, Pharaoh continues to harden his heart and refuses to let Israel go. His refusal sets the stage for the tenth and final plague.

The description of the tenth plague is different in that it is intimately connected with the institution of the Passover. Exodus 11:1–13:16, therefore, should be understood as a single unit of text.[12] In Exodus 11, God reveals to Moses that after the final plague Pharaoh will let Israel go (v. 1). God tells Moses that he is going to come in person into the midst of Egypt and that every firstborn will die, but God reassures Moses that he will make a distinction between Egypt and Israel (vv. 4–7). As Alec Motyer explains, "when Yahweh entered Egypt as absolute Lord and Judge, Israel's problem was no longer how to escape Pharaoh but how to be safe before such a God."[13]

In chapter 12, God gives Moses the instructions for the Passover ceremony that will distinguish Israel from Egypt. God tells Moses that this month will now be the first month of the year for Israel (v. 2). This night will commemorate Israel's birth as a nation.[14] Each household is to take a lamb without blemish and keep it until the fourteenth day of the month at which point it shall be killed (vv. 3–6). The lamb's blood is then to be placed on the doorposts and lintel of the houses, and the families in the houses are to eat the roasted flesh of the lamb (vv. 7–11). God tells Moses that on this night he will pass through Egypt and strike down the firstborn of the Egyptians, but he will pass over the houses marked with the sign of the lamb's blood (vv. 12–13). In earlier plagues, the Lord had distinguished between Egypt and Israel without any action on the part of Israel. Now Israel "must take a stand, self-declared as the people under the blood of the

11. Hail, locusts, and darkness become regularly associated with God's judgment throughout Scripture (Deut. 28:38; Josh. 10:11; 2 Chron. 7:13; Ps. 18:12; Isa. 8:22; 28:2, 17; 30:30; Ezek. 13:11–13; 38:22; Joel 1:1–12; 2:2).

12. Enns 2000, 244.

13. Motyer 2005, 132.

14. Sailhamer 1992, 259; Durham 1987, 153.

lamb."[15] The Passover lamb, then, becomes a substitute for Israel, God's firstborn son (cf. 4:22; 1 Cor. 5:7).[16]

In Exodus 12:14–20, God instructs Israel regarding how to commemorate this redemptive event throughout her generations. On the appointed day, Moses commands the people of Israel to do as the Lord had instructed them and to kill the Passover lamb (vv. 21–28). At midnight God himself comes into Egypt and strikes down every firstborn in Egypt including the firstborn of Pharaoh (vv. 29–30; cf. 4:22–23). Pharaoh summons Moses and Aaron and finally consents to let Israel go (vv. 31–32). After 430 years, Israel is brought up out of Egypt by God (vv. 33–42).[17] God then gives Moses final instructions regarding the Passover, telling him that no foreigner may partake of it unless he is circumcised. Those foreigners who are circumcised shall be considered as a native of the land (vv. 43–51).

Exodus 13 describes the consecration of all the firstborn of Israel, the feast of unleavened bread, and God's guidance of Israel through the wilderness by means of a pillar of cloud by day and fire by night. Exodus 14 then tells of Israel's crossing of the Red Sea and the destruction of the pursuing Egyptian armies.[18] The redemption of Israel from Egypt is celebrated in song in Exodus 15. God is there described as a warrior fighting for Israel (15:3).[19] Throughout the remainder of the Old Testament, the exodus event is seen as the birth of the nation of Israel, as a paradigm of God's past and future saving acts, and as a permanent part of Israel's self-identity.[20] The covenantal unity of the people is such that later generations are spoken to as if they were the ones who experienced the exodus event firsthand (see, e.g., Amos 2:10; 3:1).

15. Motyer 2005, 127.

16. Motyer 2005, 137.

17. The exact dating of the exodus from Egypt is disputed among historians. Some argue for a date in the thirteenth century B.C. Others, including the present author, believe the exodus occurred in the fifteenth century B.C. If 1 Kings 6:1 is taken literally (and there is no compelling reason why it should not be), a date in the fifteenth century is required. For an explanation of this and other arguments in support of the fifteenth century date, see Dillard and Longman 1994, 59–62.

18. The precise route of the exodus and the exact location of the "Red Sea" are not certain because many of the locations cited in the description of Israel's journey have not been conclusively identified.

19. For more on this important theme, see Longman and Reid 1995.

20. There are literally dozens of such passages (e.g., Josh. 24:6; Judg. 6:8; 1 Sam. 10:18; 2 Sam. 7:23; 2 Kings 17:36; Pss. 66:1–7; 81:10; 105:37–38; Isa. 11:16; 43; Jer. 16:14–15; 23:7–8).

God's Law for Israel (Ex. 19–24)

Three months after the exodus, the people of Israel finally arrive at Mount Sinai (19:1–2; cf. 3:12).[21] They will remain there for almost a year (Num. 10:11). The Sinai narrative is central to the Pentateuch. It occupies a total of a little over fifty-eight chapters (Ex. 19–Num. 10:10). There are sixty-eight chapters preceding the Sinai narrative in the Pentateuch and a little over 60 chapters following it. The events that occur at Sinai, therefore, occupy approximately the entire middle third of the Torah.[22]

After arriving at Sinai, Moses ascends the mountain, and in Exodus 19:4–6, God tells him what to say to Israel: "You yourselves have seen what I did to the Egyptians, and how I bore you on eagles' wings and brought you to myself. Now therefore, if you will indeed obey my voice and keep my covenant, you shall be my treasured possession among all peoples, for all the earth is mine; and you shall be to me a kingdom of priests and a holy nation." God has kept the promises he made to Abraham concerning his people. He has now made of Abraham a great nation (cf. Gen. 12:2). He has now brought that nation up out of Egypt (cf. Gen. 15:13–14). This great nation is now to be a kingdom of priests and a holy nation. As a holy nation, Israel is to demonstrate through her holiness what it means to be God's people.[23] As a kingdom of priests, Israel is also to be a mediator of God's blessing to the nations.[24] In order to be a kingdom of priests, Israel must be a holy nation because in order to be a blessing to the nations, Israel must live in a way that is different from the nations (Deut. 4:6–8).

The words "for all the earth is mine" in Exodus 19:5 are important because they indicate the purpose for which Israel was chosen. As William Dumbrell explains, "Such a concept would draw us back to the intent of the Abrahamic covenant which this section restates, namely that Israel is the agent used by God to achieve the wider purposes which the Abrahamic covenant entails, purposes which involve the redemption

21. The precise location of Mount Sinai/Horeb is also unknown. Based on biblical descriptions of Midian, it could be located somewhere in the present-day Sinai peninsula, or it could be located east of the Gulf of Aqaba in present-day Saudi Arabia (see Gal. 4:25).

22. Dempster 2003, 100–101.

23. Dumbrell 1994, 45; Durham 1987, 263.

24. Christopher J. H. Wright (2005, 65) explains: "As the people of YHWH they would have the historical task of bringing the knowledge of God to the nations, and bringing the nations to the means of atonement with God."

of the whole world."[25] We recall that God's creational purpose involved the establishment of his kingdom throughout the earth. The nation of Israel is to be a manifestation of God's kingdom in one small corner of the earth as well as a type of the worldwide eschatological kingdom that he will later establish. God is to be Israel's King, and Israel is to be his people.

It is important to remember that God has already made a covenant with the people of Israel in the covenant he made with Abraham and his offspring. The giving of the law in the following chapters of Exodus does not annul or replace the Abrahamic covenant (Gal. 3:15–20).[26] God had promised Abraham that he would make him a great nation (Gen. 12:2). Now that Israel, the offspring of Abraham, is a great nation, God will give the law that Israel will need as a nation under his reign.[27] The law will serve a number of functions. It will serve, for example, as a "guardian" until Messiah comes (Gal. 3:24–25). The law will also define "the holiness demanded of the covenant people."[28] The Abrahamic covenant promised the realm and the people for the kingdom of priests. The Mosaic covenant provides the law for this manifestation of the kingdom as well as the tabernacle for the presence of the divine King.

Moses sets before the people of Israel all that God reveals to him, and the people promise that they will do these things (Ex. 19:7–8). God then tells Moses to consecrate the people because he is going to "come down on Mount Sinai in the sight of all the people" (v. 11). The people are to prepare for the coming of the Lord. On the third day, a loud trumpet blast sounds, and God descends on the mountain in smoke and fire (vv. 16–20). This is a crucial theophany in the Old Testament, and it is continued in Exodus 20.[29]

25. Dumbrell 1984, 89.

26. Robertson 1980, 174; Fretheim 1990, 209; Baker 2005, 25.

27. The Hebrew word translated "law" is תּוֹרָה (*torah*). In the Old Testament, the word is used in a variety of ways. It is used to refer to ceremonial regulations (e.g., Lev. 7:7; Num. 15:29); civil, social, and legal regulations (e.g., Deut. 17:11; 2 Chron. 19:10); and instruction for godly living (e.g., Ps. 78; Prov. 3:1; 13:14). It is also used more generally to refer to the content of the book of Deuteronomy (e.g., Deut. 4:44) or to the Mosaic legislation as a whole (e.g., Josh. 1:7). Torah, then, "is instruction, whether cultic or civil, whether in the form of specific legal stipulations or less formal words of guidance from parent to child, whether a clearly defined corpus such as the book of Deuteronomy or *tôrôt* that are less easy to define precisely" (*NIDOTTE*, 4:897).

28. Childs 1974, 383.

29. On this important theme, see Niehaus 1995.

In Exodus 20:1–17, God reveals the Decalogue, the Ten Commandments. The prologue to the commandments in verse 2 is significant. God says, "I am Yahweh your God, who brought you out of the land of Egypt, out of the house of slavery." As Motyer explains, "The people were given the law not in order that they might become the redeemed, rather it was because they had already been redeemed that they were given the law."[30] God had graciously redeemed Israel from Egypt because, as O. Palmer Robertson notes, Israel "already was in a covenantal relationship with the Lord through Abraham."[31] The law, then, expresses God's will for Israel at this point in her history. It was the tool God would use to teach Israel how to live as a holy people in his presence.[32] And because it expressed the nature of God, Israel's obedience to the law was to be a witness to the nations of God's holy character (Deut. 4:6–7; Ps. 147:20).[33]

The first four commandments explain God's will for Israel's relationship with himself. The first commandment forbids the worship of any other gods (Ex. 20:3). The second commandment forbids idolatry (vv. 4–6). The third commandment forbids the misuse of God's holy name (v. 7). The fourth commandment requires Israel to observe the seventh day as a Sabbath (vv. 8–11).[34] The final six commandments explain God's will for social relationships. The fifth commandment requires the honoring

30. Motyer 2005, 213; see also Vos 1948, 127.

31. Robertson 1980, 171. Dumbrell 1984, 91, elaborates, "When given, the ten commandments are an elaboration of what is involved in the keeping of the relationship to which 19:4 has referred. The point here is that the giving of the law presupposes the framework of grace in which it can be received. This much is clear from 20:2–3 where appeal is made firstly to the fact of redemption before the demands to which the relationship points are advanced. Thus the law cannot be received by Israel unless Israelites are first addressed and are reminded of the state of grace in which they stand. Covenant loyalty is now specified in the ten commandments (the Decalogue) in terms of the life goals which must be implemented if covenant experience is to be enjoyed and maintained. The divine commitment to Israel will be unvaried and unvariable, but Israel's experience of divine blessing within her national life will depend upon the measure by which the divine will expressed through law is realised in her national experience. The call of the Decalogue is thus to translate faith into action, and the ten commandments will have no force unless they serve always to point back to the redemption which is their presupposition."

32. VanGemeren 1988a, 176.

33. Poythress 1995, 56.

34. The Israelites are told to remember the Sabbath because "in six days Yahweh made heaven and earth, the sea, and all that is in them, and rested the seventh day" (v. 11). As Dumbrell (1984, 35) explains, the Sabbath "which brings to an end the week becomes for Israel an invitation to enter into, and rejoice in, the blessings of creation." And, "in pointing back to creation, the Sabbath points also to what is yet to be, to the final destiny to which all creation is moving."

of parents (v. 12). The sixth commandment forbids murder (v. 13). The seventh commandment forbids adultery (v. 14). The eighth commandment forbids theft (v. 15). The ninth commandment forbids the bearing of false witness against a neighbor (v. 16). Finally, the tenth commandment forbids covetousness (v. 17).

Exodus 20:22–23:33 is commonly referred to as the Book of the Covenant. This section of Scripture contains a number of laws on a diverse range of subjects including altars (20:22–26), slaves (21:1–11), restitution (21:33–22:15), social justice (22:16–23:9), and the Sabbath (23:10–12). Exodus 24 then narrates the story of the confirmation of the covenant. After Moses reveals all of the words of God to the people, they answer in unison, "All the words that Yahweh has spoken, we will do" (24:3). Burnt offerings and peace offerings are sacrificed, and the blood is sprinkled on the altar (vv. 4–6). Moses then reads the Book of the Covenant to the people, who agree once again to do what the Lord has required. He then sprinkles blood on them, saying, "Behold the blood of the covenant that Yahweh has made with you in accordance with all these words" (vv. 7–8). Moses, Aaron, Nadab, Abihu, and seventy elders of Israel then ascend the mountain and partake of a covenant meal in the presence of the Lord (vv. 9–11).[35]

The law of God is "holy and righteous and good" (Rom. 7:12; Ps. 119). But the true nature and purpose of the law were not always understood in Israel. Those who believed that men were redeemed by keeping the law misunderstood the law. God gave the law to a people he had already graciously redeemed. The law described the righteousness that God required of this already redeemed nation. It explained what it meant for his people to be a holy nation and a kingdom of priests. In doing so, it also revealed sin (Rom. 3:20; 7:7). Those who rejected the transitory nature of the Mosaic administration of the law also misunderstood it.[36] The law was a guardian until Christ came (Gal. 3:19, 24). As Robertson explains, many Israelites were so impressed with the real glories of God's law that they became blind "to the temporary character of the Mosaic administration of law."[37] The law pointed forward to Christ, and it is only in Christ that we understand the law's true nature, purpose, and goal.

35. Enns 2000, 492.
36. Robertson 1980, 194.
37. Robertson 1980, 197.

God's Tabernacle in Israel (Ex. 25–40)

The remaining chapters of Exodus focus primarily on the tabernacle. Exodus 25–31 contains God's instructions to Moses regarding the plans for the tabernacle. Chapters 35–40 contain the record of its actual construction. Between these two accounts is the story of Israel's idolatrous worship of the golden calf and the renewal of the covenant following this act of rebellion (Ex. 32–34). The importance of the tabernacle for Israel rests in the fact that it was to be a sanctuary for the presence of the divine King in the midst of Israel, his kingdom of priests and holy nation.[38] It was the place where God would dwell among his chosen people (Ex. 25:8; 29:45–46).[39] It is important to recognize the relationship between the law and the tabernacle. The tabernacle, along with its priesthood and sacrifices, was part of the law revealed through Moses. God's provision of the tabernacle in this context meant that "those who were called to obey had at the centre of their life an established availability of grace to cater for their lapses from obedience."[40] The sacrifices available in the tabernacle, however, were only shadows. They could not, in themselves, take away sin (Heb. 10:4).

Exodus 25–31, which outlines God's instructions for the tabernacle, contains seven distinct sections. Each begins with the words "Yahweh said to Moses . . ." (25:1; 30:11, 17, 22, 34; 31:1, 12).[41] The seventh such section contains instructions regarding the Sabbath. This may be an attempt by the author to connect the tabernacle with the creation narrative in Genesis 1:1–2:3. Others have noted similarities between the tabernacle and the garden of Eden. T. D. Alexander, for example, observes that God walks in Eden as he does in the tabernacle (Gen. 3:8; Lev. 26:12; Deut. 23:14; 2 Sam. 7:6–7); that Eden and the later sanctuaries are both entered from the east and guarded by cherubim (Gen. 3:24; Ex. 25:18–22; 26:31; 1 Kings 6:23–29); that the lampstand is possibly a symbol of the tree of life (Gen. 2:9; 3:22; Ex. 25:31–35); that the verbs used in God's command to work and take care of the garden (Gen. 2:15) are used in combination elsewhere in the Pentateuch only to describe the duties of the Levites in the sanctuary (Num. 3:7–8; 8:26; 18:5–6); that the river flowing from Eden (Gen. 2:10) is similar to the river seen flowing from the future temple in

38. Dumbrell 1984, 104.
39. Motyer 2005, 251; VanGemeren 1990, 87.
40. Motyer 2005, 261.
41. Sarna 1996, 213.

Ezekiel 47:1–12; and that the gold and onyx found in the garden (Gen. 2:11–12) are used in Exodus (25:7, 11, 17, 31) to decorate the sanctuary and the priestly garments.[42] Noting these kinds of parallels, John Sailhamer describes the tabernacle as "a reconstruction of God's good creation."[43]

According to Exodus 25:9, Moses is instructed to build the tabernacle according to the pattern that God will reveal to him (25:40; 26:30; 27:8). The tabernacle, then, is a symbol that points to a greater reality. As Hebrews 8:5 explains, the tabernacle is "a copy and shadow of the heavenly things." Vern Poythress suggests that "the tabernacle as a whole is a replica of heaven."[44] Gregory Beale, however, argues that the Holy of Holies alone specifically represents the heavenly dwelling place of God and that the tabernacle as a whole symbolically represents the entire cosmos.[45] Beale also argues that the tabernacle serves a specific eschatological purpose in that it was "designed to point to the cosmic eschatological reality that God's tabernacling presence, formerly limited to the holy of holies, was to be extended throughout the whole earth."[46] What is beyond question is that the tabernacle "showed what God was like and what was needed to deal with sin."[47] At the very least, then, we may affirm that the tabernacle foreshadows the redemptive work of the Messiah.

The tabernacle is divided into three sections (fig. 1). At the center is the Most Holy Place, a room measuring 10 cubits by 10 cubits.[48] It contains the ark of the covenant (Ex. 25:10–22; 26:34). Separated from the Most Holy Place by a veil is the Holy Place, a room measuring 10 cubits by 20 cubits and containing the table for bread, the golden lampstand, and the altar of incense (26:33–35; see also 25:23–40; 30:1–10). The Most Holy Place and the Holy Place are within a tent, and surrounding this tent is a courtyard measuring 50 cubits by 100 cubits (27:9–19). The courtyard contains the bronze altar (27:1–8) and the bronze basin for washing (30:17–21). At the east end of the courtyard is the entrance (27:16).

42. Alexander 2002, 131; see also Beale 2004, 66–80.

43. Sailhamer 1992, 299.

44. Poythress 1995, 15.

45. Beale 2004, 31–38.

46. Beale 2004, 25.

47. Poythress 1995, 10.

48. A cubit was approximately 18 inches (or 45 centimeters). Ten cubits would equal approximately 15 feet.

Fig. 1. The tabernacle.

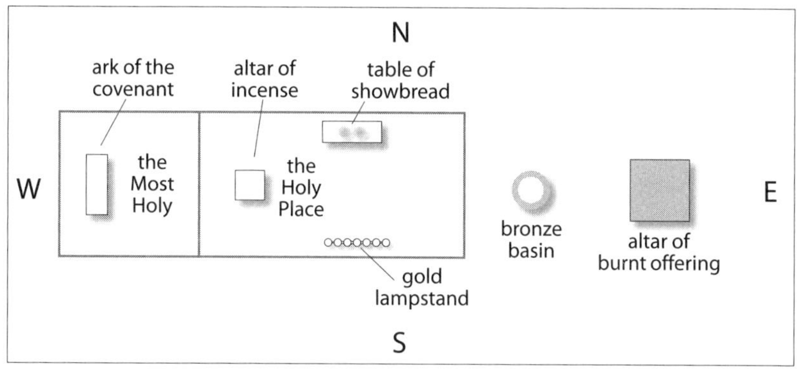

The sacrifices that are to be made on the bronze altar "are the means for cleansing and removing defilement of the people and of the tabernacle itself."[49] They maintain the holiness of God's people. The sacrifices also pointed forward to the final sacrifice that would be made by Christ (Heb. 9:11–10:18). The instructions for the priesthood are found in Exodus 28–29. These men served as mediators between God and the people of Israel. As such they prefigured Christ, pointing forward to the one ideal high priest and mediator between God and man (Heb. 4:14–5:10; 7:11–8:13; 1 Tim. 2:5).

In the final part of the section regarding the tabernacle, God provides further instructions concerning the Sabbath (Ex. 31:12–18). God tells Moses that the Sabbath is to be "a sign forever between me and the people of Israel" (v. 17). Just as God made circumcision the sign of his covenant with Abraham, he makes the Sabbath a sign of the Sinai covenant with Israel (vv. 13, 16–17).

While Moses is on the mountain receiving the instructions for the tabernacle, the people of Israel commit a grave sin. Exodus 32–34 recounts the story of the golden calf. Because of the amount of time Moses had been on the mountain, the people ask Aaron to make gods for them (32:1). Aaron then fashions a calf of gold and declares a feast day (vv. 2–6). The people of Israel, in effect, are creating their own false religion and breaking at least the first three of the Ten Commandments.[50] Their rebellion almost results in their complete destruction at the hand of God, but Moses intercedes on

49. Poythress 1995, 42.
50. Enns 2000, 571.

their behalf and has all who participated in the idolatrous worship put to death (vv. 7–35). God is merciful to the people, and he renews the covenant that Israel has broken (Ex. 34). He promises that he will continue to dwell in the midst of Israel (vv. 9–24; see also 33:15–17).

Exodus 35–40 details the construction of the tabernacle and its furnishings. The common refrain throughout these chapters is that all of these things are done as God has commanded Moses.[51] The construction of the tabernacle demonstrates that despite Israel's sin, God still intends to dwell with his people. After the tabernacle is constructed and the priests are consecrated, "the glory of Yahweh filled the tabernacle" (40:34). The glory cloud covers the tent of meeting and initially prevents Moses from entering (vv. 34–35; see also Lev. 1:1). God's dwelling with his people, initially fulfilled here by the filling of the tabernacle with the glory of God, will be more completely fulfilled in the coming of Christ (John 1:14) and in the church (Eph. 2:22). Its ultimate fulfillment, however, awaits the new heavens and earth (Rev. 21:3, 22; 22:3). The book of Exodus ends by describing how the glory cloud of God guided Israel throughout her journeys beginning the push toward the Promised Land of Canaan (Ex. 40:36–38).[52]

Leviticus

The final chapters of Exodus, recounting the construction of the tabernacle, naturally lead to the opening chapters of Leviticus, which describe in detail the various sacrifices to be offered there. Christian readers of Scripture often neglect Leviticus because of the seeming obscurity of its contents regarding animal sacrifices and various other ritual ceremonies. The difficulty of understanding the book, however, is lessened if its overarching point is remembered. The central theme of this third book of the Pentateuch is the holiness of God. In connection with this is the requirement that God's people reflect his holiness in all of their lives and in their worship (Lev. 11:45).[53] God had promised to dwell in the midst of his people, his kingdom of priests, meaning that all of Israel's life would be lived in the presence of a holy God. The prescriptions for holiness found throughout

51. Ex. 39:1, 5, 7, 21, 26, 29, 32, 42, 43; 40:16, 19, 21, 23, 25, 27, 29, 32.

52. Enns 2000, 599.

53. Harrison 1980, 14.

Leviticus thus ensure the continuing presence of God with his covenant people, his holy nation.[54]

The book of Leviticus may be divided into four major sections. Chapters 1–7 outline laws regarding various sacrifices. Chapters 8–10 deal with the consecration of the priests. Chapters 11–16 outline various rituals designed to deal with uncleanness. Finally, chapters 17–27, sometimes termed the Holiness Code, describe the practical holiness required of the people of Israel. The eschatological significance of Leviticus may not be as obvious as in the case of Genesis or certain other biblical books, but as we will see, Leviticus does contain much that is important for a biblical understanding of eschatology.

The first seven chapters of Leviticus provide the instructions for several kinds of sacrifices: the burnt offering (ch. 1; 6:8–13), the grain offering (ch. 2; 6:14–18), the peace offering (ch. 3; 7:11–36), the sin offering (4:1–5:13; 6:24–30), and the guilt offering (5:14–6:7; 7:1–10).[55] In order to understand the nature and purpose of these sacrifices, it is necessary to understand what Leviticus teaches regarding cleanness and uncleanness. Gordon Wenham provides a helpful explanation:

> Everything that is not holy is common. Common things divide into two groups, the clean and the unclean. Clean things become holy, when they are sanctified. But unclean objects cannot be sanctified. Clean things can be made unclean, if they are polluted. Finally, holy items may be defiled and become common, even polluted, and therefore unclean.[56]

He provides a diagram that graphically illustrates the point (fig. 2).[57]

Fig. 2. The holy and unclean, separate.

As the figure indicates, the holy and the unclean cannot come into contact. Sin and various infirmities defile the holy and pollute the clean. The solution that God has provided to cleanse the unclean and to sanctify

54. Harrison 1980, 26. See also Wenham 1979, 17.

55. For a detailed discussion of these sacrifices, see Wenham 1979, 47–128.

56. Wenham 1979, 19.

57. Wenham 1979, 19.

the clean is sacrifice.[58] This is illustrated in figure 3.[59] By means of the proper sacrifices, purity could be restored. Repentant Israelites could offer a sacrificial substitute that would bear the penalty for sin and restore the covenant relationship.[60] Although not explicitly prophetic, the sacrifices of Leviticus 1–7 do point forward to the sacrificial death of Jesus (Heb. 9:11–10:18). He is the one who fulfills all that they symbolize by dealing with the problem of sin once and for all.

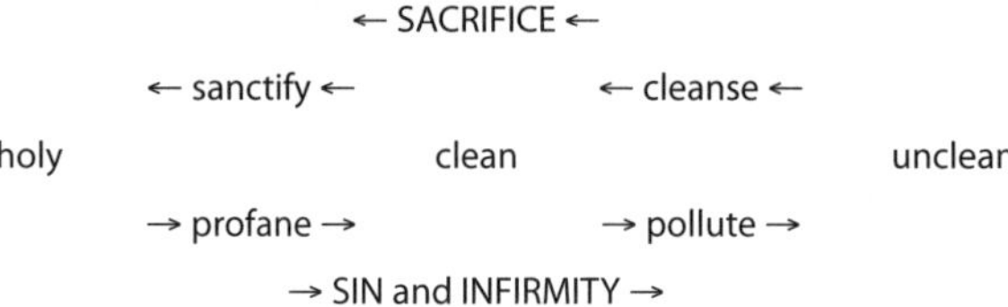

Fig. 3. The unclean, cleansed and made holy.

Leviticus 8–10 describes the Aaronic priesthood. The ordination of Aaron and his sons is described in chapter 8 (see also Ex. 29). Leviticus 9 describes Aaron's first sacrifices and God's acceptance of those sacrifices, while chapter 10 tells of the judgment of God upon Aaron's sons Nadab and Abihu for their presumptuous unauthorized offering. Leviticus reveals that the central task of Israel's priesthood was to protect the holiness of God.[61] The priests were mediators between God and Israel. Like the sacrifices that were offered, the priesthood itself also foreshadowed Christ. The priesthood pointed to the need for a perfect mediator between God and man. Ultimately, Christ fulfills all that the Israelite priesthood symbolized (Heb. 4:14–5:10; 7:11–8:13; 1 Tim. 2:5).

In Leviticus 10:10, God instructs Aaron, "You are to distinguish between the holy and the common, and between the unclean and the clean." Chapters 11–15 of Leviticus enable Aaron to fulfill his duties by describing all kinds of uncleanness as well as the rituals required for cleansing. Chapter 16 then describes the Day of Atonement ceremony in which the tabernacle itself was purified from ritual uncleanness. By distinguishing between the clean and the unclean, God reminds the people that he has made a distinction

58. Dillard and Longman 1994, 77.

59. Wenham 1979, 26.

60. The substitutionary nature of the sacrifices is indicated by the sinner's laying of his hands on the head of the animal (1:4; 3:2; 4:4).

61. Dillard and Longman 1994, 80.

between Israel and all other nations.[62] Israel was to be a holy nation, set apart for God. Only in this way could Israel ultimately be a blessing to the other nations.

The Day of Atonement, outlined in chapter 16, was the holiest day of the year for Israel. As Allen Ross explains, "Once a year, at the end of the year, all their sins and defilements were taken care of and they could start anew."[63] After describing the animals needed for the ceremony (vv. 3–5), Leviticus provides a brief summary of the rites (vv. 6–10) before proceeding to detail the necessary ceremonies (vv. 11–28). After bathing himself, the high priest was to sacrifice a bull as a sin offering for himself (v. 11). He was to take the blood of the bull along with coals and incense into the Holy Place (vv. 12–13). He was then to take the blood of the bull and sprinkle it on the ark inside the Most Holy Place (v. 14). The high priest would then take one of two goats already chosen by lot, sacrifice it as a sin offering for the people, and sprinkle its blood on the ark as well as on the tent of meeting itself (vv. 15–16).[64]

After exiting the Holy Place, the high priest would take some of the blood of the bull and the goat and sprinkle it on the altar (16:18–19). He would then lay his hands on the head of the remaining goat and confess over it the sins of the people of Israel (vv. 20–21). The goat would then be sent away into the wilderness, bearing the sins of the people (v. 22). Finally, after changing into his regular priestly clothes, the high priest would sacrifice burnt offerings for himself and for the people of Israel (vv. 23–24). In this way, atonement was made for the sanctuary, the tent of meeting, the altar, the priests, and the people (v. 33).

Like the other sacrifices and temple rituals, the Day of Atonement was eschatologically significant because it was a shadow of greater things to come (Heb. 9:6–28; 13:11–13). It too pointed forward to Christ, who by means of his own blood secured an eternal redemption (Heb. 9:12). It pointed forward to his perfect high priesthood (Heb. 8:1–7; 9:11). It also pointed forward to his substitutionary atonement (Heb. 9:12–28). The original Day of Atonement ceremonies were copies of heavenly things

62. Wenham 1979, 180.

63. Ross 2002, 313.

64. Apparently, the high priest entered the Holy Place twice, once to sprinkle the blood of the bull and then again to sprinkle the blood of the goat (see Bruce 1990, 207).

(Heb. 9:23). Christ's high-priestly offering of himself as a sacrifice was the reality (9:24).

Leviticus 17–27 is sometimes referred to as the Holiness Code.[65] These chapters outline the practical holiness required of the people of Israel. Within these chapters there are instructions regarding food, sexual behavior, criminal offenses, religious festivals, and numerous other issues. For our purposes, one text requires brief attention. Leviticus 25 describes the year of jubilee. Every seventh year was to be a Sabbath of rest for the land (25:1–8; Ex. 23:10–11). After seven Sabbath years (forty-nine years), the fiftieth year was to be a jubilee (25:8–12). The jubilee is significant because in that year "the land reverts to its original owner and the slave is given his freedom."[66] With a mighty hand, God had redeemed his people from oppression and slavery in Egypt. The jubilee "is thus a guarantee that no Israelite will be reduced to that status again, and it is a celebration of the great redemption when God brought Israel out of Egypt."[67] According to the New Testament, Christ is the fulfillment of all that the jubilee foreshadowed. It is he who was sent to proclaim liberty to the captives (Luke 4:18), to those in bondage to sin and death. The messianic age, then, is the true jubilee.

Numbers

The fourth book of the Pentateuch is titled Numbers in English, but its Hebrew name, "in the wilderness," is a more accurate description of its contents. The book is largely concerned with the forty years Israel spent in the wilderness on their journey from Mount Sinai to the plains of Moab. Numbers is integral to the overall structure and story of the Pentateuch. It describes "the transition from the old generation that left Egypt and sinned in the desert to the new generation that stands on the brink of the Promised Land."[68] The transitional nature of Numbers may be seen in its basic structure, which is formed around the taking of two distinct censuses. The first major section of the book, chapters 1–25, begins with a census

65. Wenham 1979, 241.

66. Wenham 1979, 317. The reversion of land to its original owners was to remind the people of Israel that the land truly belongs to God and that they were simply tenants (Lev. 25:23–24). The Promised Land too was a shadow of something greater to come (Heb. 11:14–16).

67. Wenham 1979, 323.

68. Dillard and Longman 1994, 83.

and describes the end of the old generation that had been brought up out of Egypt, a generation that continually rebelled against Moses and God. After the death of this first generation, a new census is taken, beginning the second major section of the book in chapters 26–36. These chapters describe the preparations of the new generation to enter Canaan.

The book of Numbers is closely connected to Exodus and Leviticus, but it has a different emphasis. Exodus is primarily concerned with the exodus from Egypt, the covenant at Sinai, and the tabernacle. Leviticus is primarily concerned with the nature of the holiness required to live in God's presence. Numbers, on the other hand, is primarily concerned with the land that God promised Abraham and with Israel's slow journey toward possession of that land.[69] As Wenham observes, "The whole book of Numbers looks forward to the occupation of the land of Canaan."[70] It is the land God has given to Israel for a permanent possession (32:7; Gen. 17:8).

The first ten chapters of Numbers describe Moses' preparations of the people of Israel for their journey from Mount Sinai to Canaan. This takes place over a period of approximately fifty days. Numbers 1–4 describes Moses' census of the people, the arrangement of the tribes around the tabernacle, a census of the Levites, and the duties of the Levites in carrying and assembling the tabernacle. Chapter 5 is devoted primarily to describing the purification of the camp. Chapter 6 then describes the vows of the Nazirites, those who voluntarily consecrated themselves to an exceptional degree of holiness and sanctification. Numbers 7–9 describes the consecration of the tabernacle and the altar, the cleansing of the Levites for service, and the observance of the second Passover. And although Israel was to be guided by God in a cloud (9:15–23), God also instructs Moses to construct two silver trumpets, which will be used primarily to summon the congregation and to break camp (10:1–10).

The next section of Numbers recounts the journey of Israel from Sinai to Kadesh (10:11–12:16; 13:26). After almost a year at Sinai, Israel finally departs for the Promised Land (10:11–36). However, no sooner does Israel depart than the people begin to grumble (11:1–15; cf. Ex. 15:22–17:7).[71]

69. Wenham 1981, 39; *NIDOTTE*, 4:989.

70. Wenham 1981, 43.

71. Stephen Dempster (2003, 112–13) notes the difference in the way God treats Israel's grumbling and other sins before and after Sinai. Before Sinai, Israel's murmuring causes Moses grief but is not judged (Ex. 15:22–25; 17:1–7). After Sinai, it is severely judged (Num. 11:1–3). Before

Grumbling and disobedience remain a common refrain throughout the first section of Numbers (12:1–2; 13:1–14:45; 16:1–40; 20:1–13; 21:5–9; 25:1–5). Because of the great burden that leading the people has become for Moses, God instructs him to gather seventy elders at the tent of meeting to share the burden (11:16). After Moses has done as the Lord instructed him, God takes some of the Spirit that is on Moses and gives it to the seventy elders. As soon as the Spirit rests on them, they begin to prophesy (vv. 24–25). Two of the elders had remained in the camp, however; and when they begin to prophesy, Joshua informs Moses (vv. 26–27). When he asks Moses to stop them, Moses replies, "Are you jealous for my sake? Would that all Yahweh's people were prophets, that Yahweh would put his Spirit on them!" (v. 29). These words of Moses anticipate the prophecy of Joel that is ultimately fulfilled on the day of Pentecost (Joel 2:28–29; Acts 2:15–21).

Numbers 13–14 is crucial in the story of Israel's journey to the land. Israel has made it to the border of the land promised by God to their fathers so long ago. God now instructs Moses to send spies into the land (13:1–2). Moses chooses twelve men, one from each tribe (vv. 3–16), and gives them their instructions (vv. 17–20). After forty days the spies return (v. 25). They tell the people of Israel that the land flows with milk and honey, but they then claim that the people in the land are too strong to conquer (vv. 26–33). Only two of the spies, Joshua and Caleb, argue that Israel can conquer the land (13:30; 14:6–9). Upon hearing the report of the spies, the people despair and grumble against Moses (14:1–12). Their rejection of the land is a failure to believe God's promise, and it is the "cardinal sin" they commit.[72] It is comparable to the sin the people committed when they worshiped the golden calf in that, again, God threatens to utterly destroy them and begin anew with Moses (14:11–12; Ex. 32:10). Once again, however, Moses intercedes on behalf of the people and averts God's wrath (Num. 14:13–19).

God pardons the people because of Moses' intercession, but he also passes judgment. Aside from Caleb and Joshua, no one above the age of twenty will be allowed to enter the land.[73] Instead, this generation will be forced

Sinai, gathering food on the seventh day results in a rebuke (Ex. 16:27–29), but after Sinai, gathering sticks on the seventh day results in the execution of the offender (Num. 15:32–36).

72. Budd 1984, xxv.

73. No Levites or priests were included among the spies, and for that reason they were apparently not included in this judgment. If Aaron's son Eleazar was over the age of twenty, which would seem

to wander in the wilderness for forty years (14:20–38). There they will die (vv. 29, 32, 33, 35; cf. v. 2). They are instructed to turn back toward the Red Sea (v. 25). They had constantly complained that it would be better to return to Egypt (e.g., 14:1–4), and here God grants their request. When the Israelites realize what they have done, they determine that they will now go into the land. Moses informs them it is too late for that, and if they attempt to go into the land they will be defeated (vv. 39–43). Despite Moses' warning, the people do proceed to enter the land and are quickly driven back by the Canaanites (vv. 44–45).

In Numbers 15, God gives Moses various laws concerning sacrifices. He tells Moses that these laws are for the people when they "come into the land" (v. 2). This indicates that in spite of Israel's sin, God has not forsaken his promise. He will bring Israel into the land that he promised to Abraham. Numbers 16–19 includes the story of Korah's rebellion (ch. 16), the proof of Aaron's priestly authority (ch. 17), the duties of the Levites (ch. 18), and various laws concerning purification (ch. 19). Numbers 20 tells the story of the disobedience of Moses and Aaron at Meribah. Because of their act of unbelief, neither Moses nor Aaron will be permitted to enter into the Promised Land (v. 12). God also tells Moses and Aaron that because of their lack of faith, Aaron will be gathered to his people. In other words, he will die (vv. 23–24). Upon his death, his son Eleazar assumes his office (vv. 25–28).

The grumbling of the people becomes an issue again in Numbers 21, and as a judgment God sends poisonous serpents among the people. When the people repent, God instructs Moses to make a bronze serpent and set it on a pole. He promises that those who are bitten and look upon the bronze serpent shall live (21:8–9). To look upon this bronze serpent for healing was an act of faith in God's promise. As such it foreshadows faith in Christ (John 3:14–15).

The story of Balaam is found in Numbers 22–24. Israel has camped at the plains of Moab, and Balak the king of Moab is overcome with fear (22:1–4). As a result, he summons Balaam, a pagan prophet from Mesopotamia, to curse the Israelites (vv. 5–8).[74] God, however, does not allow Balaam to curse Israel, but commands him to bless Israel instead. In chapters 23–24,

---

to be certain since he had already been consecrated as a priest (Lev. 8; 10:6–7), this inference would seem to be justified, since we know that he later entered the land (Num. 34:17; Josh. 14:1). See Allis 1951, 114, 124.

74. Wenham 1981, 170.

to Balak's dismay, Balaam delivers four oracles of blessing upon Israel. The fourth oracle is particularly notable because of its structure and content. It is the second of three instances in the Pentateuch where a lengthy poetic section is introduced by someone calling an audience and proclaiming what will happen in the latter days (Num. 24:14; cf. Gen. 49:1; Deut. 31:28–29).[75] Balaam foresees the coming of a king, but the coming is not to be immediate: "I see him, but not now; I behold him, but not near" (Num. 24:17). The coming king is described as a star coming out of Jacob and a scepter rising out of Israel (v. 17; Gen. 49:10). This king will utterly defeat his enemies (Num. 24:18). This prophecy would find its initial fulfillment in the reign of David, but its ultimate fulfillment awaited the coming of the Messiah.[76]

The section of Numbers concerning the first generation of Israel ends with an act of total apostasy by the people (ch. 25). The people of Moab successfully encourage the Israelites to worship Baal of Peor (vv. 1–3). This idolatry results in a death sentence being passed on those who participated as well as a plague that kills twenty-four thousand (vv. 4–9; cf. Ex. 32:35). The plague is stopped because of the zeal of Eleazar's son Phinehas who puts to death an Israelite man and Midianite woman who were showing flagrant contempt for the holiness of the camp (Num. 25:7–15). God then passes judgment upon the Midianites for tempting Israel to idolatry and orders Moses to strike them down (vv. 16–18). With this final act of blatant rebellion against God, the story of the first generation to come out of Egypt ends. Because of their unbelief and disobedience, God did not permit them to enter the land. He did not allow them to enter his rest (Heb. 3:16–19).

The second major section of Numbers begins in chapter 26 with a census of the new generation of Israel on the plains of Moab almost forty years after the first census. Such a census was necessary because the conquest of Canaan was imminent, and the size of the tribes was to determine the amount of territory in the land that each would inherit (26:52–56). Chapter 27 describes the anointing of Joshua as Moses' successor. Because Moses has been told that he will not enter the land, he asks God to appoint someone to lead the people into Canaan, and God chooses Joshua (27:12–23).

75. Sailhamer 1992, 36.
76. *NIDOTTE*, 4:987.

Various laws regarding offerings and vows are given to Moses in chapters 28–30 before we read of the fulfillment of God's command to strike down the Midianites (31:1–54; cf. 25:16–18). Numbers 32 then tells of the decision of Reuben and Gad and the half tribe of Manasseh to settle in the land east of the Jordan River. Moses gives them permission to do this on the condition that they assist the other tribes in conquering the Promised Land west of the Jordan (vv. 20–22). The book of Numbers ends with a summary of Israel's journeys between Egypt and the plains of Moab (ch. 33), a statement of the boundaries of the Promised Land (ch. 34), and laws concerning cities for the Levites, cities of refuge, and the rights of female heirs (chs. 35–36). After so many years, Israel now stands on the brink of her promised inheritance.

Deuteronomy

The book of Deuteronomy is one of the four most frequently cited Old Testament books in the New Testament.[77] Its basic subject matter is the renewal of the covenant on the plains of Moab immediately prior to Israel's entrance into the Promised Land. The death of Moses was approaching, and he needed to prepare the people for a transition in leadership. In addition, he needed to prepare the people for the wars of conquest they were about to undertake. The book of Deuteronomy, then, is something of a constitution for the people of God now set up as a theocratic nation.[78] It is also a call for Israel to make a decision. Will they obey and enjoy God's blessing? Or will they disobey and experience the curses of the covenant?

Much of the book of Deuteronomy consists of three addresses by Moses to the people of Israel (1:6–4:43; 4:44–29:1; 29:2–30:20). These three addresses, however, are placed within a larger structure that is very similar to the structure of ancient Near Eastern suzerain-vassal treaties.[79] These ancient treaties included several distinct elements: a title/preamble, a historical prologue, basic and detailed stipulations, deposition of the text, reading arrangements, witnesses, blessings, and curses. Deuteronomy shares these features and this basic treaty structure. It has a preamble (1:1–5), a historical prologue (1:6–3:29), basic stipulations (4:1–11:32), detailed stipulations

77. The others are Genesis, Psalms, and Isaiah.

78. McConville 2002, 34.

79. See Kline 1963.

(12:1–26:19), provisions for the deposition of the text (31:24–26), reading arrangements (31:9–13), witnesses (31:19–22, 26), blessings for obedience (28:1–14), and curses for disobedience (28:15–68).[80] Although perhaps not immediately apparent on the surface of the text, there is much within this book that is significant for understanding biblical eschatology.

Preamble and Historical Prologue (Deut. 1–3)

The first verses of Deuteronomy set the stage and link the book to Numbers (Deut. 1:1–5; Num. 36:13). The tribes of Israel are in Moab on the borders of the Promised Land, and these are the words Moses spoke to them. Moses begins by recounting all that has happened from the time God brought the people up out of Egypt until they arrived in Moab (Deut. 1:6–3:29). His historical summary recounts God's faithfulness as well as Israel's constant stubbornness and lack of faith. Moses' emphasis throughout these chapters is upon Israel's initial faithless refusal to enter the land and the resulting judgment of forty years of wandering in the wilderness. This is to serve as a reminder of what God has done in the past and as a warning of the kind of judgment that will befall Israel in the case of future rebellion against her divine King.

Legal Stipulations (Deut. 4–26)

Deuteronomy 4–26 is a lengthy collection of legal stipulations, laws that Israel is to obey in the land (4:1). Many of these laws are repetitions and expansions of laws found in Exodus in the Book of the Covenant (Ex. 20:22–23:33). Understandably, the land is a significant emphasis throughout these chapters.[81] It is obedience to the law that will allow Israel to enter and possess the land. But obedience to the law would not merely result in blessings for Israel. Her obedience to the law was also to be a witness to the nations of the righteousness and wisdom of God (Deut. 4:6–8). The establishment of Israel as a nation was never intended to be an end in itself.

In Deuteronomy 4, Moses introduces the legal stipulations with a warning against idolatry (vv. 15–31). The penalty for idolatry will be exile from

80. For more on the significance of the relationship between the structure of Deuteronomy and these ancient Near Eastern treaties, see Kitchen 2003, 283–94.

81. E.g., 4:5, 21; 6:18; 7:1; 8:1; 9:1, 5; 11:8, 10, 29, 31; 12:9; 15:4; 19:10; 20:16; 21:23; 24:4; 25:19; 26:1.

the land (vv. 26–28). But Moses also holds out hope by insisting that even if Israel commits idolatry God will not forget his covenant and that the people will return to God (vv. 29–31). In the fifth chapter of Deuteronomy, Moses reaffirms the Ten Commandments, recontextualizing them for this new generation.[82] The Shema, a text of great importance to successive generations of Israelites, is found in chapter 6:4–9. It begins with a declaration about God and concludes with a statement of the greatest commandment: "Hear, O Israel: Yahweh our God, Yahweh is one. You shall love Yahweh your God with all your heart and with all your soul and with all your might" (vv. 4–5; see also Matt. 22:36–37). This is the heart of Israel's confession.

After outlining Israel's policy of holy war (Deut. 7) and warning Israel not to forget God (ch. 8), Moses elaborates at length on Israel's stubbornness (chs. 9–10). He informs the people that the Canaanites are being driven out of the land because of their own wickedness, not because of Israel's righteousness (9:1–5). In fact, far from being righteous, Israel is a stubborn people who have continually provoked God from the day they came out of Egypt (vv. 6–7). Gordon McConville explains the problem: "By placing this elaboration of Israel's failure at this point, before the long series of laws that they are required to keep, Deuteronomy seems deliberately to sharpen the dilemma that it sees, namely, how it can be that a people who cannot keep covenant should be given a land on the express condition that they do so."[83] Israel's consistent inability to obey God presents a significant problem. An answer to the problem will not be found until chapter 30.

82. Enns 2000, 428. The only significant difference between the Ten Commandments as they are listed in Deuteronomy 5 as opposed to their listing in Exodus 20 is the rationale given for the observance of the Sabbath. In Exodus 20:8–11, the Sabbath is to be observed because God rested from his creative work on the seventh day. In Deuteronomy 5:12–15, the Sabbath is to be observed in remembrance of the fact that Israel was a slave in Egypt. Dumbrell (1984, 122–23) helps explain the reason for the difference: "In the parallel presentation of the ten commandments in Ex. 20:8–11 the Sabbath was understood to prefigure the rest which the completion of creation had foreshadowed for mankind." He explains that the present rationale for the Sabbath in Deuteronomy 5 does not contradict the rationale in Exodus 20. Instead, it complements it "since it is the Exodus redemption which makes the new life in the land, and thus the Edenic values recaptured, possible. Israel in Canaan is a microcosm of mankind as blessed, an illustration of what is intended for the whole world. Of course, we know that the expectation of 'rest' was not realised in Israel's experience and that finally she was driven from the land. The Epistle to the Hebrews in the New Testament makes much of this Old Testament failure, reminding us that while Israel failed to enter this rest, (Heb. 4:8–10) there still remains for the believers a Sabbath rest as the fulfillment of creation's purpose."

83. McConville 2002, 134.

Moses reminds the nation of her past faithlessness at Horeb/Sinai when she built and worshiped the golden calf (9:8–10:11). He tells the people that what God requires is "to fear Yahweh your God, to walk in all his ways, to love him, to serve Yahweh your God with all your heart and with all your soul, and to keep the commandments and statutes of Yahweh, which I am commanding you today for your good" (10:12–13). Because God has chosen Israel, Moses commands them: "Circumcise therefore the foreskin of your heart, and be no longer stubborn" (v. 16). They are to purify their hearts, to remove everything that hinders true faithfulness and love of God. Outward circumcision alone will not result in their receiving the blessings of the covenant. The inner reality signified by circumcision is required as well. If Israel is to maintain possession of the land, she must love and serve God (ch. 11).

Chapters 12–26 of Deuteronomy contain a large number of detailed laws intended for Israel's life and worship in the land. Some of these are particularly significant for an understanding of biblical eschatology. In Deuteronomy 17:14–20, for example, Moses incorporates legislation pertaining to kings into the covenant. He anticipates that there will come a time when Israel will demand a king, and he makes provision for this future eventuality. Because Israel is a theocracy, with God as her one true King, any human king must be one that God himself chooses from among Israel (v. 15). Moses warns of the dangers of autocratic rulers and stipulates that any Israelite king must exercise his authority under God and in accordance with the stipulations of the law (vv. 16–20).[84]

The establishment of the prophetic office is the subject of Deuteronomy 18:15–22.[85] After outlining forbidden ways of trying to know the will of God (vv. 9–14), Moses proceeds to explain the nature of prophecy, the legitimate means by which God would communicate his word to his people (vv. 15–22). He declares to the people, "Yahweh your God will raise up for you a prophet like me from among you, from your brothers—it is to him you shall listen" (v. 15). God here provides for the continuation of the prophetic office after the death of Moses.[86]

It is important to remember, however, that Moses was unique among the prophets as a minister of God's covenant (Num. 12:6–8; Deut. 34:10–

84. Thompson 1974, 204.

85. For a helpful discussion of this passage, see Young 1952, 20–37.

86. Craigie 1976, 262.

12). He was, as Willem VanGemeren observes, "the fountainhead of the prophets."[87] As we shall see, the message of the prophets was rooted in the Mosaic covenant.[88] Jeffrey Niehaus explains:

> The prophetic ministry was of two kinds: the prophet as covenant mediator (Moses only); the prophet as covenant lawsuit messenger (subsequent prophets). God had raised up the prophet Moses to mediate his covenant to Israel; he would raise up other prophets to bring covenant lawsuit—to recall the people to covenant obedience or to announce covenantal punishments incurred by their disobedience.[89]

God's promise to raise up another prophet like Moses was later understood by the Israelites to be a messianic prophecy (John 1:21, 45; 6:14; 7:40). Ultimately this prophetic promise points to Jesus, the unique mediator of the new covenant (Acts 3:20–22).

Moses explains the origin of the prophetic office in terms of the events at Mount Sinai when the people had demanded that Moses bring the word of God to them (Deut. 18:16–17). He tells the people that God will put his words in the mouth of the prophet, and the prophet will speak all that God commands him to speak (v. 18). Israel is to listen to God's prophet (v. 9). This requirement raises an important question. How are the people to distinguish between a true prophet and a false prophet? Moses provides the answer. First, a true prophet will urge the people to be faithful to the covenant. If he urges disobedience or speaks in the name of other gods, he is a false prophet (v. 20). Second, the words of a true prophet will come to pass (v. 22).[90]

Blessings, Curses, and Covenant Ratification (Deut. 27–30)

Deuteronomy 27–30 is important for an understanding of biblical eschatology because it contains God's pronouncement of the blessings

87. VanGemeren 1990, 28.

88. VanGemeren 1990, 28.

89. *NIDOTTE*, 4:538.

90. This final requirement must be interpreted carefully because, as Jeremiah teaches (Jer. 18:7–10; 26:2–3), many true prophecies contain either explicit or implicit conditions (see Calvin 1960, 1:227). Prophecies of coming judgment, for example, are often accompanied by implicit or explicit calls for repentance. If those to whom the prophecy is given do truly repent, the judgment may be averted. An example of this phenomenon is seen in Jonah 3:4, 10. See Craigie 1976, 263.

that will result from obedience to the stipulations of the Mosaic covenant and the curses that will result from disobedience (cf. Lev. 26). In Deuteronomy 27, Moses commands the people to set up plastered stones at Mount Ebal upon which they are to write all the words of the law (vv. 1–8). After the people enter the land, six of the tribes are to stand on Mount Gerizim and six are to stand on Mount Ebal (vv. 11–13). The Levites are then to recite a summary of the curses of the covenant (vv. 14–26). Chapter 28 outlines in great detail the blessings for obedience to God's covenant stipulations (vv. 1–14) and the curses for disobedience (vv. 15–68). Among the curses is the ultimate punishment, namely exile from the land (vv. 36, 64–65).

The lengthy recitation of blessings and curses is followed in chapters 29–30 by Moses' third major address to the people. In this final address, he reminds them of all that God has done for them and appeals for covenant faithfulness (ch. 29). He then places before them a choice between life and death and demands a decision (ch. 30). In his final address, Moses foresees that the people will not remain true to God and that the curses of the covenant, including exile, will ultimately fall upon them (30:1). But he also foresees that Israel will eventually repent and be restored from exile (vv. 2–10).[91] This foreseen restoration from exile, however, raises an important question. Gordon McConville explains:

> Deuteronomy 30:2–3 pictures the people's repentance in exile, which in turn precipitates a restoration of their fortunes, here explicitly involving a return to the land. This structure immediately raises the question how that new restored situation might be any different from the old, the one that had had such wretched and apparently inevitable results.[92]

In other words, even if Israel repents and is restored from exile, what is to prevent the entire cycle of disobedience and curses from occurring again?

An answer to the problem is found in Deuteronomy 30:6 where Moses declares, "And Yahweh your God will circumcise your heart and the heart of your offspring, so that you will love Yahweh your God with all your heart and with all your soul, that you may live." What God had com-

91. Alexander 2002, 275.
92. McConville 1993, 136.

manded in Deuteronomy 10:16, he promises that he himself will do in 30:6. The answer to the problem of Israel's stubborn infidelity ultimately rests in God himself. "He will somehow enable his people ultimately to do what they cannot do in their strength, namely, to obey him out of the conviction and devotion of their own hearts."[93] God's promise to circumcise their hearts anticipates the promise of a new heart and new covenant found in the prophets (Jer. 31:31–34; Ezek. 36:22–28). In effect, God is telling Israel in Deuteronomy that she cannot in her own strength obey the very law that he is giving her. Because of Israel's stubborn self-confidence, however, this is something that she will have to learn the hard way.

Succession Arrangements (Deut. 31–34)

The final chapters of Deuteronomy are concerned primarily with succession arrangements. In chapter 31, the Levites are commanded to read the law to the people of Israel every seven years (vv. 9–13). The reading of the law will remind Israel of her obligations and will also be a means of teaching the younger generations. Deuteronomy 31:14–30 tells of the commissioning of Joshua as the successor of Moses (31:1–8). These verses are also prophetic in that Moses foresees that Israel will not remain faithful to the covenant. Israel will commit idolatry (vv. 16–18, 20–21), and her rebellion will result in judgment from God (vv. 27–29).

God also commands Moses to write a song that will stand as a witness against the people of Israel (31:19, 22). The words of the song are found in chapter 32. This song is to stand as a perpetual warning to Israel. Within the song itself, there is an affirmation about the power of God that is important for this study. Verse 39 reads, "See now that I, even I, am he, and there is no god beside me; I kill and I make alive; I wound and I heal; and there is none that can deliver out of my hand." God here introduces a theme that will continue to be developed throughout Scripture, namely, his power to raise the dead (1 Sam. 2:6). Chapters 33–34 conclude the book of Deuteronomy and the Pentateuch with the final blessing of Israel by Moses (ch. 33) and the record of Moses' death (ch. 34). Joshua is now the leader of the people as the nation stands poised to enter the land promised them by God.

93. McConville 1993, 137.

Summary

The importance of the Pentateuch for a proper understanding of biblical eschatology cannot be overstated. The themes introduced in these books are foundational. The significance of Genesis has already been discussed. Exodus–Deuteronomy continues the story begun there. In Exodus, the promises God made to Abraham begin to see fulfillment as God redeems his people from slavery in Egypt. The exodus from Egypt is the birth of the holy nation of Israel, and this event becomes for Israel a paradigm of God's acts of salvation.[94]

The calling out of Israel to be a theocratic kingdom of priests is another stage in God's purpose to establish his kingdom and to bless the nations of the earth. After the exodus from Egypt, God establishes the Mosaic covenant, revealing to Moses the law for his kingdom people and the instructions for the tabernacle. In the tabernacle, God the Great King is present again in the midst of his people as he was in Eden. His law reveals the righteousness and holiness required of a people in whose midst God is present.

The holiness required of God's people is elaborated further in the book of Leviticus where the laws concerning sacrifices and the priesthood are given in detail. Sacrifices provided a means for the people of Israel to be cleansed when they committed sin, and the priests who offered these sacrifices stood as mediators between God and his people. Both the priesthood and the sacrifices pointed forward to a greater eschatological reality to come in the person and work of Jesus the Messiah. The book of Numbers is a book that details the forty years of wilderness wandering that resulted from Israel's disobedience and the transition from the old generation to the new generation. Its emphasis is the land of promise, God's initial step in the process of establishing his kingdom on earth.

Deuteronomy is both part of the Pentateuch and a link to the historical books that follow. As part of the Pentateuch, Deuteronomy is a distinct covenant document that sets forth God's law for the theocratic kingdom of Israel as well as the blessings that will follow from obedience and the curses that will follow upon disobedience. The historical books of Joshua, Judges, Samuel, and Kings will outline Israel's history in this light, showing

94. Bruce 1968, 32. The prophets will use the imagery of the exodus to describe the future restoration of Israel following exile.

clearly that obedience resulted in blessing, while disobedience resulted in the curses of the covenant.[95] As Deuteronomy ends, Israel is on the border of the Promised Land and has been called to make a choice between obedience and disobedience. In the historical books, we will see Israel's response.

95. Thompson 1974, 73–74.

3

The Historical Books

In the Protestant Old Testament, the books of Joshua through Esther are referred to as the "historical books." The historical narrative in these books spans a period of approximately one thousand years, recounting the history of Israel from the conquest of Canaan in the late fifteenth and early fourteenth centuries B.C. to the restoration from exile beginning in the late sixth and early fifth centuries B.C. In the Tanakh, the Hebrew Bible, the books of Joshua, Judges, Samuel, and Kings are found in the second section of the canon called the *Nebi'im*, or "Prophets," and are referred to collectively as the "Former Prophets."[1] The books of Chronicles, Ezra, Nehemiah, Ruth, and Esther are found in the third section of the canon called the *Ketubim*, or "Writings."

Scholars today often refer to the Former Prophets (Joshua–Kings) as the deuteronomic history because of their thematic connection with the book of Deuteronomy.[2] These books tell the story of Israel's history from the conquest to the exile in terms of their obedience or disobedience to

1. In the Hebrew canon, the "Latter Prophets" are the books of Isaiah, Jeremiah, Ezekiel, and the twelve Minor Prophets.

2. See, for example, Noth 1981; Fretheim 1983; and Campbell and O'Brien 2000.

the stipulations of God's covenant. Faith in God manifested itself in obedience and resulted in God's blessing, while lack of faith manifested itself in disobedience—particularly in the worship of false gods—and resulted in God's judgment.

The books of Chronicles, Ezra, and Nehemiah were written in the late fifth century or early fourth century B.C., after the Israelites returned from exile. They tell the history of Israel from a different perspective and for a different purpose, namely in order to reestablish the roots of the postexilic community. However, whereas the history recounted in the Former Prophets ends at the exile, Chronicles, Ezra, and Nehemiah extend that history to the return from exile and the beginnings of the restoration of the community around the rebuilt temple.[3] The additional historical books of Ruth and Esther are short stories that were to be read at major religious festivals. Ruth was to be read during the feast of weeks, and Esther was to be read during the feast of Purim.

The historical books of the Bible may be described as theological history.[4] However, it is important to remember the fact that although biblical history is theological history, it is not fiction. Biblical history is not mythology, as some critical scholars claim. It is the true story of Israel.[5] However, as Dan McCartney and Charles Clayton explain, theological history does other things in addition to telling Israel's story. It demonstrates to the people of Israel how the past establishes their identity, and it demands a response.[6] "Biblical history not only records the events of redemptive history, but explains the redemptive meaning of those events."[7] It is "proclamation *and* history."[8] Theological history demonstrates that God is moving history toward his intended goal. It is primarily in this respect that the historical books contribute to our understanding of biblical eschatology.

3. Blenkinsopp 1988, 36.

4. The different ways that the same history is told in the deuteronomic history and in Chronicles lend support to this idea. The Former Prophets provide a prophetic interpretation of Israel's past (see Foulkes 1958, 20).

5. Provan, Long, and Longman 2003, 36–74.

6. McCartney and Clayton 1994, 211.

7. McCartney and Clayton 1994, 213.

8. House 1995, 70.

Joshua

The book of Joshua describes the conquest of the Promised Land under Joshua (ca. 1400 B.C.). The author of the book, like the author or authors of the other books in the Former Prophets, is unknown. If the author of all of these books is a single person, as some have suggested, their completion would have to be dated sometime during or after the exile since the book of 2 Kings concludes in the exilic era (2 Kings 25:27–30). On the other hand, if the book of Joshua was written independently, then its composition should probably be dated sometime during the period of the judges.

If the book was, in fact, written during the period of the judges, one of its original purposes would have been to remind Israel of the way God had fulfilled his promises under Joshua and to encourage them to anticipate another leader like Joshua.[9] If the book of Joshua was written, along with the other Former Prophets, during the exile, its purpose would have been the same as that of those other books, namely to answer the kinds of questions that the exilic generation would likely have raised, such as, Are we still the people of God? Why did this happen? Is there any reason for hope? Have God's promises been nullified?[10]

The book of Joshua stands at a point of transition in the biblical narrative. It serves as a fitting conclusion to what has been revealed in the Pentateuch, yet as David Howard observes, it also stands "at the head of the books whose history is played out in the Promised Land."[11] In the book of Joshua, the Promised Land is conquered; in the book of 2 Kings, it is lost. Joshua's link to both the Pentateuch and the following historical books is also evident on the surface of the text. Just as Deuteronomy ends with the death of Moses, the book of Joshua ends with the death of Joshua. And just as Joshua begins with the words "After the death of Moses . . ." (Josh. 1:1), the book of Judges begins with the words, "After the death of Joshua . . ." (Judg. 1:1; cf. 2 Sam. 1:1). These literary details tie the narratives together into a unified whole.

9. Even if the book of Joshua was written originally to the people of Israel during the period of the judges, its literary and thematic connection with Judges, Samuel, and Kings indicates that the author or authors of those later books consciously saw their narratives as continuations of the narrative in the book of Joshua and incorporated them into a larger whole that directly addressed their own time.

10. For similar questions that would likely have been raised by the people of Israel during the exile, see Fretheim 1983, 46–47; Provan, Long, and Longman 2003, 195–96.

11. Howard 1993, 80.

The book of Joshua is generally optimistic, and it recounts one of the high points in the history of Israel. Marten Woudstra observes that its keynote "is the fulfillment of the promise made to the forefathers regarding the possession of the land of Canaan."[12] The land promised to Abraham (Gen. 12:7) and forfeited by the previous generation (Num. 13–14) is now being given to the people of Israel (Josh. 1:2). The narrative of Joshua may be divided into four major sections, and it is significant that the theme of each section is related to the land. The preparations for entrance into the land are found in Joshua 1:1–5:12. The actual conquest of the land is recounted in 5:13–12:24. Chapters 13–21 then detail the distribution of the land to the several tribes of Israel. Finally, chapters 22–24 deal with covenant obedience to the Lord in the land.

The first chapter of the book of Joshua records God's commissioning of Joshua as the new leader of the people of Israel. Several themes are introduced in this chapter, but the most important is found in verses 2–4. God tells Joshua, "Moses my servant is dead. Now therefore arise, go over this Jordan, you and all this people, into the land that I am giving to them, to the people of Israel" (v. 2). The inheritance of the Promised Land was one of the primary goals to which the Pentateuch had looked forward.[13] And it was the one major element of the patriarchal promises that remained outstanding at the end of the Pentateuch.[14] Moses had prepared the people to take possession of the land in the book of Deuteronomy, but it is under the leadership of Joshua that the land finally begins to be conquered and distributed to the people.

Joshua 1:2 is one of many places in the book indicating that the land is God's gift.[15] The land is also described as Israel's "inheritance."[16] It is a place of rest for God's people (1:13; Heb. 3:16–18). After encouraging Joshua that Israel will soon be given the land, God instructs him to remain faithful to the covenant (Josh. 1:7–8). Although the land is a gift promised in the Abrahamic covenant, continued possession of the land is a blessing of the Mosaic covenant, and may be forfeited by disobedience

12. Woudstra 1981, 32; see also Chisholm 2006, 89.

13. Howard 1993, 90.

14. Provan, Long, and Longman 2003, 166.

15. Provan, Long, and Longman 2003, 149–50; see Josh. 1:3, 6, 11, 13, 15; 2:9, 24; 11:23; 18:3; 21:43; 23:13; 24:13.

16. Josh. 11:23; 13:6, 7, 8, 23, 28; 14:1, 2, 3, 9, 13; 15:20; 16:5, 8, 9; 17:4; 18:2, 4, 7, 20, 28; 19:1, 2, 8, 9, 10, 16, 23, 31, 39, 48, 49, 51; 23:4.

(Josh. 23:16; Deut. 28:63). All of this raises a significant question. Is the land promise a conditional or unconditional promise? There are many texts that seem to present the promise unconditionally (e.g., Gen. 12:7; 13:15, 17; 15:7, 18–21; 28:13, 15; 35:12; Ex. 3:8, 17; 6:8). However, other texts seem to indicate that the promise is qualified by conditions (e.g., Ex. 20:12; 23:23–33; 34:24; Lev. 18:3; Deut. 4:1–5, 40; 5:33; 6:18; 8:1; 16:20; 18:9–14; 19:8–9; 21:23; 24:4; 25:15; 30:16; 32:47). How are these texts to be reconciled?

In order to understand all that the book of Joshua reveals about the nature of the land promise, it is important to remember first that the land belongs to God (Lev. 25:23). Because the land belongs to God, Israel's continued residence in it is linked to God's covenantal relationship with Israel. The promise of land is a unilateral promise, but disobedience to the covenant stipulations defiles the land and makes it unclean (Lev. 18:27). If the people defile the land by their disobedience, the land will vomit them out (Lev. 18:24–30). The promise, then, is everlasting, but "participation in it is not *guaranteed* to every person or generation."[17] The people of the wilderness generation, for example, were heirs of the promise. The promise was made to them, but they did not believe it. They were not allowed to enjoy the land because of their faithlessness. Their faithlessness, however, did not nullify the promise for every individual in that generation (e.g., Joshua and Caleb), nor did it nullify the promise for future faithful generations.[18]

In the second chapter of Joshua, two spies are sent into the land in preparation for the coming conquest. They enter the city of Jericho and are protected by a prostitute named Rahab (Josh. 2:1–7). She tells the two spies that her people have heard how God has fought for Israel since bringing the people up out of the land of Egypt, and she pleads for protection when Israel comes into her land (vv. 8–13). Because she has protected them, the spies promise her that those in her house will not be harmed when the Israelites enter the land (v. 14). The Canaanites are being judged because of their wickedness (Gen. 15:16; Deut. 9:4–5). Mercy, however, is granted to one among them who stands with God's people.[19]

In Joshua 2:10, Rahab describes how the two kings of the Amorites had been "devoted to destruction" by Israel. Here the concept of *herem* is

17. Fretheim 1983, 21; see also Waltke 1988b, 135; McComiskey 1985a, 65–66.

18. Williamson 2000, 22–24; Holwerda 1995, 88–93.

19. Hess 1996, 45.

introduced. This term refers to absolute consecration, and in the context of war, it has to do with the devotion of a city or a people to utter destruction.[20] Deuteronomy outlined the principles of such warfare (Deut. 7:1–26; 20:1–20; 21:10–14; 25:17–19). In the book of Joshua, those principles are to be put into action.[21] The theme of *herem* is closely related to another theme found in Joshua 2:10, namely, that of God as the divine warrior (cf. Deut. 31:3).[22] That God is the one who fights for Israel against her enemies is found throughout the book of Joshua.[23] This "holy war" theme is also later used in the Old and New Testaments to describe the eschatological day of the Lord (Isa. 13:1–22; Joel 2:1–11; Amos 5:4–20; Zech. 14:1–11; 1 Thess. 5:1–10; 2 Peter 3:10). The application of *herem* warfare ultimately foreshadows the final judgment and God's destruction of his enemies (Rev. 19:11–20:15).

Joshua 3:1–5:12 tells of Israel's crossing of the Jordan into the Promised Land (ch. 3), the circumcision of the new generation (5:1–9), and the celebration of the first Passover in the land (5:10–12). In Joshua 5:13–15, Joshua encounters the commander of the Lord's army, who is the Lord himself (6:2). The story is reminiscent of Moses' encounter with God at the burning bush (Ex. 3:1–6). In this theophany, the Lord appears with sword drawn, indicating his readiness for battle. He then commissions Joshua, giving him instructions for the conquest of Jericho.

The battle for the land itself is found in Joshua 6–12. Because Israel obeys the Lord's commands, the city of Jericho falls (ch. 6), but because of Achan's disobedience to the specific principles of *herem* warfare, Israel is defeated at the city of Ai (7:11–12). Achan's sin is ultimately discovered, and he receives the death penalty for his transgression (7:22–26). After his judgment, the city of Ai falls to Israel (8:1–29), and Joshua renews the covenant according to the instructions given by Moses (8:30–35; Deut. 27:2–26). Joshua 9 then explains how the Gibeonites deceived Israel and entered into a covenant with the nation. When the Gibeonites are subsequently attacked by the five kings of the Amorites, Joshua comes to their

20. *NIDOTTE*, 2:276–77.

21. For more on the way in which *herem* should be understood, especially in light of the New Testament, see Longman 2003.

22. Longman and Reid 1995, 31–47.

23. 2:10, 24; 4:23–24; 5:13–14; 6:2; 8:1, 7, 18–19; 10:8, 10, 11, 14, 19, 25, 30, 42; 11:6, 20; 21:44; 23:3, 5, 9, 10; 24:18.

assistance (10:1–28). The conquest of southern Canaan is then summarized in Joshua 10:29–43, while the conquest of northern Canaan is summarized in 11:1–23. Joshua 12 closes this section of the book with a list of the kings defeated by Moses (vv. 1–6) and Joshua (vv. 7–24).

The next major section of Joshua (chapters 13–21) tells of the distribution of the land to the various tribes. These chapters reinforce the truth that the land is a gift from God.[24] After describing the land that has yet to be conquered (13:1–7), the author of Joshua describes the inheritances of Reuben, Gad, and the half-tribe of Manasseh east of the Jordan (13:8–33). He then proceeds to describe the inheritances given to the remaining tribes west of the Jordan. He begins with the inheritance given to Caleb (14:6–15). He then describes the inheritance of Judah (ch. 15), Ephraim (ch. 16), and Manasseh (ch. 17). In each of these descriptions, the author of Joshua makes a point of noting that Canaanites remained in the land given to these tribes (15:63; 16:10; 17:12). Moses had warned of this danger (Ex. 34:11–16). They would tempt Israel to worship other gods, and such apostasy would lead to Israel suffering the same fate the Canaanites suffered (Deut. 18:9–12; 2 Kings 17:8–18; 21:3–15). What we discover here is that "the dynamics that would eventually lead to exile are already in place in Joshua."[25]

Joshua 18–19 describes the inheritances of the remaining tribes. After noting that the tabernacle was set up at Shiloh (18:1), the author of Joshua describes the inheritances of Benjamin (vv. 11–28), Simeon (19:1–9), Zebulun (vv. 10–16), Issachar (vv. 17–23), Asher (vv. 24–31), Naphtali (vv. 32–39), Dan (vv. 40–48), and Joshua himself (vv. 49–51). Joshua 20 then describes the location of the various cities of refuge, and Joshua 21 describes the cities and pasturelands given to the Levites.

The author of Joshua concludes this section by stating that God had given Israel "all the land that he swore to give to their fathers" (21:43). He states, "Not one word of all the good promises that Yahweh had made to the house of Israel had failed; all came to pass" (v. 45). This passage along with others in Joshua speaks of the land promise as if it were already completely fulfilled at this point in history (e.g., 11:23; 23:14). Other passages, however, indicate that the land was not yet fully possessed by Israel (e.g., 13:1, 6–7; 15:63; 23:4–13). Some critical scholars believe that such

24. Hess 1996, 47.

25. Dillard and Longman 1994, 113.

texts are in irreconcilable contradiction, but this is not the case. God had truly given Israel all of the land. It was now her rightful possession. The Canaanites who remained in the land were now trespassers. The different texts indicate that because some Canaanites remained in the land, Israel had to make what belonged to her "on the ground" correspond to what belonged to her by right.

The final section of Joshua (chapters 22–24) deals with the absolute necessity of covenant fidelity in the land. The return of Reuben, Gad, and the half-tribe of Manasseh to the east of the Jordan is recounted in chapter 22. Before their return, Joshua reminds them to remain faithful to the covenant (22:5). Chapter 23 records Joshua's farewell address to the elders of Israel. He tells them that God will continue to drive the remaining Canaanites out of the land (v. 5). He then exhorts them to keep the law and remain faithful to God (v. 6). They are to separate themselves from the Canaanites because of the danger the Canaanites pose (vv. 7–13). Joshua reminds them that God has blessed them with the fulfillment of the promises, but he also warns them that unfaithfulness and disobedience will result in the covenant curses, including removal from the land (vv. 14–16).

The final chapter of Joshua describes a covenant renewal ceremony at Shechem. Joshua begins by providing a summary of what God has done for Israel since calling Abraham to himself (24:1–13). He then calls the people to make a decision: "choose this day whom you will serve" (v. 15). They must decide whether they will serve the living God or false gods. The people solemnly pledge to serve the true God (vv. 16–18). Then, in a comment reminiscent of Moses' words in Deuteronomy, Joshua tells the people, "You are not able to serve Yahweh, for he is a holy God" (v. 19; Deut. 9:6; 31:16–18, 20–21). The people insist that they will serve God, and Joshua ratifies the covenant (Josh. 24:21–28). The book concludes with a brief account of the death and burial of Joshua (vv. 29–33). Although the covenant renewal ceremony offers a clear parallel with Moses (Deut. 26:16–19; 29:1–32:47), there is at least one significant difference. Unlike Moses, Joshua does not have an appointed successor. The people are in the land, but they do not have a leader like Moses or Joshua to guide them in the service of God. The result of this situation is the story of Judges.[26]

26. Dillard and Longman 1994, 113.

Judges

The book of Judges is a narrative description of the historical era between the death of Joshua and the rise of the monarchy under Samuel (ca. 1400–1050 B.C.). The book itself was written after the beginning of the monarchy, but its author is anonymous. Raymond Dillard and Tremper Longman suggest that it could have been written as early as the tenth century B.C. or as late as the sixth century B.C.[27] Daniel Block, on the other hand, believes there is good evidence for dating the composition of the book more specifically during the reign of Manasseh in the seventh century B.C.[28] The evidence for any specific date of composition, however, is not conclusive.

Like the book of Joshua, the book of Judges continues to interpret Israel's history in light of her observance of God's covenant stipulations. However, whereas Joshua recounted a period of Israel's history largely marked by faithfulness, the book of Judges recounts a period of Israel's history characterized for the most part by unfaithfulness. After the death of Joshua (Judg. 1:1), Israel begins a long downward spiral of spiritual degeneration. This can be observed in the repeated refrain "And the people of Israel did what was evil in the sight of Yahweh and served the Baals" (e.g., 2:11; 3:7, 12; 4:1; 6:1; 10:6; 13:1).[29] The people had been repeatedly warned that if the Canaanites remained in the land, they would pose a serious threat to Israel (Ex. 34:11–16; Josh. 23:12–13). The book of Judges demonstrates the truth of those warnings (Judg. 2:3). It also demonstrates the faithfulness of God to his covenant people. In spite of Israel's wickedness, and in spite of the attempts of foreign nations to destroy her, God preserves Israel.[30]

It is often suggested that the purpose of Judges is to serve as an apology or rationale for the monarchy.[31] This suggestion is based on the statement repeated four times in the final chapters of Judges, "In those days there was no king in Israel" (17:6; 18:1; 19:1; 21:25). Furthermore, in those days, "everyone did what was right in his own eyes" (17:6; 21:25). While not denying the presence of this theme, Daniel Block argues that the book is more concerned with the spiritual state of Israel than with the monarchy:

27. Dillard and Longman 1994, 121.
28. Block 1999, 66–67.
29. For a helpful analysis of the stages in Israel's degeneration, see Block 1999, 41–43.
30. Dumbrell 1984, 132.
31. E.g., Howard 1993, 120; VanGemeren 1988a, 185, 195.

> This is a prophetic book, not a political tractate. It represents a call to return to the God of the covenant, whom the people have abandoned in favor of the virile and exciting fertility gods of the land. The theme of the book is the *Canaanization of Israelite society during the period of settlement.* The author's goal in exposing this problem is to wake up his own generation. This is an appeal to the covenant people to abandon all forms of paganism and return to Yahweh.[32]

An emphasis on this aspect of Judges allows us to outline the structure of the book in a way that demonstrates its underlying unity very clearly.[33]

The first part of the book (1:1–3:6) is an introduction that shows the background and causes of the Canaanization of Israel. The tribes did not drive out the inhabitants of the land as they had been commanded (1:27–36). The main body of the book (3:7–16:31) is concerned with God's response to the Canaanization of Israel. During this period of time, Israel's history follows a downward spiral pattern. Her apostasy provokes the Lord to send judgment in the form of oppressing nations (2:11–15). Israel then cries out to God, and in response God raises up a deliverer (or "judge") who subdues the enemy (2:16–18). After a period of peace Israel again sins against God, and the downward cycle repeats (2:19). In the climactic chapters of the book, the tribes of Dan and Benjamin demonstrate the depths of the Canaanization of Israel. The Danites demonstrate the religious degeneration of Israel in their idolatry (17:1–18:31). The tribe of Benjamin demonstrates the moral degeneration of Israel by committing a sin like that of Sodom and Gomorrah (19:1–21:25, esp. 19:22–30). By the end of the book "the holy war that should have been waged against the Canaanites was directed at one of their own tribes."[34]

It should be noted that the themes of Canaanization and monarchy are not mutually exclusive. The Canaanization of Israel does in fact provide a rationale for the monarchy. The people of Israel who lived during the historical era covered in the book of Judges were being prepared for a king. God had revealed to Moses that Israel would one day have a king (Deut. 17:14–20), but under the strong leadership of Moses and Joshua, the need for a monarchy was not apparent. During the period of the judges, however,

32. Block 1999, 58; see also Block 1988, 52.
33. Block 1999, 73.
34. Block 1999, 37.

there was a steady decline in the quality of leadership. As Arthur Cundall notes, "there was no-one remotely comparable with Moses, Joshua or Phinehas until the Lord raised up Samuel."[35] But would strong leadership, such as that found in a monarchy, halt the downward spiral? Or would a monarchy further contribute to the Canaanization of Israel?

Ruth

The events described in the book of Ruth occurred during the era of the judges (Ruth 1:1). However, whereas the book of Judges portrays the nation of Israel in an almost exclusively negative light, the book of Ruth indicates that covenant faithfulness did continue to exist during these years and that in the midst of this time of turmoil God was providentially preparing to raise up a king. The book of Ruth is a beautiful story with three main characters: Naomi, Ruth, and Boaz. Naomi is an Israelite woman who journeys to Moab with her husband Elimelech and her two sons to escape a famine (1:1–2). While in Moab, Naomi is widowed, and her sons marry two Moabite women, Orpah and Ruth (1:3–4). During their ten-year stay in Moab, Naomi's two sons also die, leaving her without a husband or sons (1:5). She eventually decides to return to her home in Bethlehem. Because of her love for Naomi, Ruth insists on coming with her (1:6–22). In a well-known statement of her loyalty, Ruth declares, "Do not urge me to leave you or to return from following you. For where you go I will go, and where you lodge I will lodge. Your people shall be my people, and your God my God" (1:16).

After returning to Bethlehem, Ruth meets Boaz, a relative of Naomi's husband (2:1–23). Naomi tells Ruth that Boaz is a *go'el*, a "redeemer" (2:20). As a redeemer, Boaz had the responsibility of preserving the family name of Elimelech (Deut. 25:5–10). Naomi wants Boaz to do this by marrying Ruth, the widow of her son Mahlon (Ruth 3:1–5). Boaz indicates that he is in fact a redeemer, but he reveals that there is another redeemer, a closer relative (v. 12). He tells Ruth that if the other man will redeem her, that is his right, but if the other man will not redeem her, he will do so himself (v. 13). After settling the legal issues, Boaz does ultimately take Ruth as his wife (4:13). They bear a son named Obed, who is the father of Jesse, the father of David (vv. 14–22).

35. Cundall and Morris 1968, 40.

One of the main purposes of the book of Ruth is to reveal the absolute sovereignty of God in his hidden providence. In the lives of Naomi, Ruth, and Boaz, God is providentially preparing the family through whom David will come.[36] As part of his preparations for the monarchy, God extends his blessings to a Gentile Moabite woman and brings her into the covenant community.[37] Among the descendants of this Moabite woman will be her great-grandson David, and ultimately Jesus himself (Matt. 1:5–6). The book of Ruth clearly teaches that God has not forsaken Israel during this time of widespread apostasy, and he has not forgotten his promises.

1 and 2 Samuel

The books of Samuel deal in the broadest sense with the establishment of the monarchy in Israel in fulfillment of promises found within the Pentateuch (Gen. 36:31; 49:10; Deut. 17:14). Within this larger context, these books focus on the stories of three significant individuals in the history of Israel: Samuel, Saul, and David. The events in the lives of these men occurred over a period of approximately one and a half centuries. The book of 1 Samuel covers the period of time from the birth of Samuel (ca. 1100 B.C.) to the death of Saul (ca. 1010 B.C.), and 2 Samuel covers the period from the death of Saul to the death of David (ca. 970 B.C.).[38] Like the other books in the Former Prophets, the books of Samuel emphasize covenantal themes such as the land, and the blessings and curses that result from faithfulness and unfaithfulness respectively.

The two books of Samuel may be divided into five major sections. The rise of Samuel is related in 1 Samuel 1–7. The story of the rise and rule of Saul, a king like that of the other nations, is found in 1 Samuel 8–15. The rise to power of David, a man after God's own heart, is recounted in 1 Samuel 16–2 Samuel 4. The story of David's consolidated reign is found in 2 Samuel 5–20. The books of Samuel then conclude with an epilogue in 2 Samuel 21–24 that provides some final words about David's rule as king over Israel. The rise of the Israelite monarchy is the central theme of

36. Block 1999, 610; VanGemeren 1988a, 202.

37. The book of Ruth indicates that Deuteronomy 23:3–5, in which Moabites are excluded from the assembly of the Lord, is not an absolute prohibition. Because of her faith, the Moabitess Ruth is not only included in the people of God, she becomes the great-grandmother of David and an ancestor of Jesus Christ. See McConville 2002, 353.

38. Provan, Long, and Longman 2003, 199–202.

the books. The era of the judges had ended in complete chaos and anarchy (Judg. 21:25). Will the situation be any better under a king?[39]

The first chapter of 1 Samuel tells the story of the birth of Samuel to Hannah. Samuel is an important transitional figure in the Old Testament. As Provan, Long, and Longman observe, he is the last of the judges, he is the successor of Eli the priest, and he is at the forefront of the prophetic movement that is so pronounced during the monarchical period (Acts 3:24).[40] First Samuel 2:1–10 records the prayer of Samuel's mother Hannah.[41] This poetic section, and that in 2 Samuel 22:1–23:7, frame the entire narrative found in the books of Samuel.[42] Hannah's prayer looks forward to the rise of God's anointed king and to his victories (1 Sam. 2:10), while David's songs praise God for giving him those victories and for establishing him as king (2 Sam. 22:48–51). Notably, Hannah's prayer also includes a declaration of God's power to raise the dead: "Yahweh kills and brings to life; he brings down to Sheol and raises up" (1 Sam. 2:6; cf. Deut. 32:39).

The book of 1 Samuel continues with God's rejection of the two sons of Eli the priest because of their sinfulness (1 Sam. 2:12–34). God promises, however, that he will raise up for himself a faithful priest who shall do according to what is in God's heart and mind (v. 35).[43] The call of Samuel and his establishment as a prophet in Israel are recounted in 1 Samuel 3. First Samuel 4–7, then, recounts the story of the Philistines' capture and return of the ark of the covenant. The sons of Eli are killed in the initial battle with the Philistine army (1 Sam. 4:11), and Eli himself dies when he learns that the ark has been captured (v. 18). But after suffering a series of divine judgments, the Philistines ultimately decide to return the ark to Israel (1 Sam. 6:1–7:2). Samuel is then made a judge over Israel, and under his leadership the people are able to subdue the Philistines for a time (1 Sam. 7:3–17).

The story of the rise of Saul to the throne of Israel is told in 1 Samuel 8–15. Samuel had made his sons judges over Israel, but his sons had perverted justice (8:1–3). The elders of Israel then came to Samuel and requested

39. Dillard and Longman 1994, 145.

40. Provan, Long, and Longman 2003, 202.

41. Hannah's prayer is strikingly similar to the Magnificat of Mary (Luke 1:46–55).

42. Fretheim 1983, 43.

43. This prophecy appears to have been fulfilled, at least initially, by Zadok (1 Kings. 2:35). It is ultimately fulfilled by Jesus, the great high priest (Heb. 7–8).

that he appoint for them "a king to judge us like all the nations" (v. 5). Their request is an implicit rejection of God as their true King (v. 7). The problem, however, was not in the request per se since God himself had revealed to Moses that Israel would someday have a king (Gen. 17:6, 16; 35:11; 49:10; Num. 24:7, 17–19; Deut. 17:14–20). The problem rested in the people's motives. They wanted to be "like all the nations" (1 Sam. 8:5, 20), in spite of the fact that they had been called to be a holy nation (Ex. 19:6).

Saul, a man from the tribe of Benjamin, is chosen to be king (1 Sam. 9), and is anointed by Samuel (1 Sam. 10:1). His home is said to be Gibeah, which is not a good sign in light of recent Israelite history (v. 26; Judg. 19:22–30).[44] Initially, Saul proves his worth by defeating the Ammonites (1 Sam. 11), but Samuel warns that neither Israel nor her king will escape judgment if they rebel against God and are disobedient to him (1 Sam. 12:13–25). Saul's first major act of disobedience occurs as he is preparing to fight the Philistines. Rather than wait for Samuel, Saul offers unlawful sacrifices to God (1 Sam. 13:8–12). As a result, Samuel tells him that his kingdom will not continue (vv. 13–14). After further acts of disobedience (1 Sam. 15:9), God tells Samuel that he has rejected Saul as king (vv. 10–28).

The story of David's rise to the throne of Israel is found in 1 Samuel 16–2 Samuel 4. In 1 Samuel 16, David is shown to be God's chosen one and is anointed king by Samuel (vv. 1, 12–13). The anointing of David anticipates the founding of the Davidic dynasty, a crucial event in redemptive history.[45] The anointing of David is also crucial for understanding the Old Testament concept of the Messiah (Heb. *mashiah*). As Dillard and Longman explain, "The Hebrew term *mashiah* means 'anointed one,' and the idea of a Messiah for Israel grows out of her ideology about a righteous king, one who would be like David."[46] Throughout the books of Samuel, the "Lord's anointed" is a major theme (1 Sam. 16:3, 6, 12–13; 24:6; 26:9, 11, 16, 23; 2 Sam. 1:14, 16; 3:39; 19:21). The king is God's anointed one, that is, his "messiah." The rule of David as God's anointed one, his "messiah," is later used by the prophets to picture the coming eschatological king (Isa. 7:14–16;

44. Howard 1993, 158.
45. VanGemeren 1988a, 202.
46. Dillard and Longman 1994, 146.

9:1–7; 11:1–16).[47] The remaining chapters of 1 Samuel recount David's rise in popularity and Saul's repeated attempts to kill him (1 Sam. 17–31). The first book of Samuel ends with the ignominious death of Saul (1 Sam. 31:3–4).

After David learns of the death of Saul, and mourns for him (2 Sam. 1:4, 17–27), the men of Judah anoint him king (2 Sam. 2:4). But Abner, the commander of Saul's army, anoints Saul's son Ish-bosheth to be king over Israel (vv. 8–11). There follows a long war between the house of David and the house of Saul (2 Sam. 3:1), but Abner ultimately joins David, Ish-bosheth is murdered, and David is anointed king over all Israel (2 Sam. 5:3–4).[48] David then defeats the Jebusites and takes the city of Jerusalem, calling it the city of David (vv. 6–9). The ark of the covenant, the symbol of the throne of the divine King, is brought to Jerusalem (2 Sam. 6:1–15), and from that point onward the city becomes the religious and political center of the Davidic kingdom.[49]

A key event in redemptive history is recorded in 2 Samuel 7. According to Walter Brueggemann, this chapter "occupies the dramatic and theological center of the entire Samuel corpus."[50] The chapter records the events surrounding the establishment of the Davidic covenant. William Dumbrell helpfully explains why the events of this chapter follow those of chapter 6: "What is thus being said by the sequence of these chapters, is that Yahweh's kingship must be first provided for before the question of Israel's can be taken up. Only when such an acknowledgement of Yahweh's rule has been made may the possibility of a firmly established Israelite royal line be discussed."[51] David had captured Jerusalem and had brought the ark into the city, and God had given him rest from all his enemies (2 Sam. 7:1). At this point, David calls Nathan the prophet and expresses his desire to build a "house" (Heb. *bayit*) before God, a permanent temple instead of a tent.[52] God's response to David is found in 2 Samuel 7:4–16.

47. Dumbrell 1994, 64.

48. It is worth noting that the establishment of David's kingship occurs in progressive stages. He is anointed as the rightful king by Samuel in 1 Samuel 16. Much later, in 2 Samuel 2:4, he is anointed king over Judah. Only after a long war between his house and the house of Saul (2 Sam. 3:1) is he anointed king over all Israel (2 Sam. 5:3–4).

49. VanGemeren 1988a, 207.

50. Brueggemann 1990, 253; see also Anderson 1989, 112.

51. Dumbrell 1984, 142.

52. The word "house" is used fifteen times in this chapter, but it is used with four different denotations. It is used to refer to a king's palace (vv. 1, 2); a temple (vv. 5, 6, 7, 13); a royal dynasty (vv. 11, 16, 19, 25, 26, 27, 29); and a family (v. 18). See Hamilton 2004, 317.

God reminds David that since the time he brought Israel out of Egypt he has moved with the people in the tabernacle (2 Sam. 7:4–7). He reminds David that he has been with him wherever he went and has defeated David's enemies (vv. 8–9a). He then promises David that he will make for David a great name (v. 9b). God declares that he will give Israel rest from her enemies and that he will make a house for David (vv. 10–11). God promises that he will establish the kingdom of David's offspring (v. 12). He promises that David's offspring will build a house for God, and that he will establish David's kingdom forever (v. 13).

God promises, "I will be to him a father, and he shall be to me a son" (v. 14a). God warns that he will discipline David's offspring if he commits iniquity, but God also promises that his steadfast love will not depart from David as it was taken from Saul (vv. 14b–15). Finally, God promises David, "And your house and your kingdom shall be made sure forever before me. Your throne shall be established forever" (v. 16). David's prayer of gratitude is found in 2 Samuel 7:18–29. In this prayer, he refers to God's promise as "instruction for mankind," indicating that this covenant will involve the destiny of all mankind (v. 19).[53]

Although the Hebrew term for "covenant" (*berit*) is not found in this chapter, Scripture elsewhere does refer to this promise as a covenant (2 Sam. 23:5; Ps. 89:3). The Davidic covenant had been anticipated in God's covenant with Abraham (Gen. 17:6). It would be through the Davidic king that God's promise of blessing to the nations would be accomplished (2 Sam. 7:19; Ps. 72:8–11, 17). The Davidic covenant had also been anticipated in the Mosaic covenant (Deut. 17:14–20). The Davidic king would be the expression of God's theocratic rule in Israel.[54] He was to reflect the righteous rule of the divine King. He was also to lead Israel in the faithful observance of the Mosaic law. The Abrahamic covenant had promised a realm and a people for God's kingdom. The Mosaic covenant provided the law of the kingdom. The Davidic covenant now provides a human king for the kingdom. God's creational purpose to establish his kingdom with his image-bearer exercising dominion now reaches a new stage in its progressive accomplishment.[55]

One of the major emphases of the Davidic covenant is the idea of perpetuity. David had wanted to build for God a permanent dwelling place,

53. Dumbrell 1984, 152.
54. Wright 2005, 74.
55. Dumbrell 1984, 127.

but God instead promised that he would establish for David a permanent dynasty.[56] The Hebrew term *'ad-'olam*, or "forever," is found eight times in this chapter emphasizing the significance of this aspect of the covenant.[57] As A. A. Anderson explains, "The main feature of this kingship will be its permanent stability: it will last forever (vv 13b, 16)."[58]

In Genesis 49:10, Jacob had prophesied that the scepter would belong to the tribe of Judah until the coming of the one to whom such royal status truly belonged. This prophecy finds its initial fulfillment in the establishment of the Davidic kingship.[59] But the Davidic covenant looks not only to the fulfillment of past prophecies, it also looks forward, laying the foundation for Israel's eschatological hopes. The Davidic covenant becomes the foundation for the messianic prophecies of the later prophets.[60] As O. Palmer Robertson explains, the Davidic throne "was a typological representation of the throne of God itself."[61] The relationship is so close that the throne of David is referred to in Scripture as the "throne of Yahweh" (1 Chron. 29:23). With the coming of the Davidic monarchy, then, God's kingdom had already come to some extent, but it remained a shadow of a greater future reality.[62]

The Davidic covenant became, as Robert Bergen observes, "the nucleus around which messages of hope proclaimed by Hebrew prophets of later generations were built."[63] This covenant is mentioned or alluded to in several of the Psalms (Pss. 21, 72, 89, 110, 132). It is also alluded to in the prophetic writings. As the monarchy eventually began to slide into wickedness, the prophets began to understand the promises of the Davidic covenant eschatologically. As Joyce Baldwin notes, the prophets taught that David's "booth would be repaired (Am. 9:11); a Davidic child would establish his throne with justice and with righteousness (Is. 9:6–7); a branch from the stump of Jesse would yet create an ideal kingdom (Is. 11:1–9; cf. Je. 23:5; Zc. 3:8)."[64] The promises that had not yet been fulfilled would be fulfilled in the future (Isa. 7:13–25; 16:5; 55:3; Jer. 30:8; 33:14–26; Ezek.

56. Robertson 1980, 232.
57. Kaiser 1995, 81.
58. Anderson 1989, 122.
59. Bergen 1996, 336.
60. Bergen 1996, 336; Brueggemann 1990, 257; and Robertson 1980, 233–34.
61. Robertson 1980, 249.
62. Robertson 1980, 241.
63. Bergen 1996, 337.
64. Baldwin 1988, 213.

34:20–24; 37:24–25; Hos. 3:5; Zech. 6:12–13; 12:7–8). Ultimately, these messianic hopes would be fulfilled in Jesus, the true Son of David (Matt. 1:1; Acts 13:22–23).[65]

Some of David's many achievements as king over Israel, including his military victories over the Philistines, Moabites, Ammonites, and Syrians are found in 2 Samuel 8–10. The tragic story of David's sin with Bathsheba is then recorded in 2 Samuel 11. In his rebuke of David, Nathan declares to him, "the sword shall never depart from your house" (2 Sam. 12:10), a curse that characterizes the remainder of the deuteronomic history. David repents of his sin and is forgiven, but he still suffers many consequences. His child by Bathsheba dies (12:15–23); his son Absalom conspires against him, forcing David to flee Jerusalem; and Absalom himself is eventually killed (2 Sam. 15–19). The books of Samuel end with David's song of deliverance (2 Sam. 22:1–51) and his "last words" (23:1–7). In this poetic section, David praises God for delivering him from his enemies and for establishing an everlasting covenant with him (23:5). A question remained however. Would David's offspring remain faithful to God? This question is answered in 1 and 2 Kings.

1 and 2 Kings

The books of 1 and 2 Kings recount events that cover a period of just over four hundred years, from the death of David (ca. 970 B.C.) to the release of Jehoiachin from prison in Babylon (ca. 561 B.C.). Kings also marks the conclusion of a significant section of the Old Testament canon, the Former Prophets (Joshua, Judges, Samuel, and Kings). The books of Genesis through Samuel have described the progressive and gradual fulfillment of God's promises to give Abraham the land of Canaan and to make of him a great nation. The books of 1 and 2 Kings now describe a major reversal, a movement toward the eventual loss of land and exile.[66] The books of 1 and 2 Kings describe the rise and fall of the Davidic empire, with blame for the fall resting squarely upon the shoulders of the kings, specifically for their failure to lead the people in wholehearted devotion to God in accordance

65. Bergen 1996, 337–38. Jesus is the Son of David who will build a "house" for God, a new temple made without hands. He is the Son of David whose kingdom is established forever.

66. Alexander 2002, 85.

with the Davidic covenant. Instead of leading the people to follow God, the kings regularly lead the people into idolatry.[67]

According to Jewish tradition, the prophet Jeremiah was the author of the books of 1 and 2 Kings.[68] But because the books themselves do not name the author, it is impossible to identify him with any certainty. What is certain is that he wrote Kings during the exile and used several written sources.[69] The last event recorded in Kings is the release of Jehoiachin from prison in Babylon in 561 B.C., about twenty-five years into the exile. The book itself is an explanation of the reasons for the exile. Why has the nation that God chose and brought out of slavery in Egypt gone into exile? Have God's promises to Israel failed? The author of Kings attempts to make sense of these events for the people of Israel. The books of 1 and 2 Kings teach that God's promises have not failed. In fact, God has removed Israel from the land precisely as he promised to do if she persisted in following other gods.[70] Yet the promises have not failed. They have not been revoked.[71] There are hints throughout the books of 1 and 2 Kings that the exile will not be the final word (e.g., 1 Kings 11:39).

One of the most difficult issues involved with the books of 1 and 2 Kings is the chronology of the reigns of the kings. It is beyond the scope of this volume to address the numerous complicated issues associated with this problem.[72] The dates used in figure 4 follow David Howard's modification of Edwin Thiele's chronology.[73]

Fig. 4. The kings of Israel and Judah.

ISRAEL			JUDAH		
1.	Jeroboam I	930–909	1.	Rehoboam	930–913
2.	Nadab	909–908	2.	Abijam	913–910
3.	Baasha	908–886	3.	Asa	910–869
4.	Elah	886–885			

67. House 1995, 74.

68. Dillard and Longman 1994, 149.

69. The author uses several named sources: the "Book of the Acts of Solomon" (1 Kings 11:41), the "Book of the Chronicles of the Kings of Israel" (e.g., 1 Kings 14:19; 15:31; 16:5), and the "Book of the Chronicles of the Kings of Judah" (e.g., 1 Kings 14:29; 15:7, 23).

70. Hobbs 1985, xxvii; Dillard and Longman 1994, 161.

71. Dumbrell 1984, 153.

72. For the classic comprehensive discussion of the issues involved, see Thiele 1983. For more recent discussions, see Tetley 2005; Young 2005.

73. Howard 1993, 187.

ISRAEL			JUDAH		
5.	Zimri	885			
6.	(Tibni)	885–880			
7.	Omri	885–874			
8.	Ahab	874–853	4.	Jehoshaphat	872–848
9.	Ahaziah	853–852	5.	Jehoram	
10.	Joram	852–841		(Joram)	853–841
			6.	Ahaziah	841
11.	Jehu	841–814	7.	(Athaliah)	841–835
12.	Jehoahaz	814–798	8.	Joash	
13.	Jehoash			(Jehoash)	835–796
	(Joash)	798–782	9.	Amaziah	796–767
14.	Jeroboam II	793–753	10.	Azariah	792–740
15.	Zechariah	753			
16.	Shallum	752			
17.	Menahem	752–742	11.	Jotham	750–732
18.	Pekahiah	742–740			
19.	Pekah	752–732	12.	Ahaz	735–715
20.	Hoshea	732–723/22	13.	Hezekiah	729–686
			14.	Manasseh	697–642
			15.	Amon	642–640
			16.	Josiah	640–609
			17.	Jehoahaz	609
			18.	Jehoiakim	609–598
			19.	Jehoiachin	598–597
			20.	Zedekiah	597–586

The only significant difference between Howard's chronology and Thiele's is that Howard posits a coregency of Hezekiah and Ahaz in order to explain the overlap between Hezekiah's reign in Judah and Hoshea's reign in Israel (2 Kings 17–18).

The books of 1 and 2 Kings may be divided into seven major sections.[74] First Kings 1–2 details the end of David's reign and Solomon's accession to the throne, and 1 Kings 3–11 describes Solomon's lengthy reign. The history of the divided kingdom up to the time of the fall of the northern kingdom in 722 B.C. is found in 1 Kings 12–2 Kings 17. There are four sections within these chapters. First Kings 12–16 describes the division of

74. Following the division suggested by House 1995, 60–61.

the kingdom and the slide into idolatry. First Kings 17–2 Kings 1 describes the ministry of Elijah, while 2 Kings 2–13 describes the ministry of Elisha. Second Kings 14–17, then, recounts the final years of the northern kingdom of Israel. The final section of Kings is 2 Kings 18–25, which recounts the history of the southern kingdom of Judah up to the time of the Babylonian exile in 586 B.C.

The first two chapters of 1 Kings act as a transition between the books of Samuel and the books of 1 and 2 Kings. These chapters recount the manner in which Solomon became the king of Israel. David has now grown old, and his son Adonijah attempts to establish himself as the heir to the throne (1 Kings 1:5–10). Nathan the prophet and Bathsheba hear of Adonijah's plans, so they arrange for David to anoint Solomon as king (1:11–53). The Davidic dynasty is thus founded in fulfillment of the covenant promise God made to David (2 Sam. 7:12). Before David dies, he gives Solomon instruction, urging him to follow God by keeping his commandments (1 Kings 2:1–4). After David's death, Solomon's reign is firmly established (2:10–12).

Solomon's eventful reign (ca. 970–930 B.C.) is described in 1 Kings 3–11. His reign begins with a prayer in which he asks God for wisdom (3:3–9). God is pleased with Solomon's request and grants it (3:10–13). God then makes a promise to Solomon, saying: "if you will walk in my ways, keeping my statutes and my commandments, as your father David walked, then I will lengthen your days" (v. 14). Significantly, the establishment of Solomon's reign is described in terms that indicate it is the fulfillment of divine promises.[75] Judah and Israel are said to be "as many as the sand by the sea" (1 Kings 4:20; Gen. 22:17). The kingdom is said to extend from the river Euphrates to the border of Egypt (1 Kings 4:21; Gen. 15:18). Solomon's reign is also described in terms that the prophets would later use to describe the latter-day reign of the Messiah. During Solomon's reign it is said that Judah and Israel "lived in safety, from Dan even to Beersheba, every man under his vine and under his fig tree" (1 Kings 4:25; Mic. 4:4).[76]

The most significant event to occur during the reign of Solomon is the building of the temple at Jerusalem. Its construction fulfills Moses' words concerning God's chosen place of worship (Deut. 12:5, 11, 14; 14:23; 15:20; 16:2). Like the tabernacle, the temple is to be the place of God's presence

75. Dumbrell 1994, 75.
76. Dempster 2003, 148.

in the midst of his people. Solomon's preparations for the construction of the temple are found in 1 Kings 5, while the actual construction is recorded in 1 Kings 6. The construction of the temple began in 966 B.C., the fourth year of Solomon's reign, 480 years after the exodus from Egypt (6:1). It took seven years to complete (6:38).[77]

After the completion of the temple, the ark of God is brought into the Holy of Holies, and the glory of God fills the temple (8:1–11). Solomon then blesses the Lord for fulfilling his promise to David (v. 15) and offers a prayer of benediction (vv. 22–61). He acknowledges that this earthly temple cannot contain God, but he asks that God make known his presence in this place (vv. 27–29). Significantly, Solomon's prayer also assumes that Israel will ultimately disobey God and be exiled from the land, yet it also assumes that restoration is possible if the people repent and turn back to God (8:33–34, 46–50; cf. Deut. 30:1–3). The temple is also to be a means of blessing the nations in fulfillment of the promise to Abraham (1 Kings 8:43, 60; Gen. 12:3).[78] God hears Solomon's prayer and consecrates the temple by putting his name there forever (1 Kings 9:1–3). God then promises Solomon that if he walks in faithful obedience, his dynasty will continue, but if he turns away from God, Israel will go into exile from the land (vv. 4–9). God has established David's "house," and Solomon has built God's "house." As Robertson explains, "The merger of these two 'houses' in one place on Mount Zion established the reality of God's kingdom on earth."[79]

The final part of the narrative concerning Solomon is found in 1 Kings 9:10–11:43 and recounts his fall into idolatry. 1 Kings 10 recounts the visit of the queen of Sheba and details Solomon's great wealth. Solomon's tragic downfall is then described in chapter 11. He marries many foreign women, ignoring Moses' warning (11:1–2; Ex. 34:16). These foreign wives eventually succeed in turning Solomon's heart away from God (1 Kings 11:3). He begins to worship other gods and builds altars to the false gods Chemosh and Molech (vv. 5–8). Solomon's idolatry provokes God's anger, and God tells Solomon that the kingdom will be taken from him (vv. 9–11). He promises Solomon, however, that for the sake of David, the entire kingdom will not be taken (vv. 12–13). First Kings 11:29–39 records the

77. Note that the construction of Solomon's own palace took thirteen years to complete (1 Kings 7:1). This may be an early indication in the text of Solomon's wrong priorities.

78. Dempster 2003, 149; Provan 1995, 82.

79. Robertson 2004, 3.

prophecy of Ahijah concerning the division of the kingdom. His prophecy also includes a word of hope, "I will afflict the offspring of David because of this, but not forever" (v. 39). The kingdom will ultimately be restored to the offspring of David.[80] God remains faithful to his covenant promises despite the sins of those to whom the promises were given.

The remainder of 1 and 2 Kings recounts the history of the divided kingdom up to the fall of the northern kingdom of Israel to Assyria in 722 B.C. and the fall of the southern kingdom of Judah to Babylon in 586 B.C. After the death of Solomon, his son Rehoboam becomes king over Israel (1 Kings 11:43). Rehoboam's folly, however, results in the division of the kingdom (1 Kings 12:1–24). Jeroboam becomes king over the ten northern tribes of Israel, while Rehoboam remains king over the southern kingdom consisting of the tribes of Judah and Benjamin (vv. 20–21). Jeroboam immediately proceeds to establish a rival religion for the northern kingdom, building golden calves in Bethel and Dan (vv. 25–33; cf. Ex. 32). A man of God from Judah confronts Jeroboam with his sin (1 Kings 13:1–10), even predicting the reign of Josiah almost three hundred years beforehand (13:2; 2 Kings 23). Ahijah prophesies against Jeroboam in 1 Kings 14:7–16. He promises that Israel will be exiled for her sin (v. 15). The wicked reign of Jeroboam is significant. His idolatrous transgression is the standard by which all of the northern kings will be measured in the remaining chapters of 1 and 2 Kings.[81]

It is significant that during the era of the divided kingdom, prophetism became quite prominent. VanGemeren explains how it developed in two ways during this time:

> First, with the ministry of Elijah, the prophet became God's appointed *covenant prosecutor*. Second, in the eighth century, prophetic oracles began to be written down. The writing, editing, collecting, and organizing of the prophetic oracles mark the beginning of *classical prophetism* as a distinct development in Israelite prophetism.[82]

The books of 1 and 2 Kings provide the historical context for these developments, and the significance of prophecy is a repeated theme in these books (1 Kings 13:1–2, 5; 15:29; 2 Kings 1:17; 7:1; 9:36; 10:17).

80. VanGemeren 1988a, 251.

81. Dillard and Longman 1994, 162–63; see 1 Kings 15:26, 34; 16:19, 26, 30–31; 2 Kings 3:3; 10:29; 13:2, 11; 14:24; 15:9, 24, 28.

82. VanGemeren 1988a, 255.

The ministry of the prophets Elijah and Elisha occupies more than a third of the total chapters found in the books of 1 and 2 Kings. First Kings 17–2 Kings 1 recounts Elijah's ministry, while 2 Kings 2–13 recounts Elisha's ministry. Elijah is one of the greatest Old Testament prophets, and as Donald Wiseman observes, he "is presented as Moses *redivivus* fighting for the purity and continuance of the worship of the LORD amid idolatry and the intrusive syntheistic acknowledgement of foreign gods."[83] Van Gemeren explains Elijah's significance in the development of the prophetic ministry in Israel:

> Elijah is the beginning of a long line of prophets who charged God's people with breaking the covenant and pronounced God's judgment on them. Though Elijah primarily directed his message to the king, his ministry extended beyond Ahab to *all* Israel. He was God's first covenant prosecutor, for he charged Israel with its failures to conform to the covenant expectations (1 Kings 18:21).[84]

Much of Elijah's ministry involves confrontation with the idolatry of Ahab and Jezebel. This conflict reaches a climax in 1 Kings 18 with a contest between Elijah and the priests of Baal. The conflict reveals to the people not only that Baal is powerless, but also that he does not exist. In 1 Kings 19, Elijah flees from the wrath of Jezebel to Mount Horeb, the mountain of God (v. 8; cf. Ex. 3:1–3). There God reveals to him that he is not alone. There are seven thousand left in Israel who have not worshiped Baal (1 Kings 19:18). This text is important because, as Dumbrell observes, it "is the first biblical attestation of a group of believers within the nation, different from the nation itself."[85] In other words, this text introduces the concept of the faithful remnant.

Elisha's story begins with the account of Elijah's ascent into heaven in 2 Kings 2. Elisha had already been chosen to take Elijah's place (1 Kings 19:16–21), and he proves himself to be a worthy successor. Elisha's ministry is characterized by the working of many miracles. He miraculously provides for a widow (2 Kings 4:1–7), raises the dead (vv. 8–37), purifies contaminated food (vv. 38–41), and feeds a multitude with only a few loaves of

83. Wiseman 1993, 45. For some of the parallels between Moses and Elijah, see Dillard and Longman 1994, 167.

84. VanGemeren 1990, 37.

85. Dumbrell 1994, 78; see also Hasel 1974, 159–73.

bread (vv. 42–44). He also heals the Gentile army commander Naaman, reminding the reader again that God's grace and blessing are ultimately to be extended to all the nations (5:1–14).

Following the account of Elisha, 2 Kings 14–17 describes the remaining history of the northern kingdom of Israel to the time of its fall to Assyria in 722 B.C. These chapters focus on the reigns of the last kings of Israel, namely Jeroboam II (793–753), Zechariah (753), Shallum (752), Menahem (752–742), Pekahiah (742–740), Pekah (752–732), and Hoshea (732–722). All of these kings did evil in the sight of God and did not depart from the sins of Jeroboam.[86] It was during this period of time that Amos and Hosea prophesied in the northern kingdom warning the people of judgment to come.[87] The fall of Israel to Assyria in 722 B.C. is recorded in 2 Kings 17:6.[88] The author of Kings informs his readers that all of these things occurred because the people sinned against God by committing idolatry (2 Kings 17:7–23). Moses had warned the people that exile would be the punishment for such sin (Lev. 26:33; Deut. 28:64). The prophets had warned them as well, and finally the judgment had come. Would the southern kingdom of Judah learn from Israel's mistake and repent? That question is answered in the final chapters of 2 Kings.

The king of Judah at the time of Israel's fall was Hezekiah (729–686). During his reign, Isaiah and Micah both prophesied.[89] Hezekiah is described as one who did what was right in the eyes of God (2 Kings 18:3). The author of Kings declares, "there was none like him among all the kings of Judah after him, nor among those who were before him" (v. 5).[90] It is said of Hezekiah that "Yahweh was with him" (v. 7), words previously used only of David (e.g., 1 Sam. 16:18; 18:12; 2 Sam. 5:10). Through the mighty power of God, Judah is delivered from the fate that befell the northern kingdom

86. The repeated judgment on all of the northern kings and many of the southern kings, namely, that they "did evil in the sight of Yahweh," is the same judgment that repeatedly fell upon the Israelites during the period of the judges (e.g., 1 Kings 15:26, 34; 16:25, 30; 22:52; 2 Kings 8:18, 27; 13:2, 11; 14:24; 15:9, 18, 24, 28; 17:2; 21:2, 20; 23:32, 37; 24:9, 19; cf. Judg. 2:11; 3:7, 12; 4:1; 6:1; 10:6; 13:1). The presence of a king did not solve the problem of Israel's waywardness.

87. See chapter 5 for a full discussion of the message of these prophets.

88. It is important to note that a remnant of the ten northern tribes came to Judah before the exile and became part of the covenant community in the southern kingdom (2 Chron. 30:1, 6–9, 26–27; 31:1). They did not completely cease to exist. See VanGemeren 1988a, 259.

89. For more on the message of these prophets see chapters 5 and 6.

90. The same is said of Josiah in 2 Kings 23:25. The description is evidently a figure of speech used to indicate Hezekiah's (and later Josiah's) exceptional righteousness.

(2 Kings 18:13–19:37). Soon after the miraculous defeat of Assyria, however, Hezekiah becomes ill and near death (20:1a). Isaiah delivers God's word to Hezekiah, telling him "Set your house in order, for you shall die; you shall not recover" (v. 1b). Hezekiah, however, prays to God and is told by Isaiah that he will be healed and live another fifteen years (vv. 5–6).[91] Tragically, during his illness Hezekiah receives envoys from Babylon and shows them all the great treasures of Jerusalem (20:12–15). Upon discovering what Hezekiah has done, Isaiah prophesies the coming judgment of Judah by the Babylonians (vv. 16–18).

The wicked reigns of Manasseh (697–642) and Amon (642–640) are recorded in 2 Kings 21.[92] Of Manasseh it is said that he led the people to do more evil than the Canaanites had done (v. 9). As a result of his wickedness, God denounces him and promises that the judgment of exile is coming (vv. 10–16). Three hundred years earlier, a man of God had confronted Jeroboam and prophesied the birth of a king named Josiah who would destroy the idols in Israel (1 Kings 13:2). Josiah's accession to the throne and his reign (640–609) are recorded in 2 Kings 22–23. Both Jeremiah and Zephaniah began their prophetic ministries during the reign of this godly king.[93]

According to 2 Kings, Josiah did what was right in the eyes of God (22:2). He repairs the temple and when Hilkiah the high priest finds a copy of the book of the law, Josiah repents for the sins of his fathers (vv. 3–13). God declares through the prophetess Huldah that judgment will still come upon Judah, but it will not occur during Josiah's life (vv. 14–20). Josiah's reforms are recounted in 2 Kings 23. He begins by tearing down all idols and high places (23:1–20). He then restores the Passover (vv. 21–27). It is said of Josiah that he "turned to Yahweh with all his heart and with all his soul and with all his might" (v. 25; cf. Deut. 6:5). Yet despite all of Josiah's reforms, judgment would not be averted (2 Kings 23:26–27).

After the death of Josiah, his son Jehoahaz becomes king (609 B.C.), but he does evil in the eyes of God (2 Kings 23:28–32). He is captured by Pharaoh

91. This dramatic text demonstrates that some prophetic pronouncements are not definite fixed decrees but instead a means to elicit prayer and repentance (see Jer. 18:1–10; 26:2–3; Amos 7:1–6; Jonah 3:4, 10).

92. Nahum's prophecies against Assyria were delivered during the latter years of the reign of Manasseh.

93. For more on the message of these prophets see chapter 7.

Neco who places Eliakim on the throne in his place (609–598). Neco also changes Eliakim's name to Jehoiakim (vv. 33–35).[94] Jehoiakim also does evil in the sight of God (vv. 36–37). He becomes a vassal of Nebuchadnezzar, the king of Babylon, but he rebels, and God sends the Chaldeans against Judah just as he had warned (2 Kings 24:1–2; cf. 20:17; 21:12–14; 23:27). Jehoiakim's son Jehoiachin reigns for three months in Jerusalem (598–597), and he does evil in the sight of God just as his father had done (24:8–9). During his reign, in 597 B.C., Babylon besieges Jerusalem and he is taken captive along with many others to Babylon (vv. 10–16).[95] Nebuchadnezzar then makes Mattaniah king in his place and changes Mattaniah's name to Zedekiah (v. 17). Zedekiah, however, also eventually rebels against Babylon (v. 20), and as a result Babylon destroys Judah in 586 B.C.

Jerusalem is conquered, the temple is burned, and more prisoners are taken captive to Babylon (2 Kings 25:1–21). The Babylonians then appoint Gedaliah as a provisional governor in Judah, but he is assassinated by some of the remaining Israelites (vv. 22–26). As the book ends, Jehoiachin is released from prison (561 B.C.) and is shown favor by the king of Babylon (vv. 27–30). The end of the book of 2 Kings marks the beginning of the Babylonian exile, one of the defining moments in Israel's history. The people had been warned repeatedly since the time of Moses that exile from the Promised Land would be the ultimate judgment that would befall them if they turned from God to idols. Now that judgment had come.

1 and 2 Chronicles

In the Tanakh, Chronicles is one book and is found in the third section of the canon called the Writings. It is, in fact, the final book of the Hebrew Bible. In the English Bible, Chronicles is divided into two books and is included among the historical books after the books of 1 and 2 Kings. The order of these books in the English Bible follows the arrangement of the Septuagint. Although the book of Chronicles spans a period of history from creation to the exile, the bulk of its content focuses on the period of Israelite history from the time of David to the end of the exile.

94. Habakkuk's prophetic ministry coincides with the first years of Jehoiakim's reign. For more on the message of Habakkuk see chapter 7.

95. On this event, see Bruce 1963, 88–89. The prophet Ezekiel was among this group of exiles.

First Chronicles 1–9 is a lengthy genealogical prologue to the book. The period of the united monarchy under David and Solomon is recounted in 1 Chronicles 10–2 Chronicles 9. The history of the divided monarchy is then recorded in 2 Chronicles 10–36. Because this historical period has been examined in some detail in the previous sections of this chapter, our focus here will be upon the distinctive contribution of Chronicles to an understanding of God's purpose in this history.

The author of Chronicles is anonymous, and is usually referred to simply as the Chronicler. There is no consensus regarding the dating of the composition of Chronicles. Suggestions range anywhere from 515 to 200 B.C.[96] The content of the book requires a postexilic date, and most conservative scholars suggest a date sometime in the fifth or fourth centuries.[97] The Chronicler's postexilic concerns are evident throughout his work. Unlike the author of Kings, who addressed an audience of exiles still in captivity, the Chronicler addressed exiles who were either returning to the land or who had already returned.[98] The questions his audience would be asking are different. As Brian Kelly explains, "The Chronicler is not so much concerned, as the Deuteronomist was, with accounting for the exile and loss of land, as he is with stressing the fact of the resumption of Yahweh's saving activity towards Israel, and what the people's appropriate response should be."[99] His primary concern, therefore, is to demonstrate the continuity of the priesthood and of the Davidic dynasty.[100]

Central to his message and to the eschatology of the book is the Chronicler's emphasis on the importance of the Davidic covenant. The Davidic covenant "provides the possibility of Israel's future existence, through the promises of divine forgiveness, restoration and protection."[101] The Davidic covenant is the means by which the Chronicler emphasizes the continuity of Israel as the people of God.[102] The Davidic covenant established the Davidic kingdom, and the Chronicler understands the Davidic kingdom

96. Howard 1993, 235.

97. See, for example, Pratt 1998, 10–11; Selman 1994a, 71; and Howard 1993, 235.

98. Provan, Long, and Longman 2003, 196.

99. Kelly 1996, 182; Selman 1994a, 63; and Pratt 1998, 13.

100. VanGemeren 1988a, 249; Howard 1993, 253.

101. Kelly 1996, 156.

102. Selman 1994a, 45.

to be "the earthly expression of Yahweh's kingdom."[103] The connection between the kingdom of David and the kingdom of God is found in several passages in Chronicles (e.g., 1 Chron. 28:5; 29:23; 2 Chron. 9:8; 13:8). God's kingdom is expressed through the Davidic dynasty and through the temple. In other words, God's kingdom is expressed through the two "houses" of the Davidic covenant (2 Sam. 7:11, 13; 1 Chron. 17:10–12).[104]

Also important to the Chronicler is the idea of the unity of Israel, demonstrated through his repeated use of the phrase "all Israel."[105] As Brian Kelly explains, "the Chronicler does not treat Israel as he knew it, viz. the land and people of the post-exilic community, as a completed entity but instead projects a larger ideal that awaits future realization."[106] In other words, while the restoration has already begun, it is far from being complete (1 Chron. 9:3; 2 Chron. 30:6–9).[107] As Richard Pratt observes, those who had returned to the land "needed to remember that the restoration was incomplete so long as some of the tribes remained exiled from the land."[108] The unity of Israel is also directly addressed in the genealogies of 1 Chronicles 1–9. These genealogies not only address the unity of the tribes of Israel with each other, but they demonstrate the continuity of postexilic Israel with preexilic Israel. They also show the distinctive place of Israel within created humanity.[109]

Finally, two specific passages that are of particular importance for our purposes are 2 Chronicles 7:13–14 and 2 Chronicles 36:22–23. Second Chronicles 7:13–14 records part of God's response to Solomon's prayer at the dedication of the temple. Here God says to Solomon, "When I shut up the heavens so that there is no rain, or command the locust to devour the land, or send pestilence among my people, if my people who are called by my name humble themselves, and pray and seek my face and turn from their wicked ways, then I will hear from heaven and will forgive their sin and heal their land" (cf. Lev. 26:40–42). Raymond Dillard describes this

103. Kelly 1996, 156; Williamson 1982, 26; and Pratt 1998, 24.

104. Kelly 1996, 165; Robertson 2004, 3.

105. David Howard observes that of the 105 uses of the phrase "all Israel" in the Hebrew Old Testament, 40 are found in 1 and 2 Chronicles (Howard 1993, 255).

106. Kelly 1996, 175.

107. Kelly 1996, 183.

108. Pratt 1998, 16.

109. Dillard and Longman 1994, 173; Dumbrell 2002, 324; and Kelly 1996, 177.

text as "a program for Israel's future."[110] God promises that if the people humble themselves and repent of their sin, he will hear them and forgive them. As Martin Selman explains, this "is actually Chronicles' summary of the essential message of the Old Testament."[111]

Second Chronicles 36:22–23 contains the final words of Chronicles.[112] This text contains the proclamation of the Persian king Cyrus in 538 B.C. for the exiles to return to the land.[113] Jeremiah had prophesied that the exile would last seventy years (Jer. 25:11–12), but he had also prophesied that at the end of this time, the exiles would return (29:10; 33:10–11). Over a century earlier, the prophet Isaiah had even given the name of the king who would send the exiles back to the land (Isa. 44:24–45:2). The words of Cyrus that were proclaimed throughout his kingdom are recorded in 2 Chronicles 36:23: "Thus says Cyrus king of Persia, 'Yahweh, the God of heaven, has given me all the kingdoms of the earth, and he has charged me to build him a house at Jerusalem, which is in Judah. Whoever is among you of all his people, may Yahweh his God be with him. Let him go up.'"[114] The book of Chronicles, then, ends with the hopeful prospect of a second exodus from slavery in a foreign land.[115]

Ezra-Nehemiah

The books of Ezra and Nehemiah were originally a single document. Origen, in the third century A.D., was the first to divide the book into two separate books.[116] Ezra-Nehemiah records the last historical events during the canonical Old Testament era.[117] The events occurred over a period of

110. Dillard 1987, 78.

111. Selman 1994b, 337.

112. These are also the final words of the Hebrew Bible in the traditional canonical order.

113. Persia conquered Babylon in 539 B.C. For more on the Persian Empire, see Allen 2005.

114. Beale (2004, 176–77) observes some interesting parallels between this proclamation at the end of Chronicles and Jesus' Great Commission at the end of Matthew (28:18–19). Both Cyrus and Jesus assert authority over the earth, both commissions include a command to "go," and both commissions include assurance of the divine presence. Beale argues that the parallels indicate that in Matthew, Jesus is commissioning the remnant, "true Israel," to build a greater temple, his church.

115. Dillard 1987, 302; Dumbrell 2002, 332.

116. Fensham 1982, 1.

117. Dillard and Longman 1994, 179.

approximately a hundred years, from Cyrus's proclamation in 538 B.C. to some time after Nehemiah's return to the Persian kingdom in 433 B.C. The books, then, describe events in the immediate postexilic period. This period of time is important because it is a new opportunity for Israel, but it is also a time during which the people of Israel had many questions concerning their relationship with God and their status as his chosen people.

Ezra-Nehemiah may be divided into seven major sections.[118] Ezra 1–6 recounts the exiles' return to Jerusalem and the rebuilding of the temple. Ezra's return to Jerusalem and his reforms are recorded in Ezra 7–10. Nehemiah 1–6 tells of Nehemiah's return and the building of the wall around the city. Nehemiah 7:1–72a is a genealogy of the returnees, while Nehemiah 7:72b–10:39 records more of Ezra's reforms. Internal problems within Jerusalem are recorded in Nehemiah 11:1–13:3, and the reforms of Nehemiah's second administration are found in Nehemiah 13:4–31.

Ezra begins as Chronicles ends, with the decree of Cyrus (538 B.C.) allowing the Jews to return to their land and rebuild the temple (Ezra 1:2–4; cf. 2 Chron. 36:23). The language of these first verses of Ezra portrays the return from exile in terms of a second exodus.[119] Thousands of exiles took advantage of the opportunity and returned under the leadership of men such as Zerubbabel, a descendant of David, and Joshua the priest (Ezra 2).[120] The foundation of a new temple was laid in 536 B.C., but opposition caused delays. The prophets Haggai and Zechariah arose at this time (Ezra 5:1), and the temple was finally completed on March 12, 515 B.C. Prominent throughout the first six chapters of Ezra is the theme of restoration. God had sent the people into exile (5:12), and it was God who was bringing them back (1:1).[121] The restoration, however, is not complete. Although some of the exiles are back in the land, the land itself remains a Persian province.[122]

Ezra came to Jerusalem to teach the people in 458 B.C. leading a second wave of returnees (Ezra 7).[123] Ezra 9 records his prayer regarding Israelite intermarriage with foreign women. In this prayer, Ezra introduces another

118. Fensham 1982, 27–30.

119. Dumbrell 2002, 312; Howard 1993, 304.

120. Blenkinsopp 1988, 39.

121. *NIDOTTE*, 4:636.

122. *NIDOTTE*, 4:637; VanGemeren 1988a, 284.

123. The prophet Malachi was very likely a close contemporary of Ezra and Nehemiah (see chapter 9).

major theme of these books: the remnant (9:8, 13–15). The prophet Isaiah had said that only a remnant of Israel would return from exile (Isa. 10:22). God had destroyed the nation of Israel, but out of the ruins he raised up a small remnant who remained the heirs of the covenant promises.[124] Ezra prayed because this tiny remnant was endangering itself by marrying foreign women (cf. Ex. 34:16). Ezra's demand that the returnees keep themselves from foreign wives echoes the similar command Joshua made when Israel first entered the land (Josh. 23:12–13). If the returnees were to avoid the fate of their forefathers, they had to keep themselves separate from anything that might tempt them to commit idolatry.[125]

The book of Nehemiah begins with Nehemiah's return to Jerusalem in 445 B.C. after he hears reports that the wall of the city is in disrepair (Neh. 1–2). He brings a third wave of returnees with him, and despite opposition completes the building of the wall in just fifty-two days (Neh. 6:15). Nehemiah 8 records Ezra's reading of the law to the people, and Nehemiah 9 describes their prayer of confession. This prayer is significant because it reveals that the return of the exiles from foreign lands was only the beginning of restoration. The temple and the priesthood had been restored. The wall of the city had been rebuilt. Judah had been repopulated. But in spite of all these blessings, the people declare to God in their prayer, "we are slaves this day; in the land that you gave to our fathers to enjoy its fruit and its good gifts, behold, we are slaves" (Neh. 9:36).[126] The reality did not yet conform to the fullness of what the prophets had proclaimed. The books of Ezra-Nehemiah, then, point forward to a greater and fuller restoration.

Esther

The book of Esther describes events that happened among the postexilic Jews of the Diaspora, that is, those Jews who did not return to Judah.[127] In the Tanakh, the book of Esther is found in the third section of the canon, the Writings. It is the last of the five scrolls (Ruth, Song of Songs, Ecclesiastes, Lamentations, Esther), and is read at the feast of Purim. In

124. VanGemeren 1988a, 283.

125. Kidner 1979, 21.

126. VanGemeren 1988a, 305; Williamson 1985, lii; and Clines 1984, 198.

127. Jobes 1999, 26.

the Septuagint and in the Protestant canon, on the other hand, Esther is listed among the historical books. According to the first verse of Esther, the events described in the book occurred during the reign of King Ahasuerus (486–465 B.C.), known as Xerxes by the Greeks. In other words, the broad historical context of the book of Esther is the period of the Persian Empire (539–330 B.C.).[128]

While the general historical context is the period of the Persian Empire, the author of Esther also places the story within the more specific redemptive historical context of Scripture. The author does this by describing the ancestry of two of the major characters in the story. Mordecai the Jew is described as being from the tribe of Benjamin, the tribe of King Saul (Esth. 2:5). Haman, the enemy of the Jews in this story, is described as an Agagite (3:1). Agag was the Amalekite king defeated by Saul, but not devoted to destruction according to God's command (1 Sam. 15:1–33). The Amalekites were the first nation to oppose Israel after Israel's miraculous deliverance from Egypt (Ex. 17:8–16). As a result of the actions of the Amalekites, God declared a state of perpetual war with them that continued over the generations (Ex. 17:16; Deut. 25:17–19; Judg. 3:13; 6:3; 7:12; 10:12; 1 Sam. 27:8; 30:13–18; 1 Chron. 4:43). God's judgment of the Amalekites was in fulfillment of his promise to Abraham to curse those who dishonored Abraham (Gen. 12:2–3). As Barry Webb explains, "through Mordecai and Esther, Yahweh continues the war with Amalek he began with Moses."[129]

The story recounted in the book of Esther is uncomplicated. The Persian king chooses Esther to be his queen (Esth. 1–2). When Haman plots to destroy the Jews because of his hatred of Mordecai, Esther agrees to intercede because she is also a Jew (Esth. 3–5). Haman's plot is ultimately revealed, and in a "reversal of destiny" the fate he planned for the Jews falls upon him and the other enemies of the Jews (Esth. 6–9:19).[130] The festival of Purim is established as a memorial, and Mordecai becomes a national hero (Esth. 9:20–10:3). The basic message of the story is that "God's plans for Israel cannot be thwarted by those who hate the Jews."[131] God's deliverance of

128. There are those who question the historicity of Esther, considering it a fictional story. For a good overview of the case for the historicity of Esther, see Jobes 1999, 30–32.

129. Webb 2000, 127.

130. Jobes 1999, 40–41.

131. House 1998, 496.

his people, however, is only partial at this time. Ahasuerus is still the king, and the Jews are still under Persian domination. The final restoration of the people has not yet occurred. An even greater deliverance was yet to come.[132]

Significantly, the author of Esther gets the message across without ever mentioning the name of God. The book of Esther reveals that God is protecting his people even at a time when he seems most absent.[133] The book, therefore, is "perhaps the most striking biblical statement of . . . *the providence of God*."[134] What appears in the book of Esther to be blind coincidence is, in fact, God providentially fulfilling his covenant promises to his chosen people.[135]

Summary

The books of the Pentateuch looked forward to Israel's inheritance of the Promised Land of Canaan. The historical books of the Old Testament describe Israel's conquest of the land, their possession of it, exile from it, and eventual restoration to it. These books clearly reveal that God is providentially moving redemptive history toward his intended goal, the establishment of his kingdom. The books of Joshua, Judges, Samuel, and Kings tell the story of Israel from the conquest to the exile in terms of their faithfulness or unfaithfulness to the stipulations of the Mosaic covenant. These books demonstrate that Israel's obedience resulted in blessing, while their disobedience resulted in the curses of the covenant just as Moses had warned (Deut. 28).

The book of Joshua describes the conquest of the land in fulfillment of God's promises, but it also indicates that the conquest was incomplete. Many Canaanites remained in the land, sowing the seeds that would eventually result in judgment on the people of Israel. The book of Judges describes the downward spiral into spiritual degeneration that followed the death of Joshua. It describes the Canaanization of Israel, the result of Israel's failure to rid the land of idolatrous influences. The period of the judges ends in anarchy, but hope still remains.

132. Duguid 2006, 96.
133. Webb 2000, 124.
134. Jobes 1999, 43.
135. Jobes 1999, 38.

The book of Ruth reveals that during this period of time God was providentially preparing the way for the coming of a king by extending his blessing to a humble Gentile woman. The books of Samuel then describe the actual establishment of the monarchy in Israel and even more significantly the establishment of the Davidic covenant. The kingdom of God on earth was to be manifested in two houses, the Davidic dynasty and the temple. Both houses were established in Zion. The Davidic covenant would therefore become the foundation of Israel's eschatological hopes.

The books of 1 and 2 Kings recount the history of the rise and fall of the Davidic dynasty. David's son Solomon built the temple, but he later fell into idolatry and as a result, the kingdom was divided. The book of 2 Kings provides the historical context for most of the canonical prophetic books. The prophets spoke the Word of God to the people of Israel, calling them back to covenant faithfulness and warning them of the judgment to come if they continued in their disobedience. Ultimately, the northern kingdom of Israel fell to Assyria, and the southern kingdom of Judah, despite attempts at reformation by a few good kings, was sent into exile in Babylon.

The exile, however, is not the final word in the Old Testament historical books. The books of Ezra and Nehemiah and the conclusion of Chronicles describe the beginnings of the restoration of Israel. As the prophets had said, a remnant of Israel would return from exile to the land in a second exodus. They would rebuild the temple and repopulate the land. This had occurred. But the prophets had also said that a greater Son of David would come as king to restore the throne and the kingdom, bringing blessing to Israel and all the nations of the earth. The reality in the days of Ezra and Nehemiah was far from reflecting the fullness of all that the prophets had declared. Many exiles had indeed returned, but even those who had returned were slaves in their own land, remaining under foreign domination. The restoration of Israel had begun, but there was much more to come.

4

The Psalms, the Wisdom Books, and the Song of Songs

In the Hebrew Bible, the Former Prophets (Joshua, Judges, Samuel, and Kings) are immediately followed by the Latter Prophets (Isaiah, Jeremiah, Ezekiel, and the Twelve Minor Prophets). The books of Psalms, Job, Proverbs, Song of Songs, and Ecclesiastes are located in the third section of the Hebrew Bible, the *Ketubim*, or "Writings." In the Protestant Old Testament, on the other hand, the books of Job, Psalms, Proverbs, Ecclesiastes, and Song of Songs immediately follow the historical books. Because many of the writings included among these books were authored before the earliest prophetic books, our survey here will follow the order of the Protestant Old Testament.

The Genre of the Psalms

The genre of the Pentateuch and the historical books is primarily historical prose narrative. Within this historical narrative, poetry is found on occasion, but those occasions are typically few and far between. The substantial examples are found in the following eleven texts: Genesis 49;

Exodus 15; Numbers 23–24; Deuteronomy 32; 33; Judges 5; 1 Samuel 2:1–10; 2 Samuel 1:19–27; 22; 23:1–7; 2 Kings 19:21–28. When we turn to the book of Psalms, however, we encounter something quite different. The book of Psalms contains 150 songs of varying length, but all of these songs have one thing in common. They are all poetic. In order to read the Psalms, therefore, we must have some understanding of the nature of Hebrew poetry and how it differs from Hebrew prose.

An important preliminary observation that must be made is that there is no hard and fast line between Hebrew prose and Hebrew poetry. Instead, Hebrew prose and poetry are on a continuum.[1] Between pure prose and pure poetry, we encounter types of language that may best be described as poetic prose and others that may best be described as prosaic poetry.[2] This does not mean that the distinction between prose and poetry is unnecessary. Hebrew poetry does have characteristics that distinguish it from Hebrew prose. If there were no such distinguishing characteristics, it would be impossible to observe any differences along the continuum.

What, then, are the characteristics that distinguish Hebrew poetry from Hebrew prose? David Noel Freedman notes that one long-recognized distinctive of Hebrew poetry is the rarity of certain particles that occur frequently in Hebrew prose, namely the relative pronoun *'asher*, the sign of the definite direct object *'et*, and the definite article *ha*.[3] Careful studies of biblical texts in which the number of these particles in a passage is compared to the total number of words indicate that when these particles are 5 percent or less of the total, the text in question is poetry. When these particles are 15 percent or more of the total, the text is prose.[4]

Probably the most commonly recognized distinguishing characteristic of Hebrew poetry is what is usually referred to as parallelism. Hebrew poetry typically consists of pairs of lines in which the second line develops in some way the thought found in the first line.[5] Although there are no strict mechanical rules, it is possible to categorize several basic kinds of parallelism. Tremper Longman helpfully outlines six basic types:[6]

1. Petersen and Richards 1992, 28; Freedman 1997, 2:216.

2. Freedman 1997, 2:216.

3. Freedman 1997, 2:171; see also 2:213–26.

4. Freedman 1997, 2:215. Texts in the intermediate range (5–15 percent) may either incline toward poetry (5–10 percent) or toward prose (10–15 percent).

5. Longman 1988, 98.

6. Longman 1988, 99–102.

1. Synonymous parallelism—the second line is a near synonym of the first line (e.g., Ps. 2:2a).
2. Antithetic parallelism—the second line expresses the same idea from an antithetical perspective (e.g., Prov. 10:1).
3. Emblematic parallelism—this type of parallelism draws an explicit analogy (e.g., Ps. 42:1).
4. Repetitive parallelism—the second line partially repeats the first line, but carries the thought further ahead than in synonymous parallelism (e.g., Ps. 29:1).
5. Pivot pattern—the first line contains a word or clause in the middle of the line that should also be read in the second line (e.g., Ps. 98:2).
6. Chiasm—the second line stands in an inverted relation to the first line (e.g., Ps. 1:1).

These six kinds of parallelism are not intended to be an exhaustive taxonomy. They do, however, provide a helpful frame of reference for discussion. The regular use of parallelism distances poetry from everyday prose language.[7]

Another distinguishing characteristic of Hebrew poetry is its heightened use of figurative imagery. The Psalms are filled with similes (e.g., 1:3–4; 31:12) and metaphors (e.g., Ps. 19:1–2). In the Psalms, wicked nations are dashed to pieces like pottery (2:9) and melt like wax before God (68:2). Wicked men are pregnant with mischief (7:14) and have venom like serpents (58:4). God lifts the righteous from miry pits (40:2) and shelters them in his wings (17:8). The soul of the righteous is like a deer panting for water (42:1). The Lord himself is a rock, a fortress, a shield (18:1–2), and a shepherd (23:1). The rivers clap their hands, and the mountains and trees sing for joy (96:12; 98:8). The sun, moon, and stars, along with sea creatures, beasts, and birds praise the name of the Lord (148:3, 7, 10). By means of such artistic imagery, poetry engages our intellect, imagination, and emotions in a way that is different from prose.

It is important to observe that in the case of the psalms, while all are written in the form of poetry, not all are of the same type. Within the

7. Longman 1988, 93.

Psalter there are actually several major types of psalms.[8] There are hymns, which are characterized by their calls to praise the Lord (e.g., Pss. 103, 113, 145–150). Laments, on the other hand, are cries of distress (e.g., Pss. 3, 5, 17, 22, 42, 43). One type of lament is the imprecatory psalm in which the psalmist calls upon God to judge his enemies (e.g., Pss. 109, 137, 140). Thanksgiving psalms are, as their name indicates, psalms in which the psalmist expresses his gratitude to God (e.g. Pss. 18, 30, 40, 65, 124). Psalms of remembrance focus on God's past actions within redemptive history (e.g., Pss. 78, 89, 132). Psalms of confidence are those psalms in which the psalmist expresses his trust in the Lord (e.g., Pss. 11, 23, 62, 91, 121). Wisdom psalms resemble Proverbs in that they extol a life of wisdom (e.g., Pss. 1, 49, 73, 112, 119). Finally, kingship or royal psalms are, as their name indicates, concerned with kings, whether the earthly king or the divine King (e.g., Pss. 2, 45, 72, 110). Royal psalms are of particular significance to an understanding of biblical eschatology.

The Book of Psalms

The book of Psalms consists of 150 separate psalms. If the titles attached to many of these psalms are taken to be genuine indicators of their original setting and/or authorship, then the composition of the psalms spans a period of approximately one thousand years. Psalm 90, for example, is attributed to Moses, while others, such as Psalm 126, originated during the postexilic era. Of the 150 psalms, 116 have titles of one sort or another attached to them.[9] Many of these titles appear to indicate authorship. The named authors are: David (73 total psalms), Solomon (Pss. 72, 127), the sons of Korah (Pss. 42–49, 84, 85, 87), Asaph (Pss. 50, 73–83), Heman the Ezrahite (Ps. 88), Ethan the Ezrahite (Ps. 89), and Moses (Ps. 90).

Each of the individual psalms appears to have been written by persons or groups under specific historic conditions, yet the language of the majority of the psalms is sufficiently general that they may be sung by people in all times and places. Many of these songs were apparently adopted for liturgical use by the worshiping community many years after their original

8. See Gunkel and Begrich 1998 for an exhaustive study of the types of psalms; see also Longman 1988, 23–35; Osborne 1991, 181–85.

9. Craigie 1983, 31.

composition.[10] Some of the songs were gathered into smaller collections, which were then later incorporated into our present book of Psalms. It is not known exactly when the final compilation of the entire book of Psalms was completed, but the evidence indicates the early postexilic period (ca. fourth century B.C.).[11]

The editor or editors who compiled the book of Psalms divided it into five sections or books: Book 1 (Pss. 1–41); Book 2 (Pss. 42–72); Book 3 (Pss. 73–89); Book 4 (Pss. 90–106); and Book 5 (Pss. 107–50). But whether this was thematically significant or merely for the sake of liturgical convenience is contested. Some have suggested that the Psalter was divided into five books to correspond with the five books of the Pentateuch.[12] However, aside from the number five, there does not appear to be any obvious internal thematic correspondence between the five books of Moses and the five books in the Psalter. The question remains, however, whether there is any overarching formal structure at all to the book of Psalms. One recent suggestion is that the individual psalms were purposefully arranged to correspond to an eschatological outline.[13] Others argue that there is no evidence for this or any other such formal thematic structure.[14] While there are smaller collections within the Psalter that are based on a common theme or a common author, it is possible that there simply is no larger formal structure that would be destroyed had the individual psalms been arranged in a different order.[15] If there is such a structure, it has yet to be definitively identified.

A wide variety of themes are found throughout the Psalter. Many of the psalms in the first part of the book, for example, highlight the theme of distress.[16] The psalmist cries out to God expressing his anguish and despair. Praise of the Lord is, however, another central theme that is found even within the lament psalms. Such praise is crucial to the covenant people of God because, as Claus Westermann rightly observes, "Forgetting God and turning away from God always begins when praise has been silenced."[17]

10. See *NIDOTTE*, 4:1109.
11. Craigie 1983, 31.
12. E.g., Wilson 2005, 231.
13. See Mitchell 1997.
14. E.g., Whybray 1994.
15. Craigie 1983, 30.
16. Johnston 2005, 63.
17. Westermann 1980, 6.

Many of the psalms reflect on the theme of Israel's covenant history.[18] Many of the psalms also dwell on the failure of Israel throughout their history to remain faithful to the covenant.[19] It is in the light of this past faithlessness that the forward-looking eschatological themes in the psalms come into focus.

The lament psalms provide a good introduction to the eschatological themes of the Psalter because in the lament psalms, the psalmists indicate that things are not the way they are supposed to be. They call upon God to do something about sin and death and injustice.[20] Their appeal to God is, however, one that is based on faith. The psalmists' hope for the future is based on a confident trust in God's past covenant promises. They express hope "that in the end the wicked will be no more; that the kingdom of God will be fully established; and that theirs will be the freedom, peace, and joys of which they have been deprived in life."[21]

Within this general hope for the future, the psalmists express several specific hopes. The psalmists, for example, expect the restoration of Jerusalem (e.g., Pss. 85:9; 102:16–22; 147:2). They express their expectation that in the end God will judge the wicked nations (e.g., Pss. 2:9; 9:17; 96:13). Many of the psalms look beyond the present to a future Davidic king, through whom salvation will come. These messianic psalms express confidence in the fulfillment of the Davidic promises. These psalms portray the Messiah as a king and a priest (e.g., Pss. 2, 18, 20, 21, 45, 61, 72, 89, 110, 132). They portray the suffering of the Messiah (e.g., Pss. 22, 35, 41, 55, 69, 109). Finally, they portray the coming of the Messiah to judge his enemies and redeem his people (e.g., Pss. 18, 50, 68, 96, 97, 98, 102).[22] The psalms, therefore, contribute greatly to biblical eschatology.

Psalm 1

The first psalm in the book of Psalms introduces the entire collection by pronouncing blessing upon those who are faithful to God.[23] It is a wisdom

18. Kraus 1993a, 63.

19. Pate et al. 2004, 72.

20. VanGemeren 1991, 763.

21. VanGemeren 1991, 570.

22. See VanGemeren 1991, 586; also Kidner 1973a, 24.

23. Kidner 1973a, 47. It is not possible to look at all of the psalms in the space of a single chapter. Instead I will focus on selected psalms, addressing an entire psalm if necessary, but more often simply

psalm characterized by the resemblance of its contents to those of the wisdom books (cf. Prov. 2:12–22). The first two verses read,

> Blessed is the man
> who walks not in the counsel of the wicked,
> nor stands in the way of sinners,
>   nor sits in the seat of scoffers;
> but his delight is in the law of Yahweh,
>   and on his law he meditates day and night. (Ps. 1:1–2)

As Willem VanGemeren explains, "The psalm encourages wisdom as the way of life by emphasizing the blessedness of the righteous, the adversity of the wicked, and the contrastive ways between the righteous and the wicked."[24] The Psalter, then, opens with an emphasis on the key Deuteronomic theme of blessing and its relation to covenant faithfulness, or righteousness.

Psalm 2

Psalm 2 is one of the kingship or royal psalms. As one of the messianic psalms it looks forward to the full establishment of the kingdom of God's Son. It encourages the people to trust in God and to look forward to a time when all of God's enemies will be judged and righteousness will be established. The psalm contains four subsections: the rebellion of the nations (vv. 1–3); God's response (vv. 4–6); God's decree (vv. 7–9); and the reign of the king (vv. 10–12).

2:1–3

> Why do the nations rage
> and the peoples plot in vain?
> The kings of the earth set themselves,
>   and the rulers take counsel together,
>   against Yahweh and against his anointed, saying,
> "Let us burst their bonds apart
>   and cast away their cords from us."

---

addressing those portions of a psalm relevant in some significant way to the understanding of biblical eschatology.

24. VanGemeren 1991, 52.

These first verses set the stage of the psalm. The astonished question, "Why?" points to the completely senseless rejection of the Lord and his anointed king.[25] The close relationship between the Lord and his anointed one indicates that it is impossible to submit to God without submitting to the Messiah.[26]

2:4–6

He who sits in the heavens laughs;
  the Lord holds them in derision.
Then he will speak to them in his wrath,
  and terrify them in his fury, saying,
"As for me, I have set my King on Zion, my holy hill."

God's reaction to the rebellion of the nations is not one of surprise. He is not threatened by their actions. Instead he mocks the futility of their rebelliousness. His response is to install his king in Zion. His intention to establish the messianic kingdom will not be thwarted by any earthly nations or powers.

2:7–9

I will tell of the decree:
Yahweh said to me, "You are my Son;
  today I have begotten you.
Ask of me, and I will make the nations your heritage,
  and the ends of the earth your possession.
You shall break them with a rod of iron
  and dash them in pieces like a potter's vessel."

These verses build on the promises found in the Davidic covenant, namely God's promise to David: "I will be to him a father, and he shall be to me a son" (2 Sam. 7:14). These verses anticipate the extension of the Messiah's kingdom to the ends of the earth. In the New Testament, God the Father uses words taken from this section of Psalm 2 (and Isa. 42:1) to declare that Jesus is his Son (Matt. 3:17; 17:5).

25. Kidner 1973a, 50.
26. VanGemeren 1991, 67.

2:10–12

Now therefore, O kings, be wise;
  be warned, O rulers of the earth.
Serve Yahweh with fear,
  and rejoice with trembling.
Kiss the Son,
  lest he be angry, and you perish in the way,
  for his wrath is quickly kindled.
Blessed are all who take refuge in him.

These verses declare the necessity of submitting to the king. Psalm 2 ultimately looks forward to the coronation of Jesus as the messianic King. As VanGemeren observes, "He is born of David's lineage (Matt. 1:1; Luke 2:4, 11), has a right to David's throne (Luke 1:32), is the Son of God in a unique way (Matt. 3:17; Luke 9:35; Heb. 1:5), and will ultimately subdue all enemies under his feet (1 Cor. 15:25–27; Heb. 2:5–8)."[27]

Psalm 6

Psalm 6 is a lament song. In the early church it was one of the seven "penitential" psalms (Pss. 6, 32, 38, 51, 102, 130, 143) sung on Ash Wednesday as a means of doing penance.[28] One passage of this psalm in particular (6:4–5) is important for our purposes:

Turn, O Yahweh, deliver my life;
  save me for the sake of your steadfast love.
For in death there is no remembrance of you;
  in Sheol who will give you praise?

These verses are important because they refer to death and Sheol. The word "Sheol" is a simple transliteration of the Hebrew word *she'ol*, which is found sixty-five times in the Old Testament. It refers in general to both the grave and to the underworld, although usually the latter.[29] It is where a person goes at his death.

27. VanGemeren 1991, 65–66.
28. VanGemeren 1991, 96.
29. *NIDOTTE*, 4:6. On the Old Testament concept of Sheol, see Johnston 2002.

The concept of Sheol and the afterlife is not described as fully or clearly in the Old Testament as it is in the New. As Derek Kidner explains:

> *Sheol* can be pictured in a number of ways: chiefly as a vast sepulchral cavern (*cf.* Ezk. 32:18–32) or stronghold (Pss. 9:13; 107:18; Mt. 16:18); but also as a dark wasteland (Jb. 10:22) or as a beast of prey (*e.g.* Is. 5:14; Jon. 2:2; Hab. 2:5). This is not definitive language, but poetic and evocative; and it is matched by various phrases that highlight the tragedy of death as that which silences a man's worship (as here; *cf.* 30:9; 88:10f.; 115:17; Is. 38:18f.), shatters his plans (146:4), cuts him off from God and man (88:5; Ec. 2:16) and makes an end of him (39:13).[30]

In other words, the psalmist's declaration that "in death there is no remembrance of you" should not be taken as a literal assertion that there is no conscious afterlife. It is figurative poetic language pointing out, as Kidner notes, "the tragedy of death." Such poetic language should not be pressed beyond its bounds.

Psalm 16

Psalm 16 is an expression of confidence and trust in the Lord. The basic theme of the psalm is God's goodness and his blessings to those who place their faith in him. In verses 8–10, David expresses his confidence that death will not sever his relationship with God:

> I have set Yahweh always before me;
>   because he is at my right hand, I shall not be shaken.
> Therefore my heart is glad, and my whole being rejoices;
>   my flesh also dwells secure.
> For you will not abandon my soul to Sheol,
>   or let your holy one see corruption.

The question raised by these verses is whether David is speaking of a rescue from a potentially deadly situation or of resurrection from death. Some argue that the psalmist here is merely expressing confidence that God will deliver him from mortal danger.[31]

30. Kidner 1973a, 61.
31. E.g., Kraus 1993a, 240.

This text, however, like others found in the Psalter (Pss. 17:15; 49:15; 73:24) suggests more than a rescue from danger. As Kidner observes, the language in 16:10 is too strong to be merely describing David.[32] The answer is found by examining the New Testament use of this text. According to the New Testament, this text pointed forward to the resurrection of Jesus (Acts 13:35). The apostle Paul argued that "since David died and did not rise from the grave, the psalm received a special significance in view of Jesus' death and resurrection."[33] This psalm continues to encourage believers who look forward to the day when they too will be raised incorruptible (1 Cor. 15:20–49).

Psalm 18

Psalm 18 is a song of thanksgiving. According to the title, it was written by David "who addressed the words of this song to Yahweh on the day when Yahweh rescued him from the hand of all his enemies, and from the hand of Saul." In light of its historical context, verses 6–15 are significant:

> In my distress I called upon Yahweh;
>   to my God I cried for help.
> From his temple he heard my voice,
>   and my cry to him reached his ears.
> Then the earth reeled and rocked;
>   the foundations also of the mountains trembled
>   and quaked, because he was angry.
> Smoke went up from his nostrils,
>   and devouring fire from his mouth;
>   glowing coals flamed forth from him.
> He bowed the heavens and came down;
>   thick darkness was under his feet.
> He rode on a cherub and flew;
>   he came swiftly on the wings of the wind.
> He made darkness his covering, his canopy around him,
>   thick clouds dark with water.
> Out of the brightness before him

32. Kidner 1973a, 86.
33. VanGemeren 1991, 159.

hailstones and coals of fire broke through his clouds.
Yahweh also thundered in the heavens,
and the Most High uttered his voice,
hailstones and coals of fire.
And he sent out his arrows and scattered them;
he flashed forth lightnings and routed them.
Then the channels of the sea were seen,
and the foundations of the world were laid bare
at your rebuke, O Yahweh,
at the blast of the breath of your nostrils.

What is significant to note here is the language used by David to describe the historical occasion of his rescue from the hands of Saul and other enemies. He describes it in terms of a theophany, in which God comes to earth riding on the clouds or on a cherub. He describes it in terms of dramatic cosmic upheavals in the heavens and earth. Yet the description of the events in the historical books does not indicate that the events were literally accompanied by such cosmic phenomena. David is describing the events poetically. This is important because many of the prophets and New Testament authors use similar dramatic imagery to describe events that they foresee. Care must always be taken, therefore, not to mistake poetic images for literal descriptions of events.

Psalm 22

Psalm 22 is a lament psalm. It is significant for our study because of the use of its words by Jesus during his crucifixion (Matt. 27:46; Mark 15:34). In its original context, the psalm expresses the suffering and pain of David who feels forsaken by the Lord (Ps. 22:1). It is clear that Jesus recognized in the words of this psalm a situation of suffering that paralleled his own situation. While the psalm is not written in the form of direct prophecy, there are too many similarities between the words of this psalm and the events surrounding the crucifixion for this to be mere coincidence (see vv. 7–8, 14–18). As R. T. France observes, "The amazingly close correspondence of this psalm with the suffering of Jesus in the crucifixion can hardly have escaped him, any more than it escaped later Christian thought."[34]

34. France 1982, 57.

Psalm 45

Psalm 45 is one of the kingship or royal songs. It is attributed to the sons of Korah and addressed to the Davidic king. The first five verses are straightforward expressions of honor and praise to the king. In verses 6–7, however, the psalmist appears to be looking beyond the present Davidic king.

> Your throne, O God, is forever and ever.
> The scepter of your kingdom is a scepter of uprightness;
> you have loved righteousness and hated wickedness.
> Therefore God, your God, has anointed you
> with the oil of gladness beyond your companions.

The Hebrew words translated "Your throne, O God" are *kis'aka 'elohim*. As VanGemeren notes, this phrase can be understood in several ways. It can be understood to mean: "Your throne, O God" (e.g., KJV, NIV, NASB, NRSV, ESV). It can be understood to mean: "Your throne is like God's throne" (e.g., NEB). It can also be understood to mean: "Your divine throne" (e.g., RSV).[35] The Septuagint translation supports the translation "Your throne, O God." The New Testament citation of this verse from the Septuagint supports this translation as well (Heb. 1:8).

The Davidic king is addressed here as "God," and his throne is identified with God's throne. In Psalm 45:7, however, the Davidic king is distinguished from God: "God, your God, has anointed you." As Kidner explains, this kind of paradoxical language can be understood only in light of the incarnation of Christ. "It is an example of Old Testament language bursting its banks, to demand a more than human fulfillment."[36]

Psalm 67

This psalm is a prayer for God's blessing. Its hope is based on the promises made to Abraham regarding the blessing of the nations (Gen. 12:3). Its initial words recall the Aaronic blessing.

67:1–3

> May God be gracious to us and bless us
> and make his face to shine upon us, *Selah*

35. VanGemeren 1991, 346–47.
36. Kidner 1973a, 172.

that your way may be known on earth,
  your saving power among all nations.
Let the peoples praise you, O God;
  let all the peoples praise you!

The opening words of the psalmist are very similar to the words Aaron was instructed to speak to the people of Israel as a blessing: "Yahweh bless you and keep you; Yahweh make his face to shine upon you and be gracious to you; Yahweh lift up his countenance upon you and give you peace" (Num. 6:24–26). Here the people pray that God's blessing will be spread among all nations, and they call upon all people to praise God.

67:4–7

Let the nations be glad and sing for joy,
  for you judge the peoples with equity
  and guide the nations upon earth. *Selah*
Let the peoples praise you, O God;
  let all the peoples praise you!
The earth has yielded its increase;
  God, our God, shall bless us.
God shall bless us;
  let all the ends of the earth fear him!

In these final verses, the psalmist prays for the reign of God, the inclusion of the nations, and the blessing of God. The psalm looks forward to a time when the nations will acknowledge God's rule and praise him. Israel is to understand that salvation is not limited to her borders (Ps. 68:32).

Psalm 72

Like Psalms 2 and 45, Psalm 72 is a kingship or royal psalm. It is messianic in that it looks beyond the earthly Davidic king to the reign of Jesus Christ (cf. Isa. 11:1–5). Its structure reveals six basic subsections: a prayer for the Davidic king (Ps. 72:1); an expression of hope for justice (vv. 2–4); a prayer that the king's reign will last forever and be universal (vv. 5–11); another expression of hope for justice (vv. 12–14); another prayer for a universal and eternal reign (vv. 15–17); and finally praise of the divine King (vv. 18–20).

72:1

Give the king your justice, O God,
  and your righteousness to the royal son!

The psalmist here entreats God to bless the Davidic king. He prays that God will give the king justice and righteousness because both are required in order for the king to be an instrument of God's blessing to the people.

72:2–4

May he judge your people with righteousness,
  and your poor with justice!
Let the mountains bear prosperity for the people,
  and the hills, in righteousness!
May he defend the cause of the poor of the people,
  give deliverance to the children of the needy,
  and crush the oppressor!

In these verses, the psalmist expresses hope for a righteous and just reign. Because the king is the vicegerent of God, he is to rule in a manner that reflects the justice and righteousness of God.

72:5–11

May they fear you while the sun endures,
  and as long as the moon, throughout all generations!
May he be like rain that falls on the mown grass,
  like showers that water the earth!
In his days may the righteous flourish,
  and peace abound, till the moon be no more!
May he have dominion from sea to sea,
  and from the River to the ends of the earth!
May desert tribes bow down before him
  and his enemies lick the dust!
May the kings of Tarshish and of the coastlands
  render him tribute;
may the kings of Sheba and Seba
  bring gifts!
May all kings fall down before him,
  all nations serve him!

The psalmist here looks forward to a time when the reign of the Davidic king will extend throughout all generations and from one end of the earth to the other. He expresses the same thought that is found in Psalm 2. The kingdom will be worldwide and eternal, and all will submit.

72:12–14

For he delivers the needy when he calls,
  the poor and him who has no helper.
He has pity on the weak and the needy,
  and saves the lives of the needy.
From oppression and violence he redeems their life,
  and precious is their blood in his sight.

The Davidic king was to give justice to the needy and oppressed, and here the psalmist expresses hope for such justice to exist in the Davidic kingdom. The poor and oppressed will be the special concern of the messianic King.

72:15–17

Long may he live;
  may gold of Sheba be given to him!
May prayer be made for him continually,
  and blessings invoked for him all the day!
May there be abundance of grain in the land;
  on the tops of the mountains may it wave;
  may its fruit be like Lebanon;
and may people blossom in the cities
  like the grass of the field!
May his name endure forever,
  his fame continue as long as the sun!
May people be blessed in him,
  all nations call him blessed!

Here again, the psalmist prays for the enduring blessing of the messianic kingdom. God had promised Abraham that through him all the nations would be blessed. Here the psalmist looks to the day when that promise is completely fulfilled.

72:18–19

Blessed be Yahweh, the God of Israel,
  who alone does wondrous things.
Blessed be his glorious name forever;
  may the whole earth be filled with his glory!
    Amen and Amen!

The doxology that closes this psalm also closes Book 2 of the Psalter. God had blessed his people, and his name is to be blessed forever. The psalmist anticipates the filling of the whole earth with the glory of God, and the people respond, "Amen and Amen!"

Psalm 87

Psalm 87 is very brief, but it expresses profound eschatological hope. It is one of the Zion psalms (Pss. 48, 76, 84, 122, 137). Because of its brevity, we may quote it in its entirety.

On the holy mount stands the city he founded;
  Yahweh loves the gates of Zion
  more than all the dwelling places of Jacob.
Glorious things of you are spoken,
  O city of God. *Selah*
Among those who know me I mention Rahab and Babylon;
  behold Philistia and Tyre, with Cush—
  "This one was born there," they say.
And of Zion it shall be said,
  "This one and that one were born in her";
  for the Most High himself will establish her.
Yahweh records as he registers the peoples,
  "This one was born there." *Selah*
Singers and dancers alike say,
  "All my springs are in you."

This psalm expresses hope for the fulfillment of God's promise to bless all of the nations. Zion is spoken of as the destination of all peoples. As Kidner observes, "Nothing is explained with any fullness, yet by the end there remains no doubt of the coming conversion of old enemies and their full incorporation in the city of God."[37]

Psalm 89

Psalm 89 is a hymnic reflection on the promises of the Davidic covenant (2 Sam. 7:4–17), specifically the promise of an everlasting throne. The promises found within the Davidic covenant have made the heirs of David the representatives of God's reign on earth.[38] Psalm 89 contains three main sections followed by a brief doxology. The first section praises the kingship of the Lord (vv. 1–18). The second section focuses specifically upon the Davidic covenant and the Davidic king (vv. 19–37). The third section is a lament (vv. 38–51). The psalm concludes with a very brief doxology (v. 52).

After praising the covenant faithfulness of Yahweh in the first section of the psalm, the psalmist turns to reflect on the Davidic covenant. He begins by reminding his hearers of God's choice of David (vv. 19–23). David's power and authority are founded upon God's choice of him to be his anointed servant. The psalmist then reminds his hearers that God has promised to the Davidic dynasty a universal kingdom (vv. 24–25). In these verses, the psalmist's words look forward to the messianic King. He continues by telling his hearers that the Messiah will be the "the highest of the kings of the earth" (vv. 26–27). God then renews his covenant commitment to David (vv. 28–29). The psalmist gives God's warning to David's heirs, reminding them that if they forsake the law they will be punished (vv. 30–37). Ultimately, however, God's promises to David will be fulfilled by the one who keeps God's law perfectly: "His offspring shall endure forever, his throne as long as the sun before me" (v. 36).

Psalm 95

Psalm 95 calls the people of God to worship him. God's work of creation and redemption are both prominent themes throughout. Following the initial call to worship (vv. 1–2), God is praised for his sovereignty and for his creative work (vv. 3–5). Following a second call to worship (v. 6), the psalmist praises God for his covenant relationship with his people (v. 7) and then offers an exhortation based on God's acts of judgment at Meribah

37. Kidner 1973b, 314.
38. Kraus 1993b, 211.

and Massah (Ex. 17:7). The final two verses of the psalm (Ps. 95:10–11) are significant.

> For forty years I loathed that generation
> and said, "They are a people who go astray in their heart,
> and they have not known my ways."
> Therefore I swore in my wrath,
> "They shall not enter my rest."

In the historical context of the exodus generation, the term "rest" was specifically associated with the Promised Land. Kidner, however, explains that this term has much greater eschatological significance today:

> In relation to the Exodus it meant God's land to settle in, and peace to enjoy it (*cf.* Gn. 49:15; Ps. 132:14; 1 Ki. 8:56). But Hebrews 4:1–13 argues that the psalm still offers us, by its emphatic *Today*, a rest beyond anything Joshua won, namely a share in God's own Sabbath rest: the enjoyment of His finished work not merely of creation but of redemption.[39]

The rest that God offered his people in the Old Testament was, then, but a shadow of the greater rest he would offer in the New Testament.

Psalm 110

Psalm 110 is one of the kingship or royal psalms. It is one of the most frequently quoted psalms in the entire New Testament (Matt. 22:44; 26:64; Mark 12:36; 14:62; 16:19; Luke 20:42–44; 22:69; Acts 2:34–35; Rom. 8:34; 1 Cor. 15:25; Eph. 1:20; Col. 3:1; Heb. 1:3, 13; 5:6; 7:17, 21; 8:1; 10:12–13; 12:2). According to its title, David was the author of this psalm, a fact that is crucial to its interpretation within the New Testament.

110:1

> Yahweh says to my Lord:
> "Sit at my right hand,
> until I make your enemies your footstool."

These introductory lines are important because of what they say about the messianic King. The first words of the verse following the title are: *ne'um*

39. Kidner 1973b, 346.

yhwh indicating that this is an oracle of the Lord. The words *la'doni* are translated "to my Lord." It is significant that David speaks of the king in this psalm as "my Lord." Another translation of these words is: "my master." In short, David himself expresses submission to the king who is to sit at God's right hand. The authority of this king is derived from Yahweh who promises to extend his rule by putting all of his enemies under his feet (see Ps. 2:8–9). The footstool metaphor indicates absolute control.[40]

110:2–3

Yahweh sends forth from Zion
  your mighty scepter.
  Rule in the midst of your enemies.
Your people will offer themselves freely
  on the day of your power,
  in holy garments;
from the womb of the morning,
  the dew of your youth will be yours.

The authority of the messianic King will be extended to the point that all of his enemies will be forced to acknowledge his rule. The interpretation of verse 3 is difficult but seems to indicate that the king's people will voluntarily consecrate themselves to serve him in battle.

110:4

Yahweh has sworn
  and will not change his mind,
"You are a priest forever
  after the order of Melchizedek."

To say that Yahweh has "sworn" indicates the existence of a solemn oath. In this case, the oath refers to the covenantal promises he has made to David (2 Sam. 7:13). He declares, "You are a priest forever after the order of Melchizedek." Melchizedek was a priest-king over the city of Salem (Gen. 14:18). Like him, the Davidic king was a priest-king (2 Sam. 6:14, 17–18;

40. See VanGemeren 1991, 697.

1 Kings 8:14, 55, 62–64). The perfect union of priesthood and kingship is ultimately found only in Jesus (Heb. 5:1–10; 7:1–28).

110:5–7

The Lord is at your right hand;
he will shatter kings on the day of his wrath.
He will execute judgment among the nations,
filling them with corpses;
he will shatter chiefs
over the wide earth.
He will drink from the brook by the way;
therefore he will lift up his head.

The final verses of Psalm 110 declare the coming victory of the messianic King. Hans-Joachim Kraus helpfully summarizes the significance of this psalm's statements about the anointed king.

> In summary, four points should especially be emphasized: (1) Yahweh himself exalts the king and places him at his right hand, he nominates and empowers him as the coregent; (2) the enthroned is adjudged to be of heavenly birth; (3) he is declared to be a priest (after the order of Melchizedek); (4) through him and his presence, Yahweh, the world judge and war hero, overcomes all enemies.[41]

The authors of the New Testament recognized only one figure who fulfilled all that this psalm portrayed, namely Jesus of Nazareth. This psalm would become central to their proclamation of his exaltation.

Wisdom Books

The canonical books that are normally classed as wisdom literature are Proverbs, Ecclesiastes, and Job. A few individual psalms also fall under this classification (e.g., Pss. 1, 49, 73). Outside of the biblical canon, books such as Sirach (or Ecclesiasticus) and the Wisdom of Solomon are also considered notable examples of this genre.[42] The contribution of

41. Kraus 1993b, 353.

42. Waltke 2004, 50. On the possibility of a special class of "sages" in Israel, see Crenshaw 1981, 27–28.

the canonical wisdom books to an understanding of biblical eschatology is difficult to discern because these books do not focus on redemptive history per se.[43] They simply presuppose it. The wisdom literature is, however, generally associated with Solomon, the son of David. It seems possible, then, that the wisdom described in these books does prefigure in some ways certain attributes of the Messiah, the eschatological Son of David. In the New Testament, Jesus does identify himself as "the way," a common theme in wisdom literature (John 14:6; Ps. 1:6; Prov. 2:8; 4:11; 8:20; 10:29; 15:10). Jesus is also specifically identified with the Wisdom of God several times in the New Testament (Luke 11:49; 1 Cor. 1:24, 30).[44] In other words, Jesus does not merely exhibit biblical wisdom; he is the very incarnation of God's wisdom.[45] This appears to lend support to an understanding of the wisdom literature that sees it as providing veiled glimpses of the coming Davidic King.

Much of the content of the wisdom books is based on observations of creation and of human behavior. In Proverbs 24:30–34, for example, the author indicates that one day he passed by the field of a lazy man. The field was overgrown, and the wall was in disrepair. Upon considering what he saw, he gained insight and coined the proverb: "A little sleep, a little slumber, a little folding of the hands to rest, and poverty will come upon you like a robber, and want like an armed man."[46] However, although the wisdom books assume the clarity of general revelation and the ability of the human mind to perceive and understand it, these books also make it abundantly clear that true wisdom presupposes the fear of God (Prov. 1:7). These books address all aspects of life, even the most mundane, from this basic perspective. As Raymond Van Leeuwen observes, this means that the wisdom books view "*all of life*, not just worship, as service to Yahweh."[47] The fear of God, then, is the key to true knowledge, understanding, and

43. The relationship between the wisdom literature and the covenant is not explicit. Instead, it is implicit; the wisdom books provide instruction for those who wish to live in faithfulness to the covenant. It is similar, although not identical, to torah, or law (see Longman 2006, 80–81).

44. There is some disagreement among commentators regarding whether Jesus, in Luke 11:49, uses the phrase "the Wisdom of God" as a self-designation. A comparison of Luke 11:49–51 with Matthew 23:34–36, however, appears to support the idea that "the Wisdom of God" is used in reference to Jesus.

45. See Longman 2006, 67.

46. The same Proverb is found without the explanatory context in Proverbs 6:10–11.

47. *DTIB*, 848.

wisdom. A lack of such fear, on the other hand, leads to foolishness and death.

Proverbs

The book of Proverbs is the central wisdom book of the Old Testament. Like the book of Psalms, it is a "collection of collections."[48] The individual proverbs were composed by different authors (e.g., Solomon, Agur, Lemuel) over a period of time and finally collected into a single book. Solomon, the author of most of the proverbs, lived during the tenth century B.C., reigning from 970 to 930. Nothing certain is known about Agur or Lemuel. Proverbs also mentions Hezekiah, the king who reigned in Judah from 729 to 686 B.C. According to Proverbs 25:1, "the men of Hezekiah" copied some of the proverbs of Solomon. It is not known for certain when the final collection was finished. It seems likely, however, that scribes gathered the smaller collections of proverbs into a single book during the period of the exile. The final canonical collection exhibits a somewhat obvious overarching structure. Following a brief preamble (1:1–7) is an extended discourse on the nature of wisdom (1:8–9:18). The next section is a lengthy collection of Solomon's proverbs (10:1–22:16). The sayings of the wise (22:17–24:34) are followed by another collection of Solomon's proverbs (25:1–29:27). The final three sections of Proverbs are the sayings of Agur (30:1–33), the sayings of King Lemuel (31:1–9), and a poem dedicated to the virtuous woman (31:10–31).

In order to understand the biblical proverbs it is necessary to understand first of all that they are a type of poetry.[49] In fact, most of the individual proverbs in chapters 10–22 and 25–29 are short sayings written in parallel form. In order to understand the book of Proverbs, it is also crucial to understand that in addition to being poetic, most of the proverbs are general observations, not absolute promises or commands that will obtain under every circumstance.[50] Because of their epigrammatic nature, they do not state every possible qualification. Proper application of individual proverbs requires an understanding of the specific circumstances under which they

48. Murphy 1998, xix.
49. Longman 2002, 38.
50. See *DTIB*, 847.

may apply (e.g., Prov. 26:4–5).[51] To assume that every individual proverb is an unconditional promise or an unqualified legal command is to misunderstand their genre.[52] To use them in such a way is to renounce the very wisdom they seek to provide.

As noted above, the biblical wisdom books such as Proverbs would have provided their original audience with a broad and general understanding of the nature of the wisdom that would be exhibited by the coming Son of David, just as it had been exhibited, to an imperfect degree, by the first son of David to sit on the throne of Israel. The book of Proverbs, however, does not contain much that is *explicitly* eschatological in nature. The theme of the book that is most directly related to our study is death. As Kidner observes, "Proverbs uses the words 'death' and 'die' between 20 and 30 times, and refers in a further dozen places to Sheol (1:12; 5:5; 7:27; 9:18; 15:11, 24; 23:14; 27:20; 30:16), Abaddon (destruction) (15:11; 27:20), the pit (1:12; 28:17) and the Rephaim (the shades) (2:18; 9:18; 21:16)."[53] In a number of places, Proverbs seems to imply the immortality of the righteous (e.g., 10:2, 16; 11:4, 19). A handful of proverbs, however, seem to do more than merely imply it. A brief examination of these texts is, therefore, necessary.

Proverbs 12:28 reads: "In the path of righteousness is life, and in its pathway there is no death." The translation "there is no death" is found not only in the ESV, but in the KJV, NKJV, ASV, NASB, and NRSV among others. Along the same lines, the NIV translation reads, "In the way of righteousness there is life; along that path is immortality." On the other hand, there are translations that read along the lines of the RSV: "In the path of righteousness is life, but the way of error leads to death" (cf. also NAB, NJB). The difference in translation significantly affects the interpretation of the proverb. The Hebrew words in question are *'al-mawet*, translated "no death."[54] Some commentators, such as Roland Murphy, argue that the reading *'el-mawet* ("unto death") is to be preferred and that there is no reference to immortality in this text.[55] Bruce Waltke,

51. Crenshaw 1981, 19; see also Longman 2002, 14.

52. Job's three friends provide an important example of this kind of misuse of Scripture.

53. Kidner 1964, 55. For a detailed study of these concepts, see Johnston 2002.

54. This reading is supported by the majority of Masoretic codices.

55. Murphy 1998, 92.

on the other hand, argues that the reading *'al-mawet* is to be preferred.[56] If this reading is accepted, Proverbs 12:28 "expresses in the most creative and intensive way that the righteous retain a relationship with God forever; clinical death does not separate them from a relationship with the LORD."[57]

A similar emphasis is found in Proverbs 14:32, which reads, "The wicked is overthrown through his evildoing, but the righteous finds refuge in his death." As in the case of 12:28, there are those who insist that this verse contains no hint of the concept of immortality.[58] A closer look at the text, however, reveals that the author may be expressing more than an earthly hope. As Waltke explains, "The wicked person, who perishes through his evil, does not trust in the LORD even when dying, and the righteous, who trust in the LORD when dying, are not thrown down by any evil, including death."[59] In neither proverb is immortality as clearly and explicitly affirmed as it is in later revelation, but even in these early proverbs, the idea is not absent.

A final text in the book of Proverbs that may be of eschatological significance is found in 23:18. The author has already said that the child who is disciplined "will not die" (23:13). The thought progresses from this to the idea found in verse 14: "If you strike him with the rod, you will save his soul from Sheol" or "deliver his soul from the grave" (v. 14). In verse 18, the idea reaches its culmination: "Surely there is a future, and your hope will not be cut off." Again, Waltke provides the clearest explanation of the meaning of the saying: "The metaphor *will not be cut off* (cf. Num. 13:23, 24; 1 Sam. 24:5 [6]) signifies that the hoped-for abundant life will not be annihilated. The effective motivation to observe both sides of the coin of fervor is the promise that God will fulfill the hope of the righteous for an abundant life both for time and for eternity."[60]

56. Waltke 2004, 544–45. He notes, for example, that *'al-mawet* is the more difficult reading to explain away. It is also the ordinary word for "immortality" in Ugaritic and postbiblical Hebrew. In addition, according to this reading, the relationship between 12:28 and 13:1 precisely matches the relationship between 11:31 and 12:1 and 12:14 and 15.

57. Waltke 2004, 543.

58. E.g., Murphy 1998, 107.

59. Waltke 2004, 608.

60. Waltke 2005, 255.

The idea that there will be life beyond death and that death will not sever the relationship between the righteous and God enables us to understand the general nature of the proverbs. Sometimes in this life the wicked do prosper and the righteous do suffer. This tension will be resolved only in the eschaton.

Ecclesiastes

The Hebrew title of the book known in English as Ecclesiastes is Qohelet. The translators of the Septuagint titled the book *ekklēsiastēs*, and this Greek title was followed in the Vulgate's Latin title: *Liber Ecclesiastes*. The Hebrew word "Qohelet" literally means "one who assembles."[61] It is used as a nickname of sorts for the main speaker in the book. Traditionally, Qohelet has been understood to be a nickname for Solomon. Solomon, then, has been identified as the author of the book. There is evidence both for and against the identification of Qohelet with Solomon, but more significantly, even if Qohelet is identified with Solomon, Qohelet does not seem to be identified within the book as the author of the book.[62] There is evidence of a narrator (e.g., 1:2; 7:27; 12:8). Given the evidence within the book, Michael Eaton concludes that the narrator is "an admirer of Solomon, writing up the lessons of Solomon's life in the tradition of the wisdom for which Solomon was famous."[63]

The book as a whole may be described as "a framed autobiography."[64] There are a prologue (1:1–11) and an epilogue (12:8–14) that refer to Qohelet in the third person. The bulk of the book is a lengthy autobiographical monologue written from the perspective of Qohelet (1:12–12:8). Within the monologue itself, the narrator's perspective appears in only one place (7:27). Within the book as a whole, there are several genres of literature. The book contains proverbial material (e.g., 4:5), reflections on life (e.g., 1:13–15), anecdotal stories (e.g., 4:13–16), and instructions regarding proper thinking and proper behavior (e.g., 5:1–3).[65]

The structure of Ecclesiastes is notoriously difficult to outline. There is not even agreement regarding the exact parameters of Qohelet's monologue.

61. Longman 1998, 1.

62. For a survey of the evidence, see Longman 1998, 2–7.

63. Eaton 1983, 23.

64. Dillard and Longman 1994, 252.

65. See Longman 1998, 20.

Attempts to identify a deeper structure to Ecclesiastes have resulted in even less agreement. Although there are almost as many suggested structures as there are commentators, Eaton's is particularly helpful.[66] He identifies four major sections. The first major section deals with the problem of pessimism and its remedy (1:1–3:22). Following the title (1:1) is a section introduced by the narrator's prologue that outlines the pessimist's problems (1:2–2:23). The section ends with an explanation of the solution to pessimism, namely faith in God (2:24–3:22). The second major section deals with the problem of life "under the sun" (4:1–10:20). It begins by describing life's hardships and life's companions (4:1–5:7). It continues by describing problems associated with poverty and wealth (5:8–6:12) and suffering and sin (7:1–8:1). This section concludes with a monologue on authority, injustice, and the life of faith (8:2–9:10) followed by a discussion of wisdom and folly (9:11–10:20). The third major section is a call to decision (11:1–12:7), and the book concludes with the fourth major section, the epilogue (12:8–14).[67]

The major problem facing interpreters of Ecclesiastes is the problem of understanding the apparent contradictions with other biblical texts and the frequent changes in direction of thought within the book itself. One approach is offered by Tremper Longman, who suggests the idea that the narrator uses Qohelet's monologue as a "foil" in order to instruct his son about the dangers of speculation and doubt. Longman states, "Just as in the book of Job, most of the book of Ecclesiastes is composed of the non-orthodox speeches of the human participants of the book, speeches that are torn down and demolished at the end."[68] According to this view, Qohelet is a skeptic with no hope in the future. The positive teaching of the book is to be found in the words of the unnamed narrator.[69]

A slightly different approach to the book is suggested by Michael Eaton, who sees the book as an apologetic essay. According to Eaton, "It defends the life of faith in a generous God by pointing to the grimness

66. Eaton 1983, 52–53.

67. I differ with Eaton on the parameters of the epilogue. He identifies it as 12:9–14, but the third person reference to Qohelet in 12:8 seems to indicate that verse 8 is the beginning of the narrator's epilogue.

68. Longman 1998, 38.

69. It should be noted that while Longman understands Qohelet's speech to be unorthodox, he grants that Qohelet does truly capture the despair of a world without God (Longman 1998, 39–40).

of the alternative."[70] It points out that life without God leads ultimately to futility. There are those, on the other hand, who see a more positive side to the message of Ecclesiastes. Craig Bartholomew, for example, argues that Ecclesiastes is an affirmation of life. "In line with the goodness of creation, Qoheleth celebrates life under the motifs of eating and drinking, working, and enjoying marriage."[71] While this latter view is not completely without merit, it does not do justice to the effects of the fall upon creation.

The main theme of Ecclesiastes, namely that all is vanity (Heb. *hebel*), must be understood against the background of the fall. As Barry Webb explains, "It is a judgment, a condition, imposed on the world, and on human beings in particular, by God."[72] It is when we understand that vanity is a part of God's curse upon creation that we can begin to see the eschatological relevance of Ecclesiastes. Qohelet fell into despair because he could not see any hope beyond the present futility. He could only look backward toward the fall. In the New Testament, Paul looks back to the fall as well as forward to the consummation. In Romans 8:19–24, Paul agrees that the creation was subjected to futility. But he looks forward to the day when it will be completely set free from its bondage to decay. The redemption of creation from the curse of futility is not yet completed, but it is assured.

Job

The book of Job addresses the relationship between God's justice and human suffering in a fallen world. As such it touches on a number of themes relevant to our study. The book itself does not state the name of its author, and there is also nothing within the book that would specify a precise date for its composition. Dates have been proposed for the composition of the book ranging from the time of Moses to the Hellenistic era. Evidence for a date during or soon after the reign of Solomon is compelling, but it is certainly not conclusive. Some have argued that the book was composed in a series of editorial stages, but this theory has been ably

70. Eaton 1983, 44.
71. See *DTIB*, 184.
72. Webb 2000, 104.

refuted. Norman Habel, for example, effectively argues for the unity and integrity of the book.[73]

Although the date of the book's composition is unknown, the setting of the story found within the book is certainly the patriarchal era. Job is a patriarch very similar to Abraham or Isaac. He is a wealthy man with a large family. He offers sacrifices to God as a family priest (Job 1:5). This he would not have been permitted to do had he lived after the giving of the law and the establishment of the priesthood at Sinai.[74] He is said to be from the land of Uz, which is not within the land of Israel. It is likely that he lived before Abraham and before Israel became a nation. Many scholars today reject the historicity of the story, but mention of Job elsewhere in Scripture indicates that the story is not merely an extended parable (Ezek. 14:14, 20; James 5:11).

It is somewhat difficult to specify the genre of the book because it contains examples of many genres. Dillard and Longman categorize the book as a whole as a "wisdom debate."[75] Francis Andersen argues that "Job stands closest to the epic history of early Israel, which found its golden expression in the patriarchal stories, the saga of the Exodus, the career of David, the tale of Ruth."[76] Job is like the historical narratives in many ways, yet it also shares features with the wisdom literature and the poetic books. The combination of features makes Job a unique book both within the Bible and within the context of ancient Near Eastern literature.

The book may be divided into six major sections. It begins with a prose prologue introducing Job and the background to his test (1:1–2:13). The second major section contains a series of poetic speeches by Job and his three friends (3:1–27:23). The third section is an interlude, a poem on divine wisdom (28:1–28). Job's final speech and Elihu's response is the subject of the fourth major section (29:1–37:24). God's response to Job follows in the fifth section (38:1–42:6). The sixth and final major section is a prose epilogue describing God's final verdict and Job's restoration (42:7–17).

After introducing Job (1:1–5), the author of the book turns his attention to the heavenly court. Here we encounter one who is termed "Satan"

73. Habel 1985, 35–39.
74. Dillard and Longman 1994, 200.
75. Dillard and Longman 1994, 207.
76. Andersen 1976, 36.

or "the adversary" (1:6). He asks that the righteousness of Job be tested, and God permits such a test (1:7–2:10). Satan is sometimes perceived as an all-powerful creature, but the Bible does not present such a dualistic view. According to the book of Job, Satan is not on the same level as God. He is able to do only what God permits him to do.[77] Here God permits him to test Job. These introductory verses regarding the heavenly court are important because they remind readers of Scripture that "the history of God's people is not to be seen purely in terms of the power politics of the Ancient Near East."[78] God is providentially working out his purposes whether his people fully understand those purposes or not.

A large portion of the book of Job is taken up with a series of speeches by Job and his three friends (Job 3–27). A number of themes are addressed in this section of the book, but Norman Habel helpfully focuses in on the main issue:

> The central development in Movement II of the plot is the legal action which Job pursues. He is not content to raise a typical lament bewailing his miserable condition as a mortal. Instead, he accuses his God of being the enemy, the fierce El Gibbor who has made him the target of unwarranted attacks (16:9–14). But even more boldly, he develops a program to confront his divine adversary in court and there be vindicated.[79]

Throughout these speeches, Job pursues this aim while his three friends continue to criticize and rebuke him on the basis of their incomplete understanding of God's justice. Job's suffering causes his mind to become filled with dark images of death and chaos (e.g., 3:1–26). Job has become acutely aware that all is not right with God's good creation. It has been affected by the forces of chaos.[80] These forces are represented here by the sea and by Leviathan (3:8).

Among the many statements made by Job during the course of his debate with his three friends is one that has been interpreted by some as an expression of Job's hope for a future bodily resurrection. This text, found in chapter 19 of Job, requires some comment.

77. Andersen 1976, 83.
78. Fyall 2002, 186.
79. Habel 1985, 31.
80. Fyall 2002, 91.

19:23–27

Oh that my words were written!
   Oh that they were inscribed in a book!
Oh that with an iron pen and lead
   they were engraved in the rock forever!
For I know that my Redeemer lives,
   and at the last he will stand upon the earth.
And after my skin has been thus destroyed,
   yet in my flesh I shall see God,
whom I shall see for myself,
   and my eyes shall behold, and not another.
My heart faints within me!

Both the text and the translation of this passage have proved to be the source of numerous difficulties. The difficulties, however, should not be allowed to obscure that which is clear. The key theme that is expressed is Job's hope and expectation of future vindication. There is also a strong emphasis on Job's seeing God with his own eyes, an idea expressed three times in rapid succession. Many commentators have argued that there is no concept of immortality or resurrection expressed or implied in these verses.[81] Others argue that there does appear to be some evidence in the text that Job expects to see God after his death.[82] As Andersen observes, for example, "there would be no need for Job to deposit a written testimony, if he expects to be vindicated before he dies."[83] While the implication that Job expects to live again after his death is sufficiently clear, the full New Testament doctrine of resurrection should not be read back into the text. This text is an early hint of the fuller revelation yet to come.

After the speeches by Job and his friends are completed, the Lord himself speaks to Job (38:1–42:6). He does not answer Job's questions or challenges. Instead, he interrogates Job about his knowledge of the world, and through the interrogation Job is reassured that God is in complete control. In the second half of God's speech to Job, he refers to two mysterious creatures, Behemoth and Leviathan. According to many commentators, God is sim-

81. E.g., Pope 1973, 147; Johnston 2002, 209–14. It is not only modern commentators who have denied that the text refers in any way to resurrection. In the early centuries of the church, Chrysostom appealed to Job 14:12 as proof that this text does not express hope for resurrection.

82. Andersen 1976, 194; Habel 1985, 307; Strimple 2004, 294–95.

83. Andersen 1976, 194.

ply referring here to the hippopotamus and the crocodile respectively.[84] Others, however, argue that these two creatures are symbolic of the forces of death and evil.[85]

Robert Fyall argues persuasively that Behemoth is a figure representing death (Job 40:15–24).[86] God's speech about Behemoth indicates that man cannot control this beast, but it distinctly implies that God can and does control it (v. 24). Death is firmly under God's control. According to Fyall, God's speech about the beast Leviathan (41:1–34) provides clues that this beast is a symbol of Satan himself.[87] Along with Behemoth, these two beasts represent the forces of evil opposed to God. In the opening part of the speech about Leviathan, God describes both the impressive power of this beast and the powerlessness of man before him (41:1–8). Job has been tormented by an enemy and has wrongly believed that the enemy was God. God now reveals the nature of Job's true enemy (vv. 13–29). Man cannot control this enemy, but God can and does (41:1).

If this interpretation of the identity of Behemoth and Leviathan is correct, then Job's story of suffering is an example of the struggle between the seed of the woman and the seed of the serpent that began in Genesis 3:15. Because of sin and the fall, suffering is now a part of this world. Yet the forces of evil are not out of God's control. Although man is powerless to do anything about death, evil, and Satan, God is not. The fact that these powers are under control gives hope that God will one day destroy them. The book of Job anticipates a day when death and Satan will be destroyed. The New Testament will reveal how death and Satan are overcome by Jesus the Messiah who enters into human suffering, experiences death on the cross, and defeats the enemy in his resurrection (Heb. 2:14).

The Song of Songs

The Hebrew title of the book, *shir hashshirrim*, is a superlative construction indicating the greatest in a category of things. It is best translated as "the Song of Songs." The book has also been titled the Song of Solomon and Canticles in some English translations, but these are less precise titles. In

84. E.g., Andersen 1976, 288.
85. E.g., Fyall 2002, 128–29; Habel 1985, 66.
86. Fyall 2002, 137.
87. Fyall 2002, 157.

the Hebrew Bible, the Song of Songs immediately follows Proverbs and Ruth. The order of these three books in the Hebrew canon may be based on a common theme. Proverbs concludes with a poem about a wise woman (31:10–31). The following book, Ruth, tells the story of the marriage of a virtuous woman. The Song of Solomon is a poem or collection of poems celebrating the love and intimacy between a man and a woman.

Throughout much of history, the Song of Songs has been interpreted in an allegorical manner. Jewish interpreters offered two allegorical approaches both of which understood the book to be about God's love for Israel. One approach, represented by the Targum, reads the book as an allegory of redemptive history from the time of the exodus to the messianic age.[88] Other Jewish interpreters read the book as an allegorical description of the union between God and the human soul.[89] Christian exegetes adopted this allegorical method of interpreting the Song of Songs for much of the church's history. The only difference was that Christian commentators read the book as an allegory about Christ's love for the church rather than about God's love for Israel.

The fundamental problem with allegorical interpretations of the Song of Songs has always been the arbitrary way in which specific texts are read. The only limit has been the interpreter's imagination. When the text itself is examined, it becomes evident that the Song of Songs is love poetry.[90] Whether it is a collection of loosely associated poems or a single poem is disputed, but the fact that it is a love poem is difficult to deny.[91] Notably, much of the intimacy that is expressed in the Song of Songs occurs in a garden (2:3–13; 4:12–5:1; 5:2–6:3; 6:11; 7:10–13; 8:13–14). The man and woman are intimate and without shame. In this way, the Song of Songs pictures the restoration of the human sexual relationship to what it was in Eden before the fall (Gen. 2:25).[92] However, while the sexual union of a man and woman within the context of marriage is a positive good, it must not be mistaken for the pinnacle of blessedness. The fullness of peace is accomplished only with the coming of the Messiah. In this sense, the

88. Pope 1977, 21.

89. Longman 2001, 26.

90. Longman 2001, 48.

91. Dillard and Longman (1994, 259) understand the Song to be a collection of love poems. Others, such as Webb (2000, 22), believe the Song to be a single love poem.

92. Dillard and Longman 1994, 265.

author of the Song uses the deepest and most intense human relationship to prefigure the love of Christ for his people (see Eph. 5:31–32).[93]

Summary

The book of Psalms, the wisdom books, and the Song of Songs do not continue the narrative of redemptive history, but these books are set within the context of that history. The psalms were written over a period of approximately one thousand years during that history and express the deepest feelings of God's people. Many of the psalms express recognition that things are not the way they are supposed to be because Israel has forsaken the covenant. Yet the psalms also often express the hopes of Israel for restoration and blessing. Many of the psalms express the hopes of the people for the coming Davidic king, the Messiah who would one day restore Israel and judge her enemies.

The wisdom books of the Bible, namely Proverbs, Job, and Ecclesiastes, teach the people of God the proper way to think and behave in this world, but they do so by offering general observations on life. The wisdom books call all men to exercise God-fearing wisdom. As a description of true wisdom, these books provide insight into the kind of wisdom that would be exhibited by the coming Messiah, the King who would rule his people and the world with wisdom and righteousness. The Song of Songs, then, portrays the restoration of untainted human love, and in so doing it foreshadows the perfect love of the Messiah for his people.

93. Webb 2000, 34.

5

The Eighth-Century Prophets (1)

Jonah, Amos, Hosea, and Micah

Having surveyed the content of the Pentateuch, the historical books, and the poetic books of the Old Testament, we turn now to the writings of the prophets. In the Hebrew Bible, the *Nebi'im*, or "Prophets," is the second major section of Scripture. It includes the Former Prophets and the Latter Prophets. The Former Prophets are the books of Joshua, Judges, Samuel, and Kings. The books of Isaiah, Jeremiah, Ezekiel, and the Twelve are referred to as the Latter Prophets. In the Protestant Old Testament, the books of Joshua, Judges, Samuel, and Kings are included among the historical books, while Isaiah, Jeremiah, Lamentations, Ezekiel, Daniel, and the Twelve are the prophetic books. Our survey of the prophetic books will include the Hebrew Latter Prophets as well as the books of Lamentations and Daniel. In addition, while recognizing that the dating of the ministries and the writings of some of the prophets is uncertain, this study will address these books in a chronological rather than canonical sequence.[1]

1. I have chosen to approach the prophetic books in chronological rather than canonical sequence in order to trace the development of the prophetic message in relation to the exile and restoration of

Introduction: Prophets and Prophecy

The interpretation of the prophetic books is not a simple matter, and in order to understand these books, they must be approached with care and caution.[2] They cannot be approached as if they were little more than collections of arcane predictions. As we shall discover, they are much more than this, but before proceeding to an examination of the individual prophetic books, we must answer some preliminary questions. First, what is a prophet? In the Old Testament, the word used most frequently to refer to a prophet is *nabi'*. The general meaning of the word is "spokesman." In the Old Testament, a prophet "was *a spokesman for God* with the distinct call to be the ambassador of God."[3] In fact, it was the call of God that gave the true prophet his legitimacy.[4] Other titles used to describe prophets are *ro'eh*, meaning "seer"; *hozeh*, also meaning "seer"; and *'ish-ha'elohim*, meaning "man of God." Pieter Verhoef explains, "These titles together define the prophet as a man who has been called to communicate the revealed word of God, a man who has an intimate relationship with God as his servant and messenger, and as one whose task it is to keep watch over God's people."[5]

According to Scripture, the prophetic office originated with Moses in the events at Mount Sinai (Deut. 18:15–16; Hos. 12:13). The office of the prophet, then, is directly associated with the Sinai covenant.[6] After the exodus from Egypt, Moses had led the people of Israel to the mountain. Upon their arrival, Moses ascended the mountain, and it was revealed to him that God would descend in a thick cloud in order that the people might hear and believe that which he would speak to Moses (Ex. 19:9). On the morning of the third day God descended on the mountain in smoke and fire (vv. 16–20). There he gave the Ten Commandments (Ex. 20:1–17). In fear, the people then said to Moses, "You speak to us, and we will listen; but do not let God speak to us, lest we die" (v. 19). The people asked Moses

---

Israel. The centrality of the exile and restoration to the prophetic message will be discussed in more detail below.

2. For a helpful introduction to the subject, see VanGemeren 1990; Robertson 2004.

3. Van Gemeren 1990, 42; see also Sawyer 1993, 1.

4. For a complete discussion of the divine call and commissioning of the prophet, see Robertson 2004, 67–90.

5. *NIDOTTE*, 4:1068; see also Robertson 2004, 23; Young 1952, 13.

6. Cf. Dumbrell 1984, 136–37.

to be a mediator of God's word. All of the prophets who followed Moses shared this role.[7]

A second important issue that must be raised is the broad historical context of the prophetic books. The ministries of all of the writing prophets can be dated from the eighth to the fifth centuries B.C.[8] The books of 2 Kings, Ezra, and Nehemiah, therefore, provide the redemptive-historical context for these prophets. It will be recalled that these historical books recount the events leading to the exile, the exile itself, and the early stages of restoration after the exile. As O. Palmer Robertson explains, "the writings of Israel's prophets eventually must be seen as centering primarily around two events of immeasurable significance: Israel's exile and restoration."[9] The redemptive-historical context of the writing prophets, then, is "the death and resurrection of Israel" (Ezek. 37:1–14).[10]

In addition to understanding the historical context of the prophetic books, it is also necessary to understand the nature of the language they used. Although other genres are found in the prophetic books, including biographical and autobiographical narrative, the most common form of prophetic speech found in these books is the oracle.[11] The term "oracle," as John Sawyer observes, "is applied to all manner of prophetic utterances from lengthy 'oracles concerning foreign nations' (e.g. Isa. 13:1; 14:28; 15:1; 17:1; 19:1; 21:1; 23:1) and whole books (e.g. Nahum, Habakkuk, Malachi) to shorter prophecies addressed to specific situations (e.g. Ezek. 12:10)."[12] The prophetic oracles may be distinguished according to their content as either oracles of judgment or oracles of salvation.[13]

The prophetic oracles tend to employ poetic language rather than prose.[14] This is significant because, as we have seen, Hebrew poetry is a highly stylized form of literature. It is characterized largely by its extensive use of figurative language and striking imagery. Hebrew poetry uses numerous metaphors and other figures of speech. When it is understood that the

7. Robertson 2004, 25. Moses was unique in being the mediator of God's Word and God's covenant. All of the prophets were mediators of God's word.

8. Wolff 1987, 15.

9. Robertson 2004, 195; see also 453–98.

10. Gowan 1998, 9; Baldwin 1972, 91.

11. Bullock 1986, 29; Westermann 1967.

12. Sawyer 1993, 28.

13. VanGemeren 1990, 78.

14. Bullock 1986, 31; McCartney and Clayton 1994, 217.

biblical prophets make extensive use of poetic language, it becomes evident that those parts of the prophetic books that are poetic in nature are not to be interpreted in the same manner that prose is interpreted.

A final topic that must be examined before proceeding to the individual books of the prophets concerns the nature of the prophetic message. Undergirding the message of all the prophets is their understanding of the law and the covenant. The blessings and curses of the Mosaic covenant found in texts such as Leviticus 26 and Deuteronomy 28 are the foundation for the prophets' messages of judgment and restoration.[15] As Douglas Stuart explains, "Nearly all of the content of the classical (writing) prophets' oracles revolves around the announcement of the near-time fulfillment of covenantal curses and the end-time fulfillment of covenantal restoration blessings."[16] Robertson observes how the connection between the Abrahamic and Mosaic covenants explains some of the apparent paradoxes in the prophetic message. "The binding together of these two covenants explains how the prophets of Israel could anticipate both disaster and blessing for Israel. Disaster must come because of violation of covenant law. But blessing can be promised as the final end because of the sovereign commitment on the part of God to bless his people despite their deserving nothing."[17] The Davidic covenant also provides a foundation for the message of the prophets. God's promise in this covenant to preserve a descendant of David on the throne and to defend Jerusalem "provides the strongest basis for hope in a future messianic king beyond the judgment of exile."[18]

The basic message of the prophets included both oracles of judgment and oracles of salvation. In the oracles of judgment, the prophets condemned Israel for violating the covenant law and declared the imposition of the covenant curses.[19] Many of the oracles of judgment take the form of a prophetic lawsuit at the end of which God pronounces his sentence on Israel (Jer. 2:5–9; Hos. 2:2–23; 4:1–3; Mic. 6:1–8).[20] Exile was the ultimate judgment because it was, in effect, a death sentence for Israel.[21] A significant part of the prophetic message of judgment was the proclamation of

15. Robertson 2004, 122.
16. Stuart 1987, xxxii.
17. Robertson 2004, 178.
18. Robertson 2004, 180–81.
19. VanGemeren 1990, 78–79; Bright 1976, 42.
20. For a helpful explanation of the prophetic lawsuit, see VanGemeren 1990, 400–407.
21. von Rad 1967, 12.

the coming day of Yahweh or day of the Lord. In the prophets, the day of Yahweh is a complex idea that encompasses both judgment and salvation. This concept is best examined in the context of its usage in the individual prophetic books of Scripture in which it is found.

There is some controversy regarding the purpose of the oracles of judgment. Were they intended to produce repentance and avoid judgment, or were they intended to be understood as predictions of unavoidable judgment? Using the terminology of speech-act theory, Walter Houston asks whether these oracles are "calls for repentance (which would fall into the category of directive acts), or announcements of coming doom (which would presumably be assertive)?"[22] O. Palmer Robertson rightly concludes that these oracles were intended to lead to repentance and to avert the prophesied judgment (Jer. 26:2–3).[23] As he explains, the prophetic word "does not primarily involve prediction regarding future events."[24]

In addition to oracles of judgment, the basic message of the prophets includes oracles of salvation. These oracles proclaim the coming of a new era following judgment. Like the oracles of judgment, the oracles of salvation are also rooted in the covenants (Lev. 26:40–45; Deut. 4:30–31; 30:1–10). John Bright observes the significance of these messages of restoration:

> Virtually all of the pre-exilic prophets, albeit by no means in identical ways, looked beyond the judgment they were compelled to announce to a farther future when God would come once again to his people in mercy, restore their fortunes, and establish his rule over them in righteousness and peace. This promise of future salvation is one of the most distinctive features in the message of the prophets, and it is this perhaps more than anything else that serves to bind the Old Testament unbreakably with the New in a single canon of Scripture.[25]

The preexilic prophets looked forward to the restoration of Israel following the exile. As we shall discover, however, the postexilic prophets view the return from exile as only the beginning of the eschatological restoration.

22. Houston 1995, 145. Houston argues that these judgment oracles should be understood as declaratives, in that they initiate "an objective state of condemnation." For an explanation of speech-act terminology, see Searle 1969 and 1979. See also Vanhoozer 2002, 127–203.

23. Robertson 2004, 94.

24. Robertson 2004, 26; see also 407–51.

25. Bright 1976, 15; see also VanGemeren 1990, 89.

One of the most significant elements found in the prophetic message of salvation is the establishment of God's kingdom through a descendant of David, a Messiah.[26] The roots of the messianic idea are found in several texts in the Pentateuch (Gen. 17:6, 16; 35:11; 49:10; Num. 24:17; Deut. 17:14–20).[27] The primary foundation of this concept, however, rests in the covenant God made with David (2 Sam. 7). According to the prophets, the coming Messiah will establish God's kingdom, transforming creation and bringing blessing to all the nations, thereby fulfilling the purpose of God's covenant with Abraham (Gen. 12:3; Ps. 72:17).[28]

The transformation of creation associated with the coming of the kingdom of God ties together God's creational purposes and his redemptive purposes. According to the prophets, "there is no redemption unless it affects the whole of creation."[29] The prophets recognize that there is something radically wrong in the present creation, but unlike the followers of many pagan religions, they do not assert that the physical world is itself inherently evil. The present corruption of God's creation is due to sin. The prophets therefore affirm that all of creation will be transformed and what is wrong will be set right in the eschatological victory over evil.[30]

Jonah

The history of the northern kingdom of Israel in the eighth century is found in 2 Kings 14–17. It was a time of great wickedness and idolatry that would eventually result in the destruction of Israel by the Assyrians in 722 B.C. According to 2 Kings 14:25, Jonah the son of Amittai prophesied during the lengthy reign of Jeroboam II (793–753). All else that we know of the prophet Jonah from the book of 2 Kings is that he had prophesied the expansion of Israel's borders "from Lebo-hamath as far as the Sea of the Arabah." The book of Jonah itself provides no more specific information about the identity of the prophet than that already found in 2 Kings. Furthermore, although the general time period of Jonah's prophetic ministry is known, the date at which the canonical book of Jonah was written is

26. VanGemeren 1990, 232; Childs 1985, 119.
27. Block 2003, 37.
28. VanGemeren 1990, 233.
29. VanGemeren 1990, 86.
30. Gowan 2000, 2.

unknown.[31] Dates have been suggested ranging from the eighth to the third century. Although there is no absolutely certain evidence, T. D. Alexander makes a good case for a preexilic date of composition.[32]

The book of Jonah provides a good transition to a discussion of the prophets because the style of the book itself is distinctive among the prophetic books. Aside from portions of the book of Jeremiah and Daniel, all of the other prophetic books focus primarily on the message of the prophet. The book of Jonah, on the other hand, is a biographical prose narrative focusing almost exclusively on the prophet himself.[33] The book of Jonah, in fact, includes only one very brief oracle (Jonah 3:4). The predominantly narrative style of the book of Jonah has more in common with the historical narratives about Elijah and Elisha than it does with the other prophetic books.

The distinctive style of the book of Jonah has raised questions concerning its genre. Many recent scholars have questioned whether the book was intended to be understood as a factual historical narrative. Those who question the book's historicity have suggested that it might be a parable or an allegory. Leslie C. Allen suggests a certain combination of these two, saying, "It is best to confine the definition of the literary form of the book to that of a parable with certain allegorical features."[34] Other scholars, however, have observed that the reasons given for rejecting the historicity of Jonah are generally based on unproven naturalistic assumptions.[35] These same scholars have made a strong case for the historicity of the book.[36] The most important, and finally decisive, evidence for the historicity of the book of Jonah is, of course, the fact that Jesus assumes its historicity (Matt. 12:39–41; Luke 11:29–32).

The book of Jonah may be divided into four major sections. In chapter 1, Jonah receives his commission from God to go to Nineveh, but he disobeys. Chapter 2 reveals Jonah's response to the divine mercy shown to him after his disobedience. In chapter 3, Jonah again receives his commission from God to go to Nineveh, and this time he obeys. Chapter 4

31. Craigie 1984–85, 1:211.
32. Alexander 1988, 61–63.
33. Stuart 1987, 431; Dillard and Longman 1994, 391.
34. Allen 1976, 181.
35. See, for example, Stuart 1987, 440.
36. Stuart 1987, 440–42; Alexander 1988, 69–77.

then reveals Jonah's response to the divine mercy shown to the people of Nineveh. By means of this brief literary masterpiece, God reveals truths about his sovereignty and mercy that are as important today as they were in the eighth century B.C.

In the first three verses of the book of Jonah, the author sets the stage by informing the reader who Jonah was, what God commissioned him to do, and what Jonah's initial response was. Jonah, as we have seen, was an eighth-century prophet in the northern kingdom of Israel during the reign of Jeroboam II. God's commission to Jonah was straightforward, "Arise, go to Nineveh, that great city and call out against it, for their evil has come up before me" (Jonah 1:2). Nineveh, it should be noted, was a large city in the Assyrian Empire that occasionally served as the capital.[37] Jonah's response to God's commission is striking. He flees in the opposite direction, finding a westward-bound ship in the coastal port city of Joppa.

The ship does not proceed far before God intervenes, hurling a great wind upon the sea that causes a mighty tempest (1:4). The sailors are frightened and do all in their power to save the ship (v. 5). Eventually, the captain discovers Jonah sleeping in the inner parts of the boat (v. 6). The sailors decide to cast lots in order to discover who has brought this calamity upon them, and the lot falls on Jonah (v. 7). After questioning him and discovering what he has done, the sailors ask him what to do (vv. 8–11). Jonah instructs them to cast him into the sea (v. 12). The sailors are initially hesitant and make another attempt to get back to shore (v. 13). Finally, however, they hurl Jonah into the sea at which point the storm calms (vv. 14–15). Their response is profound: "Then the men feared Yahweh exceedingly, and they offered a sacrifice to Yahweh and made vows" (v. 16). As Joyce Baldwin notes, "The sailors have made a life-changing discovery because they have come into contact with the living God."[38]

Contrary to what he expects, Jonah does not drown in the raging sea. Instead, God causes a great fish to swallow Jonah, and he remains in the belly of the fish for "three days and three nights" (1:17). Whether or not the "three days and three nights" is meant to be understood literally has been the subject of some discussion among biblical commentators. Some have suggested that the phrase might have been an ancient figure of speech. As Douglas Stuart observes, "there may have been a sort of popular notion

37. Craigie 1984–85, 1:215.
38. Baldwin 1993, 563.

or cliché of expression in ancient times that the journey from the land of the living to Sheol (or vice versa) took three full days."[39] Whether "three days and three nights" is understood literally or as a figure of speech, it is clear that the fish is God's appointed means to deliver Jonah from death by drowning.

The second chapter of Jonah contains Jonah's psalm of thanksgiving (2:2–9). In this psalm, he thanks God for graciously saving him from the sea. As Stuart explains, thanksgiving psalms typically follow a five-part structure, and Jonah's psalm contains all of these five parts: the introduction to the psalm is found in 2:2; the description of past distress is found in 2:3–6a; the appeal to God for help is found in 2:7; the reference to the rescue God provided is found in 2:6b; and the vow of praise and/or testimonial is found in 2:8–9.[40] This psalm becomes significant as the difference between Jonah's response to the mercy shown him and his response to the mercy shown Nineveh is later revealed. Chapter 2 ends with God causing the fish to vomit Jonah out upon the shoreline.

The third chapter of Jonah finds the prophet back where he started. In fact, the first five words of the Hebrew text are exactly the same as the first five words of the first chapter.[41] This time, however, Jonah obeys and goes to Nineveh (3:3). Verse 4 contains the oracle of judgment that Jonah has been commissioned to speak: "Yet forty days, and Nineveh shall be overthrown!" In the Old Testament, forty days is often a period of particular importance. It is the amount of time that the floodwaters continued on the earth in the days of Noah (Gen. 7:17). It is the number of days Moses spent on the mountain with God after the confirmation of the covenant (Ex. 24:18). It is also the number of days that it took Elijah to journey to Mount Horeb/Sinai (1 Kings 19:8).

The word translated "overthrown" in verse 4 is a form of *hapak*, meaning "turn" or "overturn." The word has a wide semantic range. It is often used in contexts of judgment. It is used, for example, to describe the judgment of Sodom and Gomorrah (Gen. 19:25), the judgment of Jerusalem (2 Kings 21:13), and the eschatological judgment of the nations (Hag. 2:21–22). However, in some contexts, it can refer to a turning or change for the bet-

39. Stuart 1987, 474; see also Landes 1967b.

40. Stuart 1987, 472.

41. Baldwin 1993, 576.

ter (Esth. 9:22).[42] Stuart suggests that the wide semantic range of the verb leaves a measure of ambiguity about the meaning of Jonah's oracle.[43] The context of the oracle, however, appears to remove much of that ambiguity. In this context, the word would most naturally refer to judgment.

The response of the people of Nineveh to the preaching of Jonah is immediate. From the greatest to the least, they repent (Jonah 3:5–9). Even the king of Nineveh repents, saying, "Who knows? God may turn and relent and turn from his fierce anger, so that we may not perish" (v. 9).[44] The same kind of response is expressed elsewhere in the prophets (Joel 2:14). It assumes that the catastrophe mentioned in an oracle of judgment may be averted if there is sincere repentance. The prophet Jeremiah expressly states that this is possible (Jer. 18:7–8). God, in fact, did relent of the judgment proclaimed in Jonah (3:10). God's response lends weight to the idea that oracles of judgment are primarily intended to produce repentance. His response indicates that Jonah's oracle of judgment was not a simple prediction of what was certainly going to happen. Instead, his oracle contained the implicit condition described in Jeremiah 18:7–8. Because Nineveh repented, judgment was averted.[45]

Jonah's response to the mercy shown to Nineveh is revealed in chapter 4. He is not pleased. In fact, he is furious (v. 1). In verse 2, the reason for his initial attempt to flee from God's call is now revealed. Jonah says, "O Yahweh, is not this what I said when I was yet in my country? That is why I made haste to flee to Tarshish; for I knew that you are a gracious God and merciful, slow to anger and abounding in steadfast love, and relenting from disaster." In other words, Jonah was angry because he knew God might show mercy to the people of Nineveh if he preached to them. His confession of the nature of God's mercy is taken from Exodus 34:6, a context in which God has just shown great mercy to Israel after the sin of the golden calf. Jonah knows that God is merciful; he simply does not want God's mercy shown to the Assyrians. God asks Jonah in 4:4 and 4:9, "Do you do well to be angry?" This question is central to the book's message. Although Jonah

42. See *NIDOTTE*, 1:1048–50; *TWOT*, 221–22; *HALOT*, 1:253–54; BDB, 245.

43. Stuart 1987, 489.

44. Stuart suggests that the king referred to here may have been Aššur-dān III, who reigned from 773 to 756 B.C. (Stuart 1987, 486).

45. Nineveh would, however, eventually be destroyed by the Medes and Babylonians in 612 B.C., and the Assyrian Empire would fall completely in 605. See Calvin 1960, 1:227.

asserts that he has every right to be angry (4:9), the obvious answer to the question is no. Jonah pities a plant that protected him from the scorching heat (4:4–10). Should not God (and Jonah) have the same kind of pity for an entire city filled with people created in God's image (v. 11)?

Regarding Jonah, Raymond Dillard and Tremper Longman observe, "One of the most striking characteristics of the book in its Old Testament setting is its attitude toward those outside of the covenant community."[46] Jonah's attitude toward Assyria reflects a mutual antagonism between Israel and the surrounding nations. The book of Jonah serves as a guard against any kind of nationalistic particularism that could arise in such a context. The book of Jonah would not allow Jews to easily assume that they alone were to be the recipients of God's mercy. God is sovereign, and as Stuart explains, "God has every right to show mercy to all nations and peoples."[47] Against his will, Jonah becomes a source of blessing to Gentiles, thereby providing (in an ironic way) a glimpse of the eschatological fulfillment of the Abrahamic promises.

Amos

The prophet Amos ministered during the overlapping reigns of Jeroboam II in Israel (793–753) and Uzziah in Judah (792–740). There is a general consensus that his ministry occurred sometime between 760 and 755 B.C.[48] Amos prophesied at a unique time in the history of the divided kingdom. From approximately 780 to 750, Egypt, Syria, and Assyria did not pose a serious threat to Israel. During this time, Jeroboam II was able to expand the borders of Israel (2 Kings 14:25), and his successes created economic prosperity for many and a sense of security as well.[49] This situation would change dramatically with the rise of Tiglath-pileser III (744–727) in Assyria.[50] During these intervening years, however, Israel prospered, and a powerful and wealthy upper class emerged who exploited the poor and perverted justice.

Although a native of Judah, Amos prophesied to the northern kingdom of Israel.[51] He preached to an affluent society that was deeply involved in false

46. Dillard and Longman 1994, 394.
47. Stuart 1987, 500.
48. Hubbard 1989b, 90.
49. *NIDOTTE*, 4:373–74; Andersen and Freedman 1989, 22.
50. Blenkinsopp 1996, 66.
51. Mays 1969a, 3; Dillard and Longman 1994, 375.

worship and in the mistreatment of the poor. These wealthy and powerful Israelites were confident and secure. However, as S. M. Paul notes, "Blinded by their boundless optimism, which was posited on false premises, they were oblivious to the clouds of wrath and recompense swiftly gathering all about them."[52] Into the midst of this society comes Amos, declaring that Israel has broken God's covenant.[53] As Paul explains, Amos

> constantly and consistently called the upper class to task for their bribery and extortion, for their corruption of the judiciary, for perversion and dishonesty, for injustice and immorality, for exploitation of the impoverished and underprivileged, for resolute dissolute behavior, for pampered prosperity and boisterous banquetry, for greed and arrogant security, for self-indulgence and a life of carpe diem, and for pride and prejudice.[54]

God's response to Israel's breaking of the covenant is to send Amos as a "covenant-lawsuit messenger." The covenant-lawsuit was a means by which the stipulations of a covenant were enforced.[55] As Dillard and Longman explain, "In the prophetic lawsuits of the Bible, as in their extrabiblical counterparts . . . , the suzerain or lord in a treaty relationship sends a messenger to remind the disobedient vassal or client of his obligations under the terms of their covenant and of his failure to keep those terms."[56] The judgments threatened by Amos, like those in the other prophets, are based on the list of covenant curses found in texts such as Leviticus 26 and Deuteronomy 27–28.[57] Amos, however, has the distinction of being the first to bring the devastating message that the end is coming for Israel.[58] The covenant curse of exile will be imposed (Lev. 26:33; Deut. 28:24–68).[59] Judgment, however, is not Amos's final word. The same covenant that threatens exile for covenant breaking declares the

52. Paul 1991, 2.

53. House 1998, 363.

54. Paul 1991, 2.

55. For more on the covenant-lawsuit form, see Niehaus 1992, 318–21; VanGemeren 1990, 400–407.

56. Dillard and Longman 1994, 380.

57. Dillard and Longman 1994, 383; House 1998, 363; Niehaus 1992, 322–23; Stuart 1987, 288.

58. Mays 1969a, 1–8.

59. If Amos prophesied around 760 B.C., this prophecy was fulfilled about forty years later in 722 when Israel fell to the Assyrians and the population was taken into captivity.

possibility of restoration for a believing remnant.[60] Amos declares that restoration after the coming judgment is not merely a possibility but a certainty.

The book of Amos may be divided into three main sections. Amos 1–2 is a collection of oracles against the nations, including Judah and Israel. Amos 3–6 contains additional judgment oracles addressed to Israel. Finally, Amos 7–9 is a collection of five visions and an oracle of salvation. The first two verses of the first section of Amos are introductory. They provide some basic information about the context of Amos's ministry and introduce his book. Amos 1:1 informs us that the prophet was from Tekoa, which was a small town several miles south of Jerusalem in Judah. We are told that Amos prophesied during the reigns of Jeroboam II and Uzziah "two years before the earthquake." The exact date of this earthquake is unknown, but it was strong enough to be remembered centuries later (Zech. 14:5). Following this biographical information, the curse announcement in verse 2 serves as a prelude to the remainder of the book.[61]

Oracles against the Nations (Amos 1:3–2:16)

The first major section of the book, in 1:3–2:16, is a collection of oracles against the nations surrounding Israel, concluding with an oracle against Israel itself. There are eight oracles addressed consecutively to Damascus (1:3–5); Gaza (1:6–8); Tyre (1:9–10); Edom (1:11–12); Ammon (1:13–15); Moab (2:1–3); Judah (2:4–5); and Israel (2:6–16). The first seven oracles are very similar in structure and form. The eighth oracle begins in the same way as the first seven, but then follows a different structure. The form of these oracles is that of a messenger speech, in which the prophet delivers verbatim the words given to him by God (Isa. 7:7; Jer. 2:1–2; 10:1–2; Ezek. 3:10–11).[62] All eight of the oracles begin with the same introductory formula: "Thus says Yahweh: 'For three transgressions of . . . , and for four, I will not revoke the punishment" (1:3, 6, 9, 11, 13; 2:1, 4, 6).[63]

60. Dillard and Longman 1994, 383; Andersen and Freedman 1989, 7.

61. Stuart 1987, 300.

62. Stuart 1987, 308.

63. Paul (1991, 27) explains, "The pattern of the graded numerical sequence, commonly referred to as x/x+1, is a stylistic device well known from the literature of the Bible and the ancient Near East."

Following the introductory formula in the first seven oracles are a statement of the crimes for which each nation is being judged and a statement of the decreed judgment. The crimes for which the first six nations are judged are all generally civil in nature: war crimes, treaty violations, and wanton cruelty. The crimes for which Judah and Israel are judged are specifically religious in nature. Judah is charged with rejecting the law of God (2:4). Israel is charged with idolatry and with violating numerous stipulations of the Mosaic covenant, particularly those forbidding the exploitation of the poor (2:6–8). In six of the first seven oracles, God's stated judgment is: "I will send a fire." In the oracle against Ammon, the stated judgment is slightly different: "I will kindle a fire" (1:14). The stated judgment against Israel is much more detailed in nature. Israel's judgment will involve the imposition of the covenant curses, including exile.

The oracles against the nations demonstrate clearly that God is not only the God of Israel. He is the God of heaven and earth and all nations.[64] Every nation on earth stands before God and is responsible to him for their deeds (Ps. 2:10–12).[65] The message of the first two chapters of Amos is a message of judgment, not only for Israel and Judah, but for all of the nations surrounding them. As Francis Andersen and David Noel Freedman explain, "The picture, then, in Amos 1–2 is one of the wholesale liquidation of the small kingdoms in the Syro-Phoenician-Palestinian region."[66] Although the complete judgment of all of these nations was accomplished over a number of centuries, their judgment began with the rise of the Assyrian Empire only a few decades after Amos prophesied.[67]

Additional Oracles against Israel (Amos 3–6)

Amos 3–6 contains additional oracles addressed specifically to Israel. In Amos 3:1–5:17, Amos addresses three judgment oracles to the nation, including one in the form of a lamentation (5:1–17). In 5:18–6:14, he addresses two "Woe" oracles to the nation. Amos chapter 3 begins with a striking statement in verses 1–2:

64. Andersen and Freedman 1989, 89.

65. Craigie 1984–85, 1:129.

66. Andersen and Freedman 1989, 357.

67. The fulfillment of the prophesied judgment against Damascus (Amos 1:5) is clearly revealed elsewhere in Scripture (2 Kings 16:9). This particular judgment occurred ca. 734 B.C.

> Hear this word that Yahweh has spoken against you, O people of Israel, against the whole family that I brought up out of the land of Egypt:
>
> "You only have I known
> of all the families of the earth;
> therefore I will punish you
> for all your iniquities."

This oracle stresses the fact that the coming judgment is not in spite of God's covenant relationship with Israel, but because of it.

God had chosen Israel and established his covenant with her (Ex. 4:22; 19:5–6). And it is precisely because Israel had been chosen that she will be held responsible for her covenant violations. Andersen and Freedman helpfully summarize what God is saying to Israel in Amos 3:1–2: "Yahweh has done these things for you in the past, and Yahweh will do this thing to you in the future. You did not deserve the first, but he did them for you anyway; you certainly deserve the second, and in spite of every effort on his part, he finally cannot and will not avert it."[68] All of the prophets agree that the covenantal bond between God and Israel did not exempt Israel from God's judgment. The very terms of the covenant demanded judgment for violations of the covenant stipulations. God declares in the covenant that violations of its stipulations will result in the curses of the covenant.[69]

In the first judgment oracle of this section of Amos (3:1–15), the prophet declares that God is the one bringing this disaster, that it has been revealed by God to him, and that he must proclaim the message that God has given to him (3:3–8).[70] Amos then calls pagan witnesses against Israel (3:9), and declares the nature of the coming judgment (3:11–15). An adversary will surround the land (v. 11), and the wealthy will die a violent death (v. 12). The illegitimate altars at Bethel will be destroyed (v. 14), along with the great houses of the rich and powerful (v. 15). Israel's present wealth and security is contrasted with its coming destruction. As Stuart explains, "A city of pleasure seekers will see its wealth stolen, its comforts ruined, its cult annihilated and its people captured, killed, and exiled."[71]

68. Andersen and Freedman 1989, 32–33.
69. Andersen and Freedman 1989, 81.
70. Stuart 1987, 326.
71. Stuart 1987, 333.

The second judgment oracle of this section focuses on Israel's impenitence (4:1–13). In verses 1–5, Amos sarcastically condemns Israel's social and religious sins. He declares that their judgment is certain. Amos then lists a number of covenant curses that God has already visited upon Israel, including hunger, drought, and crop failure (vv. 6–11). These past judgments have not led to repentance, thus the repeated refrain, "yet you did not return to me" (vv. 6, 8, 9, 10, 11). As a result, God declares, "Therefore thus I will do to you, O Israel; because I will do this to you, prepare to meet your God, O Israel!" (v. 12). Just as Pharaoh ignored the plagues, Israel has ignored the previous judgments that God has sent. Because Israel has not returned to the Lord her God, God is preparing to send the ultimate covenant judgment, destruction of the nation and exile.

The third judgment oracle of this section of Amos is in the form of a proleptic funeral lamentation (5:1–17).[72] A lament was sung after the death of a loved one. Here, Amos laments the death of Israel before the judgment has come. This indicates that the judgment is as good as done.[73] In the midst of this lament, there is a glimmer of hope as the Lord calls to Israel, "Seek me and live" (5:4, 6). This hope is more fully expressed in verses 14–15:

> Seek good, and not evil,
>   that you may live;
> and so Yahweh, the God of hosts, will be with you,
>   as you have said.
> Hate evil, and love good,
>   and establish justice in the gate;
> it may be that Yahweh, the God of hosts,
>   will be gracious to the remnant of Joseph.

This text introduces the important concept of the remnant.[74] The remnant are those who seek the Lord and have faith in him. They are those whose faith in God bears the fruit of righteousness.[75] Judgment is coming, but judgment is not the final word. The covenant promise of restoration is held out for the remnant (Deut. 30:1–10).

72. Stuart 1987, 350.

73. Niehaus 1992, 409; Gowan 1998, 25.

74. See Hasel 1974, 190–206.

75. VanGemeren 1990, 136.

Amos 5:18–27 is the first of two "Woe" oracles against Israel in this section of the book. This first oracle is addressed to those "who desire the day of Yahweh" (v. 18). The day of Yahweh, or the day of the Lord, is a central theme in the prophetic books, and this use of the concept in Amos as a technical term is the first among the writing prophets.[76] The concept likely originated from the tradition of *herem* warfare, or "holy war" during the period of the conquest under Joshua. The day of Yahweh would be the time when God, as the great divine warrior, would go into battle against his enemies, defeating them on behalf of his people.[77] Amos's audience lived in the expectation that the day of Yahweh would be a time of national vindication for Israel.[78] Amos turns their expectation on its head, telling them that the day of Yahweh will be a day of judgment for Israel. Israel itself had become an enemy of God, and God had now declared war on his own people.[79] Israel was expecting the day of Yahweh to be "light." Amos explains that it will be "darkness." As Andersen and Freedman put it, "The truth is that the Day of the Lord will be the Night of the Lord."[80] Amos uses the terms "darkness" and "gloom" to characterize what the day of Yahweh will be for Israel. These terms are often used as metaphors for trouble, distress, misery, and death (1 Sam. 2:9; Job 3:6; 5:14; Pss. 35:6; 91:6; Prov. 2:13; Isa. 5:30; 49:9).[81]

The second "Woe" oracle is addressed to "those who are at ease in Zion" (Amos 6:1). In this oracle Amos condemns the wealthy and powerful who are not grieved about Israel's sin (6:1–6). They will be the first to go into exile (v. 7). In verses 8–14, Amos condemns the pride and unrighteousness of Israel. God declares that he will deliver Israel up in judgment (v. 8). The nation will be shattered and utterly devastated (vv. 9–11). God will raise up a nation (Assyria) that will oppress Israel throughout the length of her land (v. 14; cf. 2 Kings 14:25).

Five Visions (Amos 7–9)

The final section of Amos is dominated by five visions of judgment against Israel (7:1–9; 8:1–3; 9:1–4), but it also includes a short biographical narra-

76. Andersen and Freedman 1989, 521.
77. Stuart 1987, 353; Mays 1969a, 104; Paul 1991, 184.
78. Dillard and Longman 1994, 383–84.
79. Blenkinsopp 1996, 76; Paul 1991, 184.
80. Andersen and Freedman 1989, 57.
81. Stuart 1987, 354. The verses cited are those referenced by Stuart.

tive (7:10–17), more oracles of judgment (8:4–14; 9:5–10), and an oracle of salvation (9:11–15). The first two visions are visions concerning judgment by locusts (7:1–3) and judgment by fire (7:4–6). When Amos intercedes in response to both of these visions, God relents and suspends the judgments (vv. 3, 6). In Amos's third vision he sees the Lord "standing beside a wall built with a plumb line, with a plumb line in his hand" (7:7–9).[82] There is no record of intercession after this vision. The judgment is said to be inevitable (v. 9). In his fourth vision, Amos sees a basket of summer fruit (8:1–3). God declares here, "The end has come upon my people Israel" (v. 2). Again, there is no suspension of the judgment. Amos's final vision is one of the Lord standing beside the altar (9:1–4). This vision portrays God's complete destruction of the nation of Israel. Amos's five visions demonstrate God's determination to bring judgment and exile upon Israel.[83]

A few comments are necessary regarding some of the passages interspersed among the five visions. First, the brief biographical narrative in Amos 7:10–17 reveals that those in power considered Amos's prophecies to be a threat.[84] The priest Amaziah accuses Amos of conspiracy against the king (v. 10). He tells Amos to return to Judah (v. 12). Amos responds by pronouncing the judgment that will befall Amaziah himself (v. 17). Second, in the judgment oracle following the fourth vision, Amos describes the coming catastrophe in dramatic terms: "I will make the sun go down at noon and darken the earth in broad daylight" (8:9). It should be observed that this kind of cosmic language is found elsewhere in the prophets to describe judgments upon Israel and the nations (e.g., Isa. 13:10; 34:4–5; Ezek. 32:7; cf. Deut. 28:29). This language is used in the way that we might use the phrase "earth shattering" to describe a historical event with momentous consequences. In short, this kind of language is figurative. Finally, the last judgment oracle in the book once again establishes the possibility of escape for a remnant. God declares that he will not utterly destroy the house of Jacob (9:8).[85] This leaves open the possibility of restoration, which is declared to be more than a possibility in the final verses of Amos.

82. The meaning of the word translated "plumb line" is uncertain. The word may mean "tin." See Stuart 1987, 372–73; Niehaus 1992, 456; Andersen and Freedman 1989, 754–59.

83. VanGemeren 1990, 132.

84. Clements 1996, 32.

85. Stuart 1987, 394.

Amos 9:11–15 is an oracle of salvation. Whereas restoration following the coming judgment was merely hinted at as a possibility in earlier chapters of the book, here it is explicitly affirmed. God is not punishing Israel merely for the sake of punishment. Paul explains, "The prophet's chastisement is meant to serve as a transitional stage to a period of future restoration, at least for the surviving remnant."[86] These final verses look forward to the restoration of David's kingdom and the renewal of creation. His kingdom will rise and inaugurate a new era of abundant blessing for Israel and the nations.

In Amos 9:11–12, the prophet writes,

> In that day I will raise up
>   the booth of David that is fallen
> and repair its breaches,
>   and raise up its[87] ruins
>   and rebuild it as in the days of old,
> that they may possess the remnant of Edom
>   and all the nations who are called by my name,
>   declares Yahweh who does this.

These verses anticipate the restoration of the Davidic dynasty. The phrase "In that day" does not mean that the coming restoration will occur at the same time as the coming judgment. As David Hubbard observes, the role of this phrase "was not so much to connect the restoration with the acts of judgment announced in the previous oracles (vv. 8, 9–10) as to lift the eyes of the hearers to a more distant but undefined future."[88]

The Hebrew word translated "booth" is *sukkat*. Stuart argues that the word should be vocalized *sukkot* and that it is a reference to the city of Succoth (see Judg. 8:5–16), which was possibly used by David as a military headquarters.[89] Jeffrey Niehaus, on the other hand, argues for the translation "booth" or "hut."[90] The translation "Succoth" is lacking in sufficient evidence, and the translation "booth" can be understood in the context. According to Amos, David's booth is "fallen." The participle may also be

86. Paul 1991, 289.
87. A more precise translation of the masculine singular pronominal suffix would be "his."
88. Hubbard 1989b, 239.
89. Stuart 1987, 396–98.
90. Niehaus 1992, 490.

translated "is collapsing" or "is falling."[91] As Paul explains, "The reference here . . . is not to the later destruction of Jerusalem in 587/6 B.C.E. but rather to the 'fallen' or 'falling' state of the Davidic empire, which was the concomitant result of the rupture of the United Kingdom."[92] The references to Edom and all the nations in Amos 9:12 look back to the promises given to Abraham at the time of his call and given to the nation of Israel during the conquest. The citation of this passage in Acts 15:16–17 indicates that the conquest of these nations would be a conquest by which a remnant of them would become the people of God.[93] The restoration of the Davidic kingdom will involve blessings for the nations.

Amos 9:13–15 describes the renewal of the land of Israel and the creation in terms of agricultural bounty. Such bounty was one of the many covenant blessings enumerated by Moses (Lev. 26:5; Deut. 28:4, 11; 30:9). Amos, however, describes a bounty so great that the harvesters of one crop have not completed their work before the planters of the next crop are ready to begin (v. 13). God declares that he will restore the fortunes of his people Israel, and that they will rebuild their cities and vineyards (v. 14). God will plant them in their land, and they shall never again be uprooted from the land that he has given them (v. 15). Despite the coming judgment, God's promise remains.

Hosea

Hosea's prophetic ministry to the northern kingdom of Israel likely began soon after the ministry of Amos (ca. 752–750). Unlike Amos, however, Hosea prophesied up to the point in time just prior to the destruction of Israel (ca. 725–722).[94] His ministry, then, spanned a period of approximately three decades. Although little is known about the prophet himself outside of what can be learned from the book that bears his name, his basic message of judgment and hope is clear.[95] Moses had promised that blessing would be the result of obedience to the stipulations of the covenant, while curses would be the result of disobedience (Lev. 26; Deut. 27:9–28:68). Hosea comes with the announcement that God intends to

91. Niehaus 1992, 490.

92. Paul 1991, 290.

93. Niehaus 1992, 491.

94. Craigie 1984–85, 1:5; Mays 1969b, 3; Wolff 1974, xxi.

95. Hubbard 1989a, 51.

enforce the terms of his covenant.[96] The blessings and curses he announces are taken directly from those announced in the Mosaic law. There are, however, no blessings announced for the immediate future of Israel. The immediate future for Israel is one of judgment. Blessing is announced for the more distant future, after Israel has suffered the punishment required for breaking the covenant.[97] Judgment is coming, but God's love for Israel will not fail. His covenant mercy shines throughout the book of Hosea.[98]

The book of Hosea is divided into two main sections. Chapters 1–3 contain prophecies against Israel set within the context of Hosea's family experiences. Chapters 4–14 contain a series of prophetic messages for Israel. The fundamental theme of chapters 1–3 is Hosea's marriage, which is symbolic of God's relationship to Israel. This symbolic use of the idea of marriage becomes a more frequent theme in the later prophetic books.[99] Hosea is commanded by God to take "a wife of whoredom and have children of whoredom, for the land commits great whoredom by forsaking Yahweh" (1:2). This kind of dramatic prophetic activity, or "sign act," is not uncommon in the prophets (Isa. 8:1–4; Jer. 27; Ezek. 4:1–5:4). Gomer, the unfaithful wife, becomes a symbol of unfaithful Israel.

Hosea's naming of his three children is also a dramatic prophetic activity that is intended to send a message to Israel. Hosea is commanded to name his first son Jezreel (Hos. 1:4). The reigning king of Israel at this point in time was Jeroboam II, who belonged to the house of Jehu. It was at Jezreel that the house of Jehu had massacred the house of Omri (2 Kings 9–10). The naming of Hosea's first son subtly indicates that the same kind of bloodshed is soon to be visited on the house of Jehu (Hos. 1:4–5).[100] Hosea's next child is a daughter, and God commands him to name the child "No Mercy" for God's mercy for Israel was about to come to an end (1:6). The name of the third child is the most fearful of all. After the second child had been weaned, a son is born, "And Yahweh said, 'Call his name Not My People, for you are not my people, and I am not your God'" (1:9).

96. Stuart 1987, 7.
97. Stuart 1987, 18.
98. VanGemeren 1990, 114.
99. Dumbrell 2002, 174.
100. McComiskey 1992, 19.

This name, in effect, is a declaration of the end of God's special covenant relationship with Israel (cf. Ex. 6:6–7).[101]

A dramatic shift in tone occurs at Hosea 1:10, but this is not unusual in the book, which often moves suddenly from oracles of judgment to oracles of salvation. "Total despair [in Hosea] alternates with unbounded hope."[102] This kind of sudden shift occurs often in Hosea because the prophet regularly moves from oracles concerning the near future to oracles concerning the more distant future without explicitly indicating that he is doing so. Hosea 1:10–2:1 is an oracle of salvation, a prophecy of future restoration. Hosea declares that "the number of the children of Israel shall be like the sand of the sea" (1:10a). This oracle hearkens back to the ancient patriarchal promises (Gen. 22:17). Here "the promise to the patriarchs has become a new eschatological promise of salvation."[103]

Those who are "not my people" shall be called "Children of the living God" (1:10b). According to Hosea, "the children of Judah and the children of Israel shall be gathered together, and they shall appoint for themselves one head. And they shall go up from the land, for great shall be the day of Jezreel" (1:11). The day of Jezreel will be the time when Israel regains the Promised Land.[104] This time of restoration is described as a time when Israel "shall go up from the land." It is possible that this phrase carries a dual connotation, meaning both return from exile and resurrection.[105] Derek Kidner observes that the promise of restoration has been fulfilled to only a small degree on a literal level. Remnants of the northern kingdom "took refuge with Judah, and although King Hezekiah's overtures to the northern tribes were scorned at first, we read of elements from at least five of them which joined him at Jerusalem for his great Passover (2 Chron. 30:11, 18)."[106] The restoration that began with the decree of Cyrus in 538 B.C. was only the beginning of the fulfillment of the restoration promises.[107]

101. Hubbard 1989a, 65. As Blenkinsopp observes, the Hebrew of the last phrase in Hosea 1:9 could be translated, "You are not my people, and I am not your I AM." The Hebrew word אֶהְיֶה (*'ehyeh*) is the same as that used in Exodus 3:14 (Blenkinsopp 1996, 86).

102. Andersen and Freedman 1980, 199.

103. Wolff 1974, 26.

104. Mays 1969b, 33.

105. Stuart 1987, 39.

106. Kidner 1981, 25; see also 1 Chronicles 9:3, which mentions some of the northern tribes returning from exile.

107. Hubbard 1989a, 70–71.

Chapter 2 of Hosea includes oracles of both judgment and salvation. God promises that he will have mercy on No Mercy and he will say to Not My People, "You are my people" (2:23). In chapter 3, Hosea is commanded to redeem his wife, just as God redeems Israel (3:1–3). He then declares that the children of Israel will be without their basic political and religious institutions for "many days" (v. 4). The phrase "many days" is not specific. It refers to a long and indeterminate amount of time during which Israel will suffer.[108] Hosea then declares, "Afterward the children of Israel shall return and seek Yahweh their God, and David their king, and they shall come in fear to Yahweh and to his goodness in the latter days" (v. 5). This "afterward" points to hope following judgment.[109] The reference to "David their king" is the kind of messianic announcement that becomes more prominent in the later prophets (Jer. 30:9; Ezek. 34:23–24). As David Hubbard explains, "Hosea connected Yahweh's future victory to the renascence of David's rule."[110] The phrase "in the latter days" "denotes a period of time that, from the writer's standpoint, is in the indefinite future (Gen. 49:1; Deut. 31:29)."[111]

The second major section of Hosea, chapters 4–14, addresses Israel's moral, religious, and political transgressions in a series of prophetic judgment oracles.[112] Although it is difficult to discern a clear structure to these oracles, Willem VanGemeren outlines fourteen prophetic speeches in these chapters:[113]

1. *Rîb* ("lawsuit") against the Israelites who lack knowledge of the Torah, 4:1–19
2. Judgment (*mišpa̱t*) against the priests, king, and people, 5:1–15
3. Warning against pragmatic repentance, 6:1–11
4. Case against the kings and leaders, 7:1–16
5. Case against self-reliant Israel, 8:1–14
6. Case against pagan Israel, 9:1–9
7. Case against unfaithful Ephraim, 9:10–17
8. The fall of Samaria, 10:1–8

108. Andersen and Freedman 1980, 305.
109. Mays 1969b, 59.
110. Hubbard 1989a, 95.
111. McComiskey 1992, 54; see also Ross 1988, 700.
112. *NIDOTTE*, 4:711.
113. VanGemeren 1990, 109.

9. Israel's fall due to its longstanding apostasy, 10:9–15
10. Yahweh's love for Israel, 11:1–11
11. Israel's long history of rebellion, 11:12–12:14
12. Ephraim's helplessness, 13:1–11
13. Ephraim's fall and Yahweh's promise to redeem, 13:12–16
14. Call to repentance and promise of restoration, 14:1–8

Hosea 14:9 is a brief concluding epilogue. Some of the passages found in these chapters are particularly relevant to this study and require a few comments.

Hosea 6:1–11 warns Israel of the danger of simply pragmatic repentance. Within this oracle, we read the following words:

> Come, let us return to Yahweh;
> for he has torn us, that he may heal us;
> he has struck us down, and he will bind us up.
> After two days he will revive us;
> on the third day he will raise us up,
> that we may live before him. (vv. 1–2)

The phrases "after two days" and "on the third day" are synonymous expressions. The phrases "revive us" and "raise us up" are, as Hubbard observes, "frequent expressions for resuscitation and resurrection."[114] This language "anticipates the clearer accounts of national resurrection after death in exile or through persecution found in Ezekiel chapter 37 and Daniel 12:1–2."[115]

In Hosea 8:1–14, the prophet makes his case against self-reliant Israel. Within the prophetic oracle Hosea declares that Israel "shall return to Egypt" (8:13). The same idea is expressed in several other oracles within the book (e.g., 7:16; 9:3). This judgment is based on one of the specific curses mentioned in the Mosaic law (Deut. 28:68). The "return to Egypt" is a figurative way of saying that Israel will once again be slaves in a foreign land. The coming destruction of Israel by Assyria and the exile of the people will be, in one sense, a reversal of Israel's redemptive history.[116] This, however, is not

114. Hubbard 1989a, 125.

115. Hubbard 1989a, 125; see also Andersen and Freedman 1980, 420. Although Ezekiel 37:1–14 refers to national restoration, it should be noted that Daniel 12:1–2 is likely a prophecy of personal resurrection. For more on these two texts see chapter 8.

116. Mays 1969b, 123; McComiskey 1992, 117; Gowan 1998, 42.

the final word. As Hosea makes clear throughout his book, the destruction of Israel by Assyria will not mean the end of Israel's existence. Hosea's own generation will be judged, "but beyond that looms a bright prospect, the prospect of thousands upon thousands of redeemed Jews and Gentiles who will form a new people of God (Jer. 31:31, 34; Rom. 9:25–26)."[117]

Micah

The ministry of the prophet Micah began during the reign of the Judean king Jotham (750–732) and lasted until the reign of Hezekiah (729–686). His ministry, unlike that of Amos or Hosea, overlapped the fall of the northern kingdom. He prophesied the fall of Israel and lived to witness it. The Assyrian king Shalmaneser V attacked Israel from 725 until 722, and Israel finally fell to his successor Sargon II in 722. Following the fall of the northern kingdom, Micah prophesied to the southern kingdom of Judah. These facts are significant because the prophetic oracles found within the book bearing his name were not spoken all at one time. They are messages given over the entire course of his prophetic ministry.[118]

The general theme that runs through all of these messages is that Israel and Judah will fall because they have broken the covenant, yet a remnant of believers will remain who will be the heirs of the covenant promises.[119] Although these messages span a number of decades, the book may be divided into three main sections. Bruce Waltke's descriptions of these sections are most helpful.[120] Following a superscription (1:1), Micah 1:2–2:13 announces God's gathering of the elect remnant into Jerusalem. In chapters 3–5, Micah prophesies about God's restoration of Jerusalem's former dominion to the purified remnant. Finally, in chapters 6–7, Micah prophesies concerning God's forgiveness of the remnant of his sinful people.

God Gathers the Remnant (Mic. 1:2–2:13)

The first prophecy in the book of Micah is a judgment oracle against Samaria (1:2–7). Micah calls the nation to stand trial (v. 2). He declares that God will come down and that as a result the mountains will melt and the

117. McComiskey 1992, 224.
118. Dillard and Longman 1994, 400.
119. Dumbrell 1994, 78; *NIDOTTE*, 4:938.
120. Waltke 1993, 597–98.

valleys will split open (vv. 3–4). This language echoes the language found in the song of Deborah and Barak in the book of Judges (Judg. 5:4–5) and language found in the book of Psalms (e.g., Ps. 97:5). The language is poetic and highly figurative. In Judges, this language was used to describe God's going forth to fight against Israel's enemies. Micah uses the same language to describe God's going forth to fight against Israel herself.[121] Both Samaria (Israel) and Judah have broken the covenant with God (Mic. 1:5). Therefore both Samaria (v. 6) and her idols (v. 7) will be destroyed.

Micah 1:8–16 is a lament over the towns of Judah that uses a number of striking wordplays (vv. 10–15). This oracle concludes with a declaration that Judah will go into exile. This prophecy likely anticipated the invasion of Judah by Sennacherib in 701 B.C., an invasion that reached the very walls of Jerusalem (2 Kings 18:13–19:13). Many years later the prophet Jeremiah would explain that Judah was spared from judgment at this time because of Hezekiah's repentance (Jer. 26:18–19; 2 Kings 19:14–37). Following this oracle is another prophecy of judgment, which sentences the corrupt landowners to exile (Mic. 2:1–5). Just as they had seized land from the poor, their land will be seized from them. False prophets are denounced in yet another judgment oracle (2:6–11). They condemn true prophets (v. 6), and they themselves will be condemned. Following these four judgment oracles, the first section of the book of Micah ends on a note of hope (2:12–13). Micah promises that God will gather the remnant of his people and protect them. This is likely a prophecy of God's miraculous deliverance of Jerusalem from Sennacherib's siege, but it may also look forward to the restoration following the Babylonian exile.

God's Restoration of Jerusalem to the Remnant (Mic. 3–5)

The second main section of Micah begins with three oracles of judgment. The first oracle condemns the wicked rulers of Judah and graphically compares them to cannibals (3:1–4). The second oracle condemns false prophets who are preaching for monetary gain (3:5–8). The third and climactic oracle sentences Jerusalem to destruction (3:9–12). Jerusalem's sentence is comparable to that of Samaria. Both shall become a "heap" (v. 12; cf. 1:6). The wicked rulers and greedy religious leaders have incurred God's wrath.

121. Waltke 1993, 618.

They do not believe God will destroy Jerusalem, but Micah declares that judgment is coming (vv. 11–12).

In chapters 4–5, the prophet Micah dramatically moves from proclamations of judgment to announcements of hope. As revealed in our examination of Hosea, such shifts from oracles of judgment to oracles of salvation are not uncommon in prophetic books. In these two chapters of Micah, "seven oracles of hope revolve around the Messiah, who will rule over the remnant."[122] The first of these oracles describes the exaltation of Zion in "the latter days" as a result of God's reign on earth (4:1–5).[123] The phrase "in the latter days" or "in days to come" is generally used to introduce prophecies regarding an undetermined time in the future (e.g., Gen. 49:1; Num. 24:14; Deut. 4:30; 31:29; Jer. 23:20; 30:24; 48:47; 49:39; Ezek. 38:16; Hos. 3:5).[124] This prophecy reaches its ultimate fulfillment in the coming of the new Jerusalem from heaven to earth (Rev. 21:1–2, 10).

The second oracle of salvation in this section describes the Lord's restoration and rule over Israel in the future (Mic. 4:6–7). God will gather those who have been driven away (v. 6). He will restore them as a strong nation and will reign over them in Mount Zion forever (v. 7). As Waltke explains, "The *remnant*, that which remains after most of Israel is destroyed in judgment (v. 6), now becomes the goal of history."[125] Micah 4:8 follows with a brief oracle declaring the restoration of Jerusalem's dominion. The fourth oracle of salvation in this section (4:9–13) declares that God will rescue his people from exile in Babylon and that God plans to judge those who have mocked Israel.

The fifth oracle of salvation is significant because of its clear prophecy of the coming Messiah (5:1–6). The prophecy moves from Israel's present distress (v. 1) to the coming victory of the messianic King (vv. 2–6). In fact, it is only the coming of the Messiah that will bring about the complete restoration of Israel. The Messiah will come forth from Bethlehem, the birthplace of David (v. 2; 1 Sam. 16:1). Just as God sent David to rescue his people after the failure of Saul, so too will he send the Messiah to rescue his people after the failure of David's descendants.[126] The Messiah, however,

122. *NIDOTTE*, 4:939.
123. Mays 1976, 93.
124. Mays 1976, 96; Ross 1988, 700; Wenham 1994, 471.
125. Waltke 1988a, 176.
126. Waltke 1988a, 182.

will be greater than David. His "origin is from of old, from ancient days" (v. 2), indicating his association with God from eternity.[127] The Messiah will shepherd his people, and they will dwell in security and peace (vv. 4–5). This prophecy is fulfilled in the coming of Jesus (Matt. 2:1).

The sixth oracle in these chapters is a prophecy of the expansion of the Messiah's kingdom "among the nations" (Mic. 5:7–9). The fulfillment of this prophecy is connected with the coming of the Messiah described in 5:2–5. The final oracle in these chapters is a declaration by the Lord that he will protect his kingdom (5:10–15). He will purge all of those things from his kingdom that cause his people to stumble (vv. 10–14). He will also judge those nations that do not submit to his authority (v. 15).

God's Forgiveness of the Remnant (Mic. 6–7)

The final major section of Micah moves from various judgment oracles to a song of victory. The first oracle in this final section of the book of Micah is an indictment against Israel (6:1–8). The book has shifted from a focus on the future of Israel back to her present situation. God reminds his people of the grace he has shown to Israel from the beginning of her history (vv. 4–5). He then reveals to his people that what is required from them is not empty rituals, but justice, kindness, and humility (vv. 6–8). The second oracle declares that the curses of the covenant will be brought upon Israel (6:9–16). The third oracle is a lament for the nation (7:1–7). This lament includes both sorrow (vv. 1–6) and hope (v. 7). The book then concludes with a song of victory (7:8–20). Micah calls upon God to shepherd his people (v. 14) and on the basis of his faith in the covenant promises, he declares that God will once again have compassion and mercy on his people (vv. 18–20).

Summary

The eighth-century prophets prophesied during a time of great spiritual decline in Israel and Judah. Each of the four prophets we have examined in this chapter contributes to our understanding of biblical eschatology. The message of the prophet Jonah warns against any nationalistic view of God. The Lord is willing and able to show mercy to any nation. In fact, the

127. Andersen and Freedman 2000, 468.

Abrahamic promises declare his ultimate intention to bless the nations. Amos prophesied to a wealthy and powerful elite who were oppressing the poor and worshiping idols. He declares to Israel that her time is short. God had promised exile as the ultimate punishment for breaking the covenant, and Amos declares the imminence of exile. The day of Yahweh that the people desire will come, but it will be a day of judgment rather than salvation. Despite the judgment, however, hope remains. A remnant will be saved.

Hosea prophesied during the final decades leading up to the fall of the northern kingdom in 722 B.C. God used Hosea's family situation to dramatically illustrate his relationship with Israel. Through Hosea, God warns Israel that he is going to enforce the terms of his covenant. Judgment is coming soon, but this judgment will not be the end of God's relationship with his people. God's love for his people will not fail, and after the judgment God will restore and bless his people once again. Micah prophesied to the northern kingdom until its fall and then prophesied to the people of the southern kingdom, warning that the same fate would befall them if they failed to repent. He declares that Israel and Judah will be judged for breaking the covenant, but a remnant will be restored. Micah points to the future restoration and exaltation of Jerusalem and to the coming of a Messiah who, like David, would come from the obscure little town of Bethlehem.

6

The Eighth-Century Prophets (2)

Isaiah

Of all the eighth-century prophetic books, none matches the sheer scope of the book of Isaiah. Although his ministry took place during approximately the same period of time as that of the prophet Micah, his written work covers a much wider range of ideas. In addition to common prophetic themes regarding impending judgment and the future restoration of the faithful remnant, Isaiah also focuses much of his attention on the coming messianic King, the Servant of God. The significance of Isaiah's prophecies for a proper understanding of biblical theology may be seen in the fact that his book is quoted in the New Testament more than all of the other Old Testament prophets combined.

Isaiah

Traditionally, the book of Isaiah has been understood to be the unified work of one eighth-century author, Isaiah the son of Amoz (Isa. 1:1). With the rise of theological liberalism and higher criticism in the nineteenth century, this traditional view regarding the unity and authorship of Isaiah was called into serious question. The theory of the multiple authorship of Isaiah is now among the most dominant views within critical biblical scholarship. The book of Isaiah, it is claimed, consists of at least two major sections that were composed by different authors over a period of several centuries. According to this critical theory, chapters 1–39 were largely composed before the exile. Chapters 40–66 ("Deutero-Isaiah") were then later composed during the exile. Some critical scholars further divide the later chapters, positing the existence of a "Trito-Isaiah" (chapters 56–66) that is said to have been composed after the exile.

It is beyond the scope of this study to set forth in any great detail the arguments for and against the unity of Isaiah.[1] However, several points may be noted briefly. In the first place, the major argument for the multiple authorship of Isaiah is that the later chapters of the book assume an exilic or postexilic historical context. As John Oswalt and others have pointed out, however, this argument is not as weighty as its proponents assume. It is not uncommon for prophets to address historical contexts other than their own (e.g., Ezek. 37–48; Dan. 7–11; Zech. 8–13).[2] The preexilic material in the book of Isaiah "is made to serve pre-exilic, exilic, post-exilic and eschatological purposes."[3]

Critical assumptions regarding the multiple authorship of Isaiah also reduce much of the book to self-refuting nonsense. One of the major arguments throughout the book of Isaiah is that Yahweh may be distinguished from false gods and idols by virtue of the fact that Yahweh alone is able to reveal what will happen in the future. False gods and idols, on the other hand, are incapable of predictive prophecy. If the prophecies of Isaiah were actually written after the events they claim to predict, then this argument found throughout the book proves the very opposite of the author's stated intention. Granted that difficult questions remain, the so-called assured results of higher criticism have (again) been too hastily adopted.[4]

1. For more on the higher-critical view, see Allis 1950; Young 1958; Oswalt 1986, 17–28; Motyer 1993, 25–30; and Robertson 2004, 227–40.

2. Oswalt 1986, 26.

3. Motyer 1993, 31.

4. It should also be noted that there is no evidence that the book of Isaiah ever existed in any other than its present form. There is no manuscript evidence for the existence of a separate Deutero-Isaiah.

Isaiah's prophetic ministry spanned a period of time from approximately 740 to 686 B.C.[5] The immediate historical context for much of the book of Isaiah is a series of crises, each involving the Assyrian Empire to one degree or another. The first major crisis occurred in 735 when Syria and the northern kingdom of Israel joined forces against Judah in an attempt to force Judah into an anti-Assyrian coalition.[6] Ignoring Isaiah's call for trust in God, King Ahaz of Judah turned to Tiglath-pileser III, the king of Assyria, for assistance. Assyria deposed Pekah, the king of Israel, in 732 and replaced him with a vassal king. Assyria also invaded Syria. In 729, Hezekiah took the throne of Judah. When Tiglath-pileser died a few years later in 727, Israel's vassal king Hoshea led an insurrection. Israel's rebellion led to an attack by the Assyrian king Shalmaneser V, which lasted from 725 until 722. Shalmaneser died in 722, the same year that the northern kingdom of Israel finally fell.

Shalmaneser's death led to troubles all over Assyria's empire, troubles that kept his successor Sargon II occupied for many years. After subduing his enemies in the east, Sargon turned west and decisively defeated a confederation against Assyria that had been formed between 715 and 713 by the Philistines and others. In 710, Sargon defeated the Babylonians, but in 705, he was killed in battle. Sargon's death led to more revolts against Assyrian rule across the empire. Ignoring Isaiah's warning that such an action would bring disaster, Hezekiah himself formed an anti-Assyrian coalition composed of Judah, Philistia, Edom, and Moab. Sargon's successor Sennacherib began a series of campaigns that ended with the siege of Jerusalem in 701. Jerusalem was spared destruction only by the miraculous intervention of God.[7] It is against this historical backdrop of recurring historical crises that Isaiah's original messages must be heard.

The book of Isaiah moves from declarations of impending judgment against Judah, to reminders of the Deuteronomic promise that return from exile is possible, to glorious visions of a new heavens and earth under the rule of the messianic King. As Oswalt explains, "no other book explores in such depth the ways in which the tragedy of the dissolution of the two kingdoms and the ensuing Exile could be understood as serving God's

5. See Motyer 1993, 18. Motyer notes that Isaiah ministered from the year King Uzziah died (740) through the end of the reign of Hezekiah (686).

6. On the historical background, see Bruce 1963, 62–65.

7. For a more detailed survey of the historical context, see Oswalt 1986, 4–13.

larger plans rather than as destroying those plans."[8] Isaiah shows how Israel's judgment becomes, in God's hands, a means of salvation.[9]

The content of the book of Isaiah has been outlined in a number of ways. This study follows the particularly helpful structural outline of Alec Motyer.[10] The first major section of the book (Isa. 1–37), termed the Book of the King by Motyer, comprises four subsections, which are labeled here according to their major theme or purpose: the author's preface (1–5); the coming King (6–12); the universal kingdom (13–27); and the Lord of history (28–37). The second major section, the Book of the Servant (38–55), comprises five subsections: Hezekiah's decisive sin (38–39); the consolation of the world (40:1–42:17); the redemption of Israel (42:18–44:23); the great deliverance of Cyrus (44:24–48:22); and the greater deliverance of the Servant (49–55). The third and final major section, the Book of the Conqueror (56–66), comprises three subsections: the ideal and the actual (56:1–59:13); the coming conqueror (59:14–63:6); and the new heavens and new earth (63:7–66:24).

The Book of the King (Isa. 1–37)

The first thirty-seven chapters of Isaiah, the Book of the King, focus on several significant themes. Foremost is Isaiah's portrayal of the Lord, who in contrast to idols, is the sovereign and holy Lord of history. The Book of the King also introduces the prominent Isaianic theme of the Davidic Messiah, who will restore Zion. Finally, the reconciliation of the remnant of Israel by means of atonement is another prominent theme.[11] Each of these themes and motifs will be examined in more detail as we proceed.

The Author's Preface (Isa. 1–5)

The first five chapters of Isaiah, containing messages likely preached after Isaiah's call (see Isa. 6), introduce the book by depicting the situation in Judah at the time of that call (i.e., 740 B.C.). According to these introductory chapters, Jerusalem is disobedient and her sin will be judged, but there remains a future hope for the people of God. Isaiah begins by charg-

8. *NIDOTTE*, 4:725.

9. *NIDOTTE*, 4:725.

10. Motyer 1999, 36–40. I have adopted his section and subsection titles, in some cases making slight alterations.

11. Motyer 1993, 29–30.

ing Judah with forsaking the Lord (1:2–9). Comparing Judah to Sodom and Gomorrah, he condemns the hypocritical rituals of the people (vv. 10–15; cf. Hos. 6:4–6; Amos 4:4–5; 5:21–25) and calls them to purity (Isa. 1:16–17). Isaiah challenges the people to choose faithfulness instead of rebellion (vv. 18–20). The final verses of chapter 1 describe the present condition of Judah and declare what God's response will be (vv. 21–31). The "city has become a whore" (v. 21), and will be judged (v. 25), but Zion will ultimately be redeemed and called "the city of righteousness, the faithful city" (vv. 26–27).

In chapters 2–4, Isaiah describes a striking contrast between what Zion should and will be (2:2–4) and what she actually is at the present time (2:5–4:1). Isaiah 2:2–4 is a vision of the exaltation of Jerusalem as the center of worldwide blessing (Gen. 12:3; 22:18). Verses 2–4 are almost identical with Micah 4:1–3. In both books, the prophecy "serves to promise that Yahweh's threat of judgment (Isa. 1; Mic. 1–3) is not the final word."[12] These verses begin with the phrase "It shall come to pass in the latter days . . ." As we have seen repeatedly, "the latter days" refers to an unspecified time in the future (e.g., Gen. 49:1; Num. 24:14; Deut. 4:30; 31:29; Hos. 3:5).[13] The inclusion of the Gentiles that is so prominent a feature of this prophecy (Isa. 2:3) will be a recurring theme throughout the book of Isaiah (e.g., 11:10; 14:1; 18:7; 24:14–16; 25:6–8; 40:3, 5; 49:6; 55:5; 56:7–8; 60:3, 10; 66:19–21). It looks forward to the complete fulfillment of God's promise to Abraham.

Isaiah 2:6–4:1 describes the judgment of God that is coming upon a haughty people. Judah has adopted the idolatrous and prideful ways of its neighbors (2:6–11). The day of the Lord, however, will demonstrate that God alone is exalted (2:12–17). Idolaters will flee in terror before the face of God, hiding themselves in the rocks and cliffs (2:18–22). Judah and Jerusalem will be judged, according to the oracle in Isaiah 3:1–15. This section ends with a declaration of judgment against the women of Jerusalem (3:16–4:1; cf. Amos 4:1–3; Jer. 44:15–30).

In Isaiah 4:2–6, the prophet returns to the theme of hope. Not only will God not abandon his people, he will use the very judgment that is coming as a means of saving his people (vv. 3–4). The word translated "branch" in verse 2 comes from the same Hebrew root (*tsmh*) as the word translated

12. Goldingay 2001b, 42.

13. See Ross 1988, 700; Wenham 1994, 471.

"prosper" in 2 Samuel 23:5, which itself is part of a passage described as "the last words of David" (2 Sam. 23:1–7). Isaiah may be consciously alluding to this passage. The term "branch" is clearly used to denote the Messiah in later prophetic books (Jer. 23:5; 33:15; Zech. 3:8; 6:12). The immediate context indicates that Isaiah is also referring to the Messiah. The concept of the remnant is introduced here as well (Isa. 4:2–3), but the primary thrust of this text is that God will rule over a purified Zion and will manifest his presence as he did during and after the exodus, that is, in a cloud by day and a fire by night (vv. 4–5; cf. Ex. 13:21–22; 40:34–38).

Isaiah 5 returns to the present condition of Israel and Judah, describing the coming destruction of the nation in a parable (5:1–7). Isaiah describes Israel and Judah as a vineyard that has been lavishly cared for by its owner but has failed to produce good fruit (vv. 1–2). God, therefore, will destroy his vineyard (vv. 3–7). Isaiah 5:8–23 specifies the bad fruit produced by Israel and Judah in a series of "Woe" oracles. The bad fruit that has been produced includes greed (vv. 8–10); drunkenness (vv. 11–12); arrogance (vv. 18–19); lying (vv. 20–21); and injustice (vv. 22–23).[14] As a result, destruction is coming, and God will use the nations as his means of judging Israel and Judah (v. 26).

The Coming King (Isa. 6–12)

The unifying theme of Isaiah 6–12 is the coming messianic King. Chapters 6 and 12 frame the entire subsection, with chapter 6 telling of the call and cleansing of Isaiah and chapter 12 recording the song of salvation sung by the saved community. The subsection begins with the death of King Uzziah, the embodiment of the Davidic house. Chapters 7–11 then center on the coming of a holy and divine monarch. The two kingships, the divine and the Davidic, will ultimately merge in a messianic King from the house of David (7:14; 9:6–7; 11:1–10).

The call of Isaiah is narrated in Isaiah 6. The chapter serves as an important transition because the previous chapters have raised a serious question. How is sinful and rebellious Israel ever to be the center of worldwide blessing (Isa. 2:2–4)? What will it take for a city that is now described as a "whore" (1:21) to become "the city of righteousness, the faithful city" (1:26)? In Isaiah's personal experience of having his guilt taken away and his

14. Oswalt 1986, 157.

sin atoned for (6:7), we find the first hints of the answer. Isaiah's experience must become Israel's experience.[15]

In the year that King Uzziah died, Isaiah sees a vision that shapes the entire course of his ministry (6:1–7). Isaiah sees the Lord sitting exalted upon a throne, surrounded by seraphim who continuously sing: "Holy, holy, holy is Yahweh of hosts; the whole earth is full of his glory!" (6:3). The holiness of God is the focal point of Isaiah's vision. The Hebrew language expresses superlatives by means of repetition, but this is the only place in the Old Testament where a threefold repetition is found. As Motyer explains, it is as if to say that "the divine holiness is so far beyond anything the human mind can grasp that a 'super-superlative' has to be invented to express it."[16] The impact of this vision on Isaiah can be seen in the dominance of the theme of holiness in his work. In fact, the adjective "holy" is used in Isaiah more than it is used in the remainder of the Old Testament combined.[17]

The commission given to Isaiah is striking. God says to Isaiah,

> Go and say to this people:
> "Keep on hearing, but do not understand;
> keep on seeing, but do not perceive."
> Make the heart of this people dull,
>   and their ears heavy,
>   and blind their eyes;
> lest they see with their eyes,
>   and hear with their ears,
> and understand with their hearts,
>   and turn and be healed. (6:9–10)

Through the prophetic ministry of Isaiah, God is going to prevent the repentance of the people in order that judgment might come. They have already rejected the truth repeatedly. Now they have passed the point of no return, and judgment is certain. However, as verse 13 indicates, judgment is not the final word. A stump, or remnant, will remain.

The historical context of chapters 7–12 is the threat to Judah caused by the alliance of Syria and Israel in 735 B.C. This anti-Assyrian coalition

15. Oswalt 1986, 174–75.

16. Motyer 1999, 71.

17. It is used 33 times in Isaiah and 26 times in the remainder of the Old Testament.

invaded Judah, but was unable to overpower it (2 Kings 16:5; cf. 2 Chron. 28:5–8). In their second invasion of Judah, Syria and Israel determined to replace Ahaz with a king of their own choosing (Isa. 7:6). Because Ahaz is tempted to turn to Assyria for assistance (2 Kings 16:7–9), Isaiah comes to him telling him that he need not fear Israel and Syria and that he must trust in God (7:3–9). The issue, as Motyer explains, is clear: "will Ahaz seek salvation by works (politics, alliances) or by simple trust in divine promises?"[18]

It is in this context that the Lord offers to give Ahaz a sign of his trustworthiness (7:10–11). Ahaz feigns piety and refuses the proffered sign (vv. 12–13). Apparently, he has already decided to place his trust in Assyria, but the Lord promises a sign anyway in verses 14–17:

> Therefore the Lord himself will give you a sign. Behold, the virgin shall conceive and bear a son, and shall call his name Immanuel. . . . Before the boy knows how to refuse the evil and choose the good, the land whose two kings you dread will be deserted. Yahweh will bring upon you and upon your people and upon your father's house such days as have not come since the day that Ephraim departed from Judah—the king of Assyria.

Because of Ahaz's refusal to trust God, the sign is no longer a sign inviting faith. It is a sign confirming God's displeasure.

The "you" to whom the sign is to be given is plural, suggesting that the sign is to be given to the house of David (see v. 13).[19] It should also be observed that the time of the birth of Immanuel is not explicitly stated in this text. What Isaiah's words do indicate is that however soon Immanuel is born, the existing threat posed by Israel and Syria will have passed before the child is even able to be aware of it. According to Matthew 1:18–23, the birth of Jesus to Mary fulfilled this prophecy.[20] That this is true, we can be

18. Motyer 1993, 82.

19. The Hebrew is לָכֶם (*lakem*), a preposition with a second masculine plural pronominal suffix.

20. Much debate has centered on the meaning of the Hebrew word עַלְמָה (*'almah*) translated "virgin" in the ESV. Some have argued that *'almah* simply means "a young woman of marriageable age" and should be translated "young woman" because had Isaiah meant "virgin," he would have used the more specific term בְּתוּלָה (*betulah*). We do not know why Isaiah chose one term instead of the other, but as Oswalt (1986, 210) demonstrates, the translation is appropriate. "It would be axiomatic in Hebrew society that such a woman be a virgin." Other scholars have also ably demonstrated the propriety of the translation "virgin" (Motyer 1999, 78–79).

certain. The question remains, however, whether there was any preliminary or initial fulfillment in Isaiah's day.

The similarities between Isaiah 8:1–4 and 7:14–16 suggest that a child was born in Isaiah's time as a preliminary fulfillment of the prophecy. In 7:14, Isaiah says, "the virgin shall conceive and bear a son." In 8:3, Isaiah says that he went to the prophetess and "she conceived and bore a son."[21] In 7:16, Isaiah says, "For before the boy knows how . . ." In 8:4, he uses the identical phrase.[22] Finally, in both texts, Isaiah declares that something is going to happen to Israel and Syria before the child reaches a certain age (cf. "two kings you dread" in 7:16; "Damascus" and "Samaria" in 8:4). The similarities between these two texts do not appear to be coincidental. This would seem to indicate that in some sense the child born to the prophetess served as a kind of preliminary fulfillment of the prophecy.[23]

After declaring that the nation in whom Judah trusted for deliverance would turn against Judah (8:5–10), and after calling upon Judah to trust in God (8:11–22), Isaiah again points forward to the coming Messiah (9:1–7). Verses 2–3 describe the unbounded joy of the people. This joy is due to their deliverance from oppression (v. 4), and their deliverance from oppression is due to the end of all war (v. 5). But how will God end war? He will accomplish this through the birth of a child (vv. 6–7):

> For to us a child is born,
>   to us a son is given;
> and the government shall be upon his shoulder,
>   and his name shall be called
> Wonderful Counselor, Mighty God,
>   Everlasting Father, Prince of Peace.
> Of the increase of his government and of peace
>   there will be no end,
> on the throne of David and over his kingdom,
>   to establish it and to uphold it
> with justice and with righteousness
>   from this time forth and forevermore.
> The zeal of Yahweh of hosts will do this.

21. Forms of הָרָה (*harah*), יָלַד (*yalad*), and בֵּן (*ben*), occur in both verses.

22. The phrase is כִּי בְּטֶרֶם יֵדַע הַנַּעַר (*ki beterem yeda' hanna'ar*). What the child will know how to do is different in the two texts, but in both cases, the ability is one that is normally learned at a young age.

23. See Blomberg (2007, 4) for more evidence of a preliminary fulfillment.

This prophecy looks forward to the ultimate fulfillment of the Immanuel sign with the coming of Jesus (Matt. 1:18–23). As Motyer explains, "The perfection of this King is seen in his qualifications for ruling (*Wonderful Counselor*), his person and power (*Mighty God*), his relationship to his subjects (*Everlasting Father*) and the security his rule creates (*Prince of Peace*)."[24] The reign of this messianic King will have no end. He will be the final King who will once and for all replace unfaithful kings like Ahaz.[25] God's creational purpose to establish his kingdom on earth will be accomplished through this messianic King.

In chapter 10, Isaiah describes the coming judgment upon Assyria (vv. 5–19) and the return of a remnant of Israel (vv. 20–27), before turning in chapter 11 to another messianic prophecy. In this prophecy, the Messiah, a "shoot from the stump of Jesse" (11:1), is not merely depicted as coming; he is depicted as ruling (vv. 3–5).[26] His reign will be one marked by justice (vv. 3–4).[27] His reign will also be characterized by a transformation of creation. Old hostilities will be ended (v. 6); nature will be transformed (v. 7); the curse will be removed (v. 8); and the knowledge of the Lord will fill the earth (v. 9).[28] The Messiah will also restore God's people from every corner of the earth (vv. 10–16). This restoration is described in terms of a second exodus (vv. 10–11). A brief song of salvation follows, in which the saved community gives joyful thanks to God (12:1–6).

The Universal Kingdom (Isa. 13–27)

Isaiah 13–27 turns from an emphasis upon the coming king to an emphasis on his worldwide empire. These chapters proclaim the important truth that the Lord has authority over history and nations and is truly in control, working all things out in the interests of his faithful people. These chapters point out the folly of trusting in nations whose judgment is certain. Yet these chapters also demonstrate that judgment is not the last word, declaring that when the messianic kingdom is established, the Gentiles will know the

24. Motyer 1999, 89.

25. Childs 2001, 81.

26. It is worth noting that the one who is designated a "shoot" from the stump of Jesse in verse 1 is designated the "root" of Jesse in verse 10. As a "shoot," he springs from Jesse. As the "root," he is the origin of the Davidic line. See Motyer 1993, 121.

27. Childs 1985, 184.

28. Robertson 2004, 224; Motyer 1993, 124.

Lord and will worship on his holy mountain. At that time, God's purpose to bless the nations will be fulfilled.

This section of Isaiah consists of three series of oracles. The first series, in Isaiah 13:1–20:6, consists of five oracles relating to specific historical peoples: Babylon (13:1–14:27); Philistia (14:28–32); Moab (15:1–16:14); Damascus and Ephraim (17:1–18:7); and Egypt (19:1–20:6). The second series, in Isaiah 21:1–23:18, also contains five oracles relating to specific historical peoples, although several of the oracles are given symbolic titles: "the wilderness of the sea"/Babylon (21:1–10); "Dumah"/Edom (21:11–12); Arabia (21:13–17); "the valley of vision"/Jerusalem (22:1–25); and Tyre (23:1–18). The third series, in Isaiah 24:1–27:13, contrasts two cities: the city of man and the city of God.

Isaiah begins the first series with an oracle concerning Babylon (13:1–14:27). Babylon was already a significant and powerful nation in the latter part of the eighth century. Isaiah may have begun this series of oracles with Babylon because of the role this nation would later play in the sixth-century destruction of Judah and Jerusalem. Isaiah's oracle concerning the judgment of Babylon is couched in terms of the coming day of Yahweh. Here the term is used to describe the time when God would go into battle against his enemies and defeat them on behalf of his people.

The day of Yahweh is said to be "near" (13:6).[29] It is also described with the kind of "cosmic" judgment language found throughout the prophetic books (v. 10; Amos 8:9; Isa. 34:4–5; Ezek. 32:7; Joel 2:10). In 13:19–22, Isaiah uses the judgment of Sodom and Gomorrah as an illustration of the judgment that will befall Babylon, a judgment that finally came to pass in 539 B.C. The fact that the judgment of Babylon did not occur until almost two hundred years after this prophecy and the fact that the fall of Babylon was not accompanied by the literal darkening of the sun, moon, and stars demonstrate the figurative nature of this prophetic language.

The second section of the oracle concerning Babylon is largely a taunt against her fallen king (14:3–23). Verses 4–8 depict the joy that results from this tyrant's downfall, and verses 9–15 describe the descent of this king into Sheol. His arrival is greeted with sarcasm and astonishment (vv. 9–11). The arrogant pride of the king of Babylon is described in verses 12–15. He is

29. The Hebrew word translated "near" is קָרוֹב (*qarob*). It commonly designates close spatial or temporal proximity and is often used by the prophets in reference to the impending day of the Lord (Ezek. 30:3; Joel 1:15; 2:1; 3:14; Obad. 15; Zeph. 1:7, 14).

described as one who aspired to divinity, saying in his heart that he would ascend to heaven and make himself like the Most High (cf. 2 Thess. 2:4). Some have suggested that this passage refers to Satan, but as John Calvin observes, "the context plainly shows that these statements must be understood in reference to the king of the Babylonians."[30] He aspired to divinity, but he is brought down to the grave.[31]

Following the oracles concerning Philistia (Isa. 14:28–32), Moab (15:1–16:14), and Damascus and Ephraim (17:1–18:7), all of whom were nations surrounding Judah, Isaiah turns his attention to Egypt (19:1–20:6). The oracle concerning Egypt is in three distinct sections. The helplessness of Egypt before the coming judgment of God is described in 19:1–15. The future blessing of Egypt, along with Assyria and Israel, is described in 19:16–25. Finally, the foolishness of trusting Egypt is proclaimed in 20:1–6.

The oracle concerning Egypt begins, "Behold Yahweh is riding on a swift cloud and comes to Egypt" (19:1). Isaiah may have had Psalm 18:10–15 in mind. Psalm 18 pictures the Lord riding on a cloud to rescue David from Saul. Now Egypt poses an indirect threat to Israel, and Isaiah uses similar figurative language to describe God's judgment of Israel's old enemy (see also Deut. 33:26; Ps. 104:3). The second section of the oracle moves from impending judgment to eschatological blessing. Isaiah goes so far as to apply to Egypt and Assyria terms that had previously been used only of Israel (Isa. 19:24–25). Isaiah says that God will call Egypt "my people" (cf. 10:24; 43:6–7; Hos. 1:10; 2:23; Jer. 11:4) and will call Assyria "the work of my hands" (cf. Isa. 60:21; 64:8; Ps. 119:73; 138:8). Israel itself is called "my inheritance" (Isa. 19:25). Again we are reminded that God's promise of blessings to the nations of the earth will be fulfilled.

Like the first series of five oracles, the second series in this section also concerns five historical peoples: Babylon (Isa. 21:1–10); Edom (21:11–12); Arabia (21:13–17); Jerusalem (22:1–25); and Tyre (23:1–18). The oracle concerning Tyre contains a notable time indicator. The prophet declares, "In that day Tyre will be forgotten for seventy years" (23:15), and "At the end of seventy years, Yahweh will visit Tyre . . ." (v. 17). As Oswalt observes, the

30. Calvin 2003, 7:442.

31. Although the passage uses poetic language, it appears to indicate that in Sheol the dead are conscious and able to recognize one another. See Motyer 1993, 143–44; Johnston 2002, 69–83, 128–30.

general nature of the oracle concerning Tyre makes it difficult to determine with certainty when it was fulfilled. Between Isaiah's time and 332 B.C., Tyre was attacked five separate times. Only the final attack by Alexander the Great succeeded in overthrowing the city.[32] It should be noted that a time span of seventy years will become a significant part of Jeremiah's prophecy concerning the exile of Judah (Jer. 25:11–12).

The third series of oracles in this section of Isaiah contrasts the city of man and the city of God (Isa. 24–27). There are no clear references to contemporary eighth-century historical events in these chapters. In fact, the focus of these chapters is very much upon the final eschatological defeat of evil and the ultimate restoration of God's people, to the extent that some refer to these chapters as a "little apocalypse."[33] Chapter 24 vividly describes judgment to come upon the whole earth. Echoes of the flood narrative clearly intend to paint a picture of complete destruction (24:18; cf. Gen. 7:11). This chapter ends with a description of the Lord reigning from Mount Zion and Jerusalem (Isa. 24:21–23).

In chapter 25, those who have been delivered from destruction sing praise to God. Verses 6–8 explain that one purpose for judgment is the ultimate redemption of God's people from death. Before any part of humanity can enjoy God's feast (v. 6), God must do something about this universal curse. Isaiah reveals that God "will swallow up on this mountain the covering that is cast over all peoples, the veil that is spread over all nations. He will swallow up death forever" (vv. 7–8a).

Isaiah 26 is a song of thanksgiving in which the people sing of their security in their "strong city"—God's salvation (vv. 1–4), and of their security from God's wrath (vv. 20–21). The "lofty city" of man has been judged (v. 5), but God has prepared a smooth pathway for the righteous (vv. 7–9). The wicked are blind (vv. 10–11), but God has ordained peace for his people (vv. 12–15). The sure hope of victory over death will be seen in the resurrection (vv. 16–19). Isaiah 25:7–8 looked forward to the removal of the curse of death. Isaiah 26:19 explains that this will involve the resurrection of the body. The "little apocalypse" concludes with an oracle leading up to the final ingathering of God's people. After describing the defeat of the serpent (27:1), Isaiah declares that the vineyard Israel will blossom and

32. Oswalt 1986, 428.

33. E.g., House 1998, 283.

bear fruit and fill the world (vv. 2–6).[34] Isaiah describes the Lord's dealings with his people in the past (vv. 7–11) and then turns to describe the eschatological blessing of his people as they are gathered together in Jerusalem to worship the Lord (vv. 12–13).

The Lord of History (Isa. 28–37)

In the preceding chapters, Isaiah has predicted that Egypt and Assyria would be incorporated into the people of God and that these nations would one day submit to the Lord. In the eighth century, this might have appeared to some of Isaiah's hearers as wishful thinking. Was it realistic for the people of Judah to hope in such promises? In the present section, Isaiah answers this implied question and "offers the greatest of his interim fulfillments, a period of history in which divine sovereignty over Judah, Egypt and Assyria would be demonstrated before their very eyes."[35] Isaiah thereby demonstrably proves God's sovereignty over history.

The historical context of this entire section is a period of time between 705 and 701 B.C. during which King Hezekiah rebelled against Assyria (2 Kings 18:7) and made an alliance with Egypt (Isa. 30:1–7). In chapters 28–29, Isaiah outlines basic principles concerning God's relation to his people. These chapters are a prophecy of judgment to befall Jerusalem, most likely referring to Sennacherib's siege in 701 B.C. In chapters 30–32, Isaiah deals specifically with Egypt and Assyria, warning Judah against trusting in Egypt and interweaving prophecies of the coming messianic kingdom with prophecies of Assyria's impending downfall. In chapters 33–35, Isaiah uses God's acts in history as a paradigm of his eschatological acts. Chapter 34 describes God's judgment upon the nations, while chapter 35 describes the coming of God and its salvific results. Finally, in chapters 36–37, Isaiah points to specific historical events as reason to hope in God's promises.[36]

Isaiah 36–37 is a historical narrative paralleling the narrative in 2 Kings 18–19. This narrative recounts a critical point in Judah's history. Sennacherib has invaded Judah and has come to the gates of Jerusalem (Isa. 36:1–3). The Rabshakeh, an Assyrian state official, comes to the "conduit

34. The word translated "serpent" in 27:1 is the same term used in Genesis 3:1. This indicates that this prophecy looks forward to the ultimate restoration.

35. Motyer 1993, 227.

36. Motyer 1993, 227.

of the upper pool on the highway to the Washer's Field" and blasphemes God (v. 2). This is the exact location where Isaiah had urged Ahaz to trust God (7:3). Ahaz's failure to trust God is what had ultimately led to this present crisis. Now Hezekiah is going to be faced with a similar choice. Will he trust God?

After hearing the challenge of the Rabshakeh, Hezekiah turns to Isaiah for help (37:1–4). Hezekiah prays to the Lord for deliverance (vv. 14–20). The Lord responds through Isaiah, promising Hezekiah that Assyria will not take Jerusalem (vv. 21–35). The crisis is averted only by virtue of the miraculous intervention of the Lord, who strikes down 185,000 Assyrian soldiers (v. 36). Sennacherib is forced to return to Nineveh (v. 37), and is ultimately murdered by his own sons (v. 38). Where Ahaz failed because of doubt, Hezekiah triumphed because of faith.

The Book of the Servant (Isa. 38–55)

The second major section of Isaiah, the Book of the Servant, begins with Hezekiah's terminal illness, his miraculous healing, and his sin against God. The remaining chapters of this section of Isaiah deal with the ramifications of that sin and God's response to it. The Book of the Servant addresses a number of significant themes including the superiority of Yahweh over all false gods, the possibility and reality of Israel's future restoration, and the coming of a Servant who will deliver God's people.

Hezekiah's Decisive Sin (Isa. 38–39)

Isaiah's narrative of Hezekiah's illness and healing (38:1–8) is paralleled in 2 Kings 20:1–11. After hearing God's word concerning his impending death, Hezekiah prays in desperation, and God determines to add fifteen years to his life. Upon hearing of Hezekiah's recovery, Merodach-baladan, the king of Babylon, sends envoys with letters and a gift (Isa. 39:1). Hezekiah gladly receives these visitors and shows them all the wealth of his kingdom (v. 2). Upon hearing what Hezekiah has done, Isaiah declares to him the word of the Lord: "Behold, the days are coming, when all that is in your house, and that which your fathers have stored up till this day, shall be carried to Babylon. Nothing shall be left, says Yahweh" (v. 6). Here Isaiah prophesies the coming exile of Judah.

The Consolation of the World (Isa. 40:1–42:17)

The Assyrians had already taken the northern kingdom of Israel into exile in 722. Following the military campaign of Sennacherib that ended in 701, many people from Judah are also already in exile. Now, having declared to Judah that she will be judged and taken into exile by Babylon, Isaiah turns to much needed words of comfort. Knowing that his people will reject him, God promises in advance to redeem them and restore them from the coming exile.[37] This future return from exile is repeatedly depicted as a second exodus event (42:16; 43:16–19; 49:9–11; 51:10). To restore a people from exile is something previously unheard of, and it will demonstrate the incomparable power of God.[38]

Chapter 40 marks a turning point in the book of Isaiah in that from this point forward, the primary theme is redemption and restoration rather than judgment. That God can be trusted to redeem and restore his people is the thrust of 40:1–11. Isaiah proclaims comfort to the people (vv. 1–2), and describes a "voice" that declares the coming of a new era. In fact, God himself is coming to be revealed among men (vv. 3–5).[39] God can be trusted because there is no other like him, the almighty sovereign Lord over all things (vv. 12–26). In chapter 41, Isaiah reassures Israel that she need not fear, for God will use Israel to accomplish his plans (41:1–20). In the remainder of the chapter, Isaiah demonstrates that Yahweh alone is God because he alone is able to declare what will happen in the future (vv. 21–29). To follow lifeless idols, which cannot do this and which are not gods, is futile.[40]

Isaiah 42:1–9 contains the first of four Servant Songs in the book (also 49:1–6; 50:4–9; 52:13–53:12). In Isaiah 42:1–4, God speaks about his Servant, while in verses 5–9, he speaks to his Servant. The key theme of verses 1–4 is indicated by the threefold use of the Hebrew term *mishpat*,

37. Oswalt 1998, 45.

38. Oswalt 1998, 9.

39. See Matt. 3:3; Mark 1:1–3; Luke 3:4–6. The Gospel authors quote this text from Isaiah in connection with the ministry of John the Baptist. He is the voice crying in the wilderness. He is the one who prepares the way of the Lord. Jesus, then, will be the one who inaugurates the time of restoration and redemption foreseen by Isaiah.

40. As Oswalt (1998, 100) observes, this argument is a strong indicator of the unity of the book. "If Isaiah knows or even suspects that the predictions are not predictions at all, it is not only disingenuous of him to argue as he does here, it is completely inexplicable."

which is translated "justice."[41] This repeated term indicates the Servant's mission. Through him, God will establish his just rule, his kingdom, over the earth. Verses 5–9 are addressed to the Servant, confirming the task given to him. The Servant will be given "as a covenant for the people, a light for the nations" (v. 6). The reference to "people" is an ambiguous one and taken alone could denote either Israel or humanity as a whole. A comparison of this verse with a parallel in 49:6 seems to indicate, however, that the term "people" in this text is a reference to Israel.[42] The word "nations" refers to the Gentiles. So the Servant's mission involves both the people of Israel and the Gentile nations, but the emphasis here is on the nations. This section concludes with a song of praise in response to what has been revealed concerning the coming Servant (42:10–17).

The Redemption of Israel (Isa. 42:18–44:23)

Having proclaimed the coming of a Servant who will establish justice on earth, Isaiah turns again to address Israel's present condition (42:18–25). Israel has sinned against the Lord and broken his law (v. 24), and this is the reason for judgment (v. 25). But in spite of judgment, Isaiah declares that the people are not to fear that God has abandoned them (43:1–7). The Lord promises to bring the people of Israel back from every corner of the earth (vv. 5–6; 11:11–12; 27:13; 49:12; 60:4). He then brings another prophetic lawsuit against false gods (43:8–13). Again, Isaiah rests his case on God's ability to predict and explain future events, something idols cannot do.

God's ability to predict and explain future events is demonstrated as he declares that he is going to do a new thing for Israel, a new work of deliverance (vv. 14–21). This work of salvation will not be due to any righteousness within Israel itself (vv. 22–28). Instead, God himself will pour out his Spirit on the people with the result that they will identify themselves as God's own people (44:1–5). This section concludes with God's claims of absolute supremacy (vv. 6–8), his demonstration of the absolute foolishness of idolatry (vv. 9–20), and finally a song of redemption (vv. 21–23).

41. Goldingay 2001b, 240.
42. Oswalt 1998, 118.

The Great Deliverance of Cyrus (Isa. 44:24–48:22)

God's unique ability to predict and explain future events is revealed in the next section of Isaiah as he reveals the means by which he intends to accomplish the deliverance of Israel.[43] One named Cyrus will be called by God to deliver Israel from exile. The section begins with an announcement of coming salvation and the naming of Cyrus as the one who will fulfill God's purpose (44:24–28). Isaiah 45:1–8, then, is an oracle addressed specifically to Cyrus. He is anointed by God and will conquer nations (v. 1). The justification of what God has decreed is declared in verses 9–13. The issue is stated in terms of the right of the Creator to do what he will with his creation. The remainder of chapter 45 and all of chapter 46 are another declaration of God's supremacy over all false gods and idols (45:14–46:13). This God, who is the only God, can be trusted to do what he has promised to do. Israel has no reason to doubt his faithfulness. God calls all of the earth to turn to him and be saved (45:22) and declares that every knee will bow and every tongue will confess allegiance to him (v. 23).

Isaiah 47 is an oracle against Babylon. Because of her haughty pride, she will be brought low. Evil, disaster, and ruin shall come upon Babylon suddenly (v. 11). In chapter 48, Isaiah turns his attention once again to Israel. God reminds the people that he warned them in advance of past events in order that they might not attribute such events to their idols and images (vv. 1–5). God has revealed future things to Israel in order that she might know and trust the living God. Now, he is again warning Israel in advance of new things to come (vv. 6–11). This section concludes with God's renewed call to Israel to trust him for their redemption (vv. 12–22).

The Greater Deliverance of the Servant (Isa. 49–55)

The previous section of Isaiah has raised a significant question. Isaiah has declared that God is going to deliver Israel from exile by means of a conqueror named Cyrus, but what is going to be done about that which brought about the exile in the first place? What is going to be done about the sinfulness of Israel? How will Israel be delivered from this? Isaiah's answer is found in the present section, which itself may be divided into three smaller units involving the anticipation of salvation (49:1–52:12),

43. The following section will reveal that this deliverance is only preliminary. An even greater deliverance by a greater deliverer is coming.

the accomplishment of salvation (52:13–53:12), and the announcement of salvation (54:1–55:13).

The first of the three smaller units within this section of Isaiah describes a mounting anticipation of salvation. It begins with the second of Isaiah's Servant Songs (49:1–6). In the first Servant Song (42:1–9), Isaiah emphasized the Servant's mission to the nations. Israel's plight, however, has been brought to the fore in the intervening chapters. Therefore in this second Servant Song, Isaiah emphasizes the Servant's ministry to Israel without neglecting his mission to the world. The Servant's mission is to restore Israel (vv. 5–6).[44] The restoration in view here, however, is not like the restoration Cyrus accomplishes. It is not merely a restoration to the land. Instead, as Oswalt observes, "it is the restoration of an estranged world, along with an estranged Israel, to God."[45] The work of the Servant in restoring Israel is more fully expounded in verses 7–13.

In Isaiah 49:14–23, Zion cries out in despair, declaring that God has forsaken her and is no longer concerned for her welfare. Following God's promise that he has both the intention and the power to save Israel (49:24–50:3) is Isaiah's third Servant Song (50:4–9). This third Servant Song emphasizes the obedience of the Servant and the sufferings that result from his obedience. The Servant's suffering does not come "because of wrongdoing (as 42:24; 50:1) but through costly obedience; a suffering not merited but accepted, described in terms of the judicial act of flogging, gratuitous torture and personal humiliation."[46] As we will see, the New Testament describes the fulfillment of this prophecy in the suffering of Jesus.

Following the third Servant Song is Isaiah's call to Israel to listen to the Servant in order that she might be saved (50:10–51:8). Zion cries out for God to act (51:9–11), and God responds, telling Israel not to fear man but to fear him (vv. 12–16). God further consoles Israel by declaring to her that the cup of wrath she has been forced to drink has been taken from her and given to her tormentors (vv. 17–23). This unit concludes with a declaration to Israel that God has won the victory and that Israel has been freed (52:1–12). God's promises are so sure that their fulfillment is spoken of as

44. As McComiskey (1985a, 31–32) observes, the "Servant" here is distinguished from Israel (v. 5) and from the remnant of Israel (v. 6). Thus the Servant cannot be simply equated with Israel or with the remnant.

45. Oswalt 1998, 294.

46. Motyer 1993, 400.

having already been accomplished. The concluding song of good news and salvation proclaims the reign of God, his return to Zion, and the redemption of Jerusalem (vv. 7–9).

But if God will accomplish the salvation of Israel, how will he do so? The answer is found in the second unit of text within this section of Isaiah, the fourth and final of Isaiah's Servant Songs (52:13–53:12). The theme of the song is the Servant's taking upon himself the sin of Israel and the world.[47] The suffering, which had only been hinted at in the previous Servant Songs, is revealed to be the means by which the Servant will deliver his people from sin. This song is divided into five stanzas of three verses each.

The first stanza (52:13–15) begins with God's threefold exaltation of the Servant. He shall be "high" and "lifted up" and "exalted" (v. 13). This points to one who has great dignity and honor, but the exaltation in this first verse is immediately followed by a description of astonishment at the Servant caused by a degree of suffering so great that he is barely recognizable as human (v. 14). Somehow, the Servant's suffering will have universal effects. He will "sprinkle many nations" and kings will submit to him, for they will finally know and understand the truth (v. 15).

The second stanza (53:1–3) is the first of three describing in more detail the suffering and humiliation of the Servant. He is the "arm of Yahweh," the one who is the salvation of God personified (v. 1; 52:10). But who can believe this (v. 1)? He is born and raised as any other human child, and he is unimpressive to look at (v. 2). He is a man of sorrows who is despised and rejected by men (v. 3). The reason for his sorrow is revealed in the third stanza (53:4–6), which explains the nature and purpose of the Servant's suffering.

In the first place, his suffering is something that is uniquely his. He is alone. He bears our grief and carries our sorrows (v. 4). Upon him is laid the iniquity of us all (v. 6). Secondly, his suffering is substitutionary in nature. He is wounded for our transgressions and is crushed for our iniquities, and it is by his stripes that we are healed (v. 5). Thirdly, his suffering is the will of God. It is God who places upon the Servant all of our iniquity and sin (v. 6). This text is central to the fourth Servant Song because, as Brevard Childs observes, it demonstrates that "what occurred was not some unfortunate

47. Oswalt 1998, 377.

tragedy of human history but actually formed the center of the divine plan for the redemption of his people and indeed of the world."[48] This is how God will deal with sin, the central problem since the fall.

The fourth stanza (53:7–9) describes the Servant's voluntary acceptance of death. He is compared to a lamb led to slaughter or a sheep led to its shearers (v. 7), but what distinguishes him from a lamb or a sheep and thus from any animal sacrifices is that he goes knowingly and willingly to his death. He is "cut off out of the land of the living" (v. 8). In other words, he is executed. And his death is "for the transgression of my people" (v. 8). In other words, his death is a substitutionary sacrifice. From his death, Isaiah moves to a description of his burial (v. 9). If the first lines of verse 9 are an example of synonymous parallelism, then their meaning is: "the Servant was buried with the wicked, namely, the rich." If these lines are an example of antithetic parallelism, then their meaning is: "Although they intended to bury him with the wicked, when he died he was buried with the rich" (cf. NIV). Either reading can be understood in light of the fulfillment described in the Gospels (Matt. 27:57–60; John 19:31, 38–42). In either case, this verse concludes by emphasizing the fact that the Servant's suffering is not due to any sin on his own part. The Servant himself is without sin.

The final stanza (Isa. 53:10–12) describes the triumph of the Servant. The one who suffered, died, and was buried is now described as one who is alive. It was the will of the Lord to crush his Servant, whose suffering is described in terms of a guilt offering (v. 10ab). Now it is the will of the Lord to prosper him (v. 10c). The guilt offering of the righteous Servant removes the iniquities of his people and extends his own righteousness to them (v. 11). The Servant shall "make many to be accounted righteous." As Motyer notes, this construction is unique in the Old Testament: "The hiphil (causative) of √*ṣāḏēq* ('to be righteous') is 'to cause to be righteous' and is usually followed by a direct object (Dt. 25:1; 2 Sa. 15:4). Only here is it followed by an indirect object governed by the preposition l^{e}, hence 'bring righteousness to', 'provide righteousness for.'"[49] The great victory of the Servant is summed up in verse 12. He is the one who pours out his soul to death and bears the sin of many. In short, the problem of sin will be dealt with through the substitutionary death of a sinless Servant of God. This is a glorious prophecy of the redemptive work of Jesus.

48. Childs 2001, 415.

49. Motyer 1993, 441–42.

The third unit of text within this section of Isaiah (54–55) describes the announcement of the salvation accomplished by the Servant. In chapter 54, Isaiah outlines the effects of the Servant's redemptive work. Israel was like an estranged wife whose husband has now taken her back (54:6–8). The people who have despaired have been restored. In chapter 55, the call goes out to "everyone who thirsts" to enter into the salvation that God has accomplished. God tells his people that he will make with them "an everlasting covenant" (v. 3). Like Jeremiah, Isaiah points to the need for a new covenant after the exile (Jer. 31:31). Isaiah mentions this covenant in connection with David, thereby linking the covenant to Israel's messianic hopes. It is through the coming Davidic Messiah that the new and everlasting covenant will be established.

The Book of the Conqueror (Isa. 56–66)

Isaiah has prophesied that Judah will be exiled, but he has also promised that she will be delivered from the coming exile by Cyrus (44:24–28). An even greater deliverance, however, will be accomplished by the Lord's Servant who will bear his people's iniquities (49–55). The final major section of Isaiah, the Book of the Conqueror (56–66), addresses the situation of a people who will have been restored to the land but who will not have seen everything promised come to pass. They will have been freed from one foreign oppressor, the Babylonians, but they will remain under the foreign rule of the Persians rather than the beneficent rule of a Davidic king. Isaiah knows that questions will arise among the people, questions such as: When will we be free of foreign rule and oppression? When will we finally rest in the fullness of God's promises?

The Ideal and the Actual (Isa. 56:1–59:13)

This section of Isaiah opens with a description of the truly righteous (56:1–8). Those who are righteous are not necessarily those who are ethnically Jewish. They are those who keep justice and do righteousness (v. 1). Whether foreigners or eunuchs, the true people of God are those who have a faith in God that manifests itself in faithful living (vv. 3–6; see also Acts 8:27–39). Isaiah continues with God's promise that he will gather the outcasts of Israel and others as well (v. 8; see also John 10:16). He then declares that the nation of Israel cannot consider mere ceremonial observances to be a mark of election, especially when idolatry is running rampant (Isa.

56:9–57:13). Isaiah illustrates the difference between the faithful and the unfaithful in terms of the difference between true and false fasting (58:1–7). He concludes by describing the failure of God's people to love him and to love their neighbors (59:1–13).

The Coming Conqueror (Isa. 59:14–63:6)

Isaiah now turns to several chapters in which he will describe in some detail the future glory of the restored Israel whose salvation will draw the nations to God. The section begins and ends with a description of God as a conqueror who comes in judgment upon his enemies (59:14–21; 63:1–6). In Isaiah 59:14–21, the Lord is depicted as a warrior.[50] The coming of the divine Redeemer to Zion (59:20) will result in a glorious future that is described in 60:1–22. Zion will be characterized by the presence of the light of God, a light that will draw nations and kings (vv. 1–3). The coming of the whole world to Zion is pictured in even more detailed form in verses 4–9. They will come by land and by sea. The nations will build Zion (vv. 10, 14). It will be a secure city in which the Lord himself will dwell (vv. 11–13).

The transformation of Zion is described in Isaiah 60:15–22. She who was forsaken and hated will be "majestic forever" and "a joy from age to age" (v. 15). Israel will finally know that the Lord is her Savior and Redeemer (v. 16). Everything will be transformed for the better. Bronze and iron will be replaced with gold and silver, while wood and stones will be replaced with bronze and iron (v. 17). Violence and devastation will be no more (v. 18). That which most obviously regulated the old order, the sun and moon, will be transformed due to the presence of God who will be an everlasting light (vv. 19–20; Rev. 21:23). The people will be righteous and shall possess the land forever (Isa. 60:21). Isaiah pictures the ultimate fulfillment of the Abrahamic promises in declaring that the smallest will be made a mighty nation (v. 22; 51:2).

Isaiah turns next to the transforming work of the anointed one (61:1–9). Like the messianic figure in 11:2, the Lord has anointed this one with the Spirit. He is anointed specifically to proclaim the good news (vv. 1–2) and to bring about transformation (v. 3). This is the passage of Isaiah that Jesus cites at the beginning of his own ministry, identifying himself

50. The breastplate of righteousness and helmet of salvation worn by God here are echoed in Paul's description of the armor Christians are to wear (Eph. 6:13–17).

with the anointed Messiah (Luke 4:16–22). In 61:5–9, Isaiah expands upon the good news that the anointed one is to proclaim. Instead of Israel serving the nations, the nations will serve Israel (vv. 5–6). God's covenant with his people will result in a worldwide community, blessed by God (vv. 7–9).

A second poetic proclamation by the anointed one begins a passage describing the Savior and his people (61:10–62:12). The anointed one expresses joy at the salvation and transformation of Zion (61:10–62:7). Israel is no longer forsaken and desolate. Instead she is the Lord's delight. The security of the people is guaranteed by a divine oath (vv. 8–9). The Lord then calls both "the people" (Israel) and "the peoples" (the nations) to come through the gates of Zion (v. 10). The Lord then confirms again that salvation is coming and that the people will be redeemed (vv. 11–12). The anointed one completes his work in 63:1–6, a passage in which he is once again depicted as a warrior coming in judgment.

The New Heavens and New Earth (Isa. 63:7–66:24)

The final section of Isaiah contains an extended prayer by the people (63:7–64:12) and the response of the Lord (65:1–66:24). In 62:6–7, the anointed one had placed watchmen on the walls of Jerusalem to pray without ceasing until all is fulfilled. The watchmen were to "put Yahweh in remembrance" (v. 6). In verse 6, the verb *zakar* is plural. In 63:7, a singular form of the same verb is used. Isaiah 63:7–64:12 is the prayer of an individual "watchman" who is putting God in remembrance. The first section of the prayer involves remembrance (63:7–14). The watchman remembers the covenant love and great goodness of Yahweh (v. 7). He remembers God's past care for his people (vv. 8–9). Finally, he remembers the foundational redemptive act in Israel's history, the exodus from Egypt in which God was present with his people (vv. 10–14).

In the second section of the watchman's prayer, he asks several questions and makes numerous appeals to God (63:15–64:12). Isaiah foresees a time after the exile when God will not seem present. The watchman's prayer asks why God's compassion is far from the people (63:15–16) and why he remains alienated from his people (vv. 17–19). In the next verses, the watchman thinks longingly of what might have been (64:1–3). The words translated "Oh that you would rend . . ." in the ESV would be better translated "Oh that you had rent. . . ." The syntax indicates a wish that something had already happened in the past.[51] The watchman believes that if God had made his presence manifest, Israel's circumstances would have been different.

Israel's sinfulness causes the watchman to wonder if it is too late to hope for God's salvation (64:4–5). Israel's profound sinfulness has left her helpless before a holy God (vv. 6–7). Despite Israel's sin, however, the watchman appeals to God for mercy and forgiveness (vv. 8–9). He reminds God that Israel is the covenant people of God, his own special possession (v. 9). Finally, the watchman points to the ruins of Israel's cities and Jerusalem's temple and asks whether God is going to act (vv. 10–12). God's response to the watchman's prayer is found in the final chapters of Isaiah.

God's response is a promise of salvation for his people and judgment for those who rebel against him. Isaiah begins by describing God's judgment upon apostate Israel (65:1–7). They are described as a "rebellious people" (v. 2) who provoke God continually with their idolatry (vv. 3–7). In contrast to the judgment that is to fall upon the rebellious (vv. 11–12), God is going to pour out his blessing upon his true servants (vv. 8–10). Finally, the contrasting destinies of the rebels and the faithful are set forth (vv. 13–16).

These promises of blessing will be fulfilled in a new heaven and earth (65:17–25). The complete transformation of creation represents the ultimate consummation of God's redemptive purposes. God declares, "For behold, I create new heavens and a new earth" (v. 17). As in Genesis 1:1, "heavens and earth" represents the universe and all that is in it. All of created reality will be renewed and transformed by God. In the following verses, Isaiah uses elements of our present experience to paint a picture of what the new heavens and earth will be like.

Isaiah declares that there will be no more weeping or crying (Isa. 65:19). "No more shall there be in it an infant who lives but a few days, or an old man who does not fill out his days, for the young man shall die a hundred years old, and the sinner a hundred years old shall be accursed" (v. 20). Because Isaiah has already prophesied the complete destruction of death (25:7–8), this passage is not saying that sin and death will exist in the new heavens and new earth. It is simply a highly figurative way of indicating

51. See GKC, §151e; Motyer 1993, 518 n. 1.

that death will no longer have any power and that sin will no longer be present. Society itself will be transformed as well (vv. 21–25). It is described in the same terms that Isaiah used to describe the reign of the Messiah in 11:6–9. It is a scene of creation transformed.

Isaiah has already drawn a sharp distinction between the destinies of the righteous and the rebellious (65:1–16). In the final chapter of his book, Isaiah calls upon the people to flee from God's wrath and enter into his salvation. Those who have worshiped falsely and scorned God's people will be judged (66:1–6), and that which God has promised to do, he is able to do (vv. 7–9). Isaiah calls upon those who love Jerusalem to rejoice and be glad (vv. 10–11) for the Lord promises to extend peace to her and to comfort her (vv. 12–14).

The Lord is going to come in fire to judge the rebellious (66:15–17). The wicked and the abominable "shall come to an end together" (v. 17). The work of judgment being completed, Isaiah moves on to describe God's work of salvation, his gathering of a people into the new Jerusalem (vv. 18–24). God will set a sign among his people (v. 19). Those who are already citizens of Jerusalem are to declare the glory of God to all nations and tongues and bring believers back as "brothers" into the covenant community (vv. 19–21). That these Gentile converts will be on equal footing with the Israelites is demonstrated in Isaiah's prophecy that some of them will be priests and Levites (v. 21). The climax of God's redemptive work is the new heavens and new earth in which all nations shall worship him (vv. 22–23).

Summary

Like Micah, Isaiah's prophetic ministry witnessed the fall of the northern kingdom in the late eighth century. And like Micah, Isaiah prophesied not only the coming fall and exile of Judah but also the future restoration of Israel and the coming of a Messiah. Unlike Micah, however, Isaiah's oracles are extensive and detailed. They extend from Isaiah's immediate present into the near future and into the eschatological new heavens and new earth. Because of the detailed nature of his messianic prophecies it is hardly surprising that the New Testament writers quote his book more than that of any other Old Testament prophet.

Isaiah promises a Messiah who will be born of a virgin (7:14), a child who will be called "Wonderful Counselor, Mighty God, Everlasting Father,

Prince of Peace" (9:6). This Messiah's kingdom will have no end (9:7). His reign will be characterized by a transformation of creation and a gathering of his people from every corner of the earth (11:6–16). Isaiah also promises a coming Servant through whom God will establish justice across the earth (42:1–9). The Servant will restore an estranged Israel and an estranged world to God (49:1–6). The Servant's obedience will result in his humiliation and suffering (50:4–9). The suffering of the Servant, however, is not for nothing. The Servant will suffer as a substitutionary sacrifice for his people, bearing their sins and iniquities upon himself and providing righteousness for them (52:13–53:12).

Finally, Isaiah promises the coming of an anointed conqueror who judges his enemies and restores Israel (59:14–60:22). This Spirit-anointed conqueror will proclaim the good news of salvation to his people (61:1–9). He will judge all mankind and reign over a new heavens and new earth in which the people of God are gathered (65–66). According to the New Testament, all of these prophecies are fulfilled in and through one person, the Lord Jesus Christ.

7

The Seventh-Century Prophets

Nahum, Zephaniah, Habakkuk, Joel, and Jeremiah/Lamentations

The first half of the seventh century B.C. was a low point in the history of the kingdom of Judah. The wicked king Manasseh reigned for most of this period (697–642). The first ten years of his reign were apparently a coregency with his father Hezekiah, but following the death of Hezekiah, he reigned over Judah alone for another forty-five years.[1] According to 2 Kings 21:1–18 and 2 Chronicles 33:1–20, Judah was marked by widespread idolatry and apostasy under Manasseh's rule. Judah was following the same path that Israel had followed and was inviting the same judgment.

The first half of the seventh century also witnessed the continued dominance of the Assyrian Empire in the ancient Near East, and this dominance

1. Reconstructions of the chronology of the kings indicate a coregency with his father Hezekiah between 697 and 686. See Thiele 1983; Young 2005.

remained a constant threat to Judah. Sennacherib had laid siege to Jerusalem in 701, and Jerusalem had been delivered only because of the miraculous intervention of God. But this reprieve did not remove the Assyrian threat completely. Following the death of Sennacherib in 681, Esarhaddon took the throne and reigned until 669. He was followed by Assurbanipal who ruled from 668 until 627. Each of these kings continued Assyria's brutal policies.

The latter half of the seventh century witnessed a brief period of religious reformation in Judah during the thirty-year reign of the godly king Josiah (640–609). Sadly, Josiah's policies would not outlast his death as his sons led Judah back into idolatry, thereby sealing the nation's fate. Josiah's reign also witnessed another important development, the downfall of the Assyrian Empire and the rise of Babylon to a position of dominance in the region. The prophets Nahum, Zephaniah, Habakkuk (and possibly Joel) all ministered within this late-seventh-century context. The prophetic ministry of Jeremiah began during the same period but lasted longer, extending into the early sixth century. These seventh-century prophets ministered at a significant time in redemptive history when a large part of God's people had already been exiled and the remainder were on the verge of experiencing the same.

Nahum

The prophetic oracles found within the book of Nahum concern Nineveh, the capital of the Assyrian Empire. Approximately a century earlier, Jonah had been sent to the Ninevites, and they had repented upon hearing the prophetic word. Their repentance, however, was apparently short-lived because Nahum now addresses a wicked and brutal empire. From the content of the book itself, it is possible to determine that Nahum's oracles were delivered sometime between the years 663 and 612. The fall of the Egyptian capital of Thebes in 663 is referred to as a past event in Nahum 3:8, and the fall of Nineveh, which Nahum predicts throughout, occurred in 612. Although it is difficult to date Nahum with much more precision than this, there is some evidence that we can place the date of the oracles in the last years of Manasseh's reign (i.e., 650–642).[2]

2. This is Robertson's position (1990, 31), but because the evidence is not conclusive, conservative scholars offer a range of suggestions. Richard D. Patterson (1991, 7), for example, suggests that the

The book of Nahum may be divided into five main sections preceded by an introductory superscription (1:1). The book begins with a divine-warrior psalm in 1:2–8. Oracles of judgment and salvation follow in 1:9–2:2. A dramatic vision of the fall of Nineveh is found in 2:3–13. Nahum 3:1–7 then contains a lament for Nineveh, and 3:8–19 contains a taunt of the wicked city. As a whole, Nahum's prophecy is characterized by some of the most vivid poetic language found anywhere in the prophets. His vision of the fall of Nineveh, for example, carries the reader into the midst of the battle with all of its sights and sounds.

The superscription (1:1) introduces the subject of the book. It is an "oracle concerning Nineveh," the capital city of the Assyrian Empire. It is also described as "the vision of Nahum of Elkosh." All that is known about Nahum is his name for he is not mentioned anywhere else in Scripture outside of this prophetic book. He is said to be from Elkosh, and although scholars have suggested a number of possible locations, the site of this city has not yet been determined with any certainty.

Following the superscription is a divine-warrior psalm in which the victory of God over his enemies is celebrated.[3] The celebration of victory before the battle has even begun indicates that Nineveh's judgment is certain.[4] The tone for the entire prophecy is set in 1:2 with the three occurrences of the words *noqem YHWH* meaning "Yahweh is an avenger." In verse 3, Nahum indicates that God's patience is great, but that he will eventually judge the guilty. The prophet here echoes Moses' words following the golden calf incident (Ex. 34:6–7). According to Nahum, the Lord's judgment results in cosmic upheaval (1:4–6). He "rebukes the sea and makes it dry" (v. 4; cf. Ex. 14:21; Ps. 106:9). The mountains quake, the hills melt, and the rocks are broken into pieces (1:5–6). Nahum's point in this section is that by means of judging his enemies, God saves his people (vv. 7–8).

Nahum 1:9–2:2 is a collection of oracles of judgment interspersed with oracles of salvation. Nahum 1:9–11, 14, and 2:1 are oracles of judgment, while 1:12–13, 15, and 2:2 are oracles of salvation. The oracle of salvation

setting for the oracles is a date between 660 and 654. Dillard and Longman (1994, 405), on the other hand, suggest that the setting is most likely the years between 652 and 626. VanGemeren (1990, 164) argues for a much narrower range of possibility, suggesting that the setting is shortly before the death of Assurbanipal in 627.

3. One of the debates surrounding this section of Nahum concerns the possible existence of an acrostic. For a discussion of the topic see Longman 1993, 773–75.

4. Longman 1993, 788.

in 1:15 echoes a similar proclamation by Isaiah (Isa. 52:7) in which the prophet beholds the feet of him who brings good news. In Isaiah, the feet belong to those who proclaim the peace associated with the reign of God. In Nahum, the feet belong to those who proclaim the judgment of Nineveh, the capital of a nation that had long oppressed God's people. As O. Palmer Robertson explains, the use of the same imagery by Isaiah and Nahum is appropriate: "These two elements, the destruction of God's enemies and the salvation of God's people, must be combined if the kingdom of God is to be actually realized on earth."[5]

The last line of 1:15 is significant. Nahum declares, "never again shall the worthless pass through you; he is utterly cut off." This prophecy raises an important question. If it means that after Nineveh is judged, wicked nations will never again oppress Judah, it is false because in only a few decades Babylon would become Judah's oppressor. Read in context, however, the last line of verse 15 is intended to be a specific reference to Assyria, the target of Nahum's entire prophecy. In this case, Nahum's prophecy is of course vindicated because after 605 B.C. Assyria would never again oppress Judah or anyone else.[6]

Nahum proceeds with a vision of the fall of Nineveh in 2:3–13. The vision is extremely dramatic and vivid.[7] The events he foresees were fulfilled in 612 B.C. when the combined forces of the Medes and Babylonians overthrew the city of Nineveh. But Nahum reminds us that behind these human instruments of judgment is God himself who is the divine warrior fighting against the Assyrians (2:13). In a lament for Nineveh, Nahum indicates that the city's judgment is certain because of her great sinfulness (3:1–7). He then proceeds to taunt Nineveh because the city's population is self-deluded into thinking that the city is secure (3:8–19). Nahum promises that the city will be judged despite her strength (vv. 14–19). Not many years after Nahum prophesied, this divine judgment came to pass.

Zephaniah

The book of the prophet Zephaniah indicates that he ministered during the reign of Josiah (640–609), the last of the godly kings of Judah (Zeph. 1:1).

5. Robertson 2004, 259.
6. See Longman 1993, 800.
7. Craigie 1984–85, 2:68–69.

There is little dispute regarding this general time frame. There is debate, however, regarding the specific period of Josiah's reign during which Zephaniah prophesied. The debate centers on whether Zephaniah prophesied before or after the discovery of the book of the law in 622 B.C. Conservative biblical scholars may be found on both sides of the debate. Both Richard Patterson and Peter Craigie, for example, argue that Zephaniah prophesied before 622, in the earlier part of Josiah's reign.[8] Robertson, on the other hand, argues that Zephaniah prophesied after 622.[9] Raymond Dillard and Tremper Longman argue that there is simply not enough evidence to determine a more precise date.[10] Although the evidence is not conclusive, what evidence there is seems to favor slightly a date in Josiah's reign sometime between 622 and 612 B.C.

The structure of the book of Zephaniah is straightforward. Following the superscription (1:1), the book is divided into three main sections. Zephaniah 1:2–2:3 contains an extensive prophecy concerning the day of the Lord. The second section, 2:4–3:8, is a series of oracles against the nations and against Judah. The final section of the book, 3:9–20, is an oracle of salvation. Although the first section of the book in particular focuses on the day of the Lord, the theme pervades the entire book. Just as Amos had prophesied about the imminent coming of the day of the Lord upon Israel (Amos 5:18–27), Zephaniah now predicts its imminent coming upon Judah. The past destruction of Israel by Assyria in 722 and the coming destruction of Judah by Babylon are both instances of the day of the Lord, a day of decisive judgment. Both historical acts of judgment, however, also foreshadow the eschatological day of the Lord, the day of final judgment.[11]

Throughout the first major section of Zephaniah, the prophet connects his oracles of judgment regarding the day of the Lord to God's ancient covenants. The book opens with a declaration of judgment so sweeping in nature that it hearkens back to the days of Noah:

> "I will utterly sweep away everything
> from the face of the earth,"
> declares Yahweh.

8. See Patterson 1991, 276; Craigie 1984–85, 2:105.

9. Robertson 1990, 10, 32. Robertson bases his argument largely upon the many linguistic parallels between Zephaniah and Deuteronomy, the book presumably found in the temple (1990, 254–57).

10. Dillard and Longman 1994, 416.

11. Dillard and Longman 1994, 419.

"I will sweep away man and beast;
  I will sweep away the birds of the heavens
  and the fish of the sea,
and the rubble with the wicked.
  I will cut off mankind
  from the face of the earth,"
    declares Yahweh. (Zeph. 1:2–3; cf. Gen. 6:7)

This is one of the most dramatic declarations of coming judgment found anywhere in the prophets.

The specific object of God's wrath is declared to be Judah (Zeph. 4–6). Zephaniah proclaims that God's own people will experience the curses of the covenant that he promised would be the result of disobedience (Deut. 28:15–68). He declares, "Be silent before the Lord Yahweh! For the day of Yahweh is near; Yahweh has prepared a sacrifice and consecrated his guests" (Zeph. 1:7). Here the prophet forcefully indicates the imminence of the coming day of judgment (see also v. 14). He uses the language of sacrifice in verses 7–8 to depict this judgment, language that echoes the events surrounding the inauguration of the Abrahamic covenant and language that is found in other prophetic oracles of judgment (Gen. 15:9–11; Isa. 34:5–8; Ezek. 39:17–20).[12]

Zephaniah expands on the consequences of the coming day of the Lord in 1:8–14. It will be a time of punishment and wailing. Zephaniah further describes this coming day:

A day of wrath is that day,
  a day of distress and anguish,
a day of ruin and devastation,
  a day of darkness and gloom,
a day of clouds and thick darkness,
  a day of trumpet blast and battle cry
against the fortified cities
  and against the lofty battlements. (vv. 15–16; cf. Joel 2:1–2)

This language echoes the description of the divine theophany that accompanied the giving of the Mosaic law at Mount Sinai (Ex. 20:21). By making

12. Robertson 1990, 268.

this literary association, Zephaniah indicates that the day of the Lord is the day on which the terms of God's covenant will be enforced.[13]

The first section of Zephaniah ends with an admonition:

> Gather together, yes, gather,
> O shameless nation,
> before the decree takes effect
> —before the day passes away like chaff—
> before there comes upon you
> the burning anger of Yahweh,
> before there comes upon you
> the day of the anger of Yahweh.
> Seek Yahweh, all you humble of the land,
> who do his just commands;
> seek righteousness; seek humility;
> perhaps you may be hidden
> on the day of the anger of Yahweh. (2:1–3)

The threefold use of the word "before" in verse 2 indicates the urgency of the situation. There is not much time before judgment falls. The threefold use of "seek" in verse 3 indicates that all hope is not lost. In verse 3, Zephaniah holds out some hope for the "humble of the land" who seek the Lord, seek righteousness, and seek humility. These are the remnant, and while they will not avoid the day of the Lord, they may be "hidden on the day" (v. 3).

The second major section of Zephaniah is a series of oracles of judgment against the nations and against Judah. His oracles of judgment against the nations cover all four points of the compass. There is an oracle against Philistia to the west (2:4–7). This is followed by an oracle against Moab and Ammon to the east (vv. 8–11). Zephaniah then turns to Cush in the south (v. 12). Finally, he turns to the north with an oracle against Assyria (vv. 13–15). Following the oracles against the nations is an oracle against Jerusalem (3:1–8). Zephaniah condemns Jerusalem for being an oppressive and faithless city (vv. 1–2). He condemns her officials, judges, prophets, and priests for their treachery (vv. 3–4), a treachery made all the more odious because of the fact that the Lord who is within the city is righteous

13. Robertson 1990, 270.

and just (v. 5). Because of Jerusalem's faithlessness, her judgment is coming (vv. 6–8).

The final section of Zephaniah (3:9–20) indicates that devastating judgment is not the final word. This section contains two oracles, an oracle concerning God's purification of a faithful remnant (vv. 9–13) and an oracle concerning God's rejoicing with his people (vv. 14–20). Zephaniah declares that a faithful remnant will remain and that from this remnant, God will create a new people. This new people will contain not only the faithful remnant from Israel (vv. 11–13), it will also contain the faithful from among the nations (vv. 9–10). Together, all of the faithful will worship the Lord.

The final oracle in Zephaniah is an oracle concerning God's love for his people. God calls upon his people to sing and rejoice (3:14) for he has taken their judgments away (vv. 15–16). Then we read, "Yahweh your God is in your midst, a mighty one who will save; he will rejoice over you with gladness; he will quiet you by his love; he will exult over you with loud singing" (v. 17). Robertson refers to this verse as "the John 3:16 of the OT."[14] Yahweh, the one who is in the midst of his people, is the "mighty one who will save" (cf. Isa. 7:14; 9:6). Just as he called upon his people to sing and rejoice out of love for him, the Lord promises that he will sing and rejoice out of love for his people.[15] So the prophetic book that begins with one of the most awe-inspiring descriptions of God's judgment concludes with one of the most awe-inspiring descriptions of God's love.[16]

Habakkuk

The prophet Habakkuk lived at the end of the seventh century during the period of time when the Assyrian Empire was faltering and the Babylonian Empire was on the rise (625–605). He likely prophesied between 609 and 605, during the reign of the Judean king Jehoiakim in the last days of Assyria's long period of imperial dominance.[17] Assyria's downfall had begun in earnest in 626 with the rise of Nabopolassar to the throne of Babylon. He drove the Assyrians completely out of Babylon in 623. After the fall of

14. Robertson 1990, 339.
15. Motyer 1998b, 957–58.
16. Robertson 1990, 334.
17. Robertson 1990, 13, 37; Craigie 1984–85, 2:77; Dillard and Longman 1994, 411.

the Assyrian city of Asshur in 614, Nabopolassar formed an alliance with Cyaxares, the king of the Medes. Together, they sacked the Assyrian capital of Nineveh in 612. The Assyrians then relocated their seat of government westward to Haran, but by 609 Nabopolassar had driven them from that city as well. The remaining Assyrian stronghold of Carchemish was defeated by Nabopolassar's son Nebuchadnezzar in 605. He defeated Assyria and forced the Egyptians out of northern Syria and Judah, driving them back to Egypt. The kingdom of Judah now fell under Babylonian control, and the first deportation of Judeans to Babylon occurred (Dan. 1:1–4).[18]

In Judah, Jehoahaz had become king in 609 after the death of his father Josiah, but unlike his father, he was a wicked ruler. His reign, however, lasted only three months before the Egyptian Pharaoh Neco took him captive and set his brother Jehoiakim on the throne of Judah (2 Kings 23:31–35). Jehoiakim's wicked reign would last a full decade. Habakkuk prophesied during the first part of Jehoiakim's reign, a time when the nation was rejecting the reforms of Josiah and returning to blatant apostasy, a time when one wicked empire was being replaced by another, and a time when Judah was on the verge of destruction.

The book of Habakkuk has a unique structure among the prophetic books with its inclusion of prophetic dialogues with God and its inclusion of a complete psalm. Habakkuk understands why God is punishing his disobedient people, but he does not understand why God is using a wicked nation as his instrument of judgment. The book deals with this question and the required response of faithful trust in God. Following the superscription (Hab. 1:1) is Habakkuk's first prayer of protest (1:2–4). This is followed by Yahweh's first response (1:5–11). The book continues with Habakkuk's second prayer (1:12–2:1) and Yahweh's second response (2:2–20). The Lord's second response consists of a vision (2:2–5) and a judgment oracle (2:6–20). The book then concludes with Habakkuk's psalm (3:1–19).

The book begins with Habakkuk's plaintive cry, "O Yahweh, how long shall I cry for help" (1:2). All he sees around him is violence and wickedness (1:2–4). He cries out to God because he sees justice being perverted. The Lord's response makes two basic points. He declares that he is about to act, and he names the nation through whom he will act. He declares that he will raise up the Chaldeans (v. 6). The Chaldeans were the tribes in southern

18. For a helpful account of the history, see Merrill 1996, 447–50; see also Bruce 1993, 833–34.

Babylon who took control of the state and then overthrew the Assyrian Empire.[19] God will use the Babylonians as his instrument in bringing judgment, not only upon Assyria, but upon Judah as well (vv. 6–11).

The Lord's response leads to Habakkuk's second question. He acknowledges that God's people are wicked, but he points out that the Babylonians are far worse (vv. 12–17). He wants to know why God is using such an evil people to judge Judah. In 2:1, Habakkuk declares that he will stand at his post and await an answer from God. The Lord's response is in two parts. First, the Lord tells Habakkuk to "write the vision" (2:2). Habakkuk had asked, "How long?" Now God reveals to Habakkuk that divine action will come in God's good time (2:3). God's promise brings forth two contrary responses from the people. The wicked are puffed up, "but the righteous shall live by faith" (2:4).[20]

The second part of the Lord's response is a series of taunting woe oracles directed at the Babylonians (2:6–20). God here promises Habakkuk that although he is using the Babylonians as his instrument of judgment, they too will be judged for their own wickedness (vv. 6–8). In contrast to the Babylonian Empire, the Lord's kingdom will someday fill the earth (v. 14; cf. Isa. 11:9). The book of Habakkuk concludes with a psalm in which the coming of God in judgment is depicted in terms that echo the theophany at Mount Sinai (3:3–4).[21] Habakkuk describes the results of God's coming in terms of cosmic convulsions (vv. 6, 10, 11). He concludes by declaring that no matter what occurs, he will rejoice and trust in the Lord (vv. 17–19).

Joel

While Nahum, Zephaniah, Habakkuk, and Jeremiah are known seventh-century prophets, Joel cannot be dated to this era with absolute certainty. Unlike these other prophets, Joel does not include anything in his book that helps to date it with confidence.[22] Therefore, establishing a date for the book of Joel is notoriously difficult, and suggestions have been offered ranging from the ninth century to the second century B.C.[23] Among con-

19. Craigie 1984–85, 2:85.

20. For more on the interpretation of this verse, see Robertson 1990, 175–83.

21. Baker 1988a, 70.

22. Dillard and Longman (1994, 365–67) survey some of the internal evidence that provides clues but not certainty.

23. For a good survey of the various suggestions, see Allen 1976, 19–25.

servative scholars, three main views are suggested. Some suggest an early preexilic date in the late ninth or early eighth century.[24] Others suggest a late preexilic date in the seventh century.[25] Still others argue that a postexilic date in the late sixth to the mid-fifth century best explains the content of the book.[26] While evidence for each of these views has been presented, no one has yet established a decisively compelling argument for any of them. In the judgment of the present writer, however, the case for a late preexilic date is the most persuasive.

The book of Joel may be divided into four major sections. Following the superscription (1:1) are a description of a locust plague and a call to lament (1:2–20). Joel then describes the coming day of the Lord and issues a call to repentance (2:1–17). He moves from oracles of judgment to oracles of blessing in the second half of his book. First, he proclaims the coming restoration of Israel and all of creation as well as the outpouring of the Spirit upon all of the people (2:18–32). He then concludes with a promise of judgment against the enemies of Israel (3:1–21). The overarching theme that ties the book together is the day of the Lord. This concept is found in each major section of the book.

Joel begins his book with a description of a locust plague (1:2–12). Many argue that the description in the first chapter is a description of a literal plague of insects.[27] If Joel is describing a literal plague of locusts, then this present ecological disaster is a springboard that provides the metaphor for his prophecy in chapter 2 of a worse judgment to come. There is, however, the possibility that Joel's description of the locust plague in chapter 1 is itself a symbolic description of an invading human army.[28] According to Douglas Stuart, chapter 1 describes in figurative language the invasion of the land by a human army, probably that of the Babylonian armies in the late seventh or early sixth century. "More than just one plague among many (cf. Ex. 10:1–18) this was *the* plague par excellence, the destructive, unstoppable invasion unleashed to consume Israel as locusts consume a field."[29] While it is quite possible that Joel is describing a literal locust

24. E.g., Robertson 1995, 10–13.

25. E.g., Stuart 1987, 224–26, 250; Dumbrell 2002, 187.

26. E.g., Dillard 1992, 240–43.

27. E.g., Allen 1976, 48–55; Wolff 1977, 25–32; Hubbard 1989b, 41–48; Finley 1990, 21; Dillard 1992, 254–62; Dumbrell 2002, 186.

28. Stuart 1987, 232–34, 241–42.

29. Stuart 1987, 242.

invasion in chapter 1, the broader context seems to indicate that this is in fact a figurative description of the Babylonian armies.

Because of the threat posed by this army, Joel calls upon the people to lament and repent (1:13–20). He calls upon the leaders of the nation to fast and cry out to God (vv. 13–14). He then explains the reason for his call: "For the day of Yahweh is near, and as destruction from the Almighty it comes" (v. 15). The day of the Lord is the day of Yahweh's holy war against his enemies.[30] Because of her idolatrous rebellion, Judah was now facing the coming wrath of God. This section ends with Joel's brief prayer to God, beginning the communal period of lamentation that he has called (vv. 19–20).

In chapter 2, Joel turns to a vivid description of the coming day of the Lord (2:1–17). The people are to tremble in fear for the day of the Lord is near (v. 1). It is to be "a day of darkness and gloom, a day of thick clouds and thick darkness!" (v. 2a; cf. Amos 5:18–20; Isa. 8:22; 13:10; Zeph. 1:15). Joel describes a great number of people spread out on the mountains before Judah, a fearful prophecy of a coming invasion (2:2b). The destruction the invasion causes is described in horrifying imagery (vv. 3–11). It will be like a ravaging fire, destroying everything before it (v. 3). Joel ends by calling upon the people to repent (vv. 12–17).

The oracles of judgment in the first half of Joel are followed by oracles of blessing in the second half of the book. Joel begins with a prophecy of the coming restoration of Israel and all of creation (2:18–32). The Lord will have pity on his people (v. 18). The covenantal curses that have come upon the people will be replaced by blessings (vv. 19–27). Joel declares,

> And it shall come to pass afterward,
>   that I will pour out my Spirit on all flesh;
> your sons and your daughters shall prophesy,
>   your old men shall dream dreams,
>   and your young men shall see visions.
> Even on the male and female servants
>   in those days I will pour out my Spirit. (vv. 28–29; cf. Ezek. 39:29)

Moses had longed for the day when all of the Lord's people would be prophets (Num. 11:29). Joel promises that this hope is a part of God's

30. Dillard 1992, 266.

purpose for the future. As Dillard observes, Joel here promises a day when the "prophethood of all believers" will be a reality.[31]

The final chapter of Joel promises the future judgment of Israel's enemies (3:1–21). God himself will assemble the nations for judgment (v. 2; cf. Zeph. 3:8). Joel uses the imagery of a gathering army to describe the preparation for God's judgment of the nations (3:9–16). This judgment against the nations, like the judgment against Israel, is described as the day of the Lord (v. 14). It is the day when the wrath of God is poured out on his enemies. The judgment of the nations will be for the benefit of God's people. Their destruction will allow God's people to live in peace and security in his presence (vv. 17–21).[32]

Jeremiah

Although Jeremiah's prophetic ministry began before Habakkuk's and probably before Zephaniah's as well, it lasted far longer than either of their ministries, extending well into the sixth century. His prophetic ministry spanned a little over forty years from his call in 626 B.C. to a few years after the fall of Jerusalem in 586 B.C.[33] His prophetic call occurred in the thirteenth year of the reign of King Josiah (1:2). There are some who argue that this verse refers to the date of Jeremiah's birth rather than to the date of his prophetic call.[34] Although there are some weighty arguments for this interpretation, ultimately its proponents cannot do justice to the words of Jeremiah 1:2 and 3:6, and as John Hill observes, they are forced either to emend or ignore 25:3.[35]

As in the case of the other prophetic books, it is necessary to have some grasp of the historical context in order to understand Jeremiah.[36] As noted above, Josiah was the last good king of Judah. Following his death in 609, his son Jehoahaz reigned for three months before being taken into captivity by the Egyptians who then replaced him with his brother Jehoiakim

31. Dillard 1992, 295.

32. Stuart 1987, 265–67.

33. Dillard and Longman 1994, 302.

34. E.g., Holladay 1989, 25–26; Dumbrell 2002, 133.

35. Hill 1999, 52. For a full discussion of the issues, see Thompson 1980, 50–56.

36. Several of the standard commentaries offer helpful summaries of the historical background. See Thompson 1980, 9–27; Bright 1965, xxvii–liv; Harrison 1973, 13–21; and the chronological chart in Lundbom 2004b, 579–81.

(609–598). In 605, soon after Nebuchadnezzar routed the Assyrians and Egyptians at Carchemish, Judah was forced to become a Babylonian vassal (2 Kings 24:1–2). Nebuchadnezzar also deported some Judeans to Babylon at this time (Dan. 1:1–4). In 601, Nebuchadnezzar met strong Egyptian resistance at Egypt's frontier outposts. After Nebuchadnezzar returned to Babylon to regroup, Jehoiakim aligned himself with the Egyptians and rebelled against Babylon. Nebuchadnezzar responded in 598 by marching on Judah. Three months before the fall of Jerusalem, Jehoiakim died and was replaced by his son Jehoiachin (2 Kings 24:6).

In 597, Jerusalem fell to the armies of Nebuchadnezzar, and Jehoiachin and many of the people of Judah were taken into exile. Judah again became a Babylonian vassal, and Nebuchadnezzar set Josiah's son Mattaniah on the throne, changing his name to Zedekiah (2 Kings 24:10–17). In 595, an uprising began in Babylonia, which encouraged representatives from Edom, Ammon, and Moab to come to Jerusalem to discuss the possibility of rebelling against Babylonian rule. In 589, when Hophra became pharaoh of Egypt, Zedekiah did rebel against Babylon (2 Kings 24:20). The Babylonians marched into Judah, and in 586, Jerusalem fell, the city and temple were destroyed, and many more Judeans were taken into exile.[37] To all of this, Jeremiah was a witness.

Jeremiah declares the end of one era and announces the beginning of another. The law of God given to Moses had decreed that violations of the covenant would result in the removal of God's blessings and the imposition of the sanctions of the covenant (Lev. 26; Deut. 28). Jeremiah's ministry both announces and witnesses the imposition of the final covenantal curse upon Judah, the curse of exile (Lev. 26:33; Deut. 28:24–68). Jeremiah, however, also bears witness to God's intense love for his people.[38] Judgment is not God's last word for Judah according to Jeremiah, and he consoles his readers with numerous prophecies of restoration and salvation beyond exile. He prophesies both the imminent death of Israel and her future resurrection.

Although the structure of the book of Jeremiah is not always easy to discern, a basic outline is clear. The book begins with a narrative of the

37. There is some debate over whether Jerusalem fell in 587 or 586. Provan, Long, and Longman (2003, 382 n. 12) cite an interesting discussion of the debate in Edwards 1992, 101–6. Thus although I refer to the date of the destruction of Jerusalem as 586 B.C. throughout the book, I am aware of the dispute.

38. Brueggemann 1998, 5.

prophet's call (ch. 1). This call narrative is followed by Jeremiah's early oracles exhorting Judah to repent (chs. 2–6). Jeremiah then condemns Judah's false worship and declares inevitable judgment (7–20). In the fourth section of the book, the prophet proclaims the failure of Judah's kings and prophets (21–25). The stubbornness of the people and inevitability of exile are the subject of the next major section of the book (26–36). Tucked within this major section is the so-called Book of Consolation (30–33). The fall of Judah is the subject of the sixth major section of the book (37–45). Finally, the book concludes with Jeremiah's oracles against the nations (46–51) and an appendix concerning the fall of Jerusalem (52).[39]

The Call Narrative (Jer. 1)

The prophet Jeremiah was the son of a priest from Anathoth, a city approximately two to three miles north of Jerusalem (1:1). To Jeremiah, "the word of Yahweh came in the days of Josiah the son of Amon, king of Judah, in the thirteenth year of his reign" (1:2). As noted above, there are some who argue that this is a reference to the date of Jeremiah's birth rather than to the date of his call.[40] However, despite the strong arguments that are made for the date-of-birth view, it requires a strained interpretation of this verse as well as others. It must be noted, for example, that the same words used to describe the call of Jeremiah here are also used to describe the call of several other prophets (e.g., Hos. 1:1; Mic. 1:1; Zeph. 1:1; Zech. 1:1). In each of these other cases, the words clearly refer to the date of the prophet's call. The fact that Jeremiah uses the same formulaic words provides a strong reason to interpret Jeremiah in the same way. In addition to having problems with 1:2, the date-of-birth interpretation is also unable

39. This outline is based on the Masoretic text of Jeremiah. The Masoretic text differs rather significantly from the LXX text. The LXX is much shorter (by approximately 2,700 words) and is arranged differently. The oracles against the nations, which are found at the end of the Masoretic text, are inserted after 25:13 in the LXX. The order of the individual oracles against the nations is also different. Fragments of Jeremiah found at Qumran have not solved the problem because some support the Masoretic text, while at least one supports the Hebrew text behind the LXX. There is no consensus at this time regarding the reason for the different versions. J. A. Dearman, however, has offered what seems to be the most likely explanation. He observes that after the fall of Jerusalem there were communities of Jews in Palestine, Babylon, and Egypt. These geographically diverse communities could explain the existence of the different manuscript traditions. As Dearman (2002, 19) explains, "Probably it goes back to the exilic communities who received and transmitted collections of Jeremiah's oracles that the prophet had delivered repeatedly in previous years."

40. See, for example, Holladay 1989, 25–26.

to explain adequately other passages in Jeremiah that speak of some of his prophetic work occurring during the reign of Josiah (3:6; 25:3).

The content of the prophetic call itself is found in 1:4–10 and is in the form of a dialogue. God declares that he has appointed Jeremiah to be "a prophet to the nations" (v. 5; cf. Rom. 11:13). Jeremiah's reluctance to accept the call is reminiscent of what happened with Moses (Ex. 4:10–17). The Lord, however, touches Jeremiah's mouth and says,

> Behold, I have put my words in your mouth.
> See, I have set you this day over nations and over kingdoms,
> to pluck up and to break down,
> to destroy and to overthrow,
> to build and to plant. (Jer. 1:9–10)

This statement is significant because these six verbs occur repeatedly throughout the book of Jeremiah at critical moments (12:14–16; 18:1–10; 24:6; 31:27–28, 38, 40; 42:10; 45:4).[41]

The dialogue between Jeremiah and Yahweh concludes with two visions (1:11–16).[42] First, Jeremiah sees an almond branch, and God says, "You have seen well, for I am watching over my word to perform it" (v. 12). The connection between God's statement and the vision is unclear in English translations. In the Hebrew, the connection is based on a wordplay with the words translated "almond" (*shaqed*) and "watching" (*shoqed*). In the second vision, Jeremiah sees "a boiling pot, facing away from the north" (v. 13). The Lord explains the meaning of this vision, "Out of the north disaster shall be let loose upon all the inhabitants of the land" (v. 14). The reference here is to the coming invasion of the land by the Babylonian armies. And what is the reason for this coming judgment? God's people have broken his covenant (vv. 15–16).

Oracles of Judgment and Exhortations to Repent (Jer. 2–6)

The oracles found in Jeremiah 1–25 explain the problems with Judah including her idolatry, externalism, and corruption. Most of these oracles were delivered during the reign of Jehoiakim (609–598). Chapters 2–6 are among Jeremiah's earliest oracles of judgment against Judah, and they focus

41. Robertson 2004, 270.

42. These visions are similar to those seen by other prophets (e.g., Amos 8:1–2).

on Judah's continual apostasy. The heart of the Lord's grievance against the people is succinctly stated in 2:7: "And I brought you into a plentiful land to enjoy its fruits and its good things. But when you came in, you defiled my land and made my heritage an abomination." Jack Lundbom explains, "Graciously he brought his people from a desert into the veritable garden land they now inhabit, reversing the tragedy of Eden, as it were, but they repaid the favor by making the place an unspeakable mess."[43] The problem is that Judah has forsaken God and polluted the land by going after idols (2:5, 8, 11, 13, 20, 23, 28).

In chapter 3, Jeremiah begins by comparing Judah's unfaithfulness to adultery (3:1–5) and calling Judah to repentance (3:6–4:4). Jeremiah then looks beyond the exile to a time of restoration when all nations shall be gathered to God (3:17). The Lord promises that Israel's repentance will have worldwide consequences:

> If you return, O Israel,
> declares Yahweh,
> to me you should return.
> If you remove your detestable things from my presence,
> and do not waver,
> and if you swear, "As Yahweh lives,"
> in truth, in justice, and in righteousness,
> then nations shall bless themselves in him,
> and in him shall they glory. (4:1–2)

This prophecy contains echoes of the words of the Abrahamic covenant in which blessings are promised to the nations (Gen. 12:3).

Chapter 4 continues with another oracle of judgment declaring again that judgment is coming from the north (Jer. 4:5–10). Jeremiah describes the coming devastation of Judah in cosmic terms (vv. 23–28). He writes, "I looked on the earth, and behold, it was without form and void . . ." (v. 23). The words translated "without form and void" are *tohu wabohu*, the same words used in Genesis 1:2. To Jeremiah, the coming devastation of Judah is of such significance that it is comparable to a return to the primeval

43. Lundbom 1999, 262.

chaos.[44] It can be described in terms of "de-creation."[45] Despite the extent and severity of the devastation, however, God will not make a full end of Judah (Jer. 4:27). There is hope that a remnant will survive.

In Jeremiah 5, the author uses imagery from the Genesis narrative of Sodom and Gomorrah to describe Jerusalem (Gen. 18:22–33). In Genesis, Abraham pleaded with the Lord, and God promised to spare Sodom and Gomorrah if only ten righteous people could be found. Now the Lord rhetorically asks Jeremiah whether there is even one righteous person in Jerusalem (5:1). Because Jerusalem has refused to repent, the Lord declares his judgment upon the city (5:14–31). Jeremiah declares that great destruction is coming from the north (6:1), and it is Yahweh himself who will fight against Jerusalem (6:2).

Condemnation of False Worship and Oracles of Judgment (Jer. 7–20)

Jeremiah 7:1–8:3 is a sermon given in the gate of the temple. For the sake of better understanding, it may be divided into five sections. In the first section (7:1–15), Jeremiah criticizes the people's superstitious view of the temple. The people believed that the presence of God's temple in the city guaranteed its inviolability. Jeremiah tells them, "Do not trust in these deceptive words: 'This is the temple of Yahweh, the temple of Yahweh, the temple of Yahweh'" (v. 4). Jeremiah warns them that the temple will be no protection if they continue in their violent and apostate ways (vv. 8–12). Using words that will be echoed years later by Jesus, the Lord condemns the way in which the people have profaned the temple, saying, "Has this house, which is called by my name, become a den of robbers in your eyes?" (v. 11; Matt. 21:13).

In the following section of the sermon, Jeremiah attacks the worship of the queen of heaven (7:16–20). This is a reference to the idolatrous worship of the Babylonian goddess Astarte.[46] Next, focusing on a theme that other prophets have addressed previously, Jeremiah indicts those who

44. Thompson 1980, 230.

45. This is important because later prophecies, including some in the New Testament, will also describe coming historical judgments in terms of cosmic de-creation. The application of such language to the sixth-century judgment of Judah makes it clear that this kind of imagery should not automatically be assumed to refer to the end of redemptive history.

46. Thompson 1980, 284.

have substituted ceremonialism for obedience (7:21–28; Amos 5:21–24; Hos. 6:6; Mic. 6:6–8; Isa. 1:11–14). In the fourth section of the sermon, Jeremiah condemns abominable practices, such as child sacrifice, which the people have done (7:29–34). Finally, Jeremiah condemns those who have worshiped the sun, moon, and stars (8:1–3). This sermon, then, focuses on the people's breaking of the first and most important commandment, the prohibition against the worship of other gods.

Jeremiah 8:4–10:25 is a collection of oracles focusing on Judah's stubborn rebellion and the inevitability of her coming judgment. In chapter 8, Jeremiah is scathing in his denunciation of Judah's treachery against God, and yet his grief for his people is deep (8:18–9:3). The Lord declares that Jerusalem will become "a heap of ruins" and the cities of Judah will become "a desolation" (9:11). Her judgment is due to the fact that she forsook the law of God (vv. 12–14). The people will, therefore, be scattered among the nations according to the stipulations of the covenant they have broken (v. 16; Lev. 26:33; Deut. 28:64). Israel's worship of powerless idols will result in exile (Jer. 10:1–25).

Jeremiah 11–15 contains a series of warnings as well as a declaration of judgment against Judah. The primary focus of chapter 11 is the broken covenant. Jeremiah makes several points. Those who break the covenant are cursed (vv. 1–5). Hearing the words of the covenant is not enough. The words must be obeyed (vv. 6–8). Finally, in spite of everything, the people are engaged in the same sins their fathers committed. They are going after other gods and serving them (vv. 9–13).[47] Because of their stubborn refusal to repent, Jeremiah is told not to pray for the people any longer (vv. 14–17). Intercession is now pointless.

Jeremiah's preaching resulted in a plot against his life, which he discovers (11:18–23). The men of Anathoth tell Jeremiah that if he continues to prophesy, they will kill him (v. 21). The Lord responds by declaring their coming judgment (vv. 22–23). In a section reminiscent of Habakkuk and even Job, Jeremiah complains to the Lord, "Why does the way of the wicked prosper? Why do all who are treacherous thrive?" (12:1; Job 21:7; Hab. 1:4, 13). The Lord's response to Jeremiah does not include a direct answer to his complaint (12:7–17). Instead, the Lord laments what has become of his inheritance Israel. Yet although they will experience exile, the Lord

47. Lundbom 1999, 625–26.

declares that he will again have compassion on them and restore them to the land (vv. 14–15).

Jeremiah 13 is a series of five warnings.[48] The first warning is a symbolic parable in which the people of Israel are compared to a ruined loincloth (13:1–11). The second warning compares God's people with earthenware jars (vv. 12–14). Just as the jars are filled with wine, so the people will be filled with the wrath of God and smashed. Jeremiah's third warning is a warning against the pride and arrogance that will bring destruction (vv. 15–17). The fourth warning is a lament for the king and the king's mother (vv. 18–19). Jeremiah's fifth and final warning reminds the people that shame and destruction will be the result of continued apostasy (vv. 20–27).

In chapter 14, Jeremiah intercedes with God during a time of severe drought. In spite of the drought, Judah has failed to repent, and Jeremiah prays for the people (vv. 1–6). He confesses their sins (vv. 7–9), but God forbids Jeremiah to intercede (vv. 11–12). Jeremiah attempts to place some of the blame on the false prophets (v. 13), but the Lord declares that both the people and the lying prophets will be judged (vv. 14–16). Finally, Jeremiah acknowledges Judah's wickedness and asks whether God has utterly rejected his people (vv. 17–22). God's final answer is that he will not relent from his purpose to judge Judah (15:1–9). Jeremiah's response is a lonely lament (vv. 10–21).

Chapters 16–20 contain additional sermons as well as symbolic personal actions. In chapter 16, Jeremiah is instructed not to take a wife (vv. 1–2). His life is a symbolic mirror of his oracles of judgment. His refusal to take a wife symbolizes Judah's future desolation. When the people ask why God has decreed such a horrible judgment, Jeremiah tells them that it is because they have forsaken the Lord (vv. 10–13). The coming judgment, however, will not be the end according to Jeremiah. The days are coming when the people will experience a new exodus, an exodus from exile that will make the exodus from Egypt pale in comparison (vv. 14–15). The result of this new exodus will be the turning of the nations to God (vv. 19–21).

After another oracle concerning Judah's sin and its dire consequences (ch. 17), Jeremiah tells the parable of the potter (18:1–12). This parable includes a passage that is important for the understanding of the nature

48. Harrison 1973, 98.

of biblical prophecy. Jeremiah is instructed by God to go to the potter's house (vv. 1–2). As Jeremiah watches, the potter remakes a spoiled vessel into a new vessel (v. 4). From this he learns that God, the divine potter, is dealing with a type of clay (Israel) that is resistant to his purposes. He also learns that God will sovereignly rework this clay (vv. 5–6).[49]

Following the assertion of God's sovereignty over the clay that he is working, the Lord makes the following declaration to Jeremiah:

> If at any time I declare concerning a nation or a kingdom, that I will pluck up and break down and destroy it, and if that nation, concerning which I have spoken, turns from its evil, I will relent of the disaster that I intended to do to it. And if at any time I declare concerning a nation or a kingdom that I will build and plant it, and if it does evil in my sight, not listening to my voice, then I will relent of the good that I had intended to do to it. (18:7–10)

This text provides significant insight into the nature of biblical prophecy. Its primary purpose is not the bare prediction of future events. Instead, as O. Palmer Robertson notes, its primary purpose is to lead to repentance.[50] This principle was dramatically illustrated in the book of Jonah when Nineveh's repentance averted the judgment that had been prophesied (Jonah 3:4, 8–10; cf. 2 Kings 20:1–6).[51] Now Judah is warned that her response to the prophetic word will have consequences.[52]

Jeremiah uses another symbolic parable to condemn Judah in chapter 19. He is commanded to purchase an earthenware flask and to proclaim judgment upon the people (vv. 1–9). The Lord then commands him to shatter the flask to symbolize the shattering judgment that is coming upon Judah (vv. 10–12). Jeremiah's words lead to his persecution. Pashhur the chief officer of the temple has him beaten and placed in the stocks (20:1–2). Upon his release, Jeremiah tells Pashhur that he too will suffer judgment from God (vv. 3–6). Having delivered God's word to the people, Jeremiah

49. Thompson 1980, 433.

50. Robertson 2004, 94.

51. Almost three hundred years ago, Jonathan Edwards (2005, 169) already observed this element of biblical prophecy, saying, "all threatenings of this nature had a condition implied in them according to God's known and declared manner." See also Calvin (1960, 1:227).

52. Brueggemann 1998, 168.

reveals his internal conflict over having to deliver such news to his own countrymen (vv. 7–18).

The Failure of Judah's Kings and Prophets (Jer. 21–25)

Most of the oracles up to this point were delivered during the reign of Jehoiakim. Chapters 21–36, however, are not in chronological order. Within this small section of the book, chapters 21–24 are dated near the end of the reign of Zedekiah (597–586), while chapter 25 is dated to 605, the fourth year of Jehoiakim's reign. The first chapter of this section, chapter 21, is an oracle delivered at a point in time during Zedekiah's reign when Babylon is warring against Jerusalem (vv. 1–2). In other words, this oracle was delivered after Nebuchadnezzar's invasion in 587, in the final months before Judah's destruction. Jeremiah tells the people that God will bring the Babylonians into the midst of the city (v. 4). In fact, the divine warrior himself will fight against his own people (v. 5). Finally, the Lord pronounces his sentence of judgment on the royal house (ch. 22).

Chapter 23 begins with the conclusion of Jeremiah's condemnation of Judah's kings (vv. 1–2). The Lord then promises that he will bring his people back and that he will set godly shepherds over them (vv. 3–4). Jeremiah then states, "Behold, the days are coming, declares Yahweh, when I will raise up for David a righteous Branch, and he shall reign as king and deal wisely, and shall execute justice and righteousness in the land. In his days Judah will be saved, and Israel will dwell securely. And this is the name by which he will be called: 'Yahweh is our righteousness'" (vv. 5–6). This prophecy echoes that of Isaiah 11:1–16. In both cases, the prophet tells of the coming of a righteous king from the line of David. Jeremiah is speaking here of the Messiah. The chapter ends with a lengthy oracle concerning the false prophets and their lying ways (Jer. 23:9–40).

The oracle found in chapter 24 was delivered before the oracles in chapters 21–23. It was delivered soon after the events of 597 B.C. when Nebuchadnezzar took Jehoiachin into exile (24:1). In the oracle, Jeremiah tells of his vision of the good and bad figs (vv. 2–3). The good figs are those Judeans who have been taken into exile (vv. 4–7). They will be restored and built up. The bad figs are those who remain in the land under King Zedekiah (vv. 8–10). They will suffer utter devastation by means of sword, famine, and pestilence.

Chapter 25 is dated to 605, the fourth year of Jehoiakim. It was during this year that Nebuchadnezzar led the Babylonians to victory at Carchemish. Judah then became a vassal state, and the first Judean deportees were taken to Babylon (2 Kings 24:1; Dan. 1:1–4). Jeremiah reminds the people that even after twenty-three years of prophesying, the people have failed to repent (25:3–7). Therefore the Lord will bring the Babylonians against Judah and the surrounding nations (vv. 8–10). Jerusalem will be devoted to destruction, the same fate suffered by the Canaanites who inhabited the land during the conquest (v. 9; Deut. 7:1–2). Jeremiah then declares, "these nations shall serve the king of Babylon seventy years" (25:11). After seventy years, Babylon herself will be judged (vv. 12–14).

The number seventy is likely a round number.[53] It is used, for example, in Psalm 90:10 to describe a full lifespan. In this passage, seventy is declared to be the number of years the nations will serve Babylon (cf. Jer. 29:10). Babylon's empire did in fact last approximately seventy years. If the starting point is taken to be the fall of Nineveh, then her empire lasted from 612 to 539, or seventy-three years. If the starting point is taken to be the Babylonian victory at Carchemich, then her empire lasted from 605 to 539, or sixty-six years. Jeremiah's prophecy, dated in the year 605, seems to favor the second option (i.e., 605–539). Not only was 605 the year in which Babylon gained control over the nations in and around Palestine, it was also the year in which the first Judeans were exiled to Babylon; thus it was the first year of Jerusalem's "desolations" (Dan. 9:2).

Exile and Restoration (Jer. 26–36)

Like the chapters in the preceding section, the chapters in this section of Jeremiah are not in chronological order. Chapter 26 is a narrative of events surrounding a sermon Jeremiah preached at the temple in the early years of Jehoiakim's reign (ca. 609–607). As a result of his preaching, Jeremiah was threatened with death (vv. 7–9). The following chapters (27–29) recount Jeremiah's conflict with the false prophets. Chapter 27 is a prophecy from 594 B.C., in the early years of Zedekiah's reign. In this prophecy, Jeremiah warns the people against forming a coalition against Babylon (27:1–11). They are instructed to submit to Babylonian rule.

53. Thompson 1980, 513; Harrison 1973, 126.

The events narrated in chapter 28 also occurred in 594 B.C. This chapter recounts Jeremiah's conflict with the false prophet Hananiah who was telling the people that God would remove the Babylonian yoke within two years (28:2–3, 11). Because he lied to the people in God's name, he suffered the penalty of death (vv. 15–17). Chapter 29 is a letter that Jeremiah wrote to those Judeans who had been sent into exile in 597. He encourages them to be fruitful, to pray for the city of Babylon because they will be in exile for many years to come (vv. 4–9). At the end of this time, God will bring them back and restore them to the land (v. 10).[54]

Commentators often refer to chapters 30–33 of Jeremiah as the Book of Consolation.[55] This section of the book has been given this name because, as J. A. Thompson explains, "it gives expression to hopes for the future rather than judgment which characterizes earlier chapters."[56] Earlier chapters of Jeremiah were not without occasional references to future restoration after the judgment of exile, but the theme was not prominent. Here the themes of restoration and hope move to the forefront and are developed extensively. This section of the book reaches its climax in Jeremiah's prophecy of a new covenant in chapter 31.

Although this section of Jeremiah has a unified theme, it comprises different literary genres. Chapters 30 and 31 are almost completely poetic, while chapters 32 and 33 are prose narrative. In chapter 30, the Lord assures the people that he will restore them to the land. Jeremiah writes, "For behold days are coming, declares Yahweh, when I will restore the fortunes of my people, Israel and Judah, says Yahweh, and I will bring them back to the land that I gave to their fathers, and they shall take possession of it" (30:3). The expression "days are coming" is fairly common among the prophets, and it simply refers to an unspecified future time (Isa. 39:6; Jer. 7:32; Amos 8:11; 9:13).[57] The Lord also promises to renew his covenant relationship, telling the people that in that day, "you shall be my people, and I will be your God" (Jer. 30:22).

Jeremiah 31 contains one of the most significant prophecies in the Old Testament, the promise of a new covenant (vv. 31–34). Jeremiah begins the chapter by describing Israel's captivity, using the imagery of the wilderness

54. Lundbom 2004a, 359.

55. Lundbom 2004a, 368; Thompson 1980, 551; Harrison 1973, 133.

56. Thompson 1980, 551.

57. Thompson 1980, 553.

wandering (31:1–6). He then celebrates the coming restoration of Israel to her homeland (vv. 7–14). Jeremiah uses the imagery of Rachel weeping for her children to describe the extreme grief caused by the exile (v. 15). But the promised restoration of Israel from exile means the end of Rachel's mourning (vv. 16–22). "There is hope for your future, declares Yahweh, and your children shall come back to their own country" (v. 17). Following another promise of restoration (31:23–26), Jeremiah speaks of the days to come, using the six verbs found in 1:10: "And it shall come to pass that as I have watched over them to pluck up and break down, to overthrow, destroy, and bring harm, so I will watch over them to build and to plant, declares Yahweh" (31:28).

One of the most fundamental teachings found within the preexilic prophets is that Israel has failed to keep God's covenant and that due to this failure to obey, judgment is coming. The history of Israel from the time of Moses onward is a history of almost continual disobedience and apostasy. Both Moses and Joshua had indicated that Israel was incapable of obeying God's law, and Israel had proven them correct (Deut. 31:16–18, 20–21; Josh. 24:19). Now exile is imminent, but God is promising restoration. If the covenant relationship is to be restored, how will this happen?

Isaiah had hinted at the prospects of a new covenant many times (Isa. 42:6; 49:8; 54:10; 55:1–5; 59:21; 61:1–9). Now Jeremiah brings the nature of this covenant into clearer focus in 31:31–34:

> Behold the days are coming, declares Yahweh, when I will make a new covenant with the house of Israel and the house of Judah, not like the covenant that I made with their fathers on the day when I took them by the hand to bring them out of the land of Egypt, my covenant that they broke, though I was their husband, declares Yahweh. But this is the covenant that I will make with the house of Israel after those days, declares Yahweh: I will put my law within them, and I will write it on their hearts. And I will be their God, and they shall be my people. And no longer shall each one teach his neighbor and each his brother, saying, "Know Yahweh," for they shall all know me, from the least of them to the greatest, declares Yahweh. For I will forgive their iniquity, and I will remember their sin no more.

As R. K. Harrison rightly observes, "The prophecy of Jeremiah marks a watershed in Hebrew religious and cultic life."[58]

58. Harrison 1973, 138.

Jeremiah places the inauguration of the new covenant at an unspecified time in the future: "the days are coming" (v. 31). All that is certain, in light of the context, is that it will not occur until after the time of exile. The *concept* of a "new covenant" is found elsewhere in the prophets (Ezek. 37:26). However, the specific *term* (*berit hadashah*) is found only here in the Old Testament. The need for this new covenant is evident. The covenant that was established at Sinai has been broken by Israel. It must, as O. Palmer Robertson explains, be superseded by another covenant.[59] This is precisely what the Lord promises to do. The covenant will be made with "the house of Israel and the house of Judah." In other words, a new covenant will be made with those who broke the old covenant.[60]

The emphasis in Jeremiah 31:32–33 is upon the discontinuity between the old covenant and the new covenant, but the discontinuity is not total. The Lord emphasizes discontinuity when he declares that the new covenant is "*not like* the covenant that I made with their fathers" (v. 32). Both discontinuity and continuity are evident in the next verse, "I will put my law within them, and I will write it on their hearts" (v. 33). Under the old covenant, the law was written on tablets of stone (Ex. 24:12; 34:1). Under the new covenant, the law will be written on the hearts of God's people. Herein lies one major element of discontinuity. Yet the continuity is evident in that it is "the law" that is written on the hearts of his people.[61] God himself will make the necessary changes within the hearts of his people (Deut. 30:6).[62]

Under the old covenant, the people had to be continually instructed to do the law and to remember the law (Deut. 4:23; 5:1, 32; 6:3, 12; 8:11; etc.). In Jeremiah 31:34, the Lord declares that with the law inscribed on the people's hearts, this will no longer be necessary because all will know the

59. Robertson 1980, 272; see also Dumbrell 1984, 164.

60. In our examination of the New Testament, the relationship between "Israel" and believing Gentiles will be explored in more detail. Here it is necessary to make only a few observations that will prepare for that discussion. First, it is evident from our reading of the history of God's people that any Gentile could become a part of "Israel" by confessing faith in Yahweh (e.g., Ruth). Gentiles could become "my people" and Jews could become "not my people" (Ex. 12:43–48; Hos. 1:9). However, although this is an important truth, it must also be remembered that in Jeremiah's day, at this stage in the progress of God's revelation, "Israel" was primarily understood as the ethnic community descended from Abraham, Isaac, and Jacob. "Israel" was a people distinguishable from the surrounding Gentile peoples, whether they were Assyrians, Egyptians, or Philistines. This is how Jeremiah uses the term here.

61. Robertson 1980, 281–82.

62. Thompson 1980, 581.

Lord. Finally, in one of the most profound promises involved with the new covenant, the Lord says, "I will forgive their iniquity, and I will remember their sin no more." Under the old covenant, provisions were made for the forgiveness of sin by means of the various sacrifices. But these sacrifices had to be constantly repeated, indicating that they had no inherent power within themselves to remove sin (Heb. 10:1–10). Under the new covenant, the shadows will be replaced by the reality, and God will not only "forgive their iniquity" but also "remember their sin no more."

Following the prophecy of the new covenant is a declaration of the inseparable bond between God and Israel. The permanence of God's relationship with Israel is compared to the permanence of the created order.

> Thus says Yahweh,
> who gives the sun for light by day
> and the fixed order of the moon and the stars for light by night,
> who stirs up the sea so that its waves roar—
> Yahweh of hosts is his name:
> "If this fixed order departs
> from before me, declares Yahweh,
> then shall the offspring of Israel cease
> from being a nation before me forever."
> Thus says Yahweh:
> "If the heavens above can be measured,
> and the foundations of the earth below can be explored,
> then I will cast off all the offspring of Israel
> for all that they have done,
> declares Yahweh." (Jer. 31:35–37)

This promise is noteworthy because it is stated in absolutely unconditional terms. For those facing the prospect of seventy years of exile, it is a source of great hope for the future of Israel.[63]

The remaining chapters of the Book of Consolation are prose narratives centered on Jeremiah's purchase of a field in Anathoth. The narrative is dated to the tenth year of Zedekiah (32:1). In other words, the events described in the narrative take place during Babylon's final siege of Jerusalem in 586 B.C. Jeremiah's purchase of the field is described in 32:1–15. The purchase

63. It is a hope that will also be echoed in the New Testament in the writings of the apostle Paul (Rom. 11:1, 28–29).

is a visible demonstration of Jeremiah's faith in God's promise of future restoration. The second half of the chapter is a dialogue between Jeremiah and Yahweh (vv. 16–44). The focus is upon the future that awaits God's people (vv. 36–40). Chapter 33 concludes the Book of Consolation with further promises regarding the restoration of Judah, including a restatement of the promises made to David (vv. 14–22; 2 Sam. 7:16).

Jeremiah 34–36 contains narratives of events that occurred during the reigns of Jehoiakim and Zedekiah. Chapter 34 contains a prophetic message given to Zedekiah during the final Babylonian siege of the city (vv. 1–7) as well as an account of events that occurred during a brief respite in the siege (vv. 8–22). The story recounted in chapter 35 about the righteous Rechabites occurred near the end of Jehoiakim's reign. In it, Jeremiah contrasts the righteousness of the Rechabites with the unrighteousness of Israel. Chapter 36 recounts Jeremiah's writing of the scroll containing all of the words that God had spoken to him. This event occurred in 605, the fourth year of Jehoiakim's reign (v. 1). After Jeremiah's scribe Baruch wrote the scroll (vv. 2–8), it was read to all the people (vv. 9–10). However, when it was read before Jehoiakim, the king had the scroll destroyed (vv. 11–26). Because of this, the Lord instructs Jeremiah to rewrite the scroll and to pronounce judgment upon Jehoiakim (vv. 27–32).

The Fall of Judah (Jer. 37–45)

The fall of Judah and its aftermath are the subject of the prophetic narrative in chapters 37–45. In chapter 37, Jeremiah warns Zedekiah that Egypt will not come to Judah's rescue. Jeremiah's arrest, imprisonment, and rescue are recounted in chapter 38, while chapter 39 describes the actual fall of Jerusalem to the Babylonians (cf. 2 Kings 25:1–12). After the fall of the city, Jeremiah himself remains in Judah under the Babylonian appointed governor Gedaliah (40:1–12). However, soon after the new governor's appointment, a plot is hatched to take his life (vv. 13–16), and he is assassinated (41:1–3).

Gedaliah's assassin Ishmael escapes, but those remaining fear Babylonian reprisal and consult Jeremiah to find out whether they should flee to Egypt (42:1–6). Jeremiah tells them that they will be blessed by God if they remain, and he warns them against fleeing (vv. 7–22). Despite Jeremiah's warning, the leaders of the survivors in Judah decide to go to Egypt, and they take Jeremiah with them (43:1–7). Their decision is, in effect, a symbolic reversal of the exodus. Chapter 44 contains an oracle of judgment against the people who fled to Egypt. Like their fathers, they are declared to be unrepentant idolators (vv. 15–19). This section of Jeremiah concludes with the record of a brief message given to Baruch during Jehoiakim's reign (45:1–5). He is instructed not to despair because he will survive the coming judgment of Judah.

Oracles against the Nations (Jer. 46–51)

The Lord had appointed Jeremiah to be a prophet to the nations (1:5), and like many of the other prophetic books, his book contains a collection of oracles directed against the nations surrounding Israel (46:1; Isa. 13–23; Ezek. 25–32; Amos 1:3–2:5). Chapter 46 contains Jeremiah's oracle against Egypt dated soon after the battle of Carchemish, a battle in which Egypt was defeated by the Babylonians. Jeremiah declares that Egypt will experience the day of the Lord, the day of God's vengeance (46:10; Deut. 32:34–42). The oracle against the Philistines in chapter 47 should probably be dated around 604, prior to Nebuchadnezzar's attack on Ashkelon, one of the nation's chief cities. Jeremiah's oracle against Moab is found in chapter 48, while chapter 49 contains his oracles against Ammon, Edom, Damascus, Kedar, Hazor, and Elam. In these oracles, it is significant that Jeremiah speaks of a restoration of the nations "in the latter days" (48:47; 49:39).

The lengthiest oracle is the oracle against Babylon found in chapters 50–51. The primary thrust of this oracle is that Babylon will be overthrown and the Israelites will be restored to their land.[64] Jeremiah declares that a nation will come against Babylon from the north (50:3). She will be utterly destroyed (51:1–11). The language Jeremiah uses echoes that of Isaiah when he writes, "Suddenly Babylon has fallen and been broken" (51:8; Isa. 21:9). The fulfillment of this prophecy would occur within a short period of time. Nebuchadnezzar died in 562, and was followed by Evil-Merodach who reigned over Babylon until his assassination in 560. Neriglissar reigned from 560 to 556. His son Labashi-Marduk reigned only a few months before being supplanted by Nabonidus (556–539). Babylon was finally overthrown by the Persian king Cyrus in 539.

64. Thompson 1980, 731.

Appendix: The Fall of Jerusalem (Jer. 52)

The final chapter of Jeremiah is very similar to 2 Kings 24:18–25:30.[65] It may have been added to the book by Jeremiah's scribe Baruch in order to testify that all of Jeremiah's prophecies concerning the fall of Judah had come to pass (see 51:64).[66] This would provide encouragement to the readers and hearers of the book to trust also in Jeremiah's prophecies concerning the future restoration of Israel. The release of Jehoiachin from prison in 561 B.C. provided a visible reminder that God was not finished with Israel (52:31–34). The same God who had brought judgment upon his people promised that he would soon judge the nation that had enslaved them and that he would bring them back and restore them to the land.

Lamentations

The book of Lamentations consists of five poems of lament traditionally ascribed to the prophet Jeremiah.[67] These poems were written soon after the destruction of Jerusalem and the temple in 586 B.C. In the Hebrew Bible, the book of Lamentations is found in the Writings. It is one of the five scrolls (Ruth, Song of Songs, Ecclesiastes, Lamentations, Esther), and it is read by Jews on the ninth of Ab. According to Jewish tradition, this is the day on which the temple was destroyed. In the Septuagint and in the Protestant canon, the book of Lamentations is included among the prophetic books immediately following Jeremiah.

The historical context of the book of Lamentations is the destruction of Jerusalem and the temple by the armies of Babylon and the deportation of the people into exile. This was, by far, the most devastating event in the history of Israel to this point. For those who survived, "It was as if all the covenant promises, all the past deliverances, all the stories of Yahweh's intervention on behalf of his people, had gone up in smoke."[68] The overarching theme of the book is the grief of the survivors. For those who wondered whether the destruction occurred in spite of God's covenant with Israel, Lamentations reminds them that the judgment occurred because of the

65. It does not include, however, the material found in 2 Kings 25:22–26, the narrative about Gedaliah's assassination.

66. VanGemeren 1990, 294.

67. Dillard and Longman 1994, 304. The book itself is anonymous and does not indicate the name of its author.

68. *NIDOTTE*, 4:885.

covenant (Deut. 28:15, 49–50). However, although grief is the primary theme of Lamentations, the book is not without expressions of hope.

The five poems in the book of Lamentations, corresponding to the five chapters in the book, follow an acrostic structure. Chapters 1, 2, 4, and 5 each contain twenty-two stanzas corresponding to the twenty-two letters of the Hebrew alphabet. In chapters 1 and 2 (containing three-line stanzas), and in chapter 4 (containing two-line stanzas), the first word of each stanza begins with the next letter of the alphabet. In other words, the first word of the first stanza begins with the Hebrew letter alef, the first word of the second stanza begins with the letter bet, and so forth. Like chapters 1 and 2, chapter 3 also contains three-line stanzas, but in chapter 3 all three lines in each stanza begin with the necessary letter of the alphabet. Thus all three lines in the first stanza of chapter 3 begin with the letter alef, and all three lines in the second stanza begin with bet. Interestingly, although the stanzas of chapter 5 do not follow the acrostic structure, the poem does consist of twenty-two stanzas.

In order to understand the basic themes of the poems in the book of Lamentations, it is necessary to understand that Lamentations is an example of lyric poetry. Such poetry is not structured in the same way that other genres are structured. There is no plot structure as there is in narrative. It is not structured along the lines of a systematic logical argument. Instead, it is paratactic. Various words and images are placed side by side without coordinating or subordinating connectives.[69] It is also highly metaphorical. In other words, it uses figurative rather than literal language to communicate the truth.

The theme of Lamentations 1 is the desolation and isolation of Jerusalem, a city with none to comfort her (1:2, 9, 16, 17, 21). The poet laments, "How lonely sits the city that was full of people! How like a widow has she become" (1:1). Lamentations 2 focuses on the anger of the Lord. The divine warrior who once fought on behalf of Israel has now fought against her (2:4–5). He has done exactly what he promised that he would do if Israel persisted in apostasy (v. 17). Chapter 3 continues the lament, but in this chapter the first signs of hope appear (v. 21). The poet appeals to the love and mercy of God, placing hope in him (vv. 22–24). He will wait on God because God "will not cast off forever" (v. 31). Chapter 4 focuses

69. See Dobbs-Allsopp 2002, 12–13.

on the guilt of Israel's leaders, while chapter 5 turns again to hope for the future. The book concludes with the prayer:

> Restore us to yourself, O Yahweh, that we may be restored!
>   Renew our days as of old—
> unless you have utterly rejected us,
>   and you remain exceedingly angry with us. (5:21–22)

Summary

The prophets of the late seventh century ministered to the people during a period of intense political and spiritual turmoil. On the international scene, the Assyrian Empire was declining while the Babylonians were gaining power. In Palestine, aside from a brief period of reformation under Josiah, Judah was sliding deeper and deeper into idolatry and apostasy. Moses had warned the people that their covenant with God required obedience and that disobedience would lead to the imposition of curses rather than blessings. If apostasy persisted, God would send the people into exile. The northern kingdom of Israel had already suffered this fate, but Judah was failing to learn from what had happened. The Lord, therefore, sent prophets to the people to warn them of the consequences of such disobedience and to call them to repentance.

Assyria had been used of God as an instrument to bring judgment upon Israel. However, Assyria itself was profoundly wicked and would not go unpunished. The prophet Nahum foretold the destruction of Assyria's capital city of Nineveh, destruction that occurred in 612 B.C. This destruction dramatically prefigures the eschatological destruction of all of God's enemies. The divine judgments upon the wicked nations are acts of divine judgment against the kingdom of evil. They look forward to the full establishment of the kingdom of God and the overthrow of all of God's enemies.

Zephaniah prophesied during the reign of Josiah, the last godly king of Judah. He warned the people that the day of the Lord was going to come upon Judah, and that it would be a day of terrible judgment. The curses of the covenant would be poured out upon the people just as Moses had warned. However, in spite of the fact that great judgment was coming, all hope was not completely lost. A remnant would remain, a remnant that God would purify for himself, a beloved remnant over whom he would rejoice.

During the reign of Jehoiakim, the prophet Habakkuk found himself faced with a troubling question. Yes, his people were wicked, but why was God using the Babylonians, an even more wicked people, as the instrument of judgment? God informs Habakkuk that the Babylonians themselves will be judged soon enough. Their kingdom, like all human kingdoms, will fall. The kingdom of God, on the other hand, will fill the earth. Upon hearing the message of the prophet, the wicked will be puffed up in their pride and arrogance, but the righteous will live by faith. Judgment is coming at the hands of the Babylonians, but the faithful among the people are to rejoice and trust in God.

If Joel's prophecy is properly dated in the late preexilic period, then his message was a final appeal to the people of Judah. With the hammer of judgment about to fall, Joel warned that the day of the Lord was near, and that unless the people repented, they would be destroyed. He used a contemporary crisis (either a literal locust plague or one of Babylon's early incursions into the land) to warn the people of worse to come. Yet, like the other prophets, Joel did not end on a note of despair. He too looks forward to a time of restoration. He looks forward to a time when God's Spirit will be poured out upon all of the people, a time when the enemies of God's people will be judged and they themselves will live securely in the presence of God.

The prophetic ministry of Jeremiah began during the reign of Josiah, and it lasted until soon after the destruction of Jerusalem. Jeremiah announces the end of a significant era in redemptive history and the beginning of another. His early prophecies urge the people to repent, but when they stubbornly refuse, he warns them that the final curse of the covenant will soon be imposed. The city will be destroyed, and they will be taken into exile. There will be a remnant, however, whom God will bring back to the land. Most significantly, Jeremiah announces God's intention to establish a new covenant with Israel and Judah. It is such promises of hope that will sustain the faithful remnant after the horrors of 586 B.C.

8

The Exilic Prophets

Obadiah, Ezekiel, and Daniel

In 586 B.C., approximately 135 years after the fall of the northern kingdom of Israel to Assyria, the southern kingdom of Judah fell to Babylon. The Babylonians had already taken some Judeans into captivity in 605 during the reign of Jehoiakim (Dan. 1:1–4). A second deportation had occurred in 597 during the reign of Jehoiachin (2 Kings 24:10–17). The final major deportation occurred, however, at the time of the fall and destruction of Jerusalem in 586 (2 Kings 25:11–12). The destruction of Jerusalem and the exile of the sixth century were the greatest calamities to befall the descendants of Jacob. It was the death of Israel, and it was into this situation that the prophets of the exile were called. The earlier prophets had warned of impending judgment, but they also bore witness to future restoration. The prophets of the exile turned their focus more and more toward the future. They declared to the exiled remnant that God continued to have a purpose for Israel.

Obadiah

Before turning to the major exilic prophets Ezekiel and Daniel, a few words concerning Obadiah are necessary. The book of Obadiah, the shortest in the Old Testament, is a brief oracle against the nation of Edom. Its date is uncertain. Scholars have proposed dates ranging from the ninth century to the postexilic period. Two possible dates, however, receive the most support. Some scholars date Obadiah in the ninth century during the reign of Jehoram (848–841).[1] Others date Obadiah in the early exilic period (ca. 585–580).[2] The ninth-century date is based on biblical narratives concerning an Edomite revolt during the reign of Jehoram (2 Chron. 21:8–20). The exilic date is based on biblical passages regarding the actions of the Edomites toward Judah during and after her destruction by the Babylonians (Lam. 4:21–22; Ezek. 25:12–14; 35:5, 12–15).[3] When all the evidence is examined, an early exilic date seems to provide the most likely context for Obadiah's prophecy.

The land of Edom was located southeast of the Dead Sea and was also known as Seir. The Edomites themselves were descendants of Esau, the brother of Jacob (Gen. 32:3; 36:1, 9). A long history of conflict between Israel and Edom existed by the time of Obadiah. It was a history of conquest, rebellion, and reconquest (Num. 20:14–21; 1 Sam. 14:47; 1 Kings 9:26–28; 2 Chron. 21:8–10; 25:11–12; 28:17). In the wake of the Babylonian destruction of Jerusalem, the Edomites seized Judean lands. As a result of this, the prophet Obadiah brings God's word of judgment against Edom. Like all oracles against the nations, Obadiah's prophecy indicates that God rules over all nations. Edom represents all nations that are hostile to God and to his kingdom.[4] Such nations will always be judged.

Obadiah declares that Edom will be made an insignificant nation because of her pride (vv. 2–4). Those who plunder Edom will leave nothing behind (vv. 5–7). Even her renowned wisdom will be taken away (vv. 8–9). Edom is being punished because of the violence she committed against Judah and her failure to aid the desperate Judeans (vv. 10–11). Rather than assisting Judah, Edom instead joined the plunderers (v. 11). Edom is therefore warned not to gloat over Judah (v. 12). Obadiah declares that the day of the Lord is

1. E.g., Young 1964, 260; Niehaus 1993, 499.
2. E.g., Stuart 1987, 404.
3. See Bruce 1963, 92.
4. VanGemeren 1990, 143.

near upon all the nations and that Edom will be judged according to how she treated Judah (vv. 15–16). Obadiah concludes his oracle by contrasting the message of judgment given to Edom with a message of restoration given to Israel (vv. 17–21). That which Israel lost through disobedience, she will regain by grace.[5]

Ezekiel

Like Jeremiah, Ezekiel ministered in the years immediately preceding and immediately following the fall of Jerusalem in 586. However, unlike Jeremiah, who remained in Judah, Ezekiel ministered primarily to the exiles in Babylon. Ezekiel, a priest of the Jerusalem temple, was one of the many Judeans taken to Babylon in the deportation of 597 (Ezek. 1:1–3; 2 Kings 24:8–17). His prophetic call came only a few years after his deportation, and the prophetic oracles within his book can be dated between 593 and 571 B.C.[6]

As we have seen, the destruction of Jerusalem and the exile of the people were devastating events. The people of Israel had assumed that the presence of the temple and the promises of the covenant guaranteed God's perpetual favor and their perpetual residence within the land. They had forgotten that the covenant also contained warnings about what would happen if they broke its stipulations. The ultimate punishment would be exile (Lev. 26:33; Deut. 28:63–65). This ultimate punishment was now upon them. Ezekiel's primary purpose, therefore, is to give hope to the exiles.[7] Ezekiel wants to do this by transforming the people's understanding of God. He desires that they know the true nature of Yahweh and respond accordingly.[8]

Ezekiel handles the themes of exile and restoration by focusing in particular upon the glory of God. The beginning of the exile is represented by a vision of the departure of the glory of God from the Jerusalem temple (ch. 10). Likewise, Ezekiel's vision of future restoration climaxes with the return of God's glory to the temple (ch. 43).[9] The book of Ezekiel emphasizes

5. Niehaus 1993, 538.

6. Greenberg 1983, 12.

7. Stevenson 1996, 163.

8. Note the repeated use of the phrase "then they will know that I am Yahweh" (e.g., Ezek. 6:14). Within the book of Ezekiel, "the recognition formula with *yada'*, 'to know' occurs 54 times in its pure form, and an additional 18 times in expanded form" (Block 1997, 39).

9. Cf. Robertson 2004, 291.

the exiles' future hope throughout. This future hope has many features. There will be a new exodus, in which the people will be regathered from the nations (11:16–17; 34:11–13). The people will be brought back to a cleansed land (11:17–18). God will make a new covenant with his people (36:25–28). He will restore the Davidic dynasty (37:22–25). Israel will be blessed and secure (34:25–29). Most importantly, God will reestablish his presence in Israel (40–48).[10] All of these things are written that the exiles might not despair in their present situation.

The meanings of most of the prophecies contained in the books of the preexilic prophets are relatively noncontroversial. The same cannot be said for many of the prophecies in the book of Ezekiel.[11] The latter chapters in particular contain prophecies the interpretations of which are highly disputed. Among conservative scholars, much of the debate hinges on whether these prophecies are understood to be using literal or figurative language.[12] Each of these controversial prophecies will be discussed in more detail below.

The book of Ezekiel as a whole has a relatively uncomplicated structure. Following the account of Ezekiel's call and commission in chapters 1–3, the book is divided into three main sections. Chapters 4–24 contain oracles of judgment against Judah delivered prior to Jerusalem's fall. Chapters 25–32 contain oracles of judgment against the nations that have persecuted and oppressed Israel and Judah. Finally, chapters 33–48 contain prophecies of future restoration delivered to the people after the fall of Jerusalem.

Ezekiel's Call and Commission (Ezek. 1–3)

The narrative of Ezekiel's call and commission to the prophetic ministry is found in chapters 1–3. This call, in which Ezekiel is confronted with the glory of God, is foundational to all that follows.[13] The record of Ezekiel's call begins with a superscription (1:1–3) that reveals precisely when it happened. According to Ezekiel, it occurred on the fifth day of the fourth

10. *NIDOTTE*, 4:625.

11. They are controversial because they are difficult. In fact, Ezekiel was considered so difficult by the rabbis that they restricted the reading of some sections to those over the age of thirty (see Tuell 1992, 2).

12. For an introductory discussion of the issues involved in the interpretation of prophecy, see chapter 5.

13. See Zimmerli 1979, 139.

month in the fifth year of Jehoiachin's exile. This date reference has been established as July 31, 593 B.C.[14]

Ezekiel's initial vision of God is recorded in 1:4–28. The vision is overwhelming to the prophet, and Ezekiel's account of what he saw reflects its almost indescribable nature.[15] He sees four living creatures, each having four faces and four wings (vv. 5–14). Beside each of the creatures, he sees wheels within wheels with rims full of "eyes" (vv. 15–21).[16] Above the creatures, he sees a platform and a glorious throne (vv. 22–25). Seated on the throne, he sees "a likeness with a human appearance" surrounded in brightness (vv. 26–27). Upon seeing this vision of God, Ezekiel falls on his face and hears God's voice (v. 28).

Ezekiel's commission is found in 2:1–3:11. He is sent to the rebellious people of Israel and is instructed to speak God's word to them whether they listen or not (2:3–7). Ezekiel then sees a vision of a scroll, which he is instructed to eat (2:8–3:3).[17] Ezekiel is instructed to go to the exiles and speak all that God tells him to speak (3:4–11). The commissioning of Ezekiel so overwhelms him that he sits speechless for seven days (3:12–15). After seven days, however, the Lord instructs Ezekiel again, commanding him to be a watchman for Israel and to speak whatever word from God he is given (3:16–21; see also 33:1–9). Finally, the Lord appears to Ezekiel informing him that he will be mute except when God gives him a word to deliver to the people (3:22–27).

Oracles of Judgment against Judah (Ezek. 4–24)

The first major section of Ezekiel is a collection of oracles, visions, and prophetic "sign acts" delivered in the years leading up to the fall of Jerusalem. They are all messages of judgment against Judah intended to remove the people's false sense of security. The section begins with a dramatic sign-act portraying the judgment to come. In chapter 4, Ezekiel is commanded to enact the siege of Jerusalem. He is told to lie on his left side for 390 days to "bear the punishment of the house of Israel," and he is told that the

14. Block 1997, 87. The reference in verse 1 to the "thirtieth year" has caused some confusion, but it is likely a reference to Ezekiel's age at the time of his calling (Taylor 1969, 52–53; Block 1997, 82).

15. A similar description of the glory of God is found in Psalm 18:7–15.

16. The word translated "eyes" may mean "eye-shaped pebbles" (Block 1997, 100).

17. Cf. Rev. 10:8–11.

390 days are "equal to the number of years of their punishment" (v. 5). Ezekiel is also commanded to lie on his right side for 40 days to "bear the punishment of the house of Judah" (v. 6).

Commentators have offered a wide variety of interpretations of this passage, a fact that illustrates its inherent difficulty.[18] One possible clue to its interpretation may be found in the similarity between verse 6 and Numbers 14:34. The text in Numbers is found in the narrative of God's judgment of Israel after the spies had convinced the people that they could not conquer the inhabitants of the Promised Land. In verse 34, God delivers his judgment: "According to the number of the days in which you spied out the land, forty days, a year for each day, you shall bear your iniquity forty years, and you shall know my displeasure." As in Ezekiel 4:6, there is a correspondence between forty days and forty years of judgment. Both passages speak of bearing "punishment" or "iniquity."[19] Both verses also contain the phrase *'arba'im yom yom lashanah yom lashanah*, which is literally: "forty days, a day for the year, a day for the year." Numbers 14:34 is the only other passage in the Hebrew Old Testament containing this exact phrase. It seems very likely, therefore, that Ezekiel is consciously alluding to it.

If Ezekiel is consciously alluding to the passage in Numbers, it appears he is saying that the judgment that is about to come upon his generation will be like the judgment that fell upon the exodus generation. The forty years of wandering in the wilderness removed that wicked generation and paved the way for a new generation to enter the land. In the same way, the exile will mark a turning point that sees the end of one generation and the emergence of another that will (re)enter the land.

If the 40 days/40 years judgment is a conscious allusion to the wilderness wandering, what is the meaning of the 390 days/390 years of punishment or iniquity?[20] Unlike the reference to 40 years, there is no other passage in the

18. In addition to the inherent difficulties connected with understanding the chronology, textual variants compound the problems even further. The LXX reads "190" rather than "390" in verses 5 and 9, and it inserts the number "150" in verse 4.

19. The word עָוֺן (*'awon*), which is translated "iniquity" in Numbers 14:34, is the same word translated "punishment" in Ezekiel 4:6.

20. There is a wide diversity of opinion among commentators. Assuming that the Masoretic text is correct, most calculate 390 years forward or backward from 586 B.C. in an attempt to demarcate a 390-year period of time with a significant beginning and ending point. The problem is that there is no agreement in identifying a significant event either 390 years prior to 586 or 390 years after 586. The LXX reading (190) is no more successful in pointing to a significant date. It may be that

Old Testament that speaks of a 390-year or 390-day period of judgment. A possible explanation for the number 390 may be found when we recall that Ezekiel was to lie on one side for 390 days and then on the other side for 40 days (4:6). This means that the total number of days he was to lie down was 430 days, corresponding to a total of 430 years of judgment. While there is no other Old Testament text that speaks of a 390-year or 390-day period of time, there is a passage that speaks of a significant 430-year period of time. In Exodus 12:40–41, the passage describing the beginning of the exodus, we learn that the Israelites had lived in Egypt for 430 years.

Perhaps when Ezekiel spoke of the 390 days/years first (4:5), his original audience was as puzzled as his modern audience. Then when he spoke of 40 days/years in the language of Numbers 14, his audience would have recognized the allusion to the wilderness generation. If they put two and two together (or more precisely, put 390 and 40 together), they may also have recognized an echo of Exodus 12. The reference to 40 years would be telling them that they were about to experience a judgment much like that of the wilderness generation. The combined reference to 430 years would be telling them that this time of judgment was going to be like their years of affliction in Egypt—long and difficult.[21] It would, however, also invite hope of a new exodus and a new entry into the Promised Land.[22]

Ezekiel is instructed next to perform two further sign-acts indicating that the siege of Jerusalem, the destruction of the city, and the deportation of its inhabitants are coming. First, he is to eat unclean food (Ezek. 4:9–17).

---

586 is an incorrect reference point. Ezekiel tends to date his prophecies in relation to the date of Jehoiachin's exile in 597. Unfortunately, calculating 390 years forward or backward from 597 B.C. also fails to provide a period of time with an obviously significant beginning and ending point. An additional problem is that some of those who seek a literal 390- (or 190-) year period take the 40 years to be symbolic of the time of the exile. Yet the exile lasted much longer than 40 years. Also, there does not seem to be any adequate reason for taking 390 literally while taking 40 to be symbolic of a period longer than 40 years. Some suggest that the number 390 is a round number, but this is not really any more helpful because 390 is not an obviously round number in this context. Why 390 and not 400?

21. Obviously, the possible interpretation I have suggested takes the numbers in the passage to be symbolic. This seems to be more consistent, however, than taking one to be symbolic and the other to be literal. Consistency would seem to require that all of the numbers in these verses are to be understood either literally or symbolically. A literal understanding of the numbers is not absolutely ruled out, but given the fact that after more than two thousand years of effort among both Jews and Christians, there is still no consensus whatsoever on what literal 390- and 40-year periods of time are referenced, a symbolic interpretation of the numbers should be considered as a possibility.

22. Cf. Duguid 1999, 91.

Then he is to cut and divide his hair, burning one third, cutting one third with a sword, and scattering one third to the wind. These actions indicate the fate of the population (5:1–4). Ezekiel's description of the fate of the people indicates that they will suffer the curses of the covenant (5:5–17; Lev. 26:17–39). Ultimately, a third of the population will die of pestilence and famine; a third will fall by the sword; and a third will be deported (Ezek. 5:12). Ezekiel declares that God's coming judgment upon Jerusalem is due to idolatry (ch. 6), but the destruction will not be total. A remnant will escape (6:8–10). This coming destruction is expressed in terms of the imminence of the coming day of the Lord (7:1–27; cf. Zeph. 1:7–18). For Israel, the end has come (7:1–2; cf. Gen. 6:13; Jer. 51:13).

The vision of Ezekiel 8–11 is a unified whole focusing on the Jerusalem temple.[23] In this vision, Ezekiel learns about the abominations occurring in the temple back in Jerusalem. Ezekiel 8:1–4 serves as an introduction to the vision. It occurred in "the sixth year, in the sixth month, on the fifth day of the month" (8:1), or September 18, 592 B.C.[24] The abominations occurring in the temple are outlined in 8:5–18. Ezekiel sees an idolatrous statue in the temple (vv. 5–6), seventy Jewish elders worshiping images on the interior walls of the temple (vv. 7–13), women weeping for Tammuz (vv. 14–15),[25] and men worshiping the sun (vv. 16–18).

Ezekiel 9 concerns Yahweh's response to the idolatry occurring in the temple precincts. The Lord brings forth executioners as well as a scribe who is instructed to go through the city and place a mark on the foreheads of faithful Israelites (vv. 1–4; cf. Rev. 7:2–3).[26] The executioners are then instructed to kill any found without the mark on their forehead (Ezek. 9:5–7). After the executioners complete their task, Ezekiel sees Jerusalem burned, and he sees the glory of God depart from the temple (ch. 10). He then watches as Yahweh pronounces judgment upon those who have given wicked counsel to the inhabitants of Jerusalem (11:1–13). The vision con-

23. Duguid 1999, 130.

24. Block 1997, 278.

25. As Duguid (1999, 133) explains, "Weeping for Tammuz was a Babylonian ritual, marking the death and descent into the underworld of the god Dumuzi."

26. The Hebrew text indicates that the foreheads of the faithful are to be marked with the letter taw, the last letter of the Hebrew alphabet. "In the archaic cursive script it had the shape of an X or a cross, a form that remained essentially unchanged from the early stages of the evolution of the alphabet until the adoption of the square Aramaic script" (Block 1997, 307; see also 310–14). Also see GKC, "Table of Alphabets."

cludes with a declaration of good news (vv. 14–21). God declares that he himself has been a "sanctuary" for those in exile (v. 16).[27] As Daniel Block explains, "Here Yahweh promises to be for the exiles what the temple has heretofore been for them in Jerusalem."[28] God also promises that he will give the people a new spirit and a new heart (v. 19).

Ezekiel 12–24 contains a varied assortment of prophecies. Within these chapters there are, for example, dramatic sign-acts, disputation oracles, woe oracles, covenant lawsuits, parabolic prophecies, and lamentations. Ezekiel 12 begins with a sign-act depicting the coming exile (vv. 1–16) and another depicting horrible fear (vv. 17–20). Ezekiel then addresses scoffers who say that the fulfillment of these prophecies will not occur for a long time. He informs them that the fulfillment will, in fact, be very soon (vv. 21–28). In chapter 13, Ezekiel condemns the false prophets, while in chapter 14 he condemns the idolatrous elders, telling them that judgment is now unavoidable (v. 14).[29] He tells them that the curses of the covenant are about to fall upon Jerusalem (14:12–23) because Jerusalem has become as useless as wood from a vine (15:1–8).

In chapter 16, Ezekiel issues a scathing condemnation of Jerusalem. After tracing the people's spiritual history, Ezekiel uses intensely graphic and deliberately shocking language to compare the city to an adulterous wife. The language symbolizes Jerusalem's choice to trust in foreign alliances rather than in the Lord. Ezekiel repeatedly refers to Jerusalem as a whore (vv. 15, 16, 17, 26, 28, 34, 41). He declares that Jerusalem has been worse than a prostitute because prostitutes receive money from men in exchange for sexual intercourse, whereas Jerusalem is a whore who has paid men to fornicate with her (vv. 30–34). Because of her sinful acts, Jerusalem is sentenced to death (vv. 35–43) just as Israel had been sentenced to death a century before (vv. 44–52). Amazingly, this most scathing of condemnations concludes with an oracle of blessing. Jerusalem will be

27. The Hebrew word translated "sanctuary" is מִקְדָּשׁ (*miqdash*). It is the word used elsewhere in the Old Testament for the place where the Israelites worshiped the Lord. It is used, for example, to refer to the tabernacle (Ex. 25:8), Solomon's temple (1 Chron. 22:19), and the second temple (Neh. 10:39).

28. Block 1997, 349.

29. Traditionally, the Daniel of Ezekiel 14:14 has been identified with the biblical Daniel. More recently, scholars have argued that the Daniel here is a heroic figure from Ugaritic history known as Danel. There is no compelling reason, however, to reject the traditional interpretation. For a discussion of the issues, see Block 1997, 447–50.

restored, and God will establish his covenant once again with the people (vv. 53–63).

Block describes the content of chapters 17–22 as "messages of sin and retribution."[30] Chapter 17 is a parable about Zedekiah's treacherous rebellion against Nebuchadnezzar. His treachery is the immediate cause of Babylon's march on Jerusalem. Chapter 18 expounds upon the justice of God. The Lord promises that sons shall not suffer for the iniquity of their fathers, nor fathers for the iniquity of their sons (cf. Deut. 24:16). The righteous son of a wicked father will live, but the wicked son of a righteous father will be condemned. This chapter is a warning to those who are presumptuous toward God, and it is a message of hope to those who might despair.

Ezekiel 19 is a lament for the Davidic dynasty, which has become a caged lion (v. 9; cf. Gen. 49:8–9). In chapter 20, Ezekiel recounts the history of Israel as a history of continual apostasy. Rebellion and apostasy characterized Israel's distant past (vv. 5–26), and her recent past (vv. 27–31). In the future, however, there will be a new exodus, and Israel will be transformed (vv. 32–44). In chapter 21, Ezekiel returns to the theme of judgment, declaring that Nebuchadnezzar is the instrument God will use to judge Jerusalem. Chapter 22 announces that the day of judgment for Jerusalem is imminent.

The graphic and shocking language of chapter 16 is raised to a new level in chapter 23, an allegorical covenant lawsuit against Judah. In verses 2–35, Ezekiel explains the crimes of the sisters Oholah (Israel) and Oholibah (Judah). The declaration of judgment is then found in verses 36–49. The graphic nature of the language is intended to shock the original audience out of their apathy and pride.[31] The final prophecy of this section contains the word of the Lord that came to Ezekiel in "the ninth year, in the tenth month, on the tenth day of the month" (24:1; 2 Kings 25:1), or January 5, 587.[32] This prophecy is the final word of judgment to the city of Jerusalem. The city's final end is now in sight (Ezek. 24:25–27).

Oracles of Judgment against the Nations (Ezek. 25–32)

Like almost all of the prophetic books, the book of Ezekiel contains a series of judgment oracles against various foreign nations. In the book of

30. Block 1997, 522.
31. Zimmerli 1979, 489.
32. Block 1997, 773.

Ezekiel, these oracles are located after the oracles of judgment against Judah and before the oracles of blessing for Judah. They serve as more than a transition, however, for all of the nations addressed are the enemies of God's covenant people, and oracles of judgment directed against the enemies of God's people are implicitly messages of hope for God's people.[33] The two most extensive oracles against the nations are against Tyre and Egypt. The reason, as Walther Zimmerli notes, is likely due to the fact that in 587 these were the only two nations, aside from Judah, that were in rebellion against Babylon.[34] Because Babylon was God's chosen instrument of judgment, any nation that resisted would be punished.

This section begins with a series of brief oracles against the nations of Ammon, Moab, Seir, Edom, and Philistia (ch. 25). The lengthy oracle of judgment against Tyre is found in Ezekiel 26:1–28:19. In this oracle, Tyre is condemned to the underworld, or place of the dead (26:20). Chapter 27 is a lament for Tyre, the great city that has fallen.[35] The oracle against Tyre concludes with a declaration of judgment against the "prince of Tyre" (28:1–19). This king has claimed to be divine (v. 2). For his arrogance he will be thrust down into the pit (v. 8).

In the lament over the prince of Tyre (vv. 11–19), some interpreters have seen a veiled reference to the fall of Satan.[36] The Lord says of the prince, "You were in Eden" (v. 13), "an anointed guardian cherub" (v. 14), "blameless in your ways . . . till unrighteousness was found in you" (v. 15), "you were filled with violence . . . and you sinned" (v. 16a). For this reason God cast the prince "as a profane thing from the mountain of God" (v. 16b). Is such language a description of the sin and fall of Satan? While such an interpretation is not necessarily impossible, it must be remembered that the context of this lament is a prophetic oracle against the historical city of Tyre, and the lament is specifically addressed to the "king of Tyre" (v. 12). The nature of prophetic language must also be remembered. Hebrew prophecy often contains hyperbole and other figurative language. In the immediately preceding context of chapter 27, for example, Ezekiel has already described Tyre as a merchant ship, and this is certainly not a claim that the city of Tyre is a literal boat. The poetic language seems

33. Block 1998, 4.
34. Zimmerli 1983, 24.
35. Cf. vv. 30–33 and Rev. 18:15–19.
36. Chafer 1948, 2:39–44; Ryrie 1986, 141–42.

to indicate that the pride and sin of the prince of Tyre echo the story of man's primeval fall.[37]

Following a brief oracle against Sidon (28:20–24) and a promise that God's people will experience a new exodus (28:25–26), is a lengthy collection of oracles against Egypt and Pharaoh (chs. 29–32). These oracles are not presented in chronological order. The first oracle, dated January 7, 587, is an oracle against Pharaoh (29:1–16). The second, dated April 26, 571, describes Egypt as Nebuchadnezzar's prize (29:17–21). In the third (undated) oracle, Ezekiel declares that the day of the Lord is near for Egypt (30:1–19). Ezekiel declares in the fourth oracle, dated April 29, 587, that God will break the arms of Pharaoh (30:20–26). The fifth oracle, dated June 21, 587, describes Egypt as a great tree that God will bring down (31:1–18). In the sixth oracle, dated March 3, 585, Ezekiel laments Pharaoh, describing his coming doom (32:1–16). Finally, in the seventh oracle, dated March 18, 585, Ezekiel describes Egypt's destruction and fall into Sheol (32:17–32).[38] With this, Ezekiel's oracles against the nations come to an end.

Prophecies of Future Restoration (Ezek. 33–48)

The last major section of Ezekiel's book contains messages of hope for the exiles. The transition between the oracles of judgment and the oracles of blessing is found in chapter 33. In this chapter a messenger arrives among the exiles informing them that Jerusalem has fallen (v. 21). Ezekiel's prophecies of judgment against Judah have been fulfilled, and the way is now paved for his declarations of coming restoration. These prophecies of future restoration include some of the most well known prophecies in the Old Testament.

As already noted, these latter chapters of Ezekiel contain several prophecies, the interpretations of which are commonly disputed. Much of the difficulty is due to differences of opinion regarding the correct principles for interpreting biblical prophecy. Some argue that all biblical prophecies should be interpreted literally and claim that any other approach is inconsistent.[39] Others argue that the language used in biblical prophecy is

37. Zimmerli 1983, 95.

38. In Ezekiel, as in other Old Testament books, Sheol is a massive place of the dead where the deceased live on. See Johnston 2002.

39. E.g., Ryrie 1995, 82.

often metaphorical and thus not intended by the author to be understood literally.[40] Like the other prophets, Ezekiel often uses poetic language, filled with symbols and metaphors (cf. Num. 12:6–8). What this means is that while the events Ezekiel foresees are literal events, his descriptions of those events are not always literal descriptions.[41] In other words, like the other prophets, Ezekiel commonly uses symbolic language to speak of spiritual and earthly realities.

In order to understand the contents of Ezekiel 34–48, it is helpful to realize that all of the prophecies found in these chapters speak of different aspects of God's work of restoration.[42]

1. The restoration of divine kingship (ch. 34).
2. The restoration of the land (35–36).
3. The restoration of the people and the covenant (37).
4. The restoration of Israel's security (38–39).
5. The restoration of God's presence with his people (40–48).

These prophecies of restoration use highly idealized language to communicate their basic themes. Chapters 38 and 39, for example, use the genre of an oracle against a foreign nation to speak of God's restoration of Israel's peace and security. Chapters 40–48, on the other hand, regularly echo language found in Moses' instructions for the tabernacle. Ezekiel's use of such familiar language to depict in a symbolic manner coming new realities accounts for much of the difficulty in interpreting his prophecies.

In chapter 34, Ezekiel condemns the oppressive shepherds (leaders) of Israel, and in the process announces the restoration of the Lord's kingship through the reestablishment of the Davidic king. Those who believed that the Davidic covenant had been revoked are now assured that the house of David will be restored (vv. 23–24). The coming king "is the servant of the Lord, represented as an idealized David."[43] At the time of the restoration of the Davidic king, God will also establish a "covenant of peace" with Israel (vv. 25–30; Isa. 54:7–10).

40. E.g., McCartney and Clayton 1994, 219–21.
41. Block 1998, 57.
42. Block 1998, 272.
43. Taylor 1969, 223.

The focus of Ezekiel 35–36 is the land. Chapter 35 explains the reason for the desolation of the land, while 36:1–15 looks forward to the restoration of the land. The nations will be judged, and God will bring his people home. God will also restore his covenant with his people (36:16–38). He will do so in order to vindicate his name (vv. 22–23). God will transform the people, sprinkling them with clean water and giving them a new heart and a new spirit (vv. 25–27; 11:19).[44] He will transform society by restoring Israel to the land as a witness to the nations (36:24, 28, 33–36). God will also transform creation itself (vv. 30, 35).[45]

One of Ezekiel's most memorable prophecies is found in chapter 37. The vision of the valley of dry bones is a prophecy of the restoration of God's people from exile. In verses 1–2, Ezekiel sees a valley full of bones.[46] The macabre scene is a fulfillment of the covenant curse described in Deuteronomy 28:25–26 (see also Jer. 34:17–20). Ezekiel is commanded by God to prophesy over the bones, and the Lord says that he will cause the bones to live (37:3–6). Ezekiel obeys and prophesies over them. The bones then come together and are covered by sinews and flesh (vv. 7–8). Ezekiel is commanded to prophesy over these bodies, and when he does so, they receive breath and live (vv. 9–10).

There are some who see in this prophecy a reference to the resurrection of individual believers.[47] The majority of commentators, however, understand this to be a prophecy regarding the restoration of Israel.[48] Hosea had anticipated a national resurrection over a century earlier (Hos. 6:1–3). Now Ezekiel presents the same concept in much more detailed and graphic language. The interpretation of the prophecy as a figurative picture of the restoration of Israel to the land is confirmed by Ezekiel's own interpretation in 37:11–14. According to Ezekiel, "these bones are the whole house of Israel" (v. 11), which will be brought back into the land (vv. 12–14).

44. The language of "sprinkling clean water" echoes the symbolism of Israel's ancient ritual washings (Ex. 30:17–21; Lev. 14:48–52; Num. 19:17–19). The promise of a new heart looks back to Moses' words in Deuteronomy 30:6. Only a "heart transplant" would solve the problem of Israel's sinfulness (Allen 1990, 180).

45. Gowan 2000, 2.

46. The valley contrasts with the "very high mountain" in 40:2. One is the place of exile, while the other is the land of life (Duguid 1999, 426).

47. See Robertson 2004, 304.

48. See, for example, Taylor 1969, 236; Feinberg 1969, 212–14; Zimmerli 1983, 264; Block 1998, 386–87; Duguid 1999, 430; Johnston 2002, 224.

The restoration of the covenant is the subject of the second half of chapter 37 (vv. 15–28). The kingdoms of Israel and Judah will again be one (vv. 22–23). God will restore his covenant relationship with his people as well (vv. 24–28). In speaking of the restored covenant, Ezekiel uses language that echoes elements of the Abrahamic covenant (v. 25—the land), the Mosaic covenant (v. 24b—rules and statutes), and the Davidic covenant (v. 24a—the king). The fivefold use of the Hebrew word *'olam*, meaning "forever," points to the new relationship between God and his people.[49]

The restoration of Israel's security is the focus of chapters 38–39. In this prophecy Ezekiel witnesses the invasion of Israel by Gog and his allies and the complete destruction of these forces by God.[50] According to some interpreters, this prophecy must be understood literally as a reference to a battle that will take place in the years immediately preceding the second advent of Christ.[51] Others argue that Ezekiel is employing largely symbolic language.[52] In the judgment of the present writer, Ezekiel uses a common form of prophetic language, the oracle against a foreign nation, to depict in a figurative manner God's restoration of Israel's security. According to Ezekiel, in the coming age Israel will live securely in peace because God will completely destroy all of her enemies.[53]

The prophecy begins with a word from the Lord to Ezekiel telling him to set his face toward "Gog, of the land of Magog, the chief prince of Meshech and Tubal, and prophesy against him" (38:2). The name "Gog" may be derived from Gyges, the name of the king of Lydia in the western part of Asia Minor (present-day Turkey).[54] The term "Magog" is likely a reference to the land of Gog, namely Lydia.[55] The phrase "the chief prince" is translated "the prince of Rosh" in some English translations (e.g., ASV, NASB, NKJV). This is an unfortunate translation, however, because it

49. Block 1998, 415–16. In the ESV, the Hebrew word *'olam* is translated "forever" two times (v. 25), "forevermore" two times (vv. 26, 28), and "everlasting" one time (v. 26).

50. Block 1998, 424.

51. Feinberg 1969, 218–19; Ryrie 1986, 469. According to dispensationalist theology, the seven-year period of time immediately preceding the second coming of Christ is the great tribulation (Chafer 1948, 4:360; Walvoord 1959, 261; Ryrie 1986, 464–77).

52. E.g., Robertson 2004, 308. Robertson cites several passages within the prophecy as evidence of its essentially symbolic nature (38:19–20; 39:17–18, 20).

53. Dumbrell 1994, 105.

54. See Block 1998, 433; Allen 1990, 204; *NIDOTTE*, 4:685. This king was known to the Assyrians as Gugu (Allen 1990, 204).

55. Block 1998, 434.

implies that "Rosh" is a nation under the rule of Gog. "Rosh" simply means "chief" and is in apposition to the word translated "prince." In short, Gog is the chief prince of Meshech and Tubal, two tribal nations also located in Asia Minor.

Gog is allied with a number of other nations besides Meshech and Tubal. With him are the armies and hordes of Persia, Cush, Put, Gomer, and Beth-togarmah (38:5–6). "Gomer" is likely a reference to Gimmeraia, a tribe located north of the Black Sea, while "Beth-togarmah" refers to a tribe from the remote north bordering Tubal. Moving to the south, "Cush" refers to Ethiopia, while "Put" refers to Libya. The seven nations are all on the outer edges of the region with which Israel is familiar. The fact that they are from the extreme north and the extreme south, the very ends of the earth, points to the universal nature of the threat against Israel.

According to Ezekiel, the attack on Israel by Gog and his allies is to occur "in the latter years" (38:8) or "in the latter days" (38:16). The second phrase is found in numerous places in the Old Testament (Gen. 49:1; Num. 24:14; Deut. 4:30; 31:29: Isa. 2:2; Jer. 23:20; 30:24; 48:47; 49:39; Dan. 10:14; Hos. 3:5; Mic. 4:1). In general it refers to an unspecified time in the future.[56] The phrase "in the latter years," on the other hand, is found only here in Ezekiel. The context, however, indicates that it is simply a synonym for "in the latter days."

Gog's attack will not succeed. God will completely destroy the armies of Gog and his allies and restore Israel to safety (Ezek. 38:17–39:29). This destruction is depicted in terms of a sacrificial feast in which the birds and beasts feast on the slain bodies of the destroyed armies (39:17–20; cf. Isa. 34:6–8; Zeph. 1:7). Ezekiel depicts the final destruction of Israel's enemies and the restoration of her security as an eschatological event. The context indicates that this eschatological restoration of Israel's security is closely connected with the restoration of the Davidic kingship, the restoration of the covenant, and the restoration of God's presence with his people.[57] When God's work of restoration is complete, the enemies of God's people will no longer pose any threat. His people will live in peace and security in his presence under the rule of the Messiah.

56. Ross 1988, 700; Wenham 1994, 471.

57. Ezekiel does not indicate with specificity how all of the aspects of God's restorative work will fit together. This will become clearer in the New Testament.

The promise of the restoration of God's presence with his people is found in the final chapters of Ezekiel (40–48). These chapters, which contain a detailed description of a temple, have been interpreted in a variety of ways. John Taylor discerns four main interpretive approaches: (1) the literal prophetic approach, which understands the prophecy to be a blueprint for the postexilic temple; (2) the symbolic Christian approach, which understands it to be a symbol of the Christian church; (3) the dispensationalist approach, which understands it to be a blueprint for a future temple; and (4) the apocalyptic approach, which understands it to be a pattern for the messianic age.[58]

Of the many approaches to Ezekiel 40–48, the dispensationalist approach is among the most popular. According to proponents of this interpretation, Ezekiel's prophecy is to be understood as referring to a literal temple that will be rebuilt and that will be the center of worship during the millennium.[59] Dispensationalist commentators believe that the intricate detail in Ezekiel's description of the temple precludes anything other than a literal interpretation.[60] Dispensationalist commentators sometimes also argue that the lack of unanimity among those who interpret the prophecy in a nonliteral manner is a telling argument against the strength of those views.[61]

Those who reject the idea that Ezekiel's prophecy refers to a literal physical temple to be built in the future generally do not do so because they doubt that such a structure could be built.[62] The real difficulty with the dispensationalist interpretation is Ezekiel's description of the temple sacrifices associated with the temple (43:18–46:24). According to the book of Hebrews, the once-for-all sacrifice of Christ abolished animal sacrifices (Heb. 9–10). Dispensationalists are well aware of this difficulty and have offered several possible solutions to the problem.[63]

58. Taylor 1969, 251–53. Taylor identifies the fourth view as his own.

59. Ryrie 1953, 151; Walvoord 1959, 309–10; Feinberg 1969, 263; Rooker 1997, 128–29. According to dispensational theology, the millennium is the thousand-year earthly reign of Christ following his second advent (Ryrie 1986, 508–11).

60. Feinberg 1969, 263; Rooker 1997, 130.

61. Rooker 1997, 130.

62. There are difficulties, of course, such as the fact that the present topography of the land is incompatible with the details of the structure described by Ezekiel, but it is not beyond the power of God to change topography if he so desires.

63. Walvoord 1959, 310–11.

Some dispensationalists have argued that the sacrifices to be performed in the millennial temple are merely memorials of Christ's sacrifice, much like the Lord's Supper.[64] The problem with this interpretation, however, is that it violates dispensationalism's fundamental hermeneutical principle. In other words, it is not a literal interpretation. Ezekiel speaks literally of atoning sacrifices, not memorials (Ezek. 45:15, 17, 20). If the temple prophecy must be interpreted literally, it is arbitrary to interpret this significant detail of the prophecy nonliterally. A second dispensationalist interpretation of the sacrifices understands them to refer to ceremonial or temporal forgiveness. In other words, these millennial temple sacrifices would function in much the same way as the Mosaic sacrifices functioned.[65] The problem with this interpretation is that these kinds of sacrifices are precisely the kinds that have been abolished according to the book of Hebrews.

A third dispensationalist interpretation understands Ezekiel to be speaking of future worship and using concepts and terminology with which the exilic Jews would be familiar. Mark Rooker explains:

> Since the NT has ruled out the future existence of sacrifices after the once-for-all sacrifice of Jesus Christ (Heb. 10:18), we should expect no other and understand Ezekiel to be generally speaking of a future worship practice in the millennial age. The same could not be said of the erection and existence of the Temple, as we are not told in the NT that this promise has been fulfilled.[66]

This interpretation is consistent with Hebrews. But it does not appear to be consistent with dispensationalist hermeneutical claims regarding prophecy.

The problem with this interpretation is its seeming arbitrariness. If, in regard to the sacrifices, Ezekiel is using terminology familiar to his audience to refer to future (nonsacrificial) worship practices, why is it not possible that he is doing something similar with the entire temple prophecy? Rooker says that it is because there is nothing in the New Testament indicating that the temple prophecy has been fulfilled. That statement, however, is debatable (John 2:18–22; 1 Cor. 3:16; Eph. 2:19–22). Dispensationalists claim

64. Walvoord 1959, 312–14; Feinberg 1969, 243.

65. For a description of this view (which is not his own), see Rooker 1997, 132–33.

66. Rooker 1997, 134.

that the strongest argument for a literal interpretation of Ezekiel 40–48 is its mass of details. However, if one of those many details may (and in fact must) be interpreted figuratively, then there is no reason to presume that the other details, or the whole prophecy, should not be interpreted figuratively.

If the dispensationalist approach to Ezekiel 40–48 presents insurmountable problems, how are these chapters to be understood? Daniel Block argues that the prophecy should be interpreted "ideationally." In other words, Ezekiel employs familiar idioms to portray spiritual realities.[67] This is essentially the approach that Rooker takes with the temple sacrifices. Block simply applies the same hermeneutical principle to the entire prophecy. He argues that the genre, the context, and the contents of the prophecy demand such an approach.[68]

Some have offered a sociological interpretation of Ezekiel 40–48. Proponents of this view argue that the prophecy is a picture of radical social change.[69] Kalinda Stevenson observes that in contrast with the detailed description of the tabernacle and of Solomon's temple, there is no specific command to build Ezekiel's temple (cf. Ex. 25:9; 1 Chron. 28:10–12, 19).[70] Furthermore, there are very few vertical measurements given in the entire prophecy. The only vertical measurements provided in the entire prophecy are the heights of the outer wall (Ezek. 40:5), the altar (41:22; 43:13–17), and the tables (40:42). Stevenson argues that the reason for the vertical measurements is found in Ezekiel 42:20. It is to indicate a separation between the holy and the common.[71] The other dimensions given in the prophecy place the altar at the center of the temple compound.[72] The centrality of the altar points to its significance in the cleansing of Israelite society.[73] While some aspects of the sociological approach provide insight, it does not seem to do justice to the entirety of the prophecy and its context.

One of the most helpful discussions of the meaning of the temple prophecy in Ezekiel 40–48 is provided by Gregory K. Beale, whose approach is

67. Block 1998, 505–6.
68. Block 1998, 495–506.
69. Stevenson 1996, 151; Levenson 1976, 124.
70. Stevenson 1996, 17.
71. Stevenson 1996, 37.
72. Block 1998, 508.
73. Stevenson 1996, 43.

similar to that of Block.[74] Beale finds a clue to the meaning of the symbolism of the prophecy by examining similarities between this vision and the visions of Ezekiel 1 and 8–11:

> The geographical symbolism is enhanced from noticing that the threefold introductory vision phraseology of Ezekiel 40:1–4 occurs in the book only at chapter 1 (1:1–3) and chapter 8 (8:1–3): (1) an initial comment about the specific date on which the experience occurred; (2) "the hand of Yahweh came upon him"; (3) and Ezekiel "saw . . . visions." Two additional common elements are that the visions occur by "the river Chebar" (1:1, 3; 10:15, 22; 43:3) and that "the glory of God" is an essential component of all three vision episodes (1:28; 8:4; 9:3; 10:4, 18–19; 11:22–23; 43:2, 5). What is unique about the uses in Ezekiel 1 and 8 is that each introduces a vision in which the prophet receives a glimpse of part of a heavenly temple.[75]

Ezekiel 1 focuses on the heavenly temple. Chapters 8–9 focus on the heavenly temple in the midst of the physical temple. Finally chapters 10–11 focus on the departure of the heavenly temple from the physical temple. God himself becomes the invisible temple for the exiled remnant (11:16).[76]

If the unique introductory formula connects all three visions, then the question is whether the temple vision in chapters 40–48 "refers to the purely heavenly temple dimension that descends in the midst of the faithful saints on earth (as in chapters 1 and 11), or the heavenly dimension in the midst of another (new) earthly temple in structural form, as in chapters 8–9."[77] In either case, the emphasis is upon the heavenly dimension of the temple dwelling in the midst of God's people. Beale concludes that the vision of Ezekiel 40–48 is "a figurative vision of a real heavenly temple that would descend and be established on earth in non-structural form in the latter days."[78] But what of the mass of details in the vision? Some of these details portray future realities in the figurative manner typical of Old Testament prophetic books. Other details are similar to the detailed brush strokes of an impressionistic painting. They are necessary in order to paint the big picture.[79]

74. Beale 2004, 335–64.

75. Beale 2004, 337.

76. Beale 2004, 337.

77. Beale 2004, 338.

78. Beale 2004, 353.

79. The only other possible option is what Taylor (1969, 251–52) describes as the "literal prophetic approach," which understands Ezekiel 40–48 to be a blueprint for the postexilic temple. In this case,

A few comments on the content of the prophecy are in order. The vision may be divided into four sections: the new temple (40:1–43:11); the new law (43:12–46:24); the new land (47:1–48:29); and the new city (48:30–35). As in the vision of chapter 8, Ezekiel is here led on a tour, during which he takes precise measurements of the temple complex (40:3 ff.; cf. Rev. 11:1). In the second section of the vision, Ezekiel sees the glory of God return to the temple he had abandoned in chapters 8–11 (43:1–4). In this section Ezekiel functions as a new Moses, renewing God's covenant.[80]

Just as Joshua's division of the land followed Moses' giving of the law, so too does Ezekiel's division of the new land follow his giving of a new law (47:1–48:29). This new land is greatly blessed. Ezekiel witnesses a stream flowing from the temple through the land, ever increasing in depth until it reaches the sea (47:1–12). The river produces abundant life (v. 9). Here Ezekiel sees Zion as the source of blessing (cf. Joel 3:17–18; Zech. 14:8). Finally, Ezekiel sees a vision of a new city with twelve gates bearing the names of the twelve tribes of Israel (48:30–35; cf. Rev. 21:10–13). This vision of the temple in Ezekiel 40–48 is a wonderful picture of God's restoration of his presence among his people.

Daniel

In the Hebrew Bible, the book of Daniel is included in the Writings rather than in the Prophets. In the Septuagint, however, Daniel is included among the prophetic books.[81] The inclusion of Daniel among the Writings in the

---

the prophecy would have to be understood as that which would have occurred had Israel repented prior to the advent of the Messiah (after the coming of the Messiah, literal sacrifices would no longer be possible). In such a case, it would have to be understood as an example of the kind of implicit conditional prophecy described in Jeremiah 18:9–10. If not, it would be a false prophecy. The problem with this approach is that it is not by any means certain that Ezekiel 40–48 can be understood as an example of the kind of prophecy described in Jeremiah 18:9–10.

80. Ezekiel is the only person in Scripture apart from Moses to communicate divine legislation to the people (Levenson 1976, 39). There are, however, numerous differences between Ezekiel's legislation and the law of Moses, differences that have perplexed commentators for centuries. It must be remembered, however, that this is "vision in the form of legislation, not legislation in the form of vision" (Duguid 1999, 522).

81. The Greek versions also contain three additions that are not found in the Hebrew text. The Prayer of Azariah and the Song of the Three Jews are found between Daniel 3:23 and 3:24 in all of the Greek versions. The Septuagint adds the stories of Susanna and of Bel and the Dragon to the end of the book after chapter 12, while Theodotion's Greek translation adds Susanna to the beginning of the book and Bel and the Dragon to the end of chapter 6. The Roman Catholic Church and the

Hebrew Bible is likely due to the book's distinctive character.[82] It differs to a certain degree from the other prophetic books. Most of the other prophetic books consist primarily of various oracles that were spoken to the prophet by God and then declared to the people.[83] The first six chapters of Daniel, on the other hand, are stories about Daniel and his friends narrated in the third person. The last six chapters of Daniel are first-person descriptions of Daniel's unusual visions. In addition, Daniel, unlike the other prophetic books, is written in two distinct languages. Daniel 1:1–2:4a and 8:1–12:13 are written in Hebrew, while chapters 2:4b–7:28 are written in Aramaic.

Like Ezekiel, the book of Daniel contains a number of enigmatic prophecies. And like Ezekiel, the difficult nature of these prophecies has resulted in a wide variety of conflicting interpretations. The lack of hermeneutical consensus presents a challenge for the reader, but it is not necessarily an insurmountable one. The confusion surrounding many of the prophecies of Daniel does, however, mean that it is particularly important to understand the genre and context of the book.

Daniel uses two overarching genres to communicate his message. The first six chapters are narratives and have been described more specifically as "court narratives," which detail the interaction between the protagonist of the story and a foreign court.[84] The genre of the last six chapters of Daniel, on the other hand, is often characterized as "apocalyptic." But what is "apocalyptic," and how does it differ from "prophecy"? As William Dumbrell explains, one key difference concerns the mode of revelation:

> Though apoc[alyptic] is closely associated with prophecy, the mode of the revelation in apoc[alyptic] differs. While prophecy was primarily concerned with communication from God regarding the implications of his relationship with his people, apoc[alyptic] literature was oriented towards the future and expressed its message in vivid symbolism encoded in dreams and visions.[85]

Orthodox church accept these additions as canonical. Protestants, on the other hand, include them among the apocryphal books.

82. Its inclusion in the Writings does not necessarily mean, as critical scholars contend, that it was written in the second century (see Baldwin 1978, 71).

83. The notable exception is the book of Jonah.

84. Dillard and Longman 1994, 341; Collins 1993, 42.

85. *NIDOTTE*, 4:394.

It is the use of such symbolic images by Daniel that is the source of much of the difficulty in interpreting the book.

Other features are prominent as well in apocalyptic literature. John J. Collins provides a helpful summary of these features.[86] In apocalyptic literature, a narrative framework describes the revelation that is given in a dream or visionary journey. The revelation is supplemented by discourse or dialogue. And finally, there is an angel or other supernatural figure who interprets the vision. Given the traits found in this kind of literature, the Society of Biblical Literature has proposed the following definition of "apocalyptic": It is "a genre of revelatory literature with a narrative framework, in which a revelation is mediated by an otherworldly being to a human recipient, disclosing a transcendent reality which is both temporal, insofar as it envisages eschatological salvation, and spatial insofar as it involves another, supernatural world."[87] Hints of the apocalyptic genre may be seen in earlier biblical prophetic books such as Isaiah (chs. 24–27) and Ezekiel (chs. 40–48), and the genre is also found in the postexilic prophetic book of Zechariah, but the last half of Daniel is the most obvious Old Testament example of the genre.

While recognition of the apocalyptic genre of Daniel is crucial to understanding the book, the historical context of the book is also important. The book of Daniel is set within the context of the sixth-century exile. The events narrated in the first six chapters date from the year Nebuchadnezzar deported Daniel and his friends (605) to the third year of Cyrus (536). This spans the entire period of the Babylonian exile. As we have seen, the exile was one of the key events in the history of Israel, and the book of Daniel is set in the midst of this important time of transition for the people of God. The visions found in the last six chapters of Daniel extend beyond the Babylonian exile, although how far they extend into the future is a matter of intense debate that will be discussed in connection with the prophecies themselves.

The historical setting of the book raises the question of authorship and date. Critical scholars generally argue that the book is a pseudonymous work

86. Collins 1998, 5.

87. Cited in Collins 1998, 5. Examples of apocalyptic literature include *1 Enoch*, *4 Ezra*, and *2 Baruch*.

written sometime between 167 and 163 B.C.[88] The prophecies found in the book are considered by these scholars to be instances of "prophecy after the fact." While recognizing that the book itself does not name its author (anonymity), more conservative scholars have rejected the suggestion that the work is an example of an author using a false name (pseudonymity).[89] These scholars argue that the first six chapters are narratives of real sixth-century events and that Daniel himself is the source of the vision accounts in chapters 7–12.[90] The final composition of the book is dated to the late sixth century. It is beyond the scope of the present work to examine all of the issues related to these questions. Suffice it to say that new discoveries and continued study have added weight to the traditional arguments.[91]

As noted above, the book of Daniel contains two major sections, a series of stories (chs. 1–6) and a series of visions (chs. 7–12), and the book is also written in two languages (Hebrew and Aramaic). There is not a precise correlation between the two major sections and the use of the two languages, however. Daniel 1:1–2:4a is written in Hebrew. The author then shifts to Aramaic in 2:4b–7:28. In the final chapters of the book (8:1–12:13), the author returns to the use of Hebrew. This use of Aramaic across both major sections of the book ties them together and also provides a clue to the book's structure. The inclusion of chapter 7 in the Aramaic section indicates its strong thematic connection with the previous passages.

An examination of the content of the Aramaic section of Daniel actually reveals an overarching chiastic structure. Both chapters 2 and 7 contain prophetic descriptions of four human kingdoms followed by God's establishment of an everlasting and worldwide kingdom. Chapters 3 and 6 contain narratives in which God delivers his faithful servants from death. Chapters 4 and 5 contain God's judgment on arrogant rulers. Within the overarching division between the stories and visions, then, a basic threefold structure

88. E.g., Collins 1993, 61; Hill 2002, 102. To be more precise, critical scholars are in agreement that chapters 7–12 are to be dated in the second century. Among these scholars, however, the dating of chapters 1–6 is still debated (see Collins 1998, 88).

89. Longman 1999, 22–23. As Longman demonstrates, for pseudonymous "after the fact" prophecy to achieve its purpose, the audience has to be deceived into thinking that the author really predicted the events before they occurred. Such deliberate deception is incongruous with the ethical standards of the covenant.

90. Baldwin 1978, 17–29, 35–46; Dillard and Longman 1994, 330–31.

91. Although he does not come down firmly on either side, Lucas (2002, 306–12) provides a good discussion of the issues involved in the dating of the book.

is evident.[92] Daniel 1 is a prologue that describes the historical setting of the book. Daniel 2–7 concerns the nations in relation to the living God. Finally, Daniel 8–12 contains visions related to the last three of the four human kingdoms described in chapters 2 and 7.

Prologue: Historical Setting (Dan. 1)

The opening chapter of Daniel sets the stage for the remainder of the book by informing the reader of the historical context. According to 1:1–7, Daniel and his friends were deported to Babylon by Nebuchadnezzar in the third year of the reign of Jehoiakim (i.e., 605 B.C.).[93] Daniel 1:2 reveals that Judah's defeat at the hands of Babylon was not due to the superiority of the Babylonian gods. It is the Lord who has delivered Judah into the hand of Nebuchadnezzar. He is in control of all that is happening. Upon arrival in Babylon, Daniel and his friends begin training for service in the royal court (vv. 3–7). The remainder of the opening chapter narrates the story of Daniel's determination to avoid defilement (vv. 8–16). He and his friends succeed and are blessed by God (vv. 17–20). Nebuchadnezzar considers them to be the wisest of his wise men. The closing verse of this chapter informs the reader that Daniel remained in Babylon until the days of Cyrus. In other words, he remained in Babylon throughout the entire length of the exile.

The Nations and the Living God (Dan. 2–7)

Daniel 2 begins with a dream. Nebuchadnezzar has been having a troubling dream, which is causing him sleepless nights (v. 1). He calls for his magicians and wise men in order that they might interpret the meaning of the dream, but as a test he commands them to reveal the dream before they reveal the interpretation (vv. 2–9). The wise men complain that no

92. Robertson 2004, 330.

93. The deportation spoken of in these first verses of Daniel is likely the same deportation that is described in 2 Chronicles 36:4–8 (see also Jer. 46:2). Critical scholars have long accused the author of an error at this point because the timing of the event described here is said to contradict Jeremiah 25:1. Jeremiah places the first year of Nebuchadnezzar's reign in the fourth year of Jehoiakim's reign while Daniel places it in Jehoiakim's third year. However, as other commentators have demonstrated, different methods of reckoning the time of a king's reign were in use at the time. If Daniel and Jeremiah were each using a different method, the discrepancy between them is removed (Longman 1999, 43–45; Lucas 2002, 50).

man can do such a thing (vv. 10–11). This infuriates Nebuchadnezzar, who orders that all of the wise men be executed (vv. 12). Because Daniel and his friends are included in the decree, Daniel asks for time in order that he might reveal the dream and its interpretation to the king (vv. 13–16). Daniel and his friends pray, and the Lord responds, revealing the dream to Daniel (vv. 17–24). Daniel then goes to the king, informing him that God has done what no mere man could do (vv. 25–30). Finally, he reveals the dream and its interpretation to the king and is promoted to a position of high honor in the kingdom (vv. 31–49).[94]

Central to this chapter is the dream itself, in which God reveals to the Babylonian king things that were to come (vv. 28–29). In the dream, Nebuchadnezzar has seen a huge image with a head of gold, chest and arms of silver, belly and thighs of bronze, legs of iron, and feet of mixed iron and clay (vv. 31–33). As he watches, a stone cut by no human hand strikes the image on its feet, shattering it to dust (v. 34). The stone then becomes a great mountain that fills the earth (v. 35). Daniel reveals to Nebuchadnezzar that he, the king of Babylon, is the head of gold (vv. 36–38). The other parts of the image are kingdoms that will follow him (vv. 39–43). Finally, Daniel reveals the meaning of the stone that struck the feet of the image: "In the days of those kings the God of heaven will set up a kingdom that shall never be destroyed, nor shall the kingdom be left to another people. It shall break in pieces all these kingdoms and bring them to an end, and it shall stand forever" (v. 44).

The vision of a great image made of four metals provoked a sense of distress in the heart of Nebuchadnezzar.[95] Wading through the numerous interpretations of it found in the commentaries can easily bring about a similar response. The identification of the head of gold is not difficult because Daniel himself identifies it with Nebuchadnezzar, the ruler of the Babylonian Empire (v. 38). The identification of the remaining kingdoms, however, has been the source of endless debate because Daniel himself did not clearly identify them in his interpretation of the dream.

Most conservative interpreters identify the four kingdoms as Babylon (Nebuchadnezzar), Medo-Persia, Greece, and Rome.[96] A variation of this

94. The parallels with the story of Joseph are obvious (Gen. 41).

95. There are ancient parallels in which successive eras are envisaged in terms of different metals (for examples of these parallels, see Collins 1993, 163, and Goldingay 1989, 40).

96. E.g., Robertson 2004, 324–25; Young 1949, 275–94.

(Roman) interpretation is the dispensational premillennial view that sees the "ten-toes stage" of the Roman Empire as yet to be fulfilled.[97] Despite the prevalence of the "Roman" view among conservative scholars, a few have argued that the fourth kingdom is the Greek empire, thus identifying the four kingdoms as Babylon, Media, Persia, and Greece.[98] Most critical scholars have also adopted this (Greek) view.[99] One moderately critical evangelical scholar, John Goldingay, has taken a different approach, arguing that the four kingdoms are the reigns of the four Gentile rulers mentioned by name in the book, namely Nebuchadnezzar, Belshazzar, Darius the Mede, and Cyrus.[100] While these interpretations do not exhaust every possible view, they do summarize the most representative interpretations. Because of the close parallels between chapters 2 and 7, our final evaluation of the various interpretations must await an examination of the contents of that chapter.

According to Daniel, the stone that strikes the feet of the image represents a kingdom to be established by God himself. Here, one of the central themes of Daniel, the kingdom of God, is introduced. The point at which the stone impacts the image seems to indicate that the establishment of God's kingdom is to occur in the time of the fourth kingdom, but God's establishment of his kingdom is also said to occur "in the days of those kings" (v. 44). In other words, the stone element of the dream seems to ignore the successive chronological sequence established in the description of the sections of the great image.[101] The discrepancy is only a problem, however, if the details of the dream are pressed too literally, but recognition of the apocalyptic genre of the book cautions us against such a practice.[102]

Daniel declares that the kingdom established by God will grow until it fills the earth (v. 35; Isa. 2:2). Craig Evans explains the importance of Daniel's description of the kingdom:

97. Chafer 1948, 4:334; Walvoord 1971, 72; Barker 1997, 136–39.

98. Gurney 1977; Walton 1986.

99. E.g., Collins 1993, 166.

100. Goldingay 1989, 51. Goldingay is also distinctive in that he does not identify the four kingdoms of Daniel 2 with the four kingdoms of Daniel 7 (1989, 175).

101. Collins 1998, 97.

102. If the details were pressed too literally, there would also be chronological discrepancies between chapter 2 and chapter 7. In chapter 2, God's kingdom is said to smash all of the four human kingdoms. In chapter 7, the fourth beast/kingdom is destroyed, but the first three are given a reprieve for a time (7:11–12).

> In Daniel . . . the kingdom of God is understood as the sphere of divine authority. This kingdom is eschatological in that it brings to an end all previous human kingdoms and it is eternal in that it will never end. It constitutes the sphere into which God invites humans to enter and which God imposes upon the world, regardless of both human response and Satanic opposition to it.[103]

The fact that this coming kingdom of God fills the earth is significant. As Goldingay observes, "*History* is not destroyed; other sovereignties are."[104] The heart of Nebuchadnezzar's dream, therefore, is a revelation of the coming kingdom of God, which is to be established after a succession of four human kingdoms. The establishment of God's kingdom will mark the climax of human history.

Daniel 3 recounts the famous story of Daniel's friends and the fiery furnace. After building a huge golden image, Nebuchadnezzar gathers his officials and orders them to fall down and worship the image (vv. 1–5). Whoever does not fall down and worship the image is to be cast into a fiery furnace (vv. 6–7). Daniel's three friends, who are present, refuse to worship this idol (vv. 8–12), and a furious Nebuchadnezzar orders them to be cast into the fire, asking them, "Who is the god who will deliver you out of my hands?" (vv. 13–15). The three are cast into the furnace. Nebuchadnezzar is then astonished to see four men in the furnace walking around unharmed (vv. 16–25). The three friends are removed from the furnace, and Nebuchadnezzar praises their God, decreeing that no one shall speak anything against the God of Israel (vv. 26–30).

Daniel 4 and 5 are both narratives recounting specific acts of divine judgment against arrogant human rulers. Chapter 4 is in the form of a letter written by Nebuchadnezzar himself. It tells of another dream that Daniel interpreted for the king. The dream, which foresaw the judgment and restoration of Nebuchadnezzar, was fulfilled, resulting in Nebuchadnezzar's doxology in praise of the living God (vv. 34–37). The events narrated in chapter 5 occur several decades later in the closing moments of the Babylonian Empire. Belshazzar is holding a feast when he sees a hand write mysterious words on the wall (vv. 1–5).[105] The king is alarmed and

103. Evans 2001, 510.

104. Goldingay 1989, 60.

105. For many years, Belshazzar was cited by critical scholars as an example of one of Daniel's many historical errors, for no record of such a person existed outside Scripture. Today, however,

calls his wise men who are unable to interpret the words (vv. 6–9). Finally, Daniel is called in, and he interprets the words, telling Belshazzar that God has brought his kingdom to its end (vv. 10–29). That very night the Babylonian kingdom fell (v. 30).

In Daniel 6, another Gentile ruler, Darius the Mede, becomes prominent in the narrative.[106] Now in charge of Babylon, he places Daniel in a position of great authority, but because of this promotion, jealous officials begin to plot against Daniel (vv. 1–6). Knowing Daniel's devotion to God, they lay a trap by convincing the new king to decree that no petition shall be made to any god or man other than Darius himself for thirty days (v. 7). These men soon catch Daniel praying and report him to the king, who is distressed at what he must now do (vv. 8–15). He reluctantly casts Daniel into the lions' den, asking Daniel's God to deliver him (vv. 16–17). After a sleepless night, the king returns to the lions' den and finds Daniel unharmed (vv. 18–22). After freeing Daniel, the king casts the plotters into the lions' den and decrees that all people fear the God of Daniel (vv. 23–28).

With chapter 7, the narrative section of the book ends, and the apocalyptic section begins. The vision recorded in the seventh chapter of Daniel is central to the book, and understanding it is crucial to grasping the meaning of a number of otherwise obscure passages in the New Testament. Daniel received this vision in the first year of Belshazzar (v. 1), so it occurred sometime after the events of chapter 4 but before the events of chapter 5. In the vision, Daniel sees the winds of heaven stirring up the sea (7:2). From the sea, he witnesses four great beasts arise, each different from the other (v. 3). The first beast is like a lion with eagles' wings (v. 4). Its wings are removed and it is made to stand on two feet like a man. The second beast is like a bear (v. 5). It is raised up on one side and has three ribs in its

---

archaeological discoveries have provided abundant evidence that Belshazzar was the son of Nabonidus and was in charge of Babylon during his father's lengthy absence (see Longman 1999, 135; Lucas 2002, 126).

106. Critical scholars argue that the author of Daniel has become confused at this point because there are no extrabiblical records of any Darius the Mede (e.g., Collins 1993, 30–31; Grabbe 1988). The most plausible explanation seems to be that Darius the Mede is another name for Cyrus the Persian (see Wiseman 1965; Bulman 1973; Shea 1982, 1991; Colless 1992). The argument, as first proposed by Wiseman, suggests that the conjunction *waw* in Daniel 6:28 is a *waw* explicative and should be translated the way it is translated in 1 Chronicles 5:26. In 1 Chronicles 5:26, the *waw* explicative indicates that Pul is another name for Tiglath-pileser. If the *waw* in Daniel 6:28 is also explicative, the verse should be translated, "So this Daniel prospered during the reign of Darius, *even* the reign of Cyrus the Persian."

mouth. The third beast is like a leopard (v. 6), but it has four wings and four heads. The fourth beast is almost indescribable (v. 7). It is terrifying and strong. It devours with its iron teeth and crushes what is left with its feet. It also has ten horns. As Daniel considers the horns, he sees a little horn arise among the ten (v. 8). The little horn has the eyes of a man and a mouth speaking great things.

In the remainder of the vision, Daniel witnesses a scene of divine judgment at the very throne of God. As he looks on, the Ancient of Days takes his seat on his throne (v. 9). As tens of thousands stand before God, the books are opened and the court sits in judgment (v. 10). As the little horn is speaking, the fourth beast is killed and its body given over to be burned with fire (v. 11). The dominion of the remaining beasts is taken away, but their lives are spared for a time (v. 12). Daniel then sees "one like a son of man" coming with the clouds of heaven to the Ancient of Days (v. 13). The one like a son of man is presented before the Ancient of Days, and to him is given "dominion and glory and a kingdom, that all peoples, nations, and languages should serve him" (v. 14a). His is "an everlasting dominion, which shall not pass away, and his kingdom one that shall not be destroyed" (v. 14b). In the remainder of the chapter, an angelic being interprets Daniel's vision, giving particular attention to the fourth beast (vv. 15–28).

The parallels between the vision of chapter 7 and the dream in chapter 2 are obvious. In both cases, a symbolic image is used to reveal a succession of four earthly kingdoms, which are judged and followed by an everlasting kingdom established by God. As noted above, in our discussion of chapter 2, there is much debate over the identity of the four kingdoms. The traditional view is represented by John Calvin, who identifies the four beasts as the Babylonian, Medo-Persian, Greek, and Roman Empires respectively.[107] Calvin identifies the little horn of 7:8 with the line of the Caesars, while admitting that this interpretation of the little horn is not universally held.[108] According to Calvin, then, the establishment of God's kingdom occurred at the first advent of Christ.[109] The conservative twentieth-century Old Testament scholar E. J. Young agrees with Calvin on the identity of the four kingdoms, but he identifies the little horn as the antichrist, whose

107. Calvin 2003, 13:11–25.
108. Calvin 2003, 13:26–31.
109. Calvin 2003, 13:31–34.

power is to be manifested at the end of the present age.[110] A variation of the Roman view is the dispensationalist interpretation. According to this view, the fourth beast, or Roman Empire, is to be revived in some form at the end of the present age. According to the dispensationalist interpretation, the coming of the one like a son of man to receive the everlasting kingdom will occur at Christ's second advent.[111]

Not all conservative scholars have adopted the Roman view of the four kingdoms. Both Robert Gurney and John Walton, for example, have proposed that the four beasts should be identified as the Babylonian, Median, Persian, and Greek Empires.[112] Gurney argues that most conservatives have rejected the Greek view because the coming of Christ occurred during the period of the Roman Empire.[113] He observes, however, that the Roman Empire did not end for many centuries after Christ's first advent. In support of his position, he notes that Christ was born around 6 B.C., "very soon after the final obliteration of the Greek empire in 27 BC, when Egypt was made a Roman province."[114] Others who argue for the Greek view point out the similarity between the little horn on the fourth beast (7:8) and the little horn on the goat in Daniel 8:9.[115] The little horn of chapter 8 is universally identified as the Greek Seleucid ruler Antiochus IV Epiphanes. If the two little horns are identical, it adds weight to the argument that the fourth beast is to be associated with the Greek Empire.[116]

110. Young 1949, 150, 163; Baldwin 1978, 161–62, also defends the Roman view.

111. Barker 1997, 139–43.

112. Gurney 1977; Walton 1986. Neither argues for this position on the basis of the critical presupposition that Daniel is a second-century composition. Both argue that the prophecy is a genuine sixth-century prophecy.

113. Gurney 1977, 44.

114. Gurney 1977, 39.

115. Lucas 2002, 188; Goldingay 1989, 174–75.

116. Another conservative interpretation of the four kingdoms is suggested by Tremper Longman, who proposes that the vision was never intended to provide definite historical identification of the final three beasts. Instead the vision simply indicates that an unspecified number of evil kingdoms will continue until the end of time (Longman 1999, 184, 190). This view would be less difficult to accept if the first beast were not specifically identified with the concrete historical empire of Babylon. Granted, the imagery describing the final three beasts is often ambiguous and the numbers in the book can surely be symbolic, but some kind of definite historical referent for the final three beasts of this vision seems to be demanded by the admittedly definite historical referent of the first beast. It also seems to be demanded by the concrete historical referents of the beasts in the related visions of chapter 8, which are universally acknowledged to be Medo-Persia and Greece (8:20–21).

The two interpretations of the four beasts, then, are: (1) the traditional Roman view, which identifies the four beasts as Babylon, Medo-Persia, Greece, and Rome, and (2) the Greek view, which identifies the four beasts as Babylon, Media, Persia, and Greece.[117] Each has its own strengths and weaknesses. A strength of the Greek view is the similarity between the little horns of chapters 7 and 8. A strength of the Roman view is the use in chapter 8 of a single symbolic animal to represent the Medo-Persian Empire (8:3–4, 20). A weakness of the Greek view is a lack of explanation for Daniel's failure to say anything here about the empire that was to be in power at the first advent of Christ. A weakness of the Roman view is the continuation of the Roman Empire for centuries following the first advent of Christ.[118] While not without its difficulties, the Roman view is stronger.[119]

The coming of one like a son of man to the Ancient of Days (7:13–14) is the climactic section of this vision, and it is of crucial importance. Much confusion has been caused by the assumption that this text is a prophecy of the second coming of Christ. The context precludes such an interpretation. As this section of the vision begins, Daniel sees the Ancient of Days take his seat upon his throne (7:9). The Ancient of Days is God, and the scene is set in his heavenly throne room. While Daniel himself experiences this vision on earth from his bed (7:1), the vision itself is a vision of the heavenly throne

117. The dispensationalist view, which posits a future renewed Roman Empire, does not seem to have any warrant in the text. There is nothing in the text itself that gives any indication of two incarnations of the same fourth beast/kingdom separated by a gap of thousands of years. A revived fourth beast is posited by dispensationalists only because it is assumed that the coming of one like a son of man to the Ancient of Days (7:13) is a prophetic reference to the second coming of Jesus (Walvoord 1959, 267). Of course, if it is a reference to the second coming, and if it occurs in the days of the fourth beast, and if the second coming has not occurred yet, then the fourth beast must exist in some capacity at the time of the future second coming. It is not necessary, however, to assume that the coming of one like a son of man to the Ancient of Days in 7:13 is a prophetic reference to the second coming of Jesus. If instead it is a prophetic reference to something that occurred in connection with Christ's first advent, then there is no need to posit a future revived Roman Empire.

118. The coming of Christ "in the days of those kings" is compatible with either view. If the fourth beast is the Greek Empire, his first advent occurred after its collapse, which is similar to the implied chronology of Daniel 7:12–14. If the fourth beast is the Roman Empire, his first advent occurred not long before its collapse, which is similar to the implied chronology of Daniel 2:44. The implied chronologies should not be pressed too literally, however, because of the nature of the symbolic language.

119. This view seems to be confirmed by John's understanding of Daniel as expressed in the book of Revelation.

room.[120] After God is seated at his throne, the court sits in judgment and the books are opened (v. 10). The fourth beast is then judged and destroyed, while the remaining beasts are given a temporary reprieve (vv. 11–12). This sets the stage for Daniel's vision of the one like a son of man.

In verse 13, Daniel witnesses "one like a son of man" come with the clouds of heaven to the Ancient of Days to be presented before him.[121] The Aramaic phrase *bar 'enash*, literally translated "son of man," is a Semitism that simply means "human being."[122] What Daniel sees, then, is one "like a human being," as opposed to another beast "like a bear" or "like a leopard." This one like a son of man comes to the Ancient of Days and is presented before him (v. 13). The "coming" that is seen in this vision, then, is not a coming of God or a coming of the one like a son of man from heaven to earth. It is a coming of one like a son of man to God who himself is seated in heaven on his throne.[123] The direction of the coming is not *from* heaven but *toward* heaven. It is for this reason that this vision is not a prophecy of the second coming of Jesus from heaven to earth. Rather, as Calvin long ago explained, it is better understood as a prophecy of Christ's ascension to the right hand of God after his resurrection (Acts 1:9–11; 2:33; 5:31).[124]

The one like a son of man is presented before the Ancient of Days for the purpose of his investiture.[125] When he is presented before the Ancient

120. Contra Goldingay (1989, 167), who asserts, "The court is seated on earth." For an explanation of one problem with Goldingay's view, see Lucas 2002, 181.

121. See Shepherd 2006, 99, for the argument that the one like a son of man is an individual.

122. Goldingay 1989, 167. The Hebrew equivalent is בֶּן־אָדָם (*ben 'adam*). Ezekiel is addressed over ninety times as "son of man" in the book of Ezekiel. Earlier uses may also be found in Psalm 8:4 and 80:17.

123. France 1982, 169. Beasley-Murray (1986, 28–29) argues that the vision is a theophany in which God is seen riding the clouds to earth, where the beast/kingdoms are to be judged. Goldingay (1989, 167) concurs. The problem with this interpretation is that the vision is not one of God coming with the clouds to earth, but of one like a son of man coming with the clouds to God. The Ancient of Days (God) is seated on his heavenly throne. It is the one like a son of man who is coming with the clouds to him.

124. Calvin 2003, 13:44. Those who object to the idea that Christ was given the kingdom at his first advent because the Roman Empire continued to exist must keep in mind the possible typological parallels between the anointing of David as king and the anointing of Jesus as king. The establishment of the Davidic kingdom occurred in stages. He was anointed the true king by Samuel even though Saul was not immediately removed from the physical throne (1 Sam. 16:1, 12–13). He was later anointed king over Judah (2 Sam. 2:4). It was only after a long war (2 Sam. 3:1) that he was anointed king over all Israel (2 Sam. 5:3–4).

125. Lucas 2002, 185; Robertson 2004, 334.

of Days, he is given a dominion and a kingdom that all should serve him (Dan. 7:14a). There seems to be an allusion here to the event described in Genesis 1:26, when the first man was given dominion over all the creatures (Ps. 8:4–8).[126] The establishment of the kingdom will restore God's creational purposes. This kingdom given to one like a son of man is to be everlasting (Dan. 7:14b). As in the vision of Daniel 2, we see here a depiction of four human kingdoms followed by the establishment of God's eternal kingdom. Both texts seem to indicate that God's kingdom will be established sometime near the end of the fourth human kingdom.

The remaining section of Daniel 7 contains the angel's interpretation of the vision (vv. 15–28). The angel declares that the four beasts are four kings who shall arise, and that "the saints of the Most High shall receive the kingdom and possess the kingdom forever" (vv. 17–18). Daniel then asks about the meaning of the fourth beast, the ten horns, and the little horn (vv. 19–22). He is told that there will be a fourth kingdom, and that out of this kingdom ten kings will arise and another after them (vv. 23–24). This last king will speak against God and persecute the saints, who will be "given into his hand for a time, times, and half a time" (v. 25). The court will judge this king, taking his dominion and giving the eternal kingdom "to the people of the saints of the Most High" (v. 27; cf. v. 18).

If the fourth kingdom is the Greek Empire, then the little horn's persecution of the saints likely refers to the persecution of the Jews by Antiochus IV Epiphanes. If the fourth kingdom is the Roman Empire, then the little horn's persecution may refer to the persecution of faithful Jews by the Romans prior to the coming of Christ. The reference to a "time, times, and half a time" (v. 25) has been understood by some to be a reference to a period of approximately three and a half years, but it seems more likely to be a symbol of an indefinite period of time that is cut short by God's intervention.[127] After the judgment of the little horn, the kingdom is given to the saints of the Most High (vv. 18, 27).[128] This interpretation of verse

126. Baldwin 1978, 143.

127. Young 1949, 161–62; Baldwin 1978, 146; Goldingay 1989, 181; Longman 1999, 190–91; Lucas 2002, 194.

128. See Poythress 1976 for a discussion of the debates surrounding the identification of these "holy ones."

14 indicates a close relationship between the one like a son of man and the saints of the Most High.[129] That which is his is theirs as well.

Apocalyptic Visions (Dan. 8–12)

The final chapters of Daniel contain visions related to the last three of the four human kingdoms. Chapter 8 is a record of a vision Daniel saw in the third year of Belshazzar (8:1). There is little controversy surrounding the meaning of most of this chapter. In this vision, Daniel first sees a ram with two horns, one longer than the other (v. 3). This ram symbolizes the Medo-Persian Empire (v. 20). Daniel then sees, coming from the west, a male goat with a horn between its eyes (v. 5). The goat with the horn is a symbol of the Greek Empire and Alexander the Great (v. 21). The goat strikes the ram, breaking its two horns (v. 7), but after the goat becomes great, the horn itself is broken, and in its place four horns grow up (v. 8). The rise of the four horns represents the division of the Greek Empire after Alexander's death into four smaller Greek kingdoms under his powerful generals: Macedonia under Cassander, Thrace and Asia under Lysimachus, Syria under Seleucus, and Egypt under Ptolemy (v. 22).

Out of one of the four horns a little horn arises who persecutes the saints and disrupts the temple worship (vv. 9, 24). The little horn represents the Seleucid king Antiochus IV Epiphanes. At the end of the vision, the disruption of worship under the little horn is described as "2,300 evenings and mornings" (v. 14). This has been interpreted by some as 2,300 days (i.e., a little more than six years) and by others as 2,300 evening and morning sacrifices, or 1,150 days (i.e., a little more than three years). Either number can be approximately correlated with a different part of Antiochus's reign in the second century B.C.[130]

Daniel 9 is somewhat different from the other chapters in the latter half of Daniel. The chapter begins with a lengthy prayer (vv. 1–19) and concludes with an enigmatic visionary answer to the prayer (vv. 24–27). The vision

129. Baldwin 1978, 146.

130. It simply depends on which events are taken as the starting and ending points of the desolation. The starting point is considered by some to be the removal of the high priest Onias III in 171 and by others to be the prohibition of sacrifices in late 167. The ending point is considered by some to be the reconsecration of the priesthood in 164 and by others to be the death of Antiochus in 163 (see Longman 1999, 207). It was a little more than six years between the removal of Onias III and the reconsecration of the priesthood. It was a little more than three years between Antiochus's prohibition of the sacrifices and his death.

is dated in the first year of Darius (i.e., 539 B.C.). Daniel is reading the prophecies of Jeremiah and discerns that seventy years were to pass "before the end of the desolations of Jerusalem" (vv. 1–2; Jer. 25:11–12; 29:10). He then prays a lengthy prayer of confession and supplication for the Lord to forgive his people (Dan. 9:3–19; cf. 1 Kings 8:33–34, 46–51). The angel Gabriel brings God's answer to his prayer (Dan. 9:20–23). His relatively brief answer in verses 24–27, which speaks of a coming period of "seventy weeks," is one of the most difficult passages in the book of Daniel.

A number of commentators have surveyed in detail the main interpretations of these verses.[131] Essentially, among Christian scholars there are three main views: the messianic view, the Antiochene view, and the dispensationalist view.[132] There are also variations of each of these three main views. In brief, the messianic view understands the prophecy of the seventy weeks to be fulfilled at the first advent of Jesus.[133] The Antiochene view understands the prophecy to be fulfilled at the time of Antiochus IV Epiphanes in the second century B.C.[134] According to the dispensationalist view, the first sixty-nine weeks were fulfilled at some point during the ministry of Jesus, but there is an indefinite time gap between the sixty-ninth and seventieth week. According to the dispensationalist view, the seventieth week will be fulfilled at some point in the future.[135]

Gabriel begins by telling Daniel, "Seventy weeks are decreed about your people and your holy city, to finish the transgression, to put an end to sin, and to atone for iniquity, to bring in everlasting righteousness, to seal both vision and prophet, and to anoint a most holy place" (v. 24). In order to understand this vision, it is necessary to understand the covenantal context. Moses had long before promised that if the people were exiled because of their sin but repented, they would be restored (Lev. 26:40–45). He had also warned, however, that if their exile failed to result in their repentance, they would be punished "sevenfold" (Lev. 26:18, 21, 24, 28). Daniel has realized that he is living near the end of the seventy-year period prophesied by Jeremiah, but he has also realized that the people have not repented of

131. See Young 1949, 191–95; Baldwin 1978, 172–78; Collins 1993, 112–23.

132. See Lucas 2002, 246–47, for a summary of the messianic and Antiochene views.

133. E.g., Young 1949, 192; Baldwin 1978, 175; Robertson 2004, 338.

134. E.g., Goldingay 1989, 266–67; Lucas 2002, 248.

135. E.g., Chafer 1948, 4:339; Walvoord 1971, 231–37; Price 1994, 141–61; Barker 1997, 143–46.

their sin (Dan. 9:13–14). Because of this lack of repentance, "seventy weeks" (or "seventy sevens") have now been decreed for the people.[136] Israel is now being punished "sevenfold." In other words, the complete end of the exile has been delayed due to persistent rebellion (Jer. 18:7–10).[137]

Gabriel indicates that six things will be realized within this period of seventy weeks. Three have to do with resolving the problem of sin that Daniel has been praying about (i.e., to finish transgression, to put an end to sin, and to atone for iniquity), and three are positive goals related to the restoration of the people (i.e., to bring in everlasting righteousness, to seal both vision and prophet, and to anoint a most holy place). As noted above, proponents of the three major views place the fulfillment of this prophecy at different times. The position taken here is that the prophecy found its fulfillment at the first advent of Christ. It is through the death and resurrection of Christ that all of these six goals are accomplished.[138]

In Daniel 9:25, Gabriel continues, telling Daniel, "Know therefore and understand that from the going out of the word to restore and build Jerusalem to the coming of an anointed one, a prince, there shall be seven weeks. Then for sixty-two weeks it shall be built again with squares and moat, but in a troubled time."[139] Here Gabriel announces that the seventy weeks are to begin with "the going out of the word to restore and build Jerusalem." But what "word" or "decree" (NIV) is meant? Numerous suggestions have

136. Since the context is Jeremiah's prophecy of seventy years, the "seventy sevens" are often understood to mean seventy times seven years, or 490 years (Goldingay 1989, 257). This time is also equivalent to ten jubilees (Lev. 25:8–12).

137. See McComiskey 1985b, 44.

138. Through Christ's sacrifice, iniquity is atoned for, sin and transgression are finished, and everlasting righteousness is brought in. He sealed the vision by accomplishing everything that was promised. The anointing of a most holy place could be referring to the same action mentioned in Heb. 9:11–14.

139. English versions differ in their translation of this difficult verse, depending upon whether they follow the punctuation in the Masoretic text or one of the Greek versions. The Masoretic text indicates that the time between the decree and the coming of an anointed one is seven weeks (RSV, NAB, ESV). Theodotion's Greek version indicates that the time between the decree and the coming of an anointed one is seven weeks and sixty-two weeks (ASV, NKJV, NASB, NIV). The ESV translation follows the Masoretic text. The NIV, on the other hand, follows the punctuation of Theodotion's Greek version and translates the verse as follows: "Know and understand this: From the issuing of the decree to restore and rebuild Jerusalem until the Anointed One, the ruler, comes, there will be seven 'sevens,' and sixty-two 'sevens.' It will be rebuilt with streets and a trench, but in times of trouble." It is beyond the scope of this work to get into the details of this textual issue. The implications for our interpretation will be discussed below.

been made including Jeremiah's prophecy in 605 B.C. (Jer. 25:12), Jeremiah's prophecy in 597 B.C. (Jer. 29:10), Gabriel's own announcement here to Daniel (539 B.C.), Cyrus's decree in 538 B.C. (Ezra 1:1–4), Darius's decree in 521 B.C. (Ezra 6:1–12), Artaxerxes' decree in 458 B.C. (Ezra 7:12–26), and Artaxerxes' decree in 445 B.C. (Neh. 2:7–8).

Conservative commentators are generally divided between two of these options.[140] Some argue that the decree foretold in Daniel 9:25 is the decree of Cyrus in 538 B.C.[141] Others argue that the decree is the decree of Artaxerxes given in 445 B.C. since the biblical record of Cyrus's decree does not explicitly mention the rebuilding of the city (2 Chron. 36:22–23 and Ezra 1:1–4).[142] The position taken in this work is that when Daniel 9:25 is compared with certain prophecies of Isaiah and historical narratives of Ezra, it must be concluded that the decree to restore and rebuild Jerusalem is the decree of Cyrus in 538 B.C. Isaiah had prophesied that Cyrus would be the one who would say of Jerusalem, "She shall be built" (Isa. 44:23–28). Isaiah had also prophesied of Cyrus, "he shall build my city and set my exiles free" (45:13). If Cyrus's decree in 538 was not the decree to rebuild the city, when were these prophecies of Isaiah regarding Cyrus ever fulfilled? While the biblical record of Cyrus's decree does not explicitly include mention of the city, it seems evident later in Ezra that rebuilding Jerusalem was understood (Ezra 4:12). The decree of Cyrus in 538, then, marks the beginning of the seventy "sevens."

The period of time between the decree and the coming of the "anointed one" mentioned in Daniel 9:25 is disputed because of textual variations. The punctuation of the Masoretic text separates the seven sevens and the sixty-two sevens, indicating that the time between the decree and the anointed one of verse 25 is only seven sevens.[143] Those who follow this punctuation tend to identify the decree as one of Jeremiah's prophecies and identify the anointed one as someone associated with the return from exile (e.g., Cyrus,

140. But see McComiskey 1985b for a relatively recent conservative argument in favor of the "decree" being the prophecy of Jeremiah 29:10 in 597 B.C. In favor of this view is the similarity between the language of Dan. 9:25 and Jer. 29:10. The main problem with this view is that the passage in Jeremiah is not an actual command to restore and rebuild Jerusalem.

141. E.g., Young 1949, 202.

142. E.g., Robertson 2004, 341; Walvoord 1971, 226.

143. The Masoretes added the punctuation to the consonantal text in the last half of the first millennium A.D., and some have suggested that this added punctuation may simply be in error (Young 1949, 205).

Zerubbabel, or Joshua).[144] The punctuation of Theodotion's Greek translation of Daniel indicates that the time between the decree and the anointed one of verse 25 is seven sevens and sixty-two sevens, or a total of sixty-nine sevens. Those who follow this punctuation tend to identify the decree with one of the Persian decrees and identify the anointed one of verse 25 with Jesus. If the decree is the decree of Cyrus in 538 B.C., and if the punctuation of the Masoretic text is followed, then an anointed one, different from the "anointed one" of verse 26, was to appear early in the postexilic era (after the seven sevens).[145] If the punctuation of Theodotion's Greek text is followed, then the anointed one of verse 25 is apparently the same as the anointed one of verse 26 who is "cut off" after the sixty-two sevens.

One significant objection to the idea that Daniel 9:25 refers to the decree of Cyrus is based on a certain literal interpretation of the "sevens" in the text. If there are to be sixty-nine sevens (seven and sixty-two) from the decree until the anointed one who is cut off (v. 26), and if the sevens are understood as weeks of literal years, this would equal 483 years. But the time between the decree of Cyrus in 538 B.C. and the death of Jesus was more than 483 years. For many, this is the decisive factor in concluding that the decree mentioned by Gabriel must be the decree of Artaxerxes in 445 B.C.[146] The question remains, however, whether it is necessary to interpret the sevens in such a literalistic manner in the context of apocalyptic literature.[147]

If one begins with the assumption that these numbers in Daniel are to be understood in a literal mathematical sense, then one must ignore the

144. E.g., Lucas 2002, 243; McComiskey 1985b, 25–27.

145. Probably around the time of the completion of the temple.

146. E.g., Walvoord 1971, 230; Pentecost 1958, 248; Robertson 2004, 341. From a starting point in 445 B.C., 483 years would conclude much closer to the time of Christ. It would, however, conclude almost a decade after the death and resurrection of Christ, so the difficulty is not completely resolved.

147. Even in historical narratives, there is precedent for a nonliteral interpretation of such prophecies. In Genesis 15:13, for example, God tells Abram that his offspring will be servants in a foreign land for 400 years. In Exodus 12:40–41, however, Moses states that the people of Israel lived in Egypt for 430 years. The prophecy in Genesis must be understood as a round number. The time references "seven weeks" and "sixty-two weeks" are much more ambiguous than the number 400. If the prophecy found in the historical narrative of Genesis 15, which uses a clear and unambiguous time reference, can be fulfilled in a nonliteral manner, then it is not inconceivable that a prophecy found in an apocalyptic work, using an admittedly symbolic time reference, can be fulfilled in a nonliteral manner.

several biblical prophecies that seem to point unambiguously to Cyrus as the one who would issue the decree to restore and rebuild Jerusalem. The biblical evidence that the decree is Cyrus's decree indicates that the sevens are apparently not intended to be understood as literal years. In fact, there is no reason to expect that they should be so understood within apocalyptic literature. A. Berkeley Mickelsen helpfully suggests that these numbers could instead be understood as epochal years, approximate periods of time that provide only a general idea of the time frame involved.[148] In short, after the decree of Cyrus, ending the initial period of exile, Israel will undergo a sevenfold extension of her punishment by the end of which the six goals of verse 24 will be accomplished. But we cannot calculate the period of time with mathematical precision.[149]

In verse 26, Gabriel continues, "And after the sixty-two weeks, an anointed one shall be cut off and shall have nothing. And the people of the prince who is to come shall destroy the city and the sanctuary. Its end shall come with a flood, and to the end there shall be war. Desolations are decreed." Advocates of the Antiochene interpretation generally understand this verse to be a reference to the murder of the high priest Onias III in 171 B.C.[150] This interpretation faces a difficulty, however, in that Antiochus IV Epiphanes did not destroy the city of Jerusalem in the second century. Proponents of the messianic view understand the "cutting off" of an anointed one here to be a reference to the death of Christ (Isa. 53:8).[151] Proponents of the dispensationalist view also see a reference to the death of Christ here, but they believe that "after the sixty-two weeks" does not mean "in the seventieth week." Dispensationalists see evidence here for an indefinite gap between the sixty-ninth and seventieth week.[152] There is more agreement regarding the last part of Daniel 9:26. The destruction

148. Mickelsen 1984, 198. Goldingay argues that what is being presented is not so much chronology as it is "chronography: a stylized scheme of history" (1989, 257). See also Baldwin 1978, 171. The reference to various units of sevens, rather than to years seems deliberately vague and symbolic, lending weight to the idea that these phrases are to be understood as symbolic approximations of time.

149. Even Jeremiah's original "seventy year" prophecy does not appear to have been fulfilled in an absolutely literal manner.

150. Goldingay 1989, 262.

151. Young 1949, 207. If the Masoretic punctuation of verse 25 is correct, then the "anointed one" of verse 25 and the "anointed one" of verse 26 are not the same person since one would appear after the first "seven weeks" (v. 25), and the second would be "cut off" after the "sixty-two weeks" (v. 26).

152. Pentecost 1958, 248; Walvoord 1971, 229–37.

of the city and sanctuary by "the people of the prince who is to come" is usually understood to be a reference to the destruction of Jerusalem by the Roman armies of Titus in A.D. 70.[153]

Gabriel concludes in verse 27, "Then he shall confirm a covenant with many for one week; but in the middle of the week he shall bring an end to sacrifice and offering. And on the wing of abominations shall be one who makes desolate, even until the consummation, which is determined, is poured out on the desolate" (NKJV).[154] According to the Antiochene view, this verse refers to the covenant made between certain Jews and Gentiles in the second century B.C. (1 Macc. 1:11, 41–59).[155] According to the messianic interpretation, the antecedent of "he" is the "anointed one" of Daniel 9:26, namely Jesus, who fulfilled the covenant made with the patriarchs.[156] According to the dispensationalist view, the antecedent of "he" is "the prince who is to come" (v. 26), the future antichrist, who will make a covenant with the Jews at the beginning of the tribulation period.[157]

The context supports the messianic interpretation. The "anointed one" was to bring an end "to sacrifice and offering." If the "anointed one" is a prophetic reference to Jesus, then the fulfillment of this text occurred at his death when he offered the final sacrifice for sin (Heb. 10:5–10).[158] The seventy sevens, then, were fulfilled in the events surrounding the ministry,

153. Some argue that the mention of this destruction of the city proves the necessity of a gap between the sixty-ninth and seventieth week because the destruction of the city occurred some forty years after the death of Christ and could not fit within a literal understanding of the seventy weeks as 490 years. Two points are necessary in response. First, as mentioned above, the nature of the apocalyptic language and the identification of the decree in Daniel 9:25 with Cyrus's decree already indicate strongly that these "sevens" or "weeks" are not to be interpreted in a literalistic manner. Second, Daniel nowhere states that the destruction of the city and sanctuary occurs within the seventy weeks. Daniel does not state exactly when this event will occur.

154. The difficulty of this verse is evident from the variety of subtle differences in the translations. I have used the NKJV here because it is a better translation of this particular verse.

155. Goldingay 1989, 262.

156. Young 1949, 208–21.

157. Walvoord 1959, 259; 1971, 233. The fundamental problem with the dispensationalist interpretation is that it requires the unwarranted insertion of a gap of at least two thousand years between the sixty-ninth and seventieth week. For a critique of this interpretation, see Allis 1947, 111–23; LaRondelle 1983, 170–82.

158. Some object that Jesus could not have brought an end to sacrifice and offering since animal sacrifices continued in the temple until it was destroyed in A.D. 70. The fact of the matter remains, however, that with the death of Christ, sacrifices and offerings were abolished (Heb. 10:9). Christ's death put an end to the appropriateness of the old covenant and its sacrificial provisions. After the death of Christ, the sacrifices in the temple amounted to nothing.

death, and resurrection of Jesus.[159] The desolation referred to in the second half of Daniel 9:27 is a prophetic reference to what would occur during the destruction of Jerusalem and the temple by Titus's armies in and around A.D. 70. As in verse 26, this is not said to happen in the seventieth week. Instead it appears to be a consequence of the events of the seventieth week.[160]

Despite the many difficulties involved with the interpretation of Daniel 9:24–27, the basic message seems clear: The exile has not resulted in the repentance of God's people. Therefore God is extending Israel's punishment sevenfold. By the end of this period of time, he will atone for his people's sin through the death of an anointed one. The city of Jerusalem, which will be rebuilt at the beginning of the seventy sevens, will be destroyed once again as a consequence of the events surrounding the cutting off of the anointed one.

The fourth and final vision in the book of Daniel is found in chapters 10–12. The introduction to the vision is found in 10:1–11:1, while the vision itself is found in 11:2–12:3. God's instructions for Daniel are found in 12:4–13.[161] In chapter 10, Daniel sees a vision of a man who tells him that he has come to make Daniel understand what is to happen to his people in the latter days (vv. 1–14).[162] As we have observed in connection with its usage elsewhere, the phrase "in the latter days" is simply a reference to an unspecified time in the future.

The detail of the vision itself in 11:2–12:3 is unprecedented in biblical prophecy.[163] Some see in the detail evidence that this is prophecy written after

159. One important objection that is often raised against the messianic interpretation is that it cannot point to any significant event closing the seventieth week, three and a half years after the death of Christ (Walvoord 1959, 259). This objection, however, requires that the sevens refer to literal years. That point is highly debatable. However, even granting a more literal interpretation of the sevens, this objection also overlooks the fact that Daniel 9:24–27 does not mention a specific event closing the seventieth seven. Daniel mentions the event that marks its beginning—the decree to restore and rebuild Jerusalem, but he does not mention a specific event that clearly marks its end. Furthermore, if the punctuation of the Masoretic text is adopted, and it is by most of those who raise this objection, there is also no mention in Daniel of a specific event marking the division between the seven sevens and the sixty-two sevens.

160. Young 1949, 218–19. Daniel will later speak of an "abomination that makes desolate" (11:31) in connection with events of the second century B.C. Jesus will, however, refer to it in the future tense (Matt. 24:15). The abomination spoken of in Daniel 11:31, then, appears to be a preliminary fulfillment of the prophecy in Daniel 9, while the abomination spoken of by Jesus appears to be the ultimate fulfillment of it.

161. Longman 1999, 245.

162. Young suggests that the description of the man in verses 5–6 indicates that it was a theophany, a vision of the Lord (1949, 225).

163. Baldwin 1978, 184.

the fact.[164] It is the view of the present author, however, that the book contains a genuine prophecy of events from the time of the Persian Empire onward.[165] The last two centuries of the Persian Empire are passed over with little comment in 11:2. In verses 3–4, Daniel foresees the rise of the Greek Empire under Alexander the Great and its division into four smaller kingdoms after his death (see also 8:8, 22). The beginnings of conflict between the "king of the south" (the Ptolemaic kingdom) and the "king of the north" (the Seleucid kingdom) are described in 11:5–9. The ongoing battles between the Ptolemaic kingdom and the Seleucid kingdom are described in detail in verses 10–20.

Daniel 11:21 introduces a "contemptible person." This is generally acknowledged to be a prophetic reference to the Seleucid king Antiochus IV Epiphanes, who reigned from 175 to 163 B.C. (1 Macc. 1:10; 6:16). This section of the prophecy raises a question, however. Why so much attention devoted to this second century B.C. king? Many have suggested that the detail is due to the fact that some or all of this chapter is a prophecy of a coming antichrist.[166] Joyce Baldwin has suggested that it is due to the fact that this is the beginning of the era of the persecution of God's people.[167] The persecution of the Jews by Antiochus is well known (1 Maccabees).[168] His military exploits and persecution of the Jews are prophesied in detail at least through 11:35. In verses 29–31, Daniel declares that after his forced retreat from Egypt, this contemptible king shall set up "the abomination that makes desolate." This probably refers to the altar that Antiochus built on the temple altar (1 Macc. 1:54, 59).[169] In 11:32–35, Daniel foresees the persecution unleashed by Antiochus against the faithful remnant in Jerusalem. These verses likely have in view the Maccabean resistance.[170]

At verse 36, Daniel refers to "the king." Interpreters differ widely in their understanding of the identity of this king. Many believe Daniel is continu-

164. E.g., Collins 1993, 25–26.

165. For a good survey of the historical background, see Lucas 2002, 37–42.

166. Jerome taught that from verse 21 on, there is a double reference to Antiochus and to the antichrist. Hippolytus and Theodotion taught that verse 36 is the transition point at which the antichrist is introduced. Young agrees that verse 36 marks the transition (1949, 246).

167. Baldwin 1978, 192.

168. On the reign of Antiochus Epiphanes, see Bruce 1963, 134–46.

169. Jesus refers to an abomination of desolation spoken of by Daniel as something still future in his own day (Matt. 24:15). If Daniel 11:29–31 does refer to Antiochus, then Jesus' words open up the possibility of double fulfillment.

170. Baldwin 1978, 197.

ing to refer to Antiochus. On the other hand, many believe he is referring to a future antichrist figure. Other suggestions include Herod the Great, Constantine the Great, the Roman Empire, and the pope.[171] Those who see here a continuing reference to Antiochus face a difficulty in verses 40–45. Verse 40 provides no indication that the subject has changed, but unlike the prophecies from verses 21–35, which were fulfilled by Antiochus, the prophecies of verses 40–45 were not fulfilled by him.[172]

These factors have led most conservative interpreters to identify the king of verses 36–45 with a future antichrist figure.[173] In favor of this interpretation is the fact that verses 40–45 do not correspond to the events in the life of Antiochus. Also in favor of this interpretation is the fact that Daniel 12:1–3 is a prophecy of a resurrection of many occurring "at that time," apparently meaning at the time of that king. The weak point in this interpretation is the lack of any clear textual indication of a gap of thousands of years. The most plausible alternative to the antichrist interpretation seems to be that "the king" in 11:40–45 refers to Herod the Great and his line.[174] Edward J. Young notes that some aspects of the Herodian interpretation are plausible, while ultimately rejecting it in favor of the antichrist interpretation.[175]

In favor of the Herodian interpretation is the fact that while verses 40–45 do not correspond with any known events in the life of Antiochus, there are possible correspondences in the life of Herod the Great and his descendants.[176] The weak point in the Herodian interpretation is the reference in 12:1–3 to the resurrection of many "at that time," a resurrection which most scholars rightly understand to be a reference to the bodily resurrection of believers. Daniel 12:1–3 leaves four possibilities open for the Herodian view, the first two of which deny that Daniel 12:2 refers to a bodily resurrection and the second two of which affirm it.

171. See Young 1949, 246–47, for a list of prominent interpretations.

172. Lucas 2002, 290–91. Many advocates of this view believe that to this point the author was writing history in the guise of prophecy but that in verses 40–45 he attempted real prophecy and failed.

173. E.g., Young 1949, 247–53.

174. This view is presented in Mauro 1965.

175. Young 1949, 248.

176. Mauro, for example, argues that verses 40–43 correspond with the events marking the beginning of the Actian war (1965, 149–50). He also argues (p. 157) that verse 44 corresponds with events surrounding Herod's discovery of and reaction to the birth of Christ (Matt. 2:1–3, 16).

On the one hand, the Herodian view could be maintained by denying that Daniel 12:2 refers to a bodily general resurrection: (1) It could be argued that the resurrection in Daniel 12:2 is not a prophecy of the bodily general resurrection of believers, but is instead a prophecy regarding regeneration.[177] (2) It could be argued that the resurrection in Daniel 12:2 is a prophecy of the general resurrection of believers, and that this general resurrection did occur in the days of the Herodians. It was, however, a nonbodily resurrection, and no bodily resurrection of believers is to be expected.[178] Both of these interpretations must be rejected for their failure to do justice to the text of Daniel 12:2.

Conceivably, the Herodian view could also be maintained while affirming that Daniel 12:2 does refer to a bodily general resurrection: (3) It could be argued that the words "At that time" in Daniel 12:1 are used in a way similar to the phrase "In that day" in Amos 9:11, a text requiring a time delay. Thus, the bodily general resurrection would not be understood as having to occur in the days of the Herodians. (4) It could be argued that the reference to Jesus' resurrection as the firstfruits (1 Cor. 15:20) is an indication that his resurrection and the future general resurrection of believers should be seen as a unity (one "harvest") despite the period of time between the two.[179] In this case, the resurrection of Jesus the firstfruits in the days of the Herodians could be seen as the beginning of the fulfillment of Daniel 12:2. As Young noted, certain aspects of the Herodian interpretation seem plausible. However, little detailed study of this option has been attempted.[180] At the present time it can be mentioned only as a possible interpretation of this disputed text. If it is adopted, however, then one of the latter two explanations of Daniel 12:1–3 is required, the second being the more plausible. Otherwise, the king in 11:40–45 must be understood to be a future antichrist.

Daniel 12:4–13 contains God's final instructions for Daniel. He is instructed to "shut up the words and seal the book, until the time of the end" (v. 4a). He

177. This is Mauro's position (1965, 168ff.).

178. Such a view of the general resurrection may be found in the writings of full preterists. For a critique of the full-preterist doctrine of the resurrection, see Strimple 2004, 287–352.

179. In speaking of those passages that refer to Jesus as the "firstfruits" or the "firstborn" from the dead, Ridderbos (1975, 56) explains, "Here the picture of the harvest is in the background. The firstfruits are not only its beginning, but its representation. In the firstfruits the whole harvest becomes visible."

180. Skeptical scholars would likely not consider it as a possibility because it would demand that Daniel contains genuine prophecy regardless of the date assigned to it.

is told that "many shall run to and fro, and knowledge shall increase" (v. 4b). This seems to be a reversal of the judgment oracle in Amos 8:12. Daniel then asks how long it will be until "the end of these wonders" (12:6). He is told "that it would be for a time, times, and half a time, and that when the shattering of the power of the holy people comes to an end all these things would be finished" (v. 7; cf. 7:25). As mentioned in connection with 7:25, the reference to "a time, times, and half a time" seems to be a symbol of an indefinite period of time that is cut short by God's intervention. If the reference is to a future antichrist, then the "shattering of the power of the holy people" is likely referring to a persecution of believers prior to the second coming of Christ. If the reference is to the first century, then the reference may be to the destruction of the city and temple in A.D. 70.

Daniel says that he does not understand and asks for clarification (v. 8). He is reminded that the words are shut up and sealed until the time of the end (v. 9). He is told that many will purify themselves, but the wicked will continue to be wicked. They will not understand, but the wise will understand (v. 10). He is then told that "from the time that the regular burnt offering is taken away and the abomination that makes desolate is set up, there shall be 1,290 days. Blessed is he who waits and arrives at the 1,335 days" (vv. 11–12). As Ernest Lucas observes, "No one has been able to suggest a satisfactory explanation of the two time periods given in vv. 11–12."[181] The reference to the "abomination that makes desolate" (cf. 11:31) seems to indicate that these numbers refer to some period of time during Antiochus Epiphanes' persecution of the Jews. Regardless of their precise meaning, however, it is clear that these verses urge readers to persevere in faithfulness.

Summary

The exile marked a turning point in redemptive history. After centuries of prophetic warnings, the ultimate curses of the covenant had been imposed upon God's chosen people. They had been removed from the Promised Land and scattered to the nations. But even worse, God had removed his presence from them. Israel's sin had led to the death of the nation. The survivors were left with many questions. Had God totally forsaken his people? Were

181. Lucas 2002, 297. Lucas himself lists several of the interpretations that have been suggested, but none is obviously correct.

the ancient promises null and void? Did any hope remain for the future? Into this situation God sent the prophets of the exile.

The small book of Obadiah reminded the people who were suffering in a foreign land that all of the nations were accountable to God, and that all would be judged. It also hinted that hope remained, promising that what Israel through her sin had lost, God would by grace give back someday. The prophet Ezekiel ministered to the exiles in Babylon in the years immediately preceding and following the fall of Jerusalem. Prior to the city's fall, he warned that judgment was imminent. After the fall of the city, he turned his attention to the future. Like a new Moses, he proclaimed the coming of a new exodus. He promised that the people would be regathered from the nations, that the Davidic throne would be restored, that God would renew his covenant, and that he would dwell in the midst of his people once again.

The prophet Daniel lived most of his life in exile in Babylon. He was among the first of the exiles to be deported, yet he lived to witness the fall of Babylon and Cyrus's decree to restore and rebuild Jerusalem and the temple. The book of Daniel demonstrated to the people how to live faithfully in exile. His mysterious visions bore witness to the coming of the kingdom of God. After a series of human kingdoms, the climax of history would witness the establishment by God of a righteous kingdom that would fill the earth. However, the visions of Daniel also warned the people that their lack of repentance would entail a sevenfold extension of their exilic punishment. By the end of this period, the problem of sin would be dealt with and the Messiah would come.

9

The Postexilic Prophets

Haggai, Zechariah, and Malachi

The exile was a major turning point in the history of Israel. Judah and Jerusalem had fallen to the armies of Nebuchadnezzar. Many of the people of the land had been taken captive to Babylon, while others had fled to Egypt and parts unknown. A small number of the poor had remained behind in Judah. The ultimate curse of the covenant had been realized. After centuries of prophetic warnings, the death penalty had been carried out on Israel. The land was in ruins, and the people were in exile. In 539 B.C., however, Babylon fell to the Persians, and in 538 Cyrus issued a decree permitting the exiled Jews to return to Judah and rebuild the temple. Were the prophecies of restoration now to be fulfilled? Would the messianic kingdom of God now be established? These are the questions faced by the postexilic prophets Haggai, Zechariah, and Malachi.

In order to understand the postexilic prophets, some historical context is necessary.[1] The Babylonian king Nebuchadnezzar had died in 562, and

1. For helpful surveys, see Merrill 1996, 475–515; Provan, Long, and Longman 2003, 278–303.

his death had precipitated the rapid decline of his empire. His reign was followed in quick succession by the reigns of Evil-Merodach (562–560), Neriglissar (560–556), and Labisi-Marduk (556) before any semblance of stability was reached with the reign of Nabonidus (555–539). Yet even under Nabonidus there was trouble because of religious controversies. Due to these problems, Nabonidus was absent from the capital for lengthy periods of time. His son Belshazzar was the effective ruler of Babylon during these periods. In 539 B.C., Belshazzar was present in the city when Babylon fell to Cyrus the Persian.

Cyrus had a policy, unusual for the time, of allowing captive peoples to return to their homelands, so in 538 he issued a decree allowing the exiled Jews to return to Judah (Ezra 1:1–4). Tens of thousands returned with Zerubbabel and Joshua, but an even larger number remained behind, not willing to give up the life they had established in Babylon over the previous decades (Ezra 2). Those who did return to the land were faced with numerous hardships.[2] The land was in poor shape for farming, and many buildings were in need of repairs. In addition, the Jews who had remained in Judah had taken the land of those who had been exiled. Furthermore, Judah's neighbors were adamantly opposed to the rebuilding program. All of this caused widespread discouragement. Thus after rebuilding the altar in 537 (Ezra 3:1–7) and preparing the foundation of the temple in 536 (Ezra 3:8–13), opposition and despair caused work to come to a standstill for over fifteen years (Ezra 4:1–5).

To the northeast of Judah, Cyrus had continued to expand the Persian Empire until his death in 530. He was followed by Cambyses II (530–522), and Gaumata (522), before Darius Hystaspes (522–486) came to the throne. After receiving complaints from the enemies of the Jews and researching the royal archives, Darius discovered the decree of Cyrus. In 520 B.C. he ordered opposition against the Jews to cease in order that they might complete the temple (Ezra 5:1–6:12). It was near the beginning of his reign that the prophets Haggai (520 B.C.) and Zechariah (520–518 B.C.) arose in Judah to bring God's word to the people.

After much work, the temple was finally completed in 515 B.C. In Persia, Darius's lengthy reign was followed by that of Xerxes (486–465) and then Artaxerxes I (464–424), during whose reign Ezra led a second group of

2. Dillard and Longman 1994, 422.

returnees to Judah in 458 (Ezra 7:1–28). Nehemiah returned to Jerusalem with a third group of returnees in 445 to finish rebuilding the wall of the city (Neh. 1–2). He returned to Persia in 433. The ministry of the prophet Malachi likely occurred sometime in the period soon after Nehemiah's departure but before his second visit (Neh. 13:6).

The postexilic prophets faced a daunting task. Earlier prophets had foreseen a glorious restoration following the judgment of exile (Amos 9:11, 14–15; Mic. 4:6–7). Daniel, on the other hand, had borne witness to a sevenfold extension of the punishment of exile (Dan. 9:24–27). Yet Cyrus had now permitted the Jews in Babylon to return to their land. Was this the promised time of restoration or not? The postexilic prophets reveal an eschatological tension in their writings. They bear witness to the inauguration of eschatological restoration, but also proclaim that the fullness is yet to come.[3] They provide the first hints that the promised restoration from exile is not to occur all at once.

Haggai

It had been almost twenty years since the decree of Cyrus when the prophet Haggai was called to bring the word of God to the people of Jerusalem in 520 B.C. Following the return from Babylon, the people had begun well, completing the rebuilding of the altar in 537 and preparing the temple foundation in 536. Opposition and other problems, however, had caused discouragement to set in, and work on the temple had ceased for over fifteen years.[4] The people became occupied with their own personal concerns, and the temple remained in ruins. Haggai called on the people to get their priorities straight.

All of the oracles in the book of Haggai are precisely dated to the last several months of the year 520 B.C.[5] The first oracle (1:1–11), calling on the people to rebuild the temple, is dated August 29, 520. The second oracle (1:12–15), encouraging the workers with the promise of God's presence, is dated September 21, 520. The third oracle (2:1–9), encouraging the people with the promise of God's presence in the future, is dated October 17, 520. The fourth oracle (2:10–19), describing the blessings that will

3. Van Gemeren 1990, 87.
4. Baldwin 1972, 37.
5. Verhoef 1987, 5.

result from the rebuilding of the temple, is dated December 18, 520. The fifth and final oracle (2:20–23), looking forward to the rebuilding of the Davidic house, is also dated December 18, 520.

The book of Haggai begins by declaring when the first oracle was given, "In the second year of Darius the king . . ." (1:1). The Darius in question is Darius Hystaspes who ruled Persia from 522 until 486 B.C. The second year of Darius the king is 520 B.C. It is now some eighteen years after the return of the first group of exiles to Jerusalem, and the temple has still not been rebuilt. Haggai's commission from God is to urge the people to complete the temple. But why is it necessary to rebuild the temple? Joyce Baldwin helpfully explains: "The rebuilding of the Temple was at once an act of dedication and of faith. It was a symbol of the continuity of the present with the past, and expressed the longing of the community that despite the exile, the old covenant promises still stood."[6] The people were saying that "the time has not yet come to rebuild the house of Yahweh" (1:2). On the contrary, according to Haggai, the temple should have already been rebuilt. The people had put themselves and their own personal comfort ahead of honoring God (1:4).[7] Because of their neglect of the temple, they were experiencing some of the curses of the covenant (1:6; Deut. 28:38).

Haggai's prophetic words have their intended effect. "Then Zerubbabel the son of Shealtiel, and Joshua the son of Jehozadak, the high priest, with all the remnant of the people, obeyed the voice of Yahweh their God, and the words of Haggai the prophet, as Yahweh their God had sent him. And the people feared Yahweh" (Hag. 1:12). With their repentant faith and obedience comes God's promise, "I am with you, declares Yahweh" (v. 13). The people finally get their priorities straight and begin the work of rebuilding the temple (v. 14).

Haggai's third oracle comes several weeks after construction on the temple has actually begun (2:1–9). It had become apparent to many that the second temple was not going to be anywhere near as grand as the first temple built by Solomon (v. 3). Haggai encourages the people with the promises of God's presence: "Work, for I am with you, declares Yahweh of hosts" (v. 4). "My Spirit remains in your midst" (v. 5). God promises that he will soon "shake the heavens and the earth and the sea and the dry land" (v. 6). He declares, "And I will shake all nations, so that the treasures of all nations

6. Baldwin 1972, 21.

7. Motyer 1998a, 976.

shall come in, and I will fill this house with glory" (v. 7).[8] In short, Haggai is continuing to point the people toward the future. The ancient prophecies of restoration still await their complete fulfillment.

Haggai begins his fourth oracle with a question about sanctity and defilement (2:10–19). He wants to make it clear to the people that although defilement is transferable by contact, holiness is not. Being in the Promised Land would not make the people holy. Building the temple would not make them holy. The people have been unholy and for that reason have suffered judgment. However, as Moses had promised, their renewed obedience would result in blessing (2:19; Deut. 28:1–14).

Haggai's book ends with a somewhat enigmatic oracle to Zerubbabel (2:20–23). The Lord declares that he is about to shake the heavens and earth and overthrow kingdoms (v. 22). Haggai then says, "On that day, declares Yahweh of hosts, I will take you, O Zerubbabel my servant, the son of Shealtiel, declares Yahweh, and make you like a signet ring, for I have chosen you, declares Yahweh of hosts" (v. 23). Zerubbabel was a descendant of David, and just as David was associated with the coming Messiah in earlier prophecies, here Zerubbabel is associated with the coming Messiah (see also Ezek. 34:23). But what does this have to do with the rebuilding of the temple? "The rebuilding of the temple meant the reestablishment of the kingship of God and not of man."[9] Just as God had promised to build David's house in the context of building the first temple, so here he promises to rebuild David's house in the context of building the second temple.

Zechariah

The book of Zechariah is the lengthiest of the so-called Minor Prophets and one of the most difficult books in the Old Testament. The historical context of the book is identical to that of Haggai. The first eight chapters of Zechariah contain date references ranging from October of 520 B.C. to December of 518 B.C. Chapters 9–14 do not contain any date references. This combined with several other factors has led most critical scholars to conclude that a different author wrote chapters 9–14 in a different cen-

8. Some translations imply that this verse is a reference to the coming Messiah. The verb, however, is a third person common plural verb, so, as Calvin indicated long ago, it is doubtful that this particular verse is speaking of the Messiah.

9. Meyers and Meyers 1987, 82.

tury.[10] Suggestions range from the eighth century to the second-century Maccabean period. However, despite the consensus among critical scholars, the evidence does not demand a different author for the last six chapters of Zechariah.[11]

Zechariah deals with a number of important themes, the most significant being the restoration of Israel. He encourages the people with the promise that Jerusalem and the temple will be rebuilt and that this rebuilding will have worldwide significance. God will once again manifest his presence among his people and cleanse them from their sin. He will overcome their sin and rebellion through a coming Messiah. Zechariah's visions and oracles teach the people that although the restoration from exile has already begun, it has not yet reached its full consummation.[12]

The book of Zechariah has a fairly self-evident five-part structure. The book begins with an introductory superscription (1:1–6). The superscription is then followed by the second major section of the book, a series of eight visions interspersed with oracles (1:7–6:8). The third major section of the book is a prose narrative recounting the symbolic crowning of Joshua the high priest (6:9–15). The fourth major section of the book is largely a prose narrative involving questions about fasting and Zechariah's response (chs. 7–8). The fifth and final major section of the book contains two lengthy oracles. The first oracle prophesies the coming of God against Israel's enemies (chs. 9–11). The second and final oracle prophesies the coming of Zion's Messiah (chs. 12–14). These final two oracles move from the immediate concerns of the postexilic community toward more apocalyptic future-oriented imagery.

Superscription (Zech. 1:1–6)

The word of the Lord came to Zechariah in "the eighth month, in the second year of Darius" (1:1). This was in the year 520 B.C., approximately two months after the word of God came to Haggai (Hag. 1:1). Zechariah is described as "the son of Berechiah, son of Iddo" (Zech. 1:1). This language differs from that of Ezra 5:1 and 6:14 in which Zechariah is referred to as "the son of Iddo." The apparent discrepancy should be understood in

10. On the issues involved, see Dillard and Longman 1994, 429.
11. See Baldwin 1972, 68–69.
12. Van Gemeren 1990, 194.

light of the fact that the word "son" was occasionally used to refer to the grandson of a person. In the books of Kings, for example, Jehu is referred to as the "son of Nimshi" (1 Kings 19:16; 2 Kings 9:20) and as the "son of Jehoshaphat, son of Nimshi" (2 Kings 9:2, 14).

Zechariah begins by proclaiming, "Yahweh was very angry with your fathers" (1:2). The previous generations of Israelites had broken the covenant, and God's wrath had come upon them in the form of the covenant curses, including the exile. Subtly implied in this statement is the idea that the present generation may also be subject to God's anger if it too forsakes God. Zechariah calls upon the people to repent and return to the Lord (v. 3). He warns them not to respond to his word in the way their fathers responded to the preexilic prophets (v. 4). They ignored the prophets and went into exile (v. 5). The punishment of the exile led the previous generation to acknowledge the truth of the prophets' warnings (v. 6). Zechariah urges the present generation to learn from the example of their fathers.

Those Jews who returned to Jerusalem from exile lived in difficult times. Many probably wondered whether the covenant between Israel and God was permanently shattered. Although many of the people had returned, many had not. In addition, the temple was in ruins. Had God forever abandoned them? The word of God that came through Zechariah affirmed that the possibility of a restored relationship with God still existed.[13] Zechariah takes up where the preexilic prophets had left off, calling the people to repentance. These introductory verses characterize the entire history of Israel in terms of the way each generation heeded or failed to heed God's prophetic word.[14]

The Night Visions (Zech. 1:7–6:8)

The immediate historical concern of Zechariah is the rebuilding of the Jerusalem temple. The visions that dominate the first six chapters, however, place the rebuilding of the temple into a larger context. As Michael Floyd explains, this section of the book "persuasively describes Zechariah's claim that Yahweh's intention to restore and bless his people will be realized through the completion of the temple rebuilding project."[15] In other words,

13. Craigie 1984–85, 2:160.
14. Floyd 2000, 322.
15. Floyd 2000, 307.

the rebuilding of the temple is not merely a local Jewish concern. It is something tied to the outworking of God's redemptive historical purposes.[16]

The First Vision

The beginning of Zechariah's night visions is precisely dated on "the twenty-fourth day of the eleventh month . . . in the second year of Darius" (1:7). This is exactly five months to the day after the people had resumed work on the temple as a result of Haggai's preaching (Hag. 1:14–15). The word of God comes to Zechariah in the night, and he sees a man on a red horse among myrtle trees. Behind him are other horses of various colors (Zech. 1:8). He asks what this means, and the angel tells him, "These are they whom Yahweh has sent to patrol the earth" (v. 10). The riders then say to the angel, "We have patrolled the earth, and behold, all the earth remains at rest" (v. 11). The report that the world is at peace would appear to be good news for the postexilic Israelites, but the angel of the Lord will have a different perspective.

After hearing the report of the riders, the angel of the Lord cries out, "O Yahweh of hosts, how long will you have no mercy on Jerusalem and the cities of Judah, against which you have been angry these seventy years?" (v. 12). Although the Lord's precise response is not revealed, it is said to be "gracious and comforting" (v. 13). As Thomas McComiskey explains, this "signals the fact that God will again have compassion on his people."[17] The angel reveals that the Lord is exceedingly jealous for Jerusalem (v. 14). The Lord's loyalty to his people is not to be doubted. He is angry with the nations that are at peace, for although he used them to chastise Israel, they went beyond what was right (v. 15).[18] The Lord declares that he has returned to Jerusalem with mercy. He promises that his temple will be rebuilt, and that his blessings will be restored to the people (vv. 16–17).

The first night vision answers a question that was likely troubling the returned exiles. They had been judged for their sins, and rightly so, but what about the nations who had sinned even more wickedly? The fact that these nations were at peace raised questions concerning God's justice. This

16. See *NIDOTTE*, 4:1304.

17. McComiskey 1998, 1041.

18. It is noteworthy that Zechariah says here that God was only "angry but a little" with Israel in the years leading up to the exile. This is evident in the fact that Israel was not completely destroyed for her apostasy.

vision reveals that God is watching over all of these nations. He knows what they are doing, and he is angry with them. His justice will prevail. More importantly, however, this first vision reveals that God still has compassion for his people. Zechariah reveals God's promise to restore not only the temple building but all the blessings of prosperity.[19]

The Second Vision

In his second vision, Zechariah sees four horns (1:18). He asks the meaning of what he has seen, and the angel explains, "These are the horns that have scattered Judah, Israel, and Jerusalem" (v. 19). Zechariah then sees four craftsmen (v. 20). When he asks the meaning of these, the angel tells him, "these have come to terrify them, to cast down the horns of the nations who lifted up their horns against the land of Judah to scatter it" (v. 21). Thus, as Ralph Smith observes, "The second vision takes up the theme of the wrath of God on the nations which was set out in vision 1."[20]

Were it not for the fact that the angel describes the four horns as the horns that have scattered the people, it might be possible that what Zechariah sees are the four horns of an altar (e.g., Ex. 27:2).[21] The explanation of the angel, however, indicates that the horns represent hostile national powers (Dan. 7:24; 8:22). The four craftsmen are "God's personal emissaries, sent to destroy those who have exiled Judah."[22] The vision is meant to encourage Israel. Though hostile powers continued to surround her in her vulnerable state, God would defend her from attack.

The Third Vision

Zechariah's third night vision is of a man with a measuring line in his hand (2:1). Zechariah asks where he is going, and the man says, "To measure Jerusalem, to see what is its width and what is its length" (v. 2). The man symbolizes the ongoing rebuilding process. An angel is instructed to give a message to the man, saying, "Jerusalem shall be inhabited as villages without walls, because of the multitude of people and livestock in it" (v. 4). He continues, "And I will be to her a wall of fire all around, declares

19. Smith 1984, 191.
20. Smith 1984, 193.
21. See Sweeney 2000, 582.
22. Meyers and Meyers 1987, 148.

Yahweh, and I will be the glory in her midst" (v. 5). This is an assurance of divine protection. Jerusalem will not need defensive walls because the Lord himself will be her defense. It is also a promise of God's presence with his people. He will again dwell in her midst.

The third vision is followed by a brief oracle (vv. 6–13). This oracle, as Baldwin explains, "is addressed to the Jews who remained in exile, urging them to *flee from the land of the north*, and to return to strengthen the hands of those rebuilding the community in Jerusalem."[23] Zechariah proclaims, "Up! Escape to Zion, you who dwell with the daughter of Babylon" (v. 7). The nations that took Israel captive shall become plunder to those they enslaved (v. 9). Again the Lord promises that he will dwell in the midst of his people as he did in the days of old (v. 10). Echoes of the promise to Abraham are then heard as the Lord promises that "many nations shall join themselves to Yahweh in that day, and shall be my people" (v. 11). Jerusalem's large population, then, will be the result of the return of many more Jewish exiles along with an ingathering of people from the Gentile nations.

The Fourth Vision

In his fourth vision, Zechariah witnesses a scene involving a legal dispute. "Then he showed me Joshua the high priest standing before the angel of Yahweh, and Satan standing at his right hand to accuse him" (Zech. 3:1). The Lord rebukes this accuser, saying, "Yahweh who has chosen Jerusalem rebuke you! Is not this a brand plucked from the fire?" (v. 2). The high priest represents the people. Here Joshua represents the entire postexilic community.[24] He is depicted as standing before the angel of the Lord and clothed with filthy garments (v. 3).

Zechariah continues, "And the angel said to those who were standing before him, 'Remove the filthy garments from him.' And to him he said, 'Behold, I have taken your iniquity away from you, and I will clothe you with pure vestments'" (v. 4). McComiskey explains the significance of this: "The removal of the filthy garments silenced the accuser, making his charge baseless, because the supreme Judge has done the unthinkable: he has removed the guilt of the people by a sovereign act of grace."[25] Zecha-

23. Baldwin 1972, 108.
24. McComiskey 1998, 1069.
25. McComiskey 1998, 1071.

riah's vision demonstrates that God accepts Joshua and the people and that he has removed their sin from his sight. Having clothed Joshua with pure vestments, the angel of the Lord now speaks to him, "Thus says Yahweh of hosts: If you will walk in my ways and keep my charge, then you shall rule my house and have charge of my courts, and I will give you the right of access among those who are standing here" (v. 7).

The final verses of this vision contain a prophecy that hearkens back to preexilic messianic prophecies. The Lord will send one who will be the means by which God removes the people's guilt.

> Hear now, O Joshua the high priest, you and your friends who sit before you, for they are men who are a sign: behold, I will bring my servant the Branch. For behold, on the stone that I have set before Joshua, on a single stone with seven eyes, I will engrave its inscription, declares Yahweh of hosts, and I will remove the iniquity of this land in a single day. In that day, declares Yahweh of hosts, every one of you will invite his neighbor to come under his vine and under his fig tree. (vv. 8–10)

Zechariah uses the same word for "servant" that is found within the Servant Songs of Isaiah (Isa. 52:13; 53:11). He also uses the same term for "Branch" that is found in Jeremiah (Jer. 23:5; 33:15). The stone is possibly a symbol of the temple that is being rebuilt. If so, the seven eyes likely symbolize the fact that God is watching over the rebuilding process. Through the ministry of God's servant the Branch, Israel's iniquity will be removed, and the people will enjoy abundance and security.[26]

The Fifth Vision

In his fifth vision, Zechariah is awakened by the angel of the Lord and asked what he sees. Zechariah replies, "I see, and behold, a lampstand all of gold, with a bowl on the top of it, and seven lamps on it, with seven lips on each of the lamps that are on the top of it. And there are two olive trees by it, one on the right of the bowl and the other on its left" (Zech. 4:2–3). He asks what the meaning of this vision is, and the angel replies, "This is the word of Yahweh to Zerubbabel: Not by might, nor by power,

26. Zechariah's statement that everyone will invite his neighbor to come under his vine and under his fig tree is a symbol of the kind of abundance and security that Israel enjoyed under Solomon (1 Kings 4:25).

but by my Spirit, says Yahweh of hosts. Who are you, O great mountain? Before Zerubbabel you shall become a plain. And he shall bring forward the top stone amid shouts of 'Grace, grace to it!'" (vv. 6–7). The words of the angel are not a direct answer to Zechariah's question, but their sense may be inferred. Zerubbabel was a descendant of David, who had returned to the land after the decree of Cyrus (Ezra 2:1–2). The vision indicates, through a message to Zerubbabel, that the task of rebuilding the temple will be accomplished not by human strength, but by the power of God.

Zechariah continues, "Then the word of Yahweh came to me, saying, 'The hands of Zerubbabel have laid the foundation of this house; his hands shall also complete it. Then you will know that Yahweh of hosts has sent me to you. For whoever has despised the day of small things shall rejoice, and shall see the plumb line in the hand of Zerubbabel'" (Zech. 4:8–10). Here is an assurance that the present difficult labor of rebuilding the temple is not futile. The temple will be completed, and the people will rejoice.

Zechariah remains curious about the meaning of one element of his vision, so he asks the angel the meaning of the two olive trees to the right and left of the golden lampstand (v. 11). He then asks the meaning of the two branches from the olive trees from which oil is poured out into the lampstand (v. 12). The angel answers, "These are the two anointed ones who stand by the Lord of the whole earth" (v. 14). The two olive trees, then, represent Joshua the high priest and Zerubbabel.[27] They are specially equipped for the task to which they have been called. The vision is intended to encourage these two leaders in their task as well as to vindicate their leadership to the people. In addition, as Baldwin explains, there is also messianic significance to the passage.

> Though it is not defined, that significance is connected with the two "sons of oil," Joshua and Zerubbabel, priest and Davidic prince, who together are the means of bringing new hope to the community. Through the high priest acquittal is pronounced and access to God's presence made possible; through the prince the Temple is completed and the lampstand allowed to shine out to the world. Two "messiahs" or anointed ones have their roles co-ordinated; neither is adequate without the other.[28]

27. See Baldwin 1972, 119.
28. Baldwin 1972, 125.

In the coming of Jesus, these two functions—that of the high priest and that of the prince—will be brought together in one person.

The Sixth Vision

Zechariah's sixth vision is as unusual as all of the preceding visions. When asked by the angel what he sees, he replies, "I see a flying scroll. Its length is twenty cubits, and its width ten cubits" (5:2).[29] The angel then replies:

> This is the curse that goes out over the face of the whole land. For everyone who steals shall be cleaned out according to what is on one side, and everyone who swears falsely shall be cleaned out according to what is on the other side. I will send it out, declares Yahweh of hosts, and it shall enter the house of the thief, and the house of him who swears falsely by my name. And it shall remain in his house and consume it, both timber and stones. (vv. 3–4)

The angel clarifies the meaning of the vision by telling Zechariah that the flying scroll is "the curse." The curse is the curse of the covenant (Deut. 29:18–20). Covenant breakers in the land were under the judgment of God. God himself would purge evil from among the people, and no lawbreaker could flee from God's sight. And, as Baldwin explains, "None could plead ignorance, for the scroll was large enough for all to see, and none could escape its judgment."[30] This vision is an encouragement to the postexilic people of Israel for it affirms that in spite of the problems they witness all around, a restored covenant community was part of God's plan.

The Seventh Vision

In his seventh vision, Zechariah again sees something unusual. The angel comes to him and tells him to lift his eyes and look at what is "going out" (Zech. 5:5). Zechariah asks what it is, and the angel replies, "This is the basket that is going out." He then adds, "This is their iniquity in all the land" (v. 6). As Zechariah looks on, "the leaden cover was lifted, and there was a woman sitting in the basket!" (v. 7). The angel then declares, "This is Wickedness." He thrusts the woman back into the basket and replaces the lid (v. 8). Zechariah then sees two women with wings like a stork who

29. In other words, approximately thirty feet by fifteen feet.
30. Baldwin 1972, 127.

proceed to lift up the basket (v. 9). He asks the angel where they are taking the basket, and the angel replies, "To the land of Shinar, to build a house for it. And when this is prepared, they will set the basket down there on its base" (v. 11). The vision addresses the concern of persistent evil in the community—the greatest obstacle to restoration. The problem is not just individual sinful acts, but a spirit of evil or wickedness that threatens at all times to "break out."[31] As in the fourth vision, this vision reveals that God will sovereignly and graciously act to remove evil (3:1–10).

The Eighth Vision

In the eighth and final vision, Zechariah lifts his eyes and sees four chariots drawn by different-colored horses come out from between two mountains of bronze (6:1). When he asks the meaning of the vision, the angel tells him, "These are going out to the four winds of heaven, after presenting themselves before the LORD[32] of all the earth" (v. 5). The angel continues, "The chariot with the black horses goes toward the north country, the white ones go after them, and the dappled ones go toward the south country" (v. 6). Zechariah reveals that the horses are impatient to patrol the earth, so the angel commands them to go (v. 7). Finally the angel says, "Behold, those who go toward the north country have set my Spirit at rest in the north country" (v. 8).

Like the meaning of the others, the meaning of the eighth vision is not immediately apparent. The forces symbolized in this vision are used by God to accomplish his ends.[33] Baldwin provides a helpful summary: "The steeds are, like the winds, God's messengers (Ps. 104:4), and like the winds they travel over the face of the whole earth. All the earth belongs to the Lord whether the inhabitants acknowledge Him or not, and He gives orders concerning it all."[34] The basic point of the vision, then, is that the affairs of all the nations of the world are under God's control. This should encourage the returned exiles who have been at the mercy

31. Craigie 1984–85, 2:184.

32. The ESV translates the Hebrew here as "LORD," the usual way in which modern English versions translate the divine name *YHWH*, but the Hebrew here is *'adon*, which should be translated "Lord."

33. McComiskey 1998, 1071.

34. Baldwin 1972, 131.

of the world's empires. They can rest assured that God is in control of these empires.

The Crowning of Joshua the High Priest (Zech. 6:9–15)

The third major section of Zechariah is a brief account of a symbolic action rather than an oracle or vision. The word of the Lord again comes to Zechariah, and he is told, "Take from the exiles Heldai, Tobijah, and Jedaiah, who have arrived from Babylon, and go the same day to the house of Josiah, the son of Zephaniah. Take from them silver and gold, and make a crown, and set it on the head of Joshua, the son of Jehozadak, the high priest" (6:10–11). Here we witness something previously unheard of in the Jewish tradition: a crown is to be placed on the head of the high priest. Zechariah is then given instructions to say the following: "Thus says Yahweh of hosts, 'Behold, the man whose name is the Branch: for he shall branch out from his place, and he shall build the temple of Yahweh. It is he who shall build the temple of Yahweh and shall bear royal honor, and shall sit and rule on his throne. And there shall be a priest on his throne, and the counsel of peace shall be between them both'" (vv. 12–13). This is a significant text because nowhere else in the Old Testament is it revealed as clearly that the coming messianic King will be both a king and a priest.[35]

The crown is to be placed in the temple of the Lord as a commemorative reminder to the people that the messianic King is coming and that God has not forgotten his people.[36] Zechariah concludes this section, saying, "And those who are far off shall come and help to build the temple of Yahweh. And you shall know that Yahweh of hosts has sent me to you. And this shall come to pass, if you will diligently obey the voice of Yahweh your God" (v. 15). It seems evident that the temple in question here and in verses 12–13 is not Zerubbabel's temple because the construction of that temple had been under way for some time.[37] The temple to be built by the Messiah and by "those who are far off" will be something new (1 Cor. 3:16–17; 2 Cor. 6:16; Eph. 2:19–22). Those who are far off are the Gentiles who will join in the building of the kingdom. In doing so

35. Baldwin 1972, 137.
36. Craigie 1984–85, 2:188.
37. Baldwin 1972, 137.

they will be blessed in fulfillment of the ancient promise given by God to Abraham (Gen. 12:3).

Questions about Fasting (Zech. 7–8)

The fourth major section of Zechariah is a narrative section detailing questions that were being asked regarding the propriety of certain fasts as well as the response of the Lord. Zechariah indicates that men came to the priests of the temple with a question: "Should I weep and abstain in the fifth month, as I have done for so many years?" (7:3). They were asking about the propriety of continuing to fast and mourn for the destruction of the temple, an event that had occurred in the fifth month of 586 B.C. (2 Kings 25:8–15). Now that a new temple was almost complete, was such mourning necessary? The response of the Lord given through Zechariah turns the people's attention to their motives: "When you fasted and mourned in the fifth month and in the seventh, for these seventy years, was it for me that you fasted? And when you eat and when you drink, do you not eat for yourselves and drink for yourselves?" (Zech. 7:5–6).

Zechariah continues, saying, "Thus says Yahweh of hosts, Render true judgments, show kindness and mercy to one another, do not oppress the widow, the fatherless, the sojourner, or the poor, and let none of you devise evil against another in your heart" (vv. 9–10). Zechariah then explains in verses 11–14 that the exile had occurred because the former generations had failed to heed the prophets and had refused to repent: "they refused to pay attention and turned a stubborn shoulder and stopped their ears that they might not hear" (v. 11). Zechariah's words reveal an important truth to the people. Mourning and fasting in remembrance of the destruction of the temple was easy. Changing the attitudes that led to its destruction in the first place was the real issue.

In chapter 8, Zechariah proclaims the coming restoration of Jerusalem. He suddenly switches from descriptions of God's past wrath (7:12–14) to assurances of God's continuing love for his people (8:2). God says to his people, "I have returned to Zion and will dwell in the midst of Jerusalem, and Jerusalem shall be called the faithful city, and the mountain of Yahweh of hosts, the holy mountain" (v. 3). The restored presence of God among his people will mark the beginning of a new day in which God's covenant blessing is poured out fully on the people (vv. 4–8). "And they shall be my people, and I will be their God, in faithfulness and righteousness" (v. 8).

Following the promise of a coming new era, the Lord declares that he will not deal with the remnant of his people as he did in the former days (8:11):

> For there shall be a sowing of peace. The vine shall give its fruit, and the ground shall give its produce, and the heavens shall give their dew. And I will cause the remnant of this people to possess all these things. And as you have been a byword of cursing among the nations, O house of Judah and house of Israel, so will I save you, and you shall be a blessing. Fear not, but let your hands be strong. (vv. 12–13; cf. Gen. 12:3)

Zechariah continues declaring the word of the Lord to the people:

> As I purposed to bring disaster to you when your fathers provoked me to wrath, and I did not relent, says Yahweh of hosts, so again have I purposed in these days to bring good to Jerusalem and to the house of Judah; fear not. These are the things that you shall do: Speak the truth to one another; render in your gates judgments that are true and make for peace; do not devise evil in your hearts against one another, and love no false oath, for all these things I hate, declares Yahweh. (Zech. 8:14–17)

Zechariah then answers the original question concerning fasts. He declares that the days of fasting that were done in remembrance of the destruction of the temple are now to become days of joy and gladness. The fast days are to become feast days (vv. 18–19).

This section of Zechariah concludes with a reiteration of the promise of blessing to the nations. The Lord declares:

> Peoples shall yet come, even the inhabitants of many cities. The inhabitants of one city shall go to another, saying, "Let us go at once to entreat the favor of Yahweh and to seek Yahweh of hosts; I myself am going." Many peoples and strong nations shall come to seek Yahweh of hosts in Jerusalem and to entreat the favor of Yahweh. Thus says Yahweh of hosts: In those days ten men from the nations of every tongue shall take hold of the robe of a Jew, saying, "Let us go with you, for we have heard that God is with you." (vv. 20–23; cf. Isa. 2:2–4; 66:18–21)

The Lord had promised Abraham, "In you all the families of the earth shall be blessed" (Gen. 12:3). Here the Lord declares once again that this promise will be fulfilled.

Two Oracles (Zech. 9–14)

The fifth and final major section of Zechariah consists of two oracles. The previous visions and narratives have dealt primarily with issues of immediate concern to the postexilic community in its work of rebuilding the temple. The final two oracles of the book focus more on the distant eschatological horizon. The prophet reveals that Israel will again suffer upheaval and turmoil because of the disobedience of the people. Yet he also reveals the coming of the consummate restoration.

The First Oracle

In the first section of the first oracle, Yahweh is presented as the divine warrior marching toward Jerusalem from the north, defeating Israel's enemies as he goes, and finally setting up camp in Jerusalem to protect his people (9:1–8).[38] The cities he destroys are located in Syria, Tyre, Sidon, and Philistia. Yahweh's triumphant march from the north may be seen in contrast to earlier invasions from the north by Israel's enemies (Isa. 41:25; Jer. 1:14; Ezek. 26:7).[39] In 9:7, Zechariah describes what will happen to the nation of Philistia: "I will take away its blood from its mouth, and its abominations from between its teeth; it too shall be a remnant for our God; it shall be like a clan in Judah." As the territory of the nations is conquered by God, many of the people are graciously brought into the covenant community.[40]

The Lord's reign in Jerusalem (v. 8) will be through the messianic King (vv. 9–13). Zechariah proclaims, "Rejoice greatly, O daughter of Zion! Shout aloud, O daughter of Jerusalem! Behold, your king is coming to you; righteous and having salvation is he, humble and mounted on a donkey, on a colt, the foal of a donkey" (v. 9). This is perhaps a deliberate allusion to Jacob's prophetic blessing in Genesis 49:10–11. The New Testament authors describe Jesus' triumphal entry into Jerusalem as the fulfillment of this prophecy (Matt. 21:4–5; John 12:14–15). This coming King will

38. Dumbrell 1994, 129.
39. Baldwin 1972, 157.
40. Smith 1984, 254.

destroy the weapons of war, and "his rule shall be from sea to sea, and from the River to the ends of the earth" (Zech. 9:10; Ps. 72:8). The messianic King's dominion and the peace resulting from it will not be limited to the old boundaries of Israel. It will encompass the entire earth.

Because of God's covenantal bond with Israel, he promises, "I will set your prisoners free from the waterless pit" (Zech. 9:11). This perhaps refers to the restoration of those Israelites who have not yet returned to the land. God will restore the losses Israel sustained in the exile and establish her security (vv. 12–13). Verse 13 depicts the Lord using Israel as a weapon against foreign nations, specifically Greece. It is possible, although not certain, that this verse had an initial fulfillment in the defeat of the Seleucid Greeks by the Jews in 165 B.C.

In the remaining part of the first oracle, Zechariah deals with problems of leadership in the community and uses the metaphor of a shepherd (10:1–11:17).[41] He begins by lamenting the lack of a shepherd for the people: "the people wander like sheep; they are afflicted for lack of a shepherd" (10:2). Zechariah proclaims the Lord's extreme displeasure with the current leadership, saying, "My anger is hot against the shepherds, and I will punish the leaders; for Yahweh of hosts cares for his flock, the house of Judah" (v. 3). The imagery suddenly changes as the flock of sheep are transformed into a mighty army under the leadership of God: "They shall be like mighty men in battle, trampling the foe in the mud of the streets; they shall fight because Yahweh is with them, and they shall put to shame the riders on horses" (v. 5). Once again the imagery changes as the Lord himself is presented as a good shepherd who will guide his flock back to their home (vv. 6–12).

The concluding part of the first oracle begins with a description of the grief that will follow the fall of the world's great powers, symbolized by various trees.[42] Zechariah declares:

> Open your doors,
>   O Lebanon,
>   that the fire may devour your cedars!
> Wail, O cypress, for the cedar has fallen,
>   for the glorious trees are ruined!

41. Sweeney 2000, 657.
42. Craigie 1984–85, 2:208.

Wail, oaks of Bashan,
  for the thick forest has been felled!
The sound of the wail of the shepherds,
  for their glory is ruined!
The sound of the roar of the lions,
  for the thicket of the Jordan is ruined! (11:1–3)

God offers one last chance (vv. 4–6), but he, the good shepherd, is rejected (vv. 7–14).[43] In judgment, the Lord then gives the people a worthless shepherd (vv. 15–17). The first oracle concludes with a final denunciation: "Woe to my worthless shepherd, who deserts the flock! May the sword strike his arm and his right eye! Let his arm be wholly withered, his right eye utterly blinded!" (v. 17).

The Second Oracle

The second oracle in the final section of Zechariah begins with a description of a siege against Jerusalem (12:1–3). The Lord declares, "Behold, I am about to make Jerusalem a cup of staggering to all the surrounding peoples. The siege of Jerusalem will also be against Judah" (v. 2). However, despite the fact that the nations of the world are gathered against Jerusalem, God has made the city impregnable (vv. 4–6). The Lord intervenes on behalf of his people, protecting them, and giving them unimaginable strength (vv. 7–8). Yahweh, the divine warrior, will destroy the nations that come up against Jerusalem (v. 9).

This victory, however, does not give way to celebration because the citizens have killed someone, and now they are overwhelmed by guilt and grief (12:10–13:1). The Lord will pour out on them a spirit of grace "so that, when they look on me, on him whom they have pierced, they shall mourn for him, as one mourns for an only child" (12:10). It is highly significant that the Lord says they will "look on me." Here, the Lord indicates that he himself will somehow be the one whom the people will "pierce."[44] All of the families of Israel shall mourn when they realize their guilt (vv. 11–14). Then Zechariah proclaims, "On that day there shall be a fountain opened for the house of David and the inhabitants of Jerusalem, to cleanse them from sin

43. Some see here a prophecy of the events surrounding the destruction of Jerusalem and the temple by the Romans in A.D. 70 (see McComiskey 1998, 1201–5).

44. See McComiskey 1998, 1214.

and uncleanness" (13:1). In short, Zechariah declares that the forgiveness of the people's sins will be connected somehow to the "piercing" of God himself (Isa. 52:13–53:12). In the New Testament, it will be revealed that Zechariah's prophecy is fulfilled with the death of Jesus, the Word who was with God and who was God (John 1:1; 19:37; Rev. 1:7).

Zechariah continues by telling of the Lord's intention to destroy idols and false prophets:

> And on that day, declares Yahweh of hosts, I will cut off the names of the idols from the land, so that they shall be remembered no more. And also I will remove from the land the prophets and spirit of uncleanness. And if anyone again prophesies, his father and mother who bore him will say to him, "You shall not live, for you speak lies in the name of Yahweh." And his father and mother who bore him shall pierce him through when he prophesies. (Zech. 13:2–3)

In this way the land will be cleansed. The Lord then calls on a sword to strike the shepherd (v. 7). This will result in the sheep being scattered, but it will also result in the purification of a remnant for the Lord (vv. 8–9).

In the final section of the second oracle Zechariah gives a symbolic description of the future (ch. 14). He begins with a declaration: "Behold, a day is coming for Yahweh, when the spoil taken from you will be divided in your midst. For I will gather all the nations against Jerusalem to battle, and the city shall be taken and the houses plundered and the women raped. Half of the city shall go out into exile, but the rest of the people shall not be cut off from the city" (vv. 1–2). This chapter begins in a way very different from the beginning of the oracle in chapter 12. There the city is impregnable. Here the city is taken. The striking contrast indicates that Zechariah is either discussing two separate future events or using this war imagery in a more general way to communicate broader ideas.[45]

45. McComiskey, as we have seen, understands some of the earlier prophecies to have particular reference to events of the first century. The attack described in chapter 14, he argues, is different. It portrays in symbolic language the final eschatological onslaught against the people of God (McComiskey 1998, 1227). Wolters (2004, 284), on the other hand, argues that Zechariah 14 "has had, and will have, multiple historical fulfillments, perhaps coming to a climax at the consummation of the biblical story."

In the next part of the oracle, the Lord himself intervenes as the divine warrior fighting on behalf of his people.[46]

> Then Yahweh will go out and fight against those nations as when he fights on a day of battle. On that day his feet shall stand on the Mount of Olives that lies before Jerusalem on the east, and the Mount of Olives shall be split in two from east to west by a very wide valley, so that one half of the Mount shall move northward, and the other half southward. And you shall flee to the valley of my mountains, for the valley of the mountains shall reach to Azal. And you shall flee as you fled from the earthquake in the days of Uzziah king of Judah. Then Yahweh my God will come, and all the holy ones with him. (14:3–5)

The text here pictures the divine warrior Yahweh standing astride the ridge known as the Mount of Olives to the east of Jerusalem. The mountain range splits, creating a valley into which the Lord calls his people in order to protect them. The imagery of a giant man standing astride the mountain indicates that the language is not to be understood in an absolutely literal sense. The symbolism of the text affirms that "God will not allow his people to perish but will enter into time to preserve a remnant."[47]

Zechariah continues, "On that day there shall be no light, cold, or frost. And there shall be a unique day, which is known to Yahweh, neither day nor night, but at evening time there shall be light" (vv. 6–7). This is a turning point in the text because from this point forward, Jerusalem becomes the source of light and blessing to the world. In verses 6 and 7, Zechariah foresees great cosmic changes associated with the new era. The description of the new conditions continues, echoing one of the prophecies of Ezekiel. "On that day living waters shall flow out from Jerusalem, half of them to the eastern sea and half of them to the western sea. It shall continue in summer as in winter" (v. 8; Ezek. 47:1–12). Zechariah's description of these waters does not match Ezekiel's in its details because it is not intended to be a literal description of hydrological phenomena. It symbolically describes

46. Longman and Reid 1995, 71.

47. McComiskey 1998, 1230. It should be noted, however, that the topographical change, the mountain splitting, is compared to an actual historical earthquake, lending credence to the idea that the way the Lord will intervene to protect his people may involve some kind of unprecedented earthquake.

Jerusalem as the source of blessing. Zechariah also declares that under the Lord's reign, Jerusalem will dwell in security (14:9–11).

Zechariah turns next to a vivid description of the Lord's judgment against the nations that attacked Israel:

> And this shall be the plague with which Yahweh will strike all the peoples that wage war against Jerusalem: their flesh will rot while they are still standing on their feet, their eyes will rot in their sockets, and their tongues will rot in their mouths.
>
> And on that day a great panic from Yahweh shall fall on them, so that each will seize the hand of another, and the hand of the one will be raised against the hand of the other. (vv. 12–13)

The plague will also fall on all the animals within their camps (v. 15). In short, God will utterly destroy Israel's enemies.

The book of Zechariah concludes with a description of redeemed Gentiles worshiping with redeemed Jews in a holy and clean land (vv. 16–21). The survivors among the Gentiles will become subjects in the kingdom of God, and they will worship the Lord (v. 16). Those who do not go up to worship the Lord will be subject to the same plague that fell upon the enemy nations (vv. 17–19). There will no longer be anything unclean or unholy in Jerusalem. Holiness will not be the special status of a few people or places. Instead all of Jerusalem and everything in it will be holy (vv. 20–21; cf. Ex. 28:36). Jerusalem will finally be what she had originally been called to be, a holy nation (Ex. 19:6; Jer. 2:3).

Malachi

The book of Malachi is the last of the twelve Minor Prophets, and little is known of the author himself aside from what may be inferred from the contents of his book.[48] Unlike Haggai and Zechariah, Malachi prophesied some time after the completion of the temple in 515 B.C. In fact, it appears that Malachi prophesied over fifty years after Haggai and Zechariah. There is a general consensus that Malachi was a close contemporary of Ezra and Nehemiah in the middle of the fifth century. It is difficult, however, to be more precise with the dating of the book. Some argue that the prophecy

48. In fact, there is debate about whether Malachi is even the author's name, since the word can also be translated as "my messenger."

should be dated from approximately 460 B.C., that is, a few years prior to Ezra's return.[49] Others argue that Malachi's prophecies date from the period of time shortly after the end of Nehemiah's first visit to Jerusalem, that is, not long after 433 B.C.[50] The evidence seems to favor slightly a date around 433 B.C.

Like Haggai and Zechariah in the previous century, Malachi ministered during a difficult period of time, but the problems he faced were slightly different.[51] It had been decades since the temple had been completed, yet the glories of the messianic kingdom had not arrived as expected. But neither had the people lived up to the stipulations of God's law (see the book of Nehemiah). Politically, Israel was a minor province in the massive Persian Empire. The nation was suffering from economic and agricultural problems. The most serious problem, however, from the prophet's perspective was spiritual. Idolatry was apparently no longer a serious problem, but the people lacked zeal for the Lord. Spiritual discouragement and apathy were rampant. Malachi was called into this situation to explain the delay in the fulfillment of God's restoration promises.[52] Like the prophets who came before him, Malachi informs the people that God's blessings have been withheld because of the people's failure to adhere to the stipulations of the covenant. Like the prophets before him, Malachi calls upon the people to fulfill the covenant stipulations.

The structure of the book of Malachi is among the most obvious in the prophetic corpus.[53] Following a superscription (1:1), there are six "prophetic disputation speeches" (1:2–5; 1:6–2:9; 2:10–16; 2:17–3:5; 3:6–12; 3:13–4:3).[54] The final three verses (4:4–6) may be a part of the final disputation speech, or they may be a summary to the entire book. As Douglas Stuart explains, "The disputation (more fully, rhetorical disputation) speech form has four elements: assertion, questioning, response, and implications."[55] All six disputations in Malachi contain these four elements.

49. E.g., Stuart 1998, 1252–53; Craigie 1984–85, 2:225.

50. E.g., Verhoef 1987, 160.

51. For a helpful summary of the historical context, see Stuart 1998, 1253–54.

52. VanGemeren 1990, 202.

53. The modern chapter divisions unfortunately obscure the structure of the text. When reading Malachi, it is best to ignore these chapter divisions and focus instead on the structural markers within the text itself.

54. Stuart 1998, 1247.

55. Stuart 1998, 1248.

The book opens with a simple superscription: "The oracle of the word of Yahweh to Israel by Malachi" (1:1). This may also be translated: "A burden: The word of Yahweh to Israel through Malachi." The noun transliterated "Malachi" may be understood as a proper noun (i.e., the name Malachi), or it may be understood as a common noun with a pronominal suffix, in which case it would be translated "my messenger" (cf. 3:1). The context here indicates that the noun should be understood as the proper noun Malachi, the name of the prophet to whom the word of the Lord came.

The first disputation speech (1:2–5) addresses one of the lingering questions harbored by the returned exiles: Had Yahweh abandoned Israel? In this first disputation, Malachi reassures the people of the Lord's continuing love for them. As William Dumbrell notes, "These verses serve as a reminder that Israel stands in covenant with Yahweh, and affirm that Yahweh has remained faithful."[56] The disputation begins with the Lord's assertion "I have loved you" (1:2a). The people, however, question this assertion, saying, "How have you loved us?" (1:2b). The Lord then responds by describing his judgment of Edom, Israel's longtime enemy.[57] Malachi concludes with the implication, "Your own eyes shall see this, and you shall say, 'Great is Yahweh beyond the border of Israel'" (1:5). The fact that Judah has survived the exile "and now knows the possibility of restoration tangibly signals that Yahweh continues to love his people as he continues to govern the world."[58]

The second disputation speech addresses the priests' unfaithfulness to the legal stipulations for worship (1:6–2:9). The Lord asserts that the priests despise his name (1:6b). When the priests ask how they have despised the Lord's name (1:6c), the Lord responds, "By offering polluted food upon my altar" (1:7a). The priests then ask, "How have we polluted you?" (1:7b), to which the Lord responds, "By saying that Yahweh's table may be despised. When you offer blind animals in sacrifice, is that not evil? And when you offer those that are lame or sick, is that not evil?" (1:7c–8a). By allowing the offering of sick and blemished animals, the priests were violating the Mosaic law and defiling the sanctuary (Lev. 22:17–25). The implication of

56. Dumbrell 2002, 238.

57. In this sense, the response in the first disputation speech is similar to the oracles against foreign nations found throughout the prophetic books.

58. Floyd 2000, 585.

the oracle is found in Malachi 1:8b–2:9, in which the priests are rebuked by God.

Malachi tells the priests that it would be better if the temple were closed than to continue offering sick and blemished animals (1:10). He continues with the proclamation of the word of the Lord: "For from the rising of the sun to its setting my name will be great among the nations, and in every place incense will be offered to my name, and a pure offering. For my name will be great among the nations, says Yahweh of hosts" (1:11). Some have argued that this verse indicates that the Gentile nations, despite their ignorance, were actually worshiping and acknowledging the true God.[59] The context of Malachi, the other prophets, and the entire Old Testament, however, weighs against such an interpretation. Malachi is not condoning heathen worship. He is comparing the present flawed worship of the Jerusalem priesthood with the future reverent worship God will receive across the world. As Stuart explains, "we must appreciate here the presence of eschatological messianic universalism, that is, the common Old Testament doctrine that the true God would one *future* day reign over all peoples, who would have no choice but to acknowledge his sovereignty."[60]

Malachi's third disputation speech addresses the people's unfaithfulness to the covenant. It primarily addresses the issues of intermarriage between Jews and pagans, false worship, and divorce. Like the other disputation speeches, this one begins with an assertion (2:10–13). Malachi claims that Judah has been faithless and has profaned the covenant and that because of this, God no longer regards their offerings. When the people ask, "Why?" (2:14a), Malachi responds, "Because Yahweh was witness between you and the wife of your youth, to whom you have been faithless, though she is your companion and your wife by covenant" (2:14b). The implications are spelled out in verses 15–16, in which the Lord declares his hatred of divorce and calls his people to faithfulness.

The fourth disputation speech addresses an issue that would have been in the minds of many returned exiles. The returned exiles expected God to reestablish his presence in the temple (Ezek. 43:2–4). Due to the people's continued covenant breaking, this had yet to occur. The fourth disputation addresses the question. It begins with an assertion: "You have wearied Yahweh with your words" (Mal. 2:17a). The people ask, "How have we

59. E.g., Craigie 1984–85, 2:232.

60. Stuart 1998, 1306.

wearied him?" (2:17b), and Malachi responds: "By saying, 'Everyone who does evil is good in the sight of Yahweh, and he delights in them.' Or by asking, 'Where is the God of justice?'" (2:17c). The people, in other words, had grown disillusioned and cynical.

The Lord's response to this cynicism is to declare: "Behold, I send my messenger and he will prepare the way before me. And the Lord whom you seek will suddenly come to his temple; and the messenger of the covenant in whom you delight, behold, he is coming, says Yahweh of hosts" (3:1). Although the specific term is not used, the prophecy here is messianic. The specific identity of the messenger is not provided by Malachi. However, as Baldwin correctly observes, it is unlikely that Malachi identified this messenger with himself.[61] The New Testament, of course, identifies the messenger who prepares the way before the coming of the Lord as John the Baptist (Luke 7:24–28). The "messenger of the covenant" who follows will judge and purify his people (Mal. 3:2–5).

Malachi's fifth disputation speech concerns Israel's unfaithfulness with her tithes (3:6–12). The Lord declares: "From the days of your fathers you have turned aside from my statutes and have not kept them. Return to me, and I will return to you, says Yahweh of hosts" (3:7a). In response, the people ask, "How shall we return?" (3:7b). The Lord declares, "Will man rob God? Yet you are robbing me" (3:8a), to which the people reply, "How have we robbed you?" (3:8b). The Lord declares that they have robbed him in their tithes and contributions. "You are cursed with a curse, for you are robbing me, the whole nation of you" (3:9). In order for the people's sin to be forgiven, they must repent, but the people do not even recognize their guilt.[62] In this disputation speech, Malachi is calling the people to repent, for the fullness of the kingdom cannot come if the people remain rebellious.

The final disputation speech addresses the people's failure to fear God, and it warns of the coming day of the Lord (3:13–4:3). The Lord declares to Israel, "Your words have been hard against me" (3:13a), but the people ask, "How have we spoken against you?" (3:13b). The Lord responds, "You have said, 'It is vain to serve God. What is the profit of our keeping his charge or of walking as in mourning before Yahweh of hosts? And now we call the arrogant blessed. Evildoers not only prosper but they put God to

61. Baldwin 1972, 242.
62. Smith 1984, 332.

the test and they escape'" (3:14–15). In short, the people are saying that it is futile to follow God. The Lord responds by giving assurance to the faithful (3:16–18) and by warning of the coming day of the Lord (4:1–3).

The final verses of the book challenge the people to keep the law of Moses and to be prepared for the day of the Lord (4:4–6). The Lord instructs the people, "Remember the law of my servant Moses, the statutes and rules that I commanded him at Horeb for all Israel" (4:4). He then declares, "Behold, I will send you Elijah the prophet before the great and awesome day of Yahweh comes" (4:5). As Baldwin explains, the references to Moses and Elijah are significant: "In the references to the law of Moses and to Elijah the prophet . . . there is a backward glimpse to the covenant requirements and a forward look to one who will work for their fulfillment. The promise of the coming of 'Elijah' ensured one more prophetic voice before the end came."[63] Before the coming of the great day of the Lord, God will send Elijah. Does this mean that God will send a reincarnation of the prophet Elijah or an Elijah-type prophet? The New Testament provides the answer by identifying John the Baptist as the one who fulfilled this prophecy (Matt. 11:13–14; 17:10–13). He is the one who prepared the way for the coming of Jesus the Messiah.

Summary

The postexilic prophets were the last in a line of writing prophets who ministered to the covenant people of God between the eighth and fifth centuries B.C. Haggai and Zechariah were called to preach the word of God to the people approximately twenty years after the first group of exiles had returned from Babylon. Opposition to their work and preoccupation with their own affairs meant that the temple was being neglected. Haggai and Zechariah encouraged the people to complete the rebuilding of the temple. Haggai declared that the Lord would be present with his people and that the completion of the temple would result in God's blessing. Zechariah also encourages the rebuilding of the temple by pointing to the worldwide significance it will have.

Ultimately the second temple was completed in 515 B.C., but the fullness of the restoration promises was not realized at that time. What the people were expecting was not what they were experiencing. As the decades passed,

63. Baldwin 1972, 251.

disillusionment set in. During the time of Ezra and Nehemiah, the prophet Malachi was called to address the people's doubt and unfaithfulness. He reassured the people that they were still the objects of God's love, but he also called them to repent of their sins and reminded them that the fullness of God's blessing could not come as long as they remained unrepentant. He declared that the Lord would come back to his temple, but that he would be preceded by a messenger who would prepare the way for him. The New Testament reveals the fulfillment of this prophecy in the coming of John the Baptist and Jesus.

As we observed in chapter 5, all of the writing prophets may be dated between the eighth and fifth centuries B.C. These were the centuries that witnessed the final downfall of Israel and Judah, the exile, and the initial stages of restoration. The writings of the prophets centered on these key events. O. Palmer Robertson explains the significance:

> The gigantic task of the prophets was to anticipate the exile by predictive declarations and thus prepare the people for this unimaginable shock. At the same time, their task was to maintain hope in the Covenant LORD's long-term redemptive purposes by predicting a return from the abyss of the exile. These two great events of exile and restoration therefore became the focal point of the predictions of the prophets.[64]

The chosen people of God would become "not my people" in the exile, and it was the calling of the prophets to explain the redemptive-historical significance of these events.

Building on the covenantal foundation set down in the Pentateuch, the preexilic prophets lamented that the people were breaking God's covenant and called on them to repent. They warned the people that if they did not repent, God would pour out upon them the curses of the covenant, including the ultimate curse of exile. Yet even in the midst of their dire warnings, judgment is not their final word. Although they anticipate that their warnings will not be heeded and that exile will be the result, they also look beyond the exile with hope toward a period of restoration.

The exilic prophets were given the task of explaining to the people why such a disaster had befallen God's chosen ones. The exilic prophets point to the repeated violations of the covenant. The exile occurred because

64. Robertson 2004, 453.

Israel sinned against God. Yet judgment is not the final word for the exilic prophets either. Hope remains. The exilic prophets also look forward to restoration beyond the exile. Finally, the postexilic prophets witness the first stages of the promised restoration, but they also have to explain to the people why restoration has not come in its fullness. They too call the people to covenant faithfulness, reminding Israel that continued disobedience will result in judgment rather than blessing. They continue to look forward to further restoration, to the coming of the Messiah, and to the establishment of his kingdom in its fullness.

The problem that all of the prophets face is Israel's inability to remain completely faithful to the terms of the covenant. Sin brought about judgment and exile. In order for Israel to experience the fullness of the blessings of restoration, the problem of sin must be dealt with. Ultimately, according to the prophets, this will be accomplished through the establishment of a new covenant in the messianic kingdom. God's promises to Abraham were given with the ultimate goal of bringing blessing to all the nations of earth. The fullness of Israel's restoration will witness the complete fulfillment of that ancient promise. As Robertson explains, "Israel's restoration includes the forgiveness of sins; it involves the new life of grace; it includes the Gentile nations; and it involves the rejuvenation of the earth, culminating in resurrection from the dead."[65] The Old Testament ends, therefore, on a note of anticipation. The Messiah is coming to establish his kingdom. His coming will be preceded by an "Elijah" who will prepare the way before him. But for how long will the people of Israel have to wait?

65. Robertson 2004, 486.

Excursus

The Intertestamental Period

The historical narrative of the Old Testament ends soon after Nehemiah's return to Persia around 433 B.C., and the final prophetic book, Malachi, was written around this same time period. The first events of the New Testament, on the other hand, occur at the beginning of the first century. There is, therefore, a period of over four hundred years between the final events recorded in the Old Testament and the first events recorded in the New Testament. These four centuries between the end of the Old Testament and the beginning of the New Testament have often been referred to by Christians as the intertestamental period.[1]

1. Because the New Testament is not accepted as divine revelation in Judaism, Jewish scholars do not use the term "intertestamental," which implies a second testament (see Cohen 1987, 20). Instead, Jewish scholars today tend to refer to the period between the rebuilding of the temple in 515 B.C. and its destruction in A.D. 70 as "Second Temple Judaism" (i.e., the period during which the second temple stood). Many Christian scholars now also use this term. Each term is useful in specific contexts. The "intertestamental period" is a useful description of the period of time between the end of the Old Testament and the beginning of the New Testament. "Second Temple Judaism" is a useful term to describe one stage in the development of Judaism. It distinguishes the Judaism of this era from that which existed before the exile as well as from the Rabbinic Judaism that developed after the destruction of the temple in A.D. 70.

Those who read the Old Testament and then turn to the New Testament will immediately notice that the political, cultural, and religious context has changed dramatically. At the end of the Old Testament, many Israelites had returned to Jerusalem, but the nation remained under the domination of the Persian Empire. At the beginning of the New Testament, Israel is part of the Roman Empire. The language of the books of the New Testament is different as well. While the books of the Old Testament were originally written almost entirely in Hebrew, the books of the New Testament are written in Greek and often quote a Greek translation of the Old Testament. The New Testament also describes Jewish institutions such as the synagogue and the Sanhedrin and Jewish sects such as the Pharisees, Sadducees, and Zealots that are nowhere mentioned in the Old Testament. What happened to account for these changes?

In order to fully understand the New Testament, it is necessary to have some grasp of the historical context in which it was written. This means that we must be familiar with the history of Israel, not only in the first century itself, but also in the years leading up to the first century. It also means that we must be familiar with the Jewish writings that provide insight into the thinking of pious Jews of the time. The primary sources for an understanding of the intertestamental period are the apocryphal books, the pseudepigraphal books, the Dead Sea Scrolls, and the writings of Philo and Josephus. It is important to understand that these writings are neither inspired nor canonical.[2] They do not have the same authority as do the inspired writings of the Old and New Testaments, and they do contain errors. However, just as we can gain important insight into history by reading the works of the ancient Greek and Roman historians, so too can we gain insight into this important period by reading these Jewish works.

A Survey of the History of the Intertestamental Period

The intertestamental period may be divided into four major eras. It began during the Persian era of Israel's history (539–331 B.C.). It continued through the tumultuous Greek (331–164 B.C.) and Hasmonean (164–63 B.C.) eras,

2. The Roman Catholic and Eastern Orthodox churches include within their canons certain of the books described in this chapter as either apocryphal or pseudepigraphal. These churches often distinguish these books from the universally acknowledged books by referring to them as the deuterocanonical books. On the subject of the canon, see Bruce 1988b.

and it ended during the Roman era (63 B.C.–A.D. 135). The history of these four centuries is often complex. Here we will summarize only some of the most important developments.[3]

The Persian Era

Although the Israelites existed as a part of the Persian Empire for approximately two centuries, very little is known for certain about what was happening in Israel during the period of time between Nehemiah's return to Persia (ca. 433 B.C.) and the rise of Alexander the Great (336–331 B.C.).[4] As we know from the books of Ezra and Nehemiah, the Jews in and around Judea were moving more and more toward a policy of religious and racial exclusivity, and this seems to have continued throughout the Persian era.[5] The law was becoming the focus of Jewish piety. The institution of the synagogue, which centered on the reading and study of the law, may have originated at this time, although it is also possible that it originated during the Babylonian exile.

It is likely that during this period some Jews came into contact with the dualistic religion of Zoroastrianism, the official religion of the Persian Empire from the time of Darius I onward.[6] Whether and to what extent any Jews adopted Zoroastrian ideas is more difficult to determine.[7] The language of the Israelites also changed during the Persian era as Aramaic gradually replaced Hebrew.[8] Aside from these general statements, however, little more can be said with certainty. It appears that for much of this period, Israel was considered to be an insignificant province in the enormous Persian Empire.

The Greek Era

In 338 B.C., Philip II, the king of Macedonia, succeeded in forcefully unifying the city-states of Greece. He planned to lead a united army against

3. For a more thorough introduction to the era, see Bruce 1963, 97–196, and Scott 1995. For a recent comprehensive study of the history of these centuries, see Sacchi 2000.

4. In his *Antiquities of the Jews*, Josephus briefly discusses a few events that may have occurred early in this period. See *Ant.* 11.7.1–2 §§297–303 (all citations from Josephus include the numbering found in the Whiston translation followed by the numbering system used in the LCL edition).

5. Bruce 1963, 117.

6. Scott 1995, 78.

7. On Zoroastrianism, see Yamauchi 1997, 395–466.

8. Scott 1995, 77.

the Persians, but he was assassinated in 336 B.C. His twenty-year-old son Alexander inherited his ambition. Under Alexander the Great, the Greek army pushed eastward, and conquered much Persian territory without a fight. The decisive battle came in 331 B.C., when Alexander met the Persian army at Gaugamela and defeated it. This defeat marks the end of the Persian Empire. Alexander's conquests led him as far as India, but before he was able to consolidate his empire he died of a fever in 323 B.C. in Babylon. Alexander's sudden death led to a power struggle between his generals, with the empire ultimately being divided among several of them. After a number of years of fighting, several dynasties were established. The two most significant for an understanding of the history of Israel are the Ptolemaic dynasty in Egypt and the Seleucid dynasty in Asia.

One of the most significant effects of Alexander's conquest of the Persian Empire and much of the known world was the influence of Hellenism. D. S. Russell explains:

> The word "Hellenism" is commonly used to describe the civilization of the three centuries or so from the time of Alexander the Great (336–323 B.C.) during which the influence of Greek culture was felt in both East and West. It was the cherished desire of this ruler to found a world-wide Empire bound together in a unity of language, custom and civilization and, in his great military conquests, he did much to realize this idea.[9]

Hellenism, then, was a new way of life and thought brought about by Alexander's conquests. Alexander's heirs in Egypt and Asia did not abandon the goal of Hellenization, and ultimately, this was to have profound effects on Israel as Jews sought to preserve their identity within the culture of the Greek Empire.

When the dust finally settled following the battles among Alexander's successors, Israel had fallen under the dominion of the Ptolemaic kingdom. Israel would remain under Ptolemaic control for a little over a century (ca. 320–198 B.C.).[10] According to Josephus, Ptolemy I took Jerusalem and Judea deceitfully by pretending that he wanted to enter the city only in order to offer sacrifices in the temple.[11] He also transported many Jews to

9. Russell 1960, 14.
10. See Hayes and Mandell 1998, 28–38.
11. Josephus, *Ant.* 12.1.1 §§1–10.

Egypt and settled them in the city of Alexandria. The Jewish community in Alexandria grew to become one of the most important in the Diaspora. According to legend, it was for the Greek-speaking Jews of Alexandria that the Septuagint translation of the Old Testament was made.[12] Despite the initial deportation of many Jews to Egypt, Israel appears to have enjoyed a relatively peaceful existence under Ptolemaic rule. The same would not be true under the Seleucids.

Israel fell under Seleucid control two years after the Seleucid king Antiochus III defeated Ptolemy V at the battle of Panion in 200 B.C.[13] Initially, some Jews welcomed Seleucid sovereignty, but things would soon change. When Antiochus IV Epiphanes came to the throne in 175 B.C., he was determined to enforce the spread of Hellenism throughout his realm. This caused many difficulties for pious Jews. Further problems were created because of the political maneuvering of those vying for the position of high priest in Israel. Onias III, from the Oniad family, was the high priest at the time Antiochus IV took the throne. The Oniads were respected for their stand against the Hellenizing tendencies supported by other prominent Jewish families such as the Tobiad family. Conflicts between the Oniads and Tobiads were to play a significant role in the troubles to come.

When Antiochus IV Epiphanes took the throne, Onias's brother Jason appealed to the new king for the office of high priest. He promised to promote Hellenism and bribed the king as well. Antiochus duly appointed Jason high priest, and Jason began instituting Hellenizing reforms that offended many of the Jews.[14] In 172 B.C., matters were further complicated when Jason sent his tribute to the king in the hands of one Menelaus. Menelaus, who was supported by the Tobiad family, offered Antiochus even more money than Jason and was appointed high priest in his place.[15] Many Jews had been outraged that Jason had bought the high priesthood, but Jason was at least from the Zadokite line and therefore eligible for the high priesthood. Menelaus did not belong to any priestly family, and he knew that the pious Jews in Jerusalem would always consider the Zadokites the true high priests. Jason fled across the Jordan, but Menelaus's other

12. Bruce 1963, 125. See the *Letter of Aristeas* (in Charlesworth 1985, 12–34).
13. Hayes and Mandell 1998, 39.
14. Bruce 1963, 134–35.
15. deSilva 2002, 50.

rival Onias was less fortunate. Menelaus had him assassinated, further outraging the Jews.

In the winter of 170–169 B.C., the Ptolemies declared war on Antiochus, and Antiochus attacked Egypt. His campaign was largely successful, but it was financially draining. At that time, one means by which a king could raise money would be to plunder the various temples within his kingdom. One such temple was located in Jerusalem, and when Antiochus arrived, Menelaus escorted him into the sanctuary to retrieve money and costly vessels (1 Macc. 1:20–24). In 168 B.C., Antiochus began a second campaign against Egypt. Upon hearing a false rumor of Antiochus's death, Jason seized the opportunity to retake the high priesthood. He gathered his forces and attacked Menelaus in Jerusalem. Menelaus appealed for help to Antiochus, who interpreted the events as a revolt against his kingdom. His response was brutal. He slaughtered thousands, and because he believed the Jewish religion to be at the heart of the perceived revolt, he attempted to eliminate it. He stopped the temple ritual, ordered copies of the Scriptures destroyed, and prohibited Sabbath observance, Jewish food laws, and circumcision. He erected a new altar in the Jerusalem temple, dedicated it to Zeus, and offered a pig as a sacrifice on it.[16]

Not surprisingly, Antiochus's actions resulted in armed revolt. The story of this revolt is narrated in the books of 1 and 2 Maccabees.[17] According to the books of Maccabees, Mattathias, a priest, and his five sons lived in Modein (1 Macc. 2:1–2). After killing an official of the king who was attempting to force compliance with Antiochus's decrees, Mattathias, his sons, and numerous followers took to the hills and began a guerilla campaign against the forces of Antiochus (1 Macc. 2:15–70). When Mattathias died, he left his son Judas Maccabeus in command.[18] Over the course of the next several years, Judas's military skills combined with Antiochus's troubles in the eastern part of his empire made it possible for Judas and his followers to secure peace terms in 164 B.C. The ban on the Jewish religion was lifted. Judas and his followers then proceeded to cleanse the temple and rededicate it to the service of God.[19]

16. Josephus, *Ant.* 12.5.1–4 §§237–56; 1 Macc. 1:29–61.

17. See also Josephus, *Ant.* 12.6.1–4 §§265–86.

18. The term "Maccabees" is taken from Judas's surname, which probably means "the hammer." The term is sometimes used to refer to the descendants of Mattathias, but "Hasmonean" is the more accurate term for the family. The name "Hasmonean" is derived from the name Hasmon, an ancestor of Mattathias.

19. This rededication of the temple is commemorated by Jews every year in the eight-day festival of Hanukkah.

The Hasmonean Era

Although Judas and his followers won significant religious freedom in 164 B.C., Israel was still a part of the Seleucid kingdom, and other problems remained. Jews who lived outside of Judea faced the constant threat of attack, and the despised Menelaus remained in the office of high priest. Judas and his followers thus began a lengthy fight for political freedom. After numerous battles, the Seleucids removed Menelaus and appointed Alcimus as high priest.[20] He was not a member of the Oniad family, but he was a descendant of Aaron.[21] Unfortunately, Alcimus was also a Hellenizer and an opponent of Judas Maccabeus.

Judas was killed in battle in 160 B.C. and was succeeded by his brother Jonathan (1 Macc. 9:18–31). Jonathan was a skillful diplomat who exploited troubles within the Seleucid kingdom to expand Jewish freedoms, but he was assassinated in 143 B.C. (1 Macc. 12:46–48). Upon Jonathan's death, he was succeeded by his brother Simon, the last living son of Mattathias. The Seleucid king at the time was Demetrius II Nicator, who was facing problems caused by other claimants to the Seleucid throne. Because he needed Simon's help against these other claimants to the throne, he freed the Jews from tribute in 142 B.C. This was a virtual declaration of independence for the Jews (1 Macc. 13:41–51). Simon was then entrusted with both political and religious leadership. He was made Israel's leader and high priest (1 Macc. 14:25–49).

Simon was killed in 134 B.C. and was succeeded by his son John Hyrcanus. The disorder that resulted from the death of Simon gave the Seleucids an opportunity to retake control of Israel in 133 B.C. For five years, Israel was again a tributary of the Seleucid kingdom, but after the death of Antiochus VII in 128 B.C., Israel was able to regain its independence. John Hyrcanus then set out to conquer lands surrounding Judea. He conquered Idumea to the south, Samaria to the north, and much land east of the Jordan. According to Josephus, Eleazar, a member of the separatist lay sect called the Pharisees, urged John to give up the high priesthood, but John refused and aligned himself with the aristocratic priestly sect of the Sadducees.[22] The Pharisees were enemies of the Hasmoneans from this point forward.

20. Josephus, *Ant.* 12.9.7 §§382–88.

21. Scott 1995, 84.

22. Josephus, *Ant.* 13.10.5–6 §§288–98. On the Pharisees and Sadducees, see *NIDNTT*, 2:810–14; 3:439–41; Ferguson 2003, 514–20; Scott 1995, 202–8; Bruce 1971b, 71–81.

John's program of conquest continued under his son Aristobulus I, who conquered much of Galilee. When he took the throne in 104 B.C., he imprisoned his mother and half brothers, and also became the first of the Hasmoneans to take the title "king." Aristobulus, however, reigned only a year before dying. When he died, his widow Salome Alexandra freed his half brothers and married one of them, Alexander Jannaeus. This marriage enabled him to become both king and high priest. Alexander, however, faced both external and internal opposition. At one point during his reign, the Pharisees persuaded the Seleucid king Demetrius III Eukairos to fight against Alexander, but the sight of a Jewish king fleeing a Greek ruler caused many of Alexander's Jewish enemies to come to his aid. His retaliation against the Pharisees was harsh. He crucified eight hundred of them in Jerusalem, and before they died, he had their wives and children killed before their eyes. His reprisals were effective. He faced no further internal resistance during his reign.

When Alexander Jannaeus died in 76 B.C., he was succeeded by his widow Salome Alexandra.[23] Salome's reign was relatively peaceful. Her son Hyrcanus II was appointed as high priest, and her son Aristobulus II was made the leader of the military. Aristobulus, however, wanted more. When Salome died in 67 B.C., Aristobulus, with the backing of the Sadducees, jumped at the opportunity. Hyrcanus was the legitimate heir of Salome, but Aristobulus gathered his forces and attacked Hyrcanus. Hyrcanus fled the city and surrendered both the royal title and the high priesthood to Aristobulus. Hyrcanus, who was not a man of ambition, simply asked that he be permitted to live in peace on his estate. He would not be able to enjoy peace for long.

Aristobulus was not the only ambitious man in the region. Alexander Jannaeus had appointed a man named Antipater as governor of Idumea at the beginning of his reign. Antipater had remained governor of Idumea during Alexander and Salome's reigns. He now sought more power, and decided to use Hyrcanus to accomplish his plans. He began to stir up support for Hyrcanus among the Jews. He also gained support from the Nabateans. He eventually persuaded Hyrcanus that his brother would always consider him a threat and that his life was therefore in danger. In 65 B.C., the combined forces of Antipater, Hyrcanus, and the Nabateans

23. Josephus, *Ant.* 13.15.5 §§398–404.

attacked Aristobulus and soundly defeated him. Aristobulus was forced to flee to the temple complex for safety. There he was besieged by the forces of Hyrcanus. Events, however, were about to take an unexpected turn.

The Roman Era

By 200 B.C., Rome had been steadily growing in strength for many years. With the defeat of Carthage at the end of the Second Punic War in 202 B.C., Rome had gained control of Spain and North Africa.[24] The alliance between the Macedonians and the defeated Carthaginians led to a series of wars between Rome and the Macedonians, which finally ended in 146 B.C., with Macedonia becoming a Roman province. In 88 B.C. the first of a series of wars began between Rome and Mithridates VI of Pontus in northeast Asia Minor.

The first Mithridatic war (88–84 B.C.) ended in defeat for Mithridates, but he retained his kingdom. The second Mithridatic war (83–81 B.C.) ended in defeat for Rome. In the third and final Mithridatic war (75–65 B.C.), the Romans sent Lucius Lucullus, who was unable to achieve a decisive victory. In 66 B.C., the Romans sent Pompey to fight the war. This Roman general crushed the enemy armies, and Mithridates committed suicide. Tigranes, who was the king of Armenia, had gained control of much of the territory of the Seleucid Empire by this time. He submitted to Rome and retained his title. Pompey then sent his lieutenant Scaurus to Syria to settle the affairs there.

While in Syria, Scaurus received word of the conflict in Jerusalem and journeyed to the city. Both parties offered substantial sums of money to the Romans in exchange for their support. Scaurus decided to support Aristobulus and ordered the Nabateans to lift the siege against him. In 63 B.C., Pompey traveled to Damascus where both Aristobulus and Hyrcanus appealed to him. A third group, representing the Jewish people, also came appealing to him to abolish the Hasmonean dynasty and reestablish Jerusalem under a temple constitution. Upon returning to Jerusalem, Aristobulus decided to resist the Romans, but when Pompey advanced on the city, he chose to give himself up. Many of his followers chose to continue to resist. Hyrcanus and his followers seized the opportunity. He gained control of the city and opened the gates to Pompey's armies. Aristobulus's followers

24. For a history of this era, see Polybius, *The Histories*.

barricaded themselves in the temple compound and held out against the Roman siege for three months.[25]

After defeating the last resistance in the city, Judea was made a tributary of the expanding Roman Empire. Aristobulus and his family were brought to Rome. Hyrcanus regained the leadership of the nation and the high priesthood, but he was not allowed the title of king. Antipater, who had orchestrated Hyrcanus's attack on Aristobulus, was now in position to exploit the situation to his own advantage. He and his sons Phasael and Herod made it their policy to support the Romans regardless of who might be in power in Judea. Eventually, due to his support of Rome, Antipater was given the title of procurator of Judea in 47 B.C. Antipater appointed his son Phasael military prefect of Judea and his son Herod military prefect of Galilee.[26]

Antipater died in 43 B.C., and in 41 B.C., his sons Phasael and Herod were appointed joint tetrarchs of Judea. Not long afterward, the Parthians invaded Judea, and Aristobulus's son Antigonus who had escaped from Rome claimed the crown. He had the ears of his uncle Hyrcanus clipped in order to disqualify him from the high priesthood. Phasael committed suicide, but Herod escaped to Rome where he convinced the Romans that their cause could be furthered if he were placed in power instead of Antigonus. The Romans declared Herod the king of the Jews, and after a siege of Jerusalem, he took control in 37 B.C.[27] He spent the first several years of his reign (37–30 B.C.) securing control and settling internal political disputes. The next twenty years of his reign (30–10 B.C.) were more peaceful and allowed Herod to accomplish numerous goals, including a massive building program that included cities, fortresses, pagan temples, and roads.[28] His most significant building project, however, was the rebuilding of the Jerusalem temple, which he began in 19 B.C.[29]

During this same period of time, Rome itself was nearing the end of a long series of crises. The republic had effectively ended when Julius Caesar had been declared perpetual dictator in 44 B.C. Following the murder of Julius

25. Hayes and Mandell 1998, 107.

26. Witherington 2001b, 52.

27. Josephus, *Ant.* 14.15–16 §§394–491. On the reign of Herod the Great, see Richardson 1996; Hayes and Mandell 1998, 125–46.

28. Witherington 2001b, 59–60.

29. Josephus, *Ant.* 15.11 §§380–425; Bruce 1971b, 21.

Caesar on the 15th of March in 44 B.C., Rome suffered years of internal strife before his great nephew and heir Octavian consolidated control with the defeat of Antony and Cleopatra at the battle of Actium in 31 B.C. From this date until his death in A.D. 14, Octavian was the undisputed ruler of the Roman Empire.[30] In 27 B.C., Octavian was given the title Augustus by a decree of the Roman senate. Augustus had restored peace to Rome after a century of civil wars. Inscriptions from this era dedicated to Augustus refer to him as the "savior" (*sōtēr*) of the human race and to his birthday as the beginning of the "gospel" (*euangelion*) of peace.[31]

A Survey of the Literature of the Intertestamental Period

As we have seen, the intertestamental period was a time of far-reaching changes for the people of Israel. Numerous crises threatened their very existence. During this time, the voice of prophecy was silent, but the Jewish people themselves were not. The events of the times impacted Jewish thought and religion, and a sizable body of literature was written. Eschatology was a significant theme in many of these books. An examination of these writings provides important insight into the development of Jewish thought on the subject during the centuries leading up to the birth of Jesus.

In terms of general themes, the people continued to look forward to the prophesied time of full restoration. There is evidence in some of the intertestamental literature that a time of great tribulation and trouble was expected to precede the advent of the final age (*1 Enoch* 1:3–8; *2 Baruch* 26–29; 2 Esdras 4:52–5:13).[32] Furthermore, on the basis of their reading of Malachi, many Jews expected the prophet Elijah to appear as a forerunner of the Messiah (e.g., Sir. 48:1–11; cf. Mal. 4:5–6). However, although the coming kingdom was associated with the coming of a Messiah, the nature and work of the Messiah were disputed. J. Julius Scott explains:

> Diverse views abounded among the various groups and individuals. Some looked for the Messiah to be a specific person or group of persons. Some thought the Messiah might be a spirit or maybe only an idealized concept. Some intertestamental Jews expected the Messiah to be a human being,

30. Goodman 1997, 38.
31. Klauck 2003, 296–98; Ferguson 2003, 46.
32. For a summary of the evidence on this theme, see Pitre 2005, 41–130.

> others a supernatural or divine person. Moreover, there was little consensus regarding what the Messiah was to accomplish.[33]

The final age itself is sometimes pictured as a renewed Eden (e.g., *2 Baruch* 4; 2 Esdras 7:36–44; *Testament of Levi* 18:10–14) or as a renewed Davidic kingdom (e.g., 2 Esdras 12:31–32; *Psalms of Solomon* 17:4–10). It was expected to be a time of peace and joy (e.g., *1 Enoch* 10:17–22; 45:4–5; *Sibylline Oracles* 3:371–80, 767–95).[34]

Because the Jewish literature of these centuries is not inspired, there is not always a consistency of thought among the different authors. There was, for example, no unanimity on the chronology of expected eschatological events. Following Emil Schürer, however, Scott, provides a helpful list of the major eschatological topics discussed at various places in the literature of the time.[35]

1. The final ordeal and confusion
2. Elijah as precursor
3. The coming of the Messiah
4. The last assault of the hostile powers
5. Destruction of hostile powers
6. The renewal of Jerusalem
7. The gathering of the dispersed
8. The kingdom of glory in the Holy Land
9. The renewal of the world
10. A general resurrection
11. The last judgment, eternal bliss, and damnation

Although the details and order of these events were not always clear, God was expected to intervene in some dramatic way to bring in the final age, the age of the kingdom.

The Apocrypha

It is somewhat difficult to define precisely the contents of the Apocrypha because different collections contain different books. The Septuagint, for

33. Scott 1995, 287.
34. Scott 1995, 289.
35. Scott 1995, 285.

example, contains thirteen books not included in the Hebrew Old Testament. The Latin Vulgate used by the Roman Catholic Church and the Old Testament canon of the Eastern Orthodox churches both contain additional books. For the purposes of this study, the term "Apocrypha" will be used to designate only those writings preserved in almost all manuscripts of the Septuagint.[36] The Apocrypha, therefore, includes the following works: 1 Esdras, Tobit, Judith, the Additions to Esther, the Wisdom of Solomon, Sirach (or Ecclesiasticus), Baruch, the Epistle of Jeremiah, the Prayer of Azariah, the Song of the Three Young Men, Susanna, Bel and the Dragon, 1 Maccabees, and 2 Maccabees. We will not examine each of these books, but will look at only a few that contribute to our understanding of the eschatology of the intertestamental period.[37]

The book of Tobit, which was written sometime between 250 and 175 B.C., is a rather complex short story about a faithful Jew living in exile in Assyria.[38] He served his foreign ruler, but because of his faithfulness to Jewish law he is persecuted and removed from his office (Tobit 1:16–20). In a darkly humorous twist, he is also blinded while resting outside when bird droppings fall into his eyes (2:9–10). In his despair he prays for death. At the same time, his relative Sarah is also praying for death because a demon has killed each of her seven successive husbands on their wedding night (3:7–15). God hears both prayers and sends the angel Raphael to heal Tobit and to give Sarah as a wife to Tobit's son Tobias (3:16–17). Ultimately, Tobit is healed, and Sarah and Tobias are married. At the end of the book, Tobit offers a lengthy prayer of thanksgiving to God in which he develops some important eschatological themes.

Speaking to the children of Israel, Tobit declares that they will someday be regathered from the nations (13:5). He also speaks of the coming of the Gentile nations into the kingdom (13:11; cf. Zech. 14:16). He declares that Jerusalem will be rebuilt and restored with gold and precious jewels (Tobit 13:16–17; cf. Isa. 54:11–14). In chapter 14, the author of Tobit describes the last days in even greater detail. Everything that was spoken by Israel's prophets will come to pass (14:4). God will bring back the exiled Israelites to the land, and they will rebuild Jerusalem and the temple (14:5). The

36. See Charlesworth 1983, xxvii.

37. For a good introduction to these books, as well as those contained in the Vulgate, see deSilva 2002.

38. deSilva 2002, 69.

nations will be converted and will worship God (14:6). Finally all believing Jews will be gathered to Jerusalem where they will live in peace and safety forever (14:7). The eschatological themes of Tobit, then, are not contrary to the themes found in the canonical Old Testament.

Unlike Tobit, the Wisdom of Solomon is not a narrative, but instead it is a didactic discourse on the superiority of wisdom. The Wisdom of Solomon presents a dramatic contrast between the destinies of the righteous and the wicked. As David deSilva explains:

> Despite the apparent success of apostates in this life and despite the insult and abuse that they might heap on the righteous, Wisdom of Solomon assures the audience that God will honor the righteous with the prize of immortality (2:21–3:9) while showering disgrace and punishment on those who have not kept to God's ways (3:10; 4:17–19). The vivid description of the scenes beyond death, in which the apostates and all the Gentiles will confess their error and acknowledge the lasting honor of the loyal Jew, helps the audience grasp anew the reality of those eschatological events and live with them in view as a primary compass point in their lives.[39]

In one text, Wisdom of Solomon hints at the doctrine of resurrection, saying of God, "For you have the power over life and death; you lead mortals down to the gates of Hades and back again" (Wisdom of Solomon 16:13). Whether this text teaches the doctrine of resurrection or not, it is undeniable that the book offers great insight into the way some Jews of this period understood individual eschatology.

While the doctrine of resurrection is vague in books such as Wisdom of Solomon, it is a central theme in 2 Maccabees. This book tells the story of the crisis under Antiochus IV Epiphanes. Chapters 5–8 describe the persecutions unleashed on Jews within Jerusalem and tell the story of several faithful martyrs. Chapter 6, for example, recounts the story of the martyrdom of the elderly scribe Eleazar. Chapter 7 then turns to the story of the martyrdom of a mother and her seven sons. As the king threatens each brother with torture and death, each proclaims his faith in God, and several proclaim their explicit faith in a future resurrection.

The second brother to die proclaims to the king: "You accursed wretch, you dismiss us from this present life, but the King of the universe will raise us up

39. deSilva 2002, 143.

to an everlasting renewal of life, because we have died for his laws" (2 Macc. 7:9; see also 7:14, 23; 12:44; 14:46). The third brother stretches forth his hands and, expressing his belief in a future bodily resurrection, declares, "I got these from Heaven, and because of his laws I disdain them, and from him I hope to get them back again" (7:11). When the youngest brother is about to be killed, his mother leans over and reminds him, "Do not fear this butcher, but prove worthy of your brothers. Accept death, so that in God's mercy I may get you back again along with your brothers" (7:29). In addition to this emphasis on the future resurrection, 2 Maccabees also continues to look forward to the future regathering of Israel from the nations (2:18).

The Pseudepigrapha

While it is difficult to define the Apocrypha precisely, it is almost impossible to define the Pseudepigrapha. Despite the difficulties, however, James Charlesworth helpfully lists some distinguishing characteristics of these works. The Pseudepigrapha are those works

> 1) that, with the exception of Ahiqar, are Jewish or Christian; 2) that are often attributed to ideal figures in Israel's past; 3) that customarily claim to contain God's word or message; 4) that frequently build upon ideas and narratives present in the Old Testament; 5) and that almost always were composed either during the period 200 B.C. to A.D. 200 or, though late, apparently preserve, albeit in an edited form, Jewish traditions that date from that period.[40]

Our focus in this study is only upon those writings that can be dated with a high degree of certainty to the two centuries before the birth of Christ and to the first half of the first century. Books written later than that may preserve earlier Jewish thinking, but the possibility that they were affected by Christian preaching or the New Testament writings renders their value for this study more questionable. Many of the pseudepigraphal works are apocalyptic works, and eschatological themes are very prominent in many of them.[41] Several contain teaching on the resurrection and the kingdom of God.

40. Charlesworth 1983, xxv. All quotations from the Pseudepigrapha are taken from Charlesworth 1983, 1985.

41. Surburg 1975, 126.

One of the most important of the pseudepigraphal books is *1 Enoch*. This book is not a single work by a single author, but instead it is a collection of writings dating from the second century B.C. to the first century A.D. In the first section of the book, which is unquestionably early (ca. 175 B.C.), there is a vivid description of the coming of God for judgment:

> And I took up with a parable (saying), "The God of the universe, the Holy Great One, will come forth from his dwelling. And from there he will march upon Mount Sinai and appear in his camp emerging from heaven with a mighty power. And everyone shall be afraid, and Watchers shall quiver. And great fear and trembling shall seize them unto the ends of the earth. Mountains and high places will fall down and be frightened. And high hills shall be made low; and they shall melt like a honeycomb before the flame. And earth shall be rent asunder; and all that is upon the earth shall perish. And there shall be a judgment upon all, (including) the righteous. And to all the righteous he will grant peace. He will preserve the elect, and kindness shall be upon them. They shall all belong to God and they shall prosper and be blessed; and the light of God shall shine unto them. Behold, he will arrive with ten million of the holy ones in order to execute judgment upon all. He will destroy the wicked ones and censure all flesh on account of everything that they have done, that which the sinners and the wicked ones committed against him." (1:3–9)

The language is that of apocalyptic. It is filled with graphic imagery of coming divine judgment. The similarity with the language of some prophets is clear (e.g., Isa. 13:10; 34:4; Amos 8:9; Joel 2:2, 6, 10).

A second major section of *1 Enoch* is found in chapters 37–71. This section, often called the Book of the Similitudes, is notoriously difficult to date. Common arguments for a late date are just as problematic as common arguments for an earlier date.[42] These chapters could have been written anytime between the late first century B.C. and the late first century A.D. If this section of *1 Enoch* was composed in the first century B.C., it would be significant because these chapters contain references to a coming Son of Man who is worshiped by the Gentiles and who judges all people following their resurrection from the dead (45:1–51:5). In other words, it would show that at least some Jews of the time interpreted Daniel 7 in a way similar to that of the New Testament. However, since this section of *1 Enoch* may

42. Nickelsburg 1981, 221–23.

have been written in the late first century, it is also possible that the author wrote these sections having been influenced by Christian teaching.[43]

The third section of *1 Enoch* (chapters 72–82) is an astrological treatise, while the fourth section (chapters 83–90) contains the Dream Visions. Important for our purposes, however, is the fifth section of Enoch (chapters 91–104), which is known as Enoch's Testament. This section contains Enoch's Apocalypse of Weeks (91:11–17 and 93:1–10), which describes the events that are to occur during consecutive world weeks. In these texts, Enoch foresees a time of great trouble and tribulation to be followed by the time of righteousness. The outline of the events of the first seven world weeks is described in 93:1–10. The events of weeks 8–10 are described in 91:12–16. Because of its significance, this lengthy section is quoted here in full along with some of its context.

> For I know that the state of violence will intensify upon the earth; a great plague shall be executed upon the earth; all (forms of) oppression will be carried out; and everything shall be uprooted; and every arrow shall fly fast. Oppression shall recur once more and be carried out upon the earth; every (form of) oppression, injustice, and iniquity shall infect (the world) twofold. When sin, oppression, blasphemy, and injustice increase, crime, iniquity, and uncleanliness shall be committed and increase (likewise). Then a great plague shall take place from heaven upon all these; the holy Lord shall emerge with wrath and plague in order that he may execute judgment upon the earth. In those days, injustice shall be cut off from its (sources of succulent) fountain and from its roots—(likewise) oppression together with deceit; they shall be destroyed from underneath heaven. All that which is (common) with the heathen shall be surrendered; the towers shall be inflamed with fire, and be removed from the whole earth. They shall be thrown into the judgment of fire, and perish in wrath and in the force of the eternal judgment. Then the righteous one shall arise from his sleep, and the wise one shall arise; and he shall be given unto them (the people), and through him the roots of oppression shall be cut off. Sinners shall be destroyed; by the sword they shall be cut off (together with) the blasphemers in every place; and those who design oppression and commit blasphemy shall perish by the knife.
>
> Then after that there shall occur the second eighth week—the week of righteousness. A sword shall be given to it in order that judgment shall be executed in righteousness on the oppressors, and sinners shall be delivered

43. On the Similitudes, see Collins 1998, 177–93.

> into the hands of the righteous. At its completion, they shall acquire great things through their righteousness. A house shall be built for the Great King in glory for evermore. Then after that in the ninth week the righteous judgment shall be revealed to the whole world. All the deeds of the sinners shall depart from upon the whole earth, and be written off for eternal destruction; and all people shall direct their sight to the path of uprightness. Then, after this matter, on the tenth week in the seventh part, there shall be the eternal judgment; and it shall be executed by the angels of the eternal heaven—the great (judgment) which emanates from all of the angels. The first heaven shall depart and pass away; a new heaven shall appear; and all the powers of heaven shall shine forever sevenfold. Then after that there shall be many weeks without number forever; it shall be (a time) of goodness and righteousness, and sin shall no more be heard of forever. (91:5–17)

The details of this enigmatic text are not always clear, but the overall idea is evident. Here the author foresees a great time of trouble to be followed by the coming of the final age of righteousness. There are also hints here that he associates the coming of the age of righteousness with the coming of a messianic figure, a Great King.

Like *1 Enoch*, the *Sibylline Oracles* are a collection of writings that can be dated over a period of several centuries—in this case from the second century B.C. to the seventh century A.D. Book 3 of the *Sibylline Oracles* was written sometime between 163 and 145 B.C. in Egypt.[44] Book 3 looks forward to the coming of an ideal king and kingdom following a time of trouble. In 3:635–56, for example, we read:

> King will lay hold of king and take away territory.
> Peoples will ravage peoples, and potentates, tribes.
> All leaders will flee to another land.
> The land will have a change of men and foreign rule
> will ravage all Greece and drain off
> the rich land of its wealth, and men will come
> face to face in strife among themselves because of gold and silver.
> Love of gain will be shepherd of evils for cities.
> All will be unburied in a foreign country.
> Vultures and wild beasts of the earth
> will ravage the flesh of some. Indeed when this is completed

44. Verses 350–80, however, are likely an interpolation written sometime shortly before 31 B.C.

> the huge earth will consume the remains of the dead.
> It itself will be completely unsown and unplowed,
> wretched, proclaiming the curse of innumerable men,
> (for many lengths of yearly recurring times—
> light shields, long shields, javelins and diverse weapons
> and not even wood will be cut from a thicket for the flame of the fire).
> And then God will send a King from the sun
> who will stop the entire earth from evil war,
> killing some, imposing oaths of loyalty on others;
> and he will not do all these things by his private plans
> but in obedience to the noble teachings of the great God.

Further on, the author describes the salvation of the elect (3:702–31) and the day of judgment for all mankind (3:741–61). He then describes the eschatological kingdom of God (3:767–95). He concludes by providing the readers with signs that will signify that the end is near (3:796–808). They will see a great battle in the heavens (3:805), and dust will darken the earth (3:800–803).

Book 4 also speaks of the last days. There will be great wickedness (4:152–61). God will destroy the whole earth with fire (4:171–78). Finally, there will be a resurrection of all men, who will be judged according to their deeds (4:179–92).

The *Testaments of the Twelve Patriarchs* were written during the second century B.C. These works claim to be the final words of Jacob's twelve sons to their respective families just prior to their deaths. They reflect on their own lives, confess their sins, exhort their children, and offer predictions about the future. As H. C. Kee explains:

> Levi and Judah are central figures in the eschatology of the Testaments (TReu 6:8, 11; TSim 7:1; TIss 5:7–8; TJos 19:11; TNaph 5:1–5; 6:7; 8:2) with Judah as king (TJud 1:6; 24:1–6) but with Levi as his superior (TJos 19:4). As God's anointed priest, Levi will be the agent of redemption (TLevi 18:1–11) and will overcome Beliar (TLevi 18:12). After the temple has been destroyed in judgment (TLevi 10:3; 15:1; 16:4–5), it will be rebuilt in the end (TBenj 9:2), while in other texts there is a single agent "from Levi and Judah" who accomplishes redemption (TDan 5:10; TGad 8:1; TBenj 4:2). Finally, God himself will be revealed to all the nations (TLevi 4:4), among

> whom Israel will stand as a light (TLevi 14:34; TSim 7:2; TJud 22:3; 25:5; TBenj 9:5).[45]

Although there is a great emphasis on Levi in these books, there are also indications in the *Testaments* that God is going to do something new. In the *Testament of Levi*, for example, we read that "the Lord will raise up a new priest" (18:2). This entire chapter (*T. Levi* 18) is very likely messianic in intent.

The Dead Sea Scrolls

The discovery, beginning in 1947, of the Dead Sea Scrolls in caves to the northwest of the Dead Sea is one of the most important archaeological discoveries of the twentieth century. To date, over 900 manuscript copies have been identified.[46] These manuscripts are copies of some 350 different literary works. They were part of a library belonging to a sect known as the Essenes who established a community at Qumran in the middle of the second century B.C.[47] There are several categories of documents found among the Dead Sea Scrolls: (1) biblical texts, (2) parabiblical texts, and (3) sectarian texts. The biblical texts are copies of the books of the Bible. The parabiblical texts include fragments of previously known apocryphal and pseudepigraphal books such as Tobit or *1 Enoch*, as well as previously unknown pseudepigraphal works. The sectarian texts are books composed by members of the Qumran community for the Qumran community. Included among these works are community rule books, hymn books, liturgical texts, commentaries, apocalyptic texts, and more.[48]

The Essenes believed that they were living in the last days, and a number of the Dead Sea Scrolls touch on eschatological themes. The War Scroll, for example, predicts a future battle between the sons of light and the enemies of God.

> The sons of light and the lot of darkness shall battle together for God's might, between the roar of a huge multitude and the shout of gods and

45. In Charlesworth 1983, 779.

46. *DTIB*, 159.

47. Ferguson 2003, 521–30.

48. For a good introduction to the Dead Sea Scrolls, see VanderKam 1994. For a good English translation of the nonbiblical texts, see García Martínez 1996. All quotations from the DSS are taken from García Martínez.

> men, on the day of the calamity. It will be a time of suffering fo[r al]l the people redeemed by God. Of all their sufferings, none will be like this, from its haste (?) until eternal redemption is fulfilled. And on the day of their war against the Kittim, they [shall go out to destr]uction. In the war, the sons of light will be the strongest during three lots, in order to strike down wickedness; and in three (others), the army of Belial will gird themselves in order to force the lot of [. . .] to retreat. There will be infantry battalions to melt the heart, but God's might will strengthen the hea[rt of the sons of light.] And in the seventh lot, God's great hand will subdue [Belial, and a]ll the angels of his dominion and all the men of [his lot.][49]

Although this text is not entirely clear, it appears that there was an expectation that the battle between the sons of light and the enemies of God would occur in seven stages. In three battles, the sons of light will be victorious. In three battles, the enemies of God will be victorious. But in the final battle God will intervene decisively.

A messianic figure also appears in several of the Dead Sea Scrolls, but the picture presented in the various documents is not entirely clear or consistent. In the Rule of the Community, for example, the author speaks of two Messiahs: "They should not depart from any counsel of the law in order to walk in complete stubbornness of their heart, but instead shall be ruled by the first directives which the men of the Community began to be taught until the Prophet comes, and the Messiahs of Aaron and Israel."[50]

Elsewhere, however, there is reference to only one Messiah. The Messianic Apocalypse, for example, declares that "[the heav]ens and the earth will listen to his Messiah."[51] This same text declares that the Messiah "will make the dead live."[52] This appears to be a clear reference to belief in a future resurrection. The War Scroll appears to picture a messianic figure defeating the forces of evil: "Thus you taught us from ancient times: 'A star will depart from Jacob, a sceptre will be raised in Israel. It will smash the temples of Moab, it will destroy all the sons of Seth. It will come down from Jacob, it will exterminate the remnant of the city, the enemy will be its possession, and Israel will perform feats.'"[53] While the specifics of the

49. 1QM I.11–15.
50. 1QS IX.9b–11.
51. 4Q521, Frag. 2, II.1.
52. 4Q521, Frag. 2, II.12.
53. 1QM XI.6–7.

Qumran community's understanding of the coming Messiah are not perfectly clear, it seems apparent that they expected him to appear and judge the world very soon.

Summary

The four hundred years between the prophet Malachi and the birth of Christ were important years in the history of Israel. During this time, the nation witnessed the fall of the Persian Empire, the rise and fall of the Greek Empire, and the rise of the Roman Empire. But Israel did not witness these events from afar. The nation was often involved in the political maneuvering and battles. During these years, the people of Israel experienced grave crises, none more threatening than the Hellenistic crisis experienced under Antiochus IV Epiphanes, who attempted to utterly eradicate the religion of Israel.

The crises and suffering experienced during these years led to the production of numerous writings. In these writings, the hopes of the Jewish people are expressed. They continue to look forward to the full restoration that had been declared by the prophets. Although many had returned to the land following the exile, they also continue to look forward to the full regathering of the people. They look forward to the coming of a Messiah, one who would judge their enemies and establish the kingdom of God forever.

PART 2

THE NEW TESTAMENT

10

The Gospel of Matthew

When we turn to the New Testament, it is important to remember that what we have in these books is a continuation of the narrative found in the Old Testament. The New Testament is not a completely separate and isolated collection of books that can be fully understood without reference to what has gone before. Certainly, it is true that there is a historical gap of over four hundred years between the last events of the Old Testament and the first events of the New Testament, but the same historical gap exists between the books of Genesis and Exodus, and yet few would read those books as if they were not part of a single continuous narrative. In the same way that Exodus continues the story begun in Genesis, the New Testament continues the story begun in the Old Testament.

The Old Testament ends on a note of anticipation and expectation. Following the decree of Cyrus in 538 B.C., many of the Jews who were in captivity in Babylon returned to Jerusalem to rebuild the city and the temple. Many of them believed that the time of restoration foretold by the prophets had finally arrived, but although the second temple was completed in 515 B.C., the anticipated restoration did not come in its fullness. Most Jews in Babylon had decided to stay in Babylon. The Jews who had returned to Judah faced apathy and opposition, and they remained under foreign domination. The tribes of the northern kingdom were still scattered and in exile.[1] The Messiah had not yet come to establish his kingdom. For over four hundred years, the prophetic voice was silent in Israel. This was the situation in the days of Herod the Great when, in the small town of Bethlehem, Jesus was born.

The Gospels

The genre of the New Testament Gospels has been disputed over the last century or so. Many have assumed that these books are sui generis, that is, an absolutely unique genre of literature. More recent and thorough studies, however, have demonstrated that the Gospels closely resemble in general content and form ancient Greco-Roman biographies.[2] As we have seen, knowing the genre of a book is crucial to its interpretation. Since the Gospels are biographical, this means that the key to their interpretation is the personal subject of their biography, namely Jesus Christ. As Richard Burridge explains, "Every passage, pericope or verse must be interpreted in the light of the biographical genre of the whole: what this story tells us about the author's understanding of Jesus."[3]

The literary relationship among the Synoptic Gospels (Matthew, Mark, and Luke) has raised a number of questions since the early centuries of the church. The questions have arisen because of the numerous similarities between the gospels as well as striking differences. What accounts for both the similarities and differences? As D. A. Carson and Douglas Moo explain, there is almost universal consent that "two of the evangelists used one or more of the other gospels in constructing their own."[4] Disagreement has arisen, however, regarding the specifics. Prior to the nineteenth century, the standard theory among those who saw literary interdependence was that

1. See Pitre 2005, 34–35. It is important to recall that the ten tribes of the northern kingdom were not completely lost or destroyed in 722 B.C. Many came to the southern kingdom of Judah before the Assyrian exile (2 Chron. 30:1, 6–9, 25–27; 31:1). Some returned, but others likely stayed. The southern kingdom of Judah consisted primarily of the tribes of Judah and Benjamin, but members of the other tribes survived there and elsewhere. In fact, the New Testament assumes the continued existence of all twelve tribes (Acts 26:7; James 1:1) and occasionally mentions by name members of tribes other than Judah and Benjamin (e.g., Luke 2:36).

2. See Burridge 2004; Aune 1987, 43; Keener 2003, 1:3–34.

3. Burridge 2004, 289.

4. Carson and Moo 2005, 91.

Matthew wrote his gospel first, that Mark used Matthew in composing his gospel, and finally, that Luke used both Matthew and Mark. This view has few advocates today, but it has not been conclusively ruled out.

One contemporary theory of interdependence suggests the priority of Matthew. This view, first proposed by J. Griesbach in the eighteenth century, suggests that Matthew was written first, that Luke was written second, and that Mark used both Matthew and Luke in the composition of his own gospel. This view gained some support in the second half of the twentieth century but is not widely held today. A more common view is the Two Source view. According to this position, Mark was written first, but there also existed a separate document (Q) that was a collection of Jesus' sayings. Both Mark and Q were used by Matthew and Luke in the composition of their respective gospels. A variation on this theory (a Four Source view) suggests that Matthew also had access to a source (M) that accounts for the material unique to his gospel, while Luke had a source (L) that accounts for the material unique to his gospel. The Four Source theory was the most dominant theory in the twentieth century, but it has also recently come under great scrutiny, and many have rejected it. The Synoptic Problem is an enormously complex issue, and it is beyond the scope of this work to address it in any further detail.[5]

The Gospel of Matthew

When the gospels are listed in the writings of the early church, the gospel of Matthew is always listed first. Probably part of the reason for this is the fact that most early Christians believed that Matthew was the first of the gospels to be written. Of more significance for our purposes, however, is the early church's realization that the New Testament was the fulfillment of the Old. More than any other gospel, Matthew emphasizes the theme of fulfillment.

5. For a helpful introductory discussion of the issues involved, see Guthrie 1990a, 136–208. For a more thorough discussion, see Stein 1987. What evidence we have indicates that the literary relationship among the Synoptic Gospels is likely far more complicated than any of the theories proposed thus far. There is strong evidence that Mark was written first and that he used eyewitness testimony. There is not strong evidence, however, for the existence of the hypothetical written document Q. Matthew and Luke each apparently had access to the gospel of Mark as well as to their own independent eyewitnesses, and Matthew was also able to recount that which he witnessed himself (Bauckham 2006). Although I am persuaded that there is strong evidence that Mark was written first, I have chosen to discuss the gospel of Matthew first. This is due to the nature of Matthew's opening chapters, which draw out the connections with the Old Testament narrative very clearly.

He continuously explains how the life and ministry of Jesus fulfill the Old Testament promises and prophecies.[6] In so doing, Matthew provides the perfect canonical transition from the Old Testament to the New.

Regarding the authorship of the gospel, there are many scholars who claim that the book was not attributed to Matthew until the second century. The gospel, however, never circulated without the title heading "according to Matthew." There is, in addition, other strong evidence supporting Matthean authorship.[7] There is no sufficient reason, then, to reject the traditional view that the author is the apostle Matthew, one of the twelve, and an eyewitness of Jesus. The dating of the composition of his gospel is more difficult to determine, but a date in the 60s before the beginning of the Jewish war appears to be the most likely date.[8]

The gospel of Matthew is well organized, but discerning its precise structure is no easy task. Commentators are agreed that the gospel follows a roughly chronological outline and that within this outline are found five major teaching discourses.[9] This general agreement, however, has not led to any consensus regarding the overall structural outline of the book.[10] Probably the most helpful structural outlines are those which emphasize the general chronological and geographical sequence. Leon Morris provides such an outline, dividing the book into eight major sections.[11] These are: (1) the birth and infancy of Jesus (1:1–2:23); (2) the preliminaries to Jesus' ministry (3:1–4:11); (3) Jesus' ministry in Galilee (4:12–13:52); (4) the end of Jesus' Galilean ministry (13:53–18:35); (5) Jesus' journey to Jerusalem (19:1–20:34); (6) Jesus' ministry in Jerusalem (21:1–25:46); (7) the passion story (26:1–27:66); and (8) the resurrection of Christ (28:1–20).

The Birth and Infancy of Jesus (Matt. 1:1–2:23)

The gospel of Matthew opens with words that immediately cause the reader to reflect on the Old Testament: "The book of the genealogy of Jesus Christ, the son of David, the son of Abraham" (1:1). The phrase "book of

6. See France 1989, 166–241.

7. For a survey of the evidence, see Carson and Moo 2005, 140–50.

8. Nolland 2005, 17.

9. Davies and Allison 1988, 58–59.

10. In fact some (e.g., Gundry 1982, 10; Davies and Allison 1988, 72) doubt whether Matthew had any specific structural outline in mind at all.

11. Morris 1992, v–ix.

the genealogy" is a translation of the Greek phrase *biblos geneseōs*, which is found in the Septuagint translation of Genesis 2:4 and 5:1. The phrase suggests the idea of a new beginning, or even a new creation.[12] Its connection with the name of Jesus indicates that the coming of Jesus is that which brings about this new beginning.

Jesus is also described in this first verse as the "son of David." By the first century, the title "Son of David" had become a common title for the expected Messiah who would sit on the throne of David, restore Israel, and establish God's kingdom.[13] By applying the title to Jesus, Matthew clearly indicates that Jesus is the promised messianic King of Israel. Jesus is also referred to in the first verse as the "son of Abraham." This title indicates not only that Jesus is a true Israelite; it also indicates that in his coming, God's ancient promise to bless the nations of the earth will be fulfilled (Gen. 12:3; Matt. 28:19).[14] As David Holwerda observes, "a new age has begun, but it is new because after centuries of Israel's failure the covenant promises of God to Abraham and David are finding fulfillment in their Son, Jesus Christ."[15]

Matthew 1:2–17 is a genealogy designed to identify Jesus not only as the heir of David, but also as the culmination of the Old Testament story of Israel.[16] The genealogy is divided into three groups of fourteen. There are fourteen generations from Abraham to David, fourteen generations from David to the exile, and fourteen generations from the exile to Jesus. Numerous explanations for the 3 × 14 structure have been suggested, but none is self-evidently correct. Regardless of the precise reason for the division into three groups of fourteen, the point of the major divisions seems clear. The first group of fourteen ends with David, the point at which the Israelite kingdom was established. The second group ends with the

12. Davies and Allison 1988, 150; Luz 1995, 24; France 2007, 28. It is also possible that Matthew is using the phrase in the same way Moses used it in Genesis. In the Septuagint, the Greek word *geneseōs* is a translation of the Hebrew word *toledot*. Moses uses this word at the beginning of the ten major sections of Genesis. Matthew may be deliberately tying his narrative to the Genesis narrative with the use of the phrase "the book of the genealogy of Jesus Christ." To those of his readers familiar with the Greek Septuagint, the language likely brought to mind the same words in Genesis. Matthew, then, may have been saying that his gospel is the eleventh *toledot*, as it were, the fulfillment of that which Moses foresaw.

13. Hagner 1993, 9.

14. Holwerda 1995, 32.

15. Holwerda 1995, 32.

16. See France 1989, 168; Keener 1999, 74.

Babylonian captivity, the point at which this kingdom was lost. The third group ends with Jesus, indicating that with the birth of Jesus the time of the restored kingdom has come.

Of great significance is the inclusion within the genealogy itself of four women. Women were not usually included in genealogies in the Near East. Even more unusual than the inclusion of the four women, however, is the identity of the women included. Matthew does not include the names of women one might expect in a genealogy of the Messiah if women were to be included at all. He does not include the names of Sarah, or Rebekah, or Leah. Instead he includes Tamar, Rahab, Ruth, and Bathsheba. But why? Several suggestions have been made, but the most plausible explanation is that their inclusion reflects Matthew's interest in the Gentiles. Rahab was a Canaanite, and Tamar was probably the same. Ruth was a Moabitess, and Bathsheba was married to a Hittite.[17] The inclusion of these women in the genealogy indicates, as Craig Keener explains, "that the Gentiles were never an afterthought in God's plan, but had been part of his work in history from the beginning."[18]

The birth of Jesus is recounted in Matthew 1:18–25. Joseph and Mary were betrothed, but before they consummate the marriage, Mary is found to be with child (v. 18). Joseph considers divorcing Mary, but an angel of the Lord appears to him instructing him to take Mary as his wife because the child in her womb is from the Holy Spirit (vv. 19–20). The angel tells Joseph, "She will bear a son, and you shall call his name Jesus, for he will save his people from their sins" (v. 21). The name Jesus is the Greek form of the Hebrew name Joshua, which is related to the Hebrew verb "to save." The prophet Jeremiah had long ago prayed, "O Yahweh, save your people, the remnant of Israel" (Jer. 31:7; cf. Ps. 130:8). Here in Matthew, the angel announces that the Old Testament hopes for the eschatological salvation of Israel will be fulfilled by Jesus.

Matthew writes, "All this took place to fulfill what the Lord had spoken by the prophet: 'Behold, the virgin shall conceive and bear a son, and they shall call his name Immanuel' (which means, God with us)" (1:22–23). Here Matthew cites Isaiah 7:14, a prophecy that had an initial fulfillment already in the Old Testament, but now has its ultimate fulfillment.[19] The

17. See Luz 1995, 26.

18. Keener 1999, 80.

19. Blomberg 1992, 60. For an explanation of the initial fulfillment of Isaiah 7:14, see chapter 6.

reference to Jesus as Immanuel indicates that in him, God's presence is manifested once again in Israel.[20] This passage (Matt. 1:22–23) is the first in a series of five brief stories in which Matthew focuses on the fulfillment of an Old Testament prophecy. This idea of fulfillment is central to Matthew's teaching.[21] As Donald Hagner explains: "Matthew contains well over sixty explicit quotations from the OT (not counting a great number of allusions), more than twice as many as any other Gospel. This heavy dependence on the OT reflects Matthew's interest in the gospel of the kingdom as the fulfillment of the OT expectation."[22] The coming of Jesus, in other words, is the fulfillment of all of the Old Testament prophecies and promises. His coming is the climactic point, the goal, of Israel's history, the event to which all of the Old Testament Scriptures looked forward.[23]

Matthew 2:1–12 tells the story of the visit of the wise men. Matthew writes, "Now after Jesus was born in Bethlehem of Judea in the days of Herod the king, behold, wise men from the east came to Jerusalem, saying, 'Where is he who has been born king of the Jews? For we saw his star when it rose and have come to worship him'" (2:1–2). After meeting with the priests and scribes and discovering where the Messiah was to be born, Herod asks the wise men to find him in order that he too might worship the newborn king (vv. 3–8). The wise men follow the star, find the newborn Christ, and worship him, but they are warned in a dream not to return to Herod, so they go back to their own country by a different route (vv. 9–12).

The wise men are Gentiles from the east, and while many Jews at the time considered Gentiles to be outside of God's purposes, this narrative demonstrates the openness of at least some Gentiles to the work of God. The Old Testament had foretold the eschatological pilgrimage of Gentiles to Jerusalem to worship the Messiah and submit to God (Ps. 72; Isa. 60). In fulfillment of Micah's prophecy, the Messiah has been born in Bethlehem (Matt. 2:1, 6; Mic. 5:2). Now, the wise men from the east are portrayed in Matthew as the first of the Gentiles from the nations to come to Jerusalem to worship the newborn Messiah in the last-days pilgrimage. In sum, the time of eschatological fulfillment has begun.

20. Another reference to the Lord's presence with his people will close Matthew's gospel (Matt. 28:20).

21. France 1989, 166.

22. Hagner 1993, liv.

23. See Vos 1948, 358; Ridderbos 1962, 465; France 1989, 197.

After the wise men depart, an angel appears to Joseph in a dream and warns him to flee to Egypt with Mary and Jesus because Herod will seek to kill the child (Matt. 2:13). Joseph obediently flees to Egypt where the family remains until the death of Herod (v. 14). This is said to fulfill Hosea 11:1, which reads: "Out of Egypt I called my son." Since Hosea 11:1 refers to Israel's original exodus from Egypt, how is Jesus' flight to Egypt a fulfillment of the prophecy? In its context, Hosea 11:1 is part of a prophecy that looks back at the original exodus in order to point forward to a new exodus.[24] Hosea promises that despite the coming exile, God will restore his people (Hos. 11:11). In Matthew's use of Hosea's prophecy, a couple of points are made. First, Jesus' flight from Israel is similar to Moses' flight from Egypt. Israel has, in a sense, become like Egypt of old. Whereas Gentile wise men from the east come to worship the Messiah, a prominent leader in Jerusalem seeks to kill him. In the second place, Matthew points to Hosea 11 to indicate that with Jesus the time of the promised new exodus has begun. The day of eschatological salvation has dawned.[25]

When Herod discovers that he has been tricked by the wise men, he becomes furious and has all of the male children in Bethlehem under the age of two murdered (Matt. 2:16–18). Some time later, after Herod's death, an angel instructs Joseph to return to Israel. Joseph does so and settles in Nazareth (2:19–23; cf. Ex. 4:19–20).[26] As W. D. Davies and D. C. Allison observe, Jesus culminates Israel's history in Matthew 1, but in chapter 2, he repeats it.[27] The parallels between the exodus narrative and the early chapters of Matthew indicate that Matthew is portraying Jesus as the new Moses-like redeemer who will inaugurate the promised final restoration by leading his people in the eschatological new exodus. The main point of the first two chapters, then, is to indicate that Jesus is the one in whom all of the Old Testament hopes find their fulfillment.[28]

24. The Old Testament prophets often described the future restoration of Israel in terms of a new exodus (Hos. 2:14–15; Isa. 10:24–26; 11:15–16; Jer. 16:14–15; Ezek. 20:33–38).

25. Keener 1999, 108.

26. France (2007, 94) suggests that the statement "He shall be called a Nazarene" (v. 23) paradoxically takes its cue from the fact that Nazareth is not mentioned in the Old Testament. The idea that the Messiah would come from Nazareth would invite ridicule and derision. France suggests the verse has to do then with derogatory name-calling (Isa. 53:1–3).

27. Davies and Allison 1988, 282.

28. France 1985, 68.

Preliminaries to Jesus' Ministry (Matt. 3:1–4:11)

The events of Matthew 3 occur approximately thirty years after the events of Matthew 1–2. Matthew writes, "In those days John the Baptist came preaching in the wilderness of Judea, 'Repent, for the kingdom of heaven is at hand'" (3:1–2). After four hundred years, the voice of prophecy is again heard in Israel. As Matthew clearly indicates, John was the prophesied forerunner of the Messiah, called to prepare the way for the coming of the Lord (Matt. 3:3; Isa. 40:3).[29] John announces the coming of the Messiah. He declares the advent of a new era. John was a prophet, but unlike the prophets of old who declared that the Messiah would come, John declared that the Messiah had come.

John appears in the wilderness preaching, "Repent, for the kingdom of heaven is at hand." This is the first explicit mention of the kingdom of heaven in the gospel of Matthew, and it is important to understand the meaning of the concept. As we have seen, part of God's original creational purpose was to establish his kingdom on earth. When man fell into sin, God did not abandon his original purpose, but the establishment of the kingdom took a circuitous route. At the time of the exodus, the new nation of Israel was constituted a "kingdom of priests" (Ex. 19:6). Israel was to be a manifestation of God's kingdom on earth. Under the rule of David, this Old Testament manifestation of God's kingdom reached its highest point. The exile, however, brought the Old Testament kingdom to an end.

Before, during, and after the exile, the prophets had looked forward to a time of restoration when the kingdom of God would be established in fullness with the coming of the messianic King. According to the prophets, the very purpose of the coming of the Messiah was to establish the kingdom.[30] When John announces that the kingdom of heaven is at hand, he is announcing the arrival of this kingdom that the faithful within Israel have been awaiting for centuries.[31] God is finally going to fulfill his original purpose for creation.[32] The kingdom is no longer something that can only be seen from a distance. The promised kingdom is now "at hand."

29. Isaiah's use of the term "way," which is quoted by Matthew, alludes to the time of the original exodus (Ex. 13:21–22; 23:20). Isaiah uses the term to point toward a future, new exodus. Matthew's quotation of Isaiah indicates that the time of the new exodus has arrived.

30. Beasley-Murray 1986, 17.

31. Bruce 1978, 15.

32. McCartney 1994, 2.

It is important to understand that in the New Testament, the kingdom of God is not to be identified with mere historical processes. It is instead "God's supernatural breaking into history in the person of Jesus."[33] It is established by God, not by man. This is important because in Jesus' day there were those who sought to establish the kingdom by human power and violence.[34] It must also be understood that the kingdom of God is not identical to the church. George Ladd provides a helpful explanation of the differences between the two:

> In biblical idiom, the Kingdom is not identified with its subjects. They are the people of God's rule who enter it, live under it, and are governed by it. The church is the community of the Kingdom but never the Kingdom itself. Jesus' disciples belong to the Kingdom as the Kingdom belongs to them; but they are not the Kingdom. The Kingdom is the rule of God; the church is a society of men.[35]

Great confusion has been caused throughout history by those who have confused the kingdom with the church. The two must be distinguished.

Finally, a word must be said about the relation between those passages of the New Testament that proclaim the presence of the kingdom and those that proclaim the future coming of the kingdom. As we shall see, some passages, such as Matthew 3:2, speak of the nearness or the presence of the kingdom. Others speak of the coming of the kingdom as something still future (e.g., Matt. 6:10). How are these teachings to be reconciled? How can the kingdom be both present and future?[36] Dale C. Allison Jr. explains:

> The seeming contradiction between the presence of the kingdom of God and its futurity is dissolved when one realizes that Jewish thinking could envision the final events—the judgment of evil and the arrival of the kingdom of God—as extending over time, and as a process or series of events that could involve the present. When Jesus announces that the kingdom of God has come and is coming, this means that the last act has begun but has not yet

33. Ladd 1974a, 189.

34. See Cullmann 1956, 24; Witherington 1990, 116.

35. Ladd 1974a, 262.

36. Some, such as Dodd (1961), attempt to ease the tension by arguing that the New Testament teaches that the kingdom of God has come and denying that it really teaches any future coming of the kingdom. Others, such as traditional dispensationalist commentators, emphasize the future coming of the kingdom.

> reached its climax; the last things have come and will come. Already, in the person and activity of Jesus, the kingdom of God is present.[37]

The incarnation, crucifixion, resurrection, ascension, second coming, and final judgment are a series of distinct events that are part of a single whole—the coming of the kingdom. In order to understand the New Testament teaching regarding the kingdom of God, it is necessary to understand that the kingdom has *already* been inaugurated, but it has *not yet* been consummated.[38]

John called the people to repentance and baptized those who confessed their sins (Matt. 3:4–6). His call to repentance echoes the Old Testament prophetic calls to the people of Israel to "turn" or "return" to their God.[39] John is calling out and identifying by baptism the remnant of Israel.[40] He declares the imminence of judgment, saying: "Even now the axe is laid to the root of the trees. Every tree therefore that does not bear good fruit is cut down and thrown into the fire" (3:10). John continues: "I baptize you with water for repentance, but he who is coming after me is mightier than I, whose sandals I am not worthy to carry. He will baptize you with the Holy Spirit and with fire.[41] His winnowing fork is in his hand, and he will clear his threshing floor and gather his wheat into the barn, but the chaff he will burn with unquenchable fire" (3:11–12). Here John proclaims the coming of the eschatological outpouring of the Spirit (Isa. 44:3–5; Ezek. 36:27; Joel 2:28–32) as well as the eschatological judgment by fire (Mal. 4:1).

The second section of Matthew concludes with a narrative of Jesus' baptism followed by his temptation in the wilderness. Matthew writes:

> Then Jesus came from Galilee to the Jordan to John, to be baptized by him. John would have prevented him, saying, "I need to be baptized by you, and do you come to me?" But Jesus answered him, "Let it be so now, for thus it is fitting for us to fulfill all righteousness." Then he consented. And when Jesus was baptized, immediately he went up from the water, and behold,

37. Allison 1985, 105–6. We recall that David's kingdom was established in stages.

38. Ladd 1993, 89–90.

39. Keener (1999, 120) cites the following Old Testament texts as examples: Isa. 31:6; 45:22; 55:7; Jer. 3:7, 10, 14, 22; 4:1; 8:5; 18:11; 24:7; 25:5; 26:3; 35:15; 36:7; 44:5; Lam. 3:40; Ezek. 13:22; 14:6; 18:23, 30; 33:9, 11; Hos. 11:5; 12:6; 14:1–2; Joel 2:12–13; Zech. 1:3–4; Mal. 3:7.

40. Meyer 2002, 128.

41. This is significant because in the OT only God could bestow the Spirit (e.g., Joel 2:28–29).

> the heavens were opened to him, and he saw the Spirit of God descending like a dove and coming to rest on him; and behold, a voice from heaven said, "This is my beloved Son, with whom I am well pleased." (3:13–17; cf. Isa. 11:2; 42:1; 61:1)

What does it mean for Jesus and John to "fulfill all righteousness"? In light of prophecies such as Isaiah 42:1, it appears that Matthew is saying that Jesus will fulfill the righteousness symbolized by John's baptism. In other words, Jesus "would actively carry out that righteousness in his life and thereby establish the righteousness of God's kingdom on earth."[42] The coming of the Spirit upon Jesus in the form of a dove at his baptism marks the beginning of his public ministry, his anointing as it were (Isa. 11:2; 61:1). The voice of God from heaven echoes the beginning of the Servant Song in Isaiah 42:1 as well as the royal messianic Psalm 2 (v. 7). Jesus is thereby identified with both the Servant of God and the messianic King.

Immediately after his baptism, Jesus is led into the wilderness to be tempted by the devil for forty days (Matt. 4:1–11). We cannot help but be reminded here of the devil's temptation of Adam (Gen. 3). However, whereas that temptation took place in a perfect garden, this temptation takes place in a desolate wilderness. Adam failed to obey, and the result was the curse. The second Adam does not fail, and the result will be the restoration of God's blessing.

The temptation of Jesus not only recalls the temptation of Adam, but in the context of Matthew's gospel, it may also be compared with the testing of Israel. As we have seen, Matthew has been drawing comparisons between Jesus and Israel throughout the early chapters of his gospel. Israel had been tested in the wilderness by God for forty years. As D. A. Carson explains, it may be that Matthew is here paralleling Jesus' experience with that of Israel.[43] In contrast with Israel, however, Jesus remains obedient. Davies and Allison reflect on the meaning of this passage:

> Jesus, as the personification or embodiment of obedient Israel, repeats the experience of Israel of old: having passed through the waters, he enters the desert to suffer a time of testing (cf. Deut 8.2). What does this signify? Why

42. Holwerda 1995, 43.
43. Carson 1984, 112.

> is the parallel important? 4.1–11 leads through 4.12–17 to 4.18–22, this last being the calling of the first disciples; and this means that the baptism and temptation of Jesus inaugurated the renewal of the people of God. Just as Israel was born in the first exodus, so is the church born in a second exodus. By repeating or recapitulating in his own person the exodus and the events thereafter, the Son of God brings a new people into being.[44]

Here again we see how Matthew draws all the various threads of Old Testament prophecy together into a coherent whole.

Jesus' Ministry in Galilee (Matt. 4:12–13:52)

Jesus' Galilean ministry is occasioned by the arrest of John the Baptist. When Jesus hears about John's arrest, he withdraws himself from Nazareth to Galilee, more specifically to Capernaum in the territory of Zebulun and Naphtali (Matt. 4:13). Matthew tells us that this is in fulfillment of prophecy (vv. 14–16). The specific prophecy cited is Isaiah 9:1–2, a prophecy that describes the unbridled joy of the people when they are delivered from oppression at the coming of the Messiah. Matthew's citation of this prophecy indicates that Jesus is the Messiah who has come to deliver the people from oppression. Matthew writes, "From that time Jesus began to preach, saying, 'Repent, for the kingdom of heaven is at hand'" (Matt. 4:17). Jesus' proclamation is the same as that of John the Baptist (3:2). Like John, Jesus announces the advent of God's kingdom. In doing so, he is declaring to the people of Israel that the prophesied time of eschatological restoration has come.

The First Disciples

In Matthew 4:18–22, Jesus calls the first disciples to follow him. Each of those he calls immediately obeys. Jesus' mission is then described:

> And he went throughout all Galilee, teaching in their synagogues and proclaiming the gospel of the kingdom and healing every disease and every affliction among the people. So his fame spread throughout all Syria, and they brought him all the sick, those afflicted with various diseases and pains, those oppressed by demons, epileptics, and paralytics, and he healed them. (4:23–24)

44. Davies and Allison 1988, 402–3.

The miraculous healings that Jesus performs indicate that the power of Satan is being broken, thus manifesting the coming of God in power in his kingdom.[45] This is also an initial manifestation of the reversal of the curse on creation. It is the beginning of the renewal and restoration of creation.[46]

Matthew writes that Jesus was proclaiming the "gospel of the kingdom." This is the first use of the term "gospel" in Matthew. The word "gospel" is a translation of the Greek word *euangelion* and means "good news."[47] When Matthew speaks here of the "good news" of the kingdom, he is evidently recalling the use of the term "gospel" in Isaiah to describe the coming time of restoration for Israel (Isa. 40:9; 52:7; 61:1). The good news of the kingdom is that the long-awaited Messiah who would establish the kingdom has finally come. The miraculous healings and exorcisms, then, are signs of the presence of the messianic kingdom age.[48]

It is instructive to note here that the word "gospel" was also used at this time in history to describe the perceived blessings brought by the emperor Caesar Augustus. Roman political propaganda hailed Augustus as a "savior" whose birth was the beginning of the "gospel."[49] An inscription, dated 9 B.C., speaks of Augustus in terms that would later be used by early Christians:

> Since the Providence [*Pronoia*] which has ordered all things and is deeply interested in our life has set in most perfect order by giving to us Augustus, whom she filled with virtue [divine power] that he might benefit mankind, sending him as a Saviour [*Sōtēr*], both for us and for our descendants, that he might end war and arrange all things, and since he, Caesar, by his appearance [*phaneis*] [excelled even our anticipations], surpassing all previous benefactors [*euergetai*], and not even leaving to posterity any hope of surpassing what he had done, and since the birthday of the god Augustus was the beginning for the world of the good tidings [*euangelion*] that came by reason of him . . .[50]

This kind of exalted language grew up in connection with the Roman emperor cult. In ancient times religion and the state were not separated as

45. Vos 1972, 53–54.
46. Ridderbos 1962, 115.
47. See BDAG, s.v. εὐαγγέλιον, 1 (p. 402).
48. Bruce 1977a, 16.
49. Bolt 1998, 53.
50. Cited in Ferguson 2003, 46.

they often are today.[51] Prior to Julius Caesar, the Roman state itself had been worshiped as the goddess Roma.[52] In the last months of Julius Caesar's life, he himself was divinized, being referred to as "the god who has appeared visibly [θεὸν ἐπιφανῆ] and universal savior of the life of human beings."[53] The same kinds of honors were accorded the later emperors, including Augustus. The declaration of the "good news" of the kingdom of Jesus Christ is, then, an implicit declaration of an alternative to the Roman emperor and Roman Empire.[54] It is the declaration of the advent of the true King of kings.

The Sermon on the Mount

Matthew's narrative of Jesus' Galilean ministry continues with the first major discourse in the book, the Sermon on the Mount (5:1–7:29). This passage begins with words that recall a specific event in the Old Testament: "Seeing the crowds, he went up on the mountain, and when he sat down, his disciples came to him. And he opened his mouth and taught them, saying . . ." (Matt. 5:1–2). In light of the exodus imagery used throughout the first four chapters of Matthew, it appears that these verses present the mountain upon which Jesus sat as analogous to Mount Sinai, the mountain on which the law of God was delivered by Moses to Israel.

The Sermon on the Mount begins with a series of Beatitudes, or declarations of blessing (5:2–12). Readers of Matthew who are familiar with the Old Testament will recall that blessing is a key theme in the book of Genesis. After the fall, the narrative of Genesis traces the initial outworking of God's plan to restore his blessing to his people. The prophets of the Old Testament indicated that the ultimate restoration of God's blessing would occur when the Messiah came. Jesus has declared that the kingdom of heaven is at hand, and now he proclaims the blessings of the kingdom. Jesus has been sent to fulfill the Old Testament promises of blessing. He is the promised Messiah, and the Beatitudes indicate that his kingdom will bring "eschatological comfort, a permanent inheritance, true satisfaction, the obtaining of mercy, the vision of God, and divine sonship."[55]

51. Gradel 2002, 12.
52. Klauck 2003, 283.
53. Klauck 2003, 290; see also Gradel 2002, 54–55.
54. Bolt 1998, 77.
55. Davies and Allison 1988, 466.

After calling his followers to be a light to the world, in short, to be what he himself is (5:13–16; cf. 4:16), Jesus makes an important statement about the law:

> Do not think that I have come to abolish the Law or the Prophets; I have not come to abolish them but to fulfill them. For truly, I say to you, until heaven and earth pass away, not an iota, not a dot, will pass from the Law until all is accomplished. Therefore whoever relaxes one of the least of these commandments and teaches others to do the same will be called least in the kingdom of heaven, but whoever does them and teaches them will be called great in the kingdom of heaven. For I tell you, unless your righteousness exceeds that of the scribes and Pharisees, you will never enter the kingdom of heaven. (5:17–20)

In order to understand this passage correctly, the broader context of Matthew must be kept in mind. As we have seen, Matthew 1–4 presents Jesus as the one who fulfills the promises and prophecies of the Old Testament. When we turn to the Sermon on the Mount (Matt. 5–7), we see Jesus addressing numerous misunderstandings of the law. Jesus is not contradicting the Old Testament in the Sermon, but the newness of his teaching could lead some of his hearers to ask whether he is abolishing the law. Thus the need for Jesus' words in 5:17–20.

Jesus says that he has not come to abolish the Law or the Prophets, but to fulfill them. What is the meaning of "fulfill" (*plēroō*) in this context? Does Jesus mean to say merely that he has come to "confirm" the validity of the Mosaic law? This is unlikely for a number of reasons. First, "to confirm" is not the normal way that the verb *plēroō* is used. As Vern Poythress explains, "Induction from other instances where the New Testament speaks of fulfilling the Scriptures indicates that the bringing to realization of forward-pointing aspects of Old Testament revelation is in view."[56] Second, confirmation of every detail of the Mosaic law would contradict not only other passages within the New Testament but Matthew's own insistence elsewhere that with the coming of Jesus there are now changes in the law's administration (e.g., Matt. 5:33–37).

When Jesus says that he has come to fulfill the law, then, he is saying that a fundamental advance has occurred in redemptive history. All that

56. Poythress 1995, 267.

the law foreshadowed and symbolized has become reality in Jesus. D. A. Carson explains:

> The best interpretation of these difficult verses says that Jesus fulfills the Law and Prophets in that they point to him, and he is their fulfillment. . . . Therefore we give *plēroō* ("fulfill") exactly the same meaning as in the formula quotations, which in the prologue (Matt 1–2) have already laid great stress on the prophetic nature of the OT and the way it points to Jesus. . . . In the light of the antitheses (vv. 21–48), the passage before us insists that just as Jesus fulfilled OT prophecies by his person and actions, so he fulfilled OT law by his teaching.[57]

Just as Old Testament prophecy looked forward, so too did the Old Testament law. Jesus will say later, "For all the Prophets *and the Law* prophesied until John" (Matt. 11:13; see also Luke 24:44).[58] Not only the prophets, but the law as well, "prophesied." It pointed forward to something greater. Jesus "fulfills" the Law and the Prophets because they pointed forward to him (Luke 24:44). Vern Poythress summarizes the significance of the passage: "Matthew 5:17–19 asserts in a sweeping and direct fashion what the rest of Matthew illustrates in detail: Jesus in His person and His ministry brings to realization and fulfillment the whole warp and woof of Old Testament revelation, including the revelation of the law."[59]

The next section of the Sermon contains Jesus' instruction on prayer (6:5–13). Jesus instructs the disciples to pray:

> Our Father in heaven,
> hallowed be your name.
> Your kingdom come,
> your will be done,
> on earth as it is in heaven.
> Give us this day our daily bread,
> and forgive us our debts,
> as we also have forgiven our debtors.
> And lead us not into temptation,
> but deliver us from evil. (6:9b–13)[60]

57. Carson 1984, 143–4.

58. See France 2007, 183.

59. Poythress 1995, 268; see also France 1985, 114.

60. The words translated "evil" are the Greek words τοῦ πονηροῦ (*tou ponērou*) and should be translated "the evil one."

We have seen that both John the Baptist and Jesus himself have proclaimed that the kingdom of heaven is "at hand" (3:2; 4:17). Why then does Jesus instruct his disciples to pray, "Your kingdom come" (6:10)? In order to understand the answer to this question, we must understand that at this point in redemptive history the kingdom is *already* being inaugurated, but it has *not yet* been consummated. The kingdom is being inaugurated in the person and ministry of Jesus, but the final consummation of the kingdom remains in the future. Therefore, as D. A. Carson observes, "To pray 'your kingdom come' is . . . simultaneously to ask that God's saving, royal rule be extended now as people bow in submission to him and already taste the eschatological blessing of salvation and to cry for the consummation of the kingdom."[61]

Jesus' Ministry of Healing

Following the Sermon on the Mount, Matthew recounts a series of Jesus' miraculous works (8:1–9:34). Jesus heals a leper, the servant of a centurion, and Peter's mother-in-law. By healing the sick, Jesus is actively reversing the effects of the curse and pointing forward to the day when all sickness will be eliminated.[62] The next several stories reveal both the authority and mercy of Jesus. First, he calms a storm on the sea (8:23–27). He then casts out demons by simply commanding them to go (8:28–34). He compassionately heals a paralytic and demonstrates the authority to forgive sins (9:1–8). Finally, he compels a complete stranger to follow him (9:9). His power is further revealed when he raises a child from death and heals the blind and the mute (9:18–34). By raising the child to life, Jesus demonstrates his authority even over death and anticipates the eschatological resurrection of the dead.[63] His healing of the blind and the mute indicates that the prophesied time of eschatological restoration has arrived (Isa. 35:5–6).

A Discourse on Mission

The second major discourse of Jesus is the instruction given to the disciples as he sends them out to the cities of Israel to proclaim the

61. Carson 1984, 170.
62. See Davies and Allison 1991, 58.
63. Hagner 1998, 101.

gospel of the kingdom. He tells his disciples, "The harvest is plentiful, but the laborers are few; therefore pray earnestly to the Lord of the harvest to send out laborers into his harvest" (Matt. 9:37–38). In the Old Testament, the imagery of harvest was sometimes used in prophecies of the last days (e.g., Hos. 6:11; Joel 3:13). By using the same imagery, Jesus frames his discourse within an eschatological context. Jesus calls to himself twelve disciples (Matt. 10:1–4). But why twelve? The answer is that Old Testament Israel was composed of twelve tribes. In calling twelve disciples, Jesus is making the point that the time of Israel's restoration has come.[64] The image here is of the disciples as the regathered remnant of Israel.[65]

In his commissioning of the twelve disciples, Jesus instructs them to go only to the cities of Israel. He commands them to "proclaim as you go, saying, 'The kingdom of heaven is at hand.' Heal the sick, raise the dead, cleanse lepers, cast out demons" (10:7–8). In short, the disciples are to participate in Jesus' ministry (4:17, 23; 9:35). Jesus tells his disciples that they will suffer persecution for their witness to him (10:16–25). Matthew's description of the persecution the disciples will suffer in this mission prior to the death and resurrection of Christ parallels Mark's description in the Olivet Discourse of the persecution the followers of Jesus will suffer after the death and resurrection of Christ (Mark 13:9–13). This indicates that Jesus sees the mission of the church as in some way connected to the time of eschatological tribulation and suffering.

At the conclusion of Jesus' prediction of persecution, he makes a striking statement, saying, "When they persecute you in one town, flee to the next, for truly, I say to you, you will not have gone through all the towns of Israel before the Son of Man comes" (Matt. 10:23). This saying has been the source of much debate. Some have argued that what Jesus means is that the disciples will not have completed their mission to Israel before he comes to join them in that mission. Others have suggested that Jesus here predicted wrongly that the disciples will not have completed their mission to Israel before the end of the world occurs. Still others believe that what Jesus is saying is that the disciples will not have completed their mission to Israel before the second coming of Christ. Finally, some believe that Jesus

64. Pitre 2005, 434.
65. Ladd 1974a, 250–51.

is saying that the disciples will not have completed their mission to Israel before he comes in judgment upon Israel.[66]

Among evangelicals, probably the most common interpretation is that Jesus is speaking here of his second coming.[67] According to proponents of this interpretation, Jesus did not make a false prophecy here because the mission to Israel has never been completed. Although such an understanding of the passage is certainly not impossible, there are several reasons why it is unlikely that Jesus is speaking here of his second advent. In the first place, this was a historically specific mission for the disciples in which they were to go only to Israelite cities. They were not to go to the cities of the Gentiles and Samaritans. These specific conditions do not apply after Pentecost. Second, at this point in Jesus' ministry, his disciples did not yet understand that Jesus was going to die, be raised from the dead, and ascend to heaven, much less come a second time. Without grasping the concept that Jesus would be going away, talk of his second coming would have been virtually meaningless to them.[68]

The third reason we must consider is that when Jesus speaks of the "coming of the Son of Man," he is deliberately alluding to Daniel 7:13–14.[69] As we have seen in our examination of that text, Daniel sees a vision of one like a Son of Man coming with the clouds of heaven up to the Ancient of Days in heaven in order to receive his kingdom.[70] Those who argue that Jesus is speaking of his second coming in Matthew 10:23 tend to argue that Daniel 7:13–14 is a vision of the coming of the Son of Man from heaven to earth.[71] This, however, is not what Daniel sees. As R. T. France explains, "The 'coming' of the Son of man in Daniel 7:13 was a coming to God to receive authority, not a 'descent' to earth."[72] When Jesus says that the disciples will not have gone through all the towns of Israel before the Son

66. For a thorough explanation and bibliography of the various interpretations, see Carson 1984, 250–52.

67. E.g., Beasley-Murray 1986, 283–91; Blomberg 1992, 176.

68. See Wright 1996, 345.

69. Wenham 1987, 132; Davies and Allison 1991, 47–52; Collins 1993, 95, 105.

70. For a full explanation, see chapter 8.

71. E.g., Beasley-Murray 1986, 28–29; Ladd 1993, 204. Ladd argues that although the Son of Man comes first to the Father to receive the kingdom, the kingdom is then given to the saints on earth, clearly implying that the Son of Man brings it to them. Such a reading, however, is unnecessary. God gives many gifts to his people on earth without being forced to leave his heavenly throne.

72. France 1982, 146; 2007, 396.

of Man comes, he is saying in effect that they will not have gone through all these towns before the prophecy of Daniel 7:13–14 is fulfilled. In other words, they will not have gone through all the towns of Israel before Jesus receives the kingdom from the Father. The "coming of the Son of Man" is a virtual synonym for the "coming of the kingdom."[73]

Jesus concludes his second major discourse by warning his disciples that what matters most is not the pain they will experience in their present service of Christ but their eternal fate (Matt. 10:26–28). He encourages the disciples by reminding them that God is sovereign even in the midst of suffering (vv. 29–33). Jesus then says, "Do not think that I have come to bring peace to the earth. I have not come to bring peace, but a sword. For I have come to set a man against his father, and a daughter against her mother, and a daughter-in-law against her mother-in-law. And a person's enemies will be those of his own household" (vv. 34–36; cf. Mic. 7:5–6). These words are given to help Jesus' disciples understand the nature of the present age. The kingdom of heaven is at hand, but so are tribulation and suffering.[74]

Responses to Jesus

While in prison, John the Baptist hears of Jesus' teaching and miracles and sends word to him, asking, "Are you the one who is to come, or shall we look for another?" (Matt. 11:3). Jesus responds, "Go and tell John what you hear and see: the blind receive their sight and the lame walk, lepers are cleansed and the deaf hear, and the dead are raised up, and the poor have good news preached to them. And blessed is the one who is not offended by me" (vv. 4–6). The words of Jesus' response are based on prophecies in Isaiah (Isa. 29:18–19; 35:5–6; 61:1–2). Isaiah's prophecy described the future time of restoration in terms of the jubilee (Lev. 25). By appealing to Isaiah's words, Jesus is telling John the Baptist that he is the coming one of whom John has spoken—the Messiah. In his words and work, Jesus is fulfilling Isaiah's messianic prophecies.

John the Baptist's question apparently raises questions in the minds of Jesus' followers about the role of John himself because Jesus begins to

73. Carson 1984, 252; Ridderbos 1962, 31. This fact will become even more evident when we look at Jesus' use of this same phrase in Matthew 16:27–28 and compare it to parallel passages in Mark 8:38–9:1 and Luke 9:26–27.

74. See Davies and Allison 1991, 218, 220.

speak about John (Matt. 11:7). He tells the crowds that John is a prophet, and more than a prophet (vv. 7–9). Jesus tells them that John is the one of whom Malachi wrote, the prophesied messenger who prepares the way for the coming of the Lord (v. 10; Mal. 3:1). Jesus tells them that for those who are willing to accept it, "he [John] is Elijah who is to come" (Matt. 11:14; Mal. 4:5). Does Jesus mean that John the Baptist is *literally* the same person as the Old Testament prophet Elijah? This is very unlikely. In the first place, John himself denies elsewhere that he is Elijah (John 1:21). In the second place, Elijah himself will make an appearance in Matthew (17:3). What Jesus apparently means here is that John is the one who has come "in the spirit and power of Elijah" (Luke 1:17).[75]

In Matthew 11:20–24, Jesus pronounces oracles of judgment upon the cities of Chorazin and Bethsaida because of their lack of repentance. He also offers eschatological rest to those who will follow him (vv. 25–30). Matthew turns next to controversies related to the Sabbath. Jesus declares himself to be the Lord of the Sabbath and greater than the temple (12:6, 8), and he angers the Pharisees by healing a man on the Sabbath (vv. 9–14). Matthew then cites a quotation from Isaiah 42:1–3 to indicate that Jesus is the prophesied Servant of Yahweh (Matt. 12:18–21).

When Jesus heals a demon-possessed man, the Pharisees declare that he does so only by the power of Satan (vv. 22–24). Jesus, however, declares that Satan cannot cast out Satan, and then says, "But if it is by the Spirit of God that I cast out demons, then the kingdom of God has come upon you" (v. 28). The exorcisms performed by Christ indicate that the kingdom of God is already present in some way.[76] The Pharisees seal their doom by

75. In the midst of his discussion of John, Jesus makes an enigmatic statement that has perplexed commentators for centuries. He says, "From the days of John the Baptist until now the kingdom of heaven has suffered violence, and the violent take it by force" (v. 12). The phrase "From the days of John the Baptist until now" means from the time of John's ministry to the time Jesus spoke these words. It does not imply anything about whether the action continues past this time. The next phrase is the source of much debate. The Greek verb *biazetai* could be either a middle or a passive voice (See BDAG, s.v. βιάζω, pp. 175–76). If it is passive, then the meaning is that the kingdom is being attacked in some sense (ESV). If *biazetai* is in the middle voice, then the meaning is that the kingdom has been forcefully advancing (NIV). The parallel passage in Luke 16:16 appears to support the latter interpretation, namely, that the kingdom has been forcefully advancing. The final phrase in this verse, "the violent [*biastai*] take it by force," simply means that the kingdom, although advancing, has been attacked by violent men (see Carson 1984, 267). This interpretation lends support to the idea that the kingdom age is also an age of conflict.

76. Carson 1984, 289; Ladd 1974a, 151.

attributing the work of Christ to Satan. Jesus then tells his followers that a tree is known by its fruits (vv. 33–37). The Pharisees may appear to be good, but their fruit indicates that they are actually evil. The Pharisees demand that Jesus show them a sign, but he refuses, telling them that the only sign they will receive is the sign of Jonah (vv. 38–42). In other words, the only sign they will receive will be Jesus' resurrection.

Teaching in Parables

Jesus' third major discourse is found in Matthew 13. Here Jesus teaches about the kingdom of God in parables. The first parable is the parable of the sower (13:1–9). Jesus tells of a sower who sowed seed, some upon a path, some upon rocky ground, some among thorns, and some in good soil. However, before explaining the parable (vv. 18–23), Jesus tells his disciples the reason he teaches in parables (vv. 10–17). Their purpose is twofold: to reveal truth to those who believe and follow Jesus, and to confirm in their hardness of heart those who reject him. Jesus quotes Isaiah 6:9–10 in support of this latter point. He then explains the parable, telling the disciples that the seed is the "word of the kingdom" (Matt. 13:19) and that the various kinds of ground upon which the seed is sown represent various kinds of people who hear the word (vv. 20–23). All people will be held responsible for their response to the word of God.

The parable of the tares (13:24–30) makes a slightly different point. Here a sower sows good seed in his field, but an enemy sows weeds among the wheat. When the wheat grows up, the weeds appear mixed in with it. The sower allows both to grow together, but at the harvest, the weeds are to be gathered and burned. Before explaining the meaning of this parable, Jesus tells the parables of the mustard seed and the leaven (vv. 31–33). In the parable of the mustard seed, he says: "The kingdom of heaven is like a grain of mustard seed that a man took and sowed in his field. It is the smallest of all seeds, but when it has grown it is larger than all the garden plants and becomes a tree, so that the birds of the air come and make nests in its branches."

The parable of the leaven is similar: "The kingdom of heaven is like leaven that a woman took and hid in three measures of flour, till it was all leavened." Several points are made in these two brief parables. First, there is the contrast between the small, almost insignificant, beginning and the grand ending.[77] Second, there is continuity between the small beginning and the future glory. As Davies and Allison put it, "The end is in the beginning."[78] Third, the kingdom of God grows over time, although this growth is almost imperceptible.[79]

Jesus explains the meaning of the parable of the tares in Matthew 13:36–43. The sower is the Son of Man. The field is the world, and the good seed are the children of the kingdom. The weeds are the sons of the evil one. At the end of the age those who are evil will be gathered, judged, and thrown into the fiery furnace. The point of the parable is to place evil in eschatological perspective. The evil that believers have to endure in this world is only for a time. At the end of the age, the problem of sin and evil will be resolved once and for all.[80]

The End of Jesus' Galilean Ministry (Matt. 13:53–18:35)

After completing his parables Jesus returns to his hometown of Nazareth and teaches in the synagogue there, but he is rejected by the people (13:53–58). Jesus tells them that "a prophet is not without honor except in his hometown and in his own household" (v. 57). His words indicate that he considers himself to stand in continuity with the long line of prophets who preceded him. Matthew 14 begins with the narrative of the death of another prophet, John the Baptist (14:1–12). His martyrdom, which is the fate of a true prophet, foreshadows the fate of Jesus.[81]

Following John's death, Jesus removes himself to a desolate place, but the crowds follow, and then Matthew recounts the story of Jesus' miraculous feeding of the five thousand (14:13–21). Echoing events in the lives of both Moses and Elisha, the story demonstrates the Messiah's provision for his people (Ex. 16:4; 2 Kings 4:42–44). It is also a foretaste of eschatological blessing.[82] The story of the feeding of the five thousand is immediately followed by the narrative of Jesus' walking on the water. As Davies and Allison observe, "Jesus here exhibits an authority which the Jewish Scrip-

77. Carson 1984, 318.

78. Davies and Allison 1991, 416.

79. Hagner 1993, 387.

80. Davies and Allison 1991, 431.

81. Davies and Allison 1991, 476. In fact, as Davies and Allison observe, there are numerous literary parallels between the story of John's martyrdom and the narrative of the death of Christ (see also France 2002, 246).

82. Hagner 1995, 419.

tures associate exclusively with the deity."[83] The Old Testament speaks of Yahweh trampling the waves of the sea (e.g., Job 9:8; Ps. 77:19). By walking on the water, Jesus identifies himself with Yahweh, the one who overthrows the forces of chaos represented by the sea and who also makes a path for his people.

Matthew 15 contains stories of both opposition and loyalty to Jesus. In Gennesaret, the scribes and Pharisees question Jesus about his observance of the law, but his response indicates that it is they who are the hypocrites, the ones truly breaking the law (15:1–20). Jesus leaves this area and travels to the region of Tyre and Sidon on the coast of the Mediterranean. Here he encounters a Gentile, a Canaanite woman, who pleads with him to heal her daughter (vv. 21–22). At this point in his ministry, Jesus' primary purpose is to proclaim the gospel of the kingdom to Israel alone, but his mercy toward the Canaanite woman provides a foretaste of the mission to the Gentiles that will begin in earnest after his resurrection. Jesus then returns to the Sea of Galilee and heals many (vv. 29–31). Here again he also feeds another large multitude (vv. 32–38). After the feeding of the four thousand, Jesus travels across the sea to the region of Magadan (15:39). While there, the Pharisees and Sadducees come to him again asking for a sign, and again he tells them that the only sign they will receive is the sign of Jonah (16:1–4).

Jesus travels next to Caesarea Philippi, a city about twenty-five miles north of the Sea of Galilee, and when he arrives he asks his disciples, "Who do people say that the Son of Man is?" (16:13). His disciples tell him who the people are suggesting he is, and he then asks, "But who do you say that I am?" (v. 15). Peter responds, "You are the Christ, the Son of the living God" (v. 16). Jesus tells Peter that he is blessed because the Father has revealed this truth to him, and then he says to Peter, "And I tell you, you are Peter [*Petros*], and on this rock [*petra*] I will build my church [*ekklēsia*], and the gates of hell shall not prevail against it" (v. 18).[84] The word *ekklēsia*

83. Davies and Allison 1991, 512; see also Edwards 2002, 198.

84. This text has been the source of much debate between Protestants and Roman Catholics. Because Roman Catholics use this text as a support for their understanding of the papacy, many Protestants have denied that Jesus is referring here to Peter as the "rock" upon which he will build his church. However, as D. A. Carson (1984, 368) observes, were it not for the historic debates, it is unlikely that many would have ever understood "rock" here to mean anything other than Peter. Carson demonstrates that the fact that Jesus makes a wordplay with the name of Peter here does not in any way support the developed doctrine of the papacy.

was a term used by the Greeks to refer to the citizen assembly in a Greek city (Acts 19:39).[85] Here Jesus uses it to describe the new community he is establishing. The church (*ekklēsia*) is the people who will share in the blessings of the kingdom of God.[86] According to Jesus, all the forces of hell will not be able to stand against his church.

The primary focus of this passage is not the person of Peter. The primary purpose of this passage is to reveal something about the establishment of God's new community, the church. The establishment of the church occurs because of the rejection of Jesus by the representatives of the nation of Israel. Although much discussion of this text has focused on the person of Peter, his role here is simply to mark a new stage in redemptive history. As Davies and Allison explain, "His significance is the significance of Abraham, which is to say: his faith is the means by which God brings a new people into being."[87] As he promised in the Old Testament, God is going to build a house upon a rock (see 2 Sam. 7:4–16). That house will be his church.

From the point of Peter's confession onward, Jesus begins to teach his disciples that he must go to Jerusalem, suffer, be killed, and on the third day be raised (Matt. 16:21). Peter rebukes Jesus for saying this, but Jesus shows him that this is the only way (vv. 22–23). Jesus tells his disciples that they must take up their cross and follow him because it is foolish to gain the world and lose one's soul (vv. 24–26). Then Jesus says, "For the Son of Man is going to come with his angels in the glory of his Father, and then he will repay each person according to what he has done. Truly, I say to you, there are some standing here who will not taste death until they see the Son of Man coming in his kingdom" (vv. 27–28).

Like Matthew 10:23, this text has also been the source of much debate. Davies and Allison survey some eight different interpretations that have been proposed.[88] Among the more prominent interpretations is the idea that "the coming of the Son of Man" in view here is the transfiguration, which is narrated in the following chapter.[89] Some suggest that Jesus is referring to his resurrection or to Pentecost. Others suggest that Jesus is

85. Ferguson 2003, 46.
86. Ridderbos 1962, 354.
87. Davies and Allison 1991, 643.
88. Davies and Allison 1991, 677–79.
89. See Blomberg 1992, 261.

referring to the destruction of Jerusalem in A.D. 70.[90] Then there are those who believe Jesus is speaking here of his second coming and of the end of history. Among those holding this view, there are those who believe Jesus was mistaken because he believed this would occur within the lifetime of his hearers, and there are those who believe that Jesus was correct because the "some standing here" refers to a later generation.[91]

In order to come to an understanding of this saying, we must again be reminded that when Jesus speaks of the "coming of the Son of Man," he is purposefully alluding to Daniel 7:13–14. And again we must recall that the coming of the Son of Man in Daniel 7 is set within a judgment scene before the throne of God (Dan. 7:9–10). Unlike the saying in Matthew 10:23, the saying in 16:28 is found in the immediate context of words regarding judgment (16:27). The point that Jesus is making when he says that there are some standing here who will not die before they see the Son of Man coming in his kingdom is that there are some to whom he is speaking who will not die before the prophecy of Daniel 7 is fulfilled, in other words, before Jesus receives the kingdom from his Father.

A comparison of Matthew 16:28 with its parallels in Mark 9:1 and Luke 9:27 lends support to this interpretation. All three sayings are set within the same context immediately before the transfiguration, yet whereas Matthew speaks of some living long enough to see the coming of the Son of Man, Mark and Luke speak of some living long enough to see the coming of the kingdom of God. The "coming of the Son of Man" then is simply another way of saying "the coming of the kingdom of God." It is the assumption that the words "coming of the Son of Man" must mean second coming that has caused much of the confusion. Once we realize that Jesus is simply using a phrase from Daniel 7 to allude to the whole prophecy, texts such as Matthew 16:28 are much more readily understood. Jesus was not predicting that his second coming would occur within the lifetime of some of his hearers. He wasn't speaking of the second coming at all.[92] He

90. See Hagner 1994, 62.

91. There are also some who believe that Jesus correctly predicted that his second coming would occur within the lifetime of some of those who were listening to him speak. They argue that the second coming of Jesus and all the events associated with it occurred already in the first century. For a critique of this interpretation, see Mathison 2004.

92. Some might ask whether this interpretation requires us to believe that nothing is said in the New Testament about the second coming of Christ. I do not believe this to be true. Jesus himself may have said very little about the second coming, but it must be remembered that his disciples were

was referring to the fulfillment of Daniel 7, his reception of the kingdom from the Father, and this was fulfilled within the lifetime of some of his hearers (Matt. 28:18).[93]

As noted above, Matthew 16:28, unlike 10:23, is set within the context of a discussion of judgment. In 16:27 Matthew speaks of the Son of Man coming with angels and judging man. If the coming of the Son of Man in verse 28 is an allusion to Daniel's prophecy of one like a Son of Man coming up to the Ancient of Days, is the coming of the Son of Man in verse 27 a different "coming"? If it is the same coming, then what is the judgment spoken of in verse 27? There are two possibilities. Since Jesus' receiving of the kingdom is part of an entire nexus of events that concludes only at the consummation and second coming, it could be that the judgment referred to in verse 27 is the final judgment. If so, Jesus speaks of the first and last events in the connected series as parts of a single whole but without mentioning the amount of time that might lapse between them. Another, more likely, possibility is that the judgment Jesus is referring to in verse 27 is the judgment referred to in Daniel 7:9–10, a heavenly judgment of the "beasts/nations" that is directly related to Jesus' receiving of the kingdom of God from the Father, an event that occurs in connection with his first advent.[94]

---

barely able to grasp the idea that he would be leaving them. It makes sense that the bulk of the New Testament's teaching on the second coming would be found after the resurrection and ascension (e.g., Acts 1:9–11; 1 Cor. 15:23; 1 Thess. 4:16–17; Heb. 9:28).

93. In our discussion of the "already/not yet" nature of the kingdom of God, we observed that the incarnation, crucifixion, resurrection, ascension, second coming, and final judgment are all distinct events, but events that are part of a single whole—the coming of the kingdom. Some of these events are associated with the kingdom's inauguration, some with its consummation. What I am arguing here does not contradict this previous assertion. I am arguing here that when Jesus speaks of the "coming of the Son of Man" he is referring specifically to the events at the beginning of the series, those associated with the inauguration of the kingdom, not to events at the end of the series that are associated with its consummation. The events associated with the inauguration and with the consummation of the kingdom cannot ultimately be separated, but they are distinguished in the New Testament. It should also be observed that some of the events associated with the inauguration of the kingdom are seen as firstfruits of a larger whole that includes events associated with the consummation of the kingdom. The resurrection of Jesus, for example, is the firstfruits of a larger harvest that includes the general resurrection of the last day. The coming of the Son of Man is to the Second Coming what the inauguration of the kingdom is to the consummation of the kingdom, closely related but distinct concepts.

94. Even if the judgment mentioned in Matthew 16:27 is the heavenly judgment of the beasts/nations found in Daniel 7, it is possible that there is a secondary reference to the final judgment since all of the events from the first advent to the second advent are part of a whole. The heavenly judgment of the beasts/nations at the first advent may be viewed as the firstfruits of the eschatological judgment.

Jesus' enigmatic saying is immediately followed by the narrative of his transfiguration (Matt. 17:1–13). Jesus leads Peter, James, and John up on a high mountain and is transfigured before them. Moses and Elijah also appear, and a voice from heaven declares, "This is my beloved Son, with whom I am well pleased; listen to him" (v. 5). Jesus then instructs Peter, James, and John to tell no one about this event until after the resurrection (v. 9). They then ask him why the scribes say that Elijah must come, and he tells them that Elijah does come and will restore all things (vv. 10–11). He then tells them that Elijah has already come but was not recognized. His disciples understand that he is referring to John the Baptist (vv. 12–13). The transfiguration narrative recalls events in the life of Moses (Ex. 24, 34), and the implication is that Jesus is the prophet of whom Moses spoke (Deut. 18:15–18). As Davies and Allison observe, "The eschatological prophet, the one like Moses and Elijah, has appeared, and the light of the resurrection and *parousia* has already shone forth."[95]

Jesus' Journey to Jerusalem (Matt. 19:1–20:34)

Having completed his ministry in Galilee (17:14–18:35), Jesus sets his face toward Jerusalem. Along his journey, he continues to be harassed by the Pharisees. They try to trap him with a question on divorce, but he reveals their lack of biblical knowledge and silences them (19:1–12). The questions of a rich young man then provide Jesus with the opportunity to teach his disciples about the dangers of wealth (vv. 16–27). When Peter observes that he and the other disciples have left all to follow Jesus, he says to them, "Truly, I say to you, in the new world, when the Son of Man will sit on his glorious throne, you who have followed me will also sit on twelve thrones, judging the twelve tribes of Israel" (v. 28). Like Matthew 10:23 and 16:28, this verse also alludes to Daniel 7, but whereas the other texts focus primarily on Daniel's prophecy of the Son of Man receiving his kingdom (Dan. 7:13–14), Matthew 19:28 alludes to those sections of Daniel 7 in which the saints are also given possession of the kingdom (Dan. 7:22, 27). That which belongs to the Son belongs to his people.

On the way to Jerusalem, Jesus again predicts his coming suffering, death, and resurrection (Matt. 20:18–19). A question from the mother of

95. Davies and Allison 1991, 705.

James and John provides Jesus the opportunity to teach the disciples that service is the nature of those who will truly be great in the kingdom (vv. 20–28). The Son of Man himself "came not to be served but to serve, and to give his life as a ransom for many" (v. 28). Here Jesus clearly declares the saving effects that his death will have. He is the Suffering Servant of Isaiah 52:13–53:12, the one who bears our iniquities.[96] The last miracle Jesus is reported to have done before his entry into Jerusalem is the healing of two blind men (Matt. 20:29–34). The blind men call out to Jesus as "Son of David" (vv. 30, 31). The irony here is that while the leaders of Israel do not recognize who Jesus is, two blind men identify the messianic Son of David.

Jesus' Ministry in Jerusalem (Matt. 21:1–25:46)

In the Old Testament, the temple was the place of God's special manifest presence (1 Kings 9:3), but at the time of the exile the glory of God departed from the temple (Ezek. 10). This, however, was not the end of the story. The Old Testament prophets foresaw a day when God would return to Jerusalem. Throughout the writings of the Old Testament prophets, the future coming of God to the city is a prominent theme (e.g., Isa. 35:3–6; 40:3–11; 52:7–10; 59:15–21; 66:14–16; Ezek. 43:1–7; Zech. 2:4–5, 10–12; 8:2–3; Mal. 3:1–4). Now Jesus enters Jerusalem (Matt. 21:1–11). He is no longer merely announcing the coming of God to the city; he is enacting it in his own person.[97]

Jesus enters the city of Jerusalem from the east, from the direction of the Mount of Olives (Matt. 21:1). He has his disciples find a donkey with a colt in order that he may ride into the city in fulfillment of the prophecy of Zechariah 9:9. The context of this prophecy describes the divine warrior marching toward Jerusalem, defeating Israel's enemies and setting up camp in Jerusalem (Zech. 9:1–8). Zechariah 9:9 then describes the coming of the messianic King through whom Yahweh will reign over Jerusalem. His rule will

96. It is worth noting here that many Old Testament prophecies of the coming new exodus incorporate the language of "ransom" and "redemption" (Isa. 43:1–19; 51:10–11; 52:7–12; Jer. 31:7–12; Mic. 4:1–10; Zech. 10:6–12). This use of "ransom" and "redemption" language in connection with prophecies of the new exodus echoes the same language used in describing the original exodus from Egypt (Ex. 6:6–8; 15:13–16; Deut. 7:8; 13:5; 15:15; Ps. 74:2; Mic. 6:4). Jesus' use of this language here indicates that his atoning death is central to the fulfillment of the Old Testament promises of a new exodus.

97. Davies and Allison 1997, 112; Wright 1996, 615.

extend to every nation (Zech. 9:10). Jesus' entry into Jerusalem in fulfillment of Zechariah's prophecy, then, is the formal presentation of the messianic King.[98] The crowds respond to Jesus' entry by proclaiming, "Hosanna to the Son of David! Blessed is he who comes in the name of the Lord! Hosanna in the highest!" (Matt. 21:9). Jesus' implicit claim to messianic kingship and the response of the crowd present a challenge to Jerusalem. Jerusalem must now answer the question "Who is this?" (21:10). The city's answer to that question will drive all that follows from this point forward.

Following his arrival in the city, Jesus enters the temple and drives out all who are selling and buying there (21:12). He condemns the people for turning the house of God into a den of robbers (v. 13; Jer. 7:11). The Pharisees are indignant, but Jesus is able to depart for Bethany (Matt. 21:15–17). The cleansing of the temple echoes Old Testament passages in which the corruption of the priesthood is tied to an expectation of the temple's destruction (e.g., Jer. 7:1–15; Ezek. 8:16–18; Mic. 3:1–12). As we shall see, Jesus will soon explicitly prophesy the destruction of the temple (Matt. 24:2). The next day, however, he returns to the city and sees a fig tree with no fruit. He says, "May no fruit ever come from you again!" and the tree withers (21:18–19). His cursing of the fig tree is a prophetic sign-act in which the barren fig tree symbolizes faithless Israel.

Jesus' authority is challenged by the chief priests and elders while he is teaching the people, but he refuses to be trapped by their questions (21:23–27). This section clearly shows that Jesus was up against wicked men. The entire passion narrative will depict a struggle between Jesus and evil men.[99] Following the challenges to his authority, Jesus tells two parables that are designed to illustrate the wickedness of the chief priests and Pharisees (vv. 28–44). He concludes his parables by saying to them, "Therefore I tell you, the kingdom of God will be taken away from you and given to a people producing its fruits" (v. 43). The language is reminiscent of the words of Samuel to Saul when God took the kingdom from him and gave it to David (1 Sam. 15:28). Jesus gives the kingdom to the faithful remnant of Israel (Dan. 7:22, 27; 1 Peter 2:9).[100] Jesus then

98. Ham 2005, 107.

99. Davies and Allison 1997, 163.

100. Jesus does not say here whether the judgment upon Israel is final (see Holwerda 1995, 149). The focus is on Israel's present rejection of her Messiah. It is Paul who will finally answer the questions regarding Israel's future (Rom. 9–11).

illustrates his point about the kingdom with his parable of the wedding feast (Matt. 22:1–14).

The Pharisees and Sadducees have not given up their hope of entrapping Jesus in his words. The Pharisees now attempt to trap him with a question about the propriety of paying taxes to Caesar, a volatile issue at this period in Israel's history when various revolutionary leaders were calling for rebellion against Roman rule. Jesus, however, skillfully deflects their attack (22:15–22). The Sadducees then attempt to trap him with a convoluted question about the nature of the resurrection. Unlike the Pharisees and most other Jews of this time, the Sadducees did not believe in the doctrine of a future resurrection of the dead.[101] Jesus deflects this attack as well by an appeal to Old Testament Scripture. The final challenge occurs when another Pharisee asks Jesus which commandment is the great commandment in the law (22:36). Jesus answers: "You shall love the Lord your God with all your heart and with all your soul and with all your mind. This is the great and first commandment. And a second is like it: You shall love your neighbor as yourself. On these two commandments depend all the Law and the Prophets" (vv. 37–40).

Having been interrogated by the Pharisees and Sadducees, Jesus turns the table by asking them a question. He asks, "What do you think about the Christ? Whose son is he?" He is pushing the most important issue—the identity of the Messiah. The Pharisees respond, "The son of David" (v. 42). Jesus then asks,

> How is it then that David, in the Spirit, calls him Lord, saying,
>
> "The Lord said to my Lord,
> Sit at my right hand,
> until I put your enemies under your feet"?
>
> If then David calls him Lord, how is he his son? (vv. 43–45)

Jesus is quoting from Psalm 110, a psalm in which David expresses submission to the messianic King who sits at God's right hand. The Pharisees are unable to answer (Matt. 22:46).

In Matthew 23, Jesus uses a series of seven woe oracles to pronounce judgment upon the Pharisees and the other leaders of Israel (Matt. 23:13,

101. Wright 2003, 131–40.

15, 16, 23, 25, 27, 29). Their fundamental sin is found in the introductory words of six of the oracles, "Woe to you, scribes and Pharisees, hypocrites!" Their hypocrisy is their chief sin. They claim that they would have never persecuted the prophets had they lived in Old Testament times (vv. 29–33). Jesus tells them that he will send prophets to them whom they will kill, "so that on you may come all the righteous blood shed on earth, from the blood of innocent Abel to the blood of Zechariah the son of Barachiah, whom you murdered between the sanctuary and the altar" (v. 35). Jesus then says, "Truly, I say to you, all these things will come upon this generation" (v. 36). The words "this generation" refer to the generation that is listening to Jesus at this point in time.[102] Upon them would fall this dreadful judgment.

Jesus laments over Jerusalem, declaring that she is desolate (23:37–38). He then says, "For I tell you, you will not see me again, until you say, 'Blessed is he who comes in the name of the Lord'" (v. 39). In the Old Testament, Israel had often been told that when she experienced judgment for her sin, her repentance would lead to her restoration (e.g., Lev. 26:40–45; Deut. 30:1–3; 1 Kings 8:33–40; 2 Chron. 7:13–14). Here Jesus expresses a similar idea, connecting Israel's repentance with his presence. The text indicates that when his people finally bless him and acknowledge who he is, he will come.[103] This is why the apostles later preached, "Repent therefore, and turn again, that your sins may be blotted out, that times of refreshing may come from the presence of the Lord, and that he may send the Christ appointed for you, Jesus, whom heaven must receive until the time for restoring all the things about which God spoke by the mouth of his holy prophets long ago" (Acts 3:19–21).[104] Israel has rejected Jesus the Messiah. Jesus has begun the work of restoration, but the fullness of restoration will not occur until Israel repents and blesses her Messiah.

The Olivet Discourse

The final major discourse in Matthew is Jesus' Olivet Discourse, so named because it was given on the Mount of Olives just east of Jerusalem. It has been the source of much disagreement among commentators. As D. A. Carson observes, "The history of the interpretation of this chapter is

102. Blomberg 1992, 349; Davies and Allison 1997, 319; Nolland 2005, 948.
103. Davies and Allison 1997, 323.
104. Allison 1985, 159.

immensely complex."[105] Critical scholars tend to see the Olivet Discourse as a patchwork of traditions with little or no internal cohesion.[106] Among those who believe that the discourse is coherent and unified, a number of interpretations have been proposed: (1) some argue that Jesus speaks about both the destruction of Jerusalem and the future second coming but that it is impossible to tell exactly where he moves from one topic to the other; (2) some argue that the entire discourse deals only with the future second coming of Jesus; (3) some argue that the entire discourse deals only with the first-century destruction of Jerusalem; (4) some argue that Jesus speaks of the destruction of Jerusalem through verse 35 and then speaks of the future second coming from verse 36 onward; (5) many dispensationalists argue that Matthew 24:4–28 speaks of a future seven-year great tribulation, that verses 29–35 speak of the second coming, and that verses 36–41 speak of a secret rapture that will precede the great tribulation.[107] The strengths and weaknesses of each view will become evident as we proceed to examine the text of the discourse itself.

As Jesus departs from the temple, his disciples point out the magnificent buildings to him. His response is disconcerting: "You see all these, do you not? Truly, I say to you, there will not be left here one stone upon another that will not be thrown down" (24:1–2). This prediction of the destruction of the temple raises serious questions in the minds of the disciples. After proceeding outside of the city and across the valley to the Mount of Olives, Jesus' disciples ask him their questions, "Tell us, when will these things be, and what will be the sign of your coming [*parousias*] and of the close of the age?" (v. 3).[108] The disciples' question indicates that in their mind the destruction of the temple and the close of redemptive history are closely related in time.[109] They do not conceive of any significant temporal delay between the destruction of Jerusalem and the end of redemptive history. Jesus' response to their question, however,

105. Carson 1984, 488. For a thorough survey of the history of the interpretation of this discourse through 1991, see Beasley-Murray 1993.

106. See Beasley-Murray 1993.

107. For a more detailed description of the various interpretations along with critiques, see Carson 1984, 491–95.

108. The word *parousia* refers to the state of being present at a place or to arrival as the first stage in presence. In other words, it can denote either presence at a place or coming to be present at a place. See BDAG, s.v. παρουσία (pp. 780–81). Its precise meaning is determined by its context.

109. See Hagner 1995, 688; Carson 1984, 495.

indicates that their understanding is in need of some correction. While the destruction of Jerusalem will occur soon, the end of redemptive history will not occur for some time.

Jesus tells his disciples:

> See that no one leads you astray. For many will come in my name, saying, "I am the Christ," and they will lead many astray. And you will hear of wars and rumors of wars. See that you are not alarmed, for this must take place, but the end is not yet. For nation will rise against nation, and kingdom against kingdom, and there will be famines and earthquakes in various places. All these are but the beginning of the birth pains. (24:4–8)

What Jesus indicates here is that certain things must take place before "the end," but he does not indicate when "the end" will be. In fact, he does not specify what end he is speaking of. Is he speaking of the end of the old covenant age? The end of redemptive history? He is not specific. Despite any lingering ambiguity, it is made abundantly clear that during this period of time before the end, Jesus' disciples must not allow themselves to be led astray by false Christs.

Jesus continues:

> Then they will deliver you up to tribulation and put you to death, and you will be hated by all nations for my name's sake. And then many will fall away and betray one another and hate one another. And many false prophets will arise and lead many astray. And because lawlessness will be increased, the love of many will grow cold. But the one who endures to the end will be saved. And this gospel of the kingdom will be proclaimed throughout the whole world as a testimony to all nations, and then the end will come. (vv. 9–14)

Here Jesus continues a general description of the time leading up to the end. It is a time of persecution and tribulation. It is a time of false prophets, lawlessness, and apostasy. It is also a time when the gospel will be preached to all nations. Here again we find a hint that the end does not come until the missionary task is completed (see also 23:39).[110] Since the missionary task has not yet been completed even in our own day, the

110. Davies and Allison 1997, 343.

implication would seem to be that the end in view here is the end of redemptive history.[111]

The overarching idea in Matthew 24:4–14 is that the period of time between Jesus' first advent and the end is to be a time of persecution and tribulation as well as a time in which the gospel will be proclaimed to every nation. The events Jesus describes are not signs pointing to anything specific. They merely characterize the entire period of time prior to the end. Jewish literature of the intertestamental period had anticipated a time of trouble, or messianic woes, that would precede the time of restoration.[112] In the New Testament, the inauguration of this time of tribulation appears to be concurrent with the inauguration of the time of the kingdom. Matthew 24:4–14, for example, views the time between the first advent and the end as a time of trouble and tribulation. Matthew 28:16–20, which features many of the same themes as Matthew 24:4–14, views the time between the first advent and the end of the age as the time when Jesus has been given his kingdom and all authority in fulfillment of Daniel 7:13–14.[113] Both view this period of time as the time when the gospel is preached to all nations.

Jesus continues the discourse with a more specific warning concerning the destruction of Jerusalem, the topic that raised the disciples' original question. He warns his disciples:

> So when you see the abomination of desolation spoken of by the prophet Daniel, standing in the holy place (let the reader understand), then let those who are in Judea flee to the mountains. Let the one who is on the housetop not go down to take what is in his house, and let the one who is in the field not turn back to take his cloak. . . . For then there will be great tribulation, such as has not been from the beginning of the world until now, no, and never will be. And if those days had not been cut short, no human being

111. If it could be demonstrated that the missionary task was completed in the first century, then the end in view here could possibly be the end of the old covenant age. In the past, I considered this as a good possibility (see Mathison 1999, 113). Although it is a possible interpretation, I am no longer convinced that it is the best interpretation. Passages adduced in support of a first-century fulfillment simply cannot prove it conclusively. Romans 10:18 merely cites Psalm 19:4. Colossians 1:6 and 23 are found in the context of a letter in which Paul sees his missionary work as ongoing (e.g., Col. 1:29). In fact, all of Paul's later epistles written in the 60s view the missionary task as still unfinished. It does not appear likely that Paul believed the task would be completed any time in his near future.

112. See Pitre 2005, 127–29; Allison 1985, 115.

113. Davies and Allison 1997, 369.

> would be saved. But for the sake of the elect those days will be cut short. (Matt. 24:15–22)[114]

The mention of the "abomination of desolation" is an allusion to Daniel 9:27; 11:31; and 12:11. Daniel's original prophecy had been fulfilled in the second century B.C. by Antiochus Epiphanes. But here, Jesus indicates a further fulfillment to come.[115] If we examine the parallel passage in Luke 21:20, the meaning of the text becomes clearer. This "abomination of desolation" will be the surrounding of Jerusalem by a foreign army.[116] This would occur in the war with Rome (A.D. 66–70).

Jesus warns that those who see these events unfold should flee without delay.[117] He warns that the surrounding of Jerusalem by armies will presage a time of tribulation "such as has not been from the beginning of the world until now, no, and never will be." Some infer that such language can only speak of a unique end-time event. It is instructive to note, however, that such language is found in the Old Testament as well and appears to be a common hyperbole. Moses uses similar language to describe the effects of the final plague on Egypt (Ex. 11:6). Ezekiel uses such language to describe the destruction that was to befall Jerusalem in 586 B.C. (Ezek. 5:9; cf. Joel 2:2). Jesus appears to be using the same kind of language to describe the destruction that will fall upon Jerusalem in A.D. 70.

Jesus again warns his disciples of false prophets (Matt. 24:23–26), and then says, "For as the lightning comes from the east and shines as far as the west, so will be the coming of the Son of Man" (v. 27). Jesus has spoken previously of the coming of the Son of Man (Matt. 10:23; 16:28). In both instances, we concluded that he was alluding to Daniel 7 and that the phrase referred to his enthronement and the inauguration of his kingdom, not to the second advent. Is the same true in Matthew 24:27? Many would argue that in this case Jesus is speaking of his second coming because he uses the

114. Interestingly, Josephus describes the suffering of Jerusalem during the war with Rome in terms of an unprecedented tribulation. According to Josephus, "neither did any other city ever suffer such miseries, nor did any age ever breed a generation more fruitful in wickedness than this was, from the beginning of the world" (*J. W.* 5.10.5 §442).

115. Hagner 1995, 700.

116. Other suggested interpretations of the "abomination of desolation" include Caligula's attempt to erect a statue of himself in the temple in A.D. 40, the actions of John of Gischala in the temple in A.D. 67–68, and a last-days antichrist figure (see France 2002, 525; Edwards 2002, 398–99).

117. Their flight recalls the flight of Lot and his family (Gen. 19:15–22).

phrase in connection with dramatic descriptions of lightning. However, if he has consistently used the phrase previously to refer to something other than his second coming, consideration should be given to the possibility that he is doing so here as well.

It appears that Jesus is combining an allusion to Daniel 7 with an allusion to Zechariah 9. In his description of the triumphal entry, Matthew has already referred to Zechariah 9:9, a prophecy of the divine warrior coming to Jerusalem. In Zechariah 9:14 we read that the coming Messiah "will appear over them, and his arrow will go forth like lightning." Zechariah 9 speaks of the coming of the messianic King to establish his worldwide kingdom. Daniel 7 speaks of one like a Son of Man coming to the Ancient of Days in heaven to receive his kingdom. Both speak in different ways of the beginning of the messianic kingdom. Matthew has already alluded to both chapters previously. It appears that in Matthew 24:27, he is combining the imagery from both Old Testament prophets to speak of the inauguration of the kingdom, not the second advent.

Jesus continues his discourse saying:

> Immediately after the tribulation of those days the sun will be darkened, and the moon will not give its light, and the stars will fall from heaven, and the powers of the heavens will be shaken. Then will appear in heaven the sign of the Son of Man, and then all the tribes of the earth will mourn, and they will see the Son of Man coming on the clouds of heaven with power and great glory. And he will send out his angels with a loud trumpet call, and they will gather his elect from the four winds, from one end of heaven to the other. (Matt. 24:29–31)

This passage often causes readers difficulty because of a lack of familiarity with the language of the Old Testament prophets. Such language does not necessarily, or even usually, refer to the end of the space-time universe.[118] As we have seen, the prophets regularly use such metaphorical language to describe historical judgments, judgments that have already occurred without involving the literal end of the world (Isa. 13:10; 34:4–5; Ezek. 32:7; Amos 8:9). In modern parlance, it would be as if we were to refer to a significant historical event as "earth-shattering."

118. Caird 1980, 256.

Jesus says these things will happen "immediately after the tribulation of those days." The tribulation in question is most likely the tribulation described in Matthew 24:15–21. That great tribulation is the most obvious antecedent of the words in verse 29.[119] If this is true, then the coming of the Son of Man is connected in some way to the events surrounding the destruction of Jerusalem in A.D. 70. Again, it is important to remember that when Jesus speaks of the coming of the Son of Man, he is not referring to the second advent. He is speaking of the fulfillment of Daniel 7, the coming of the Son of Man up to the Ancient of Days to receive his kingdom. In short, according to Matthew 24:29–30, the inauguration of Jesus' kingdom is connected in some way to the destruction of Jerusalem. What then of his sending of angels to gather his elect? The word translated "angels" in verse 31 is a form of the word *angelos*, which is sometimes used of the spiritual beings we call "angels," and sometimes used to refer to human "messengers" (Matt. 11:10; Luke 7:24; 9:52).[120] Here it most likely refers to the human messengers who are sent out into the world to proclaim the gospel, thereby gathering the elect into the kingdom.[121]

In the next section of the discourse, Jesus clarifies the significance of all that he has said in Matthew 24:15–31. He says to his disciples, "From the fig tree learn its lesson: as soon as its branch becomes tender and puts out its leaves, you know that summer is near. So also, when you see all these things, you know that he is near, at the very gates. Truly, I say to you, this generation will not pass away until all these things take place. Heaven and earth will pass away, but my words will not pass away" (Matt. 24:32–35). Jesus explains that when the events ("all these things") he has described occur, his disciples should recognize what they mean. But what does Jesus mean by "all these things"? When he says "all these things," he is likely referring to the specific events leading up to

119. Carson (1984, 504) argues that the tribulation in question is the tribulation of verses 9 and 22, which he distinguishes from the tribulation of verses 15–21. He is forced to make this argument because of his belief that the coming of the Son of Man in verse 30 is a reference to the second coming. According to this interpretation, the second coming occurs immediately after the general period of tribulation that extends from the first advent to the second. If the coming of the Son of Man is a reference to the second advent and not to the coming of the kingdom in fulfillment of Daniel 7 as I have suggested, then something like Carson's interpretation is required.

120. See BDAG, s.v. ἄγγελος (pp. 8–9).

121. France 1985, 345.

the destruction of Jerusalem (vv. 15–26).[122] Those are the only things spoken of as specific signs to do something—namely to flee. When his disciples see "all these things," they are to recognize that something "is near, at the very gates." The ESV translates this phrase "he is near," but the subject could be "he" or "it." If the phrase is read "he is near," then the implied subject is the divine warrior who is coming in judgment upon Jerusalem. If the phrase is read "it is near," then the implied subject is the judgment itself. The two ideas are not mutually exclusive. The question is only one of emphasis.

Jesus' next comment has been the source of endless debate. He says, "Truly, I say to you, this generation will not pass away until all these things take place. Heaven and earth will pass away, but my words will not pass away" (vv. 34–35). The first issue that must be addressed is the meaning of the phrase "this generation." While some have argued that the phrase refers to the generation alive at the time of Christ's second coming, or to the Jewish people in general, or to the human race in general, such interpretations go against the natural meaning of the words in their context.[123] In context, the phrase refers to the generation of Jews listening to Jesus at that time. Before they pass away, all these things will take place. This interpretation is supported by the fact that every other time the phrase is used in Matthew, it is used to refer to the generation of Jews to whom Jesus is then speaking (11:16; 12:41, 42, 45; 23:36). In fact it is used in the immediate context of the Olivet Discourse to refer to the generation of Jews to whom Jesus was speaking (23:36).

What Jesus is saying here, then, is that all of these things (the events leading up to and including the destruction of Jerusalem) will occur within the lifetime of the generation listening to him. These events will be a sign of the fulfillment of Daniel 7:13–14, the coming of the Son of Man to the Father to receive his kingdom. Jesus is not predicting here that his second coming will occur before the generation listening to him passes away. He is not speaking of his second coming at all at this point. Instead, he is speaking of the final series of events associated with the inauguration of his kingdom.[124]

122. Unlike the events described in verses 15–22, the things Jesus mentions in verses 4–14 are not signs of anything near (see v. 6).

123. Such interpretations of "this generation" are suggested because of the conviction of many that Jesus is speaking of his second coming throughout this discourse.

124. This suggests that the events of A.D. 70 are of more redemptive-historical significance than commonly recognized (similar to the events of 586 B.C.). The fulfillment of Daniel 7 in the first

In the last half of the Olivet Discourse, Jesus focuses on the need of his disciples to be vigilant. He tells them, "But concerning that day and hour no one knows, not even the angels of heaven, nor the Son, but the Father only" (24:36).[125] This verse does not contradict verse 34. As Davies and Allison explain, "Rather does the uncertainty of v. 36 interpret the certainty of the earlier verse: although the end will come upon 'this generation,' its exact time cannot be fixed."[126] In other words, from verse 15 to this point Jesus has been warning his disciples that they should be watching for certain events to occur within their lifetime, the events that will signal the impending destruction of Jerusalem. When they see these events, they are to take certain actions immediately. But here Jesus warns them that they do not know exactly when they will see these events. Because they do not know when these events will occur, there is the possibility that they could grow lax in their watchfulness if these events do not occur very soon. Much of the remainder of the Olivet Discourse is a warning to the disciples to remain watchful and vigilant.

Jesus tells his disciples that the judgment associated with the "coming of the Son of Man" will be like the days of Noah (24:37–39). N. T. Wright explains, "The days of Noah and the days of Lot were both times when devastating judgment fell on those who were failing to heed divine warning."[127] Jerusalem now faces the same dire situation. Jesus urges his disciples to remain watchful: "Therefore, stay awake, for you do not know on what day your Lord is coming" (v. 42). He tells them, "you also must be ready, for the Son of Man is coming at an hour you do not expect" (v. 44). If those listening to Jesus grow lazy and disobedient, they too will be judged (vv. 45–51). Jesus emphasizes the theme of faithfulness and watchfulness further in the parables of the ten virgins (25:1–12) and the parable of the talents (vv. 14–30).

Jesus concludes the Olivet Discourse with a description of judgment (vv. 31–46). He says to his disciples, "When the Son of Man comes in his glory,

---

century involved Christ's resurrection, ascension, and the events surrounding the destruction of Jerusalem in A.D. 70.

125. R. T. France (1985, 346–48) sees clear evidence here of a change in subject. According to France, up to this point Jesus has been speaking of events associated with the destruction of Jerusalem, and from this point until the end of chapter 25, he is speaking of events associated with his second coming. I believe the consistent use of "coming of the Son of Man" language is inconsistent with this view. For a view similar to the one that I am proposing here, see Wright 1996, 339–66.

126. Davies and Allison 1997, 378.

127. Wright 1996, 365.

and all the angels with him, then he will sit on his glorious throne. Before him will be gathered all the nations [*ethnē*], and he will separate people one from another as a shepherd separates the sheep from the goats" (vv. 31–32). Once again Jesus speaks of the coming of the Son of Man. This theme has run throughout the Olivet Discourse, and its use here raises an obvious question. Which judgment is being described in Matthew 25:31–46? If Jesus' use of the imagery of the coming of the Son of Man is a deliberate allusion to Daniel 7, as I have suggested, and if Daniel 7 is a prophecy of the inauguration of the messianic kingdom rather than the second coming, then the judgment spoken of in Matthew 25:31–46 is the heavenly judgment of the nations that Daniel associates with the inauguration of Christ's kingdom (Dan. 7:9–10).[128]

The Passion Narrative (Matt. 26:1–27:66)

All of the gospels culminate with the story of the crucifixion of Jesus, and Matthew is no exception. Jesus has predicted his coming death several times (16:21; 17:22–23; 20:17–19), and after concluding the Olivet Discourse, he predicts it again, saying, "You know that after two days the Passover is coming, and the Son of Man will be delivered up to be crucified" (26:2). As Davies and Allison observe, "Having spoken at length of the last things, it remains for Jesus to see them commence through his death and resurrection."[129] While at Bethany, Jesus is anointed with oil by a woman (26:6–13). He explains to his disciples that she has anointed him for burial (v. 12). Jesus is the anointed one, the Messiah, but the path to his throne leads to a cross.

On the first day of the feast of unleavened bread, Jesus instructs his disciples to prepare for the Passover (26:17–19). When he gathers with his disciples to eat, he informs them that one of them is going to betray

128. Most commentators understand the judgment scene in Matthew 25:31–46 to be a description of the final judgment because it is associated with the coming of the Son of Man (v. 31), and the coming of the Son of Man is generally assumed to be a reference to the second coming. The interpretation I have proposed is based on understanding the language of the coming of the Son of Man to be an allusion to Daniel 7, which is not a prophecy of the second coming. This interpretation does not mean that there is no final judgment. Such a judgment is clearly spoken of elsewhere in Scripture (e.g., Rev. 20:11–15). It simply means that it is not what Jesus is specifically referring to at this point.

129. Davies and Allison 1997, 436.

him, and Judas is identified as the traitor (26:20–25, 14–16). Matthew continues:

> Now as they were eating, Jesus took bread, and after blessing it broke it and gave it to the disciples, and said, "Take, eat; this is my body." And he took a cup, and when he had given thanks he gave it to them, saying, "Drink of it, all of you, for this is my blood of the covenant, which is poured out for many for the forgiveness of sins. I tell you I will not drink again of this fruit of the vine until that day when I drink it new with you in my Father's kingdom." (vv. 26–29)

In order to understand the eschatological significance of the Last Supper, it is important to recall that the Old Testament prophets often spoke of the coming time of restoration as a new exodus (Isa. 63:10–17; Jer. 31:7–9; Hos. 1:10–11; 11:1–12). Just as the original exodus began with the twelve tribes observing the first Passover, the new exodus will be set in motion with the twelve disciples observing a reconfigured Passover. Jesus Christ, the one who is about to be betrayed, will become the new Passover sacrifice. His blood, the blood of the new covenant, will be "poured out for many" (Matt. 26:28; 1 Cor. 11:25). "In this way the suffering servant, who offers himself willingly, inaugurates a new covenant for the new community."[130]

Jesus commands his disciples to eat the bread, saying, "This is my body" (Matt. 26:26). These words indicate that the disciples are to participate in the benefits of Christ's sacrificial death just as those who partook of the original Passover participated in the redemption from Egypt. Jesus takes the cup, telling his disciples to drink it because it is the "blood of the covenant, which is poured out for many for the forgiveness of sins" (v. 28). Jesus is here connecting his death with the establishment of the promised new covenant (Jer. 31:31–34).[131] He uses language associated with the establishment of the old covenant to describe the establishment of the new (Ex. 24:8).[132] In declaring that he will not drink of the fruit of the vine until that day when he drinks it anew with his disciples in his Father's kingdom (Matt. 26:29), Jesus indicates that the Lord's Supper is observed in anticipation of the great eschatological banquet.

130. Davies and Allison 1997, 464.

131. Robertson 1980, 144–46.

132. There may also be an indirect allusion to Zechariah 9:9–11 here.

After observing the Passover, Jesus and his disciples go to the Mount of Olives and Jesus predicts that they will all forsake him that very night (26:30–32). The reference here to Zechariah 13:7–9 ties Jesus' coming death to the beginning of a time of tribulation and trouble.[133] Peter assures Jesus that he will never deny him, but Jesus assures Peter that he too will fall away (Matt. 26:33–35). His prophecy will soon be fulfilled (vv. 69–75). Jesus then goes with his disciples to the garden of Gethsemane where he fervently prays to the Father and submits to his will (vv. 36–46). While Jesus is speaking to his disciples, Judas arrives in the garden to betray him (vv. 47–56). Jesus then allows himself to be taken in order that the Scriptures might be fulfilled (vv. 54, 56).

Caiaphas the high priest along with many scribes and elders have gathered together seeking how they might put Jesus to death. He is brought before them, but they cannot get any two false witnesses to agree (vv. 57–60). Finally, two false witnesses tell the high priest and elders that Jesus claimed he was able to destroy the temple and rebuild it in three days (v. 61).[134] Caiaphas demands that Jesus tell them whether he is the Christ, the Son of God (vv. 62–63). Jesus responds, "You have said so. But I tell you, from now on you will see the Son of Man seated at the right hand of Power and coming on the clouds of heaven" (v. 64). At this, the high priest tears his clothes and accuses Jesus of blasphemy (v. 65). The elders and scribes determine that he is worthy of death, and they begin to spit on him and strike him (vv. 66–68).

Jesus' response to Caiaphas in verse 64 has caused confusion among many commentators. How will the high priest and the elders see Jesus "seated at the right hand of Power" and "coming on the clouds of heaven"? Are not the two images mutually exclusive? The two images are difficult to reconcile if it is assumed that "coming on the clouds of heaven" is a reference to the second coming. Jesus, however, is combining imagery from Daniel 7:13–14 and from Psalm 110:1. Daniel 7, as we have seen, speaks of one like a Son of Man coming to heaven to receive supreme authority. Psalm 110:1 speaks of the messianic King sitting at the right hand of God. R. T. France explains the meaning: "The sitting at God's right hand and the coming with clouds are not, then, two events separated by an indefinite period of time, but two figures for the single idea of the vindication and exaltation of the Son

133. Pitre 2005, 456–57.

134. In his resurrection, Jesus establishes the new temple.

of man."[135] Caiaphas and the elders condemn him now, but they will soon discover that the one they condemn is the Lord.

The following morning, the chief priests and elders deliver Jesus over to Pontius Pilate, who was the Roman procurator in Palestine from A.D. 26 to 36 (Matt. 27:1–2). When Judas discovers that Jesus has been condemned, he returns the money that had been given to him in exchange for his betrayal of Jesus and then hangs himself (vv. 3–10). Jesus is taken before Pilate, who proceeds to interrogate him (vv. 11–14). Pilate finds no cause for judgment, but at the instigation of the crowds, he has Jesus scourged and delivers him over to be crucified (vv. 15–26). The Roman soldiers strip him and place a crown of twisted thorns on his head before mocking him and striking him (vv. 27–31). They then take him to Golgotha and crucify him between two thieves (vv. 32–44). It is important to remember that crucifixion in the first century was the punishment given to slaves. It symbolized shame and degradation.[136] It was something so shameful and horrible that civilized Romans were encouraged not to even mention or think about the word "cross."[137] This was the kind of punishment to which Jesus was subjected.

At midday, darkness descended across the land (v. 45). The Old Testament prophets often spoke of darkness in connection with God's judgment (Isa. 13:9–16; Jer. 13:16; Amos 5:18–20). Here the darkness of judgment is connected to the crucifixion of Jesus. At about three in the afternoon, Jesus cries out with a loud voice (Matt. 26:46). Some of those nearby think he is calling for Elijah, and they wait to see what will happen (vv. 47–49). Jesus then cries out again and yields up his spirit (v. 50). Jesus' death on the cross is the fulfillment of numerous Old Testament prophecies. He is the Suffering Servant of Isaiah who was wounded for our transgressions and crushed for our iniquities (Isa. 52:13–53:12). His death was the final offering for sin (Isa. 53:10).[138] Israel's entire history has been a history of almost uninterrupted rebellion. Amazingly, God takes Israel's final and greatest act of rebellion, the rejection and crucifixion of her Messiah, and makes it the very thing that will save his people. It is at the cross that sin and evil are definitively conquered. As Henri Blocher explains, God "makes the

135. France 1982, 141.

136. Hengel 1977, 62.

137. See the quote by Cicero cited by Hengel (1977, 42).

138. Ridderbos 1962, 172.

supreme crime, the murder of the only righteous person, the very operation that abolishes sin."[139]

After Jesus yields up his spirit, several things happen. Matthew describes the events: "And behold, the curtain of the temple was torn in two, from top to bottom. And the earth shook, and the rocks were split. The tombs also were opened. And many bodies of the saints who had fallen asleep were raised, and coming out of the tombs after his resurrection they went into the holy city and appeared to many" (Matt. 26:51–53). The tearing of the temple veil, a symbolic act of destruction, is significant because it points forward to the total destruction of the temple that will occur in A.D. 70.[140] In fact, the tearing of the temple veil is very possibly the first stage in the destruction of the temple that will culminate with the events of A.D. 70.

Matthew says that after Christ's resurrection, many saints who had fallen asleep came out of their tombs and appeared in the city (vv. 52–53). The Old Testament looked forward to the great eschatological day of resurrection (e.g., Dan. 12:2). It did not, however, see this great day separated into stages. The New Testament, on the other hand, reveals that Christ is the "firstfruits of those who have fallen asleep" (1 Cor. 15:20). He is raised first; then at his second coming, those who are his will be raised (1 Cor. 15:23). The events described in Matthew 27:52–53 are difficult to understand completely, but they seem to indicate that at least some Old Testament saints were raised after Christ was raised. Jesus' death and resurrection, then, is presented by Matthew as the eschatological turning point of the ages.[141]

After Jesus' death, his body is removed from the cross and buried in the tomb of Joseph of Arimathea. A great stone is then rolled across the entrance of the tomb (27:57–60). On the following day, the chief priests and Pharisees come to Pilate telling him that Jesus had said that he would rise from the dead after three days (vv. 62–63). They ask Pilate to make sure the tomb is secured so that Jesus' disciples will not steal his body and claim he has risen from the dead (v. 64). Pilate then instructs them to go and make the tomb secure by sealing the stone and setting guards to watch over it (vv. 65–66). All of their efforts, however, are for naught, for death will not be able to hold Jesus in its grasp.

139. Blocher 1994, 132.

140. Fletcher-Louis 1997, 164; Davies and Allison 1997, 631.

141. Meier 1976, 164; Allison 1985, 46.

The Resurrection of Christ (Matt. 28:1–20)

The scribes and Pharisees and the Roman authorities in Israel probably breathed a sigh of relief after the crucifixion of Jesus. Gone was this man who had exposed their hypocrisy. Gone was this man who had claimed to be Israel's long-awaited Messiah. Gone was this man who had been drawing multitudes to himself. They were finally rid of him. Or so they thought. On the first day of the week, Mary Magdalene and another Mary go to Jesus' tomb and discover that an earthquake had rolled back the stone (28:1–4). An angel of the Lord appears to the women and tells them, "Do not be afraid, for I know that you seek Jesus who was crucified. He is not here, for he has risen, as he said" (vv. 5–6). The angel instructs the women to tell the disciples that Jesus has risen and that they will see him in Galilee (v. 7).

As they rush to tell the disciples, Jesus appears to them, and they fall and worship him (vv. 8–9). The guards of the tomb tell the chief priests all that has taken place, but the priests bribe them to tell anyone who asks that Jesus' disciples stole his body (vv. 11–15). The eleven remaining disciples go to Galilee, and Jesus comes to them and declares, "All authority in heaven and on earth has been given to me. Go therefore and make disciples of all nations, baptizing them in the name of the Father and of the Son and of the Holy Spirit, teaching them to observe all that I have commanded you. And behold, I am with you always, to the end of the age" (vv. 18–20).

The death and bodily resurrection of Jesus mark the turning point of redemptive history. Jesus' resurrection is an eschatological event. It is the firstfruits of the great eschatological resurrection, and it marks the beginning of a new era.[142] It marks the beginning of the time of restoration. Jesus declares that all authority in heaven and earth has been given to him. His kingdom is inaugurated. His disciples are now to go teach and baptize the nations. God had promised Abraham long ago that through him all the families of the earth would be blessed. The mission of Jesus' disciples to the world will fulfill that promise. Through it all, Jesus promises to be with his disciples, for he is truly Immanuel, "God with us" (Matt. 1:23).

Summary

The book of Matthew is the story of Jesus, and it is a book of fulfillment. It is a continuation of the narrative of the Old Testament. In Matthew all

142. Ladd 1974b, 294; Allison 1985, 67.

of the promises and prophecies of the Old Testament are fulfilled in one person, Jesus of Nazareth. The early chapters of Genesis revealed that Adam's disobedience and sin resulted in God's curse and judgment upon mankind. Sin was introduced into God's good creation and became the fundamental problem in man and in the world. Satan, the archenemy of God, usurped the dominion that had been entrusted to man. But God made a promise that through the seed of the woman, Satan would be overthrown and the kingdom would be established. The birth of Jesus was the birth of the one who would finally save his people from their sins and inaugurate the kingdom of God. His exorcisms indicate his defeat of the forces of Satan, and his acts of healing are a reversal of the curse.

With the call of Abraham at the beginning of the patriarchal narratives, God introduced his plan for the restoration of blessing to man. He promised that through Abraham all the families of the earth would be blessed. In Jesus, the son of Abraham, this promise is fulfilled as the gospel is proclaimed to all nations. At the time of the exodus, the children of Abraham were in slavery in Egypt, but God sent Moses to deliver them. The Passover and exodus witnessed the birth of the nation of Israel, and at Sinai God established the Mosaic covenant, giving his people the law and the instructions for the tabernacle in which he would be present among his people. Israel, however, was unable to fulfill the demands of the law and thus faced the curses of the covenant, including exile. Jesus comes as a new Moses who leads his people in a new exodus. He recapitulates the history of Israel in his own life in order to bring about the restoration of Israel, fulfilling the law that they could not. The righteousness demanded in the law, the sacrifices provided in the law, the tabernacle described in the law—all pointed forward to Jesus, and in him they found their fulfillment.

At the time of David, the kingdom of Israel reached its historical pinnacle as a manifestation of God's kingdom on earth. God promised that he would establish the kingdom of David's offspring. God promised that David's offspring would build a house for God and that God would establish David's kingdom forever. However, as the monarchy eventually began to slide into wickedness, the prophets began to understand the promises of the Davidic covenant eschatologically. A descendant of David, a Messiah, would come to reestablish the Davidic throne with justice and righteousness. In Jesus, the Son of David, these expectations are finally fulfilled. He is the promised Messiah, the long-awaited heir to the throne of Israel.

The prophets of Israel arose during the decline of the Old Testament kingdom. They warned Israel that continued disobedience would lead to the imposition of the covenant curses, including exile. But the prophets also looked beyond the exile with hope to a time of restoration. The coming of Jesus is the beginning of the fulfillment of all the prophetic hopes. In Jesus, God's covenant presence with his people is reestablished. He is Immanuel, "God with us." He is the Suffering Servant who comes to offer himself as a sacrifice for the sins of his people, and through his atoning death, he establishes the promised new covenant with his people.

Jesus is also the Son of Man, the one who is given dominion, glory, and a kingdom. But Jesus' death and resurrection and the coming of his kingdom do not immediately usher in the end of redemptive history. They do, however, mark the great turning point within redemptive history. Israel's rebellion and rejection of her Messiah are used by God as the means by which he will save his people, but her rebellion also means that her own full restoration is delayed. God's promise to bless all nations will not be thwarted by Israel's faithlessness, but the mission to bring the good news of salvation to the nations will be met with resistance, and Israel herself will face imminent judgment. Despite resistance, tribulation, and suffering, however, all the forces of hell will not be able to stand against the church, for Jesus has overcome the powers of death and hell, and nothing will ever be the same.

11

The Gospels of Mark and Luke

The gospels of Mark and Luke are very similar to the gospel of Matthew in content and structure, thus the descriptive label "Synoptic" Gospels. The word "synoptic" means "seeing together" and was applied to these three gospels because they all present the story of Jesus in such a similar manner. The same general geographical order is evident in all three of the Synoptic Gospels: preliminaries to Jesus' ministry, ministry in Galilee, the journey to Jerusalem, ministry in Jerusalem, and the passion narrative. Many of the same events are also narrated, including the commissioning of the twelve disciples, the transfiguration, the Olivet Discourse, and so forth. Because over 90 percent of the content of Mark is found in Matthew, our focus with Mark will be upon themes that require further discussion. Luke also contains a substantial amount of material that is found in Matthew and Mark. However, Luke also contains a good amount of material distinctive to his gospel. We will, therefore, look at Luke section by section, with particular focus on his distinctive contributions.

The Gospel of Mark

The gospel of Mark is in all likelihood the earliest of the four New Testament gospels. It is difficult to date the book with precision, but the evidence generally supports a date in the late 50s or early 60s.[1] According to early Christian tradition, the gospel was written in Rome by Mark, who was a companion of Paul for part of Paul's first missionary journey and who was later a companion of Peter (Acts 12:12, 25; 13:5, 13; 15:37; Col. 4:10; 2 Tim. 4:11; Philem. 24; 1 Peter 5:13). Mark's repeated translation of Aramaic expressions and his explanations of Jewish customs indicate that his audience was primarily, if not exclusively, Gentile. Like Matthew, the overarching purpose of Mark's gospel is to tell the story of Jesus the Messiah.

The basic structure of Mark's gospel reveals several of his most general concerns. Throughout the first half of the gospel, Jesus' words and actions cause those around him to ask two important questions: Who and why? (Mark 1:27; 2:7, 16, 24; 4:41; 6:2; 7:5).[2] Who is this man who does these things? Why do his followers do what they do? The first question is answered by Peter in Mark 8. When Jesus asks his disciples, "Who do you say that I am?" Peter answers, "You are the Christ" (8:29). In other words, Jesus is the promised Messiah. From the point of Peter's confession onward, Mark begins explaining what Jesus' mission is. It is a mission that involves suffering and death (8:31; 9:31; 10:32–34). Jesus has come to suffer and die in order to give his life as a ransom for many (10:45). In other words, Jesus the Davidic Messiah is also God's Suffering Servant (Isa. 52:13–53:12). In Mark's passion narrative (chs. 11–16), the Messiah's mission is accomplished.

Although Mark does not emphasize the theme of Old Testament fulfillment to the degree that Matthew does, his opening words in 1:1–3 do set his entire gospel within the framework of the Old Testament story of redemption and restoration. Mark writes, "The beginning of the gospel of Jesus Christ, the Son of God. As it is written in Isaiah the prophet, 'Behold, I send my messenger before your face, who will prepare your way, the voice of one crying in the wilderness: Prepare the way of the Lord, make his paths straight.'" Mark's quotation combines elements of three Old Testament passages: Exodus 23:20; Malachi 3:1; and Isaiah 40:3. The use of these Old Testament texts sheds light on the way in which Mark understands Jesus and his ministry.

1. Carson and Moo 2005, 182.
2. See Witherington 2001a, 37–38.

The primary text from which Mark quotes is Isaiah 40. This Old Testament prophecy is one of a series of oracles declaring the coming restoration of Israel. Yahweh declares that he will return to reign in Zion, and a messenger announces the "good news" to Jerusalem (Isa. 40:9–11).[3] In the oracles following Isaiah 40, the coming salvation is described in terms of a new exodus (Isa. 41:18–19; 43:19–21; 44:3–4). Malachi 3:1–3, written after the return from Babylon, also prophesies the coming of the Lord to Jerusalem, but Malachi warns that this coming will involve judgment. Malachi is still awaiting the fullness of the restoration promised in Isaiah. He promises that a messenger will be sent to prepare the way for the coming of the Lord. In Exodus 23:20, set in the context of the original exodus, God promises his people that he will send his angel ahead of them into the Promised Land, and he warns them not to rebel. By alluding to these specific texts, Mark transforms "Israel's memory of her founding moment into a model for her future hope."[4] The long-awaited Old Testament promises of restoration through the coming of the Lord and a new exodus are now being fulfilled (Mark 1:14–15). The time of the kingdom has come, and the promised new order is about to be realized.[5] Thus the "good news" that Mark proclaims is the "good news" that Isaiah promised.[6]

The first half of the gospel of Mark emphasizes Jesus' ministry of healing and exorcism. His works lead to amazement among the people. They continually ask who this man is. These works also lead to rising opposition among the Jewish religious leaders. The stage for his ministry of healing and exorcism is set early. Following Jesus' baptism, he is driven into the wilderness and is tempted by Satan for forty days (1:12–13). Satan is God's original adversary. It was he who tempted the first man to sin against God (Gen. 3:1–7), and it was he whom God promised to crush through the seed of the woman (Gen. 3:15). The early chapters of Genesis set the stage for viewing redemptive history as a conflict between God and Satan. Now Jesus has come "to destroy the works of the devil" (1 John 3:8). His work begins in the wilderness where he is subjected to Satan's temptations. He

3. In Isaiah 40:9 (LXX), the word translated "good news" is εὐαγγελιζόμενος (*euangelizomenos*), the participial form of εὐαγγελίζω (*euangelizō*). The Hebrew is מְבַשֶּׂרֶת (*mebasseret*). The word translated "Gospel" in Mark 1:1 is εὐαγγελίου (*euangeliou*), the genitive form of εὐαγγέλιον (*euangelion*). For a helpful discussion, see Cranfield 1977, 35.

4. Watts 1997, 90.

5. Beasley-Murray 1986, 73; Bruce 1978, 15.

6. Edwards 2002, 24–25.

is victorious there, and his work continues as he drives out demons and heals the sick.

The first miracle recorded by Mark is the exorcism of a man with an unclean spirit or demon (1:21–28). Here the kingdom of God comes face to face with the kingdom of Satan and the spiritual powers of darkness.[7] Jesus drives the demon out of the man, amazing the people who are present. This theme continues as Jesus heals Peter's mother-in-law (vv. 29–31) and many who were sick and oppressed by demons (vv. 32–34). His fame begins to spread far and wide. He heals a leper (vv. 40–45) and a paralytic (2:1–12). His healing of the paralytic causes many to glorify God, but because he also forgives the man's sins, some religious leaders who are present accuse him of blasphemy. In doing so, they side with the forces of darkness. When Jesus heals a man with a withered hand on the Sabbath, the Pharisees begin to seek a way to destroy him (3:1–6). The Pharisees eventually accuse Jesus of casting out demons by the power of Satan, but he indicates that his exorcisms are evidence that he is in fact binding Satan (vv. 22–30).

Jesus continues to demonstrate his power by calming a storm (4:35–41), driving a legion of demons out of a tormented man (5:1–20), healing a woman with a hemorrhage (vv. 21–34), and raising a child from the dead (vv. 35–43). He feeds a multitude with a handful of food (6:30–44), walks on the surface of a lake (vv. 45–52), and heals multitudes of sick and diseased people (vv. 53–56). All of these things cause astonishment and wonder. While in the region of the Gentiles, he drives a demon out of the daughter of a Syrophoenician woman (7:24–30), heals a deaf man (vv. 31–37), and feeds another multitude with a handful of food (8:1–10). Upon returning to Bethsaida, he heals a blind man (vv. 22–26).

In his works of exorcism and healing and raising the dead, Jesus is engaged in a cosmic conflict with the ancient adversary, for demonic oppression, sickness, and death are the fruits of Satan's work. By driving out demons, Jesus is overthrowing the usurper and destroying Satan's rebellious kingdom. He is binding the strong man (3:27). Sickness and death are due to the curse on man and creation that resulted from the fall. By healing all manner of sickness and raising the dead, Jesus is demonstrating the beginnings of the reversal of the curse and the restoration of blessing. Through both, he is demonstrating that he is the Son of God and the promised Messiah.

7. Edwards 2002, 56.

As we have already observed, Jesus' ministry of exorcism and healing is accompanied by rising opposition among the religious leaders who side with the powers of darkness. The opposition begins in Mark when Jesus heals the paralytic in Capernaum (2:1–12). His ministry had been drawing larger and larger crowds, and scribes are present when the paralytic man is brought to him. When Jesus declares the man's sins forgiven, the scribes begin questioning in their hearts, "Why does this man speak like that? He is blaspheming! Who can forgive sins but God alone?" (2:7). The scribes and Pharisees also object when Jesus gathers for dinner with tax collectors and sinners (2:16). They ask Jesus why his disciples do not fast (2:18), and they strongly object when Jesus' disciples pick heads of grain to eat on the Sabbath (2:24).

The objections to Jesus' ministry take an ominous turn when Jesus heals a man with a withered hand in the synagogue on the Sabbath. The Pharisees watch to see if he will do such a thing, and when he does, the conspiracy against him reaches a new and murderous level of intensity. "The Pharisees went out and immediately held counsel with the Herodians against him, how to destroy him" (3:6). While in Nazareth, the opposition of the scribes and Pharisees reaches a dangerous point when they declare that Jesus is possessed by Beelzebul and that he casts out demons by the power of Satan (3:22). He warns them that they are uttering unforgivable blasphemy, but it does not stop them.

The scribes and Pharisees challenge Jesus and his disciples for not following their traditions, but Jesus condemns them for rejecting the Word of God in order to establish their traditions (7:1–13). They challenge Jesus to produce a sign, but he refuses (8:11–13). He then warns his disciples to beware of the kind of hypocrisy demonstrated by the scribes and Pharisees (vv. 14–21). All of this opposition comes to a head after Peter's confession, when Jesus declares that "the Son of Man must suffer many things and be rejected by the elders and the chief priests and the scribes and be killed, and after three days rise again" (8:31). In other words, the rejection of the Messiah by the religious leaders of Israel will be the immediate cause for the suffering of God's Servant, the suffering that was foreseen by the prophets. The opposition of the Jewish leaders will ultimately lead to the cross, the climax of the cosmic battle between God and Satan.

The crowds had been wondering who Jesus is throughout the first half of Mark. Peter's confession provides the answer. Jesus is the Christ, the promised Messiah. After Peter's climactic confession, Jesus turns his face decisively toward Jerusalem and begins instructing his disciples about his mission. Three times on the journey to Jerusalem, Jesus predicts his suffering, death, and resurrection (8:31; 9:31; 10:32–34). He declares that "the Son of Man came not to be served but to serve, and to give his life as a ransom for many" (10:45). But who are the many? As Herman Ridderbos explains, they are the "many" mentioned in Isaiah's fourth Servant Song (Isa. 52:15; 53:11, 12).[8]

The first three Servant Songs are found in Isaiah 42:1–9; 49:1–6; and 50:4–9. The first Servant Song emphasizes the theme of the establishment of God's just rule over all of the earth. The second Servant Song emphasizes the Servant's mission to restore Israel. The third Servant Song emphasizes the obedience of the Servant and the sufferings that result from his obedience. The fourth and final Servant Song (Isa. 52:13–53:12) indicates the manner in which God will accomplish the salvation of his people. According to Isaiah, the Servant will take upon himself the sins of Israel and the world. His suffering will be the means by which he will deliver his people from their sins. He will be wounded for our transgressions and crushed for our iniquities, and by his stripes we will be healed (Isa. 53:5). The Lord will lay on the Servant the iniquity of us all (v. 6). He will be stricken for the transgressions of his people (v. 8). His soul will make an offering for sin (v. 10). He will "make many to be accounted righteous, and he shall bear their iniquities" (v. 11). He will bear the sin of many (v. 12).

When Jesus declares that he must suffer and die and that he has come to give his life as a ransom for many, he is identifying himself with the Suffering Servant of Isaiah. The same one who is the Davidic Messiah, the long-awaited King who has come to establish the kingdom of God, is also the Servant who has come to suffer and die in order to atone for the sins of his people. Throughout the second half of Mark, it is this truth that Jesus attempts to explain to his disciples. The coming of the kingdom is not going to occur in the way that many of them expected. The Son of Man will take his throne and establish his kingdom, but before this happens the Son of Man must suffer, and be killed, and after three days rise again.

8. Ridderbos 1962, 167.

The Gospel of Luke

The gospel of Luke is unique in that Luke is the only gospel author to have written a sequel to his gospel, namely the book of Acts. The connection between the two books is self-evident. The prologues to both Luke and Acts are addressed to Theophilus, and Acts specifically refers back to the author's "first book," the gospel of Luke (Luke 1:1–4; Acts 1:1–5). There is little doubt that the same author wrote both books. However, although Luke's gospel anticipates the narrative found in the book of Acts, the genre of the two books is not identical. Like Matthew and Mark, the gospel of Luke shares many generic features with ancient biographies. The book of Acts, on the other hand, resembles ancient histories.

The gospel of Luke was likely written in the mid 60s, and according to tradition, it was written by Luke the physician and friend of Paul (Col. 4:14).[9] The gospel of Luke may have been written from either Antioch or Achaia, but there is not enough evidence to determine which with any certainty. It is addressed to one Theophilus, and while some suggest that this is a generic term referring to anyone who loves God, it is more likely a reference to a definite individual.[10] Although it is addressed specifically to an individual, Luke does seem also to have had a larger and predominantly Gentile audience in mind as well.[11]

Luke follows the same basic structural outline as the other two synoptic gospels, but he also includes material that is not found in Matthew and Mark. Luke begins with a prologue and the infancy narratives of John the Baptist and Jesus (1:1–2:52). Following this is the narrative of the ministry of John the Baptist and Jesus' preparation for his ministry (3:1–4:13). Luke then narrates Jesus' Galilean ministry (4:14–9:50). Luke's extended description of the journey to Jerusalem follows (9:51–19:44). He continues with the narrative of Jesus' ministry in Jerusalem (19:45–21:38). This is then followed by Luke's passion narrative (22:1–23:56). Luke concludes his gospel with his account of the resurrection of Christ (24:1–53).

9. Carson and Moo 2005, 203–10.

10. The Greek name *Theophilus* means "one who loves God."

11. For a thorough, if somewhat critical, discussion of these introductory questions, see Fitzmyer 1981, 3–258.

The Infancy Narratives (Luke 1:1–2:52)

The beginning of Luke's gospel is unique in that he introduces his work with a prologue (1:1–4) that is similar to the kinds of prologues found in ancient Greek and Hellenistic Jewish works.[12] In the prologue, Luke justifies the writing of his gospel by appealing to the precedent of similar narratives that have already been written (1:1). He claims to have had access to eyewitness testimony (v. 2) and to have engaged in careful study of the evidence (v. 3). His purpose "was to give an historical account which would form the basis for a sound Christian faith on the part of those who had already been instructed, perhaps imperfectly and incompletely, in the story of Jesus."[13] Luke wanted to reassure Theophilus and others that what they had been taught about Jesus was absolutely true (v. 4).

The infancy narratives of John the Baptist and Jesus following the prologue are also unique to Luke's gospel (1:5–2:52). This section of Luke sets the story of Jesus within the context of the Old Testament story. John Carroll explains:

> The language, style, and content of the narratives and speeches of Luke 1–2 converge to connect Luke-Acts as a whole with the story of Israel. The impression generated by these chapters is that one has been immersed in the continuing experience of God's people. Yet, Luke 1–2 also announces that the *closing chapter* in the history of God's people has begun. The hope of Israel is on the verge of realization.[14]

In other words, Luke uses these introductory chapters to indicate that the fulfillment of all of Israel's eschatological hopes is found in Jesus. All of the ancient promises of redemption are to be realized in him.[15]

The infancy narratives of John and Jesus both follow the pattern of promise, fulfillment, and response, but a comparison of the two reveals the superiority of Jesus to John. The narratives begin with the promise of the birth of John the Baptist in 1:5–25. Zechariah, a priest of God, and

12. Marshall (1978a, 39) notes the striking similarities with Josephus's *Against Apion*, a two-part work with a preface to the whole at the beginning of the first part and a brief recapitulation at the beginning of the second part.

13. Marshall 1978a, 40.

14. Carroll 1988, 49.

15. See Green 1997, 47. Mark L. Strauss (1995, 76) points out the specific mention of the promises to David in 1:26–38, 68–79; and 2:1–20.

his wife Elizabeth are an elderly righteous couple, but they are childless (vv. 5–7). While Zechariah is in the temple burning incense, the angel Gabriel appears (vv. 8–12, 19). He promises Zechariah that he and his wife shall bear a son whose name will be John (v. 13). Gabriel's appearance itself is already a hint of the eschatological significance of these events because Gabriel's only previous appearances in Scripture have been in the book of Daniel when he explained Daniel's eschatological visions (Dan. 8:16–17; 9:21–23). His appearance here in the infancy narratives of Luke hints that the births of John and Jesus are closely associated with the fulfillment of Daniel's eschatological visions.[16]

Gabriel tells Zechariah that the birth of John will bring him joy and gladness and that many will rejoice at his birth (Luke 1:14). The child will be great before the Lord and will be filled with the Holy Spirit. Furthermore, like the Nazirites of the Old Testament, the child is not to drink wine or strong drink (v. 15; Num. 6:2–3). Gabriel then says of John, "And he will turn many of the children of Israel to the Lord their God, and he will go before him in the spirit and power of Elijah, to turn the hearts of the fathers to the children, and the disobedient to the wisdom of the just, to make ready for the Lord a people prepared" (Luke 1:16–17). Here Luke sets forth John's role in God's redemptive plan. John is to be a prophet calling God's people to repentance. The reference to Elijah places John's work in an eschatological framework. He is to prepare a remnant for the long-awaited coming of the Lord.[17]

The promise of John's birth is followed by Luke's narrative of the promise of Jesus' birth in 1:26–38. Again Gabriel is sent to bear the news, but this time he is sent to the one who will be the child's mother, a virgin named Mary (vv. 26–28). Mary is troubled by the appearance of the angel, but he tells her not to be afraid for she has found favor with God (vv. 29–30).[18] The angel then makes his announcement: "And behold, you will conceive in your womb and bear a son, and you shall call his name Jesus. He will be great and will be called the Son of the Most High. And the Lord God will give to him the throne of his father David, and he will reign over the house of Jacob forever, and of his kingdom there will be no end" (vv. 31–33).

16. Brown 1977, 270–71.

17. Bock 1994a, 99–100.

18. The phrase "found favor" is common in the Old Testament (e.g., Gen. 6:8; 18:3; 39:21; 43:14; Judg. 6:17; 1 Sam. 1:18; 2 Sam. 15:25).

Concerning John, the angel had said, "he will be great before the Lord" (v. 15). But of Jesus, he says, "he will be great and will be called the Son of the Most High." Zechariah's child will prepare the way for the coming of the Lord. Mary's child will be the Lord.

The angel Gabriel tells Mary that her child will be given the throne of his father David and that he will reign over Jacob forever in a kingdom without end. This is not a direct quotation of any particular Old Testament verse. Instead it is a summary of several Old Testament prophetic expectations, in particular God's promise to David (2 Sam. 7:9–16; see also Ps. 89:26–29, 36; Isa. 7:14; 9:6–7; Dan. 7:14).[19] The first thing then that Luke tells us about Jesus is that in him the promises made to David will be fulfilled. All the hopes of Israel and the world rest with this child.

Upon hearing the angel's announcement, Mary asks, "How will this be, since I am a virgin?" (Luke 1:34). Gabriel responds, "The Holy Spirit will come upon you, and the power of the Most High will overshadow you; therefore the child to be born will be called holy—the Son of God" (v. 35). The angel tells Mary that her relative Elizabeth, who was barren, has also conceived a son (v. 36). Mary then humbly submits to God's will (v. 38). Although the manner of Jesus' conception is miraculous, the nature of the conception itself is not the focus of the passage. The focus is upon the identity of this unique child. The nature of his conception and the content of the angel's announcement serve to identify this child as the Son of God and the Davidic Messiah.[20]

Luke continues by recounting Mary's visit with Elizabeth (1:39–45). Upon arriving at the home of Zechariah and Elizabeth, Mary greets her relative. When Elizabeth hears the voice of Mary, her child leaps in her womb (v. 41). Elizabeth is filled with the Holy Spirit and proclaims to Mary, "Blessed are you among women, and blessed is the fruit of your womb!" (v. 42). She refers to Mary as "the mother of my Lord" (v. 43) and praises her for believing that what the Lord spoke he would certainly fulfill (v. 45). Mary responds with a song that has come to be known as the Magnificat (vv. 46–55):

> My soul magnifies the Lord,
> and my spirit rejoices in God my Savior,

19. Strauss 1995, 88–89.
20. Fitzmyer 1981, 340; Bock 1994a, 127.

for he has looked on the humble estate of his servant.
  For behold, from now on all generations will call me blessed;
for he who is mighty has done great things for me,
  and holy is his name.
And his mercy is for those who fear him
  from generation to generation.
He has shown strength with his arm;
  he has scattered the proud in the thoughts of their hearts;
he has brought down the mighty from their thrones
  and exalted those of humble estate;
he has filled the hungry with good things,
  and the rich he has sent empty away.
He has helped his servant Israel,
  in remembrance of his mercy,
as he spoke to our fathers,
  to Abraham and to his offspring forever.

The Magnificat most closely resembles Hannah's song of praise in 1 Samuel 2:1–10, but it alludes to numerous other Old Testament texts as well.[21] In the song, Mary seems to speak as the representative of the people of Israel.[22] Throughout the song, two images of God are seen. God is described as the divine warrior who delivers his people from their enemies. He is also described as the God who is great in mercy toward his people.[23]

The birth of John the Baptist and Zechariah's response are narrated by Luke in 1:57–80. The response to John's birth is Zechariah's prophecy, known as the Benedictus (vv. 68–79). Zechariah proclaims:

Blessed be the Lord God of Israel,
  for he has visited and redeemed his people
and has raised up a horn of salvation for us
  in the house of his servant David,

21. The opening verses (vv. 46–47) closely resemble Psalm 35:9 and Habakkuk 3:18. The first half of verse 48 echoes 1 Samuel 1:11, while the second half echoes Genesis 30:13. Verse 49 resembles Deuteronomy 10:21. Verse 50 is very similar to Psalm 103:17. Verses 51–53 are similar to 1 Samuel 2:7–8. And verses 54–55 echo several Old Testament texts, including Isaiah 41:8–9; Psalm 98:3; and Micah 7:20.

22. Johnson 1991, 43.

23. Green 1997, 102.

as he spoke by the mouth of his holy prophets from of old,
that we should be saved from our enemies
  and from the hand of all who hate us;
to show the mercy promised to our fathers
  and to remember his holy covenant,
the oath that he swore to our father Abraham, to grant us
  that we, being delivered from the hand of our enemies,
might serve him without fear,
  in holiness and righteousness before him all our days.
And you, child, will be called the prophet of the Most High;
  for you will go before the Lord to prepare his ways,
to give knowledge of salvation to his people
  in the forgiveness of their sins,
because of the tender mercy of our God,
  whereby the sunrise shall visit us from on high
to give light to those who sit in darkness and in the shadow of death,
  to guide our feet into the way of peace.

In the announcement of John's birth, the angel Gabriel had spoken of John as the one who would prepare the way for the Messiah. In the Magnificat, Mary had spoken of Jesus as the one in whom Israel's eschatological hopes rest. In the Benedictus, Zechariah speaks of both John and Jesus, tying their redemptive roles together.[24] Jesus will be the "horn of salvation" (Ps. 18:2; 132:17; Ezek. 29:21). Jesus is the Messiah, and he will come to the people who sit in darkness and death and will be a light of salvation for them.

The birth of Jesus and the immediate responses to it are narrated in Luke 2:1–40. Luke places the birth of Jesus in its specific historical context. He writes, "In those days a decree went out from Caesar Augustus that all the world should be registered. This was the first registration when Quirinius was governor of Syria" (2:1–2).[25] Augustus had restored peace to Rome after a century of civil wars. He is referred to in inscriptions from the era as "savior." His birthday is referred to as the beginning of the "gospel."[26]

24. Nolland 1989, 91.

25. A number of historical questions surround these verses. For a helpful discussion, see Bock 1994a, 903–9.

26. Klauck 2003, 296–98; Ferguson 2003, 46.

Luke's infancy narratives indicate that Jesus is the true Savior. His advent is the true "good news."[27]

Because of the census, Joseph and Mary travel from Nazareth to Bethlehem to be registered (2:3–5). While in Bethlehem, Mary gives birth to Jesus (vv. 6–7). Luke then describes the appearance of an angel to some shepherds, who were watching over flocks in a field. The angel declares, "Fear not, for behold I bring you good news of a great joy that will be for all the people. For unto you is born this day in the city of David a Savior, who is Christ the Lord" (vv. 10–11). The angel is proclaiming the fulfillment of Isaiah 9:6–7. Jesus is the promised child. He is the Savior. He is the Christ, or Messiah. And he is the Lord. After declaring all of these titles of the child, the angel tells the shepherds, "And this will be a sign for you: you will find a baby wrapped in swaddling cloths and lying in a manger" (Luke 2:12). The paradox here is that Israel's long-awaited Messiah is to be found lying in a feeding trough.

According to the law of Moses, a woman was considered unclean for forty days following the birth of a child (Lev. 12:2–4). After the forty days, Joseph and Mary brought Jesus to Jerusalem to present him to the Lord as was necessary with all firstborn sons (Luke 2:22–23; Ex. 13:2, 12, 15; Num. 18:15–16). In Jerusalem, they encounter a righteous man named Simeon, to whom it had been revealed that he would not die before he had seen the Messiah (Luke 2:25–27). When Joseph and Mary present Jesus in the temple, Simeon takes the child, blesses God, and says,

> Lord, now you are letting your servant depart in peace,
> according to your word;
> for my eyes have seen your salvation
> that you have prepared in the presence of all peoples,
> a light for revelation to the Gentiles,
> and for glory to your people Israel. (vv. 29–32)

Simeon here speaks of Jesus as not only the salvation of Israel, but of the Gentiles as well. He is the one who will bless the nations in fulfillment of the ancient promise to Abraham.

Having offered his blessing to God for the birth of the Messiah, Simeon blesses the child's parents (vv. 33–35). He tells Mary, "Behold, this child

27. Fitzmyer 1981, 394.

is appointed for the fall and rising of many in Israel, and for a sign that is opposed (and a sword will pierce through your own soul also), so that thoughts from many hearts may be revealed." Simeon's first statement recalls the Isaianic prophecy of the stone of offense upon which many will stumble (Isa. 8:14–15). Many will stumble over the claims of Jesus. He will also be a sign that will be opposed. Simeon tells Mary of the anguish she will suffer because of the rejection of her son, a rejection that will culminate in his death.

Preparation for Ministry (Luke 3:1–4:13)

The second major section of Luke's gospel describes John's ministry and the preparations for Jesus' ministry. John's ministry begins in the fifteenth year of Tiberius Caesar, in other words, sometime between August of A.D. 28 and August of A.D. 29.[28] He comes preaching a baptism of repentance for the forgiveness of sins. As Mark does in the opening verses of his gospel, Luke here places the beginning of John's ministry in the context of an Isaianic prophecy of the coming new exodus (3:4–6; Isa. 40:3–5).[29] John's ministry, then, is set within the larger framework of God's redemptive work, and his promise of forgiveness comes with a warning to those who fail to repent (Luke 3:7–14). John makes it clear that his own work is preliminary. His work is only a baptism with water as opposed to the baptism with the Holy Spirit and fire to be performed by the one for whom he prepares the way (vv. 15–17).

Luke's narrative of Jesus' baptism (vv. 21–22) is followed by a genealogy of Jesus that goes back to Adam (vv. 23–38).[30] By tracing Jesus' genealogy back to Adam, Luke ties all of mankind together. It is not merely the fate of Israel that rests on Jesus; it is the fate of the world. As Darrell Bock observes, this genealogy indicates that Jesus "represents the focal point of history."[31] The genealogy of Jesus is followed by Luke's narrative of the temptation

28. Augustus Caesar died on August 19 in A.D. 14. Although there is some debate, I would suggest that the fifteenth year of Tiberius's reign should be calculated from this date.

29. As Pao (2002, 39) explains, Luke's inclusion of the line "and all flesh shall see the salvation of God" (3:6) is significant for an understanding of Luke-Acts. It "points to the wider Isaianic program lying behind the narratives of both Luke and Acts." The Isaianic "new exodus" shapes the way Luke structures his narrative.

30. For a discussion of the relationship between Luke's genealogy and Matthew's genealogy, see Bock 1994a, 918–23.

31. Bock 1994a, 360.

of Jesus in the wilderness (4:1–13). Here Jesus demonstrates his absolute obedience and complete faithfulness to God.

The Galilean Ministry (Luke 4:14–9:50)

Like Matthew and Mark, Luke contains a lengthy section narrating Jesus' ministry in Galilee. In this section, Luke focuses on Jesus' training of his followers to be true disciples. Luke begins this section with the story of Jesus' reception at the synagogue in Nazareth (4:14–30). At the synagogue, Jesus is given the scroll of the prophet Isaiah. He opens it and reads the following passage from Isaiah 61:1–2:

> The Spirit of the Lord is upon me,
> because he has anointed me
> to proclaim good news to the poor.
> He has sent me to proclaim liberty to the captives
> and recovering of sight to the blind,
> to set at liberty those who are oppressed,
> to proclaim the year of the Lord's favor. (Luke 4:18–19)

As was the case with John the Baptist, Jesus' public ministry is introduced by Luke with a citation from Isaiah (cf. 3:4–6). After reading the text, Jesus tells the people, "Today this Scripture has been fulfilled in your hearing" (v. 21). Jesus is announcing the beginning of a new era, an eschatological turning point.[32] The quote from Isaiah speaks of the salvation that the Messiah brings in terms of the year of jubilee (Lev. 25:8–12).[33] According to Jesus, this time of deliverance has arrived with his coming. Jesus demonstrates the fulfillment of Isaiah's prophecy by healing the sick and casting out demons (Luke 4:31–41).

After calling his first disciples to follow him and become fishers of men, Jesus' ministry of healing continues as he heals a leper and a paralytic (Luke 5:1–26). The Isaiah prophecy quoted by Jesus at the synagogue in Nazareth had focused on those who would be considered outsiders—the poor, the blind, and the oppressed. So far, Jesus has dealt closely with lepers and demoniacs. His focus on social outsiders continues when he calls a tax col-

32. Marshall 1988, 119; Bock 1994a, 420; Pao 2002, 74–84.

33. Lincoln 1982b, 201; Green 1997, 212.

lector named Levi to follow him (vv. 27–28).[34] Tax collectors were despised by the Jews of the first century. They were considered to be extortionists as well as collaborators with the Roman government. Not only does Jesus call a tax collector to be a disciple, he attends a feast arranged by Levi at which a large number of other tax collectors are present (v. 29). The Pharisees do not understand why Jesus would associate himself with such people, but Jesus makes it clear that he has been sent to call such sinners to repentance (vv. 30–31).

After choosing twelve apostles from among his disciples (6:12–16), Jesus goes with them to a plain where a great crowd has gathered to hear him teach and to be healed of their afflictions (vv. 17–19). Luke then narrates Jesus' Sermon on the Plain (6:20–49). There are many parallels between this sermon and Matthew's account of the Sermon on the Mount (Matt. 5:1–7:29). While some suggest that the same sermon lies behind both accounts, there are also numerous differences between the two. It is much more reasonable to assume that Jesus, in his role as a teacher, would have repeated many of his teachings at numerous times during his ministry and that this is just such an instance.[35]

The sermon begins with a series of four beatitudes (or blessings) and four woes (6:20–26). The blessings and woes are surprising because Jesus blesses those whom the world despises (the poor and oppressed) and curses those whom the world values highly (the rich and satisfied). The blessed ones are those who are poor and oppressed "on account of the Son of Man" (v. 22). In the eyes of the world, Jesus' disciples are a pitiful lot, but according to Jesus, they are blessed. Those who are truly cursed are the self-satisfied, those who are content with riches and the praise of men and who have no concern for the things of the kingdom.

The heart of this sermon is found in Jesus' admonition to his disciples to love their enemies (6:27–36). He tells them:

> But I say to you who hear, Love your enemies, do good to those who hate you, bless those who curse you, pray for those who abuse you. To one who strikes you on the cheek, offer the other also, and from one who takes away your cloak do not withhold your tunic either. Give to everyone who begs

34. Levi's name is given as Matthew in the first gospel (Matt. 9:9), and he is also referred to as Matthew in Luke's list of the twelve (Luke 6:15).

35. See Morris 1988, 138–39.

> from you, and from one who takes away your goods do not demand them back. And as you wish that others would do to you, do so to them.
>
> If you love those who love you, what benefit is that to you? For even sinners love those who love them. And if you do good to those who do good to you, what benefit is that to you? For even sinners do the same. And if you lend to those from whom you expect to receive, what credit is that to you? Even sinners lend to sinners, to get back the same amount. But love your enemies, and do good, and lend, expecting nothing in return, and your reward will be great, and you will be sons of the Most High, for he is kind to the ungrateful and the evil. Be merciful, even as your Father is merciful.

Here Jesus sets forth the radical nature of true discipleship. The kingdom has come with the advent of Christ, and even though the consummation of the kingdom is still future, the ethics of the kingdom are to be put into practice by the disciples today.

Jesus' followers are to love those who are ungrateful and evil because God has loved those who are ungrateful and evil. Jesus' followers are to be merciful because God is merciful. Jesus instructs his disciples not to judge or condemn but to forgive (6:37–42). Jesus' followers are not to be hypocrites. He tells them that their actions demonstrate the state of their hearts (vv. 43–45) and urges them to be both hearers of his word and doers. Those who hear him and do what he says are likened to a wise man who builds a sturdy house on a rock (vv. 47–48). Those who hear him and do not do what he says are like a foolish man who built a house with no foundation only to have it collapse (v. 49).

The eschatological ethics of Jesus are a challenge to the status quo. Jesus' true followers are to demonstrate a radical unselfish love for others, just as God has done by sending his only begotten Son. Jesus' followers are not to respond to hatred in the way that the world responds or even in the way that the outwardly religious respond. They are to demonstrate the ethical character of the Messiah by showing forth the mercy and love of God through their own mercy and love toward those who treat them with hatred, abuse, and contempt.

Jesus' fame continues to spread throughout the remainder of his Galilean ministry. His healing of a Gentile centurion's servant in 7:1–10 provides a foreshadowing of God's plan to bless the nations.[36] His raising to life of

36. Bock 1994a, 644.

the widow's son reveals his power and authority and causes reports of him to be spread throughout the land (vv. 11–17). A meal with a Pharisee provides Jesus with the opportunity to teach him the nature of true love and forgiveness, but his actions and words raise the eyebrows of some who are present (7:36–50). They ask one another, "Who is this, who even forgives sins?" (v. 49).

Luke 8 introduces readers to some of the women who followed Jesus, including Mary Magdalene, Joanna, and Susanna (8:1–3). These women were important to the ministry of Christ because they provided material support for him and the disciples (v. 3). Luke's gospel is unique in the emphasis it places on the role of women. There are a large number of references to women in the gospel of Luke, many of which are unique to Luke.[37] As Leon Morris notes, the role of women in Jesus' ministry is striking because other first-century rabbis did not teach women and assigned them an inferior place. Jesus, on the other hand, had numerous women disciples.[38] This again demonstrates his focus on those who were accorded lower status by the social standards of the day.

While in Galilee, Jesus gathers the twelve apostles together, gives them power to cast out demons and heal diseases, and then sends them out to proclaim the kingdom of God and to heal those who are afflicted (9:1–2). To this point, the disciples have for the most part been accompanying Jesus and observing his ministry. Now they begin to participate in his ministry as their missionary endeavor becomes a means by which God builds his kingdom. Jesus' ministry is expanded here to include those who will be his witnesses in the book of Acts.[39] At this point, Luke does not describe in any detail what happened to the disciples on their mission. Luke simply says that they went through the villages preaching the gospel and healing everywhere (v. 6). The apostles tell Jesus all that they did, but Luke does not tell his readers (v. 10).

37. Among the references that are unique to Luke's gospel are the references to Elizabeth (1:5–7, 13, 24–25, 36, 40–45, 56–61); the annunciation to Mary (1:26–56); Anna (2:36–38); the widow of Nain (7:11–17); the sinful woman (7:36–50); the ministering women (8:1–3); Mary and Martha (10:38–42); the crippled woman (13:10–17); the parable of the woman with the lost coin (15:8–10); the parable of the widow and the judge (18:1–8); and the report of the women at the tomb (24:22–24).

38. Morris 1988, 164.

39. Bock 1994a, 809.

The Journey to Jerusalem (Luke 9:51–19:44)

Luke's narrative of the journey to Jerusalem is substantially longer than the parallel accounts in Matthew and Mark, and much of the material in these chapters is unique to Luke. In contrast with the previous section of Luke, which focused primarily on Jesus' deeds, these chapters consist primarily of instruction and parables indicating that the teaching of Jesus is Luke's major concern here.[40] Jesus has set his face toward Jerusalem. He is going there to suffer and die in order to fulfill God's plan, so he is now preparing his disciples for the mission they will be given after his death and resurrection.

The duties of true disciples are introduced first. Jesus appoints seventy-two disciples and sends them out ahead of himself, two by two, into every town where he is planning to go (10:1).[41] Jesus tells them that there is much work to do: "The harvest is plentiful, but the laborers are few" (v. 2). Their work will not be an easy task, but will be fraught with danger (v. 3). When they find a place to lodge, they are to receive the hospitality offered with thankfulness, but they are not to go from house to house overstaying their welcome because they need to press on with their work (vv. 4–8). They are to proclaim the gospel of the kingdom and to heal the sick (v. 9). Those who reject them will be judged (vv. 10–12). Jesus concludes his commission by identifying the mission of the disciples with his own mission: "The one who hears you hears me, and the one who rejects you rejects me, and the one who rejects me rejects him who sent me" (v. 16).

After the disciples return from their mission, they declare to Jesus with joy, "Lord, even the demons are subject to us in your name!" (10:17). Jesus responds, "I saw Satan fall like lightning from heaven" (v. 18). What Jesus sees is the effect of the disciples' mission. Their activity manifested his victory over the power and kingdom of the enemy. As Joseph Fitzmyer explains, "Jesus summarizes the effects of the mission of the seventy (-two) in terms of the fall of Satan."[42] By identifying the disciples' mission with his own work, and by associating it with the fall of Satan, Jesus establishes

40. Bock 1996, 960.

41. There is a difficult text-critical problem here involving the number of people that were sent out by Jesus. Is it seventy or seventy-two? The manuscript evidence is almost evenly divided. The problem, however, does not seriously affect our interpretation. For more on the textual evidence see Metzger, *TCGNT*, 126–27.

42. Fitzmyer 1985, 860.

the eschatological nature of his disciples' work. The proclamation of the gospel by the disciples of Jesus is God's means of spreading the eschatological kingdom of Christ and tearing down the strongholds of the enemy.

Having explained some of the basic duties of true disciples, Jesus turns his attention to the character of true disciples (10:25–11:13). A lawyer's question provides the opportunity for Jesus' first teaching on the subject, the telling of the parable of the good Samaritan (10:25–37). Here again, Jesus will outline the radical nature of eschatological kingdom ethics. The followers of Jesus are not to extend mercy and love on the basis of racial, ethnic, or nationalistic categories. Mercy and love are to be shown to all men. When told by Jesus that he must love the Lord with all his heart and love his neighbor as himself, the man asks, "And who is my neighbor?" (vv. 25–29). In his response, Jesus tells a parable in which the uncaring and unloving actions of a priest and Levite toward an injured man are compared to the merciful actions of a Samaritan (vv. 30–35). Jesus asks the lawyer to tell him which of the three proved to be a neighbor, and the lawyer acknowledges that the one who showed mercy was the one who was the neighbor. Jesus then tells him to go and do likewise (vv. 36–37).

The radical nature of the parable becomes more apparent when it is recalled that Samaritans were despised by the Jews of Jesus' day (John 4:9). They were considered racially and religiously impure. And the Samaritans were not the only ones disdained by many Jews at that time. Some Jewish teachers restricted the law of neighborly love to the covenant people Israel.[43] In the parable, both a priest and a Levite pass by a wounded man in need of help. Priests and Levites were religious leaders in Israel. They were people of high status. Yet in the parable they do not demonstrate love and compassion. The person who does demonstrate mercy is a Samaritan. He is the one who demonstrates what it means to be a true neighbor. And Jesus tells the lawyer to behave in the same manner as the Samaritan in his story. By means of this parable, Jesus turns the world's ethics on its head. Jesus' followers are to demonstrate love and mercy to all men, even those who may have been labeled "not one of us."

Luke's narrative concerning Martha and Mary illustrates the primary importance of listening to Jesus (10:38–42). Jesus' disciples are not to allow the everyday demands of life to prevent them from hearing his word. Fur-

43. Bock 1996, 1027.

thermore, not only are Jesus' disciples to hear from God, they are to speak with God. Jesus' disciples are to be a people of prayer. Upon hearing him in prayer, Jesus' disciples ask him to teach them to pray (11:1). He gives them a pattern for prayer, the Lord's Prayer (vv. 2–4). He then tells them a parable that illustrates God's readiness and willingness to hear their prayers (vv. 5–8). He promises them that God will answer their prayers (vv. 9–10). Finally, he emphasizes his previous point by telling them that as much as a loving human father is ready to give his children what they request, God is even more willing and ready to answer his people's prayers (vv. 11–13).

Further opportunity for teaching is provided as Jesus engages in controversy with the Pharisees on a number of issues (11:14–54). The first point of dispute involves the authority of Jesus (vv. 14–26). Jesus' exorcism of a demon-possessed man leads some Pharisees to say that he is doing his works by the power of the devil. Jesus tells them that he casts out demons by the power of God, and the fact that he does so indicates that the kingdom of God has come (v. 20). When a woman in the crowd cries out, blessing Jesus' mother, Jesus takes the opportunity to make another point, saying, "Blessed rather are those who hear the word of God and keep it!" (v. 28).

Jesus replies to the people's request for a sign by explaining that he himself will be a sign to his generation, just as Jonah had been a sign to the people of Nineveh (Luke 11:29–30). Nineveh repented at the preaching of Jonah, but Jesus' generation has not repented at his preaching even though he is greater than Jonah. For this, his generation will be judged (vv. 31–32). Jesus' dinner with a Pharisee leads to a rebuke of Pharisaism. The Pharisee is astonished at the dinner because Jesus does not wash and ritually purify himself before eating (vv. 37–38). Jesus rebukes the Pharisees for their hypocritical concern for outward cleanliness and disdain of inward purity (vv. 39–40). He proceeds to pronounce a series of woes on the Pharisees and scribes rebuking them for their hypocrisy, for their lack of justice, for their burdening of the people with burdens they themselves do not bear, for consenting to the wicked deeds of their ancestors, and for blocking the people's access to the kingdom of God (vv. 42–52). This kind of behavior cannot characterize God's people.

Following his condemnation of the Pharisees, Jesus turns the attention of his disciples to the judgment that is coming upon this hypocritical generation and begins to prepare them for this impending crisis (12:1–13:21). Jesus tells his disciples that they are not to live hypocritically, as the Pharisees do, but are to acknowledge him openly before all men (12:1–9). Jesus' followers are to guard against an attachment to wealth and riches because these can be a snare for their souls (vv. 13–21). They are not to be anxious for their earthly needs but are to trust in God's faithful provision (vv. 22–34).

The disciples of Jesus are to remain ever vigilant and watchful because judgment may come at any time (vv. 35–48). The coming of the Son of Man spoken of in verse 40 is in a context similar to that of Matthew 24:36–44, a context of imminent judgment. The similarities indicate that Luke, like Matthew, is speaking of the impending first-century judgment of Israel, not the second coming. Jesus warns his disciples that his message brings division as it forces people to be for him or against him (Luke 11:49–53). He turns to the crowds and tells them that they should be able to interpret the significance of the present time (vv. 54–56). Israel has been spared judgment for many years, but this should not cause the people to think that everything is fine. If they do not repent they will perish (13:1–9). God's saving power is then demonstrated once again as Jesus heals a disabled woman (vv. 10–17). Her healing is an indication of the presence of the kingdom, a kingdom that begins small but will become great (vv. 18–21).

Jesus continues his instruction of the disciples by explaining various aspects of the kingdom of God to them (13:22–14:35). The first question that is raised concerns the number of those who will be in the kingdom (13:22–30). Jesus' response is to tell his hearers that the door is narrow and that they should strive to enter in. In other words, according to Jesus, his hearers' concern should not be with the number of those in the kingdom. His hearers should be concerned to make sure that they are among that number. The door is presently open, but once it is closed, it is closed for good. Ethnicity will not matter because many who are ethnic Jews, related to Abraham by blood, will not be found in the kingdom. On the other hand, many Gentiles will be found in the kingdom (vv. 28–30).

Jesus' ministry has raised the hostility of many, including Herod himself. A number of Pharisees now come to Jesus and warn him that Herod intends to kill him (v. 31).[44] Jesus' response is to set his face even more

44. There is some dispute as to whether Luke is presenting the Pharisees here in a positive light. Are these Pharisees warning Jesus because of a positive regard for him? Or are they viewing him as a troublemaker and hoping their warning will get rid of him? It is not possible to say with certainty, but the latter view seems somewhat more likely. For more, see Marshall 1978a, 570–71; Fitzmyer 1985, 1030.

firmly toward the accomplishment of the task for which he has been sent. He is not to be killed until he is in Jerusalem (vv. 32–33). The thought of his death at the hands of his own people leads Jesus to lament over the city of Jerusalem (v. 34). His lament is reminiscent of Jeremiah's lament over Israel (Jer. 22:29).

The lament is prophetic in nature and is immediately followed by a pronouncement of judgment (v. 35a), but even in the pronouncement of judgment there is a note of hope. Jesus says, "And I tell you, you will not see me until you say, 'Blessed is he who comes in the name of the Lord'" (v. 35b). This statement suggests that the rejection of Jesus by the Jews will not be permanent. Such an idea will gain further support later in Luke when he speaks of the "times of the Gentiles" (21:24), and in Paul's epistle to the Romans when Paul speaks of Israel's "hardening" as temporary (Rom. 11:7, 25). Here, however, Jesus merely hints at this idea.

Jesus uses the healing of a man on the Sabbath to introduce his followers to more truths concerning the kingdom of God and the nature of true discipleship (Luke 14:1–35). In his healing of a man on the Sabbath, Jesus makes it clear that the Sabbath is not a time to rest from compassion (vv. 1–6). Jesus also explains to his disciples that following him requires humility (vv. 7–14). He then tells them that those who do not respond to his word have no excuse (vv. 15–24). However, although there is a danger in refusing to accept Jesus' invitation, there is also a danger in underestimating the cost of accepting that invitation (vv. 25–35). The cost of discipleship is high. Those who follow Jesus must take up their cross and renounce all else.

The contents of chapter 15 are occasioned by the criticism Jesus is receiving for fellowshiping with sinners (15:1–2). The three parables that follow explain and justify his actions. The parables of the lost sheep (vv. 3–7) and the lost coin (vv. 8–10) illustrate God's love for sinners and his active initiative in seeking them.[45] Jesus' disciples should reflect the same kind of love and initiative for the lost. The parable of the prodigal son, or perhaps more correctly the parable of the forgiving father, illustrates in greater detail many of the same truths found in the previous two parables (vv. 11–32). In this parable, Jesus teaches that the repentance of a sinner is received with joy and forgiveness by God. Jesus also teaches that repentant sinners

45. Morris 1988, 261.

should not be treated the way that the religious leadership has been treating them, with revulsion and contempt. Instead, they are to be received into the family with gladness.

Luke next recounts Jesus' teachings and warnings about money as well as a few comments on other issues. Jesus begins with a parable that is among the most difficult of all the parables to interpret, the parable of the clever manager (16:1–9). The main character in the parable is a manager who is fired for dishonesty and corruption. The manager then decides to reduce the debts of his master's debtors. The master praises him for his shrewdness. The traditional interpretation argues that the manager's action in reducing the amounts owed by the debtors was dishonest. The manager was not praised for his dishonesty but for his foresight in planning for his future. Others argue that his action in reducing the debts was actually praiseworthy in a first-century context.[46] In either case, the parable pictures a man in a desperate situation. He is able to evaluate the future wisely and acts in a way to prepare for the future. Jesus' disciples are also to think ahead, to act with generosity with their wealth. In his summation following the parable, Jesus makes it very clear that we are to hold our wealth loosely because one "cannot serve God and money" (v. 13).

Because the Pharisees love money, they scoff at Jesus' teaching (16:14). Jesus rebukes them, telling them that even though they may be highly esteemed by men, God is able to see their hearts. The Pharisees need to know that what they secretly exalt is an abomination to God (v. 15). Jesus then makes a statement that points to his own time as a turning point in redemptive history: "The Law and the Prophets were until John; since then the good news of the kingdom of God is preached" (v. 16). That to which the law looked forward has come, but God's moral standards have not lessened or changed (v. 17). As an example, Jesus explains that divorce is still against the will of God (v. 18).

Jesus concludes his warnings about the dangers of wealth with the story of the rich man and Lazarus (16:19–31). There has been some discussion regarding the genre of this story. Is it a story about actual historical events? Is it a parable? Is it something else? A similar story, in which the roles of a rich man and a poor man are reversed in the afterlife, has been found in ancient Egyptian sources, but that story also differs in several important

46. For a fuller discussion of the issues involved, see Marshall 1978a, 614–17.

ways from the parable. In short, Jesus is not merely retelling a familiar folktale here.[47]

Some commentators see the story as simply another parable despite its differences with the known parables of Jesus.[48] Darrell Bock, on the other hand, considers it an "example story," a subclass of parables. An example story "teaches a lesson through comparison of a graphic hypothetical situation with true life."[49] He explains further:

> Calling the account an example story implies that its details about the afterlife are graphic portrayals, not necessarily actual descriptions of the afterlife. This does not mean that there is no afterlife or no place like Hades. It means that the conversations are simply part of the story's literary means to depict the great chasm in the afterlife between the righteous in paradise and those in Hades. Such a separation is permanent.[50]

The point is that we should not be using the story of the rich man and Lazarus to construct a geographical map of the underworld as some authors have done.[51]

The story makes a number of important points. By means of this story, Jesus teaches his followers that God does not approve of those who live in a self-indulgent way demonstrating no care or concern for others. Jesus also teaches that our eternal destinies cannot be changed once the final judgment has been made. The rich man no longer has the opportunity to repent once he has been cast into Hades. Finally, Jesus makes the important point that those who will not hear the word of God will not change their minds on account of miraculous signs. Those who desire to escape the rich man's fate are to forsake similar behavior and turn to Jesus while there is still opportunity.

Chapter 17 contains instructions to the disciples on various matters of discipleship as well as a discourse on the coming of the kingdom. Jesus begins by warning the disciples against false teaching that leads to sin (17:1–3a). He then instructs them on the necessity of forgiving repentant brothers (vv. 3b–4). On the issue of faith, Jesus tells the disciples that what

47. Morris 1988, 275; Bock 1996, 1362.
48. E.g., Geldenhuys 1952; Marshall 1978a; Morris 1988.
49. Bock 1996, 1363.
50. Bock 1996, 1363.
51. E.g., Larkin 1921, 88. See his chart "The Underworld."

is important is not the quantity of faith but its quality (vv. 5–6). He then instructs them about the nature of obedience to God. Jesus' disciples must understand that God does not owe them anything for doing what they are supposed to be doing (vv. 7–10).

After describing the healing of ten lepers, nine of whom miss the significance of what has happened (17:11–19), Luke turns to Jesus' words concerning the kingdom of God (vv. 20–37). This discourse is occasioned by a question from the Pharisees who ask Jesus when the kingdom of God would come (v. 20a). Jesus responds, "The kingdom of God is not coming with signs to be observed, nor will they say, 'Look, here it is!' or 'There!' for behold the kingdom of God is in the midst of you" (vv. 20b–21). When Jesus says that the kingdom of God is not coming "with signs to be observed," he is saying that its arrival does not involve the apocalyptic signs expected by so many first-century Jews.[52]

Jesus' final statement concerning the kingdom has been the source of much debate. What does Jesus mean when he says, "the kingdom of God is in the midst of you" (v. 21)? Several interpretations have been suggested. Many have taken the phrase to mean that the kingdom of God is "inside you." This is unlikely considering the fact that nowhere else in the New Testament is the kingdom spoken of as something internal. As I. Howard Marshall observes, "Jesus speaks of men entering the kingdom, not of the kingdom entering men."[53] Some have understood the phrase to mean that the kingdom of God is "within your grasp."[54] While this interpretation is possible, it is more likely that the meaning of the phrase is that the kingdom of God is "in your presence" or "among you." In other words, the Pharisees do not need to be looking here and there for the kingdom because it is present here and now in the person and work of Christ right before their eyes.[55]

After addressing the Pharisees, Jesus gives a lengthy discourse to his disciples (17:22–37). The interpretation of this passage is made more difficult by questions related to the parallels among the Synoptic Gospels. In Matthew and Mark, there is only one extended eschatological discourse, the Olivet Discourse, and this is paralleled in Luke (Matt. 24–25; Mark

52. Marshall 1978a, 654.

53. Marshall 1978a, 655.

54. E.g., Wright 1996, 469; Fitzmyer 1985, 1161–62; Beasley-Murray 1986, 102–3.

55. See Bock 1996, 1416–17.

13; Luke 21). Luke, however, also includes an extended eschatological discourse here in chapter 17. The difficulty arises for several reasons. First, some of the themes found in the Olivet Discourse in Matthew and Mark are not found in Luke's version of the Olivet Discourse (Luke 21) but in Luke 17 instead. Second, the sequence of the themes in Luke 17 differs from the sequence in Matthew and Mark's Olivet Discourse. Third, some of the content of Luke 17 is unique to Luke. Finally, there is no overlap between any of the content of Luke 17 and Luke's own Olivet Discourse in Luke 21.

Darrell Bock's solution to the problem seems to make the best sense out of the evidence. We know from Luke's prologue that he used sources. Bock suggests that Luke had three sources for his eschatological discourses. The numerous parallels of Luke 17 and 21 with Matthew 24–25 indicate that Luke shared a source with Matthew. Luke apparently also had access to the form of the discourse found in Mark, but chose not to use it extensively. Finally, Luke also had a unique source that included two eschatological discourses. Luke chose to follow this source and include two discourses in his gospel. He chose not to repeat the material he included in chapter 17 in his form of the Olivet Discourse.[56]

Jesus begins this eschatological discourse with a statement unique to Luke's gospel, "The days are coming when you will desire to see one of the days of the Son of Man, and you will not see it" (17:22). Throughout the Old Testament, the phrase "the days are coming" is used in prophetic announcements.[57] By using this opening phrase, Jesus makes it clear that what he is about to announce is prophecy. The phrase "days of the Son of Man" is unique to Luke 17, and is found only in verses 22 and 26. Its meaning is disputed. One of the more plausible suggestions is that the phrase is equivalent to the Jewish phrase "the days of the Messiah" (i.e., the period of the Messiah's reign).[58] If that is the meaning of the phrase, Jesus is saying that days are coming when the disciples will long for his reign or for his return. One potential difficulty with this interpretation, however, is that after the ascension of Jesus, the disciples understood themselves to be living under his reign (Matt. 28:18; Acts 2:30–36; 17:7).

56. Bock 1996, 1420–23.

57. 1 Sam. 2:31; 2 Kings 20:17; Isa. 39:6; Jer. 7:32; 9:25; 16:14; 23:5, 7; 31:27, 31, 38; 33:14; 48:12; 49:2; 51:47, 52; Amos 4:2; 8:11; 9:13.

58. Marshall 1978a, 658.

If Luke 17:22–24 is compared to the close parallel in Matthew 24:23–27, it appears that what Jesus is saying rather obscurely in verse 22 is that the days are coming when the disciples will desire to see the fulfillment of Daniel 7, namely the coming of the Son of Man.[59] Before this happens, however, the Son of Man must first suffer and be rejected by his generation (Luke 17:25; Mark 8:31). Jesus continues by comparing the days of the Son of Man to the days of Noah and the days of Lot (Luke 17:26–30). The days of Noah and Lot were days when divine judgment fell upon a population that was ignoring warnings of impending judgment. The parallels in Matthew indicate that Luke's "days of the Son of Man" are the years leading up to the destruction of Jerusalem (Matt. 24:37–39).

Jesus' warning in Luke 17:31 parallels the warning given to those who see the abomination of desolation in Matthew 24:17–18 and Mark 13:15–16. Luke 17:32–34 has no parallels in the other synoptic accounts of the Olivet Discourse, although verse 33 is similar to Mark 8:35. And although Luke 17:34 does not have an exact parallel in the other synoptic accounts of the Olivet Discourse, it is similar in content to verse 35, which does have a parallel in Matthew 24:41. Finally, at the conclusion of his discourse, the disciples ask, "Where, Lord?" and he says, "Where the corpse is, there the vultures will gather" (Luke 17:37). Jesus' answer is paralleled in Matthew 24:28. In summary, Luke 17:22–37 is speaking of the difficult years leading up to the judgment of Jerusalem in A.D. 70.[60]

59. Again it must be emphasized that the reference to the coming of the Son of Man in Daniel 7 is not a reference to the second coming of Jesus. It refers to all that is entailed with Christ's accession to the throne of his kingdom and his heavenly judgment of the beasts/nations. With hindsight, we know that the fulfillment of Daniel 7 did not occur in one day but included a number of events stretching from the resurrection and ascension to the destruction of Jerusalem in A.D. 70.

60. It should be noted that if Luke 17:22–37 is a unified discourse, then it lends support to our argument that all of the Olivet Discourse refers primarily to first-century events. As we have seen, some argue that Matthew 24:36 and Mark 13:32 are turning points in their respective accounts of the Olivet Discourse with the passages before the turning point referring to first-century events and the passages after the turning point referring to still future events (France 1985, 347; 2002, 541). In Luke 17:22–37, however, one finds material that is placed after the supposed turning point in Matthew and Mark located before material that precedes the turning point. Luke 17:22–24 contains material that is paralleled in Matthew 24:23–27 (pre–turning point). Luke 17:26–30 contains material that is paralleled in Matthew 24:37–39 (post–turning point). Luke 17:31 then contains material that is paralleled in Matthew 24:17–18 (pre–turning point). Luke 17:35 contains material that is paralleled in Matthew 24:41 (post-turning point). Luke 17:37 concludes with material that is paralleled in Matthew 24:28 (pre–turning point). If Matthew and Mark contain such a clear turning point, then Luke's sequencing of this material in chapter 17 needs to be explained. If our interpretation of

The final chapters in Luke's account of the journey toward Jerusalem focus on issues such as prayer and the nature of the kingdom. In the parable of the persistent widow, Jesus teaches his disciples that they are always to pray persistently and not lose heart (18:1). His parable illustrates a basic point: If a wicked judge will respond to persistent appeals, how much more will our loving God respond (vv. 2–6)? Jesus concludes by asking, "And will not God give justice to his elect, who cry to him day and night? Will he delay long over them? I tell you, he will give justice to them speedily. Nevertheless, when the Son of Man comes, will he find faith on earth?" (vv. 7–8).

Jesus' response raises two significant questions. What does he mean when he says God will give justice to his elect "speedily"? And what does he mean when he asks whether there will be faith on earth when the Son of Man comes? If these verses are related in any way to the previous context, which concerned the coming days of trouble leading up to the judgment on Jerusalem, then that context will help explain this text. The Greek words translated "speedily" in the ESV are *en tachei*. On the basis of the use of these words in the LXX (Josh. 8:18–19; Ps. 2:12; Ezek. 29:5; Sir. 27:3), some have suggested the translation "suddenly." However, in the New Testament, *en tachei* can also mean "soon" (Acts 25:4; Rom. 16:20; 1 Tim. 3:14; Rev. 1:1; 22:6). If the context of Luke 17 is significant, then the words should probably be translated "soon." If so, the justice God will give his elect will involve the judgment of Israel in A.D. 70.

When the Son of Man comes, will he find faith on earth (18:8)? Jesus' question presupposes the kind of difficult trials and tribulations implied in 17:22. Such trials and tribulations could tempt the disciples to give up faith and hope despite Jesus' exhortation to pray and not lose heart (18:1; see also Matt. 24:22). The question does not imply either a negative or a positive answer. It is part of an ethical exhortation to stand fast in the faith and to pray continuously. To what then is Jesus referring when he says, "When the Son of Man comes . . ."? As we have already seen in our study of Matthew, when Jesus uses these words he is alluding to Daniel 7:13–14,

---

Matthew 24–25 is largely correct, then Luke's discourse is explainable. Jesus simply spoke of the same coming judgment more than once and used many of the same phrases and illustrations each time he taught on the subject. Luke recounts two discourses. Matthew and Mark record only one. If all of the material in both of the discourses has a largely first-century reference, then Jesus would have had no reason to be concerned with always keeping the material in the same order.

a prophecy in which the Son of Man comes to the Father to receive his kingdom. It is not a prophecy of the second coming. Here too, Jesus is asking whether his disciples will remain steadfast in their faith throughout the difficult years leading up to the destruction of Jerusalem.[61]

In Jesus' next parable he continues to reflect on prayer and faithfulness (Luke 18:9–14). He tells the story of two men who went to the temple to pray, a Pharisee and a tax collector. The Pharisee prays in a self-exalting manner, thanking God that he is not like other (sinful) men. The tax collector, on the other hand, simply cries out, "God, be merciful to me, a sinner!" According to Jesus, it is the tax collector who left the temple justified. The point of this parable is to emphasize the necessity of humility before God. Prideful self-righteousness and comparison of oneself to others will not stand before a holy God.

The remainder of Luke 18 is paralleled in the other synoptic gospels. The discussion of children and faith (18:15–17) is found in Matthew 19:13–15 and Mark 10:13–16. The story of the rich young ruler (vv. 18–30) is found in Matthew 19:16–30 and Mark 10:17–31. Jesus' passion prediction (vv. 31–34) is paralleled in Matthew 20:17–19 and Mark 10:32–34. Finally, the healing of the blind beggar (vv. 35–43) is paralleled in Matthew 20:29–34 and Mark 10:46–52. Because we have already discussed these texts in our study of Matthew, we will not repeat the discussion here.

Luke 19 begins with a story unique to this gospel, the story of Zacchaeus (19:1–10). The story shows Jesus again reaching out and interacting with a hated tax collector. The story also demonstrates what the proper response

61. If there is any use of this phrase by Jesus in the New Testament that could possibly refer to his future second coming, this use of the phrase in Luke 18:8 would be a likely candidate. Jesus says, "When the Son of Man comes, will he find faith on earth?" It is not difficult to see why some would say that the question itself strongly implies that this coming of Jesus is from heaven to earth, where he will see if there is any faith remaining. While this interpretation cannot be rejected out of hand, the immediate and broader context seems to require that Jesus is using this phrase in the same way he uses it elsewhere, namely to refer to the fulfillment of the Daniel 7 prophecy. First, in the same verse (18:8), Jesus says that God will not delay and that he will give justice to his elect "soon." He then speaks of the coming of the Son of Man. If this coming is the second coming, the indication that it will occur "soon" is inexplicable. Second, the immediately preceding context is a discourse concerning the judgment on Israel and Jerusalem that would occur in a few decades (17:22–37). As we have seen in our study of Matthew, Jesus speaks of the coming of the Son of Man (not the second coming) in connection with the destruction of Jerusalem. Third, Jesus does not have to come to earth to find out whether there is faith on earth, so there is no reason this use of the phrase cannot be understood in the same manner as its other uses. In short, Jesus is asking, "When Daniel 7:13–14 is fulfilled and Jerusalem is judged, will there be any faithful disciples remaining?"

to Jesus should be: joy and true repentance. In Luke 19:11–27, Jesus tells a parable that is similar in many ways to the parable of the talents in Matthew 25:14–30. It is spoken in a different setting, however, indicating that Jesus told different versions of the same story in different settings to different people. Most traveling preachers do. The point of the parable is the same as that of the parable in Matthew 25, namely the need for the disciples to remain faithful and watchful.

All four gospels tell the story of the triumphal entry (Luke 19:28–40; Matt. 21:1–9; Mark 11:1–10; John 12:12–19). Jesus' lament over Jerusalem in Luke 19:41–44, however, is unique to Luke's gospel. Luke writes:

> And when he drew near and saw the city, he wept over it, saying, "Would that you, even you, had known on this day the things that make for peace! But now they are hidden from your eyes. For the days will come upon you, when your enemies will set up a barricade around you and surround you and hem you in on every side and tear you down to the ground, you and your children within you. And they will not leave one stone upon another in you, because you did not know the time of your visitation."

Jesus mourns the fate of the ancient city of Jerusalem here (cf. 2 Kings 8:11–13; Jer. 9:1; 14:17). His lament is a prophetic oracle of woe. The judgment oracle is similar to several Old Testament oracles of judgment (Isa. 29:1–4; Jer. 6:6–21; Ezek. 4:1–3). Because Jerusalem did not know the time of her visitation, she will now be visited with judgment.

Jesus in Jerusalem (Luke 19:45–21:38)

Having arrived in Jerusalem, Jesus faces several controversies before he is eventually arrested and executed. His first act upon entering the city is to go to the temple where he proceeds to drive out the moneychangers (19:45–48; Matt. 21:12–13; Mark 11:15–19). The chief priests and scribes as well as other leaders in the city seek to destroy him (Luke 19:47). The leaders make three different attempts to trap Jesus with questions regarding his authority (20:1–8; Matt. 21:23–27; Mark 11:27–33), the paying of taxes to Caesar (Luke 20:19–26; Matt. 22:15–22; Mark 12:13–17), and the resurrection (Luke 20:27–40; Matt. 22:23–33; Mark 12:18–27). Between the first and second challenge, Jesus tells a parable to indicate that God is making his final appeal to these leaders (Luke 20:9–18; Matt. 21:33–46; Mark 12:1–12).

After the third challenge, he asks them a question about their interpretation of Psalm 110 that proves they do not understand the identity of the Messiah (Luke 20:41–44; Matt. 22:41–46; Mark 12:35–37). Finally, Jesus compares the scribes who make an outward show of righteousness with a poor widow who demonstrates the nature of true righteousness (Luke 20:45–21:4; Mark 12:38–44).

Luke's version of the Olivet Discourse is found in 21:5–38. Much of the discourse in Luke parallels the discourse in Matthew and Mark. Luke does add several comments, however, that are of some significance. In Luke 21:5–6, Jesus predicts the destruction of the temple (Matt. 24:1–2). The disciples ask him when these things will happen (Luke 21:7; Matt. 24:3). Jesus begins his answer by first describing general signs including wars, earthquakes, famines, and persecution. These signs do not indicate the nearness of the end (Luke 21:8–19; Matt. 24:4–14).[62]

In his specific description of the destruction of Jerusalem (Luke 21:20–24), Luke makes clear what the parallel accounts mean when they speak of the mysterious "abomination of desolation" (Matt. 24:15; Mark 13:14). Where the other gospel authors speak of this "abomination," Luke says, "When you see Jerusalem surrounded by armies, then know that its desolation has come near" (21:20). This prophecy was fulfilled when the Roman armies surrounded Jerusalem in the war of A.D. 66–70 that led up to the destruction of the city and temple.

Luke's final words in this section are also significant. He writes concerning the Jews, "They will fall by the edge of the sword and be led captive among all nations, and Jerusalem will be trampled underfoot by the Gentiles, until the times of the Gentiles are fulfilled" (21:24). The prophecy is a fulfillment of the curse described in Deuteronomy 28:64. It is a prophecy of another exile similar to the Old Testament prophecies concerning the judgment of Israel and her exile (Isa. 5:5; 63:6, 18; Jer. 20:4; 21:7). Jesus says that Jerusalem will be trampled "until the times of the Gentiles are fulfilled." These words seem to set a time limit to this new exile, this new judgment of Israel. These words also suggest that Israel is not cast off permanently. In other words, Jesus holds out hope here that Israel will eventually turn to God.[63]

62. As we saw in our study of Matthew's version of the Olivet Discourse, these general signs are likely representative of the entire interadvent age.

63. The apostle Paul will develop this theme in greater detail in Romans 11.

Following his description of the coming judgment of Jerusalem, Jesus describes the coming of the Son of Man, the fulfillment of Daniel 7 (Luke 21:25–28; Matt. 24:29–31). He then uses the lesson of the fig tree to urge the people to understand the importance of what he is telling them (Luke 21:29–33; Matt. 24:32–35). Luke's account of the Olivet Discourse closes with Jesus' exhortation of his disciples to be constantly vigilant and watchful (Luke 21:34–36; Matt. 24:36–44).

The Passion Narrative (Luke 22:1–23:56)

As in the other gospels, Luke's account of Jesus' story reaches its climactic point in the passion narrative. It is here that redemptive history reaches its decisive turning point. With the death of the Messiah, the promise made so long ago to the first man and woman is finally fulfilled. The Messiah's heel is bruised, but in the process, he crushes the serpent's head (Gen. 3:15). The fundamental problem in creation since the fall has been sin. At the cross, we witness God's solution to that problem as God's Servant is wounded for our transgressions and crushed for our iniquities (Isa. 53:5). All of the shadowy types found in the Old Testament sacrifices are fully and finally fulfilled here at the cross as the true Lamb of God dies as an atonement for the sins of his people. The importance of the passion narrative to understanding God's eschatological plan cannot be overstated.

The passion narrative of Luke, as in the other gospels, begins with Judas's betrayal of Jesus to the chief priests and scribes who were seeking a way to kill Jesus. For a fee, he promised to betray Jesus to them (Luke 22:1–6; Matt. 26:2–5; Mark 14:1–2). Luke then turns to Jesus' Last Supper with the disciples (vv. 7–38). The disciples are instructed to prepare a room in which they will observe the Passover (vv. 7–13; Matt. 26:17–19; Mark 14:12–16). At the Passover meal, Jesus institutes the Lord's Supper (Luke 22:14–23; Matt. 26:26–29; Mark 14:22–25). He tells the disciples that those who would be greatest among them are to be servants and not seek to exercise lordship over the others (Luke 22:24–30). Jesus then warns Peter that Satan is seeking to destroy his faith (vv. 31–32). When Peter confidently asserts that he will die for Jesus if necessary, Jesus tells him that very soon he will deny that he even knows Jesus (vv. 33–34; Matt. 26:30–35; Mark 14:26–31). Before they leave the upper room, Jesus tells the disciples that he is about to fulfill the prophecy of Isaiah 53:12 and be numbered with the transgressors. In other words, he is declaring to them that he is the Suffering Servant of Isaiah 52:13–53:12.

After leaving the upper room, Jesus and the disciples go to the Mount of Olives to pray (Luke 22:39–46; Matt. 26:36–46; Mark 14:32–42). While there, Jesus is betrayed by Judas and arrested (Luke 22:47–53; Matt. 26:47–56; Mark 14:43–50). He is taken before the high priest where he is mocked (Luke 22:54–65; Matt. 26:57–68; Mark 14:53–65). On the following morning, he is brought before the assembly of the elders and convicted of blasphemy (Luke 22:66–71; Matt. 26:59–66; Mark 14:55–64). Jesus is then taken before both Pilate and Herod, and Pilate finally sentences him to be crucified (Luke 23:1–25; Matt. 27:1–2, 11–26; Mark 15:1–15).

Luke's account of Jesus' crucifixion is narrated in a series of steps. The journey to Golgotha is described first (23:26–32). Luke then provides his account of the crucifixion itself (vv. 33–38). Jesus' conversation with the thieves is recounted in verses 39–43. Finally his death is described (vv. 44–49). As Bock explains, "The entire presentation shows that Jesus is in control of events. He dies as an innocent sufferer who is able to save those who turn to him."[64] Luke alone contains the two declarations of Christ's innocence, one by the thief and one by the centurion (vv. 41, 47). They recognize what the people failed to see. The account of Christ's death is then followed by a brief description of his burial (vv. 50–56).

While on the cross, one of the thieves says, "Jesus, remember me when you come into your kingdom" (v. 42). Jesus replies, "Truly, I say to you, today you will be with me in paradise" (v. 43). There is some dispute regarding the thief's understanding of the afterlife. Does he mean "Remember me when you take the throne of your kingdom," whenever that may be? Or does he mean "Remember me when you go through death into your kingdom in the next world"?[65] Regardless of how the thief understood or misunderstood the nature of Christ's kingdom, Jesus assures the thief that he will be with him that very day. In other words, the thief will be with Jesus after his death.

64. Bock 1996, 1836.

65. For a discussion of the textual issues involved see Metzger, *TCGNT*, 154; Bock 1996, 1869.

The Resurrection (Luke 24:1–53)

The final chapter of Luke's gospel narrates the events of the resurrection and ascension of Jesus. This chapter, along with Acts 1, marks the transition from the story of Jesus to the story of his disciples and their ministry.[66] The first subsection of Luke's resurrection narrative is Jesus' appearance to the women at the tomb (24:1–12). The women find the stone rolled away from the mouth of the tomb and discover that Jesus' body is no longer inside (vv. 1–3). Two angels appear to them and announce that Jesus has risen. He had promised that he would be raised from death, and the promise has been fulfilled (vv. 4–8). The women report all of this to the disciples, but the disciples do not believe them (vv. 9–11). Peter, however, runs to the tomb to see for himself and is amazed that the tomb is empty (v. 12).

The second subsection of the resurrection narrative recounts Jesus' discussion with two disciples on the road to Emmaus (24:13–35). As the two disciples are walking on the road and talking with each other about all that has happened, Jesus comes alongside them, but they do not recognize him immediately (vv. 13–16). Jesus asks them what they are discussing, and they tell him about all that has occurred over the last several days (vv. 17–24). He responds, "O foolish ones, and slow of heart to believe all that the prophets have spoken! Was it not necessary that the Christ should suffer these things and enter into his glory?" (vv. 25–26). He then begins to go through Scripture and explain to the two disciples how the Scriptures spoke about the Messiah (v. 27). The focus on the fulfillment of Old Testament prophecy demonstrates that God's plan is being fulfilled. As they approach the village, the two disciples urge their guest to stay with them. As they are dining, Jesus breaks bread and gives it to them. When he does so, their eyes are opened, and they recognize him, but he suddenly vanishes (vv. 28–32). The two disciples immediately return to Jerusalem and report what has happened to the others (vv. 33–34).

In the final subsection of the resurrection narrative, Jesus appears to all of the disciples (24:36–53). As they are discussing the report of the two disciples, Jesus appears in their midst (v. 36). They believe they are seeing a ghost, but Jesus shows them his hands and feet and tells them to touch his body in order that they might know that he has flesh and bones and is not a spirit. In other words, the body that was raised is the body that was

66. Green 1997, 832.

crucified (vv. 37–40). Jesus then asks the disciples if they have any food. They offer him a piece of fish, and he eats it (vv. 41–43). After eating, Jesus speaks to the disciples, saying, "These are my words that I spoke to you while I was still with you, that everything written about me in the Law of Moses and the Prophets and the Psalms must be fulfilled" (v. 44; Matt. 5:17). He then begins to explain the Scriptures, saying, "Thus it is written, that the Christ should suffer and on the third day rise from the dead, and that repentance and forgiveness of sins should be proclaimed in his name to all nations, beginning from Jerusalem" (Luke 24:46–47). Everything from Christ's suffering to the mission of the apostles was prophesied in the Old Testament.[67] God's people, then, are given a role in the fulfillment of God's eschatological plan.

Jesus tells his disciples that he is sending the promise of the Father upon them, but they are to remain in the city until they are clothed with power from on high (v. 49). Luke's resurrection narrative ends with a brief account of the ascension. Jesus then leads the disciples out to Bethany and blesses them (v. 50). While blessing them, he is carried up into heaven (v. 51). The disciples return to Jerusalem with great joy, and we are told that they were continually in the temple blessing God (vv. 52–53).

Summary

Like Matthew, the gospels of Mark and Luke tell the story of Jesus of Nazareth, and while there is much that is similar in these gospels, each author looks at the story from a slightly different perspective. As we have seen, Matthew focuses on the idea of fulfillment. Jesus is the fulfillment of the Old Testament promises and prophecies. Mark and Luke also note that Jesus is the fulfillment of the Old Testament promises and prophecies, but each writer has different emphases. Mark's focus is on the identity of Jesus and the reason for his deeds. Mark reveals that Jesus is the long-awaited Messiah. He does the things he does because he has been sent on a mission to seek and save the lost. He is the Messiah, but he is also the Suffering Servant who must be rejected by Israel and die for the sins of his people.

Luke sets the story of Jesus within a larger context, including it with the Acts of the Apostles. In doing so, Luke indicates that his narrative is the completion of the entire biblical narrative. The Old Testament story of

67. Bock 1996, 1941.

Israel reaches its climactic point in the story of Jesus, but the story continues as Jesus' ministry is carried forward by his followers after his death and resurrection. The "end" toward which the Old Testament looked includes the time of Jesus but also extends into the time of the church. Seen from this angle, Luke's emphasis on the nature of true discipleship and the significance of missions is understandable. Because Luke looks ahead to the age following Christ's ascension, he places great emphasis on what it means to live as a true disciple of Christ in this age prior to the consummation. A true disciple reflects the character of Christ and proclaims the gospel of Christ to all people. The kingdom of God is thereby extended through the missionary work of Christ's disciples.

12

The Gospel of John

All four of the New Testament gospels are biographical works that tell the story of Jesus, but even a cursory reading will reveal that the gospel of John is somewhat different from the other three gospels. Matthew, Mark, and Luke share much of the same content and generally follow the same geographical outline. While John does follow the broad narrative outline found in the Synoptic Gospels, his work is also unique in some ways. Unlike Matthew, Mark, and Luke, John begins his gospel with a prologue identifying the incarnate Christ with the eternal Logos. John's gospel also includes accounts of Jesus' early ministry in Judea and Jerusalem as well as several lengthy discourses that are not recorded in the Synoptics. John's gospel also leaves out content that is found in the other gospels. John's gospel, for example, does not include an account of Jesus' baptism, temptation, or transfiguration. It also does not include any account of the Olivet Discourse or the institution of the Lord's Supper. The differences between John's gospel and the Synoptics do not mean that his work is incompatible with theirs. In fact, the four gospels are all complementary and mutually reinforcing.[1]

1. Carson and Moo 2005, 258–59. For questions related to the historicity of John's gospel, see Blomberg 2001.

The Gospel of John

It is difficult to date the gospel of John with any precision, and dates have been suggested from before A.D. 70 to the second half of the second century. The evidence that exists points to a date of composition some time between A.D. 80 and 95.[2] The question of the gospel's authorship is in some ways even more complicated than the question of its date. Although the fourth gospel is anonymous, traditionally it has been attributed to the apostle John, the son of Zebedee. While this position has been strongly challenged in many quarters, the evidence does appear to support the traditional view.[3] On the face of it, questions about the purpose of John's gospel are much clearer. The purpose of the gospel is stated by the author himself in the text: "Now Jesus did many other signs in the presence of the disciples, which are not written in this book; but these are written so that you may believe that Jesus is the Christ, the Son of God, and that by believing you may have life in his name" (John 20:30–31). In short, the author of the gospel writes with an overarching evangelistic purpose. His goal is to persuade his readers of the true identity of Jesus that they might believe in him.

The distinctive eschatological contribution of John's gospel requires a preliminary comment. John emphasizes what has been called "realized eschatology."[4] In other words, John emphasizes the truth that blessings associated with the end time can be experienced in the present because of the work of Christ.[5] This does not mean, however, that he excludes future eschatology. It simply means that his emphasis lies elsewhere. The advent of Jesus is for John the turning point of redemptive history. It is not, however, the end of redemptive history. It is also of the utmost importance to realize that in John's gospel, eschatology is inseparable from Christology. Eternal life, the life of the age to come, can be experienced now, but it is found only in Jesus the Messiah, who is himself the resurrection and the life.

The basic structural outline of the gospel of John is rather uncomplicated, and most commentators observe the same divisions within the text. John

2. See Kruse 2003, 30–32. Late-second-century dates have now been ruled out by the discovery of a fragment of John's gospel in Egypt dating from approximately A.D. 130 (see Carson and Moo 2005, 273).

3. For helpful overviews of the evidence, see Morris 1971, 8–30; Guthrie 1990a, 252–83; Keener 2003, 1:81–115; Carson and Moo 2005, 229–54.

4. Brown 1966, cxvii; Dodd 1965, 7; Keener 2003, 1:321.

5. Burge 1987, 116; Morris 1989, 143; Kruse 2003, 42.

begins with a prologue (1:1–18). The main body of the text is then divided into two large sections. The first section is commonly referred to as the Book of Signs and covers Jesus' public ministry (1:19–12:50). The second is commonly referred to as the Book of Glory and covers Jesus' farewell discourse and the passion narrative (13:1–20:31). The gospel then closes with an epilogue (21:1–25).

The Prologue (John 1:1–18)

The Synoptic Gospels begin their narratives with the birth of Jesus or with the ministry of John the Baptist. The gospel of John, on the other hand, literally begins "in the beginning," before creation, with one who was with God and who was God. The prologue to the gospel of John is the key to understanding the gospel as a whole. As Ben Witherington explains, "Throughout the Gospel, knowing where the Son of God came from and where he is going is the key to understanding who he is, and thus is also a key to understanding why so many misunderstand and reject him."[6] By tracing the story of Jesus to its ultimate origins in eternity, John reveals the importance of what he is about to say and what he is about to call on his readers to believe.[7]

The prologue begins with some of the most profound words in all of Scripture: "In the beginning was the Word, and the Word was with God, and the Word was God" (1:1). The words "In the beginning" (*en archē*) are a clear echo of the first words of Genesis. As A. T. Lincoln observes, John here links the life of Jesus "to the beginning of the world and beyond that to the life of the Creator."[8] The words hint at the fact that with the advent of Christ, a new beginning has come. The meaning of the term "Word" (*logos*) has been the topic of much discussion.[9] In the Old Testament, the "word" (Heb. *dabar*) is associated with creation and revelation (e.g., Ps. 33:6; Jer. 1:4). In the Old Testament, the "word" is also personified (e.g., Isa. 55:11).[10] "In short," as D. A. Carson explains, "God's 'Word' in the Old Testament is his powerful self-expression in creation, revelation and

6. Witherington 1995a, 47.

7. Ridderbos 1997, 40.

8. Lincoln 2005, 93.

9. For an introduction, see *NIDNTT*, 3:1081–1119; see also Morris 1971, 115–26; Keener 2003, 1:339–63.

10. See also Proverbs 8:22–36, in which "wisdom" is personified.

salvation, and the personification of that 'Word' makes it suitable for John to apply it as a title to God's ultimate self-disclosure, the person of his own Son."[11]

John continues, "The Word was with God" (*ho logos ēn pros ton theon*). Although the preposition *pros* often means "toward" when used with the accusative, it is not accurate to say, as some commentators do, that the words in John 1:1 literally mean "the Word was toward God."[12] The preposition *pros* has a wider range of meaning, and the context determines that meaning.[13] In many contexts, the preposition simply means "with" (e.g., Matt. 13:56; Mark 6:3; 9:19; 14:49; Luke 9:41; 1 Thess. 3:4; 2 Thess. 2:5; 3:10). Here in John 1:1, the context indicates that the best translation is "the Word was with God." In other words, the Word (*logos*) is in close relationship with God yet also distinct from God. This, however, is not all that John has to say about the relationship between the Word and God.

Not only was the Word *with* God in the beginning, "the Word was God" (*theos ēn ho logos*). John does not simply say that the Word was "divine." The Greek word meaning "divine" is *theios*. John does not say this. He identifies the Word with God (*theos*). Some have attempted to minimize the startling character of John's statement, arguing that because there is no definite article before the word "God" (*theos*), the Word is being identified here as *a* god.[14] In other words, the lack of a definite article means that the word *theos* must be translated as an indefinite noun.

Such a determination, however, cannot be made simply on the basis of the absence of the definite article. In John's prologue alone, a form of the word *theos* occurs eight times, and only twice does it occur with the definite article (1:1, 2). Yet, in the other six cases, there is no question that the reference is definite.[15] Furthermore, it is not uncommon in the New Testament for

11. Carson 1991, 116. It is also worth noting Dodd's observation (1965, 85) that "many of the propositions referring to the Logos in the Prologue are the counterparts of rabbinical statements referring to the Torah." This becomes more significant in verse 17 (see Pryor 1992, 123).

12. Morris 1971, 75–76.

13. See BDAG, s.v. πρὸς, 874–75.

14. Today the most outspoken proponents of this view are the Jehovah's Witnesses. The New World Translation of the Holy Scriptures, published by the Watchtower Society, translates these words, "the Word was a god."

15. The New World Translation demonstrates its theological bias by its inconsistent translation. The two articular instances of *theos* are consistently translated "God." The six anarthrous (i.e., without the article) instances of *theos*, on the other hand, are translated inconsistently. The anarthrous *theos* is translated "God" four times, "a god" one time, and "the . . . god" one time.

a predicate nominative lacking the definite article and preceding the verb to be definite (e.g., Matt. 27:42; John 1:49; 3:29; 10:2; Acts 13:33; Rom. 1:16; 1 Cor. 1:18; 4:4; Heb. 1:10). The significance of John's identification of the Word with God has been summed up well in the oft-quoted words of C. K. Barrett: "John intends that the whole of his gospel shall be read in the light of this verse. The deeds and words of Jesus are the deeds and words of God; if this be not true the book is blasphemous."[16] John has not only placed the Word in the presence of God in eternity past, but he has also indicated that the Word shares in the very being of God.

John continues his prologue saying, "He [the Word] was in the beginning with God. All things were made through him, and without him was not anything made that was made. In him was life, and the life was the light of men. The light shines in the darkness, and the darkness has not overcome it" (John 1:2–5). The creation motifs continue in these verses as John expands on the idea that the Word is both "with" God and yet somehow also shares in the being of God. The Word was in the beginning with God, yet he was also the one through whom all things were created, the one Genesis 1 identifies as God himself (Col. 1:16–17; Heb. 1:2). He shares in God's creative work. And as was true at the time of creation, the light shines into the darkness and is not overcome by it (John 1:5; Gen. 1:3–4). The Word is the light of the world (John 8:12; 9:5).

John briefly mentions the preparatory mission of John the Baptist (1:6–8) before describing the coming of the Word into the world. He came into the world, but the world did not know him, and he came to his people, but as in the Old Testament his people were recalcitrant and did not receive him (vv. 9–11; Isa. 65:1–5; Jer. 7:22–26). Those who did receive him he gave the right to become the children of God (John 1:12–13). In other words, the Word shares not only in God's creative work, but also in his redemptive work. But who is this Word, this *Logos* who in the beginning was with God and was God, through whom all things were created, and through whom those who believe become children of God? In the final verses of the prologue, we learn that the Word is none other than Jesus Christ.

John writes, "And the Word became flesh and dwelt among us, and we have seen his glory, glory as of the only Son from the Father, full of grace and truth" (v. 14). The entire final paragraph of the prologue (vv. 14–18)

16. Barrett 1960, 130.

echoes the imagery of Exodus 33–34 where God reveals his character to Moses in the context of a second giving of the law.[17] John now reveals that the Word who was with God and who was God "became flesh" (1:14; Phil. 2:7). This can refer to no other than Jesus Christ (John 1:17). John tells us that the Word became flesh "and dwelt among us." Here John alludes to the Old Testament tabernacle and temple where God dwelt among his people. Jesus is now the new tabernacle and new temple (2:19). In him God is present with his people.[18] The Old Testament had anticipated that God's glory would be revealed to his people again in the last days (e.g., Isa. 60:1–3). Now John says that "we have seen his glory." The glory of God has been revealed in Jesus. His glory is "glory as of the only Son from the Father."[19] The eschatological plan of God has reached a climactic point in the incarnation of the Word.

The prologue concludes with the words, "And from his fullness we have all received, grace upon grace. For the law was given through Moses; grace and truth came through Jesus Christ. No one has ever seen God; the only God, who is at the Father's side, he has made him known" (John 1:16–18). The meaning of the phrase "grace upon grace" (v. 16) is disputed. The basic meaning of the preposition *anti* is substitution or exchange.[20] As Leon Morris explains, John probably means that "as one piece of divine grace (so to speak) recedes it is replaced by another."[21] But what display of God's grace is replaced by another? The answer is given in verse 17 where John says that the law was given through Moses, but grace and truth came through Jesus. John here contrasts Moses and Jesus because Jesus is the one toward whom the law pointed and in his work it is fulfilled (vv. 1, 14).[22]

The final verse of the prologue (v. 18) is similar to the opening verse in that both contain profound declarations of the deity of Jesus Christ, the incarnate Word of God. John first declares that no one has ever seen God (see also Ex. 33:20; Col. 1:15; 1 Tim. 6:16). He then says that the one who has made God known is "the only God, who is at the Father's side."

17. Keener 2003, 1:405.

18. Walker 1996, 168.

19. For a discussion of the meaning of the term *monogenēs*, translated "only Son," see Morris 1971, 105; Carson 1991, 128; Keener 2003, 1:412–16; Kruse 2003, 70–71; Köstenberger 2004, 43–44.

20. See BDAG, s.v. ἀντί, 87–88; Wallace 1996, 364.

21. Morris 1971, 110; see also Carson 1991, 132–33.

22. Dodd 1965, 83, 295; Pryor 1992, 8, 123; Witherington 1995a, 53; Beasley-Murray 1999, 16.

There are several textual variants of the phrase translated "the only God" by the ESV. The variants are (1) *ho monogenēs*; (2) *ho monogenēs huios*; (3) *ho monogenēs theos*; and (4) *monogenēs theos*. As Murray Harris demonstrates, the evidence favors the reading *monogenēs theos*.[23] This, however, does not solve all of the problems surrounding this text, because the translation of the phrase *monogenēs theos* is also disputed.[24] Probably the best translation is "God the only Son" (NRSV). John, therefore, says here that God the only Son, who is at the Father's side, has made the invisible God known. Again, this is a clear declaration of the deity of Jesus. This understanding of who Jesus is and where he has come from shapes the remainder of John's gospel.

The Book of Signs (John 1:19–12:50)

The first major section of John's gospel begins with an account of John the Baptist and his testimony concerning Jesus (1:19–34). John the Baptist distinguishes himself from the one who is coming after him. His role is only to prepare the way for the coming Messiah (1:23). He is not the Messiah himself (1:20). When he sees Jesus approaching, he declares, "Behold, the Lamb of God, who takes away the sin of the world!" (v. 29). The entrance of sin into the world at the fall resulted in the curse falling on mankind and all of creation. Throughout all of redemptive history, God has been working toward the goal of dealing finally and conclusively with sin. John's declaration here reveals that the solution to the fundamental problem of sin is Jesus. There is some dispute regarding the background of John's use of the words "Lamb of God."[25] The most likely suggestion, however, is that John is alluding to the imagery found in Isaiah's fourth Servant Song (Isa. 52:13–53:12).[26] In Isaiah, the Servant who bears our sin is compared to a sacrificial lamb that is being led to the slaughter (Isa. 53:4–9). According to John the Baptist, Jesus is this sacrificial lamb.

Following the narrative of the testimony of John the Baptist, the gospel turns to the calling of Jesus' first disciples. After leaving the Baptist to follow Jesus, Andrew goes to his brother Peter and tells him, "We have found the Messiah" (John 1:41). Likewise, Philip goes to Nathaniel and says to him,

23. Harris 1992, 74–82.

24. Harris (1992, 88–90) fills several pages with the translations that have been suggested.

25. For a discussion of the proposed backgrounds, see Keener 2003, 1:452–54.

26. Keener 2003, 1:453; Lincoln 2005, 113; and Brown 1966, 63.

"We have found him of whom Moses in the Law and also the prophets wrote, Jesus of Nazareth, the son of Joseph" (v. 45). When Jesus reveals his knowledge about Nathaniel, the new disciple proclaims, "Rabbi, you are the Son of God! You are the King of Israel!" (v. 49). Jesus then reveals to Nathaniel by means of an Old Testament allusion that the Son of Man is the one mediator between heaven and earth (v. 51; Gen. 28:12, 17).[27] Through this narrative, John adds confirming testimony regarding the true identity of Jesus. He reveals here that Jesus is not only the fulfillment of Old Testament prophecy, but also the fulfillment of all that was symbolized by locations such as Bethel and structures such as the tabernacle and temple.[28]

The Wedding at Cana

John's narrative of Jesus' public ministry begins with an account that is unique to his gospel, the wedding at Cana (2:1–11). Jesus is at this wedding along with his disciples and his mother (vv. 1–2). When his mother comes to him to inform him that the wine has run out, Jesus says, "Woman, what does this have to do with me? My hour has not yet come" (vv. 3–4). This is the first mention in the gospel of the coming "hour." Throughout the first part of the gospel, the hour of Jesus' death and resurrection is said to be "not yet." After the triumphal entry (12:12–19), this hour is said to be present (12:23; 13:1; 17:1). This first reference to the coming eschatological hour of glory indicates that Jesus is following the predetermined plan of his heavenly Father.[29]

Jesus tells some of the servants present at the wedding to fill six stone waterpots with water (2:6–7). He then instructs them to draw from the water pots and take it to the master of the feast. The master of the feast then drinks what has now become wine (vv. 8–9). John writes, "This, the first of his signs, Jesus did at Cana in Galilee, and manifested his glory" (v. 11). The first major section of the book, the Book of Signs, contains seven "signs" as well as seven major discourses.[30] But what does the first

27. Barrett 1960, 61; Brown 1966, 91.

28. See Dodd 1965, 293; Lincoln 2005, 122.

29. Lincoln 2005, 128.

30. The "signs" are found in John 2:1–11; 4:46–54; 5:1–18; 6:1–15; 6:16–21; 9:1–41; and 11:1–57. The seven discourses are found in 3:1–21; 4:1–42; 5:19–47; 6:22–65; 7:1–52; 8:12–59; and 10:1–42.

sign mean? According to Old Testament prophecy the age to come was to be characterized by an abundance of wine (e.g., Isa. 25:6; Jer. 31:12–14; Hos. 14:7; Amos 9:13–14). The miracle at Cana is a sign indicating that with the coming of Jesus the old age is passing and the age to come has dawned.[31] The promise of abundant blessing is beginning to be fulfilled.

The Cleansing of the Temple

John turns next to Jesus' cleansing of the temple in Jerusalem (2:13–22). The Synoptic Gospels teach that Jesus cleansed the temple soon after his triumphal entry and shortly before his crucifixion (e.g., Matt. 21:12–17). John, on the other hand, says in this passage that Jesus cleansed the temple near the beginning of his ministry. Did Jesus cleanse the temple twice? Many commentators argue that this is unlikely.[32] Most of these suggest that John rearranged the chronological account found in the Synoptic Gospels for theological or narrative reasons. A. T. Lincoln, for example, suggests that the placement of the temple incident at the beginning of John's gospel "helps to structure the whole narrative of Jesus' public mission in terms of a major confrontation between his claims and the views of official Judaism."[33] Other commentators rightly argue that it is not impossible to think that Jesus cleansed the temple twice and that John recorded the first instance while the Synoptists recorded the second.[34]

After he has driven out the moneychangers, the Jews confront Jesus and ask him, "What sign do you show us for doing these things?" (John 2:18). Jesus responds, "Destroy this temple, and in three days I will raise it up" (v. 19). The Jews are stunned by this answer because they think Jesus is speaking of the literal temple, which had at the time been under construction for fory-six years (v. 20). John, however, reveals that Jesus is speaking of the temple of his body (v. 22). As C. H. Dodd explains, the main idea in this narrative is the replacement of the old temple with a new one.[35] The temple had been the place of God's unique presence among his

31. Dodd 1965, 299; Kruse 2003, 95.

32. E.g., Brown 1966, 117; Ridderbos 1997, 115; Beasley-Murray 1999, 38–39; Keener 2003, 1:518; Lincoln 2005, 141.

33. Lincoln 2005, 142.

34. E.g., Tasker 1960, 61; Morris 1971, 189–91; Carson 1991, 177–78; Köstenberger 2004, 111. Aside from the mention of John the Baptist, nothing in the first five chapters of John's gospel is included in the Synoptic narratives.

35. Dodd 1965, 301.

people. Now the incarnate Word was the place of God's manifest presence. As such, everything that had been available through the temple was now available through Jesus, the true temple of God.[36] Dodd helpfully sums up the significance of the miracle at Cana and the cleansing of the temple. Both are signs "which signify the same fundamental truth: that Christ has come to inaugurate a new order in religion."[37]

Nicodemus and the Woman from Samaria

The theme of John 2 is expanded upon in the two major discourses found in chapters 3 and 4. In chapter 3, a Pharisee named Nicodemus comes to Jesus intrigued by the signs he has performed (3:1–2). Jesus tells him, "Truly, truly, I say to you, unless one is born again he cannot see the kingdom of God" (v. 3). D. A. Carson explains, "To a Jew with the background and convictions of Nicodemus, 'to see the kingdom of God' was to participate in the kingdom at the end of the age, to experience eternal, resurrection life."[38] Jesus informs Nicodemus here that man is not by nature capable of entering the kingdom.[39] Nicodemus is confused by Jesus' words, so Jesus explains further, "Truly, truly, I say to you, unless one is born of water and the Spirit, he cannot enter the kingdom of God. That which is born of the flesh is flesh, and that which is born of the Spirit is spirit" (vv. 5–6). As Stephen Smalley explains, "The background to this passage lies in the Old Testament (rather than in Hellenism), where the gift of the Spirit—often in association with (cleansing) water—is promised to God's faithful people as a mark of the new age which will arrive in the 'last days.'"[40] The point is that the eschatological age of the Spirit is being inaugurated with the coming of Jesus (Ezek. 36:25–27).

Jesus continues his discourse, telling Nicodemus, "No one has ascended into heaven except him who descended from heaven, the Son of Man. And as Moses lifted up the serpent in the wilderness, so must the Son of Man be lifted up, that whoever believes in him may have eternal life. For God so loved the world, that he gave his only Son, that whoever believes in him should not perish but have eternal life" (John 3:13–16). "Eternal

36. Barrett 1960, 167; Walker 1996, 198.
37. Dodd 1965, 303.
38. Carson 1991, 188.
39. Barrett 1960, 172.
40. Smalley 1998, 256.

life" is literally the life of the coming eschatological age.[41] As Colin Kruse explains, "it is something that may be experienced in part in the present age and will be consummated in the resurrection."[42]

Jesus continues, saying, "Whoever believes in him is not condemned, but whoever does not believe is condemned already, because he has not believed in the name of the only Son of God" (v. 18). The present nature of salvation and judgment expressed here does not mean that John's focus is exclusively with the present. Carson explains:

> This does not collapse the notion of eschatological judgment into present, spiritual experience, since the future judgment remains (5:28–29). Rather, it is in line with the New Testament insistence that the age to come can no longer be set off absolutely from the present age, now that Jesus the Messiah has come. Believers already enjoy the eternal life that will be consummated in the resurrection of their bodies at the parousia; unbelievers stand under the looming wrath of God that will be consummated in their resurrection and condemnation.[43]

Jesus' discourse in chapter 3 emphasizes the realized aspects of eschatology. Eternal life, the life of the age to come, may be experienced now by those who believe in Jesus, but those who are to experience it must be born again, born of God (1:13). One will not inherit eternal life simply by being born a physical descendant of Abraham.

John 4 recounts Jesus' encounter with a woman from Samaria. He encounters the woman at a well in the city of Sychar and asks her for a drink (vv. 5–7). Her surprise that a Jew is speaking with a Samaritan leads him to say, "If you knew the gift of God, and who it is that is saying to you, 'Give me a drink,' you would have asked him, and he would have given you living water" (v. 10). She asks him if he is greater than Jacob who drank from this well, and he says, "Everyone who drinks of this water will be thirsty again, but whoever drinks of the water that I will give him will never be thirsty forever. The water that I will give him will become in him a spring of water welling up to eternal life" (vv. 13–14). Jesus speaks here of the fulfillment of Old Testament prophecy (Isa. 12:3; 44:3; 49:10; 55:1–3).

41. See Morris 1989, 204; Lincoln 1998, 128.
42. Kruse 2003, 43.
43. Carson 1991, 214.

The woman points out to Jesus that her people worship on Mount Gerizim while the Jews worship in Jerusalem (John 4:20). Jesus responds:

> Woman, believe me, the hour is coming when neither on this mountain nor in Jerusalem will you worship the Father. You worship what you do not know; we worship what we know, for salvation is from the Jews. But the hour is coming and is now here, when the true worshipers will worship the Father in spirit and truth, for the Father is seeking such people to worship him. God is spirit, and those who worship him must worship in spirit and truth. (vv. 21–24)

Authentic and true worship is no longer tied to the location of Jerusalem or to the physical temple. Believers must participate in the worship inaugurated by Jesus, who himself is the new temple.[44] The old is being superseded by the new as Christ's advent inaugurates the last days.

Resurrection Now and Not Yet

One of John's few explicitly eschatological passages is found in chapter 5. The occasion is the healing of a lame man at the pool of Bethesda on a Sabbath. Because Jesus heals the man on a Sabbath, the Jews persecute him (5:16). Jesus then says to them, "My Father is working until now, and I am working" (v. 17). The response infuriates the Jewish leaders even more because "not only was he breaking the Sabbath, but he was even calling God his own Father, making himself equal with God" (v. 18). Jesus then says, "Truly, truly, I say to you, the Son can do nothing of his own accord, but only what he sees the Father doing. For whatever the Father does, that the Son does likewise. For the Father loves the Son and shows him all that he himself is doing. And greater works than these will he show him, so that you may marvel" (vv. 19–20). As C. K. Barrett explains, Jesus' point here is that he is what he is "only in humble obedience to and complete dependence upon the Father."[45]

Jesus then says, "For as the Father raises the dead and gives them life, so also the Son gives life to whom he will. The Father judges no one, but has given all judgment to the Son, that all may honor the Son, just as they honor the Father" (vv. 21–23). While the Father is the source of life and

44. Lincoln 2005, 182; Dodd 1965, 316; Barrett 1960, 191.
45. Barrett 1960, 214.

judgment, he has delegated to the Son the authority to raise the dead and to judge. Jesus continues, "Truly, truly, I say to you, whoever hears my word and believes him who sent me has eternal life. He does not come into judgment, but has passed from death to life" (v. 24). Carson rightly observes that this "is perhaps the strongest affirmation of inaugurated eschatology in the Fourth Gospel."[46] The emphasis here is clearly on that which is already true of the believer. He already has eternal life. He has already passed from death to life. In other words, he has already been spiritually resurrected.

Spiritual resurrection is the subject of the following verse, as Jesus continues his discourse, "Truly, truly, I say to you, an hour is coming, and is now here, when the dead will hear the voice of the Son of God, and those who hear will live" (v. 25). The coming hour is the eschatological future age. However, because the Messiah who raises the dead is now here, the eschatological age has already been inaugurated.[47] Jesus says that hour is coming "and now is" (*kai nun estin*). He is referring, therefore, to the life that is given now to the spiritually dead. Barrett explains, "That the dead referred to in this verse are not the physically dead is confirmed by the fact that they are not (like those of v. 28) said to be in the tombs; the aorist participle ἀκούσαντες suggests those who at the time of writing have been vivified by the word of Christ."[48] The resurrection life of the future age reaches back into the present and is available now to the spiritually dead.[49] Believers now receive a foretaste of the resurrection life that they will experience in fullness on the last day.

Jesus says, "For as the Father has life in himself, so he has granted the Son also to have life in himself. And he has given him authority to execute judgment, because he is the Son of Man" (vv. 26–27). Here there is a possible allusion to Daniel 7:13–14, the Old Testament prophecy in which all authority is given to the Son of Man. Jesus continues, "Do not marvel at this, for an hour is coming when all who are in the tombs will hear his voice and come out, those who have done good to the resurrection of life, and those who have done evil to the resurrection of judgment" (John 5:28–29). Unlike verse 25, which speaks of present

46. Carson 1991, 256; see also Beasley-Murray 1999, 76.

47. Beasley-Murray 1999, 76.

48. Barrett 1960, 218.

49. Ladd 1993, 341; Carson 1991, 256.

spiritual resurrection, verses 28–29 speak of the future bodily resurrection of the dead.[50]

It is important to note, as Craig Keener explains, that the future form of verse 28 ("an hour is coming") does not include the present ("and is now here") that is found in verse 25. In other words, John does not teach a completely realized eschatology.[51] George Beasley-Murray helpfully summarizes the teaching of these verses:

> The spiritually dead who "hear" the voice of the Son of God in the days of their flesh and are raised by him to life will hear that voice again, calling them to enter upon the fullness of resurrection life for the kingdom of glory. Similarly those who are deaf to the voice of the Son of God in life must in the end respond to that voice, and rise to hear the word of condemnation pronounced upon them.[52]

The relationship between present and future eschatology is nowhere more intricately connected than it is here in these verses. The resurrection life of the age to come is experienced in part now by believers. They are no longer spiritually dead. Their bodies, however, will die. But on the last day, they will experience the fullness of resurrection life when the voice of God calls them from the grave and their corruptible bodies are raised incorruptible (1 Cor. 15:35–49).

The Bread of Life

John 6 contains the fourth gospel's account of the feeding of the five thousand as well as the Bread of Life discourse. A number of disputed issues are raised in this text, but our focus shall be on its eschatological significance.[53] The feeding of the five thousand is recounted in all of the synoptic gospels as well as by John (6:1–14; Matt. 14:13–21; Mark 6:32–44; Luke 9:10–17). After the miraculous provision of food, the people want to make Jesus king by force, but Jesus withdraws (John 6:15). Jesus then begins explaining to them that he is the Bread of Life come down from heaven (vv. 22–59). Dodd places the discourse in its broader context:

50. Barrett 1960, 219; Brown 1966, 218–21; Bruce 1983, 131–33; Carson 1991, 258.

51. Keener 2003, 1:654–55.

52. Beasley-Murray 1999, 77.

53. The Bread of Life discourse has, for example, been the focus of intense sacramental debates.

"The multitude are prepared to find in Him a second Moses, who will restore the gift of manna. This is set aside. Christ gives something better than manna; He gives bread of life: more than that, He *is* Bread of Life. He is the Ζωοποιῶν. Union with Him is eternal life."[54] Instead of bread that perishes, the people are urged to partake of the food that endures to eternal life (v. 27).

The people's response sets the stage for the remainder of the discourse, which is set in the form of a traditional synagogue homily.[55] The text for the homily is found in John 6:31 where the people say to Jesus, "Our fathers ate the manna in the wilderness; as it is written, 'He gave them bread from heaven to eat.'"[56] Jesus then tells them that it was not Moses who gave them bread from heaven, but the Father (v. 32). In other words, Moses did not give life. Jesus tells them that the bread that comes down from heaven gives life to the world (v. 33). Upon hearing this, the people ask Jesus to give them this bread always (v. 34). Jesus' response is eschatologically significant:

> I am the bread of life; whoever comes to me shall not hunger, and whoever believes in me shall never thirst. But I said to you that you have seen me and yet do not believe. All that the Father gives me will come to me, and whoever comes to me I will never cast out. For I have come down from heaven, not to do my own will but the will of him who sent me. And this is the will of him who sent me, that I should lose nothing of all that he has given me, but raise it up on the last day. For this is the will of my Father, that everyone who looks on the Son and believes in him should have eternal life, and I will raise him up on the last day. (vv. 35–40)

The eternal life that belongs to believers in the present will entail their bodily resurrection on the last day (vv. 44, 54).[57] "Here, as in 5.24–9," Barrett explains, "John balances exactly the two aspects of the Christian life, in present possession and future hope; and there is nothing to indicate that he thought one more important than the other."[58]

54. Dodd 1965, 344.
55. See Borgen 1965 for a full defense of this assertion.
56. Lincoln 2005, 223.
57. Borgen 1965, 168; Carson 1991, 292; Lincoln 2005, 230.
58. Barrett 1960, 244.

Jesus' Conflict with the Authorities

John 7–8 is dominated by the growing conflict between Jesus and the Jewish authorities. The context of the events of chapters 7–8 is the feast of tabernacles. It was the most popular of the stipulated feasts, and significantly for our purposes, it had been associated with eschatological salvation by the prophet Zechariah (Zech. 14:6–8, 16–21). Lincoln explains that during the feast of tabernacles, the men set up booths in which they ate and slept during the first seven days of the feast. "On these days there was a procession to the Pool of Siloam to gather water and four large menorahs were set up in the court of the women, providing light to enable the celebrants to dance there through the night."[59]

In the events described in John 7–8, Jesus is presented as the one who fulfills that which the feast of tabernacles symbolized through its use of water and light. As Jesus teaches in the temple, the people debate his identity amongst themselves. Some oppose him, but others believe (7:14–31). In the context of the symbolism being used, Jesus' words on the last day of the feast carry great weight. He tells the people, "If anyone thirsts, let him come to me and drink. Whoever believes in me, as the Scripture has said, 'Out of his heart will flow rivers of living water'" (vv. 37–38; Zech. 14:8). John informs his readers that Jesus was speaking about the Spirit, who had not been given because Jesus was not yet glorified. John is making the point that the Spirit's work could not begin in full until the death and resurrection of Christ. As Leon Morris puts it, "Calvary is the necessary prelude to Pentecost."[60]

Jesus' words cause division among the people as some are saying he is the Christ while others mock the very idea (John 7:40–44). Jesus declares to them, "I am the light of the world. Whoever follows me will not walk in darkness, but will have the light of life" (8:12). Keeping in mind the symbolism of light used at the feast of tabernacles in the lighting of the four menorahs, Jesus' words are particularly striking (Zech. 14:7). Isaiah had spoken of one to come who would be a light to the nations (Isa. 42:6; 49:6; 51:4). Jesus is the one who fulfills such prophecies. As Beasley-Murray makes clear, "It should not be overlooked that in these sayings Jesus presents himself to the people as Messiah and offers them the blessings associated

59. Lincoln 2005, 242.
60. Morris 1971, 427.

with the messianic age, but in terms quite different from those of popular messianic ideas."[61]

The dispute concerning the identity of Jesus comes to a head in John 8 when Jesus tells the Jewish people that the truth will set them free (8:31–32). They tell him that they are children of Abraham and have never been enslaved (v. 33). Jesus responds by saying that everyone who commits sin is a slave of sin, and he tells them that they are doing the works of their father (vv. 34–38). When they say that Abraham is their father, Jesus says that cannot be because they do not do the works of Abraham. Instead they are of their father the devil (vv. 39–47).

The people protest, but Jesus says, "if anyone keeps my word, he will never see death" (v. 51). At this, the people turn sarcastic, saying that Abraham is dead, and asking Jesus if he thinks he is greater than Abraham (vv. 52–53). Jesus tells them that Abraham rejoiced to see his day (v. 56). When the Jews ask him if he is claiming to have seen Abraham, Jesus says, "Truly, truly, I say to you, before Abraham was, I am" (v. 58). At this the Jews pick up stones to throw at him, but Jesus escapes (v. 59). They pick up stones because Jesus, by referring to himself as "I am," has identified himself as God (see Ex. 3:14). The people of Israel are at a crossroads, and the stakes could not be any higher.

Jesus, the one who brings light and life into the world, the one who is the world's light and life, continues to face rejection in chapters 9–10 of John's gospel. The coming of the light brings salvation, but it also contrasts with the darkness, creating judgment as well.[62] Chapter 9 opens with the story of the healing of a man born blind (9:1–41). His healing results in his being cast out by the Pharisees, but it also results in his salvation (vv. 34–41). The miracle indicates that Jesus is able to open the eyes of the spiritually blind (v. 41).[63] In the Old Testament, the giving of sight was associated with God (Ex. 4:11), and in the prophets it was associated with the Messiah (Isa. 29:18; 35:5; 42:7). Jesus' healing of the man born blind thus identifies him in this context as the divine Messiah.[64]

In his discourse in John 10, Jesus identifies himself as the good shepherd. The background of such language can be found in prophetic denunciations

61. Beasley-Murray 1999, 140.
62. Dodd 1965, 360; Beasley-Murray 1999, 161.
63. Tasker 1960, 122–23.
64. Morris 1971, 475.

of the failed religious shepherds under the old covenant (Isa. 56:9–12; Jer. 23:1–4; 25:32–38; Ezek. 34; Zech. 11) as well as descriptions of God as the shepherd of his people (Pss. 23:1; 80:1; Isa. 40:11). In his discourse, Jesus declares not only that he is the good shepherd, but that he "lays down his life for the sheep" (John 10:11, 15, 17–18). Here, in this final discourse of Jesus' public ministry, he points forward to his passion, to his sacrificial death for his people.[65]

The Raising of Lazarus

The story of the raising of Lazarus from the dead (John 11:1–44) marks the beginning of the transition from the confrontations between Jesus and the Jewish authorities to the narrative of Jesus' suffering and death. Jesus is informed that Lazarus, the brother of Mary and Martha, is ill, and he declares that this illness will be for the glory of God (11:1–4). Jesus purposely waits two days before heading toward Bethany, the home of Lazarus (vv. 5–7). He then informs his disciples that Lazarus has died (vv. 11–16). When he arrives in Bethany, he finds that Lazarus has been in the tomb for four days (v. 17). Martha comes to him saying that if he had been there Lazarus would not have died (vv. 20–21).

Jesus tells Martha, "Your brother will rise again" (v. 23). Martha, thinking that Jesus is speaking of the final resurrection, says to him, "I know that he will rise again in the resurrection on the last day" (v. 24). Jesus then says, "I am the resurrection and the life. Whoever believes in me, though he die, yet shall he live, and everyone who lives and believes in me shall never die. Do you believe this?" (vv. 25–26). Martha responds, "Yes, Lord; I believe that you are the Christ, the Son of God, who is coming into the world" (v. 27). Lincoln explains that by claiming to be the resurrection and the life, Jesus is claiming to be the fulfillment of Jewish eschatological expectations. In claiming to be the resurrection and the life, "Jesus is claiming to be both the one who embodies the power to raise from the dead and the one who is the source of the positive verdict of life."[66]

When Jesus comes to the tomb of Lazarus, he tells those who are nearby to remove the stone from the entrance to the tomb. Martha protests that the smell will be bad after so many days (11:38–39). After the stone is removed,

65. Lincoln 2005, 300.

66. Lincoln 2005, 323; see also Ridderbos 1997, 396.

Jesus prays to the Father and then cries out with a loud voice, "Lazarus, come out" (vv. 41–43). Lazarus then comes out of the tomb, still covered in grave clothes, and Jesus commands those nearby to unbind him and let him go (v. 44). The raising of Lazarus is a resuscitation, for Lazarus has not been raised in a glorified body. He will die again. However, the raising of Lazarus is an anticipation of the final resurrection on the last day.[67] Raymond Brown helpfully explains that "Jesus has given (physical) life as a sign of his power to give eternal life on this earth (realized eschatology) and as a promise that on the last day he will raise the dead (final eschatology)."[68]

The response of those present at the miracle is mixed. Many believe in Jesus (11:45). Others, however, report what has happened to the Pharisees (v. 46). The chief priests and the Pharisees then gather a council and say, "What are we to do? For this man performs many signs. If we let him go on like this, everyone will believe in him, and the Romans will come and take away both our place and our nation" (vv. 47–48). The irony of this statement is rich.[69] That which the chief priests and Pharisees sought to avoid, namely destruction by the Romans, they themselves ultimately caused by their rejection of Jesus. The high priest Caiaphas then says to them, "You know nothing at all. Nor do you understand that it is better for you that one man should die for the people, not that the whole nation should perish" (vv. 49–50). Caiaphas, of course, meant one thing by his statement, but unwittingly, he prophesied truth as well because Jesus would die for his people in a way that Caiaphas did not understand (vv. 51–52).

From this point forward, the Jewish authorities plan to put Jesus to death (11:53). Jesus therefore no longer travels openly among the people (v. 54). Six days before the Passover feast, Jesus comes to Bethany to dine with Lazarus, Mary, and Martha (12:1–2). While they are dining, Mary pours expensive ointment on Jesus' feet and anoints him (v. 3). Jesus tells his disciples that she is anointing him for the day of his burial (v. 7). John's narrative of the triumphal entry of Jesus into Jerusalem follows in 12:12–19. Following his entry, he is approached by some Greeks who wish to see him (vv. 20–21). There is a hint here of the prophesied eschatological gathering of the nations. Jesus says, "The hour has come for the Son of Man to be

67. Barrett 1960, 322.

68. Brown 1966, 437.

69. See Köstenberger 2004, 350.

glorified" (v. 23). From this point forward, Jesus' hour of glory is spoken of as having come.

Jesus continues speaking of his hour, saying, "Now is my soul troubled. And what shall I say? 'Father, save me from this hour'? But for this purpose I have come to this hour. Father, glorify your name" (12:27–28a). A voice from heaven then says, "I have glorified it, and I will glorify it again" (v. 28b). Jesus tells the people, "This voice has come for your sake, not mine. Now is the judgment of this world; now will the ruler of this world be cast out. And I, when I am lifted up from the earth, will draw all people to myself" (vv. 30–32). The judgment of the world is said to be "now" because the hour of Jesus' death has arrived.[70] The eschatological significance of the cross is made clear. Beasley-Murray explains:

> The most vivid expression of the death of Jesus as exaltation ("lifting up") is in vv 31–32, which is also the most notable representation in the Gospels of the death and resurrection of Jesus as the eschatological event which forms the turning point of the ages. It is alike the hour of the judgment of the world, the overthrow of Satan's power, and the exaltation of Christ as Lord of the saving sovereignty of God. As such it is the climax of the work of the incarnate Son to bring the kingdom of God to humankind.[71]

The cross is the place where Jesus' heel is bruised, but ultimately it is the place where the serpent's head is crushed (Gen. 3:15). The final judgment is inaugurated at the cross. The usurper of the kingdom will be cast out, and authority will be transferred to the Son of Man.

The Book of Glory (John 13:1–20:31)

The second major section of the gospel of John is commonly referred to as the Book of Glory. It includes Jesus' farewell discourse, his high-priestly prayer, and the passion narrative. Because the time of Jesus' death has arrived and because he will soon be going back to the Father, he gathers his disciples to prepare them for what is to come. In the farewell discourse, Jesus teaches his disciples that they will share in his sufferings and in the life of the age to come. Jesus tells them that they are to exhibit the true character of those

70. Kruse 2003, 271.
71. Beasley-Murray 1999, 219.

who share in the life of Christ.[72] The discourse itself extends from 13:31 to 16:33. Before revealing the content of the discourse, John sets it in its context in the upper room, where Jesus demonstrates the nature of servanthood by washing the disciples' feet (13:1–20). His humility is to be an example to his disciples, and they are to do as he has done (vv. 14–15).

The Farewell Discourse

Jesus begins his farewell discourse by saying,

> Now is the Son of Man glorified, and God is glorified in him. If God is glorified in him, God will also glorify him in himself, and glorify him at once. Little children, yet a little while I am with you. You will seek me, and just as I said to the Jews, so now I also say to you, "Where I am going you cannot come." A new commandment I give to you, that you love one another: just as I have loved you, you also are to love one another. By this all people will know that you are my disciples, if you have love for one another. (13:31–35)

The heart of what it means to be a disciple of Jesus is to love one another, to have the same love for Jesus' people that he has for them.

When Peter asks Jesus where he is going, Jesus says to him and the other disciples, "Let not your hearts be troubled. Believe in God; believe also in me. In my Father's house are many rooms. If it were not so, would I have told you that I go to prepare a place for you? And if I go and prepare a place for you, I will come again and will take you to myself, that where I am you may be also. And you know the way to where I am going" (14:1–4). The words here appear to allude to events associated with the original conquest of Canaan.[73] On the eve of the conquest, Moses calmed the people's fears about the Canaanites dwelling in the land by saying, "Do not be in dread or afraid of them" (Deut. 1:29; cf. John 14:1). Moses then tells the people that God "went before you in the way to seek you out a place to pitch your tents" (Deut. 1:33; cf. John 14:2). If Jesus is alluding to this Deuteronomic text, the idea is that Jesus goes before his people to prepare a place for them just as God went before the Israelites to prepare a place for them. The question is: what place is Jesus going to prepare and what does he mean

72. Dodd 1965, 398; Keener 2003, 2:893.
73. Brown 1970, 625.

when he says he is coming again? Many commentators understand Jesus to be speaking here of his second advent at the end of history.[74] This is certainly possible, but in light of the larger context, another explanation of his words is also possible.

Craig Keener suggests that the words about the going away and coming again of Jesus in these verses (14:1–4) be understood in the same sense as they are understood in 14:18–19 and 16:16–22.[75] As we shall see, most commentators understand these other passages to be referring to Jesus' departure at his death and his coming again to the disciples at his resurrection. According to Keener, Jesus' words in 14:1–4 should be understood in the same way. In other words, "Jesus is going to prepare them a place in the Father's presence and will return after the resurrection as their way to the Father's presence."[76]

> Jesus makes it plain exactly where he is going in vv. 4–6—to the Father—and in the same verses says that they will end up in the same place by coming through Jesus. After his glorification is complete, he will come to them, manifest himself to them, and impart the Spirit to them so that they may continue in his presence (vv. 7–26). This is the only coming (vv. 18, 23, 28) and dwelling place (v. 23) of which the chapter as a whole speaks.[77]

In other words, Keener argues that in this chapter, Jesus is speaking only of his imminent departure at his death and his coming back to the disciples at his resurrection. By his death and resurrection, Jesus will make it possible for believers to dwell permanently in the presence of God (14:23). In light of the broader context and despite the very real difficulties, Keener's interpretation seems to be the most consistent.

Thomas responds to Jesus' words, saying, "Lord, we do not know where you are going. How can we know the way?" (14:5). Jesus tells him, "I am the way, and the truth, and the life. No one comes to the Father except through me" (v. 6). What is the background of this language about the way? The wisdom literature of the Old Testament speaks often of the way of righteousness or wisdom (Prov. 2:20; 4:11; 8:20; 9:6; 10:29). In addition,

74. E.g., Morris 1971, 639; Carson 1991, 488; Ridderbos 1997, 489; Beasley-Murray 1999, 250; Kruse 2003, 296; Köstenberger 2004, 427; Lincoln 2005, 389–90.

75. Keener 2003, 2:930–38.

76. Keener 2003, 2:930.

77. Keener 2003, 2:938.

Isaiah's prophecies of the eschatological new exodus often use the imagery of a way being prepared by and for God (Isa. 35:8; 40:3; 42:16; 43:16, 19; 49:11; 57:14; 62:10). Jesus may be echoing both types of imagery in his identification of himself as the way.

Jesus' second statement about coming back to the disciples is made in the context of comments concerning the Holy Spirit. Jesus says, "If you love me, you will keep my commandments. And I will ask the Father, and he will give you another Helper, to be with you forever, even the Spirit of truth, whom the world cannot receive, because it neither sees him nor knows him. You know him, for he dwells with you and will be in you" (John 14:15–17). The word translated "Helper" by the ESV is the Greek word *paraklētos*. In general, the word refers to one who acts as an advocate in a legal or forensic context.[78]

Jesus continues, saying, "I will not leave you as orphans; I will come to you. Yet a little while and the world will see me no more, but you will see me. Because I live, you also will live" (14:18–19). Here, as many commentators recognize, in the context of the sending of the Paraclete, Jesus is speaking of his coming to the disciples after the resurrection.[79] Keener explains: "If the disciples keep Jesus' commandments (14:15), especially loving one another to the death (13:34–35), he will send them another Advocate to minister for them in his stead (14:16–17). Thus, when Jesus comes to them after the resurrection to give them resurrection life (14:18–19), he will in some sense remain with them—indeed, *in* them (14:20)."[80] In short, what Jesus teaches his disciples in chapter 14 is that his departure to the Father will ultimately be a benefit to them. They will continue to enjoy the presence of God, only in a different manner than when Jesus was physically present with them.[81]

The farewell discourse of Jesus continues in chapter 15 with Jesus' discourse on the true vine. He declares, "I am the true vine, and my Father is the vinedresser. Every branch of mine that does not bear fruit he takes away, and every branch that does bear fruit he prunes, that it may bear more fruit" (15:1–2). The background of this imagery is found in the Old Testament descriptions of Israel as a vine or as a vineyard (Ps. 80:8–16; Isa. 5:1–7;

78. Lincoln 2005, 393–94; Keener 2003, 2:956.

79. E.g., Morris 1971, 651; Carson 1991, 501; Keener 2003, 2:973; Lincoln 2005, 395.

80. Keener 2003, 2:971–72.

81. Barrett 1960, 378.

27:2–6; Jer. 2:21; Ezek. 15:2–6; 17:5–10; 19:10–14). Jesus is the true vine. "With Him therefore," as R. V. G. Tasker explains, "a new Israel emerges, the members of which draw their spiritual sustenance from Him alone."[82]

The concluding section of Jesus' farewell discourse begins with a warning about the persecution that will come upon the disciples. Jesus tells his disciples that they will be put out of synagogues and even killed (John 16:1–4). He recognizes that sorrow has filled their hearts because he has told them he is going away (vv. 5–7). Jesus then says, "Nevertheless, I tell you the truth: it is to your advantage that I go away, for if I do not go away, the Helper will not come to you. But if I go, I will send him to you" (v. 7). When the Helper comes, he will convict the world concerning sin and righteousness and judgment (vv. 8–11). In the Old Testament, the coming age was depicted as the age of the Spirit (e.g., Isa. 11:1–10; 32:14–18; 42:1–4; 44:1–5; Ezek. 11:17–20; 36:24–27; Joel 2:28–32). Jesus here informs the disciples that something must occur before the Spirit can come. The age of the Spirit cannot begin until Jesus has died, been raised from the dead, and been exalted to the right hand of the Father.[83] Before the Spirit can be poured out on all believers, the blood of Jesus must be poured out for all believers.

Jesus tells his disciples, "A little while, and you will see me no longer; and again a little while, and you will see me" (John 16:16). The disciples ask each other what this saying means (vv. 17–18). Jesus tells them, "Truly, truly, I say to you, you will weep and lament, but the world will rejoice. You will be sorrowful, but your sorrow will turn into joy. . . . You have sorrow now, but I will see you again and your hearts will rejoice, and no one will take your joy from you" (vv. 20, 22). Jesus is speaking here of the disciples' experience following his death and their experience when they will see him after his resurrection (20:19–29).[84] They will weep at his death, but when he is raised and appears to them, they will rejoice, and no one will be able to take that joy away from them.

The High-Priestly Prayer

Following the farewell discourse is Jesus' high-priestly prayer (17:1–26). In the prayer, Jesus continues to prepare the disciples for their future mis-

82. Tasker 1960, 174.

83. Carson 1991, 533–34.

84. Morris 1971, 702; Carson 1991, 543; Lincoln 2005, 422.

sion to a world that will persecute them. There are three major sections in the prayer.[85] First, Jesus prays for his own glorification (vv. 1–8). Second, Jesus prays for the disciples (vv. 9–19). Third, Jesus prays for those who believe and those who will believe (vv. 20–26). In the first section, Jesus twice asks the Father to glorify him (vv. 1, 5). He says that the Son has been given authority over all flesh (v. 2; Dan. 7:14; Matt. 28:18). In the second section of the prayer, Jesus requests that the Father would keep the disciples in his name (John 17:11), keep them from the evil one (v. 15), and sanctify them in the truth (v. 17). In the final section, Jesus asks the Father that the disciples and those who will believe through their word "may all be one" in order that the world may believe (vv. 20–23). He concludes by asking that those who have been given to him may be with him to see his glory (v. 24). The prayer appears to be a reference to the presence with the Father and Son spoken of elsewhere in the farewell discourse (e.g., 14:3, 20, 23).

The Crucifixion and Death of Christ

With the passion narrative, John picks up again with material that is found in all of the gospels. Jesus' lengthy farewell discourse and high-priestly prayer have prepared the disciples (and the reader) for what is to follow. As Lincoln explains, the death of Christ is the hour toward which everything in the gospel has been moving. Despite all outward appearances, it is the hour of Jesus' glory.[86] The betrayal and arrest of Jesus are narrated in John 18:1–11. His interrogation (and that of Peter) is then recorded in verses 12–27. Following his interrogation by the Jews, Jesus is tried before Pontius Pilate (18:28–19:16). Here the rejection of Jesus by the Jewish authorities reaches its climax, for when Pilate asks them, "Shall I crucify your King?" they respond, "We have no king but Caesar" (19:15). Here they renounce God's kingship and pledge allegiance to their oppressor. John's gospel has repeatedly emphasized that the rejection of Jesus entails the rejection of God. Now, as Lincoln explains, "By proclaiming their loyalty to Caesar as a way of securing Jesus' death, the chief priests end up renouncing their God."[87]

85. Lincoln 2005, 434.
86. Lincoln 2005, 441.
87. Lincoln 2005, 471.

The crucifixion and death of Jesus are recorded in John 19:17–37. Following his death, Joseph of Arimathea and Nicodemus take Jesus' body and bury it in a tomb (vv. 38–42). Dodd has helpfully summarized the redemptive-historical significance of the crucifixion of Jesus the Messiah: "Here is something that happened in time, with eternal consequence. Though individual men may miss its significance, nevertheless the thing has happened and history is different: the whole setting of human life in this world is different. It is an epoch-making event; in history, things can never be the same again."[88]

The Resurrection

John's narrative of the resurrection is in three parts. The discovery of the empty tomb and Jesus' appearance to Mary Magdalene are recorded in 20:1–18. Following this is the narrative of the appearance of Jesus to the disciples (vv. 19–23). At this appearance, Jesus breathes on the disciples and says, "Receive the Holy Spirit" (v. 22). The meaning of this verse has been the subject of much debate, but it appears to be a symbolic giving of the Spirit, with the full gift to come at Pentecost.[89] The third section is the narrative of Jesus' appearance to Thomas and Thomas's confession of the deity of Christ (vv. 24–29). The resurrection narrative concludes with John's declaration of the purpose of the gospel. John has written all of these things that his readers might believe that Jesus is the Messiah, the Son of God, and that by believing they might have life in his name (v. 31).

Epilogue (John 21:1–25)

The gospel of John concludes with an epilogue narrating a third postresurrection appearance of Jesus to some of the disciples.[90] First, he appears to seven of the disciples, providing them with a miraculous catch of fish (21:1–14). As Lincoln explains, this miracle "points beyond itself to the continuation of Jesus' mission through that of the disciples."[91] The second section of the epilogue concerns the rehabilitation of Peter (vv. 15–19).

88. Dodd 1965, 439.

89. See Köstenberger 2004, 574.

90. Many scholars argue that this chapter was added to the original gospel at a later date, but the arguments for this view are rather weak. For a critical discussion of the evidence, see Keener 2003, 2:1219–24.

91. Lincoln 2005, 515.

Peter had denied the Lord three times while Jesus was being interrogated (18:15–18, 25–27). What was to become of him? This section of the epilogue reveals Jesus' restoration of Peter. Peter is instructed to feed the sheep (21:15–17). Jesus then indicates the kind of death Peter would face (v. 18). Peter had declared that he would follow Jesus to death immediately before Jesus had predicted his betrayal (13:36–38). Jesus thus appropriately concludes his words to Peter with the command, "Follow me" (21:19).

The final section of the epilogue concerns the role of the beloved disciple (21:20–24). Peter looks at John and asks Jesus, "Lord, what about this man?" (v. 21). Jesus says, "If it is my will that he remain until I come, what is that to you? You follow me!" (v. 22). As John explains, "So the saying spread abroad among the brothers that this disciple was not to die; yet Jesus did not say to him that he was not to die, but, 'If it is my will that he remain until I come, what is that to you?'" (v. 23). Because this is a postresurrection appearance of Jesus, the coming of Jesus in question is likely his future second advent. Apparently the rumor had arisen during the lifetime of John that Jesus had promised to return before he died. With these words, John lays that rumor to rest. He makes it clear that while Jesus promised to come again, he did not promise to do so before John himself died.[92]

Summary

The primary eschatological emphasis of the gospel of John is that which is already realized. This is because the incarnation of the divine Logos is the turning point of redemptive history. The advent of the Messiah has made the blessings of the last day available in the present. However, while John's primary focus is on realized eschatology, he does not ignore the consummation. The life of the age to come is available now, but it will be received in fullness only at the resurrection on the last day. Believers have been raised from spiritual death, and on the last day, their bodies will be raised from physical death. According to John, the eschatological hour is now here, but it is also coming.

92. Köstenberger 2004, 601.

13

The Book of Acts

Luke's historical account of the history of the early church is the last strictly narrative work in the Scriptures. Most of the letters of the New Testament that follow were written by Paul and others during the events described in Acts.[1] Therefore, just as the Prophets and the Writings of the Old Testament must be understood within the narrative framework provided by the Pentateuch and the historical books, so too must the letters of the New Testament be understood within the narrative framework provided by the book of Acts. As the concluding narratives of Scripture, the Gospels and the book of Acts recount the climactic events of God's redemptive work. The Gospels narrate the life, death, and resurrection of the promised Messiah, and the inauguration of his kingdom. The book of Acts narrates the initial fulfillment of God's plan to bring salvation and blessing to all nations.

1. Paul may have written the Pastoral Epistles during a journey anticipated in Acts but not recorded there. The book of Revelation was written after the events described in Acts (i.e., some time after A.D. 62), but it is not written in the form of a historical narrative and must be dealt with separately.

The Book of Acts

The book of Acts is unique in that it is the only historical account of the first decades of the Christian church. Traditionally, the author of the gospel of Luke and the book of Acts has been understood to be Luke, a companion of Paul during part of his ministry (Philem. 24). Although critical scholars regularly challenge this traditional view today, there is no compelling reason to reject it and much to support it.[2] We have very little definite personal information about Luke himself. However, it is significant to know that if the author of Acts is Luke, a companion of Paul, he would have had access to eyewitnesses of the events he describes.[3] In fact, Luke explicitly mentions his access to eyewitness accounts in the prologue that serves to introduce his two-volume work (Luke 1:1–4).

The original recipient of both the gospel of Luke and the book of Acts is said to be Theophilus (Luke 1:3; Acts 1:1), a man about whom virtually nothing certain is known. He may have been Luke's patron,[4] but until more evidence is uncovered, all such suggestions will be mere speculation. Dating the book of Acts also involves uncertainty. New Testament scholars have suggested dates for the writing of Acts that range from A.D. 62 until well into the middle of the second century.[5] The most plausible suggested dates are those that range from the mid-60s to the mid-80s. A strong case can be made for a date somewhere in the mid-60s.[6]

Luke's prologue to his gospel helps us identify his basic purpose in writing both the gospel itself and the book of Acts. In his prologue, Luke writes:

> Inasmuch as many have undertaken to compile a narrative of the things that have been accomplished among us, just as those who from the beginning were eyewitnesses and ministers of the word have delivered them to us, it seemed good to me also, having followed all things closely for some time past, to write an orderly account for you, most excellent Theophilus, that you may have certainty concerning the things you have been taught. (1:1–4)

2. For an examination of the arguments for and against Lucan authorship, see Carson and Moo 2005, 290–96.

3. Kistemaker 1990, 7.

4. Johnson 1992, 24.

5. For a survey of the evidence for various dates, see Carson and Moo 2005, 296–300.

6. See, for example, Hemer 1989, 365–408.

Luke makes several important points in this prologue. First, he states that his purpose is to write an orderly account of the things that happened. He is aware of other written accounts of these things, and he says that he is among those to whom accounts of these things have been delivered by eyewitnesses. In other words, Luke's primary stated purpose in writing is historical.[7] His books are a record of the climactic events of redemptive history. Second, Luke is providing Theophilus with this historical account in order that he may have certainty concerning the things he has been taught (1:4). In other words, Luke is not writing history for history's sake. He is providing Theophilus with a certain historical foundation for his Christian faith. Luke intends his gospel and the book of Acts to present the true story of Jesus and the early church in order to ground the faith of his readers.

The most basic structural division in the book of Acts is the division between chapters 1–12, which narrate the early apostolic mission to the Jews, Samaritans, and Gentiles in Israel, and chapters 13–28, which narrate Paul's expanded mission to the Gentiles in Asia Minor and Europe. The book of Acts begins with a prologue that ties it to the gospel of Luke (1:1–5). The ascension of Christ and the reconstitution of the twelve apostles are recounted in 1:6–26. Luke then describes the birth of the church in Jerusalem (2:1–5:42) and its growth in the midst of persecution (6:1–9:31). This persecution leads to the spread of the gospel to the Gentiles (9:32–12:25). Luke turns his attention in the second half of the book to the missionary work of Paul. He provides details of Paul's first missionary journey (13:1–14:28) and the Jerusalem Council (15:1–35). Luke continues with an account of Paul's second (15:36–18:22) and third (18:23–21:17) missionary journeys. The events leading up to and including Paul's arrest in Jerusalem are then recounted (21:18–23:35). Luke concludes the Book of Acts with a narrative of Paul's defense before Felix, Festus, and Agrippa in Caesarea (24:1–26:32) and his journey to Rome (27:1–28:31).[8]

The Prologue (Acts 1:1–5)

The prologue to the book of Acts indicates that the book is a sequel to Luke's gospel. It ties the two books together and introduces the events to follow:

7. The historicity of the book of Acts is vigorously denied by skeptical scholars. For a thorough reply to such skepticism, see Hemer 1989.

8. The outline is borrowed, with some adaptation, from Guthrie (1990a, 400–401).

> In the first book, O Theophilus, I have dealt with all that Jesus began to do and teach, until the day when he was taken up, after he had given commands through the Holy Spirit to the apostles whom he had chosen. To them he presented himself alive after his suffering by many proofs, appearing to them during forty days and speaking about the kingdom of God.
>
> And while staying with them he ordered them not to depart from Jerusalem, but to wait for the promise of the Father, which, he said, "you heard from me; for John baptized with water, but you will be baptized with the Holy Spirit not many days from now." (Acts 1:1–5)

Luke here describes his gospel as "the first book," meaning that Acts is a second book. In the first book, Luke deals with what Jesus "began to do and teach," implying that "Acts relates what he continued to do and teach through the agency of his witnesses."[9] Luke informs his readers that Jesus appeared to the apostles over a period of forty days after his death and resurrection. He offered many proofs that he was truly alive (see Luke 24:39–43), and he spoke to them about the kingdom.[10] Jesus also commanded the apostles to wait in Jerusalem for the promise of the Father—the baptism of the Holy Spirit (Acts 1:4–5; Luke 24:49). The reference to Jerusalem is significant because in the gospel of Luke, the narrative moved ever forward toward Jerusalem and the cross. In Acts, the movement will be away from Jerusalem to the ends of the earth.[11]

The Ascension of Christ and the Reconstitution of the Twelve (Acts 1:6–26)

Acts 1:6–8 follows the brief introductory prologue and provides the immediate context for the ascension narrative:

> So when they had come together, they asked him, "Lord, will you at this time restore the kingdom to Israel?" He said to them, "It is not for you to know times or seasons that the Father has fixed by his own authority. But you will receive power when the Holy Spirit has come upon you, and you will be my witnesses in Jerusalem and in all Judea and Samaria, and to the end of the earth."

9. Marshall 1980, 55.

10. As Johnson (1992, 25) observes, the apostles will continue this proclamation of the kingdom throughout the book of Acts (Acts 8:12; 14:22; 19:8; 20:25; 28:23, 31).

11. Johnson 1992, 10.

The apostles have gathered together with Jesus on the Mount of Olives (see Acts 1:12) just east of Jerusalem. The apostles then ask Jesus a question about the kingdom, specifically whether he would "at this time" restore it to Israel.[12] His response is highly significant because it reveals the last words Jesus speaks before his ascension. He does not respond to the apostles' question with a direct yes or no. Instead, he tells the apostles that it is not for them to know "times or seasons." They are not to concern themselves with this question. Knowledge of the time of restoration belongs to God.[13]

Jesus then reminds the apostles of the promise of the Father that they are to await in Jerusalem (1:5). He tells them they will receive power when the Holy Spirit comes upon them. There is a possible allusion here to Isaiah 32:15. David Pao explains that the possible allusion is significant because in its original context, the reference to the outpouring of the Holy Spirit "signifies the dawn of the Isaianic New Exodus."[14] If Jesus is alluding to this text, he is connecting the coming outpouring of the Holy Spirit on the day of Pentecost in some way with the fulfillment of this Isaianic prophecy. This is significant because in Isaiah and other prophets the new exodus is a way of describing the coming restoration of Israel. If Jesus is alluding to Isaiah 32:15 here, then his words indicate that the restoration the apostles have asked him about is in fact coming. It will not, however, occur in the exact manner that nationalistic Jews might be expecting.

Jesus then gives the apostles their last commission, telling them they will be his witnesses in Jerusalem, Judea, Samaria, and to the end of the earth.[15] Again there are possible allusions to Isaiah (Isa. 43:10; 49:6). As Pao explains: "Acts 1:8 . . . becomes the second part of the response to the question in that it confirms the beginning of the process of the restoration of Israel. This process of restoration is portrayed through the model of the Isaianic New Exodus in which the salvation of the Gentiles becomes part of the program of the reconstitution of Israel."[16]

12. Barrett (2002, 5) explains that this is a "futuristic present." In other words, the apostles are asking, "Are you about to do this now?"

13. Marshall 1980, 59.

14. Pao 2002, 92.

15. Many commentators believe this commission acts as a kind of key to the structure of Acts with the apostles preaching in Jerusalem in Acts 1–7, in all Judea and Samaria in 8:1–11:18, and to the ends of the earth in 11:19–28:31 (see, for example, Bruce 1988a, 36–37).

16. Pao 2002, 95–96.

In short, the restoration of Israel will involve the fulfillment of the task that has been given to the apostles to accomplish. The restoration of Israel will involve their bearing witness to Christ not only in Israel but to the ends of the earth. Their commission introduces a theme that is important throughout the book of Acts, namely the progress of the gospel and the expansion of the church. The gospel of Jesus will be taken from Jerusalem to the very ends of the earth.[17]

The account of Jesus' last words to the apostles is immediately followed by the account of the ascension (Acts 1:9–11). Because of its eschatological significance, it is necessary to look at this brief account in some detail. The entire account is told very succinctly in three verses:

> And when he had said these things, as they were looking on, he was lifted up, and a cloud took him out of their sight. And while they were gazing into heaven as he went, behold, two men stood by them in white robes, and said, "Men of Galilee, why do you stand looking into heaven? This Jesus, who was taken up from you into heaven, will come in the same way as you saw him go into heaven."

Why is the account of the ascension found at this point in the narrative? What is Luke's purpose? At the most basic level, as we have seen, Luke's purpose is to write an accurate account of what happened at Jesus' final appearance to his apostles after the resurrection. The ascension narrative in Acts 1, therefore, is presented as a straightforward historical narrative.

Luke does not provide this account, however, simply to satisfy our historical curiosity. The ascension account also forms an important part of Luke's overall narrative purpose. In the context of Luke's broader narrative (Luke-Acts), this historical account of the ascension serves as a transition point, a hinge, as it were, between the Gospels and Acts, between the time of Jesus and the time of the Spirit. It is informative to observe, for example, the frequency of the term *pneuma* ("spirit") in each of the gospels in com-

17. Brian Rosner (1998, 233) makes some important points regarding the progress of the gospel and the expansion of the church in Acts: "In describing the progress of the word in Acts several general points may be made: (1) It is not progress in the triumphalistic sense that Acts portrays (*contra* Conzelmann), for opposition and persecution are pervasive and enduring; (2) the Jewish element of the mission is not removed, as might be suggested by the simple formula of the word going from Jews in Jerusalem to Gentiles in Rome; (3) God is repeatedly given the credit for progress—it is divinely ordained, planned, guided and supported expansion; and (4) the progress theme functions to include the reader in the task of spreading the word, especially with the open-ended ending of the book."

parison to its frequency in Acts. In Matthew, the word *pneuma* occurs 19 times; in Mark, 23 times; in Luke, 36 times; in John, 24 times. In Acts, however, the word is used 70 times, indicating the change in emphasis. Jesus explained to his disciples, "it is to your advantage that I go away, for if I do not go away, the Helper will not come to you. But if I go, I will send him to you" (John 16:7). According to Jesus, then, his departure (Acts 1) is a necessary condition for the sending of the Holy Spirit (Acts 2).[18] It makes perfect sense, therefore, for Luke to introduce the era of the Spirit with the account of Jesus' ascension.

The ascension also provides a turning point in the apostles' understanding of the kingdom of God. Jesus had appeared to the apostles over the previous forty days, speaking to them about the kingdom of God (Acts 1:3). Just prior to the ascension, the apostles had asked Jesus a question about the kingdom: "Lord, will you at this time restore the kingdom to Israel?" (Acts 1:6). After Jesus' ascension, whatever confusion may have remained in the apostles' minds regarding the kingdom had been dispelled. From the ascension onward, they are found confidently proclaiming the kingdom of God (Acts 8:12; 14:22; 19:8; 20:25; 28:23, 31). They are found proclaiming that Christ is now King (Acts 17:7; see also 2:36). The same proclamation is found in the books these apostles wrote after the ascension (Col. 1:13; Heb. 12:28; Rev. 1:6, 9). The book of Acts begins (1:3) and ends (28:31) on the subject of the kingdom. The ascension of Christ is what cemented the apostles' understanding of this key doctrine.

The account of the ascension follows immediately upon the account of Jesus' last words to the apostles. Jesus has just said to them that they will be his witnesses to the end of the earth. Luke continues: "And when he had said these things, as they were looking on, he was lifted up, and a cloud took him out of their sight" (Acts 1:9). Luke connects verse 9 to the previous text with the conjunction *kai* ("and") and two participles: the aorist participle *eipōn* ("after he said," or "when he had said") and the present participle *blepontōn* ("while they were looking," or "as they were looking"). As C. K. Barrett observes: "The contrast between aorist and present participles is intentional and significant. Jesus has now said all that he has to say to his disciples. The promise of the Spirit and the commission to act as witnesses complete his work on earth. The disciples however are still looking at him,

18. Johnson 1992, 30.

and are thus able to vouch for his ascent into heaven."[19] The participle *blepontōn* is a form of the verb *blepō*, which in general simply refers "to the capacity to see, of sense perception."[20] Of course, the meaning of any word is determined by its context, so the question is whether the meaning of *blepō* in the context of Acts 1:9 refers literally to perception with the eye or figuratively to some kind of spiritual perception.

Significantly, the ascension is not presented as a visionary experience. It is presented very simply as an observable historical event in the same category as the other events in the life of Jesus.[21] Furthermore, in addition to the verb *blepō*, Luke uses several other synonymous terms throughout this brief account to describe the visibility of the event. In addition to using a form of the word *blepō* twice in these three verses, Luke also uses the words *atenizō* (1:10) and *theaomai* (1:11). The normal meaning of all of these words involves literal sight. In other words, the visibility of the ascension is strongly emphasized by Luke.[22]

Luke tells us that after Jesus had said these things (Acts 1:6–8), and while they were looking on, "he [Jesus] was lifted up." The verb is the passive form of *epairō*, which simply means "to cause to move upward, *lift up*, *hold up*."[23] In other words, what Luke is describing in this passage is the visible upward motion of a person. Luke concludes verse 9 with the statement "and a cloud took him out of their sight." What does this phrase mean? The first question that must be answered in connection with the interpretation of this phrase is the precise meaning of *kai*, the Greek conjunction translated "and." The question is whether *kai* is being used here as a simple connective conjunction or as an explicative (epexegetical) conjunction.[24] In other words, is the intended meaning: "he was lifted up, *and then* a cloud took him out of their sight" (connective)? Or is the meaning: "he was lifted up; *that is*, a cloud took him out of their sight" (explicative)? In terms of what Luke says the apostles witnessed, the question is whether they saw Jesus ascend a certain distance and then disappear from their sight when he reached the cloud (ascension *to* a cloud) or whether they saw the cloud

19. Barrett 1994, 81.
20. *NIDNTT*, 3:515.
21. Metzger 1968, 82; Barrett 1994, 81.
22. Fitzmyer 1998, 208.
23. BDAG, s.v. ἐπαίρω. The passive voice does not alter the meaning of the verb.
24. BDF, 227–28 (§442); Robertson 1923, 1181–83; BDAG, s.v. καὶ.

appear to actively lift Jesus upward a certain distance before he disappeared from their sight (ascension *in* or *with* a cloud).

The only way to determine which meaning is most likely intended by Luke is to examine the context. The strongest contextual evidence for the connective interpretation is the fact that Acts 1:11 clearly states that the apostles saw Jesus going. If the explicative interpretation requires us to say that Jesus himself was not visible at all during his ascent, then the clear statement in verse 11 would seem to rule out that possibility. The strongest evidence in favor of the explicative interpretation is the apparent meaning of the verb *hypelaben* in verse 9. This is a form of the verb *hypolambanō*. According to the BDAG lexicon, the verb is used in Acts 1:9 in the sense of "to cause to ascend, take up."[25] This use of the verb would seem to imply that the cloud acted as "the vehicle of ascent."[26]

There does not appear to be enough evidence to determine conclusively whether *kai* is connective or explicative. There is some support for both views. What is important to note is that either interpretation is perfectly consistent with the remainder of the narrative. If *kai* is connective, then the apostles saw Jesus ascend to a certain point (the cloud) at which he was no longer visible to them. If *kai* is explicative, then the apostles saw Jesus ascend in and with the cloud to a certain point after which he was no longer visible to them.[27] Regardless of which interpretation is chosen, verse 9 cannot be used to say that the apostles did not see Jesus go when verse 11 explicitly says the apostles did see Jesus go.

The final question we must ask in connection with Acts 1:9 concerns the significance of the cloud. Some have seen in the reference to the cloud allusions to the biblical account of the ascension of Elijah (2 Kings 2:11) or to noncanonical accounts of the ascension of Moses.[28] While it is possible that Luke intends to bring these accounts to mind, the most obvious biblical allusion is to the glory cloud. Throughout the Old Testament, the glory cloud is used to describe and signify the presence of God (Ex. 13:21–22; 14:19–20; 19:16; 24:15–18; 33:9–10; 40:34–37; 1 Kings 8:10–11; Pss. 78:14; 99:7; 105:39; Isa. 4:5; 19:1; Ezek. 1:4). Most likely,

25. BDAG, s.v. ὑπολαμβάνω.

26. Johnson 1992, 27; Marshall 1980, 61.

27. The contextual evidence appears to favor slightly this interpretation.

28. See, for example, Josephus, *Ant.* 4.8.48 §326.

the cloud in Acts 1:9 is the same glory cloud described throughout the Old Testament.[29]

The closest Old Testament parallel to what is described in Acts 1:9 is Daniel's vision of the Son of Man (Dan. 7:13–14). Daniel describes a vision in which he sees one like a "son of man" coming with the clouds of heaven up to the Ancient of Days to receive a kingdom. As we have seen in our study of the Gospels, Jesus regularly refers to himself as the Son of Man (e.g., Matt. 11:19; 16:13; 17:9; 20:28). He also speaks often of the Son of Man coming with clouds (e.g., Matt. 24:30; 26:64; Mark 13:26; 14:62; Luke 21:27). As we have argued, when Jesus speaks of the coming of the Son of Man, he is deliberately alluding to Daniel 7 and speaking of the inauguration of his kingdom. In Acts 1:9–11, we have an account of Jesus ascending into heaven and a reference to a cloud taking him. On the day of Pentecost, Peter will declare that when Jesus ascended into heaven he was seated at the right hand of God and made both Lord and Christ (Acts 2:22–36). Since Daniel's vision is a vision of one coming with the clouds to the Ancient of Days in heaven and receiving his kingdom, it appears that the ascension of Christ is a fundamental part of what Daniel foresaw.

Luke continues in Acts 1:10, "And while they were gazing into heaven as he went, behold, two men stood by them in white robes." Luke explains here what happened while Jesus ascended. He begins the verse with the phrase "And while they were gazing" (*kai hōs atenizontes ēsan*). The word *hōs* is a temporal conjunction simply meaning "while." The following word *atenizontes* is used with the verb *ēsan* as a periphrastic participle, which is translated "they were gazing."[30] This word is a form of the verb *atenizō*, which means to "look intently at" or to "stare at" something or someone.[31] This word is used fourteen times in the New Testament, and "in each NT use (all but two of which occur in the Lucan writings) *atenizō* seems to emphasize the intensity of the look."[32] Again, Luke is emphasizing the fact that the apostles were witnessing something objectively visible.

29. Bruce 1988a, 38.

30. Barrett 1994, 82.

31. BDAG, s.v. ἀτενίζω.

32. *NIDNTT*, 3:520. Aside from its occurrence in Acts 1:10, this verb is also found in the following texts: Luke 4:20; 22:56; Acts 3:4, 12; 6:15; 7:55; 10:4; 11:6; 13:9; 14:9; 23:1; 2 Cor. 3:7, 13.

The apostles are said to be gazing "into heaven" (*eis ton ouranon*). This is the first of four uses of this exact phrase in verses 10–11.[33] The Greek word *ouranos* is used in a number of ways in Scripture. It can be used, for example, to refer to the transcendent dwelling place of God (e.g., Heb. 8:1). It can also be used to refer to that part of creation distinct from the earth, namely, the sky (e.g., Matt. 8:20; Heb. 11:12).[34] In Acts 1:9–11, these two meanings tend to overlap to some degree because of the very nature of the ascension as a transition between the visible and invisible dimensions of existence, but the emphasis is on that which is objectively visible.

It is unlikely that *ouranos* is being used in these verses to mean the transcendent abode of God, angels, and deceased saints for at least two reasons.[35] First, in two of the four places where the phrase is used in these verses, the apostles are said to be "looking" into heaven (v. 10; v. 11a), and in one place they are said to have seen Jesus go into heaven (v. 11b). Since Luke does not present the ascension event in terms of a visionary experience in which the witnesses "see the heavens opened" (e.g., Acts 7:56; 10:11; Ezek. 1:1) or in which they have their eyes opened to something that is normally invisible (e.g., 2 Kings 6:17), it seems likely that the term *ouranos* is being used to refer to the visible sky. Second, if the apostles actually saw Jesus go into the normally invisible dwelling place of God at this point, then Luke's claim that "a cloud took him *out of their sight*" (Acts 1:9) becomes inexplicable because it would have the apostles both seeing and not seeing the same thing at the same time. It is true that the ultimate destination of Jesus' ascension is the right hand of God in the heavenly places as explained elsewhere in Acts (Acts 2:32–33), but the ultimate destination does not appear to be what is described in the text of Acts 1:9–11. These verses describe that which was objectively visible to all.

The apostles stood there on the mountain gazing intently as Jesus went. The Greek word translated "went" is *poreuomenou*, the participial form of *poreuomai*. This participle is translated "as he went" in the ESV. It could

33. The third of the four uses of this phrase is not found in some Greek manuscripts. Its accidental omission, however, is more readily explainable than its accidental insertion, so all four instances of the phrase are likely original. For the textual evidence, see *TCGNT*, 245.

34. Some English translations (e.g., NASB, NIV, NAB) cause confusion by translating the four instances of this word in Acts 1:10–11 in two different ways. Other English translations (e.g., KJV, NKJV, RSV, ESV) rightly translate all four instances of the word in the same way.

35. Although it must be noted that this is the way the editors of the BDAG lexicon chose to categorize its use in Acts 1:10 and 1:11; see BDAG, 739.

also be translated "while he went." The word *poreuomai* is quite common in the New Testament, being used about 150 times. Although it is sometimes used figuratively to mean the way one lives or conducts himself (e.g., Acts 14:16; 1 Peter 4:3) and is even used on occasion to mean "die" (e.g., Luke 22:22, 33), it is normally used in the literal sense "to go, proceed, or travel."[36] Luke is using the word here in its normal sense.[37]

While the apostles are intently watching, two men (*andres duo*) in white clothing suddenly appear standing beside them. The appearance of the two men immediately brings to mind the appearance of the two men at Jesus' transfiguration (Luke 9:30) as well as the appearance of the two men in "dazzling apparel" at the empty tomb of Jesus (Luke 24:4).[38] The two men who appear at the transfiguration are identified as Moses and Elijah. The two men who appear at the empty tomb are not specifically identified. Are the two men who appear to the apostles at the ascension Moses and Elijah, or are they two other men, or two angels? The text does not explicitly tell us, so any one of these is a possibility.[39]

Luke concludes the ascension account in Acts 1:11 with the words the two men speak to the apostles. They say, "Men of Galilee, why do you stand looking into heaven? This Jesus, who was taken up from you into heaven, will come in the same way as you saw him go into heaven." The verb translated "looking" is a participial form of the verb *blepō*, the same verb used in verse 9, emphasizing once again the visibility of the ascension event. The question asked by the two men indicates that the apostles are continuing to look upward toward the sky. The two men ask them why. Jesus has commanded the apostles to await the promise of the Father in Jerusalem. He has told them that they will be his witnesses to the end of the earth. In other words, he has given them their marching orders. The necessary implication of the commands Jesus gives the apostles in Acts

36. BDAG, s.v. πορεύω. BDAG provides this definition: "to move over an area, gener. with a point of departure or destination specified." See also *NIDNTT*, 3:946.

37. Quite obviously neither of the other two meanings would make any sense in this context. The apostles were not gazing into heaven as Jesus "went about his life." Nor were they gazing into heaven as Jesus died. They were gazing into heaven as he departed, as he went from them.

38. The same words (*andres duo*) are used to describe both of these other appearances.

39. Jewish tradition asserted that both Moses and Elijah had ascended to God. (Of course, Scripture explicitly affirms that Elijah ascended; see 2 Kings 2:11–12. The alleged ascension of Moses is found only in noncanonical Jewish sources.) In addition, the Greek word *andres* usually refers to human beings rather than angels.

1:4–8 is that his return will not be immediate. Therefore, the apostles should not be standing there looking into the sky. They should be in Jerusalem awaiting the outpouring of the Spirit. They have much work to do.[40]

The two men follow their question with this assertion: "This Jesus, who was taken up from you into heaven, will come in the same way as you saw him go into heaven."[41] The words *houtos ho Iēsous* ("This Jesus") stress continuity. It is this Jesus and no other who will come. The word *analēmphtheis* is an adjectival participle translated "who was taken up."[42] The two men state that this same Jesus who has been taken up from them "will come." They do not say *when* he will come, only *that* he will come.[43] No time frame is given. The word translated "will come" is *eleusetai*, the future indicative form of the verb *erchomai*. This verb is used almost six hundred times in the New Testament, making it one of the most frequently used words in the Bible. It is most often used to describe "movement from one point to another, with focus on approach from the narrator's perspective."[44] In other words, its usual meaning is "to come." This is especially evident in cases such as Acts 1:11 where it is used opposite a form of *poreuomai*, which means "to go." The statement by the two men, then, is a clear promise regarding Jesus' second coming.

The next issue addressed by the two men in white is the manner of Christ's coming. They tell the apostles that Jesus will come "in the same way as you saw him go into heaven" (lit. "will come thus, in the manner you saw him going into heaven").[45] The word *houtōs* is an adverb meaning "in this way." The construction *hon tropon* is a compound adverbial phrase corresponding to *houtōs*. It means "in the manner in which" or "just as."[46] The use of *houtōs* together with *hon tropon* serves to emphasize the point that Jesus will come in the same way that he departed. So, in what manner did he depart?

40. Barrett 1994, 84.

41. Greek, οὗτος ὁ Ἰησοῦς ὁ ἀναλημφθεὶς ἀφ᾽ ὑμῶν εἰς τὸν οὐρανὸν οὕτως ἐλεύσεται ὃν τρόπον ἐθεάσασθε αὐτὸν πορευόμενον εἰς τὸν οὐρανόν.

42. BDAG, s.v. ἀναλαμβάνω.

43. Fitzmyer 1998, 211.

44. BDAG, s.v. ἔρχομαι.

45. Johnson 1992, 27.

46. BDAG, s.v. τρόπος. For other uses of this construction in the New Testament, see Matt. 23:37; Luke 13:34; Acts 7:28; 15:11; 27:25; 2 Tim. 3:8.

First, it should be observed that the primary emphasis throughout these verses is on the visible manner of the ascension event. The ascension of Jesus occurred "as they were *looking* on" (v. 9). As Jesus departed, they were "*gazing*" intently (v. 10). The two men in white ask the apostles why they are standing there "*looking* into heaven" (v. 11). And it is explicitly asserted that the apostles "*saw* him [Jesus] go into heaven" (v. 11). There is little more Luke could have said to describe an event that was objectively visible. Second, the ascension involved Jesus' resurrected body. The apostles are talking to the resurrected Jesus immediately prior to the ascension. They are not having a collective visionary experience. They are not talking to the incorporeal spirit of Jesus (Luke 24:39). Jesus is standing before them in his resurrected body, and he ascends as they look on. Third, and finally, Jesus departed in or with the glory cloud.

The two men in white tell the apostles that Jesus will come in the same manner that they saw him go. Since Jesus departed visibly and bodily in or with the glory cloud, the manner in which he will come will likewise be visible and bodily and accompanied by the glory cloud.[47] It must be noted, however, that the two men do not say that the immediate circumstances of Christ's coming will be the same as the immediate circumstances of his going.[48] Since the ascension and second coming have different purposes in the outworking of redemptive history, we would expect there to be different surrounding circumstances. The ascension of Christ is part of the nexus of events (e.g., the resurrection, the ascension, the destruction of Jerusalem, etc.) that marks the inauguration of the kingdom, while the second coming of Christ is part of the nexus of events (e.g., the second coming, the general resurrection, the final judgment, etc.) that marks the consummation of the kingdom. Acts 1:11 simply affirms that Christ will come in the same manner that he ascended. Acts 1:11, by itself, does not provide details regarding the specific circumstances surrounding his return.

A final comment must be made regarding the common claim that the traditional interpretation of Acts 1:9–11 necessitates the adoption of a false three-tiered understanding of the universe as well as the idea that heaven is located at some physical point somewhere in space. This objection is frequently raised in the writings of skeptics, scholarly and otherwise, who

47. Kistemaker 1990, 57; Barrett 1994, 84.

48. As an example of what I mean by immediate circumstances, it is not necessary that the eleven apostles be standing on the Mount of Olives when Jesus returns.

then conclude that the ascension narrative is a myth or a legend.[49] But does a traditional interpretation of Acts 1:9–11 require the belief that heaven is located somewhere in the sky above the clouds? The answer is no.

As Bruce Metzger explains, "the ascension, properly understood, has no more to do with Ptolemaic astronomy than does the incarnation."[50] Jesus did not have to physically ascend into the sky in order to enter the invisible heavenly dimension of existence.

> Though Jesus did not need to ascend in order to return to that sphere which we call heaven, yet in fact he did ascend a certain distance into the sky, until a cloud took him out of sight. By such a miraculous sign he impressed upon his followers the conviction that this was now the last time he would appear to them, and that henceforth they should not expect another manifestation, but should realize that the transitional period had ended.[51]

Metzger concludes, "At Jesus' final appearance to his followers he rose from their midst, not because he had to do so in order to go to the Father, but for didactic reasons, in order to make his last act symbolically intelligible."[52] In other words, Jesus could have "ascended" to the right hand of the Father without moving at all. He could have simply vanished and immediately entered into the heavenly sphere of existence. But he didn't. He chose instead to do something that would dramatically symbolize the end of the transitional period to his apostles.

Jesus' visible physical ascension symbolized other truths as well. It clearly demonstrated to the apostles that he was going back to where he was before (John 6:62). It also visibly indicated that he was going to receive his kingdom (Dan. 7:13–14). The fact that the action was symbolic, however, does not mean that it was not real. According to Scripture, Jesus was lifted up a certain distance before he entered the heavenly sphere of existence. We are not told how far Jesus was lifted up, only that he was. This does not mean that heaven, as the dwelling place of God, is located in the sky somewhere above the surface of the earth.

49. E.g., Spong 1993, 90; Harnack 1909, 156–57; Bultmann 1961, 1–3; Funk 1998, 451, 495.

50. Metzger 1968, 84.

51. Metzger 1968, 85–86.

52. Metzger 1968, 86.

Following the ascension, the apostles return from the Mount of Olives to Jerusalem (Acts 1:12). In the narrative that follows, the apostles deal with the problem caused by the treachery and death of Judas (1:13–26). The seriousness of the problem is explained by L. T. Johnson:

> One of those chosen to be among the twelve by Jesus (Luke 6:12–16) and given the authority to preach and to heal (Luke 9:1), as well as to exercise rule over the twelve tribes of Israel (Luke 22:29–30), turned into a traitor with a heart possessed by Satan (Luke 22:3) and led Jesus' enemies to arrest him (Luke 22:47). Luke has made clear from the feeding of the five thousand (9:17) as well as from his prophecy at the last supper (22:30) that the significance of the number twelve was in relation to the restored people of Israel. . . . The betrayal of Judas was therefore more than simply the failure of an individual. It splintered the numerical and symbolic integrity of that group which constituted the beginning and essential authority of the restored people of God. . . . The defection of Judas posed a unique problem and demanded a unique solution. When others of the Twelve died, there would be no need to replace them. Why? Because once the Twelve had definitively been constituted at the heart of the people *and the Spirit bestowed*, the faithful Israel would have come into existence, and the promise of God would have reached fulfillment. This is why Judas had to be replaced before Pentecost, because the integrity of the apostolic circle of Twelve symbolized the restoration of God's people.[53]

Peter stands among those who are gathered in the upper room and tells them that Judas' actions had fulfilled prophecy (Acts 1:15–20). He tells them that one of those who had accompanied the disciples from the time of John the Baptist until the ascension "must become with us a witness to his resurrection" (vv. 21–22; Luke 24:46–48). After prayer, the disciples cast lots and choose Matthias to replace Judas (Acts 1:26).

The Birth of the Church in Jerusalem (Acts 2:1–5:42)

Jesus has promised the disciples that they would be baptized with the Holy Spirit (1:5). He has promised that they will receive power when the Holy Spirit has come upon them (1:8; Luke 24:49). Ten days after the ascension of Christ, on the day of Pentecost, the promise is fulfilled as the

53. Johnson 1992, 38–39.

risen Jesus gives his people the gift of the Spirit. The outpouring of the Holy Spirit is described in Acts 2:1–4:

> When the day of Pentecost arrived, they were all together in one place. And suddenly there came from heaven a sound like a mighty rushing wind, and it filled the entire house where they were sitting. And divided tongues as of fire appeared to them and rested on each one of them. And they were all filled with the Holy Spirit and began to speak in other tongues as the Spirit gave them utterance.

We recall that at the Jordan River, the Father sent the Holy Spirit to his Son Jesus in order to equip him for his ministry (Luke 3:22). Here Jesus sends the Spirit, the gift of the Father, to his followers in order to equip them for their ministry (cf. 2 Kings 2:9–12).[54]

Pentecost publicly marks a major turning point in redemptive history, the transition from the old age to the new, the arrival of the messianic age.[55] The account of Pentecost resembles in some ways the account of the giving of the law at Sinai, another significant development in redemptive history.[56] As Sinclair Ferguson observes, "The revelation of God to Moses at Sinai had been accompanied by fire, wind and a divine tongue (Heb. 12:18–21)."[57] The outpouring of the Spirit is accompanied by similar phenomena. Additionally, by the time of the first century, the day of Pentecost had become the day on which the Jews celebrated the giving of the law on Mount Sinai.[58] At Sinai, God gave the law, which under the terms of the old covenant was written on stone tablets. Now on the day of Pentecost, he gives the Spirit, who under the terms of the new covenant writes the law on the hearts of his people (Jer. 31:31–34). The tongues of fire are an apparent fulfillment of John the Baptist's promise of one to come who would baptize with the Holy Spirit and with fire (Luke 3:16).[59]

Luke tells us in Acts 2:4 that the disciples who were filled with the Holy Spirit began to speak with "other tongues" (*heterais glōssais*). He continues by describing the reaction of the people to these events (2:5–13).

54. Gaffin 1979, 17.
55. Fee 1994, 806.
56. The similarity is particularly evident in the LXX version of Ex. 19:16–18.
57. Ferguson 1996, 61.
58. Johnson 1992, 46; Ferguson 1996, 61.
59. Gaffin (1979,18) suggests that the fire may represent purification (Mal. 3:1–4).

> Now there were dwelling in Jerusalem Jews, devout men from every nation under heaven. And at this sound the multitude came together, and they were bewildered, because each one was hearing them speak in his own language. And they were amazed and astonished, saying, "Are not all these who are speaking Galileans? And how is it that we hear, each of us in his own native language? Parthians and Medes and Elamites and residents of Mesopotamia, Judea and Cappadocia, Pontus and Asia, Phrygia and Pamphylia, Egypt and the parts of Libya belonging to Cyrene, and visitors from Rome, both Jews and proselytes, Cretans and Arabians—we hear them telling in our own tongues the mighty works of God." And all were amazed and perplexed, saying to one another, "What does this mean?" But others mocking said, "They are filled with new wine."

What does Luke mean when he reports that the disciples began to speak in other tongues? The answer is debated. Many argue that the disciples were given the supernatural ability to speak languages they had never learned but which the hearers understood.[60] Others argue that the disciples were engaged in ecstatic utterances.[61] Both of these suggested interpretations have raised almost as many questions as they have answered.[62]

A third possibility has been suggested in an article by Robert Zerhusen.[63] Zerhusen argues that from the text of Acts we can establish the fact that the "other tongues" were human languages (not ecstatic utterances). We also know they were the native languages of the Jewish crowd. From historical sources we learn that the native languages of first-century Jews, whether Palestinian or Diaspora, were Aramaic and Greek. Therefore, Zerhusen argues, the "other languages" spoken by the disciples were Aramaic and Greek, languages both they and the crowd knew. This raises two questions. First, why are Aramaic and Greek referred to as "other languages"? Second, why did the Jewish crowd react with astonishment?

Zerhusen argues that the missing piece in the puzzle is the existence of the phenomenon of "diglossia" among first-century Jews. "Diglossia" refers to the coexistence in a society of two languages, a language of high prestige that is used in more formal situations and a language of lower prestige that

60. E.g., Marshall 1980, 69–70; Kistemaker 1990, 78; Fitzmyer 1998, 239.

61. E.g., Johnson 1992, 42.

62. See Kistemaker 1990, 78–79.

63. Zerhusen 1995.

is used in informal situations.[64] Among first-century Jews, Hebrew was the sacred, holy language, the language of worship. "Other tongues" were languages other than Hebrew.[65] Jews expected to hear the sacred language of Hebrew spoken in the temple liturgy on the day of Pentecost. They were astonished when the disciples began boldly preaching in the "profane" languages of Aramaic and Greek.

The reaction of the Jewish crowd to the disciples' speaking in other tongues prompts Peter to rise and explain the significance of the events to the crowd (Acts 2:14–41). When Peter stands with the other eleven (v. 14), the twelve apostles as a group confront the twelve tribes of Israel—the whole "house of Israel" (see v. 36). Peter declares to the crowd that the disciples are not drunk and that what they are witnessing is the fulfillment of Joel's prophecy (Acts 2:15–21; Joel 2:28–32). Joel had prophesied that the outpouring of the Holy Spirit would occur in the "last days." According to Peter, Joel's prophecy has been fulfilled and those listening to him are now living in the prophesied "last days."[66] The age to come has arrived.

Peter then gives the crowd a brief account of the life, death, and resurrection of Jesus (Acts 2:22–24). He declares that this Jesus, whom the Jewish authorities had recently killed, was resurrected by God because it was not possible for him to be held by death. Peter then argues that in Psalm 16:8–11, where the Lord promises that he would not abandon his Holy One to Hades—the place of the dead, David was speaking of the resurrection of Jesus (Acts 2:25–28). Since David had died and remained buried, he was not speaking of himself in this psalm (v. 29). Instead, speaking prophetically, David foresaw the resurrection of the Messiah (vv. 30–31).[67] Jesus has been raised up and exalted to the right hand of God. Having received the promise of the Spirit from the Father, he has poured out the Spirit on his disciples, and this is what the crowd has witnessed (vv. 32–33). David did not ascend into heaven, so when he wrote Psalm 110:1, he was speaking of the Messiah (Acts 2:34–35). Peter declares, "Let all the house of Israel

64. The phenomenon still exists in several cultures.

65. Hebrew was contrasted with the languages of foreigners in the Old Testament, and Israel was warned that if she forsook God, she would be judged by nations that spoke other languages (Deut. 28:49; Isa. 28:11; Jer. 5:15). In 1 Corinthians 14:21, Paul refers to these prophetic warnings using the word ἑτερογλώσσοις (*heteroglōssois*).

66. Marshall 1980, 68; Bruce 1988a, 60–61; Barrett 1994, 135; Witherington 1998, 140.

67. Fitzmyer 1998, 249.

therefore know for certain that God has made him both Lord and Christ, this Jesus whom you crucified" (v. 36).

When the people hear Peter's sermon, they are cut to the heart and ask the apostles, "Brothers, what shall we do?" (v. 37). Peter tells them, "Repent and be baptized every one of you in the name of Jesus Christ for the forgiveness of your sins, and you will receive the gift of the Holy Spirit" (v. 38). He continues, "For the promise is for you and for your children and for all who are far off, everyone whom the Lord our God calls to himself" (v. 39). As a result of his preaching, approximately three thousand people are baptized (vv. 40–41). Mark Strauss explains the importance of Peter's sermon:

> In summary, in his Pentecost speech Peter uses scriptural proof to demonstrate that Jesus is the messianic king, now enthroned in heaven. Since neither Ps. 16.8–11 nor Ps. 110.1 concern David himself, they must be understood as prophecies concerning the resurrection and ascension-exaltation of Jesus the Christ. Together they represent the fulfillment of God's oath to David to seat his descendant upon the throne of his kingdom forever (Ps. 132.11). Through his death, resurrection and exaltation, Jesus has been vindicated and enthroned as the Davidic messiah, the king of Israel. In this exalted status, he pours out salvation blessings upon his people. All who repent receive forgiveness of sins and the gift of the Holy Spirit (v. 38; cf. 5.31).[68]

With the exaltation of Jesus the Messiah to the right hand of God and the giving of the Holy Spirit at Pentecost, the old age gives way to the new.

Acts 3–5 explains how the early witness of the church began to bring the disciples of Jesus into conflict with the Jewish authorities. The first instance of conflict is occasioned by the healing of a lame beggar (3:1–10). The astonishment of the people leads Peter to speak to them (vv. 11–26). He asks them why they are wondering at this miracle of healing (vv. 11–12) and tells them that it is through Jesus, the one whom they killed, that this lame beggar has been healed (vv. 13–16). Peter then tells them that he knows they and their rulers acted in ignorance, but that God had fulfilled what was spoken by the prophets, namely that the Messiah would suffer (vv. 17–18).

68. Strauss 1995, 147.

Peter's next comment has obvious eschatological significance, but its exact meaning is disputed. Peter tells the gathered crowd of astonished onlookers, "Repent therefore, and turn again, that your sins may be blotted out, that times of refreshing may come from the presence of the Lord, and that he may send the Christ appointed for you, Jesus, whom heaven must receive until the time for restoring all the things about which God spoke by the mouth of his holy prophets long ago" (3:19–21). The people had rejected Jesus, and Peter is now calling upon them to repent.

The structure of the sentence indicates that repentance has two consequences. The immediate personal consequence of repentance is the blotting out of sin (3:19).[69] The broader consequence of repentance is the coming of "times of refreshing" (*kairoi anapsyxeōs*) and the sending of Jesus the Messiah (v. 20).[70] What does Peter mean when he speaks of "times of refreshing" (v. 20a)? C. K. Barrett argues that the plural *kairoi* ("times") indicates that the "times of refreshing" are repeated intervals of respite between the resurrection and the parousia.[71] Hans Conzelmann and others rightly reject this idea. They argue instead that "times of refreshing" refers to the final age of salvation.[72] But is this a better interpretation?

While it is plausible that the phrase "times of refreshing" refers to the final age of salvation and is basically synonymous with the "time for restoring all the things" (3:21), a better interpretation exists. The only other place where the noun *anapsyxis* ("refreshing") is found in the Bible is in the Septuagint translation of Exodus 8:15 (LXX, 8:11). There it refers to a temporary respite from judgment that was granted to Pharaoh after he finally promised to let the people of Israel go.[73] If the word is understood in this sense, as a respite from judgment, then Peter's words in Acts 3:20 can be understood in a different way. As F. F. Bruce explains, "Repentance would bring the people of Jerusalem a respite from the judgment foretold by

69. Barrett 1994, 203. This first purpose clause is introduced by εἰς τὸ (*eis to*) with an infinitive.

70. Barrett 1994, 203. The second purpose clause is introduced by ὅπως ἂν (*hopōs an*) and contains two subjunctive verbs: ἔλθωσιν (*elthōsin*), which is translated "may come," and ἀποστείλῃ (*aposteilē*), which is translated "may send."

71. Barrett 1994, 205.

72. Conzelmann 1987, 29; Marshall 1980, 93; *NIDNTT*, 3:686.

73. Johnson 1992, 69; Fitzmyer 1998, 288; BDAG, s.v. ἀνάψυξις.

Jesus, as it brought the Ninevites a respite from the destruction announced by Jonah."[74]

Peter also says that the people must repent in order that the Lord "may send the Christ appointed for you, Jesus" (3:20b). The idea here is that the repentance of Israel will result in the return of Jesus.[75] Jesus himself hinted at the same idea when he said, "For I tell you, you will not see me again, until you say, 'Blessed is he who comes in the name of the Lord'" (Matt. 23:39; 2 Peter 3:12). Peter tells them that this Jesus is the Messiah "appointed" for Israel. As Joseph Fitzmyer explains, "This is a new Christian interpretation of existing Jewish messianic expectations, according to which the Messiah already exalted is destined to come at the parousia in his glorious advent."[76]

Peter continues, telling the crowd that Jesus the Messiah must be received by heaven "until the time for restoring all the things about which God spoke by the mouth of his holy prophets long ago" (Acts 3:21). Jesus has already ascended and is exalted at the right hand of God. He must remain there until this time of restoration (*apokatastasis*). Barrett explains the significance of this term: "The use of this word implies a creation that has diverged from the condition in which it was intended to be; it is perverted and must be put right."[77] In other words, the Lord will send Jesus the Messiah from heaven when the time for restoring the fallen creation has arrived (Rom. 8:19–21).

Peter concludes his speech by telling the people that Moses had foreseen the day when God would raise up a prophet like himself and had told the people that they were to listen to him (Acts 3:22–23; Deut. 18:15–19). This prophet is Jesus. Peter tells the crowd that all of the prophets spoke of the last days in which they are now living (Acts 3:24). He then appeals to their status as the covenant people of God, saying, "You are the sons of the prophets and of the covenant that God made with your fathers, saying to Abraham, 'And in your offspring shall all the families of the earth be blessed.' God, having raised up his servant, sent him to you first, to bless you by turning every one of you from your wickedness" (vv. 25–26). Abraham's offspring, in the ultimate sense, was Jesus Christ (Gal. 3:16). In

74. Bruce 1988a, 84 n. 38.

75. Haenchen 1971, 208; Bruce 1977b, 67; Kistemaker 1990, 135.

76. Fitzmyer 1998, 288; see also Marshall 1980, 93–94.

77. Barrett 1994, 206.

and through him all of the families of the earth will be blessed, but as Peter says, he was sent first to the Jewish people (Rom. 1:16) that they might have the opportunity to repent and turn from wickedness.

The healing of the lame beggar by Peter and John had led to an opportunity to proclaim the gospel. Peter's preaching leads to the repentance of many, but his preaching also leads to opposition from the Jewish authorities, and he and John are arrested (Acts 4:1–4). They are taken before the Jewish council where they proclaim Christ boldly to the leaders of the people (vv. 5–12). The leaders are astonished at their boldness, but they cannot deny the reality of the miracle of healing, so they release the two apostles, forbidding them to speak anymore of Jesus (vv. 13–18). Peter and John refuse to comply, saying that it is necessary to listen to God rather than to men (vv. 19–20). They are threatened some more but ultimately released (vv. 21–22). In this section of Acts, Luke has shown that official Judaism was setting itself in opposition to God, and that men would be forced to choose whether they would obey the Jewish leadership or obey God.[78] After Peter and John are released, they return to the other disciples and praise God (vv. 23–24). They observe that opposition to God can never succeed, and they pray for continued boldness in the proclamation of the gospel (vv. 25–31).

Luke pauses at this point in the story to give a brief summary of the life of the early church (4:32–37). He then recounts the story of Ananias and Sapphira, two disciples who died because they tried to deceive God (5:1–11). After describing the ongoing work of signs and wonders done by the apostles and the continued growth of the church (vv. 12–16), Luke turns to describe the second major conflict between the young church and the Jewish authorities (vv. 17–42). It begins when the high priest and the Sadducees have the apostles arrested and thrown in prison (5:17–18).

During the night, an angel appears and frees the apostles, telling them to go to the temple to proclaim the gospel (5:19–21). The priests are perplexed the next day when they discover the prisoners gone, but they are informed that the apostles have been seen teaching the people in the temple (vv. 22–25). They are brought before the council and asked why they are continuing to teach in the name of Jesus after being instructed to stop (vv. 26–28). The apostles tell the council that they must obey God rather

78. Barrett 1994, 218.

than men (v. 29). They then declare that God has raised Jesus, the one the authorities killed, and "exalted him at his right hand as Leader and Savior, to give repentance to Israel and forgiveness of sins" (v. 31). The apostles are here offering salvation to the very people who had killed Jesus.[79]

The apostles declare that they are witnesses to the resurrection and ascension of Jesus (5:32). The council is enraged, but they are advised by a Pharisee named Gamaliel to leave the apostles alone because if their message is not from God it will fail, and if it is from God it cannot be overthrown (vv. 33–39). The council heeds his advice and sends the apostles away after beating them and warning them not to speak in the name of Jesus any longer (v. 40). The apostles leave, rejoicing that they have been counted worthy to suffer for Jesus, and they continue to proclaim from house to house that Jesus is the long-awaited Messiah (vv. 41–42). He is the fulfillment of the Old Testament promises.

The Growth of the Church in the Midst of Persecution (Acts 6:1–9:31)

Acts 6 recounts the choice of seven men to distribute food among the disciples (6:1–7). The choice becomes necessary because of complaints of unfairness. Luke indicates that this problem is quickly solved and the result is the further growth of the church.[80] One of the seven men chosen to assist in the distribution of food is Stephen. He is described as a man "full of grace and power" (v. 8). He is seized by enemies of the church and brought before the council where he is accused of speaking against the law (vv. 9–15). Stephen's arrest is the penultimate crisis the church faces in Jerusalem, because it leads directly to a widespread persecution of Christians that forces them to leave for other cities and lands.[81]

The high priest asks Stephen if the accusations against him are true (7:1). Stephen's response is a lengthy speech to the council (vv. 2–53). Stephen begins by recounting the history of Israel's disobedience (vv. 2–50; cf. Ezek. 20), and he concludes with a strong condemnation of his hearers as stiff-necked, lawbreaking people who had killed the prophets and have now killed their Messiah (Acts 7:51–53). The disobedience of Israel and their

79. Marshall 1980, 120.
80. Barrett 1994, 303.
81. Fitzmyer 1998, 356.

rejection of God's chosen messengers in the past foreshadowed Israel's current disobedience and their current opposition to Jesus and his disciples.[82] Not surprisingly, the council is enraged at Stephen's speech (v. 54). When Stephen declares that he sees heaven opened and that he sees Jesus standing at the right hand of God (vv. 55–56), they cast him out of the city and stone him to death (vv. 57–58a). Present at his stoning is a young man named Saul who will become an important figure in the early church (v. 58b).

Luke tells us that Saul approved of Stephen's execution and that afterward there arose "a great persecution against the church in Jerusalem" (8:1a). Saul himself was going from house to house dragging disciples to prison (v. 3). As a result of the persecution, the disciples were scattered throughout the regions of Judea and Samaria (v. 1b). The scattering of the disciples leads to a major advance in the church's mission, namely the spread of the gospel to the Samaritans (vv. 4–25).[83] Philip begins proclaiming Christ in Samaria, casting out demons and healing the sick (vv. 4–8). Many of the Samaritans believe the gospel and are baptized (v. 12). When the apostles who had remained in Jerusalem hear of what has occurred in Samaria, they send Peter and John who pray that the Samaritan believers might receive the Holy Spirit (vv. 14–16). When they lay their hands on them, they do in fact receive the Spirit (v. 17). In another locale, Philip bears witness to Jesus when he encounters an Ethiopian eunuch reading Isaiah (vv. 26–28). Philip explains to him the meaning of the text, with the result that the eunuch believes and is baptized (vv. 29–39).

The story of the conversion of Saul, which occurred sometime in A.D. 33 or 34, is told three times in the book of Acts, indicating its importance to Luke's narrative (9:1–19; 22:6–16; 26:12–18). The story of his conversion is similar in many ways to the accounts of the calling of prophets in the Old Testament (Isa. 6:1–13; Jer. 1:4–10). Saul has sought and received permission to find disciples of Jesus in Damascus and bring them back to Jerusalem to be imprisoned (Acts 9:1–2). On his way to Damascus, a bright light flashes around him and he hears a voice saying, "Saul, Saul, why are you persecuting me?" (vv. 3–4). He asks who is speaking, and hears the voice saying, "I am Jesus, whom you are persecuting" (v. 5). Saul loses his sight during the encounter with Jesus, so he is led the rest of the way to Damascus (vv. 6–9). The Lord then appears to a disciple in Damascus

82. Fitzmyer 1998, 364; Barrett 1994, 337.

83. Marshall 1980, 152.

named Ananias and tells him to find Saul (vv. 10–12). Ananias is fearful because he has heard of Saul, but the Lord says to him, "Go, for he is a chosen instrument of mine to carry my name before the Gentiles and kings and the children of Israel" (vv. 13–15). Ananias finds Saul and lays his hands on him that he might regain his sight and be filled with the Holy Spirit (v. 17). Saul immediately regains his sight and is baptized (v. 18). As a believing Pharisee, Saul had learned about the coming Messiah. Now he knows that the Messiah is Jesus.[84]

Saul stays for some time with the disciples in Damascus, and begins preaching in all of the synagogues, declaring that Jesus is the Son of God (9:19b–20). Those who hear him preach are amazed because they know of his reputation as one who persecuted Christian disciples (v. 21). Saul, however, simply continues to preach, proving to the Jews that Jesus is the prophesied Messiah (v. 22). Saul's conversion does not go unnoticed by the Jewish authorities, however, and when they find out about it they seek to kill him (v. 23). Saul discovers the plot and with the help of some of the other disciples he escapes Damascus (vv. 24–25). In A.D. 37, he travels to Jerusalem where he attempts to join the other disciples, but they are not sure whether he can be trusted (v. 26). Barnabas then takes him to the apostles and tells them what happened on the road to Damascus and about Saul's subsequent preaching (v. 27). After preaching in Jerusalem and disputing with the Greek-speaking Jews, Paul is taken to Caesarea to protect him from further plots against his life (vv. 28–30).

The Spread of the Gospel to the Gentiles (Acts 9:32–12:25)

Jesus had told his disciples that they would be his witnesses "in Jerusalem and in all Judea and Samaria, and to the end of the earth" (1:8). Following the conversion of Saul, the next major stage in the spread of the gospel is ready to occur. The inauguration of the Christian witness to the Gentiles is introduced by two miracle stories. Luke describes Peter's healing of Aeneas (9:32–35) and his raising of Dorcas to life (vv. 36–43) before telling of Peter's witness to Cornelius (10:1–48). Cornelius, a devout Gentile centurion, sees a vision in which he is told to send for a man named Peter who is staying in Joppa (vv. 1–8). As two of Cornelius's servants are traveling to Joppa, Peter himself sees a vision in which he is instructed not to call unclean that

84. Fitzmyer 1998, 421.

which God has called clean (vv. 9–16). Peter is perplexed, but before he can figure out what the vision means, Cornelius's servants arrive, and in another vision, Peter is instructed to go with them (vv. 17–20).

Peter asks the two men why they have come, and they tell him that they were sent by Cornelius who himself was directed by God to send for Peter (vv. 21–22). The following day, Peter and some of the brothers depart and come to Caesarea (vv. 23–24). When Peter arrives, he tells Cornelius that it is considered unlawful for a Jew to associate with Gentiles, but God has shown him that he should not call any person unclean (vv. 25–28). He asks Cornelius why he was requested to come, and Cornelius tells him of the vision he saw (vv. 29–33). Peter then begins telling Cornelius and those with him of Jesus, the one who was crucified and then raised by God (vv. 34–42). He tells Cornelius that everyone who believes in Jesus receives forgiveness of sins (v. 43). While Peter is speaking, the Holy Spirit falls upon all who are hearing his word to the amazement of the Jewish believers who accompanied Peter (vv. 44–46). Upon witnessing the work of God, Peter has all of the new Gentile converts baptized in the name of Jesus (vv. 47–48).

When Peter returns to Jerusalem, he is criticized for eating with uncircumcised Gentiles (11:1–3). Peter then explains what happened, telling the others that God had poured out the Spirit upon the Gentiles and that he was not going to try to stand in the way of God (vv. 4–17).[85] When the others hear this, they are satisfied and begin to praise God, saying, "to the Gentiles also God has granted repentance that leads to life" (v. 18). In these narratives, Luke has described the fulfillment of the ancient promise made to Abraham long ago. The promises to Abraham had been made in order that God might bless all nations (Gen. 12:1–3). Now that promise is being fulfilled as the gospel of Jesus and the promise of forgiveness of sins go out to the Gentiles. Luke concludes this account by describing the arrival of Barnabas and Saul in Antioch, the place where disciples were first called Christians (Acts 11:19–26).

In Acts 12, the persecution of the church takes a new turn. Thus far, the persecution has come from the Jewish authorities. Now it begins to come from the political authorities as well. King Herod Agrippa arrests some of the leaders of the church and has James the brother of John killed (12:1–2). He

85. Fitzmyer 1998, 470.

attempts to have Peter killed as well, but an angel of the Lord rescues Peter from prison, and he returns to join the other disciples (vv. 3–19). Luke's placement of the story of Herod's death (A.D. 44) immediately after the story of his killing of James and imprisonment of Peter serves to emphasize the idea of divine judgment (vv. 20–23). Herod tries to crush the church, but he himself is crushed, and all the while the word of God increases and multiplies (v. 24). As Jesus had promised, the gates of hell do not prevail against the church (Matt. 16:18).

Paul's First Missionary Journey (Acts 13:1–14:28)

In the second half of the book of Acts, Luke turns his attention to the missionary work of Saul, who was also called Paul (13:9). The account of the first missionary journey, which occurred in A.D. 48, is found in Acts 13:1–14:28. Paul and Barnabas are sent by the Holy Spirit from Antioch, and they sail first to the island of Cyprus (13:1–4). They proclaim the word of God in Salamis and Paphos, two cities on the island, and then set sail for the northern shore of the Mediterranean Sea and the city of Perga (vv. 5–13). They travel north from Perga to Antioch of Pisidia, and on the Sabbath they go to the synagogue (v. 14). Paul will continue the strategy of preaching first at synagogues throughout his missionary journeys. The strategy is sound because at the synagogues he will find both pious Jews and God-fearing Gentiles.[86]

The rulers ask if they have any word of exhortation, so Paul stands and begins to speak (13:15–16). His speech is similar in many ways to those of Peter in Acts 2 and Stephen in Acts 7. He briefly summarizes the history of Israel and then declares that Jesus is the promised Savior (13:17–32). He declares that Jesus fulfills the promises made to David (vv. 33–37) and tells the people, "Let it be known to you therefore, brothers, that through this man forgiveness of sins is proclaimed to you, and by him everyone who believes is freed from everything from which you could not be freed by the law of Moses" (vv. 38–39).

The people beg Paul to teach them more the next Sabbath, but when the Jews see the crowds the following week, their jealousy prompts them to revile Paul (13:40–45). Paul tells them that if they are going to reject God's word, then he will bring the word to the Gentiles in fulfillment of

86. Bruce 1977b, 167.

Old Testament prophecy (vv. 46–47). The Gentiles rejoice at this, but the unbelieving Jews stir up persecution against Paul and Barnabas and drive them away (vv. 48–50). Paul and Barnabas travel southeast to Iconium, where they speak in the synagogue, but again opposition arises and the city is divided among those who side with the Jews and those who side with Paul and Barnabas (13:51–14:4).

When Paul and Barnabas discover a plot against their lives, they flee south to Lystra where they continue to preach the gospel and minister to the people (14:5–18). Jews from Antioch of Pisidia arrive in Lystra and after persuading the crowds, they stone Paul (v. 19). Paul, however, rises up and departs with Barnabas to the city of Derbe, east of Lystra (v. 20). After preaching at Derbe, they return through Lystra, Iconium, and Antioch of Pisidia in order to encourage the new disciples and appoint elders (vv. 21–23). They travel back to Perga on the southern coast of Asia Minor and then over to Attalia, from where they sail back to Antioch (vv. 24–26). When they arrive back at the church in Antioch, they tell of all that God did on their journey and how he had granted faith to the Gentiles (v. 27).

The Jerusalem Council (Acts 15:1–35)

The Council of Jerusalem in A.D. 49 is a watershed moment in the early church. As F. F. Bruce observes, it is as epoch-making "as the conversion of Paul or the preaching of the gospel to Cornelius and his household."[87] The conversion of Gentiles had raised serious questions among the original Jewish believers. The questions had to be dealt with if the church was to remain unified. The occasion for the council is the arrival in Antioch of men from Judea who begin teaching the Gentile disciples there that they must be circumcised in order to be saved (15:1). Paul and Barnabas debate these men, and eventually they are sent to Jerusalem in order to ask the apostles about this question (v. 2). When they arrive in Jerusalem, they are welcomed by the apostles and they declare all that had been done among the Gentiles. Some of the believers who were Pharisees, however, said concerning these Gentile believers, "It is necessary to circumcise them and to order them to keep the law of Moses" (vv. 4–5). The question before the apostles is thus clearly framed: Must Gentile believers be circumcised and instructed to keep the law of Moses in order to be saved, as the Pharisees claimed?

87. Bruce 1988a, 282.

After much debate among the apostles and elders, Peter stands and reminds those present that God had chosen him to be the instrument through which the Gentiles would first hear the word of the gospel (15:6–7). He reminds them that God gave the Gentiles the Holy Spirit just as he had given the Spirit to them and that God made no distinction between the Gentile believers and the Jewish believers, cleansing the hearts of both by faith (vv. 8–9). Peter's point is that God imparted the Spirit as soon as they believed, so why should any further conditions be placed upon them?[88] Peter then asks, "Now, therefore, why are you putting God to the test by placing a yoke on the neck of the disciples that neither our fathers nor we have been able to bear? But we believe that we will be saved through the grace of the Lord Jesus, just as they will" (vv. 10–11). Peter's response is a refutation of the claim made by the believing Pharisees that unless Gentiles are circumcised they cannot be saved (v. 1). In fact, Peter reverses the expectation by using the salvation of the Gentiles to reveal to the Jews the true ground of their own salvation, namely grace.[89]

After Peter finishes speaking, Barnabas and Paul describe all that God has done among the Gentiles to whom they have ministered (v. 12). Then James arises and declares that what is occurring among the Gentiles is in fulfillment of Old Testament prophecy, and he cites Amos 9:11–12, which speaks of the Gentiles seeking the Lord (Acts 15:13–17). He concludes, saying, "Therefore my judgment is that we should not trouble those of the Gentiles who turn to God, but should write to them to abstain from the things polluted by idols, and from sexual immorality, and from what has been strangled, and from blood" (vv. 19–20).[90]

What is the meaning of these prohibitions? C. K. Barrett offers one clue. He explains that there were "a group of rabbinic passages in which it is urged that, though in persecution a Jew is not expected to give his life on any minor issue, there were three matters on which no compromise was possible: idolatry, the shedding of blood and incest."[91] If such ideas accurately reflect the convictions of first-century Jews, then the point is

88. Bruce 1988a, 290; Barrett 1998, 714–16.

89. Johnson 1992, 263.

90. The description of the prohibitions makes it clear that the apostles are not saying Gentile believers are free to disregard the universally valid moral imperatives found in the law. Gentile believers are not free to murder or to commit adultery or to steal, for example.

91. Barrett 2002, 234.

that while Gentile Christians should not be forced to keep the law of Moses and be circumcised, they should avoid giving offense to Jewish believers.[92] Another possible interpretation that complements the above is suggested by Ben Witherington who makes the case that James is specifically instructing Gentile believers to avoid the one place where all of these forbidden things could be found together, namely at idol feasts in pagan temples.[93]

The account of the Jerusalem Council concludes with the description of the letter sent by the council to the Gentile church at Antioch (15:22–29) and the church's response (vv. 30–31). The council sends Judas and Silas along with Paul and Barnabas to Antioch with a letter describing their decision concerning the question of circumcision and the keeping of the law of Moses among Gentile believers. They tell the church in Antioch that "it has seemed good to the Holy Spirit and to us to lay on you no greater burden than these requirements: that you abstain from what has been sacrificed to idols, and from blood, and from what has been strangled, and from sexual immorality. If you keep yourselves from these, you will do well" (vv. 28–29). By respecting the values of the Jewish believers among them, they will preserve the unity of the church.[94]

Paul's Second Missionary Journey (Acts 15:36–18:22)

The preparations for the second missionary journey of A.D. 50–52 began soon after the Jerusalem Council (15:36–38). Paul proposes to Barnabas that they return to the cities they visited on their first journey (v. 36). After some disagreement over whether or not to take Mark, Barnabas takes Mark with him to the island of Cyprus, and Paul departs northward with Silas, journeying over land through Syria and Cilicia (vv. 37–41). Paul travels first to Derbe, and then to Lystra, where he is joined by Timothy, the son of a Jewish woman and a Greek father (16:1–5). Apparently, they return to Iconium and Antioch of Pisidia as well (v. 4), but they are prevented by the Holy Spirit from proceeding into Bithynia, so they journey to Troas

92. Blomberg 1998, 416. This view sheds light on James's otherwise obscure words in verse 21. He says, "For from ancient generations Moses has had in every city those who proclaim him, for he is read every Sabbath in the synagogues." The point seems to be that Jews are found throughout the cities of the Gentile world, and they are instructed in the law of Moses. Gentile Christians who live in these cities should be aware of this and avoid giving unnecessary offense.

93. Witherington 1998, 462–64, 650.

94. Fitzmyer 1998, 563.

on the northeastern shore of the Aegean Sea (vv. 6–8). As Joseph Fitzmyer explains, this episode stresses the Spirit-guided nature of Paul's ministry.[95] While in Troas, Paul sees a vision of a man of Macedonia urging him to come over to Macedonia (v. 9). After seeing the vision, Paul and the others with him determine to go there to preach the gospel (v. 10).

They set sail from Troas, sailing first to the island of Samothrace and then to the city of Neapolis on the northern shore of the Aegean (v. 11). From there they proceed to the city of Philippi where they remain for several days (v. 12). A woman named Lydia is one of the first converts in the city, and she opens her house to Paul and the others (vv. 13–15). Paul and Silas are thrown into the Philippian jail when they cast an evil spirit out of a slave girl (vv. 16–24). God, however, uses this occasion to spread the gospel further among the Gentiles.

An earthquake looses the prisoners from their shackles, and when the jailer awakens and discovers this, he draws his sword to kill himself (16:25–27). Paul tells him not to do this because all of the prisoners are still there, and the jailer asks them, "Sirs, what must I do to be saved?" (vv. 28–30). They tell him, "Believe in the Lord Jesus Christ, and you will be saved, you and your household" (v. 31). He and his family are baptized and rejoice in their new faith (vv. 32–34). The next day, the prisoners are released, but when the magistrates discover that Paul and some of the others are Roman citizens, they are fearful and apologetic for imprisoning them, and they ask them to leave the city (vv. 35–40).

Paul and the others travel westward through Amphipolis and Apollonia before arriving in the city of Thessalonica on the northwestern shore of the Aegean (17:1). In the synagogue, Paul reasons with the Jews, "explaining and proving that it was necessary for the Christ to suffer and to rise from the dead," and bears witness to them that "this Jesus, whom I proclaim to you, is the Christ" (vv. 2–3). The twofold nature of Paul's message to the Jews, then, is that the Old Testament foretold the death and resurrection of the Messiah and that the Messiah is Jesus of Nazareth.[96] In proving from the Old Testament that the Messiah was to suffer and be raised, it is likely that Paul used texts such as Psalms 2, 16, 110, and Isaiah 52:13–53:12.

95. Fitzmyer 1998, 577.

96. Barrett 1998, 811; Marshall 1980, 277. For a fuller treatment of the content of the apostolic message to the Jews, see Bruce 1977a, 14–31.

Some of the Jews present, as well as many Gentiles, are persuaded of the truth and join Paul and Silas (Acts 17:4). The unbelieving Jews, however, become jealous and stir up opposition among the people and civil authorities (vv. 5–9). Paul and Silas leave for the city of Berea to the west, and when they arrive they go to that city's synagogue (v. 10). There Paul and Silas proclaim the same message to the Bereans that they proclaimed to the Thessalonians, but the Bereans are more willing to search the Scriptures to see if Paul's arguments concerning a suffering and resurrected Messiah are valid (v. 11).[97] As a result, many believe, but when the unbelieving Jews in Thessalonica hear what is happening in Berea, they come there and stir up opposition in that city (vv. 12–13).

Paul is sent onward by sea to Athens, which lies about two hundred miles south-southeast of Berea, but Silas and Timothy remain behind, waiting to join Paul later (17:14–15). Athens had been the most renowned city in ancient Greece, and now Paul arrives in this great city to bear witness to Jesus.[98] He reasons in the synagogues with the Jews and in the marketplace with whoever happens to be there, including Epicurean and Stoic philosophers (vv. 16–18). Soon, the Athenians bring Paul to the Areopagus, asking him to explain the new teaching that he is presenting (vv. 19–21).[99]

Paul does not quote any Old Testament prophecies here because they would have been unfamiliar to this audience comprised largely, if not exclusively, of unbelieving Gentiles.[100] Instead, his point of contact is an inscription he saw on an altar in the city that read "To the unknown god" (17:23a). Paul takes the inscription as a declaration of the people's ignorance about the nature of God, so he proceeds to teach them about the true God (v. 23b). He tells them first that God is the Creator of all things (v. 24a). Second, he tells them that God does not inhabit man-made temples (v. 24b). The third point he makes is that God is not dependent on mankind (v. 25).

Paul then proceeds to teach the Athenians the truth about man. He tells them first that all men are descended from a single ancestor (17:26a). Second, where and when men live has been appointed by the sovereign

97. Barrett 1998, 818.

98. Fitzmyer 1998, 600.

99. For a good overview of Paul's Areopagus speech, see Bruce 1977a, 39–49. I have largely followed the details of Bruce's analysis.

100. Not all Gentiles were unfamiliar with the Old Testament. The God-fearers who attended the synagogue would have been familiar with the Jewish Scriptures to some degree.

God (v. 26b). Third, God has arranged things in the way he has in order that man might seek God and find him (v. 27a). Fourth, this is possible because God is not far from every man (v. 27b). Paul establishes this point by citing two Greek poets (v. 28). God, he says, is not like the images formed by man (v. 29). Fifth, God has overlooked man's ignorance, but now he calls all people everywhere to repent (v. 30). The reason man must repent is that God has determined a day on which he will judge the world by one he has appointed (v. 31a). As Barrett explains, "That one who has been a man should be exalted to the role of universal judge is unheard of and needs proof."[101] The proof of this one's appointment as judge is his resurrection from the dead (v. 31b). As a result of Paul's Areopagus speech, some mock, others determine to hear more, and some believe his word (vv. 32–34).

Paul eventually departs Athens and travels to Corinth, a city to the west of Athens and located just south of the narrow isthmus between the Greek mainland and the Peloponnese (Acts 18:1). He stays at the house of a Jew named Aquila who, along with other Jews, had been expelled from Rome, and he reasons in the synagogue every Sabbath, attempting to persuade all who would listen (vv. 2–4). Silas and Timothy arrive from Macedonia soon afterward, and Paul continues testifying to the Jews that the prophesied Messiah is Jesus (v. 5).

When the Jews oppose him, Paul turns to the Gentiles with the result that many believe (vv. 6–10). He stays in Corinth for a year and a half teaching the people the word of God (v. 11). During the reign of Gallio in Achaia (A.D. 51 or 52), Paul is brought before the tribunal by Jews, but their charges are dismissed (vv. 12–17). After many more days, Paul departs, sailing to Ephesus on the eastern shore of the Aegean (vv. 18–19). He reasons with the Jews in the synagogue, and although asked to remain, he declines, promising to return if God wills it (vv. 20–21). He sets sail from Ephesus and arrives in Caesarea before making the journey north to the church in Antioch (v. 22).

Paul's Third Missionary Journey (Acts 18:23–21:17)

Paul's third missionary journey from A.D. 53 to 57 begins very soon after the conclusion of the second journey. It appears that he begins the journey

101. Barrett 1998, 853.

by retracing the route of the second journey through Derbe, Lystra, Iconium, and Antioch of Pisidia (Acts 18:23). However, rather than proceeding north from Antioch of Pisidia, this time he continues west toward Ephesus (19:1). In Ephesus, Paul encounters some disciples of John the Baptist and baptizes them in the name of Jesus (vv. 2–7). He continues teaching both Jews and Gentiles in Ephesus for two years (vv. 8–10).

After a riot caused by a pagan silversmith named Demetrius (vv. 21–41), Paul finally departs from Ephesus (20:1). He travels through Macedonia and spends three months in Greece, but when a plot against his life is discovered, he decides to return through Macedonia (vv. 2–5). He and his companions sail from Philippi to Troas where they stay for seven days (v. 6). From Troas, they set sail southward along the coast, stopping at Assos and Mitylene before finally arriving at Miletus, just south of Ephesus (vv. 13–15).

While in Miletus, Paul calls for the Ephesian elders, and when they arrive he speaks to them at length to prepare them for the future (20:17–38). He reminds them of his lengthy ministry among them (vv. 18–21) and tells them of his plans to go to Jerusalem even though he knows imprisonment awaits him (vv. 22–23). He warns them to beware because after his departure fierce wolves will come in to destroy the flock, and even from among the leaders of the church men will arise who will speak falsehood (vv. 29–30). After further warnings, Paul prays with the Ephesian elders, and they accompany him to the ship (vv. 31–38). From Miletus, they sail around the coast to Patara (21:1). From Patara they sail to Tyre and then journey southward through Ptolemais and Caesarea on the way to Jerusalem (vv. 2–16). In A.D. 57, they arrive in Jerusalem and are received gladly by the brethren (v. 17).

Paul's Arrest in Jerusalem (Acts 21:18–23:35)

The events leading up to the arrest of Paul are significant. On the day after his arrival in Jerusalem, Paul meets with James and the other leaders of the church (21:18). He tells them of all that God has done among the Gentiles (v. 19). They rejoice at the news and then say to Paul,

> You see, brother, how many thousands there are among the Jews of those who have believed. They are all zealous for the law, and they have been told about you that you teach all the Jews who are among the Gentiles to forsake Moses, telling them not to circumcise their children or walk according to

our customs. What then is to be done? They will certainly hear that you have come. (vv. 20–22)

The situation is reminiscent of the one that led to the Jerusalem Council, but there are significant differences as well. In Acts 15, the problem concerned believing Gentiles. Here the problem concerns believing "Jews who are among the Gentiles." In Acts 15, the question facing the apostles was whether believing Gentiles should be circumcised and instructed to keep the law of Moses in order to be saved (15:5). Here the question is whether believing Jews among the Gentiles are being taught to forsake circumcision and the law of Moses. In both cases, the problem involved circumcision and the law of Moses, but the people involved in each case are different.

The answer to the two problems is different as well. James instructs Paul to purify himself according to the law of Moses and to take four men who have made a vow and pay their expenses. In this way all of the believing Jews in Jerusalem who are zealous for the law will know that the rumors about Paul's teaching are false and that he himself lives in observance of the law (21:23–24). Then James makes it clear that he is not speaking of the problem dealt with at the Jerusalem Council of Acts 15, saying, "But as for the Gentiles who have believed, we have sent a letter with our judgment that they should abstain from what has been sacrificed to idols, and from blood, and from what has been strangled, and from sexual immorality" (21:25). The following day, Paul does as James has requested, purifying himself and going to the temple (v. 26).

At the Jerusalem Council the apostles had decreed that believing Gentiles were not to be forced to undergo circumcision or be placed under the yoke of the law of Moses in order to be saved. Here the same apostles declare that believing Jews who are among the Gentiles should not be told to forsake circumcision or the law of Moses.[102] This does not mean, however, that Jews are saved by circumcision or the law of Moses (15:11). As we will see, the question of the Mosaic administration of the law and its implications for Jews and Gentiles in the young church will remain a source of controversy for some time.

Paul's arrest occurs when he is seen in the temple area by Jews from Asia (21:27). They stir up the crowds by declaring that Paul has desecrated the

102. Barrett 1998, 1008.

temple by bringing Gentiles into it (v. 28). The people seize Paul and are about to kill him when he is rescued by Roman soldiers who arrest him and take him to the barracks (vv. 29–36). Before he is taken into the barracks, however, Paul asks for and receives permission to speak to the crowd. He silences the crowd and to their astonishment begins addressing them in Hebrew (vv. 37–40). In his address to the crowd, Paul tells them of his Jewish background and of the events that led to his conversion (22:1–21). The riotous response of the crowd leads the tribune to order that Paul be examined by flogging to see why everyone is in such an uproar (vv. 22–24). Before he can be flogged, however, Paul asks the centurion whether it is legal for him to flog a man who is a Roman citizen (v. 25). When the tribune discovers that Paul is a Roman citizen, he is fearful and unbinds Paul (vv. 26–29).

On the following day, the tribune orders the Jewish leaders to meet, and he brings Paul before their council (22:30). When Paul proclaims that he is being persecuted on account of his hope in the resurrection of the dead, he causes a split in the council between the Pharisees and the Sadducees who differed in their opinion on this subject (23:6–8). The debate turns violent, and the tribune has Paul removed before he is hurt. He commands that Paul be brought down to the barracks (vv. 9–10). The following night, the Lord appears to Paul telling him that just as he has testified to the truth in Jerusalem, so must he do in Rome (v. 11). When a plot against Paul's life is discovered (vv. 12–22), the tribune has Paul sent under guard to Felix the governor in Caesarea (vv. 23–35).

Paul's Defense before Felix, Festus, and Agrippa in Caesarea (Acts 24:1–26:32)

After five days, Ananias and some Jewish elders arrive in Caesarea to set forth the case against Paul before Felix (24:1). The case against him is presented by Tertullus (vv. 2–8). Paul then gives his reply, arguing that he has done nothing worthy of arrest and that he is on trial merely for teaching the resurrection (vv. 10–21). Paul, however, is kept in custody for a period of two years (A.D. 57–59) because of the desire of Felix to do the Jews a favor (vv. 22–27). Soon after Festus succeeds Felix, he too is presented with the case against Paul (25:1–5). Paul is then brought before the tribunal where he defends himself against the charges, ultimately appealing to Caesar (vv.

6–12). The trial before Festus is important, then, because it is the occasion for Paul's journey to Rome.[103]

Some time after Paul's hearing before Festus, Agrippa the king and Bernice arrive in Caesarea (25:13). While they are in the city, Festus discusses Paul's case with them (vv. 14–21). Agrippa tells Festus that he would like to hear Paul himself, and the next day Paul is brought before the king (vv. 22–23). After Festus introduces the case to the larger crowd that is gathered (vv. 24–27), Agrippa tells Paul that he may speak (26:1). Paul tells the king that for a long time he had lived as a Pharisee (vv. 1–5), and then he says that he is on trial because of his hope in the promise of the resurrection (vv. 6–8). Paul describes his persecution of the Christians and the events that led to his conversion (vv. 9–18). He tells of his missionary work and declares that he is "saying nothing but what the prophets and Moses said would come to pass: that the Christ must suffer and that by being the first to rise from the dead, he would proclaim light both to our people and to the Gentiles" (vv. 19–23). At the conclusion of his speech the king tells Festus that Paul has done nothing wrong and could have been set free had he not appealed to Caesar (vv. 31–32).

Paul's Journey to Rome (Acts 27:1–28:31)

The book of Acts concludes with the story of Paul's journey to the capital of the empire, the city of Rome, in A.D. 59–60. Paul is taken with some other prisoners to a ship that is about to sail along the coast of Asia Minor, and they put to sea (27:1–2). They sail north along the coast, stopping at Sidon (v. 3), and they then proceed north of Cyprus to Myra on the southern coast of Asia Minor (vv. 4–5). In Myra, the centurion in charge of the prisoners finds a ship sailing for Italy and puts the prisoners on board (v. 6). With some difficulty they continue west and arrive in Cnidus on the southeastern shore of the Aegean Sea. They then continue on southward around the island of Crete, eventually stopping at a place on the south shore of the island called Fair Havens (v. 8).

The ship attempts to sail farther west to Phoenix, a harbor at the western end of Crete, so that they can spend the winter there, but a storm drives them to sea and continues to carry the ship along for two weeks (27:9–38). The ship is eventually wrecked on the shores of an island, but all of the

103. Fitzmyer 1998, 742.

men survive (vv. 39–44). They learn that they have been shipwrecked on an island called Malta, which is just south of the island of Sicily (28:1). They are welcomed by the people of Malta, and Paul ministers to them (vv. 2–10), but after three months they eventually find a ship to complete the journey (v. 11). They sail to Syracuse on the east coast of Sicily and from there sail to Rhegium on the southern tip of the Italian peninsula and then up the west coast to Puteoli (vv. 12–13). From Puteoli, they travel across land to Rome (v. 14). Upon arriving in Rome, Paul is greeted by the brothers in the city, and he is allowed to stay by himself with a guard (vv. 15–16).

Paul's two-year stay in Rome, from A.D. 60 to 62, is described in the final section of Acts (28:17–31). After three days in the city, Paul calls together the leaders of the Jews in Rome and tells them that although he has done nothing, he has been delivered over to the Romans by the Jews in Jerusalem (v. 17). Although the Romans have found no cause to hold him, he was forced to appeal to Caesar because of the obstinacy of his accusers (vv. 18–19). He tells the Jewish leaders of Rome that he has asked to see them because he is in chains for his belief in the hope of Israel (v. 20). The Jewish leaders tell him they have heard nothing evil about him, but they wish to hear more about this sect that is everywhere spoken against (vv. 21–22).

They appoint a day when they can come to Paul's lodging, and on that day, from morning to evening, he teaches them about the kingdom of God and attempts to persuade them about Jesus from the Scriptures (v. 23). Some believe, but others reject Paul's teaching (v. 24). Paul concludes by citing a prophecy of Isaiah in which the prophet condemned the people of Israel for their failure to hear and see the truth (vv. 26–27; Isa. 6:9–10). Paul tells them that because the Jews have rejected the truth, the salvation of God is being sent to the Gentiles because they will listen (Acts 28:28).[104] For the remainder of the time Paul spends in Rome, he continues to proclaim the kingdom of God and teach about Jesus with all boldness.

Summary

The book of Acts is the last strictly narrative book of the Bible. Along with the gospel of Luke, it tells the story of the climactic events in the history of redemption. In the gospel of Luke, there is a centripetal force, drawing everything closer and closer to Jerusalem and the death and resurrection of

104. Barrett 1998, 1246.

Jesus. The book of Acts begins with the ascension of Jesus to the right hand of the Father where he is exalted as both Lord and Christ and from where he sends the gift of the Holy Spirit. The outpouring of the Holy Spirit on the day of Pentecost indicates the arrival of the prophesied last days. From this point forward, the book of Acts bears witness to the centrifugal force of the Spirit that spreads the gospel outward from Jerusalem to the ends of the earth, expanding the church in the process.

At the ascension, the apostles are told that Jesus will return again, a clear promise of the consummative redemptive event, but in the meantime, by the power given to them by the Spirit, they are to be witnesses of Jesus to all nations. Throughout the book of Acts, the mission of the apostles brings them into conflict with both religious and political authorities, and they suffer persecution. But every attempt by its enemies to crush the church leads only to the church's further growth. With the growth of the church among the Gentiles, the promises to Abraham begin to be fulfilled in a way they have not yet been fulfilled. Through his offspring, God is blessing all nations.

The conversion of Gentiles to faith in the Messiah of Israel, however, also raises serious questions in the minds of some of the original Jewish believers concerning the applicability of the law of Moses to these converts. The issue becomes such a problem that the apostles are forced to meet in a council to resolve it. They ultimately determine that Gentile believers are not to be told that they must be circumcised or keep the law of Moses, and they remind the Jewish believers that they themselves are not saved by the law. Instead, Jewish and Gentile believers alike are saved through the grace of the Lord Jesus Christ (Acts 15:11). The epistles of Paul will make it evident that these questions about the law remained significant ones in the life of the young church.

The book of Acts begins and ends with the disciples of Jesus proclaiming the kingdom of God and declaring that Jesus is the Messiah who the Old Testament Scriptures said would suffer and die and then be resurrected and exalted. The first several chapters of Acts contain the record of decisive redemptive-historical turning points, most importantly, the ascension of Jesus and the outpouring of the Holy Spirit on the day of Pentecost.

The remainder of Acts can seem somewhat anticlimactic after these dramatic events, as these chapters contain almost day-to-day accounts of persecution and the spread of the gospel to Jews in Palestine and the Diaspora, to Samaritans, and to Gentiles all across Asia Minor and Europe. But this is the mission that Jesus has given to his disciples. The eschatological task of the church is to bear witness to Jesus to all nations. By this means the kingdom of God grows from a small stone into a mountain that fills the earth, and God's eschatological purposes are fulfilled. The open-ended nature of the conclusion of Acts indicates that the story begun there has not ended. The church's mission today remains the same as it was then. We continue to be witnesses to Jesus to the ends of the earth until he returns and restores all things.

14

The Pauline Epistles (1)

Galatians and Thessalonians

It is a striking fact that of the twenty-seven books of the New Testament, twenty-one are epistles, or letters. Epistles were a common form of communication in the Greco-Roman world just as they are today. In the first century, such letters typically consisted of an opening address with a greeting to the recipients, the body of the letter, and then some concluding remarks. Although the style of the greetings and concluding remarks has changed, the overall structure of these letters is very similar to the structure of letters today. Thirteen of the New Testament epistles were written by one man, the apostle Paul.[1] Paul wrote all of his letters over a period of

1. The accuracy of this statement is, of course, disputed by numerous critical scholars. Seven of the epistles traditionally attributed to Paul are generally undisputed and almost universally understood to be Pauline (Galatians, Romans, 1 and 2 Corinthians, 1 Thessalonians, Philemon, and Philippians). Four are strongly disputed and usually denied to be Pauline (Ephesians, 1 and 2 Timothy, and Titus). Scholarly opinion is divided in regard to two of the letters (2 Thessalonians and Colossians).

approximately twenty years (ca. A.D. 48–68). His letters were typically occasional writings, meaning that he was addressing very specific situations, which are sometimes difficult to reconstruct. Some of his letters were written to local churches (e.g., Romans, 1 and 2 Corinthians), while others were written to individuals (e.g., Philemon, Titus).

Just as the individual prophetic books of the Old Testament were written within the context of the events narrated in the historical books, most of the individual New Testament epistles were written within the context of the historical events narrated in the book of Acts. Most of Paul's epistles were written at various times during his several journeys. It is important, therefore, to keep in mind the historical events of Acts while reading these epistles. For this reason, we will look at the epistles of Paul in chronological rather than canonical order.[2]

Not only is it important to understand the historical context of Paul's writings, it is also important to understand their narrative context. As Ben Witherington explains, Paul's thought "is grounded in a grand narrative and in a story that has continued to develop out of that narrative."[3] Paul knows the Old Testament story, and he sees the advent of Christ as the climactic event in redemptive history. The long story of God's people has culminated with the coming of Jesus the Messiah. When reading Paul's epistles, therefore, it is important to remember the biblical narrative of redemptive history.

Paul's understanding of the significance of the coming of the Messiah profoundly shapes his eschatology, and his eschatology profoundly shapes everything he writes. As Herman Ridderbos explains, the whole content of Paul's preaching "can be summarized as the proclamation and explication of the eschatological time of salvation inaugurated with Christ's advent, death, and resurrection."[4] He continues, "It is from this principal point of view and under this denominator that all the separate themes of Paul's preaching can be understood and penetrated in their unity and relation to each other."[5] Paul's eschatology is obviously centered on Jesus Christ. For Paul, the christological and the eschatological are inseparably intertwined.

2. The dating of a few of the letters is disputed, but a general chronological sequence can be discerned.

3. Witherington 1994, 2.

4. Ridderbos 1975, 44.

5. Ridderbos 1975, 44. Paul's epistles explore the ramifications of the eschatological turning point for all manner of issues.

For Paul, the death and resurrection of Jesus mean that the events that were expected to occur at the end have already begun within history.[6] As Geerhardus Vos explains, "To Paul, the death and resurrection of Christ are the beginning of the world to come, and of the eschatological process."[7] Christ's resurrection is the firstfruits of the eschatological resurrection.[8] His ascension points to the inauguration of the reign of God's Messiah, and Pentecost indicates that the eschatological gift of the Spirit has been given. The importance of these events for Paul is explained by George Ladd:

> The events of the eschatological consummation are not merely detached events lying in the future about which Paul speculates. They are rather redemptive events that have already begun to unfold within history. The blessings of the Age to Come no longer lie exclusively in the future; they have become objects of present experience. The death of Christ is an eschatological event. Because of Christ's death, the justified person stands already on the age-to-come side of the eschatological judgment, acquitted of all guilt. By virtue of the death of Christ, the believer has already been delivered from this present evil age (Gal. 1:4). He or she has been transferred from the rule of darkness and now knows the life of the Kingdom of Christ (Col. 1:13). In his cross, Christ has already defeated the powers of evil that have brought chaos into the world (Col. 2:14f.).[9]

Granted all of this, is there nothing left to expect? Has everything been fulfilled? Not as Paul understands it. According to Paul, the eschatological era has dawned with the advent of Christ, but it has not reached the time of consummation. Although the age to come has begun, the present age continues. This age and the age to come overlap, as it were.[10] Vos provides a helpful diagram illustrating this overlapping of the ages (fig. 5).[11] What this means is that for Paul, the last act in the drama of redemption has already begun, but it has not yet concluded.

6. Marshall 1997, 50; Morris 1986, 88.
7. Vos 1977, 51.
8. Ladd 1993, 408.
9. Ladd 1993, 596.
10. For more on the "already and not yet" nature of Pauline eschatology, see Vos 1991.
11. Vos 1991, 38.

Fig. 5. Vos's two-age diagram.

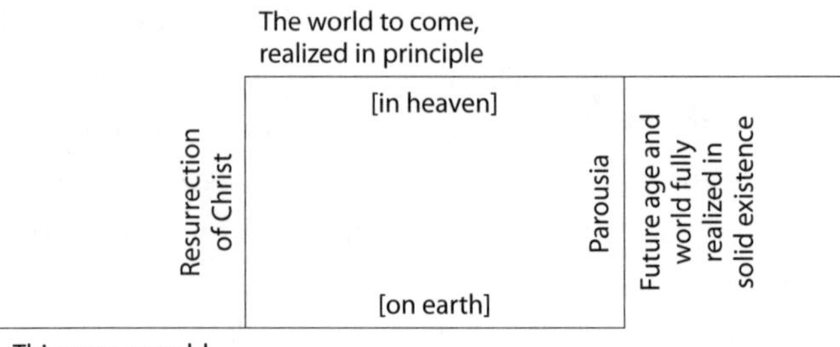

What then of Christ's return and the last judgment? When does Paul expect the last act to conclude? According to some, Paul expected all things to be consummated within his own lifetime. Albert Schweitzer, for example, claimed, "From his first letter to his last Paul's thought is always uniformly dominated by the expectation of the immediate return of Jesus, of the judgment, and the Messianic glory."[12] Is Schweitzer correct? As we will see in our study of the letters themselves, Paul may have considered the return of Christ within his lifetime to be a possibility, but he did not consider it to be a certainty.[13]

Galatians

The epistle to the Galatians is one of the most profound books in the entire New Testament, and its themes have inspired countless multitudes. It is almost universally conceded that the apostle Paul wrote this brief letter.[14] However, while the identity of the author of Galatians is the source of almost no debate, the identity of the Galatians themselves is the source of much debate. The difficulty is due to the fact that by the time Paul wrote the letter, the term "Galatia" had two meanings. The word could refer to the region in central Asia Minor inhabited by ethnic Galatians.[15] It could also refer to the entire Roman province known as Galatia, a province that included the region in central Asia Minor as well as the region to the south stretching all the way to the Mediterranean

12. Schweitzer 1953, 52.

13. See Witherington 1992, 19.

14. Longenecker 1990, lvii.

15. The ethnic Galatians were descendants of Celtic tribes who migrated from central Europe into Asia Minor. These Celts also migrated into Britain, France, and Germany (Longenecker 1990, lxii).

Sea.[16] The question is whether Paul was writing to churches in the original Galatian territory, which would entail a "North Galatian" location, or to churches in the southern part of Asia Minor that were part of the Roman province of Galatia, a "South Galatian" location.[17] If Paul was writing to churches in the southern part of Asia Minor, then the Galatian churches are likely those Paul and Barnabas planted during their first missionary journey (Acts 13:1–14:28), namely, the churches in Pisidian Antioch, Iconium, Lystra, and Derbe.

If Paul was writing to churches in the northern part of Asia Minor, then his letter could not have been written before his second visit to the region (Acts 18:23), meaning that he could not have written the letter until his third missionary journey. If Paul was addressing the churches in the south that he and Barnabas planted on their first missionary journey, then a much earlier date is possible. Although the evidence is not completely conclusive, the evidence that exists supports the South Galatian theory. Paul sent the epistle to these Galatian churches soon after the completion of the first missionary journey and just prior to the Jerusalem council (Acts 15). If this is correct, then Galatians was written sometime in A.D. 48 or 49, and it was the earliest of Paul's epistles.[18]

The occasion for the letter was the news Paul received informing him that certain Jews had visited the churches he had planted in Galatia and were telling the Gentile believers there that they must adhere to the requirements of the Mosaic law in order to be saved (Acts 15:1–2). They were telling the Gentile believers that they must be circumcised and observe special days on the Jewish calendar.[19] In order to gain a hearing, they were also questioning Paul's authority.

Paul viewed these actions as a threat to the gospel and wrote the epistle to the Galatians to counter the false teaching that was being spread through

16. For a fuller discussion of the issues surrounding the identity of the Galatians, see Bruce 1982b, 3–18; Fung 1988, 1–3; Longenecker 1990, lxi–lxxii.

17. See Bruce 1982b, 5.

18. The South Galatian theory also makes sense of several chronological problems that appear to be irresolvable in the North Galatian view. The problems involve the correlation of Paul's visit to Jerusalem described in Galatians 2:1–10 with the visits recorded in Acts. Is it the same as the visit recorded in Acts 11:30; 15:2–29; 18:22; or 21:15–16? Many modern scholars identify the visit of Galatians 2 with the visit of Acts 15, but this creates numerous problems. A more likely solution is that the visit of Galatians 2 is the visit of Acts 11:30. For a full discussion, see Fung 1988, 10–28.

19. Bruce 1982b, 19.

the churches. One of the major themes addressed in the letter, therefore, is the nature and purpose of the Mosaic law.[20] On the surface, eschatology does not appear to be a major theme in the epistle. The law is the major theme. As we will see, however, Paul's explanation of the nature and role of the law is grounded in his understanding of redemptive history and eschatology.[21] What Paul teaches regarding the law in the epistle to the Galatians would soon afterward be confirmed by the apostles at the Jerusalem Council (Acts 15).

In his opening salutation, Paul identifies himself, writing, "Paul, an apostle—not from men nor through man, but through Jesus Christ and God the Father, who raised him from the dead—and all the brothers who are with me, To the churches of Galatia" (Gal. 1:1–2). It is significant that at the very outset of his first epistle, Paul mentions the resurrection of Jesus. By doing so, he points his readers to the climactic event of redemptive history. As Moisés Silva explains, "By highlighting this truth already in the greeting, Paul effectively lays down his most basic assumption, namely, that the passage from slavery to freedom has been made possible through an eschatological event."[22] The foundational assumption of Paul's letter is that with the death and resurrection of Jesus a new era has been inaugurated.

Paul addresses the epistle to the churches (*ekklēsiais*) of Galatia. The word *ekklēsia* is regularly used in the Septuagint to translate the Hebrew word *qahal.* This word (*ekklēsia*) is used to refer to the people of God, Israel (e.g., Deut. 23:2; 31:30; Judg. 20:2; 1 Kings 8:14). It is also used, especially in the Psalms, to refer specifically to the worshiping congregation of the

20. The study of Paul's view of the law is an industry in itself resulting in dozens of monographs and articles every year. With the rise of the New Perspective(s) on Paul (NPP) in the last several decades, the scope of such studies has broadened and become even more complex. Since eschatology is the primary focus of this present study, my comments on the Pauline view of the law will be necessarily restricted. For more thorough discussions of Paul's view of the law, see Ridderbos 1975, 130–58, 170–73, 278–87; Bruce 1977b, 188–202; Schreiner 1993; Thielman 1989, 1994, 1999, 7–46. Regarding the NPP, although its proponents do not agree on every detail (see, for example, the comments critical of Sanders in Dunn 1990), the basic ideas have been expanded in a number of works (e.g., Sanders 1977, 1983; Dunn 1990, 2001a; Wright 1997). Despite its current popularity, the NPP faces serious historical, exegetical, and theological problems. For critiques of the NPP, see Carson, O'Brien, and Seifrid 2001, 2004; Kim 2002; Gathercole 2002; Westerholm 2004; Waters 2004; and Venema 2006.

21. Silva 1996a, 169.

22. Silva 1994b, 145.

people (e.g., Pss. 22:22; 35:18; 40:9; 68:26; 149:1). In the Greco-Roman world, the word *ekklēsia* was a political term used to refer to the citizens' assemblies that existed in the Greek city-states.[23] By referring to the local gatherings of believers as *ekklēsiais*, Paul reveals the continuity between them and the Old Testament people of God. They are the new congregation gathered together to worship God. Paul very likely also views the various congregations of the *ekklēsia* as an alternate society existing alongside the political societies of the world.

Paul concludes his opening salutation saying, "Grace to you and peace from God our Father and the Lord Jesus Christ, who gave himself for our sins to deliver us from the present evil age, according to the will of our God and Father, to whom be the glory forever and ever. Amen" (Gal. 1:3–5). It is significant that Paul here describes what Jesus' death accomplished in terms of individual salvation ("for our sins") and in terms of redemptive history ("to deliver us from the present evil age").[24] The age to come is no longer completely future. Believers now live during the overlap of the present evil age and the age to come. The result of this overlap is that the present age is an age marked by intense conflict because although the decisive battle has already been won, the enemy has not yet been completely removed from power.[25]

In Galatians 1:6–9, Paul reveals the problem that exists in the Galatian churches. People have arrived who are preaching another gospel, and the Galatians are being led astray. After expressing astonishment that they are so quickly turning to a different gospel, Paul explains to the Galatians that his authority does not depend on the Jerusalem apostles (1:10–2:14). He reminds the Galatians of his calling from God to proclaim the gospel (1:10–16). He reminds them of his visits with the apostles and how they added nothing to his calling (1:17–2:10). Finally, he reminds them that he even had to rebuke Peter, one of the original twelve apostles (2:11–14). This long section of the letter indicates that the Jews who were troubling the Galatian churches were challenging Paul's authority. He is forced therefore to reestablish his credentials.

The bulk of the epistle to the Galatians consists of Paul's defense of the true gospel (2:15–6:10). He begins his defense saying, "We ourselves are

23. Horsley 1997, 8.
24. George 1994, 87.
25. Martyn 1997, 101–2.

Jews by birth and not Gentile sinners; yet we know that a person is not justified by works of the law but through faith in Jesus Christ, so we also have believed in Christ Jesus, in order to be justified by faith in Christ and not by works of the law, because by works of the law no one will be justified" (2:15–16). According to some, when Paul speaks of the "works of the law," he is referring primarily to those practices that distinguished Jews from Gentiles (e.g., circumcision and food laws).[26] As we have seen in the book of Acts, a major problem in the early church was the relationship between Jewish believers and Gentile believers. It is certainly true that the Jews from Judah who were troubling the Galatian churches were claiming that Gentile believers must be circumcised, but they were also claiming that it was necessary for Gentile believers to keep the law of Moses in a broader sense (Acts 15:1, 5).[27] The phrase "works of the law," then, should not be restricted to practices such as circumcision, dietary laws, and Sabbath observance.

Gentiles cannot be justified by means of circumcision or dietary restrictions, but Paul's point is larger than that. Neither Gentiles nor Jews can be justified by means of the Mosaic law as a whole.[28] As Paul will make clear further on in his letter, the reason no one can be justified through the law is human inability to keep it (Gal. 3:10).[29] In claiming that the law cannot be kept, Paul is merely restating what had been said since the time of Moses. Moses pointed out that Israel would not be able to keep the law (Deut. 31:16–21). Joshua said the same thing when he renewed the covenant at Shechem (Josh. 24:19). The people could not obey the law because their hearts were hard. Since no one, whether Jew or Gentile, is able to obey the law, no one can be justified by the law. A person, whether Jew or Gentile, can be justified only "through faith in Jesus Christ."[30]

26. See, for example, Dunn 1993, 135–37.

27. See Calvin 2003, 21:67.

28. Schreiner 1993, 51–57. A clear inference of Paul's statement here is that no one can be justified by means of *any* good works they perform.

29. As Martin Luther wrote in thesis 26 of his *Heidelberg Disputation*, "The law says, 'Do this,' and it is never done. Grace says, 'Believe in this,' and everything is already done."

30. Some have taken the genitive in the phrase "faith in Jesus Christ" (2:16) as a subjective genitive, meaning "the faithfulness of Jesus Christ." The primary argument against this view, and for the understanding of the genitive as an objective genitive, is that in the very next phrase, Paul declares that Jesus is the object of our faith. The second phrase clarifies the meaning of the first (see Bruce 1982b, 139; Fung 1988, 115). Furthermore, when Paul defends his argument from the Old

The major point that Paul makes in Galatians 3–4 is that the Mosaic law, as an aspect of the Mosaic covenant, belonged to a stage in redemptive history that has ended with the death and resurrection of Jesus.[31] Paul first appeals to the Galatians' reception of the Holy Spirit apart from the law to prove that they need not follow the works of the law in order to be accepted by God (Gal. 3:1–5). Paul then appeals to the faith of Abraham to make his point (vv. 6–9). Abraham was justified by faith (v. 6). Therefore those who believe are the true sons of Abraham (v. 7). God has always intended to justify the Gentiles by faith, and this is why he promised Abraham that in him all nations would be blessed (v. 8).

Those who are of faith are blessed (3:9), but those who rely on the works of the law are cursed (v. 10a). They are cursed because the law requires perfect obedience, something that no human being can accomplish (v. 10b). No one can be justified by law because the righteous live by faith (v. 11). Paul contrasts the law with faith, saying, "But the law is not of faith, rather 'The one who does them shall live by them'" (v. 12). The law is contrasted with faith because the proper response to law is obedient "doing." The proper response to the promise, on the other hand, is faith.[32] Since everyone who does not perfectly obey the law is cursed (v. 10), Christ "redeemed us from the curse of the law by becoming a curse for us" (v. 13). Because Christ bore the curse of the law, the blessing of Abraham comes to the Gentiles now through faith (v. 14).

Paul turns next to an explanation of the relationship between the promise and the law. Here the effects of his eschatology on his teaching become abundantly clear. He begins by explaining that the promises were given to Abraham and his seed 430 years before the law was given as part of the Mosaic covenant (3:15–17a).[33] The law did not annul the promises previ-

---

Testament he appeals to Genesis 15:6 , showing that Abraham was justified by faith, and the faith by which Abraham was justified was his faith in God's word.

31. The relationship between the Mosaic covenant and the new covenant remains one of the most controverted and difficult topics in biblical and systematic theology. As the great American theologian Jonathan Edwards said, "There is perhaps no part of divinity attended with so much intricacy, and wherein orthodox divines do so much differ as stating the precise agreement and difference between the two dispensations of Moses and Christ" (cited in VanGemeren 1993, 14). In Galatians, because of the specific point he is making, Paul's emphasis is obviously on the points of discontinuity, but it should be remembered that Galatians does not include all that Paul had to say on the subject.

32. Bruce 1982b, 162.

33. Paul makes the point that the "seed" ("offspring") is singular and refers to Christ. As Bruce (1982b, 172) explains, the word "seed" is being used here as a "collective singular."

ously given to Abraham (v. 17b). Therefore, the inheritance promised to Abraham comes by faith in the promise, not by doing the works of the law (v. 18). This raises an obvious question: "Why then the law?" (v. 19a). Why was the law given? What was its purpose?

Paul answers his own rhetorical question by explaining that the law "was added because of transgressions, until the offspring should come to whom the promise had been made" (3:19b). What does Paul mean when he says "because of transgressions"? It may simply mean that the law came in order to produce a knowledge of sin (Rom. 3:20).[34] It may also mean that the law came in order to bring sin to its fullest development (Gal. 3:22; Rom. 5:20).[35] Both of these were part of the purpose of the law. Paul says that the law was "added . . . until the offspring should come to whom the promise had been made." Paul has already identified this offspring as Christ (Gal. 3:16), so what he is saying is that the law was added until the coming of Christ. The Mosaic covenant occupied a period in redemptive history between the giving of the promise and the arrival of the heir of that promise.[36] Paul develops this point further in the remainder of this section.

Paul first explains that the law is not contrary to the promises of God because it was not given for the same purpose as the promise (3:21–22). The law could not give life. If it could have given life, then righteousness would have been by the law (v. 21b). Instead, the law was given to imprison everything under sin so that the promise might be given to those who place their faith in Jesus Christ (v. 22). Paul then writes, "Now before faith came, we were held captive under the law, imprisoned until the coming faith would be revealed" (v. 23). Paul has just spoken of imprisonment under sin; now he speaks of imprisonment under the law. This imprisonment was to last until the coming of faith. In redemptive-historical terms, the coming of faith is another way of referring to the coming of Christ. With Christ's coming the age of imprisonment under sin gives way to the age of faith.[37]

Paul continues his argument, writing, "So then, the law was our guardian until Christ came, in order that we might be justified by faith. But now that faith has come, we are no longer under a guardian, for in Christ Jesus

34. Longenecker 1990, 138.

35. Ridderbos 1975, 149–50; Bruce 1982b, 175.

36. Silva 1994b, 152; Witherington 1994, 54; George 1994, 254; Bruce 1982b, 176.

37. Bruce 1982b, 181.

you are all sons of God, through faith" (3:24–26). The word "guardian" is a translation of the Greek word *paidagōgos*. The word does not mean "teacher" (Gk. *didaskalos*). In the first century, a *paidagōgos* was a slave who attended a young boy wherever he went until his coming of age. His function was primarily disciplinary. Until a boy reached maturity, he was little different from a slave himself.[38]

Paul's description of the law as a *paidagōgos* indicates that he sees the history of the people of God under the Mosaic covenant as their childhood, their time of immaturity. But with the coming of Christ "we are no longer under a guardian" (v. 25). The emphasis here is on the temporal sense, the succession of different times within redemptive history.[39] Those Jews who are troubling the Galatian churches do not understand what time it is in redemptive history.[40] The Mosaic covenant was given for a specific purpose for a specific time. With the inauguration of the new covenant, the Mosaic covenant comes to an end.

Now that Christ has come, the Galatians are sons of God through faith (3:26). All who were baptized into Christ have put on Christ (v. 27). There is now neither Jew nor Greek, slave nor free, male nor female, for all are one in Christ Jesus (v. 28). Anyone who is Christ's is Abraham's offspring and an heir of the promise (v. 29). Contrary to what the Jewish agitators are saying, the Galatians inherit the promises through faith in Christ, not by means of submitting to the yoke of the Mosaic law (Acts 15:10–11). Paul explains that heirs, while they are children, are no different from slaves (Gal. 4:1). They are under guardians until they reach a certain age determined by their fathers (v. 2).

Paul then explains, "In the same way we also, when we were children, were enslaved to the elementary principles of the world. But when the fullness of time had come, God sent forth his Son, born of woman, born under the law, to redeem those who were under the law, so that we might receive adoption as sons" (vv. 3–4). Here Paul points to that element of eschatology that is "already" fulfilled. The coming of Christ brings in the "fullness of time." Paul is urging his readers to understand that the redemptive-historical period of immaturity under a guardian (the Mosaic covenant) has ended.[41]

38. Bruce 1982b, 182–83; Ridderbos 1975, 148; Schreiner 1993, 78; Bell 2005, 171.

39. Longenecker 1990, 149; Burton 1921, 200; Calvin 2003, 21:106–10.

40. Martyn 1997, 104.

41. Bruce 1982b, 194.

They are no longer slaves, but adopted sons, and since they are sons, they are heirs (v. 6).

Paul appeals to the Galatians not to abandon the gospel he has proclaimed to them (4:8–20), and then illustrates the points he is making by looking at the story of Sarah and Hagar (4:21–5:1). He explains that Abraham had two sons by two women, one a slave woman, and one a free woman (4:21–22). The son of the slave woman was born according to the flesh, but the son of the free woman was born according to promise (v. 23). Paul then offers an allegorical interpretation explaining that the two women are two covenants (v. 24a). He identifies Hagar with Mount Sinai in Arabia and says that she corresponds with the present Jerusalem, for she is in slavery with her children (vv. 24b–25). Paul identifies believers as children of the Jerusalem above (vv. 26–31). On what basis, however, does Paul identify Mount Sinai (i.e., the place where the law was given) with Hagar? He points out the fact that Mount Sinai is in Arabia, the land of the Ishmaelites, and outside the Promised Land.[42] Since believers are children of the Jerusalem above which is free, Paul urges the Galatians not to submit to a "yoke of slavery" (5:1).

Paul concludes this section of the epistle by appealing to the Galatians not to abandon the gospel by accepting circumcision (5:2–12). He reminds them that they are free, but tells them they are not to use their freedom as an opportunity for the flesh (v. 13). Their liberty is not to be equated with licentiousness. Instead, through love they are to serve one another for "the whole law is fulfilled in one word: 'You shall love your neighbor as yourself'" (v. 14). The fact that they are free does not mean that they will not struggle with the desires of the flesh, but if they walk by the Spirit they will not gratify those desires (vv. 16–17).

Paul tells the Galatians that if they are led by the Spirit they are not under the law (5:18). Here life in the Spirit is contrasted with the life of the previous age, life under the Mosaic covenant.[43] Paul then describes the works of the flesh, explaining that those who do such things will not inherit the kingdom of God (vv. 19–21). He also describes the fruit of the Spirit, saying that against such things there is no law (vv. 22–23). Fruit and works are not the same thing. Law can prescribe and prohibit various works, but fruit cannot be legislated. Fruit is the result of a vine's life. A fruit tree or

42. George 1994, 341.
43. Bruce 1982b, 245.

vine produces fruit by virtue of what it is. Since believers live by the Spirit, they are to walk by the Spirit, bearing the fruit of the Spirit (v. 25).

Paul urges the Galatians to bear one another's burdens and to watch themselves lest they fall into sin (6:1–5). Paul then reminds his readers of the future judgment of God, telling them that if they sow to the flesh, they will reap corruption, but if they sow to the Spirit, they will reap eternal life (vv. 6–8). They are to take every opportunity to do that which is good (vv. 9–10). Paul concludes his epistle by appealing one final time to the Galatians not to abandon the gospel (vv. 11–16). He reminds them that neither circumcision nor uncircumcision counts for anything. What matters is the new creation (v. 15). Believers who are in Christ are a new creation, and this means that the old has passed away (2 Cor. 5:17).

The Thessalonian Epistles: Introduction

The historical context of Paul's epistles to the Thessalonians is found in Acts 17:1–10. This narrative recounts Paul's work in the city of Thessalonica during his second missionary journey. While there he spoke in the synagogue, persuading some Jews and even more God-fearing Gentiles that Jesus was the promised Messiah. Some of the Jews, however, became envious and dragged a few of Paul's converts before the city authorities, claiming that the Christians were being seditious ("saying that there is another king, Jesus"). Paul and Silas were forced to leave the city, so they made their way to Berea. Paul would soon afterward travel to Athens and then Corinth. Paul wrote the first epistle to the Thessalonians after being forced to leave the city. He was concerned for these new believers because of the persecution they were suffering. His first epistle to them was probably written while he was in the city of Corinth, sometime in the latter part of A.D. 50, or early 51. The second epistle was written not long afterward.[44]

The city of Thessalonica was located on a major Roman road, the Via Egnatia, and was a major port city on the northwestern shore of the Aegean Sea.[45] Because of its strategic location, it was the most important city in

44. See Bruce 1982a, xxxiv.

45. The Romans could reach the Via Egnatia by traveling southeast down the Via Appia from Rome to the coastal city of Brundisium. From there, they would cross the Adriatic Sea to the city of Dyrrachium. The Via Egnatia continued from Dyrrachium eastward for approximately seven hundred miles, skirting the northern shores of the Aegean Sea, until reaching its terminus in the city of Byzantium.

Macedonia. At the time of Paul's visit to the city, it was the administrative center of the province.[46] Thessalonica had closely aligned itself with Rome and had enjoyed the many benefits of loyalty. Other cities had from time to time resisted Rome and suffered the consequences. The Thessalonians were, therefore, very careful to maintain their loyalty. It is not difficult to understand, then, why the city authorities would be disturbed at the reports of someone speaking of "another king."

Like many first-century cities, Thessalonica was populated with adherents of dozens of religions and deities. Significantly, in addition to the numerous mystery religions, Thessalonica had very early on embraced the imperial cult—the worship of the Roman emperor. As early as the time of Augustus, priests of the imperial cult could be found in Thessalonica.[47] The Thessalonians had also erected a statue of Augustus and had a temple dedicated to him as well. As we have already seen, Augustus had been proclaimed the savior of the world. His coming had been heralded as the beginning of the gospel.[48] His successors were also the objects of worship. James Jeffers explains the political significance of this Roman emperor cult: "Emperor worship was a way for Roman leaders to establish their power in the eastern Mediterranean. It also served to focus the loyalty of provincials on the person of the emperor. This cult was readily accepted by the peoples of the eastern Mediterranean who for centuries had been taught to venerate their rulers as gods."[49]

It is important to realize that the emperor cult was not merely a religious phenomenon; it was political as well. Religion and politics were joined together in the public life of all ancient cities and nations, and the worship of the emperor was both a religious and a political act.[50] The significance of emperor worship in Thessalonica will become evident as we examine the eschatological teachings of the letters.

The Thessalonian epistles are unique among the New Testament epistles in terms of the relative amount of space devoted to explicitly eschatological themes. Eschatological themes are primary topics in 1 Thessalonians 4:13–18; 5:1–11; 2 Thessalonians 1:5–12; and 2:1–12. Paul speaks in these passages of the coming of the Lord, the resurrection of the dead, the timing

46. Wanamaker 1990, 3.

47. Witherington 2006a, 5; Wanamaker 1990, 5.

48. Klauck 2003, 296–98.

49. Jeffers 1999, 101; see also Klauck 2003, 261.

50. Gradel 2002, 12; Green 2002, 41.

of the day of the Lord, eschatological judgment, and the revelation of the man of lawlessness. These texts have been the source of much debate and disagreement because of their inherent difficulty.[51] Great care and humility are required, therefore, when seeking to understand what Paul meant.

1 Thessalonians

The first epistle to the Thessalonians begins with a greeting to the church (1:1). Paul then offers thanksgiving for the Thessalonian believers (vv. 2–10). He reminds them of his recent stay with them (vv. 3–5) and of their reception of the gospel (vv. 6–10). They had turned to God from idols to serve God and "to wait for his Son from heaven, whom he raised from the dead, Jesus who delivers us from the wrath to come" (v. 10). In this Paul rejoiced. The "wrath to come" (*tēs orgēs tēs erchomenēs*) that Paul mentions is a reference to divine judgment. There is some indication in this first epistle that the wrath spoken of here refers to some first-century judgment (2:16), but in light of Paul's "already/not yet" eschatology, even such contemporary manifestations of wrath must not be understood to rule out the final full manifestation of God's wrath on the wicked.[52]

Paul takes up the themes of chapter 1 again in chapter 2. The character of Paul and his companions and their ministry to the Thessalonians is his first concern (2:1–12). It is likely that Paul felt the need to include this defense of himself and his companions because of how quickly they had left the city and because he had not yet been able to return to them.[53] At the conclusion of this section, Paul makes a significant statement, saying, "we exhorted each one of you and encouraged you and charged you to walk in a manner worthy of God, who calls you into his own kingdom and glory" (v. 12). Paul speaks of a present calling to indicate that people are continually being called into God's kingdom.[54] The emphasis here, then, is on the present aspect of the kingdom.[55]

51. I cannot help but think that the eschatological sections of the Thessalonian epistles may have been in Peter's mind when he said that there are things in Paul's letters that are "hard to understand" (2 Peter 3:16).

52. See Witherington 2006a, 75.

53. Green 2002, 114.

54. Wanamaker 1990, 107.

55. Like Jesus, Paul sometimes speaks of the kingdom of God as present (e.g., Col. 1:13) and sometimes as future (e.g., 1 Cor. 6:9–10).

In 2:13–16, Paul again gives thanks for the reception of the gospel by the Thessalonians and for their steadfastness in persecution. Concerning their suffering, Paul writes:

> For you, brothers, became imitators of the churches of God in Christ Jesus that are in Judea. For you suffered the same things from your own countrymen as they did from the Jews, who killed both the Lord Jesus and the prophets, and drove us out, and displease God and oppose all mankind by hindering us from speaking to the Gentiles that they might be saved—so as always to fill up the measure of their sins. But God's wrath has come upon them at last! (vv. 14–16)

Paul's words should not be understood as being a general condemnation of Jews as Jews. Paul himself was a Jew as were many of the believers in Judea and in the churches he had planted. When Paul speaks of the Jews who displease God here, he is specifically referring to those who have rejected the gospel and who have actively hindered his mission. What he says of them is not at all dissimilar from the words used by many of the Old Testament prophets when they addressed unrepentant Israel. Paul points out to the Thessalonians that they are being persecuted in the same way that the Jewish believers in Judea have been persecuted. The Jews who are persecuting the young church are "filling up" the measure of their sins. This language is used elsewhere in Scripture to describe those who are opposing God and who must reach a certain point before they are ready for judgment (Gen. 15:16; Dan. 8:23). Jesus himself uses this language when speaking to the generation of Jews who are rejecting him (Matt. 23:32). Paul's statement indicates that Israel's sin is reaching the breaking point.[56]

Paul says that God's wrath "has come upon them" at last (1 Thess. 2:16). According to Paul, God's eschatological wrath has already begun to be poured out on the unbelieving Jews who are persecuting the church. It appears that Paul is speaking of something the readers would recognize in A.D. 50 or 51, the time that this letter was written. It is worth noting that in A.D. 49 at the Passover there was a massacre of thousands of Jews in the temple courts.[57] The same year witnessed the forceful expulsion of

56. See Beale 2003, 84–85.
57. Green 2002, 149.

the Jews from Rome by the emperor Claudius. Does Paul see such events as present manifestations of God's eschatological wrath being poured out upon those who called for Christ's crucifixion and who had continually persecuted the church? Such an idea does not seem to be out of the question. These events do not express the fullness of eschatological wrath, of course. They are indications of inaugurated eschatology. This wrath will be demonstrated much more visibly and fully when Jerusalem and the temple are destroyed in A.D. 70, but God's wrath will be expressed in its complete fullness only on the last day.

What does Paul mean when he says that God's wrath has come upon them "at last" (2:16)? The words translated "at last" are the Greek words *eis telos*. The meaning is likely similar to the meaning of the phrase in Matthew 10:22. In other words, it should be translated "to the end." The idea is that God's wrath has come upon the unbelieving Jews because of their rejection of the Messiah and will continue until the final events of human history.[58] Such an idea would coincide well with what we have seen suggested in several other places, namely, that Jesus and the apostles hold out hope for Israel's eventual repentance (e.g., Luke 21:24).

In 1 Thessalonians 2:19, Paul introduces a significant term into his discussion. He writes, "For what is our hope or joy or crown of boasting before our Lord Jesus at his coming [*parousia*]? Is it not you?" The word *parousia* occurs twenty-four times in the New Testament. Paul himself uses it fourteen times. Sometimes he uses the word to speak of his own "coming" or "presence" (2 Cor. 10:10; Phil. 1:26; 2:12). Sometimes he uses it to speak of the coming of his associates (1 Cor. 16:17; 2 Cor. 7:6, 7). Sometimes he uses it in reference to Jesus (1 Cor. 15:23; 1 Thess. 2:19; 3:13; 4:15; 5:23; 2 Thess. 2:1, 8), and on one occasion he uses it in reference to the man of lawlessness (2 Thess. 2:9). In general, the various contexts indicate that the word can be used to refer to the state of being present at a place or to the coming or arrival of someone as the first stage in their presence.[59] We will look more closely at this word in our examination of 1 Thessalonians 4:13–18.

In 1 Thessalonians 3, Paul tells the church that he had been unable to bear wondering about how they were faring in the faith and therefore sent Timothy to them to find out about them (3:1–5). He reminds them

58. Witherington 1992, 103.

59. BDAG, s.v. παρουσία.

that while he was with them he had told them that they were going to suffer affliction because they were "destined" for it. In other words, the inauguration of the kingdom does not mean the complete end of suffering and affliction.[60] In fact, the inauguration of the kingdom intensifies suffering because Satan does not readily concede defeat, and thus the conflict during the overlap of the ages between the rightful King and the usurper will be intense. Paul wants the Thessalonian believers to understand this in order that they might not be swayed but instead stand strong in their faith.

Timothy's report to Paul is encouraging (3:6–13). Paul learns that the Thessalonians have stood firm under their afflictions. He prays that he might come to them again and then says, "may the Lord make you increase and abound in love for one another and for all, as we do for you, so that he may establish your hearts blameless in holiness before our God and Father, at the coming [*parousia*] of our Lord Jesus with all his saints" (vv. 12–13). Paul seems to be alluding here to Zechariah 14:5, which itself is part of a vision of Yahweh fighting on behalf of his people as the divine warrior. If Paul is alluding to Zechariah, he is identifying Jesus as the divine warrior. Significantly, Paul here points to the coming of Jesus as an incentive for holiness and faithfulness.[61] By doing so he illustrates the fact that eschatology is not an abstract speculative topic. It should have very practical implications on the way we live.

In the remainder of the first epistle, Paul exhorts the church and answers several questions that were apparently sent back with Timothy (4:1–5:22). Paul encourages the Thessalonians to continue as they have been in steadfast faithfulness (4:1–2) and warns them to abstain from sexual immorality (vv. 3–8). To disregard this warning will be to invite judgment from the Lord (v. 6). In verse 9, Paul apparently begins answering a series of questions sent by the Thessalonians pertaining to specific topics. The first topic they ask Paul about is brotherly love, but Paul tells them that they have no need for him to write to them for they have already been taught by God to love one another (v. 9). They have already been exercising brotherly love, so Paul simply encourages them to continue to do so more and more (vv. 10–12).

60. Beale 2003, 100.
61. Bruce 1982a, 73.

The Dead in Christ

Paul turns next to a specifically eschatological question regarding believers who have died (4:13–18). He writes, "But we do not want you to be uninformed, brothers, about those who are asleep, that you may not grieve as others do who have no hope" (v. 13). A question has arisen among the Thessalonians because one or more of their fellow believers has died since Paul left.[62] Given what Paul says in this and the following verses, it appears that the Thessalonians were concerned about the position of deceased believers at the Lord's second coming.[63] Their question indicates that this was one topic that they did not understand fully. Apparently, Paul had taught them something about the resurrection of the dead but was forced to leave the city before teaching them as much as they needed to know.[64] Paul's basic response to their concern is to tell them that they have no reason to worry.

Paul tells the Thessalonians not to grieve over the dead like the unbelievers who have no hope. "For since we believe that Jesus died and rose again, even so, through Jesus, God will bring with him those who have fallen asleep" (4:14; Acts 17:3). Paul points the Thessalonians back to the resurrection of Jesus as the foundation of their hope for the dead in Christ. Jesus was raised from the dead, and those who are in Christ will be raised from the dead as well (2 Cor. 4:14). The eschatological resurrection began with the resurrection of Jesus. Believers now have hope because they know that they too will be raised to everlasting life.

Paul continues by explaining what will happen at the Lord's coming: "For this we declare to you by a word from the Lord, that we who are alive, who are left until the coming [*parousian*] of the Lord, will not precede those who have fallen asleep" (1 Thess. 4:15). The first question that must be addressed in connection with this verse is whether or not Paul taught here that he would definitely live until the time of the coming of Christ to raise the dead. According to some, Paul's use of the word "we" indicates that he definitely believed he would live to see the second coming of Jesus

62. "Sleep" is a common euphemism for death in the Jewish and Christian literature of this time period (Bruce 1982a, 95). While not stated explicitly, the death of the Thessalonian believer(s) may very well have been at the hands of those who were persecuting them.

63. Best 1986, 180.

64. Green 2002, 216.

and the final resurrection.[65] This interpretation, however, is unlikely. First, in the immediate context of this passage, Paul indicates the possibility that he might live to see these things and the possibility that he might not. He says that Christ died for us so that whether "we are awake [alive] or asleep [dead] we might live with him" (5:10). In his other letters Paul also entertains the possibility that he might die before the final resurrection (e.g., 1 Cor. 6:14; 2 Cor. 5:8; Phil. 1:20–24; 2:17).

Paul does not ever claim to know when he will die or exactly when the second coming of Jesus will occur. Therefore, as Witherington explains, he could not have said "we who are dead and not left around to see the parousia of the Lord. . . ." He does not know for sure that he will be dead, "so the only category in which he can logically place himself and the Christians he writes to here is the 'living.'"[66] The "we" is simply an expression of corporate solidarity.[67] Essentially, all that Paul means here is that those Christians who are alive at the coming of the Lord will not precede those who are dead.

The word Paul uses to refer to the coming of the Lord here is *parousia*. As we have already seen, Paul uses this word to speak of the presence or the arrival of someone, sometimes Jesus and sometimes other individuals. In the Greco-Roman world, the word was sometimes used to describe either the coming of a deity or the official visit of a ruler to a city. Such visits were important events, and the city would have great celebrations in honor of the visiting king.[68] The important city officials and the citizens would go out of the city to meet the visiting sovereign and escort him back to the city in a glorious procession. If Paul had this imagery in mind in this context, perhaps a misunderstanding of it is one reason the Thessalonians

65. E.g., Wanamaker 1990, 171–72.

66. Witherington 2006a, 134.

67. As Beale (2003, 140) explains, a similar concept is used throughout the Old Testament. A contemporary generation of Israel could be addressed as if they themselves had actually participated in the historical events of the past or would participate in historical events of the future, even if the individuals of that generation did not or would not participate. In Deuteronomy 4:20–31, for example, Moses, speaking to the second generation of Israel after the exodus, tells them that God brought "you" out of Egypt even though it was the first generation who actually experienced the exodus firsthand. He also tells this generation that they will experience exile if they disobey God and that they will be restored if they repent. Hundreds of years later, Israel was exiled, and many years after that, Israel was restored, but none of the individual Israelites to whom Moses spoke experienced these events firsthand. They had all died many years before the exile.

68. Green 2002, 223; Witherington 2006a, 91.

were confused about those who had died. It is possible they believed that those who had died would not enjoy the honor of going out to meet the coming Messiah in this official *parousia*. If that is the case, Paul puts the concern to rest, telling the Thessalonians that those who are alive "will not precede those who have fallen asleep." Those believers who have died will participate in this glorious event and will in fact have a place of honor.

Paul tells the Thessalonians, "For the Lord himself will descend from heaven with a cry of command, with the voice of an archangel, and with the sound of the trumpet of God. And the dead in Christ will rise first" (1 Thess. 4:16). It is important to observe that Paul specifically describes this event in terms of Christ's *descent* from heaven.[69] As we have already seen, Jesus often spoke of the coming of the Son of Man, alluding to the prophecy of Daniel 7:13–14. Daniel 7 spoke of one like a Son of Man coming up to the Ancient of Days. In other words, Daniel 7 used the imagery of an *ascent*. As I have argued, Daniel's prophecy of the Son of Man's ascent to receive his kingdom was fulfilled in connection with the first advent of Jesus. What Paul is speaking of here, on the other hand, is Christ's descent from heaven.

It should be recalled that when Jesus spoke of Daniel's "coming of the Son of Man," a coming up to the Father, he sometimes used the word *parousia* (e.g., Matt. 24:27, 37, 39) and sometimes used the word *erchomai* (e.g., Matt. 16:28; 24:30, 44; 26:64).[70] Paul, on the other hand, uses the word *parousia* in this context to refer to Jesus' descent from heaven, his coming to earth, and as we've already seen, he also uses the term elsewhere to refer to the presence or arrival of people other than Jesus. What all of this means is that the term *parousia*, by itself, is not a synonym for the second coming of Jesus. It is simply a word that means "presence" or "arrival" or "coming." Whose coming is meant and the direction they are coming can be determined only from the context.

Christ's descent from heaven is the fulfillment of the promise made to the apostles by the two men in white at the time of the ascension (Acts 1:11). In other words, at the time of Jesus' ascension *to* heaven (itself part of the fulfillment of Daniel 7:13–14), there is a promise of a future coming *from* heaven. The ascension to heaven and the promised coming from heaven are not the same events. In 1 Thessalonians 4:16, Paul is speaking

69. BDAG, s.v. καταβαίνω.

70. In the Olivet Discourse, Jesus alternates the terms throughout.

of the future coming *from* heaven—the second advent.[71] At the time of the second coming, Christ will call out a "cry of command" (4:16). Jesus' cry of command is likely the command to the dead calling them to rise from the grave (John 5:28–29; see also John 11:43). At his command, "the dead in Christ will rise first."

Paul continues, "Then we who are alive, who are left, will be caught up together with them in the clouds to meet the Lord in the air, and so we will always be with the Lord" (1 Thess. 4:17). The word translated "to meet" is the word *apantēsin*. This word was used in the Greco-Roman world to describe the meeting of a king or other important official who has come to visit a city.[72] As F. F. Bruce explains, "When a dignitary paid an official visit (παρουσία) to a city in Hellenistic times, the action of the leading citizens in going out to meet him and escort him back on the final stage of his journey was called the ἀπάντησις."[73]

According to Paul, after the dead in Christ are raised, those who are still alive will be caught up together with them so that all will meet the Lord in the air and then be with him forever. Paul does not explicitly say at this point where we will be with the Lord forever. Some suggest that after meeting Christ in the air, we will go with Christ into heaven.[74] However, if Paul is describing the meeting of Christians in the air with the Lord in terms of the known customs involving official visits of dignitaries and kings, then the idea is that believers will meet the coming Lord and escort him back to the earth. The Thessalonians are to encourage one another with these words (4:18).

Times and Seasons

The next question Paul addresses concerns the timing of the day of the Lord (1 Thess. 5:1–11). He writes, "Now concerning the times and the seasons, brothers, you have no need to have anything written to you" (v. 1). The words translated "Now concerning" are *peri de*. Paul uses this phrase

71. Much of the confusion on this subject is due to the fact that the word "coming" is used to describe these two different events (and other things as well). Daniel speaks of the "coming of the Son of Man" to refer to one event, while Paul and others often use the word "coming" to speak of the other event.

72. Koester 1997, 160.

73. Bruce 1982a, 102; see also Green 2002, 226–27.

74. E.g., Walvoord 1955, 70.

in 4:9 to introduce a new topic of discussion.[75] Here he uses it in the same way.[76] He has been discussing the second coming of Jesus and the resurrection of the dead. Now he turns his attention to the topic of the timing of the day of the Lord. This raises a question concerning how closely related the two topics are. In other words, how closely related are the second coming of Jesus (1 Thess. 4) and the day of the Lord (1 Thess. 5)?

According to G. K. Beale, it is evident that both chapters 4 and 5 are talking about the same events because both passages form a continuous depiction of the same narrative found in Matthew 24.[77] The problem with this line of argument is that it assumes Jesus is speaking of his second advent when he speaks of "the coming of the Son of Man" in Matthew 24 and that Paul is speaking of the same thing in 1 Thessalonians 4. As we have seen, however, there is very good reason to believe that when Jesus speaks of the coming of the Son of Man, he is alluding to the prophecy of Daniel 7:13–14 and speaking of something that was fulfilled in connection with his first advent.

The coming of the Son of Man is a coming *to* heaven to receive the kingdom. The second coming is a coming *from* heaven to raise the dead and consummate all things. If this is correct, it does not prove that 1 Thessalonians 4 and 5 are speaking of completely unrelated events. It simply means that the supposed parallels with Matthew 24 do not provide a strong argument for the contrary argument. As we will see, the relation between the events of 1 Thessalonians 4 and 5 cannot be finally decided until we examine 2 Thessalonians 2. At this point we will simply look at what 1 Thessalonians 5 says about the timing of the day of the Lord.

The Thessalonians have sent a question to Paul concerning "the times and the seasons" (*tōn chronōn kai tōn kairōn*). Paul tells them that they do not need him to write a response since they already know the answer. He tells them, "For you yourselves are fully aware that the day of the Lord will come like a thief in the night" (1 Thess. 5:2). Paul is essentially saying the same thing Jesus said in Acts 1:7 when he was asked about the timing of future

75. He uses it in the same manner a number of times in 1 Corinthians (1 Cor. 7:1, 25; 8:1; 12:1; 16:1, 12).

76. Richard 1995, 249.

77. Beale 2003, 136; see also the chart on page 137. Beale suggests the following parallels: 1 Thess. 4:16–17 (Matt. 24:30–31, 40–41); 1 Thess. 5:1–2 (Matt. 24:36); 1 Thess. 5:2, 4 (Matt. 24:43); 1 Thess. 5:3 (Matt. 24:8, 37–39); 1 Thess. 5:4–5 (Matt. 24:43); 1 Thess. 5:6 (Matt. 24:37–39); 1 Thess. 5:7 (Matt. 24:49).

things. He said to the apostles, "It is not for you to know times or seasons [*chronous ē kairous*] that the Father has fixed by his own authority."

In our examination of the Old Testament prophets we discovered that the phrase "day of the Lord" was used in numerous contexts. In general, the day of the Lord referred to that time when God, the divine warrior, would come in judgment to battle his enemies on behalf of his people. Thus it encompassed both judgment (for God's enemies) and salvation (for God's people). We are not surprised, therefore, to find prophets speaking of an imminent day of the Lord coming upon nations such as Babylon (Isa. 13:6, 9) and Egypt (Jer. 46:10), both enemies of God's people.

What the Israelites failed to understand, however, was that they too could become God's enemies if they forsook his covenant. Thus in the eighth century Amos spoke of the coming divine judgment of Israel in terms of the day of the Lord (Amos 5:18–27). In the latter half of the seventh century, Zephaniah foretold the coming judgment of Judah in the same terms (Zeph. 1:2–2:3). Ezekiel also spoke of the impending destruction of Jerusalem by the Babylonians in terms of the day of the Lord (Ezek. 7). What we see, then, is that many historical judgments that have already occurred were referred to by the prophets as the day of the Lord. The prophets, however, could also speak of a day of the Lord that was to come in the indefinite future (Mal. 4:5). In the prophetic books, then, the phrase "day of the Lord" could refer to any coming divine judgment. It did not always refer to the final eschatological judgment.

Paul had apparently taught the Thessalonians about a time of coming judgment that he referred to as the day of the Lord. They asked Paul when it would come, and he tells them that they already know it will come "like a thief in the night." Only twenty years earlier, Jesus had spoken to his disciples about a coming judgment that would arrive unexpectedly like a thief (Matt. 24:43). This judgment would be a type of the final judgment upon all mankind. Paul here uses similar language to speak of a coming judgment.

If Jesus was speaking of the judgment that would fall upon the nation of Israel during the war with Rome in A.D. 66–73, Paul may have the same judgment in mind. It is questionable, however, that the Thessalonian church would need to stay alert for that historical judgment, since they were predominantly Gentile, and since they lived hundreds of miles away from Israel. Paul may, however, be speaking of repercussions that would fall on the new churches in the wake of the Roman war with Israel. On the other hand, it is also possible that Paul is speaking of the final time of judgment that will come in connection with Christ's second advent. In any case, the point of the comparison with a thief is to encourage steadfast watchfulness.[78] Paul is telling the Thessalonians that the timing of this coming judgment is unknown, but they are to be prepared always.

Paul tells the Thessalonians, "While people are saying, 'There is peace and security,' then sudden destruction will come upon them as labor pains come upon a pregnant woman, and they will not escape" (1 Thess. 5:3). The phrase "peace and security" (*eirēnē kai asphaleia*) is not a quotation from the Old Testament. It is, however, a phrase that has been found in ancient inscriptions all over the Roman Empire. The inscription attributes the coming of "peace and security" to Rome.[79] If Paul is alluding to this bit of Roman political propaganda, he is using the power of Rome to make a point about God's coming judgment. The coming judgment of God will bring to nothing such arrogant political claims. Destruction will come like "labor pains" (Isa. 13:8; 21:3; 37:3; Jer. 6:24). Paul's point is that when God's judgment comes, the wicked will not be expecting it and will not be able to escape it.

Believers on the other hand will not be overtaken by surprise because they are to be vigilant and watchful (1 Thess. 5:4–10). The Thessalonians are not in a state of moral darkness like their pagan neighbors (v. 4). Instead, they are children of light (v. 5). For this reason, they are to stay awake (v. 6). In other words, they are to remain always ready for the day of the Lord. The Thessalonians are instructed to manifest faith, love, and hope in their lives because they have not been destined for wrath, but for salvation through Jesus Christ (vv. 8–9). The day of the Lord will be a day of judgment for unbelievers, but a day of salvation for those in Christ. Paul's point is that the way to be prepared for the coming day of the Lord, whenever it may be, is to live in faith, hope, and love.[80] Paul concludes this section of the epistle by saying that Jesus "died for us so that whether we are awake or asleep we might live with him" (v. 10). In other words, Paul does not know when the day of the Lord will come, but he does know that whether he is

78. Bruce 1982a, 109.

79. Witherington 2006a, 146; Koester 1997, 162.

80. Green 2002, 230.

alive or dead when it does come, he will live with Christ. Believers will live because Christ died for them and then rose again (4:14).

Following his words about the timing of the day of the Lord, Paul gives the church his final instructions. He asks them to show respect to those who have emerged as leaders in the body (5:12–13). He then gives them instruction regarding various duties (vv. 14–22). He prays that the Lord will sanctify them completely that they may be blameless "at the coming of our Lord Jesus Christ" (vv. 23–24). Finally, he closes, requesting that his letter be read to all the brothers (vv. 25–28).

2 Thessalonians

The second epistle to the Thessalonians was written not long after the first in order to answer some problems that had arisen in the new church. The most significant problem had to do with a misunderstanding of Paul's eschatological teaching. Paul's response to the Thessalonians contains one of the most difficult eschatological texts in the entire New Testament. The difficulty involves not only the content of the text itself but also the relationship of that content to other texts, particularly the eschatological texts found in 1 Thessalonians 4 and 5.

Revealed from Heaven

Following a brief greeting (1:1–2) and thanksgiving for the Thessalonians' spiritual growth amidst persecution (vv. 3–4), Paul turns to a discussion of their persecution in light of God's purposes (vv. 5–10). Concerning their persecutions and afflictions, Paul writes, "This is evidence of the righteous judgment of God, that you may be considered worthy of the kingdom of God, for which you are also suffering" (v. 5; cf. Phil. 1:27–28). What is the "evidence of the righteous judgment of God"? A number of suggestions have been made, but it appears that what Paul is saying is that their steadfastness and faith in all of the persecutions and afflictions they are enduring (2 Thess. 1:4) is in some way the evidence of God's righteous judgment (v. 5). Furthermore, in all of their suffering they will be counted worthy of the kingdom of God (Acts 14:22).

Paul continues, saying, "since indeed God considers it just to repay with affliction those who afflict you, and to grant relief to you who are afflicted as well as to us, when the Lord Jesus is revealed from heaven with his mighty angels in flaming fire, inflicting vengeance on those who do not know God and on those who do not obey the gospel of our Lord Jesus" (2 Thess. 1:6–8). Here Paul is using the kind of language found in the prophets to speak of the coming of the Lord in judgment upon those who have persecuted his people (Isa. 66:15). The word translated "revealed" is *apokalypsei*, which is used to refer to something being made fully known.[81] Christ's presence is presently hidden from our sight in the heavenly dimension (Acts 1:9). Paul looks forward to a day when Jesus will be revealed to all. When he is revealed, those who have persecuted his people will be judged. Paul's language is similar to the language found in the prophets when they promised future relief to God's people (e.g., Isa. 60:14; Jer. 17:18; 30:17; Ezek. 36:7). Their language was not a guarantee that such relief would come upon the generation that heard them. It was again an expression of the corporate solidarity of the people of God.

Paul writes, "They will suffer the punishment of eternal destruction, away from the presence of the Lord and from the glory of his might, when he comes [*elthē*] on that day to be glorified in his saints, and to be marveled at among all who have believed, because our testimony to you was believed" (2 Thess. 1:9–10).[82] The word translated "destruction" here is *olethron*. It is the same word Paul uses in 1 Thessalonians 5:3. It is typically found in texts that are dealing with the subject of judgment (e.g., 1 Cor. 5:5; 1 Tim. 6:9). Here Paul uses it to refer to the punishment of the wicked at the final judgment. Paul concludes this section of his letter by praying for the Thessalonians that God may glorify the name of Jesus in them according to his grace (2 Thess. 1:11–12).

The Day of the Lord and the Man of Lawlessness

The second chapter of Paul's second epistle to the Thessalonians contains one of the most difficult eschatological texts in all of Scripture. There are as many different interpretations, it seems, as there are interpreters, and even those who are in agreement concerning certain basic elements of the text disagree on secondary details. According to F. F. Bruce, "There are few New Testament passages which can boast such a variety of interpretations as

81. BDAG, s.v. ἀποκάλυψις.

82. The word *elthē* is the aorist active subjunctive of the verb *erchomai*, which simply means "to come."

this."[83] The difficulty of this chapter has long been recognized. Concerning one part of Paul's teaching in this chapter, Augustine (A.D. 354–430) wrote, "I frankly confess I do not know what he means."[84] However, despite the difficulty involved in understanding some of the details, the most basic point that Paul makes in this text is, as we shall see, relatively clear.

Because of the difficulty of the text, it will perhaps be best to look at it in its entirety before proceeding to examine its details. Paul writes:

> Now concerning the coming [*parousias*] of our Lord Jesus Christ and our being gathered together to him, we ask you, brothers, not to be quickly shaken in mind or alarmed, either by a spirit or a spoken word, or a letter seeming to be from us, to the effect that the day of the Lord has come. Let no one deceive you in any way. For that day will not come, unless the rebellion comes first, and the man of lawlessness is revealed, the son of destruction, who opposes and exalts himself against every so-called god or object of worship, so that he takes his seat in the temple of God, proclaiming himself to be God. Do you not remember that when I was still with you I told you these things? And you know what is restraining him now so that he may be revealed in his time. For the mystery of lawlessness is already at work. Only he who now restrains it will do so until he is out of the way. And then the lawless one will be revealed, whom the Lord Jesus will kill with the breath of his mouth and bring to nothing by the appearance of his coming [*parousias*]. The coming [*parousia*] of the lawless one is by the activity of Satan with all power and false signs and wonders, and with all wicked deception for those who are perishing, because they refused to love the truth and so be saved. Therefore God sends them a strong delusion, so that they may believe what is false, in order that all may be condemned who did not believe the truth but had pleasure in unrighteousness. (2 Thess. 2:1–12)

What is clear from this text is that at the time of Paul's writing (ca. A.D. 50), the day of the Lord, whatever he meant by that phrase, had not yet come (vv. 1–3). According to Paul, the day of the Lord would not come until certain other things happened first.

The main issues facing the contemporary interpreter, who lives much later than Paul, involve identifying what these things are that he said

83. Bruce 1971b, 309.

84. Augustine, *City of God* 20.19. I must confess that I take some comfort in the fact that Augustine, perhaps the greatest mind in the history of the postapostolic church, confesses difficulty in understanding this text.

must occur before the coming of the day of the Lord and discerning whether any of them have already occurred or have begun to occur since the time Paul wrote. Unfortunately, answering these questions is far from a simple matter. There are four basic options regarding the time of their fulfillment: (1) All of the preliminary signs and the day of the Lord have already occurred; (2) All of the preliminary signs have occurred, so there is now nothing preventing the coming of the day of the Lord, but the day of the Lord itself has not yet come; (3) Some of the preliminary signs have either occurred or begun to occur, but since all of them have not yet occurred, the day of the Lord cannot come yet; and (4) None of the preliminary signs has yet occurred, so the day of the Lord still cannot come. Within each of these basic overarching interpretive schemes, a number of variations in detail and nuance are possible. Before looking at the strengths and weaknesses of each basic option, we must look at the details of the text.

Paul begins by indicating the issue he will be addressing. He writes, "Now concerning the coming [*parousias*] of our Lord Jesus Christ and our being gathered together to him, we ask you, brothers, not to be quickly shaken in mind or alarmed, either by a spirit or a spoken word, or a letter seeming to be from us, to the effect that the day of the Lord has come" (2:1–2). Apparently, Paul has received word that the Thessalonians had been misled or were in danger of being misled to believe that the day of the Lord has already come.[85] He writes to reassure them that this is not true because certain events, to be mentioned in the following verses, must take place before the day of the Lord comes.

In this opening sentence, Paul indicates that the topic he is addressing is "the coming of our Lord Jesus Christ and our being gathered together to him," and he says that concerning these things, the Thessalonians are not to believe "that the day of the Lord has come." It appears, then, that there is a close relationship of some kind between the "day of the Lord" to which Paul is referring here and the "coming [*parousias*] of our Lord Jesus Christ and our being gathered together to him."[86] The word translated "gathered together" (*episynagōgēs*) is used only one other time in the New Testament. In Hebrews 10:25, it is used to refer to the assembling together of Christians. It is used once in the apocryphal books to refer to

85. Best 1986, 274.
86. Green 2002, 301.

the regathering of Israel after the exile (2 Macc. 2:7). F. F. Bruce suggests that "our being gathered together to him" in 2 Thessalonians 2:1 is a reference to the resurrection event described in 1 Thessalonians 4.[87] If that is what Paul means by these words in 2 Thessalonians, it would provide the strongest argument that the topics Paul discussed in 1 Thessalonians 4:13–18 (Christ's second coming and the resurrection of the dead) and in 5:1–11 (the day of the Lord as a time of coming judgment) are closely related in some way.

According to Paul, the Thessalonians should not be misled to believe "that the day of the Lord has come." But what does Paul mean when he says "has come"? The word translated "has come" is *enestēken*, the perfect indicative form of *enistēmi*. Some suggest the word should be translated "is about to take place" or "is in the process of coming."[88] Others reject this argument. Beale, for example, observes that "Paul's use of *enistēmi* ('to be present, come') in his other letters, in line with the typical contemporary Hellenistic usage, alludes to the present time in contrast to the future (e.g., Rom 8:38; 1 Cor 3:22; 7:26)."[89] Thus what the Thessalonians have been told is not that the day of the Lord is about to take place, but that the day of the Lord has already come, or has already begun.[90]

If the day of the Lord is associated with the second coming and the resurrection from the dead, were the Thessalonians actually being told by some that these things had already happened? If so, how could they possibly believe this since Paul had taught them that they too would be caught up to be with the Lord at this time (1 Thess. 4:15–17)? If this is what they were being told, then it is likely that they were being told that the second coming of Jesus and the resurrection of the dead had already occurred in some invisible spiritual sense.[91] We know from elsewhere in Paul's writings that similar things were being taught by others. Hymenaeus and Philetus were spreading the false teaching "that the resurrection has already happened" (2 Tim. 2:17–18). It appears that a similar false doctrine found its

87. Bruce 1982a, 163.

88. E.g., Green 2002, 305.

89. Beale 2003, 199.

90. Wanamaker 1990, 240.

91. Beale 2003, 200. Such ideas are still being taught in the present time. The Jehovah's Witnesses taught that the second coming occurred invisibly in 1914. In recent years, full preterists have taught that the second coming occurred invisibly in A.D. 70 (see Beale 2003, 201–2).

way into the midst of the church in Thessalonica. In the following verses, Paul will explain to the Thessalonians why they should not believe that the day of the Lord has already come.

Paul writes:

> Let no one deceive you in any way. For that day will not come, unless the rebellion comes first, and the man of lawlessness is revealed, the son of destruction, who opposes and exalts himself against every so-called god or object of worship, so that he takes his seat in the temple of God, proclaiming himself to be God. Do you not remember that when I was still with you I told you these things? (2 Thess. 2:3–5)

Paul indicates here that he is reminding the Thessalonians of something he had already told them during his time with them. In other words, Paul is assuming some knowledge on their part, knowledge that contemporary readers are forced to infer.

Paul reminds the Thessalonians that the day of the Lord will not come until two things occur. First, the day of the Lord will not come until the "rebellion." The word translated "rebellion" is *apostasia*. According to the standard Greek lexicon, this is an accurate translation.[92] The word, however, can refer to either political or religious rebellion, and Paul does not specify which sense he intends.[93] Josephus uses the term to speak of the Jewish political rebellion against Rome that began in A.D. 66.[94] The author of 1 Maccabees, on the other hand, uses the term to refer to the attempts by the oppressors of the Jews to force them to rebel against God (1 Macc. 2:15).

What, then, does Paul mean when he speaks of the rebellion that must come before the day of the Lord comes? Apparently he is referring to a specific coming rebellion, either religious or political, that he had informed the Thessalonians about.[95] They presumably knew exactly what rebellion he was talking about here. We, on the other hand, are left to do the best we can with the available evidence. It seems clear that whatever this rebellion

92. BDAG, s.v. ἀποστασία. Some dispensationalists (e.g., Wuest 1957, 60–69) have suggested that the word means "departure" in the sense of the church's departure from the earth (i.e., rapture), meaning that the day of the Lord will not occur until after the rapture of the church, but the word is never used in such a sense elsewhere (see Beale 2003, 204; Gundry 1973, 114–18).

93. Bruce 1982a, 166.

94. Josephus, *Life* 4 §17.

95. Morris 1984, 127.

was, it would have to be evident to witnesses when it occurred; otherwise its failure to occur at the time Paul wrote 2 Thessalonians could not be used sensibly by Paul to demonstrate that the day of the Lord had not come.

Was Paul speaking of a religious rebellion to occur at some point in the future? According to many interpreters, Paul is speaking here of a large-scale falling away from the faith by professing Christians.[96] G. K. Beale argues that such a meaning is evident here "because of the immediate context of false teaching (2:1–2, 9–12) and the clear allusions to Daniel's prediction of an end-time opponent who will bring about a large-scale compromise of faith among God's people."[97] It could also be argued that since the man of lawlessness, who is associated in some way with the rebellion, is himself killed by Jesus at his second coming, then all of these events must be events that occur at the time of Christ's second coming (2 Thess. 2:8). This interpretation of the *apostasia*, therefore, cannot be categorically ruled out. Paul may very well have been speaking of a religious rebellion, a falling away from the faith before the coming of the day of the Lord.

The primary difficulty faced by this view is that whatever Paul means when he speaks of "the rebellion," it was to be something the Thessalonians would be able to recognize if they lived to see it. Otherwise Paul could not point to its failure to occur yet as a reason to conclude that the day of the Lord had not yet come. If the rebellion is a religious rebellion, it would also have to manifest itself in a way that it had not already done. It is evident from the letters of Paul and other New Testament texts that even during the middle of the first century, there were already false teachers and religious apostasy (e.g., 2 Cor. 11:13; Gal. 1:6; 2:4; 2 Tim. 2:17–18; 2 Peter 2:1–22; 1 John 4:1). In fact, throughout the history of the church there has been apostasy from the faith. What amount of religious apostasy, then, would have to occur before it could be recognized as *the* rebellion? One potential answer is that this apostasy, as opposed to all past apostasy, would be associated with the revelation of the man of lawlessness. The only difficulty here is that the identity of Paul's "man of lawlessness" is surrounded by as much disagreement as the meaning of "the rebellion." Of course, the religious rebellion could be of such a magnitude that it would be self-evident to any biblically informed Christian that it is *the* rebellion.

96. See Hoekema 1979, 153; Venema 2000, 162–64; Green 2002, 307; Beale 2003, 203–5; Riddlebarger 2006, 125–26.

97. Beale 2003, 203–4.

What about the other possibility? Could Paul have been speaking about a coming political rebellion of some kind?[98] We know from Scripture that Jesus had foreseen that Jerusalem would be surrounded by armies (Luke 21:20), and we know from history that such invasions during this era could be the result of political rebellion. Could it be the case that Paul is speaking here of the same coming events that Jesus foresaw in the Olivet Discourse? If so, he is saying that the day of the Lord cannot come before the Jewish rebellion against Rome that would lead to the fulfillment of the prophecy found in Jesus' Olivet Discourse.

This interpretation has the advantage of being a readily observable event. In other words, the Thessalonians and everyone else would know exactly when this event occurred. The difficulty with this interpretation is that Paul later says in 2 Thessalonians 2:8 that the man of lawlessness, who seems to be closely associated in some way with the rebellion, and who is also to be revealed before the coming of the day of the Lord, will be destroyed by Jesus at his "coming" (*parousia*), an event which itself is closely associated with the day of the Lord and "our being gathered together to him." If the "rebellion" and the revelation of the man of lawlessness are fulfilled in the events of the first-century Jewish War, and if the man of lawlessness is destroyed at the time of Christ's coming, and if the time of Christ's coming is to be the time of our gathering together to him (the resurrection of the dead and the "rapture" of the living to be with the Lord forever), then Paul was mistaken because the resurrection and "rapture" did not occur at that time.[99]

Both of the proposed interpretations that we have looked at assume that the "rebellion," whatever it may be, is a relatively brief occurrence, essentially identifiable with a single event. But there is another option. It is possible that the rebellion has its identifiable beginning point during the Jewish War of A.D. 66–73, but then continues until it culminates with the revelation

98. See Gentry (1999, 103–4) for a contemporary defense of this position.

99. There are some (full preterists) who would suggest that the difficulties here can be solved simply by believing that the second coming of Jesus and the resurrection from the dead *did* occur around A.D. 70, but such a solution is comparable to getting rid of a termite infestation by burning down one's house. Such a solution would insist that the false teachers troubling the Thessalonians were not in error when they asserted the invisible spiritual nature of the second coming and resurrection from the dead. They were only in error about the *timing* of these spiritual and invisible events. For an explanation of why a proper understanding of the nature of the final resurrection of the dead is crucial to the Christian faith, see Strimple 2004.

of the man of lawlessness just prior to the second advent of Jesus and the resurrection of the dead. In other words, it is possible that the rebellion began in the first century and still continues today. Is there any evidence to support such an idea? We know that Jesus foresaw the coming Jewish War as an event that would mark the point at which Israel "filled up" the sins of their fathers (Matt. 23:32). In other words, Israel's rejection of the Messiah reached a climactic point and was judged during her rebellion against Rome. This political rebellion marks the point at which Israel had filled up the cup of her sins, and it marks the beginning of a long period of time during which she continues in her rejection of the Messiah.

Luke refers to the lengthy period of time that began during the Jewish War of A.D. 66–73 as "the times of the Gentiles," a time during which Jerusalem will continue to be trampled underfoot by the Gentiles, and a time that will come to a conclusion (Luke 21:24). In other words, he portrays the times of the Gentiles as the continuation of the judgment on Jerusalem that began with the Jewish War of the first century and continues until the last day. It is possible, then, that when Paul speaks of the rebellion, he is speaking primarily of the event that marks the culmination of Israel's rejection of the Messiah (i.e., the destruction of Jerusalem). But since this event also marks the beginning of a lengthy period of time during which Israel continues to reject her Messiah, and which Luke portrays as the ongoing "destruction" of Jerusalem ("trampled underfoot"), it is possible that Paul also has this lengthy period of time in mind as well. In order to discover which, if any, of these interpretations of the rebellion makes the best sense of the text, we will have to closely examine the remainder of Paul's words on the subject.

Paul tells the Thessalonians, "that day will not come, unless the rebellion comes first, and the man of lawlessness is revealed, the son of destruction, who opposes and exalts himself against every so-called god or object of worship, so that he takes his seat in the temple of God, proclaiming himself to be God" (2 Thess. 2:3–4). Not only must the rebellion occur before the day of the Lord will come, the man of lawlessness must also be revealed. The language Paul uses to describe the man of lawlessness is similar to the language Daniel uses in 11:36–37 to describe a coming wicked king.[100] It is also very similar to prophecies concerning the king of Babylon in Isaiah

100. As we have seen in chapter 8, it is possible that this prophecy referred to Antiochus Epiphanes, to Herod, or to a future antichrist figure.

14:13–14 and the king of Tyre in Ezekiel 28:2. In the pseudepigraphal *Martyrdom of Isaiah*, similar language is used to describe the wicked king Manasseh.[101]

What all of these texts have in common is that they all speak of political rulers who arrogated titles and honors belonging only to God. When Paul speaks of a man of lawlessness taking his seat in the temple of God and claiming to be God, he is evoking the memory of these biblical texts apparently in order to point to a coming political ruler who would do the same kind of thing. It is very likely that he was also evoking the memory of Emperor Gaius (Caligula), who only ten years earlier (A.D. 40) had attempted to have his statue set up in the Jerusalem temple. Only his murder in A.D. 41 prevented this blasphemous act from being carried out.[102] What Paul seems to be saying is that the day will come when another political ruler will do what these other wicked kings have done and tried to do. He will claim to be the manifestation of God.[103] Paul is also saying that this must happen before the day of the Lord will come.

To whom, then, is Paul referring when he speaks of the man of lawlessness? We cannot begin to answer that question until we look at 2 Thessalonians 2:6–7. Paul writes, "And you know what is restraining him now so that he may be revealed in his time. For the mystery of lawlessness is already at work. Only he who now restrains it will do so until he is out of the way." These verses raise a whole host of questions. The first question that must be answered concerns the correct understanding of *to katechon* in verse 6 and *ho katechōn* in verse 7. There are two separate questions involved here. First, we must ask whether the basic meaning of the word in this context implies hostile opposition. Second, we must discover the significance of the change from the neuter participle in verse 6 to the masculine participle in verse 7.

101. In Acts 12:21–23, we find a record of Herod Agrippa accepting divine honors. The language used to describe this event is not the same as that in 2 Thessalonians, but it is another example of a political ruler taking divine honors.

102. Klauck 2003, 304; Bruce 1982a, 168.

103. Bruce 1977b, 233. What of Paul's statement that he "takes his seat in the temple of God" (v. 4)? Does this mean that the man of lawlessness had to come before the Jerusalem temple was destroyed in A.D. 70? Or, if the man of lawlessness did not come before the temple's destruction, does this mean a new Jerusalem temple must be built? The answer to both questions is no. Paul's words must be understood against the backdrop of Old Testament texts such as Daniel 11; Isaiah 14; and Ezekiel 28, as well as the imperial cult that was so prevalent in Thessalonica at the time. There was a temple to the emperor in Thessalonica. Paul is simply painting a picture of a political ruler who takes upon himself divine honors (see Green 2002, 312).

Another question that must be answered concerns whether anything in these verses indicates that the man of lawlessness was already in existence at the time of the writing of this epistle. The answers to all of these questions are crucial to understanding the meaning of the text.

The ESV translates *to katechon* (neuter) as "what is restraining" (v. 6) and *ho katechōn* (masculine) as "he who restrains" (v. 7). Most interpreters have begun with the assumption that the word "restrain" in both verses implies a power that is opposed to the man of lawlessness and then have sought to identify who or what is restraining the man of lawlessness. The suggestions are legion. The "restrainer" has been identified as the Roman Empire and the emperor, Roman law and order, the preaching of the gospel, God, the Holy Spirit, the archangel Michael, and a host of other persons and things.[104] Probably the most likely of these interpretations is the proposal that the Holy Spirit is the one who restrains. The fact that the word for "Spirit" is *pneuma* (a neuter noun) might explain the use of the neuter *to katechon*, and the fact that the Holy Spirit is a person might explain the use of the masculine *ho katechōn*.[105]

Others have argued that it is wrong to assume that "the restraint" is being imposed by something/someone who is opposed to the man of lawlessness. Gene Green, for example, argues that the context indicates the possibility that the "restraining power/person" may also be an evil and lawless power/person that "holds back" the revelation of the man of lawlessness until it/he is ready to unleash this man upon the world.[106] In verse 7, for example, Paul seems to closely relate the restraining power to the "mystery of lawlessness," and in verse 9, he says that "the coming of the lawless one is by the activity of Satan."

104. For defenses of some of these various interpretations, see Marshall 1983, 199–200; Wanamaker 1990, 256; Beale 2003, 216; Witherington 2006a, 211.

105. There are two common objections to the idea that Paul is speaking of the Holy Spirit. First, some ask why Paul would use such obscure language to speak of the Holy Spirit. It is difficult to provide an answer to a question regarding a person's unstated motives, but we might suggest that Paul spoke of the Holy Spirit as a "restrainer" here for the same kind of reason that Jesus spoke of him as a *paraklētos*, or "Helper" (John 14:16, 26; 15:26; 16:7). In other words, he was speaking of the Holy Spirit here in terms of a particular function. A second objection raised by some is that it seems strange to speak of the Holy Spirit being taken "out of the way." However, as Beale (2003, 215) observes, this objection "is mitigated by taking the word *genētai* as a deponent middle and translating it 'he comes from the midst.'" Beale ultimately rejects this interpretation because he thinks it unlikely that the Holy Spirit would be removed from earth, but the context nowhere demands that the "restrainer" be removed from earth.

106. Green 2002, 316.

James Everett Frame suggests the possibility that *katechon* and *katechōn* refer to "a well-known spirit or person, possibly the Devil himself who is in control of the forces of evil, the prince of the power of the air that operates in the sons of disobedience."[107] Green also argues that the *katechōn* is Satan.[108] According to this understanding of the text, the *katechon* (neuter) is the evil spiritual force identified with the "mystery of lawlessness" in verse 7.[109] This evil spiritual force is personified by Satan the *katechōn* (masculine). Satanic spiritual forces are already at work at the time Paul is writing (v. 7a). Satan himself is "holding back" the revelation of the man of lawlessness until the appointed time, a time when Satan is "out of the way" (v. 7b). Ultimately this view is unpersuasive.

Another question that must be answered is whether the text indicates that the man of lawlessness was already in existence at the time Paul wrote 2 Thessalonians. According to Bruce, "It is plain . . . that both the mystery of iniquity and the restraining agency are at work at the time of the writing of the epistle; the restrainer has not yet been removed, therefore the man of lawlessness has not yet appeared, and *a fortiori* the Day of the Lord has not yet arrived."[110] With this, there can be little dispute. Paul says that the "mystery of lawlessness is already at work" (v. 7), and he also speaks of a force and a person that are presently "holding back" the revelation of the man of lawlessness (vv. 6–7). But does he say or imply that the man of lawlessness himself is already in existence?

Some argue that since the "holding back" is already occurring at the time of writing, the man of lawlessness must be an individual who is alive at that time.[111] James Stuart Russell, for example, asks, "Why should he [Paul] delineate the features of this mysterious personage to the Thessalonians if he was one with whom the Thessalonians had nothing to do, from whom they had nothing to fear, and who would not be revealed for ages yet to come?"[112] In response, it could be said that Paul did this for the same reason that Daniel revealed a similar personage in Daniel 11:36–37, one who also would not appear on the scene for centuries. In addition, Paul

107. Frame 1912, 259.
108. Green 2002, 318.
109. Wanamaker 1990, 253.
110. Bruce 1982a, 171.
111. E.g., Russell 2003, 180; Gentry 1999, 105.
112. Russell 2003, 179.

does not indicate that he knows exactly when the man of lawlessness would be revealed. It could happen at any time, so the Thessalonians needed to be prepared.

Many who believe the man of lawlessness had to have been alive at the time Paul wrote conclude that he should be identified with the emperor Nero.[113] It should be noted that Nero was identified as the man of lawlessness by some in the early church.[114] Furthermore, if one reads the ancient historical accounts of Nero's life, it is not difficult to understand how many could conclude that he was the manifestation of lawlessness on earth.[115] Considering the relatively recent actions of Caligula, it is not difficult to see how Paul's words could be understood as referring to a future Roman emperor.[116] The primary obstacle to identifying the man of lawlessness with Nero, however, is Paul's statement in verse 8 to the effect that the man of lawlessness will be killed by Jesus at his "coming" or *parousia*. If Paul is speaking of Jesus' second coming in verse 8, then Nero cannot be the man of lawlessness, since Nero died in A.D. 68, and the second coming did not occur at that time.

According to some, the language Paul uses to speak of the man of lawlessness being killed by the breath of Christ's mouth at the time of the second coming is the kind of metaphorical language found in the prophets (e.g., Isa. 11:4; 30:27–31).[117] There is no question that Paul is using prophetic metaphorical language to describe how the man of lawlessness is killed. The problem involves the *time* of his destruction. If the man of lawlessness is Nero, and if his destruction occurs at the time of Christ's *parousia*, and if Christ's *parousia* is the time at which the dead are raised and caught up to be with Christ together with those believers who are alive at his coming (1 Thess. 4:15–17), then we have to conclude one of three things: (1) Paul was wrong since the resurrection of the dead did not occur anywhere near the time of Nero's death; (2) the resurrection occurred at that time, but it was an invisible spiritual resurrection; or (3) the resurrection was for some reason delayed. None of these conclusions is acceptable. The first would call into

113. Gentry 1999, 106; Russell 2003, 182. I previously suggested the same identification (see Mathison 1999, 232), but this is a conclusion that I now question.

114. This interpretation is mentioned by Augustine (*City of God* 20.19).

115. See, for example, the account of Nero's life in Suetonius's *Lives of the Twelve Caesars*.

116. Witherington 2006a, 219.

117. Gentry 1999, 112.

question the accuracy of Scripture. The second contradicts other Scripture and is a heresy that Paul himself opposed. The third finds no support in the text. In short, it appears that the only way the man of lawlessness can be identified with Nero is to maintain that the *parousia* of Christ spoken of by Paul in 2 Thessalonians 2:8 is something different from the *parousia* of Christ spoken of by Paul in 1 Thessalonians 4:15.[118]

In order to resolve the question of the identity of the man of lawlessness, we must return to the presuppositions of the argument. In other words, does the text require that the man of lawlessness be a person who was alive when Paul wrote his epistle? That which restrains is in existence at the time of Paul's writing, and the mystery of lawlessness is already at work at the time of his writing, but Paul does not explicitly say that the man of lawlessness himself is in existence at the time of his writing. Nor does Paul say explicitly that he is not in existence. Some say the text requires that he is in existence at that time, arguing that if the restrainer is presently holding him back, he must be in existence. However, in light of the fact that Paul is using highly symbolic (apocalyptic) language, it is possible that the one who is holding the man of lawlessness back is holding him back *in his plans*. Such an idea is suggested by Paul's language concerning the revelation of the man of lawlessness "in his time" (2 Thess. 2:6).

Paul continues his letter, saying, "And then the lawless one will be revealed, whom the Lord Jesus will kill with the breath of his mouth and bring to nothing by the appearance of his coming" (2:8). The one who has held back the revelation of the man of lawlessness steps out of the way (or is taken out of the way; v. 7), and now the man of lawlessness is revealed. Whoever this arrogant political ruler turns out to be, he will not prevail. The Lord Jesus will destroy him at his second advent. In his description of the destruction of the man of lawlessness, Paul alludes to Isaiah 11:4, part of a prophecy of the coming Messiah.

After describing the destruction of the man of lawlessness, Paul describes his coming, "The coming [*parousia*] of the lawless one is by the activity

118. Such a possibility should not be completely ruled out since, as we have already seen, Paul uses the word to speak of the coming or presence of different persons and since Jesus uses the word to speak of his "coming" to the Father, a first-century event. The question, however, is how likely it is that Paul would use the term in different senses between the time of the writing of 1 Thessalonians 4 and 2 Thessalonians 2, especially when the Thessalonians were already confused about eschatological issues.

of Satan with all power and false signs and wonders, and with all wicked deception for those who are perishing, because they refused to love the truth and so be saved" (2 Thess. 2:9–10). Paul's description of the coming of the man of lawlessness as a *parousia* indicates that this man of lawlessness is Satan's parody of Christ, his counterfeit Christ. His coming will be accompanied by all kinds of false signs and wonders. Such satanic "miracles" are designed to deceive.

Paul continues, "Therefore God sends them a strong delusion, so that they may believe what is false, in order that all may be condemned who did not believe the truth but had pleasure in unrighteousness" (2:11–12). Because those who are perishing refused to love the truth, God sends his judgment upon them. God sends upon them a delusion that makes them unable to distinguish between the truth and falsehood. Scripture repeatedly speaks of God judging people by giving them over to the sin they embrace (Ps. 81:11–12; Rom. 1:24, 26, 28; 11:8). The result of believing the lie will be condemnation.

Having looked at the details of the texts, it is necessary to look briefly at the four basic options concerning the events that must precede the coming of the day of the Lord in order to observe the strengths and weaknesses of each. The first option is to conclude that all of the preliminary signs and the day of the Lord itself have already occurred. The strength of this interpretation is that it explains well Paul's use of the present tense when speaking about the restraining of the lawless one. It is also able to provide suggestions of readily observable events and persons (e.g., the Jewish War, Nero) that the Thessalonians could recognize and that would serve well as signs. It also makes sense in light of the fact that only twenty years earlier Jesus had spoken of a major judgment to come within a single generation. The weakness of this interpretation is that Paul closely relates the "day of the Lord" with the *parousia* "of our Lord Jesus Christ and our being gathered together to him" (2 Thess. 2:1–2). When read in light of what Paul has written in 1 Thessalonians, his words in 2:1 *appear* to be a reference to the second coming and the resurrection of the dead. In addition, the man of lawlessness is said to be killed by Jesus at the time of the *parousia*. If this *parousia* is the second coming, then the man of lawlessness cannot be identified with Nero or any other person who died in the first century, since Jesus' second coming did not occur in the first century.

A second option is to conclude that all of the preliminary signs have occurred, so there is now nothing preventing the coming of the day of the Lord, but the day of the Lord itself has not yet come. This option posits a delay between the preliminary signs and the coming of the day of the Lord. This view shares all of the strengths of the first view. The weakness of this view is that Paul says that the man of lawlessness is destroyed by Christ at his *parousia* (2:8), which itself is closely related to the day of the Lord (2:1–3). There does not appear to be any room in the text for a multigenerational delay between the time of the man of lawlessness and the day of the Lord/second coming of Christ, since it is at the time of the second coming of Christ that the man of lawlessness is killed.

A third option is to conclude that some of the preliminary signs have either occurred or begun to occur, but since all of them have not yet occurred, the day of the Lord has not come yet. One might suggest that the "rebellion" is that point in time when Israel filled up the cup of her sins in rejecting the Messiah. This rebellion continues concurrently with the "times of the Gentiles." In other words, the destruction of Jerusalem in A.D. 70 that marked the culmination point of Israel's rejection of the Messiah will continue as Jerusalem continues to be "trampled underfoot" by the Gentiles. This period of "rebellion" will end with the revelation of the man of lawlessness who will be destroyed at the second advent of Christ. The strength of such a view is that the "rebellion" and the "man of lawlessness" remain readily identifiable events/persons without suggesting that Paul made the mistake of saying the second coming of Jesus and the resurrection of the dead would occur in the first century. One weakness of such an idea is that Paul speaks of a power/person who is presently restraining the man of lawlessness. Although such language doesn't absolutely require that the man of lawlessness be in existence at the time Paul wrote, the idea seems to be implied.

A fourth option is to conclude that none of the preliminary signs has yet occurred, and therefore the day of the Lord has not yet come either. According to this view, the contemporary church is in exactly the same position as the Thessalonian church, still awaiting the "rebellion" and the revelation of the man of lawlessness. The strength of this view is that it maintains consistency between Paul's use of *parousia* in 2 Thessalonians 2:8 and 1 Thessalonians 4:15. It does not require the suggestion that Paul used the same term in two different ways in these letters written to confused believers. The weakness of this view is that Paul seems to suggest that the man of lawlessness is in existence at the time of the writing of the epistle. He speaks of something "restraining him now" (2 Thess. 2:6) and of one "who now restrains" (2:7).

As mentioned above, within each of these basic overarching interpretive schemes, a number of variations in detail and nuance are possible. In other words, because there are so many different ways of interpreting such things as "our being gathered together," the "day of the Lord," the "rebellion," the "man of lawlessness," the restraining force/person, and more, there are several potential versions of each of the four basic views. It is simply not possible in the space of a single chapter to examine every conceivable interpretation of this passage. Instead, a few closing hermeneutical observations are in order.

One of the most important facts to keep in mind before coming to any conclusion about the meaning of 2 Thessalonians 2:1–12 is that it is universally admitted to be a difficult and somewhat obscure text. Paul apparently assumes some prior knowledge on the part of the Thessalonians, knowledge communicated to them while he was with them, knowledge contemporary readers may not have.[119] What this means is that we should not start with the more obscure text of 2 Thessalonians 2 and then force other clearer texts to conform to our interpretation of it. It would be better to admit ignorance of the meaning of 2 Thessalonians 2 and leave it at that. The concluding observations that follow, therefore, remain somewhat tentative due to the difficulty of the text.

Paul opens this passage with the words "Now concerning the coming [*parousias*] of our Lord Jesus Christ" (2:1). Near the end of the passage, he refers again to Jesus' "coming" (*parousias*) (v. 8). Since Paul has very recently taught the Thessalonians by letter about the "coming [*parousian*] of the Lord" (1 Thess. 4:15), and since the Thessalonians are already confused about eschatology, it would seem that we should presume that the *parousia* in 2 Thessalonians 2 is the same as the *parousia* in 1 Thessalonians 4 unless there is significant evidence to the contrary. In other words, the burden of proof rests on those who would suggest that Paul is referring to two different events.[120] If the *parousia* in 2 Thessalonians 2 is the same as

119. In this sense, the content of 2 Thessalonians 2:1–12 is similar to the content of 1 Corinthians 15:29 in which Paul discusses baptism for the dead.

120. As I have mentioned, this is not inherently impossible, since the word *parousia* is not a technical term synonymous with the second coming of Jesus, and since Paul uses it elsewhere to refer to the

the *parousia* in 1 Thessalonians 4, then we have at least one solid anchor point because we know that the events described in 1 Thessalonians 4 have not yet occurred.[121]

If the *parousia* of Jesus that is mentioned twice in 2 Thessalonians 2 is in fact a reference to the second coming, then of the four basic options mentioned above, the third and fourth would appear to be the most plausible. In other words, we might conclude that although some of the preliminary signs (i.e., the rebellion) have already occurred or begun to occur, not all of them have occurred (i.e., the revelation of the man of lawlessness), and therefore the day of the Lord and the second coming have not yet occurred (Option 3). Or we might conclude that none of the preliminary signs have occurred and therefore the day of the Lord and the second coming have not yet occurred (Option 4). Although the text makes it difficult to be certain, there appears to be slightly stronger evidence for the third option.

Granted the greater plausibility of these two broad interpretive options, what about the meaning of the disputed details of the text? As I have already noted, there is a strong presumption in favor of interpreting the "coming of our Lord Jesus Christ and our being gathered together to him" (2 Thess. 2:1) as a reference to the second coming and resurrection described in 1 Thessalonians 4:13–18. If that is the case, then the day of the Lord in view here in 2 Thessalonians 2:3 is the final eschatological day of the Lord. If the third option I mentioned above is correct, then the "rebellion" may be connected with the events of the Jewish War of the first century, and it may continue into the present time. If the fourth option is correct, then the "rebellion" is more than likely some kind of major religious apostasy. It seems likely that the man of lawlessness is a political ruler. If the *parousia* of 2 Thessalonians 2 is the second coming, then this person has not yet been revealed since he is destroyed by Christ at the time of this *parousia* (2:8).[122]

The identity of the restraining force/person is one of the most difficult aspects of the text. I am persuaded that it/he is more than likely a spiritual

coming or presence of other persons in addition to Jesus. However, since immediate context plays a more crucial role in determining the use of a word, Paul's use of it in 1 Thessalonians 4, which was written not very long before 2 Thessalonians was written, carries a lot of weight.

121. See Strimple 2004 for a comprehensive critique of those who would try to get around this by suggesting that the resurrection from the dead described in 1 Thessalonians 4 was an invisible spiritual resurrection.

122. It is very possible that this end-time figure is foreshadowed by first-century figures such as Caligula, Nero, and Domitian, Roman emperors who accepted divine honors.

force/person. Since the early church, there have been those who have identified this restrainer as the Holy Spirit, and I am inclined to agree with some reservation.[123] The "mystery of lawlessness" was already at work at the time of Paul's writing. This appears to be the evil activity of Satan that continually opposes God and his people. The Thessalonians were not to let their guard down simply because the man of lawlessness had not yet been revealed, for the mystery of lawlessness was in fact already at work in their own day.

A few additional words are required concerning the remainder of the epistle. After concluding this eschatological text, Paul continues his second epistle to the Thessalonians with thanksgiving (2:13–14), an exhortation (2:15), and a prayer (2:16–17). He wraps up the epistle with a request that the Thessalonians pray for him (3:1–4), his own prayer for them (3:5), and an exhortation (3:6–15). He warns them to keep away from those who are idle (v. 6) and gives himself and his companions as an example of those who worked hard (vv. 7–10). They too are to work hard and earn a living (vv. 11–12). He exhorts them to do what is right (v. 13), and warns them to have nothing to do with those who refuse to obey (vv. 14–15). Paul then closes the letter with a benediction (3:16–18).

Summary

For the apostle Paul, the death and resurrection of Jesus were the climactic events of history. The coming of Jesus shaped how Paul viewed the past, the present, and the future. He wrote after the first advent, after Christ had died and risen again, but he wrote before the final consummation of all things. Paul realized that he lived during the overlap of the ages. The particular redemptive-historical background of his writings (between the times) explains why his eschatology is characterized by what has sometimes been called an "already and not yet" perspective.

Paul's understanding of eschatology affects everything he writes. Even in letters such as the epistle to the Galatians, in which eschatological issues are not at the forefront, they do form the basis for much of what he argues. The historical context of the letter to the Galatians is found in the narrative of Acts 15:1. Jewish converts were coming to the churches he had recently planted and telling the Gentile converts that they must be circumcised

123. The obscurity of the text makes it difficult to be absolutely certain, but it seems that the Holy Spirit makes better sense than many of the other suggested interpretations.

and they must keep the law of Moses in order to be saved (Acts 15:1, 5). Before the Jerusalem Council is held, Paul writes to these churches warning them not to fall away from the gospel by accepting the idea that they can be saved by obeying the law. One of Paul's primary arguments used to support his case is an eschatological argument. He argues that with the coming of Jesus, the age of the Mosaic covenant has come to an end. The age of the Mosaic covenant was preparatory for the present age.

In his epistles to the Thessalonian churches, eschatology is no longer in the background. It takes center stage. Paul was forced to leave this young church during his second missionary journey (Acts 17:1–10). His abrupt departure, before he had completed instructing the Thessalonians fully, resulted in a number of questions regarding eschatological issues. In his first epistle, Paul attempts to relieve the worry of the Thessalonians about fellow believers who had died, telling them that they all would be raised at the second coming of Jesus. He also tells them that the day of the Lord, a time when God would judge his enemies, will come like a thief in the night. In order to always be prepared, believers are to remain faithful.

Not long after sending his first epistle, Paul learns that the Thessalonians are being troubled by false teachers who are telling them that the day of the Lord has already come. Paul assures them first that God will judge those who have persecuted them, and then he assures them that the day of the Lord has not come because the two things that must happen before it comes (the rebellion and the revelation of the man of lawlessness) have not yet happened. They are not to be shaken by false teaching such as this. Instead they are to stand firm in what Paul had taught them and not grow weary in doing good. Such is the practical nature of Paul's eschatological teaching that even when he completes one of his most difficult eschatological discussions, he turns as always to the way believers should be living in light of the fact that Jesus is going to return to judge the wicked and grant relief to the afflicted.

15

The Pauline Epistles (2)

Corinthians and Romans

Paul's letters to the Galatians and to the Thessalonians were written within a relatively short period of time. As we have seen, Galatians was written between A.D. 48 and 49 just prior to Paul's second missionary journey, and the two letters to the Thessalonians were written between A.D. 50 and 51 during the second missionary journey. In the present chapter we will look at Paul's epistles to the Corinthians and to the Romans. These three epistles were also all written within a few years of each other (ca. A.D. 55–57) in the latter part of Paul's third missionary journey. Because of the length of these three epistles, our focus will necessarily be limited to those passages that have the most direct bearing on the topic of our study.

1 Corinthians

The city of Corinth was located on the isthmus that connects the Peloponnese with the mainland of Greece. At its narrowest point, the isthmus is approximately four miles across. To its west is the Gulf of Corinth, an inlet of the Ionian Sea, which separates Macedonia from Italy. To its east is the Saronic Gulf, an inlet of the Aegean Sea, which separates Macedonia from Asia Minor. The ancient Greek city of Corinth was destroyed by the Romans in 146 B.C. and lay desolate until Julius Caesar decided to rebuild it as a Roman colony in 44 B.C. While there were some Greek residents after the rebuilding, the population consisted primarily of Hellenized Romans.[1] Geographically the city was Greek, but culturally it was Roman.

Paul's first encounter with the Corinthians occurred during his second missionary journey (Acts 18:1–17). During this journey, Paul stayed in Corinth for eighteen months, teaching the new believers the word of God (Acts 18:11). There is a general consensus among scholars that this period of time can be dated from March of A.D. 50 to late September of A.D. 51.[2] After leaving Corinth, Paul stopped briefly in Ephesus before making his way back to his base in Antioch (Acts 18:18–22). In his third missionary journey, Paul worked his way westward through Galatia before coming again to Ephesus (Acts 18:23–19:1). He remained in Ephesus for two years (Acts 19:8–10). Paul wrote the first epistle to the Corinthians during this stay in Ephesus (1 Cor. 16:8). It was likely written in the spring of 55.[3]

Paul had already written one letter to the Corinthians, a letter that is now lost (1 Cor. 5:9). The epistle we know as 1 Corinthians is Paul's second letter to this church. Two events led to the writing of this epistle. First, Paul had received a report from Chloe's people indicating that there was trouble in the church (1 Cor. 1:11; 11:18). Second, the Corinthians themselves had written to Paul asking for his instruction on a number of matters (7:1). In chapter 15, eschatology is one of the matters explicitly addressed by Paul, but we should not be misled into thinking that this is the only place in 1 Corinthians where Paul's eschatology comes into play. As in his other epistles, the way Paul addresses almost every issue is affected in some way by his eschatology.

Paul opens his letter to the Corinthians with a greeting (1 Cor. 1:1–3) and thanksgiving (vv. 4–9). The thanksgiving contains words that set the whole epistle within an eschatological framework. Paul says that the Corinthians "wait for the revealing of our Lord Jesus Christ, who will sustain you

1. Carson and Moo 2005, 419.

2. See the discussion in Thiselton 2000, 28–29.

3. Carson and Moo 2005, 448; Thiselton 2000, 32; Garland 2003, 20.

to the end, guiltless in the day of our Lord Jesus Christ" (vv. 7–8). Richard Hays helpfully explains the significance of these verses for an understanding of the epistle:

> Paul sets his thanksgiving for the Corinthians' "giftedness" within the framework of a not-yet-fulfilled hope. . . . No matter how richly blessed the community may be in the present, Paul insists that they have not yet received that for which the church ultimately longs: the revelation (*apokalypsis*) of Jesus Christ, his final coming again to triumph over the powers of evil and death (cf. 15:20–28). Thus, the church's present existence is a time of waiting, a time in which they must be sustained and strengthened by Christ in anticipation of the end.[4]

The Corinthians must view their present situation in light of biblical eschatology, understanding that although Christ has won the decisive battle, the war continues to rage.[5]

Following his greeting and thanksgiving, Paul responds to the reports he has received about the Corinthian church (1:10–6:20). He begins by addressing the problem of division in the church (1:10–4:21). He has heard that there is quarreling among the members of the church (1:11), so he makes it clear that such things indicate they are not walking according to the Spirit but according to the flesh (3:1–4). They are walking according to the wisdom of the world rather than the wisdom that comes from above (1:18–2:16). The wisdom from above is not "the wisdom of this age," which is doomed to pass away (2:6). When Paul speaks of "this age," he is speaking in an eschatological manner, contrasting the present fleeting age with the eternal age to come.[6]

When Paul turns his attention to correcting the Corinthians' false views of church leadership and ministry, he makes a statement that has caused unnecessary confusion among many readers. After explaining that church leaders are servants (1 Cor. 3:5–9), Paul tells the Corinthians that leaders must build the church with care (vv. 10–15). Paul explains that he laid a foundation that someone else is building upon and that whoever builds upon it must take care how he builds (v. 10). The only foundation is Jesus

4. Hays 1997, 18.
5. Thiselton 2000, 99; Collins 1999, 60.
6. Barrett 1968, 70.

Christ (v. 11). Paul then writes the words that have been the cause of so much unnecessary debate:

> Now if anyone builds on the foundation with gold, silver, precious stones, wood, hay, straw—each one's work will become manifest, for the Day will disclose it, because it will be revealed by fire, and the fire will test what sort of work each one has done. If the work that anyone has built on the foundation survives, he will receive a reward. If anyone's work is burned up, he will suffer loss, though he himself will be saved, but only as through fire. (vv. 12–15)

The Roman Catholic Church has traditionally appealed to this passage as a proof-text for its doctrine of purgatory, but Paul's words here have nothing to do with purgatory or any such thing.[7] The context indicates that Paul is speaking of the work of church leaders who are building on what he started.[8] Their work will be judged on the last day.

Another crisis Paul faced in the Corinthian church was the church's apparent antagonism against Paul himself (4:1–21). Paul urges the church not to judge him before the coming of the Lord who will bring all things to light (vv. 1–5). He then describes the marks of true apostleship, contrasting the Corinthians' overbearing pride with his own weakness (vv. 6–13). He concludes with an appeal for right behavior (vv. 14–21). He warns the Corinthians that he is preparing to visit them and urges them to be imitators of him so that he may come to them in a spirit of gentleness rather than with a disciplinary rod.

Paul turns next to the problem of sexual immorality in the church (5:1–13). Someone in the church was having sexual relations with his own stepmother, and the Corinthians had done nothing about it (vv. 1–2). Paul tells them that when they are assembled they are to "deliver this man to Satan for the destruction of the flesh, so that his spirit may be saved in the day of the Lord" (v. 5). When Paul refers to the "day of the Lord" here, he is speaking of the final judgment. But what does he mean by "destruction of the flesh"? As Gordon Fee explains, Paul wanted this man put outside of the Christian church so that what was carnal in him could be destroyed.[9]

7. The *Catechism of the Catholic Church* (par. 1031), for example, cites this text as support for its doctrine of purgatory.

8. Hays 1997, 55.

9. Fee 1987, 212.

The Corinthian church was not only plagued by problems of sexual immorality, the members of the church were dragging their grievances against one another before the pagan courts (1 Cor. 6:1–11). Paul's eschatology becomes the basis for his critique of this practice. He writes, "Do you not know that the saints will judge the world? And if the world is to be judged by you, are you incompetent to try trivial cases? Do you not know that we are to judge angels? How much more, then, matters pertaining to this life!" (vv. 2–3). Paul does not specify exactly how the saints will participate in the judgment of the world, but he makes it clear that since they will in fact do so, it is absurd for them to take smaller matters before pagan courts of law.[10] He concludes this section by warning the Corinthians that "the unrighteous will not inherit the kingdom of God" (v. 9).

Paul briefly addresses the problem of sexual relations with prostitutes in 6:12–20. He appeals to the resurrection as a basis for his argument, saying, "The body is not meant for sexual immorality, but for the Lord, and the Lord for the body. And God raised the Lord and will also raise us up by his power" (v. 14). As C. K. Barrett explains, "It is because *the body* will not simply pass away but will be raised up that men must avoid using it for fornication."[11] What each of us does in our present body matters.

Following his response to the problems that had been reported by Chloe's people, Paul turns his attention to the questions raised by the Corinthians themselves in a letter they had sent to him (7:1–16:12). Their first question concerns marriage and related issues (7:1–40). Apparently the Corinthians wanted to know whether it was good to get married. Paul tells them that in order to avoid sexual immorality it is good for each man and woman to have a spouse (vv. 1–5). Not all are able to abstain (vv. 6–7). Paul says that it is better if the unmarried and the widows can remain as they are, but if they cannot exercise self-control, it is better for them to be married (vv. 8–9). He informs them that husbands and wives should not divorce (vv. 10–11), even if the spouse is an unbeliever (vv. 12–16). Paul outlines his basic principle in verses 17–24, urging the Corinthians to stay as they are.

Paul continues by addressing questions concerning the "betrothed" (7:25–40). Again, Paul's eschatology plays a major part in the way he addresses the issues. Paul writes, "Now concerning the betrothed, I have no command from the Lord, but I give my judgment as one who by the

10. Garland 2003, 201.

11. Barrett 1968, 148.

Lord's mercy is trustworthy. I think that in view of the present distress it is good for a person to remain as he is" (vv. 25–26). What does Paul mean when he speaks of "the present distress"? The word translated "present" is *enestōsan*, the perfect active participle of *enistēmi*. Although some have translated the words here as "impending distress," Paul's use of the word elsewhere (e.g., Rom. 8:38; 1 Cor. 3:22; Gal. 1:4) indicates that whatever the "distress" is, it is something the Corinthians are already experiencing.[12] Some understand the word *anankē*, translated "distress," to be the eschatological woes that are already anticipated in the sufferings of Christians.[13] However, as others point out, the word has a broad range of uses and may not be referring here to eschatological distress.[14] In either case, Paul's basic point is that believers have plenty of troubles in the present time without adding to them (1 Cor. 7:27–28).

Paul continues, saying:

> This is what I mean, brothers: the appointed time has grown very short. From now on, let those who have wives live as though they had none, and those who mourn as though they were not mourning, and those who rejoice as though they were not rejoicing, and those who buy as though they had no goods, and those who deal with the world as though they had no dealings with it. For the present form of this world is passing away. (vv. 29–31)

The verb translated "has grown short" in verse 29 is *synestalmenos*, which is the perfect passive participle of *systellō*. In this context, it appears that what Paul is saying is that "time has been compressed."[15] The death and resurrection of Jesus inaugurated the last days. Paul is reminding the Corinthians that this eschatological fact should affect the way they view their relationship to the world around them. They must understand that the present age is "passing away" (v. 31). The present age is only a penultimate age, and life should be lived in light of this fact.[16]

Paul continues responding to the Corinthians' questions by dealing with the topic of food offered to idols (8:1–13). He then defends his apostleship against apparent accusations made by some in the Corinthian com-

12. Fee 1987, 329.
13. E.g., Barrett 1968, 175.
14. Garland 2003, 323; Collins 1999, 293.
15. Fee 1987, 339; Garland 2003, 328.
16. Collins 1999, 291.

munity (9:1–27) and warns them about the ever present danger of idolatry (10:1–22). After providing Israel as an example of a people who fell into such idolatry (10:1–5), Paul says, "Now these things happened to them as an example, but they were written down for our instruction, on whom the end of the ages has come" (v. 11). What does Paul mean by this? Hays helpfully explains, "Paul reads Scripture in the conviction that its narratives and prophecies all point to his own time; the church lives in the exhilarating moment in which all of God's past dealings with Israel and the world have come to their climactic point."[17] In other words, with the death and resurrection of Jesus the last act in the drama of redemption has begun.

After addressing a question concerning men and women in worship (11:2–16), Paul addresses a question concerning the Lord's Supper (vv. 17–34). His eschatology again comes into play when he writes, "For as often as you eat this bread and drink the cup, you proclaim the Lord's death until he comes" (v. 26). The Lord's Supper looks forward as well as backward. We look back as we observe the Lord's Supper "in remembrance" of Jesus (v. 24), but we also look forward, anticipating the eschatological Supper of the Lamb.[18]

In chapters 12–14, Paul addresses questions concerning spiritual gifts. Paul first addresses the unity of the body and the diversity of spiritual gifts (12:1–31). He then places the spiritual gifts in proper perspective, comparing their temporary nature with the permanence of love (13:1–13). Finally he instructs the Corinthians about the gifts of prophecy and tongues (14:1–25) and the necessity of orderly worship (14:26–40). Paul's eschatology comes to the foreground in chapter 13 as he compares tongues, prophecy, and knowledge with love. Paul writes:

> Love never ends. As for prophecies, they will pass away; as for tongues, they will cease; as for knowledge, it will pass away. For we know in part and we prophesy in part, but when the perfect comes, the partial will pass away. When I was a child, I spoke like a child, I thought like a child, I reasoned like a child. When I became a man, I gave up childish ways. For now we see in a mirror dimly, but then face to face. Now I know in part; then I shall know fully, even as I have been fully known. (13:8–12)

17. Hays 1997, 162.
18. Thiselton 2000, 888.

Most exegetes agree that when Paul refers to the coming of "the perfect," he is referring to "the state of affairs brought about by the parousia."[19] John Calvin understood these verses in this way. He says that the perfect "will not be completely manifested until the day of judgment."[20] D. A. Carson agrees, saying that these verses are "almost certainly a reference to the new state brought about by the parousia."[21] It is difficult to dispute this conclusion. The coming of the "perfect" marks a transitional point in time. Before the coming of the "perfect" we know "in part" (13:9). After the coming of the "perfect" the "partial will pass away" (v. 10). The present time is described as a time during which "we see in a mirror dimly" and "know in part" (v. 12), but "then" (which can only be after the coming of the "perfect" described in verse 10), we will see "face to face" and "know fully," even as we have been fully known (v. 12). There is no time prior to the second advent that can be described in these terms. We do not presently see "face to face" or "know fully." We still "see in a mirror dimly." Paul's main point in this passage is that love lasts forever. On the other hand, the spiritual gifts, of which the Corinthians were so proud, belong only to the penultimate age.[22]

19. Garland 2003, 622; see also Carson 1987, 70–72; Fee 1987, 646; Blomberg 1994, 260; Collins 1999, 486. As Hays (1997, 229) explains, "In dispensationalist Christian groups, it is sometimes claimed that 'the complete [*to teleion*]' in v. 10 refers to the completion and closure of the New Testament canon." The problem with this interpretation, as numerous scholars have pointed out, is that it has no exegetical or contextual support (see Garland 2003, 622; Hays 1997, 229; Gaffin 1979, 109).

20. Calvin 2003, 20:428; see also his comments on 13:12.

21. Carson 1987, 71.

22. Since the rise of the Pentecostal and charismatic movements in the twentieth century, these verses have been at the center of the debate between those who believe that the gifts of prophecy and tongues ceased in the first century (cessationists) and those who believe they continue today. One's interpretation of "the perfect," however, does not necessarily dictate one's conclusions regarding the continuation or cessation of these gifts. For example, in his book *Perspectives on Pentecost* (1979, 109), cessationist author Richard Gaffin grants that the coming of "the perfect" (v. 10) and the "then" of the believer's full knowledge (v. 12) "no doubt refer to the time of Christ's return." Part of the difficulty of the debate is due to the lack of consensus regarding the precise nature of these gifts (particularly prophecy and tongues). As an example, many see the New Testament gift of prophecy as entailing ongoing divinely inspired revelation, while others understand it to be speech that builds up or exhorts (see Thiselton 2000, 1094). Some see the gift of tongues as a miraculous gift of heavenly language, while some argue that tongues is a nonmiraculous gift. According to Robert Zerhusen (1997, 139–52), for example, it is simply the native language of speakers in a multilingual culture like Corinth. Thiselton (2000, 956–65, 1087–94) provides a helpful overview of the debate concerning the nature of prophecy in the New Testament. He also (2000, 1098–1100, 1108–11) provides a

The Resurrection of the Dead (1 Cor. 15)

Eschatology moves from the background to the foreground in 1 Corinthians 15. Here Paul turns his full attention to the doctrine of the resurrection. The question to which Paul is responding is not stated explicitly until verse 12. Paul informs us there that some of the Corinthians were saying that "there is no resurrection of the dead." As we examine the text, it will become clear that what they were denying was the future bodily resurrection of believers. Paul makes very clear in this chapter how central the doctrine of the resurrection is to the Christian faith. His argument proceeds in two stages. In verses 1–34, he demonstrates the reality of the resurrection of the dead. In verses 35–58, he explains how it is that the bodily resurrection of believers is possible.

Paul opens the discussion by reminding the Corinthians of the gospel that he had preached to them and that they had believed (15:1). In other words, Paul begins his argument by stating a belief on which they agree, and from there he moves to the necessary consequences of that belief. Paul states the content of his gospel in verses 3–5, saying, "For I delivered to you as of first importance what I also received: that Christ died for our sins in accordance with the Scriptures, that he was buried, that he was raised on the third day in accordance with the Scriptures, and that he appeared to Cephas, then to the twelve."

The death and resurrection of Jesus are the center of Paul's proclamation of the gospel. It is by means of Christ's death and resurrection that the two evils introduced into the world at the time of the fall are overcome. Christ's death on the cross is God's solution to the problem of sin, and Christ's resurrection from the grave is God's solution to the problem of death. When Paul says that "Christ died for our sins," he is alluding to Isaiah 53:5–6 and its language of substitutionary atonement. But when Paul says that Christ died and was raised "in accordance with the Scriptures," he has more in mind than the fulfillment of specific individual texts. Rather, the death and resurrection of Christ are the climactic fulfillment of the entire Old Testament narrative.[23] This is the gospel that the Corinthians believed. They professed belief in the death and resurrection of Jesus.

---

helpful overview of the debate concerning the nature of tongues in 1 Corinthians. Ultimately, a full discussion of the cessationism debate is beyond the scope of this book. For a helpful overview of these chapters of 1 Corinthians and the related issues, see Carson 1987.

23. Thiselton 2000, 1195; Barrett 1968, 338.

Granted their faith in the resurrection of Christ, Paul asks, "how can some of you say that there is no resurrection of the dead?" (1 Cor. 15:12). The remainder of the chapter makes it clear that what the Corinthians were denying was the idea of a future *bodily* resurrection.[24] In this, they were simply expressing the beliefs of ancient paganism, which denied the very possibility of such a thing.[25] In verses 12–19, Paul explains the consequences of such a denial. Paul asserts, "if there is no resurrection of the dead, then not even Christ has been raised" (v. 13). Here Paul is showing the contradictory nature of the Corinthians' beliefs. They profess belief in the bodily resurrection of Christ while at the same time denying the possibility of bodily resurrection, but their denial of the resurrection of the dead necessitates the conclusion that Christ was not raised. Their denial of the resurrection of the dead is a denial of the very heart of Christianity.[26]

In verses 13–19, Paul expands on the consequences of their denial of the resurrection of the dead. If there is no resurrection of the dead, then Christ is not raised, and if Christ is not raised, Paul's preaching is in vain, and the Corinthians' faith is in vain (v. 14). If there is no resurrection of the dead, Christians are bearing false witness against God by claiming that he raised Jesus from the dead (v. 15). If Christ has not been raised, the Corinthians are still in their sins (vv. 16–17) and those who have died are without hope (v. 18). If there is no resurrection of the dead, Christians are the most pitiful of people for believing in a delusion (v. 19). In short, what Paul is telling the Corinthians is that if their denial of the resurrection of the dead is true, then Christianity is worthless nonsense.[27]

Paul changes course slightly in verses 20–28 by moving back to the point of agreement between himself and the Corinthians. He writes, "But in fact Christ has been raised from the dead, the firstfruits of those who have fallen asleep" (v. 20). The word "firstfruits" (*aparchē*) refers to the first and representative portion of an agricultural harvest.[28] It implies more fruit to come, and it implies a relationship between the firstfruits and the remaining harvest. As Joost Holleman explains, "The designation of the risen Jesus as the 'first-fruits of those who have fallen asleep' (v. 20) means

24. See Holleman 1996, 40; Hays 1997, 253; Garland 2003, 699; Marshall 2004, 264.

25. For a discussion of ancient pagan views of the afterlife, see Wright 2003, 32–84.

26. Barrett 1968, 346.

27. Hays 1997, 260; Thiselton 2000, 1218.

28. Collins 1999, 547–48; Holleman 1996, 50.

that Jesus has been raised as the first and the representative of those who will be raised."[29] In other words, Christ's resurrection and the future bodily resurrection of Christ's people form "an unbreakable unity."[30]

Paul continues, "For as by a man came death, by a man has come also the resurrection of the dead. For as in Adam all die, so also in Christ shall all be made alive" (vv. 21–22). Holleman helpfully explains the significance of Paul's words: "In verses 21–22 he [Paul] establishes that, just as death came into the world through Adam, resulting in the death of all people who are represented by Adam, so resurrection came into the world through Christ, resulting in the resurrection of all people who are represented by Christ."[31]

Paul elaborates on the sequence of resurrection, saying, "But each in his own order: Christ the firstfruits, then [*epeita*] at his coming those who belong to Christ. Then [*eita*] comes the end, when he delivers the kingdom to God the Father after destroying every rule and every authority and power" (15:23–24). Paul pictures Christ's resurrection as the inauguration of the eschatological resurrection; it is all one harvest. Jesus' resurrection is the first stage in the eschatological resurrection, and the resurrection of Christians is the second stage.[32] The resurrection of believers occurs "at his coming," which means that it is a future event.

Some exegetes believe that Paul's words in verse 24 indicate the existence of an interval between Christ's coming and "the end" or final consummation.[33] The argument is that Paul envisions three stages in the unfolding of these eschatological events: the resurrection of Christ, then the parousia at which believers are raised, and then the end when Christ hands over the kingdom to his Father. Some exegetes argue that since there is an indefinite interval between stages one and two, it is likely that there is also an interval between stages two and three.[34] While the grammar alone may allow for

29. Holleman 1996, 51.

30. Ridderbos 1975, 538.

31. Holleman 1996, 55. He explains further, "The parallelism between the two clauses of verse 22 does not lie in the fact that both groups are identical, but in the fact that for both groups the representative determines the fate of the group. The unity with Adam leads to death, the unity with Christ leads to resurrection. Since only Christians are united with Christ, only Christians will be made alive through Christ" (p. 53).

32. Holleman 1996, 1; Fee 1987, 746; Wright 1991, 27.

33. This interpretation is affirmed by premillennialists such as Hiebert 1997, 229–34.

34. Hiebert 1997, 230.

such an interpretation, there are several reasons why it is highly unlikely. First, these same adverbs (*epeita* and *eita*) are used in the immediate context and elsewhere to indicate nothing more than a simple sequence of events (15:5–7). They do not, by themselves, imply anything about intervals of time. Second, in the immediate context, the completion of the eschatological resurrection, which occurs at Christ's second coming, is tied to the defeat of death, which occurs at "the end" (15:24–26, 54–55). This indicates that Christ's second coming occurs at "the end," something that Paul indicates in other epistles as well (1 Thess. 4:13–18). Third, the beginning of Christ's kingdom does not await his second coming. As we have seen repeatedly, Christ's kingdom was inaugurated at his first advent (e.g., Matt. 28:18; Acts 2:29–36; Col. 1:13; Rev. 1:5).

Paul concludes this section by building on Psalm 110:1. He writes, "For he must reign until he has put all his enemies under his feet. The last enemy to be destroyed is death" (1 Cor. 15:25–26). Paul then quotes Psalm 8:6 as he envisions the subjection of all things to God (vv. 27–28). The full manifestation of the kingdom of God is Christ's ultimate goal. Through Christ, God defeats every enemy in order that his reign might be established over all.[35] The eschatological importance of the resurrection could not be made any clearer than it is in this section of Paul's epistle.

Paul concludes his argument for the reality of the resurrection of the dead in 15:29–34. He asks several rhetorical questions to add weight to his argument. The first question he asks has been the source of much discussion. "Otherwise, what do people mean by being baptized on behalf of the dead? If the dead are not raised at all, why are people baptized on their behalf?" (v. 29). Numerous interpretations of the meaning of this verse have been suggested.[36] While not without its difficulties, Thiselton's suggestion is perhaps the most plausible. He argues that baptism on behalf of the dead "refers to the decision of a person or persons to ask for, and to receive baptism as a result of the desire to be united with their believing relatives who have died."[37] In other words, dying believers would urge their unbelieving family members to become Christians in order that they might be together again. Paul, then, is referring to those unbelievers who converted to Christ for this reason as those who were "baptized on behalf

35. Collins 1999, 555; Holleman 1996, 60.

36. See the various commentaries for full discussions.

37. Thiselton 2000, 1248.

of the dead." If there is no resurrection of the dead, their conversion/baptism was for naught. Paul's second question concerns the dangers he places himself in (vv. 30–34). If there is no resurrection, then what he is doing is foolish in the extreme.

The reason behind the Corinthians' denial of the resurrection of the dead was a worldview that abhorred the idea of bodily resurrection. They may have thought that resurrection meant nothing more than the mere reanimation of a corpse. Paul turns his attention to this issue in 15:35–49. He writes, "But someone will ask, 'How are the dead raised? With what kind of body do they come?'" (v. 35). The word translated "body" is the Greek word *sōma*. Paul uses the word in relation to human beings to speak of the physical body.[38] As Robert Gundry explains, Paul uses this word "precisely because the physicality of the resurrection is central to his soteriology."[39]

Paul rebukes his hypothetical questioner (15:36a) and then uses an agricultural analogy to illustrate continuity and discontinuity between the present body and the resurrected body (v. 37). As Hays explains, "The analogy of the seed enables Paul to walk a fine line, asserting both the radical *transformation* of the body in its resurrected state and yet its organic *continuity* with the mortal body that precedes it."[40] Paul then describes the many different kinds of bodies that God has created: for humans, animals, birds, fish, heavenly bodies, earthly bodies, sun, moon, and stars (vv. 38–41). Reading Paul's list here reminds one of the creation account of Genesis.[41] The whole creation was affected by the fall (Rom. 8:20–21). By mentioning all aspects of God's creation in the context of a discussion of resurrection, Paul may be hinting at the idea of the new creation, when everything will be set free from the effects of the curse.[42]

Paul continues, "So it is with the resurrection of the dead. What is sown is perishable; what is raised is imperishable. It is sown in dishonor; it is raised in glory. It is sown in weakness; it is raised in power. It is sown a natural body; it is raised a spiritual body. If there is a natural body, there is also a spiritual body" (1 Cor. 15:42–44). Paul's words indicate both continuity

38. See Gundry 1987, 80; Dunn 1998, 61.

39. Gundry 1987, 169.

40. Hays 1997, 270; see also Thiselton 2000, 1264; Wright 2003, 341.

41. Paul's later mention of Adam adds weight to the comparison.

42. Wright 2003, 313.

and transformation.[43] The continuity is seen in the fact that the same "it" that is sown is also raised. The transformation is seen in the contrasts that Paul describes: perishable versus imperishable; dishonor versus glory; weakness versus power; natural versus spiritual.

Paul's use of the words "spiritual body" to describe the resurrection body has led some to deny the corporeal nature of the resurrection of the dead, but the words themselves lend no weight to such an argument. In verse 44, Paul says "It is sown a natural body [*sōma psychikon*]; it is raised a spiritual body [*sōma pneumatikon*]." To say that the resurrection body is a *sōma pneumatikon* does not mean that it is composed of a *pneumatic* substance.[44] The contrast Paul is making is between a "natural body" (i.e., a body animated by the breath of life given to Adam) and a "spiritual body" (i.e., a body animated by the Holy Spirit).[45] Richard Hays suggests that the Jerusalem Bible is perhaps the best translation of this phrase: "When it is sown it embodies the soul, when it is raised it embodies the spirit. If the soul has its own embodiment, so does the spirit have its own embodiment."[46]

Paul writes:

> Thus it is written, "The first man Adam became a living being"; the last Adam became a life-giving spirit. But it is not the spiritual that is first but the natural, and then the spiritual. The first man was from the earth, a man of dust; the second man is from heaven. As was the man of dust, so also are those who are of the dust, and as is the man of heaven, so also are those who are of heaven. Just as we have borne the image of the man of dust, we shall also bear the image of the man of heaven. (15:45–49)

Paul's point here is that just as our present body is like Adam's physical body, so our future body will be like Jesus' resurrection body.[47] In short, Paul is portraying Jesus as the one who inaugurates the new creation and the new humanity.[48]

The conclusion to Paul's argument in 1 Corinthians 15 ties the resurrection of the dead to God's triumphant victory over death, the last enemy

43. Fee 1987, 777.
44. See Vos 1991, 166–67; Ridderbos 1975, 544; Fee 1987, 786.
45. Wright 2003, 354; Ridderbos 1975, 541–42.
46. Hays 1997, 272.
47. Wright 1991, 32.
48. Ridderbos 1975, 56.

(vv. 50–58). Paul reiterates what he has already said, when he states that "flesh and blood cannot inherit the kingdom of God, nor does the perishable inherit the imperishable" (v. 50). These two clauses are in synonymous parallelism and indicate the same truth, namely, that our present bodies must be transformed in order to participate in the consummation of the kingdom. Paul then writes, "Behold! I tell you a mystery. We shall not all sleep, but we shall all be changed, in a moment, in the twinkling of an eye, at the last trumpet. For the trumpet will sound and the dead will be raised imperishable, and we shall be changed. For this perishable body must put on the imperishable, and this mortal body must put on immortality" (vv. 51–53). What Paul describes here is the same event he described in his first epistle to the Thessalonians (1 Thess. 4:13–18). It is the resurrection of the dead and the transformation of those still living at the time of Christ's second coming.

Paul concludes by quoting the eschatological vision found in Isaiah 25:8. He writes:

> When the perishable puts on the imperishable, and the mortal puts on immortality, then shall come to pass the saying that is written:
>
> "Death is swallowed up in victory."
> "O death, where is your victory?
> O death, where is your sting?"
>
> The sting of death is sin, and the power of sin is the law. But thanks be to God, who gives us the victory through our Lord Jesus Christ. (1 Cor. 15:54–57)

Death has wielded its reign of terror over man since the fall. The resurrection of Jesus sets into motion the eschatological events that will culminate in the resurrection of his people, an event which will mark the final defeat of death itself.

2 Corinthians

The historical circumstances behind the writing of 2 Corinthians are somewhat difficult to reconstruct. We know from the final chapter of 1 Corinthians that Paul intended to stay in Ephesus until Pentecost and then travel to Macedonia and Corinth (1 Cor. 16:5–8). Although he was not yet prepared to go himself, he sent Timothy to Corinth to assist the church (1 Cor. 16:10–11). Paul soon learns that a serious situation had arisen in Corinth due to an individual who was verbally attacking him (2 Cor. 2:5–11; 7:8–13). We do not know whether Timothy reported this situation to Paul or whether Paul found out about it another way, but upon hearing of the situation Paul immediately set sail for Corinth.

Paul's confrontation with the Corinthians was not successful, and he refers to it as a "painful visit" (2 Cor. 2:1). After this visit, Paul returned to Ephesus and sent another letter, which is now lost to us (2 Cor. 2:4; 7:8–12).[49] Paul apparently had Titus deliver this "severe letter" and arranged to meet him later in Troas (2 Cor. 2:12–13). To make matters worse, at some point during all of this, a group of self-proclaimed apostles arrived in Corinth stirring up even more trouble (2 Cor. 11:13–15). The evidence from 2 Corinthians indicates that these men may have been Judaizers who were encouraging the Gentiles to adhere to the Mosaic covenant.[50]

Paul eventually left Ephesus for Troas, hoping to meet Titus, but Titus was not there (2 Cor. 2:12–13). Paul soon left Troas for Macedonia (2:13). While he was ministering in Macedonia, Titus arrived with an encouraging report (2 Cor. 7:6–7). As a result of this report from Titus, Paul wrote the letter we know as 2 Corinthians sometime in A.D. 56.[51] He wrote the letter to express his thanksgiving for the church's renewed repentance (2 Cor. 7:15–16), to encourage them to complete their collection for the poor in Jerusalem (2 Cor. 8–9), and to defend his ministry from those who had been falsely accusing him (2 Cor. 3:1–6; 10:1–13:10).

Paul opens 2 Corinthians with a greeting (1:1–2), a benediction (vv. 3–7), and a few brief comments on the afflictions he has suffered (vv. 8–11). The key word in the benediction is "comfort" (*paraklēsis*). Paul uses variations of this word ten times in these five verses. As Paul Barnett explains, this term evokes Old Testament images of the messianic age (Isa. 40:1; 49:13;

49. There are many who believe that this letter may be identified with 2 Corinthians 10–13. Proponents of this view cite the sudden change in tone at 10:1 among other arguments. Although the arguments have persuaded many, there are good reasons to see 2 Corinthians as a literary unity. For a discussion of the issues, see Matera 2003, 29–32; and Barnett 1997, 15–23.

50. See Barnett 1997, 35.

51. For helpful reconstructions of the historical circumstances, see Carson and Moo 2005, 420–25; Martin 1986, xxxiv.

51:3, 12, 19; 52:9; 61:2; 66:13).[52] It implies a hostile situation as well as a promise of deliverance from that situation. Paul briefly mentions the extreme danger he has encountered and then says, "But that was to make us rely not on ourselves but on God who raises the dead. He delivered us from such a deadly peril, and he will deliver us. On him we have set our hope that he will deliver us again" (2 Cor. 1:9–10). This understanding of God, as the one who raises the dead, is the foundation for all that Paul writes.

In 2 Corinthians 1:12–7:16, Paul deals with the crisis that has arisen regarding his apostolic authority. He begins by giving an account of the recent events that have occurred since he sent the letter we know as 1 Corinthians. In 2:14–7:4, Paul's defense "takes the form of an extended excursus in which he grounds his ministry in the promise of a new covenant and the new creation that God has effected through Christ."[53] Paul first presents himself as a minister of the prophesied new covenant and the Corinthians as his letter of recommendation (2:14–4:6).[54] He writes, "And you show that you are a letter from Christ delivered by us, written not with ink but with the Spirit of the living God, not on tablets of stone but on tablets of human hearts" (3:3). There is a clear echo here of the prophecies of a new covenant in Jeremiah and Ezekiel (Jer. 31:31–34; Ezek. 36:26–27). What Paul is implying is that the ancient prophecies have come to pass in his ministry at Corinth. As David Garland observes, "Their conversion through the Spirit is evidence of the arrival of the new age."[55] Paul, in fact, calls himself a minister of "a new covenant, not of the letter but of the Spirit" (2 Cor. 3:6a). This new covenant was inaugurated by Christ (1 Cor. 11:25). The ancient promise has been fulfilled.

Paul tells the Corinthians, "the letter kills, but the Spirit gives life" (2 Cor. 3:6b). He then expands on this statement by examining Exodus 34:29–35, the story of Moses coming down from Mount Sinai with his face shining with glory. Paul uses this story to teach the Corinthians that although the old covenant was glorious, the new covenant is even more glorious (2 Cor. 3:7–11). The old covenant offered no power to fulfill the law. Furthermore, although the old covenant served its purpose, its purpose was temporary.[56]

52. Barnett 1997, 69.

53. Matera 2003, 2.

54. Matera 2003, 66.

55. Garland 1999, 161; see also Hughes 1962, 89.

56. Martin 1986, 73; Barnett 1997, 181.

Paul's inclusion of this section lends weight to the idea that the Corinthian church had come under the influence of Judaizers. Paul declares that the minds of the people of the old covenant are veiled, and they cannot see the true meaning of the Old Testament Scriptures (3:12–15; 4:3–4). The people of the new covenant, on the other hand, are all "beholding the glory of the Lord" and are "being transformed into the same image from one degree of glory to another" (3:18). Under the new covenant, the shattered image of God is being restored in those who behold Christ.[57]

Paul's discourse naturally raises a question.[58] If Paul is the minister of such a glorious new covenant, why is his ministry characterized by suffering and affliction? As Frank Matera explains, Paul "will argue that his apostolic sufferings on behalf of the Corinthians paradoxically reveal the eschatological power of Christ's resurrection life in his mortal body (4:7–15)."[59] Already his inner nature is being renewed (4:16–18), and he trusts that he will receive a resurrection body in the future (5:1–10). The God who raises the dead (1:9) is transforming him and will transform him.

Paul writes, "But we have this treasure in jars of clay, to show that the surpassing power belongs to God and not to us" (4:7). This term "jars of clay" designates that which the Corinthians see, namely Paul's weak and inglorious appearance. Paul continues:

> We are afflicted in every way, but not crushed; perplexed, but not driven to despair; persecuted, but not forsaken; struck down, but not destroyed; always carrying in the body the death of Jesus, so that the life of Jesus may also be manifested in our bodies. For we who live are always being given over to death for Jesus' sake, so that the life of Jesus also may be manifested in our mortal flesh. So death is at work in us, but life in you. (4:8–12)

Paul views his afflictions in light of his union with Jesus in his death and resurrection (Rom. 6:5).[60] It is significant that Paul expects the life of Jesus to be manifested "in our bodies." There is no denigration of the physical body in Paul's thought. This jar of clay will be resurrected and transformed, not cast aside.

57. Hughes 1962, 119.
58. Barnett 1997, 227.
59. Matera 2003, 105.
60. Hughes 1962, 142.

Paul expands on what he has written, saying, "Since we have the same spirit of faith according to what has been written, 'I believed, and so I spoke,' we also believe, and so we also speak, knowing that he who raised the Lord Jesus will raise us also with Jesus and bring us with you into his presence" (2 Cor. 4:13–14). Paul here explains that his faith in the resurrection is the foundation for his preaching ministry.[61] He cites verse 10 from Psalm 116, in which the psalmist praises God for delivering him from death (see Ps. 116:3–8). Like the psalmist, Paul suffers affliction, but like the psalmist, he also places his faith in the God who raises the dead.

Paul turns his attention next to the transformation that is occurring (2 Cor. 4:16–18) and that will occur (5:1–10). Key to Paul's argument in these verses is the contrast between the present age and the age to come as well as the contrast between the outer nature and the inner nature.[62] Paul begins first by explaining the transformation that is already underway. He writes, "So we do not lose heart. Though our outer nature is wasting away, our inner nature is being renewed day by day" (4:16). The "wasting away" of the outer nature refers back to the afflictions Paul mentioned in verses 8–9.

Paul continues, "For this slight momentary affliction is preparing for us an eternal weight of glory beyond all comparison, as we look not to the things that are seen but to the things that are unseen. For the things that are seen are transient, but the things that are unseen are eternal" (4:17–18). Paul here contrasts the affliction of this age with the glory of the age to come. Not only are the present afflictions temporary, they are preparatory. Paul is not minimizing the reality and pain of suffering. Instead, as Barnett explains, Paul is looking at his present suffering from the perspective of eternity. "Suffering, real though it is, is ephemeral because it belongs to this age, in contrast with the age to come, which is eternal."[63]

Having discussed the present transformation of the inner nature, Paul turns his attention to the future transformation of the body (5:1–10). Paul begins by saying, "For we know that if the tent, which is our earthly home, is destroyed, we have a building from God, a house not made with hands, eternal in the heavens" (5:1). Paul has been discussing the afflictions he has suffered. Here he states that if he does die as a result of these afflictions and

61. Barnett 1997, 242; Matera 2003, 112.

62. Barnett 1997, 246.

63. Barnett 1997, 252.

persecutions, he knows that God has something better prepared for him. He contrasts the "earthly home" (his body) with "a building from God" (the resurrection body). Although other suggestions have been made, the context indicates that the "building from God" is the resurrection body.[64]

What does Paul mean when he says that "we have" a building from God? The verb here is in the present tense. Barnett asks, "Does the 'we have' (present tense) point to (1) the *fact* of having, (2) the *permanency* of having, or (3) the *immediacy* of having in the event that death should occur prior to the Parousia?"[65] According to David Garland, Paul is likely speaking of immediacy and thus understands the believer to receive his resurrection body at the point of death.[66] The difficulty with this interpretation is that it conflicts with what Paul has already taught in 1 Thessalonians 4 and 1 Corinthians 15, namely that the believer receives his resurrection body at the time of the second coming. This interpretation also destroys what Paul says regarding the parallel between Christ's resurrection body and ours (e.g., Phil. 3:21). Christ's body was resurrected, and his grave was empty. If Christians are receiving their resurrection body at death, then their bodies are not being resurrected because their bodies remain in the grave.[67] A better explanation is offered by Matera, who explains that it is more likely "that the present tense emphasizes Paul's firm conviction in what God has in store for him at the general resurrection of the dead."[68]

Paul next expresses his desire for his resurrection body. He writes, "For in this tent we groan, longing to put on our heavenly dwelling, if indeed by putting it on we may not be found naked" (2 Cor. 5:2–3). The groaning here is an expression of the intense longing for final restoration and redemption felt by all believers (Rom. 8:23–25). That which Paul longs for is to be clothed with the resurrection body, something that occurs at the time of Christ's second coming (1 Cor. 15:53–54). Paul hopes that he will not be found naked (2 Cor. 5:3). The context indicates that Paul is referring here to the bodiless state that would occur were he to die before

64. See Matera 2003, 120; Barnett 1997, 257–58.

65. Barnett 1997, 258–59.

66. Garland 1999, 251.

67. If Christians receive their resurrection body at death, what would be happening would not actually be resurrection, since nothing would be raised at that point. What would be happening in such a case would instead be the reembodiment of the soul, a kind of immediate "reincarnation."

68. Matera 2003, 120; see also Barnett 1997, 259.

the second coming of Christ.[69] This nakedness is the state of affairs between the removal of the old garment (the present body) and the putting on of the new garment (the resurrection body).

In verse 4, Paul repeats his thoughts from verses 2–3, saying, "For while we are still in this tent, we groan, being burdened—not that we would be unclothed, but that we would be further clothed, so that what is mortal may be swallowed up by life." The echoes of Paul's words concerning the final resurrection in 1 Corinthians 15:54 are clear here, and it is this event for which Paul longs. He writes, "He who has prepared us for this very thing is God, who has given us the Spirit as a guarantee" (2 Cor. 5:5). The giving of the Spirit guarantees the future resurrection of the body. In this, Paul places his hope.

Paul continues, saying, "So we are always of good courage. We know that while we are at home in the body we are away from the Lord, for we walk by faith, not by sight" (5:6–7). This is the confident expression of faith of all who live in this present age facing the possibility of death. Paul writes, "Yes, we are of good courage, and we would rather be away from the body and at home with the Lord" (v. 8). In other words, although Paul hopes to be alive until the second coming of Christ, he recognizes the possibility that he might die first. If he does die, he may have to await the receiving of his resurrection body, but he will not have to wait to be present with the Lord.

Finally, Paul writes, "So whether we are at home or away, we make it our aim to please him. For we must all appear before the judgment seat of Christ, so that each one may receive what is due for what he has done in the body, whether good or evil" (5:9–10). Rather than getting lost in eschatological speculation on the nature of the intermediate state, Paul here brings his readers back to the basics. His point is to urge his readers toward holiness in their lives. Such holiness is important because they, and we, will stand before Jesus to give account of everything we have done.

Following his discussion of the transformation that is now occurring and the one that will occur, Paul returns to a discussion of his own ministry. In 5:11–6:10, Paul presents himself as a minister of reconciliation.[70] Paul expresses his conviction concerning the eschatological significance of Jesus Christ in 5:16–21. Here he explains that with the death and resur-

69. Barnett 1997, 262; Martin 1986, 106.

70. Matera 2003, 66.

rection of Jesus, a new age has begun. The eschatological significance of Jesus is tied to his soteriological significance. He is the one who died that his people might live (vv. 14–15). Now "if anyone is in Christ, he is a new creation. The old has passed away; behold, the new has come" (v. 17). Adam's sin wreaked havoc with God's creation, but it did not thwart God's plans. The prophets looked forward to a new creation. Here we see that the redemption accomplished by Christ is God's means of fulfilling these ancient purposes and promises.[71] He has inaugurated a new era, the "day of salvation" (6:2).

Before moving into the final sections of his epistle, Paul calls the Corinthians to reconciliation (6:11–7:4) and recounts more of the events that have transpired between him and the Corinthian church (7:5–16). In chapters 8–9, Paul appeals to the Corinthians to continue taking up the collection for the saints in Jerusalem, a collection that they had begun the previous year (8:10; 9:2). Paul concludes the epistle with a strong defense of his apostolic integrity and authority (10:1–13:10). He attacks the false apostles who have turned the church against him and sternly warns those who have not yet repented.[72]

Romans

The epistle to the Romans was likely written from Corinth during Paul's three-month stay there near the end of his third missionary journey (Acts 20:2–3). He had come to Corinth just as he had announced at the end of 2 Corinthians, the letter he sent as he was on his way to confront them (2 Cor. 13:2–3, 10). If 2 Corinthians was written in A.D. 56, the epistle to the Romans was written later in A.D. 56 or in 57.[73] The situation in Corinth seems to have improved enough by this time to allow him time to write. But what was Paul's reason for writing to the church at Rome, a church he himself did not plant? The answer can be discerned from the letter itself (Rom. 1:8–15; 15:14–33).

Paul had completed his labors in Asia Minor and Greece, and now his desire was to take the gospel further west into Spain. He hoped to visit the church at Rome on his way and to spend some time with them. He hoped

71. Hughes 1962, 201–2.
72. Matera 2003, 213–14.
73. Carson and Moo 2005, 394.

to be encouraged and to be an encouragement as well as to gain their support for his work.[74] He was also apparently aware of some issues involving Jewish-Gentile relations within the church (11:13–24). In short, Paul had a number of reasons for writing to the church at Rome.

The city of Rome was the capital of the Roman Empire. It seems likely that the church there was founded very early since visitors from Rome were among those who heard Peter's Pentecostal sermon (Acts 2:10). The church was likely founded upon their return to Rome from Jerusalem. It has been estimated that the number of Jews in Rome in the middle of the first century was between forty and fifty thousand.[75] These Jews would have been the first to hear from those who were present in Jerusalem at the time of Peter's sermon. Gentile God-fearers who were associated with the synagogues would have also been present to hear the news. By the time Paul wrote his epistle to the church at Rome, it appears that the church there was a mixed group of Jewish and Gentile Christians with the Gentile believers in the majority.[76]

Paul's epistle to the Romans is a tightly structured argument. In fact, it is the most systematic of all his letters. The structure of Paul's letter to the Romans reveals that it is all about the gospel of Jesus Christ.[77] The gospel is indicated to be the theme in the opening of the letter (Rom. 1:1–17). The first main section of the letter following the opening is about the heart of the gospel—justification by faith (1:18–4:25). In the second main section of the letter, Paul proceeds to discuss the assurance provided by the gospel (5:1–8:39). In the third main section of the letter, Paul defends the gospel by addressing the problem of Israel (9:1–11:36). Paul then turns, in the fourth main section of the epistle, to the transforming power of the gospel in the Christian life (12:1–15:13). Paul closes his letter with an announcement of his travel plans and numerous greetings (15:14–16:27).

The Letter Opening (Rom. 1:1–17)

Paul opens his epistle with a lengthy greeting to the church at Rome (1:1–7). He refers to himself as "a servant of Christ Jesus, called to be an

74. Cranfield 2004a, 22–23.

75. Dunn 1988a, xlvi.

76. Moo 1996a, 12.

77. Moo's outline of Romans is among the most helpful, and I have followed it throughout this section of the present chapter.

apostle, set apart for the gospel of God" (v. 1). Paul's life, in other words, is completely dedicated to declaring the good news. Paul elaborates on the meaning and content of the gospel in verses 2–4, saying that the gospel is that "which [God] promised beforehand through his prophets in the holy Scriptures, concerning his Son, who was descended from David according to the flesh and was declared to be the Son of God in power according to the Spirit of holiness by his resurrection from the dead, Jesus Christ our Lord."

Here Paul indicates first that the gospel was something promised in the Old Testament. It was not something completely unrelated to what had gone before.[78] He also indicates here that the gospel concerns Jesus Christ.[79] This Jesus was descended from David and is the long-awaited Messiah (2 Tim. 2:8).[80] He was declared to be the Son of God in power. As Douglas Moo explains, "What Paul is claiming . . . is that the preexistent Son, who entered into human experience as the promised Messiah, was appointed on the basis of (or, perhaps, at the time of) the resurrection to a new and more powerful position in relation to the world."[81] Paul is referring here to Christ's exaltation to the right hand of God.

Following his greeting, Paul expresses thanksgiving for the church at Rome and his desire to visit them (Rom. 1:8–15). He declares that he is eager to preach the gospel in Rome, and then explains why: "For I am not ashamed of the gospel, for it is the power of God for salvation to everyone who believes, to the Jew first and also to the Greek. For in it the righteousness of God is revealed from faith for faith, as it is written, 'The righteous shall live by faith'" (vv. 16–17). The gospel, the good news concerning Jesus Christ, which to the world appears weak and foolish, is the manifestation of the power of God directed toward the salvation of man (cf. Isa. 55:10–11).[82] This gospel reveals the righteousness (*dikaiosynē*) of God.[83]

78. Moo 1996a, 43; Fitzmyer 1993, 233.

79. Murray 1968, 5; Bruce 1985, 68; Moo 1996a, 44; Sproul 1999, 20; Cranfield 2004a, 57.

80. Cranfield 2004a, 58.

81. Moo 1996a, 48–49.

82. Cranfield 2004a, 87.

83. It is important to note that the word *dikaiosynē* (translated "righteousness" here) shares the same root (*dik-*) as the words *dikaioō* (translated "justify") and *dikaios* (translated "righteous"). The relationship between the words translated "righteous" and "righteousness" and the words translated "justify" and "justification" does not come across in English versions. For a discussion of the significance of these words in Paul's letter to the Romans, see Moo 1996a, 79–90.

The Heart of the Gospel (Rom. 1:18–4:25)

Paul has already stated that the gospel was "promised beforehand" through the prophets in the Scriptures (Rom. 1:2). Now, in the first major section of his letter, Paul explains the heart of this gospel—justification by faith (1:18–4:25). Before getting to the explanation proper, however, Paul prepares his readers by first demonstrating the fact of the universal reign of sin (1:18–3:20). Paul demonstrates that all people, Jews and Gentiles alike, are under God's wrath because all have sinned and fallen short of the glory of God.[84] Only when people understand this sobering fact can they understand why salvation must be humbly received as a gift of grace. Paul declares that the wrath of God is revealed against all unrighteousness and explains that this wrath is justified because people commit all kinds of ungodliness, and they suppress the truth (1:18–20). He then describes some of the ways in which people have suppressed the truth (vv. 21–32).

Having described the unrighteousness of pagans, Paul turns his attention to the unrighteousness of the Jews in 2:1–3:8. Why is this necessary? As Douglas Moo explains, "The literature of intertestamental Judaism, while consistently stressing the need for Jews to repent of sin, also tended to highlight Israel's favored position to the extent that its security in God's judgment was virtually unassailable."[85] It is this idea that Paul effectively dismantles in this section of his letter. He argues that God will judge all men impartially (2:6–11). He makes it clear that possession of the law will not give Jews an advantage at the final judgment (vv. 12–16).[86] Neither the law (vv. 17–24) nor circumcision (vv. 25–29) will exempt Jews from God's judgment (Jer. 9:25–26). Echoing Moses, Paul indicates that it is necessary for Jews to be circumcised in their hearts (vv. 28–29; Deut. 10:16).

Anticipating a possible objection to his teaching, Paul raises a question his readers might ask: "Then what advantage has the Jew? Or what is the value of circumcision?" (Rom. 3:1). Paul's response in verses 2–8 indicates that Jewish unfaithfulness does not nullify the faithfulness of God. C. E. B. Cranfield helpfully explains the point of these verses:

84. Schreiner 1998, 78.

85. Moo 1996a, 133.

86. Cranfield 2004a, 153; Fitzmyer 1993, 305.

> [The Jews] fundamentally misunderstood their special position when they thought of it as a ground for self-complacency and all too human glorying. But to challenge the falsehood of Jewish complacency and draw attention to the fact that the Jews were for the most part excluding themselves from an active and voluntary participation in the working out of God's gracious purpose was by no means to deny the reality of their pre-eminence which rests not on the faithfulness of men but on the grace and faithfulness of God.[87]

Paul concludes this section with a litany of Old Testament quotations demonstrating that both Jews and Gentiles are under the power of sin and guilty before God (3:9–20).

The need for the gospel demonstrated, Paul now explains that salvation is available, not through the law, but through faith in Jesus Christ (3:21–4:25). It is those who put their faith in Jesus who are justified, or declared righteous. The same justification is available for both Jews and Gentiles (3:22–24). Paul explains that Jesus was put forward by God "as a propitiation" (v. 25). His death on the cross fulfilled the symbolism of the Old Testament Day of Atonement ritual. In the remainder of this section (3:27–4:25), Paul will expand on the theme of justification.

Paul insists that we are "justified by faith apart from the works of the law" (3:28). He insists, however, that his doctrine of justification by faith does not overthrow the law; instead the law is upheld (v. 31). It is possible that Romans 8:4 is an explanation of this statement. There Paul says that the righteous requirement of the law is fulfilled in those who walk by the Spirit. At this point in his letter, however, Paul does not elaborate. Instead, he appeals to the patriarch Abraham to support his doctrine of justification by faith apart from the works of the law (Rom. 4:1–25).

Abraham was graciously justified by faith, not works (4:3–5). He was justified before he was circumcised (vv. 9–12) because the promises were to be inherited on the basis of faith not the law (vv. 13–14). Circumcision, then, is not the ground of justification. Paul insists that the inheritance is based on faith, rather than the law, in order that the promise might be guaranteed to both Jews and Gentiles (v. 16). In this way, the promise to Abraham that he would be a father of many nations is ultimately fulfilled (v. 17).

87. Cranfield 2004a, 178.

The Assurance Provided by the Gospel (Rom. 5:1–8:39)

In Romans 5–8, Paul describes the life, assurance, and hope provided by the gospel. The justified believer has peace with God (5:1), access to God's grace (v. 2a), and hope for the future (v. 2b). He is saved from wrath and has been reconciled to God (vv. 6–11). In 5:12–21, Paul declares that a new age has begun with the coming of Christ. It is through Jesus that the results of Adam's fall are being reversed.[88] Death entered the world through Adam (v. 12), but life and righteousness have come through Jesus the Messiah (vv. 15–19). What does this mean for mankind? Douglas Moo explains: "All people, Paul teaches, stand in relationship to one of two men, whose actions determine the eternal destiny of all who belong to them. Either one 'belongs to' Adam and is under sentence of death because of his sin, or disobedience, or one belongs to Christ and is assured of eternal life because of his 'righteous act, or obedience.'"[89] Paul then states the reason for the coming of the law. It was not to change the situation created by Adam's fall. Instead, the law came "to increase the trespass" (v. 20). Yet where sin increased, grace increased more, and as sin reigned through death, grace reigns through Jesus Christ (vv. 20–21).

Are we then to continue in sin that grace may abound (6:1)? Paul responds to this rhetorical question in chapter 6. He argues on the basis of the believer's union with Christ that we must not continue in sin (vv. 2–11). But what does Paul mean when he says we die and rise with Christ? Christ's death and resurrection were one-time redemptive-historical events. Believers enter into this objective redemptive-historical experience at their conversion when they are brought into union with Christ. Our union with Jesus in his death and resurrection is to form the grounds of our self-evaluation (v. 11), and it is to result in a life of obedience to God (v. 12).[90] It is not, however, until the final resurrection that we will be released completely from all of the effects of sin (v. 5). This explains why Paul can say "sin will have no dominon over you" (v. 14) and also say "let not sin therefore reign" (v. 12).[91] In the final verses of chapter 6, Paul explains that our freedom from sin entails our slavery to God and righteousness (vv. 15–23).

88. Schreiner 1998, 267.
89. Moo 1996a, 315.
90. Ridderbos 1975, 209.
91. Moo 1996a, 352.

In chapter 7, Paul turns his attention to the Mosaic law. In verses 1–6, Paul argues, using the analogy of marriage, that a person must die to the law in order to enter a new relationship with Christ (v. 4). In the remainder of the chapter, Paul indicates that the law in itself is good but that it has become a tool for evil in the hands of sin (vv. 7–25). Sin uses law to produce more sin and ultimately death (vv. 7–12). It is man's own fallen nature that allows sin to use the law in this way in spite of the law's own goodness (vv. 13–25). As Moo explains, "the law, in setting forth God's standard, arouses sins by stimulating human beings' innate rebelliousness against God."[92]

Paul picks up the theme of life in Christ again in chapter 8 (cf. 5:12–21), declaring, "There is therefore now no condemnation for those who are in Christ Jesus" (8:1). He contrasts life in the flesh with life in the Spirit (vv. 2–9). Those who live in the Spirit can look forward to having life given to their mortal bodies through the same Spirit who raised Jesus from the dead (vv. 10–11). Paul is speaking here of the future resurrection of our present bodies. These bodies will be given life and raised just as Jesus' body was raised (v. 11).[93] Paul explains that those who are led by the Spirit are sons of God and heirs with Christ who suffer with him (vv. 12–17). As heirs, believers must look to the future for the final enjoyment of the promises. The emphasis here is upon that which is "not yet."

In Romans 8:18–25, Paul looks forward to the ultimate consummation of God's plan for creation. He states that God's salvific plan involves more than the redemption of souls. It involves all of creation. It involves the reversal of the curse of the fall.[94] Paul indicates that the sufferings of the present are nothing compared to the glory that is to come (v. 18). He then describes the coming redemption of creation from its bondage to decay (vv. 19–22). Paul is referring here to the subhuman creation.[95] This present creation, like the believer himself (v. 23), is subject to decay and corruption, but Paul envisions a coming new creation, one that is set free (Rev. 21–22).[96] Paul turns his attention back to believers in the conclusion of this paragraph, promising that all of those who have been called according

92. Moo 1996a, 420.

93. Wright 2003, 256; Fitzmyer 1993, 491.

94. Bruce 1985, 160.

95. Cranfield 2004a, 411–12; Dunn 1988a, 469.

96. Witherington 2004, 223.

to God's purpose will be glorified (Rom. 8:28–30). Here we see that the foundations of biblical eschatology were established from all eternity.

The Defense of the Gospel (Rom. 9:1–11:36)

An obvious question arises in light of all that Paul has written thus far. What about Israel? What has become of God's promises to her in light of her rejection of the Messiah? Has the faithlessness of Israel negated God's promises? Has Israel been disinherited? Has the plan of God revealed throughout the Old Testament been derailed or set aside?[97] Paul's own teaching in Romans 1–8 could lend support to such a notion. He has already denied that Jews are guaranteed salvation on the basis of their distinctive privileges. He has also indicated that all who believe in Jesus are children of Abraham. As Douglas Moo says, "It seems that Israel has not only been disinherited but replaced."[98]

These significant questions indicate that chapters 9–11 of Romans are not peripheral in Paul's epistle. They are, in fact, central to an understanding of redemptive history and eschatology. Moo provides a very helpful summary of the argument of chapters 9–11, which follows in full:

> **9:1–5**—Introduction of the issue Paul seeks to resolve: the Jews' failure to embrace the gospel (vv. 1–3) calls into question the value of the privileges and promises God has given them (vv. 4–5).
>
> **9:6–29**—Defense of the proposition in v. 6a—"the word of God has not failed." Paul argues that God's word never promised salvation to all the biological descendants of Abraham (9:6b–13). Salvation is never a birthright, even for Jews, but always a gift of God's electing love (vv. 14–23), a gift he is free to bestow on Gentiles as well as Jews (vv. 24–29).
>
> **9:30–10:21**—Connected to 9:6b–29 (and esp. vv. 25–29) with the rhetorical question "What then shall we say?" Paul uses his understanding of the gospel to explain the surprising turn in salvation history, as Jews are cast aside while Gentiles stream into the kingdom.
>
> **11:1–10**—Connected to 9:30–10:21 (esp. vv. 20–21) and indirectly to 9:6b–29 with the rhetorical question "I ask, then . . . ." Paul summarizes the situation of Israel as he has outlined in the previous two sections and prepares for the next section by affirming the continuation of Israel's election.

97. As Günter Wagner (1988, 80) observes, what Paul is dealing with in these chapters is not just a question about Israel, it is also a question about God.

98. Moo 1996a, 549.

11:11–32—Connected to 11:1–10 (esp. v. 7a) with the rhetorical question "I ask then . . . ." Paul argues that Israel's current hardened state is neither an end in itself nor is it permanent. God is using Israel's casting aside in a salvific process that reaches out to Gentiles and will include Israel once again.

11:33–36—Response to the teaching of Rom. 9–11 with extolling of God's transcendent plan and doxology.[99]

As we see, the content of Romans 9–11 is a sustained argument. With this summary outline in mind, we can better follow its details.

Paul's Anguish for Israel

Paul opens this section of his epistle with a lament for Israel:

> I am speaking the truth in Christ—I am not lying; my conscience bears me witness in the Holy Spirit—that I have great sorrow and unceasing anguish in my heart. For I could wish that I myself were accursed and cut off from Christ for the sake of my brothers, my kinsmen according to the flesh. They are Israelites, and to them belong the adoption, the glory, the covenants, the giving of the law, the worship, and the promises. To them belong the patriarchs, and from their race, according to the flesh, is the Christ who is God over all, blessed forever. Amen. (9:1–5)

Paul's lament is reminiscent of the laments of the Old Testament prophets (Jer. 4:19; 13:17; 14:17; Lam. 1:12, 16; 2:11; Dan. 9:3–5). They too anguished over the stubbornness of Israel. Paul's expressed desire that he could be "cut off" instead of Israel echoes the intercession of Moses for Israel after their worship of the golden calf at Mount Sinai (Ex. 32:32). Once again Israel has rebelled against God. However, although Israel has rejected the Messiah, Paul is able to affirm that to them belong the adoption, the covenants, and the promises (Rom. 9:4). He is hinting here at the truth he will develop further in the following sections, namely, that God has not completely rejected Israel.

God's Sovereign Election

In 9:6–29, Paul defends the proposition he states in verse 6a: the word of God has not failed. In verses 6–13, he explains that the corporate elec-

99. Moo 1996a, 554.

tion of Israel never meant the salvation of every biological descendant of Abraham. He notes that "not all who are descended from Israel belong to Israel" (v. 6b). In verses 14–23, Paul expands on this, explaining that salvation was never a birthright based on biological descent. It has always been a gift based on God's sovereign election. Moo explains, "So many Jews have failed to embrace the gospel because God has so willed it: as with Pharaoh, God has hardened them, and they are now vessels on whom God's wrath rests."[100] Furthermore, as Paul explains in verses 24–29, God is free to bestow this gift of salvation on Gentiles as well as Jews. The prophets themselves foresaw the salvation of the Gentiles (vv. 25–26). They also foresaw a day when only a remnant of Israel would be saved (v. 27). In short, what is happening with Israel is all a part of God's plan.

Jesus: The Climax of Redemptive History

In 9:30–10:21, Paul elaborates on the turn that redemptive history has taken, namely that while Israel has stumbled over Jesus, Gentiles are now streaming into the kingdom. According to Paul, the current situation can be explained by references to one crucial aspect of the gospel—the necessity of faith (9:30–33; see also 3:27–4:25). Gentiles have attained a righteous standing by faith, but Israel failed to attain a righteous standing because they pursued such a standing by works of the law.

In Romans 10:1, Paul writes, "Brothers, my heart's desire and prayer to God for them is that they may be saved." As Cranfield explains, "The fact that Paul continued to pray for the unbelieving Jews, who had 'stumbled against the stone of stumbling,' is clear proof that he did not think of their present rejection as final and closed."[101] Paul states that Israel has a zeal for God, but it is a zeal without knowledge (v. 2). Rather than submitting to God's righteousness, they sought to establish their own (v. 3). Christ, Paul says, "is the end of the law for righteousness to everyone who believes" (v. 4). The era of redemptive history governed by the Mosaic covenant has been brought to a close with the coming of Christ and the establishment of the new covenant. Christ has inaugurated a new era, and until Israel recognizes this fact, she will continue to stumble over the gospel.

100. Moo 1996a, 609.

101. Cranfield 2004b, 513. Paul's example is one that the church should follow.

In 10:5–13, Paul contrasts "the righteousness that is based on the law" with "the righteousness based on faith." The righteousness based on the law depends upon doing all of the commandments (v. 5). The righteousness based on faith depends on belief, "for with the heart one believes and is justified, and with the mouth one confesses and is saved" (v. 10). The righteousness based on faith is available to both Jews and Gentiles, for everyone who trusts in the one Lord Jesus Christ will be saved (vv. 12–13). In the final verses of chapter 10, Paul reveals that the prophets foresaw a time when Israel would reject God, and the blessings of God would go forth to the Gentiles (vv. 16–21).

Israel's Rejection Is Not Total

What Paul has said thus far raises a question, which he now states, "I ask, then, has God rejected his people? By no means!" (11:1a). This is the basic theme of chapter 11, namely, that God has not rejected Israel.[102] Paul will explain the answer to his question in the remainder of chapter 11, but the question itself does not imply anything specific about the future. In fact, in verses 1–10, Paul explains his answer by appealing to what is going on in the present time. In verses 1–10, Paul demonstrates that God has not rejected Israel by distinguishing between the "remnant" and the "hardened."

Building on what he has already said in 9:6–13 and 9:27, Paul indicates that just as in the days of Elijah, there is now a believing remnant (11:2–5).[103] The significance of the remnant is sometimes overlooked. In the days of Elijah, the existence of the remnant indicated God's continuing care for Israel. It was a sign of his continuing faithfulness to the nation as a whole. Cranfield explains the significance for the present time: "The point that Paul is making is that the remnant of the present time, that is, the company of Jews who have believed in Christ, is a similar remnant, the existence of which is also based not on human deserving . . . , but on God's gracious election, and is therefore also a pledge of the continuing election of Israel as a whole."[104]

In contrast with the remnant chosen by grace (v. 5) is the rest, the nation of Israel as a whole, which has been "hardened" (v. 7). God has dulled

102. Moo 1996a, 671; Cranfield 2004b, 542. Paul's question and answer echo a number of texts in the Old Testament (1 Sam. 12:22; Ps. 94:14; Jer. 31:37).

103. Bruce 1985, 201.

104. Cranfield 2004b, 548; see also Holwerda 1995, 167.

the spiritual senses of Israel (v. 8), and they have stumbled (vv. 9–10). N. T. Wright argues that the hardening of which Paul speaks in verse 7 is permanent, like the hardening of Pharaoh.[105] Were verses 1–10 of chapter 11 all we had, this interpretation might be plausible. As we shall see, however, Paul explicitly denies that the hardening of Israel is permanent in the remainder of the chapter.

Israel's Rejection Is Not Final

Romans 11:11–32 is one of the most significant eschatological texts in the New Testament, and like most eschatological texts, its interpretation is disputed. Most commentators believe that Paul teaches here that Israel's present condition is not permanent, that Israel as a whole will come to Christ, that there will be some kind of eschatological conversion of the nation.[106] There are, however, others who strongly deny such an interpretation.[107] The only way to settle the question is to carefully examine what Paul wrote.

In the previous verses, Paul indicated that Israel as a whole had stumbled. Now he asks, "Did they stumble in order that they might fall?" (11:11a). What is his answer? "By no means! Rather through their trespass salvation has come to the Gentiles, so as to make Israel jealous" (v. 11b). O. Palmer Robertson objects to the view that Paul is here introducing a section that discusses Israel's future, saying that it would be strange if the argument of Romans 11 omitted "any reference to Israel's present significance."[108] However, as we have seen, Romans 11 does not omit any reference to Israel's present significance. Paul has already addressed it in verses 1–10, and he will continue to address it in these verses. There is no reason, however, why his discussion of Israel's present significance should rule out a discussion of Israel's future significance.

What is the present significance of Israel's stumbling? Paul explains that "through their trespass salvation has come to the Gentiles, so as to make

105. Wright 2002, 677.

106. E.g., Sanday and Headlam 1902; Murray 1968; Bruce 1985; Dunn 1988b; Vos 1991; Fitzmyer 1993; Moo 1996a; Schreiner 1998; Sproul 1999; Cranfield 2004b; Witherington 2004.

107. E.g., Ridderbos 1975, 354–61; Robertson 2000, 167–92; Wright 2002, 679–95. In order to interact with the strongest arguments against my own view, I refer repeatedly in this section to the exegetical arguments of O. Palmer Robertson and N. T. Wright. These scholars write from widely different theological perspectives, but their various arguments present the strongest challenges to the view I am presenting.

108. Robertson 2000, 168.

Israel jealous" (11:11b). The hardening of Israel is serving God's purpose. Their trespass has served as the occasion for the granting of salvation to the Gentiles.[109] Paul states, "Now if their trespass means riches for the world, and if their failure means riches for the Gentiles, how much more will their full inclusion mean!" (v. 12). Here we find a statement that for many clearly implies a future restoration of Israel. As R. C. Sproul explains, "Paul is saying that if the apostasy of Israel brought great blessings to the world, how much greater blessings will come through their restoration."[110]

In verses 11–12, Paul mentions three events: the trespass (or "failure") of Israel, the salvation of the Gentiles, and the full inclusion of Israel. The first of these leads to the second, and the second leads to the third. Israel's trespass, in other words, has started a process that will ultimately lead back to Israel's restoration.[111] This is the first of five places in this section of Romans 11 where Paul explains the purpose and future of Israel in terms of three stages. Douglas Moo provides a helpful summary:

- vv. 11–12: "trespass of Israel"—"salvation for the Gentiles"—"their fullness"
- v. 15: "their rejection"—"reconciliation of the world"—"their acceptance"
- vv. 17–23: "natural branches broken off"—"wild shoots grafted in"—"natural branches" grafted back in
- vv. 25–26: "hardening of Israel"—"fullness of Gentiles"—"all Israel will be saved" (?)
- vv. 30–31: disobedience of Israel—mercy for Gentiles—mercy to Israel[112]

109. Concerning verse 11, Calvin (2003, 19:421) writes, "Here he [Paul] justly denies that the salvation of the Jews was to be despaired of, or that they were so rejected by God, that there was to be no future restoration, or that the covenant of grace, which he had once made with them, was entirely abolished, since there had ever remained in that nation the seed of blessing." Calvin's interpretation of "all Israel" in verse 26 has led many to believe that he rejected any idea of a future restoration of Israel. However, in his comment on verse 11, he appears to affirm precisely such a restoration, saying that Paul denies there was to be no future restoration.

110. Sproul 1999, 187.

111. Moo 1996a, 687.

112. Moo 1996a, 684. Moo apparently includes the question mark at vv. 25–26 because of the disputed nature of that text.

The repeated occurrence of this three-stage process reinforces the idea that Paul is looking forward to a future restoration of Israel as a whole. Paul characterizes the present condition of Israel as "failure" (v. 12). At present only a remnant of Israel has believed. He characterizes the future condition of Israel in terms of "full inclusion." Israel is not simultaneously in the condition of failure and full inclusion. The full inclusion will follow the failure.[113]

There are those who object to this interpretation. Wright, for example, argues, "There is no reason to suppose that 'the fullness' of Israel will mean anything more than this: the complete number of Jews, many more than at present, who likewise come to faith in the gospel."[114] On the contrary, a good reason does exist to suppose that the "fullness" of Israel means more than this, namely, the entire context of Romans 11:11–32. It is not that the restoration of Israel in the future will entail anything other than their conversion to Christ. The issue is Paul's contrast between Israel's present condition and Israel's future condition. Her present condition is her failure. This is contrasted with her future fullness, not equated with it.

Robertson also rejects the idea that Israel's "acceptance" is chronologically subsequent to her "rejection." He writes, "For both Gentiles and Jews, the full cycle of movement from a state of disobedience to a state of mercy occurs in the present age."[115] For individual Jews and Gentiles this is most certainly true. However, for Israel and the Gentiles as corporate entities, it is not. In the history of redemption there was an era during which Israel (as a whole) was the chosen nation (although individual Gentiles could be saved at the time). The present era is a reversal of that situation. Now Israel (as a whole) is rejected (although a remnant of individual Jews are being saved) while the Gentiles are experiencing privileged blessings.

Paul anticipates a potential problem in verses 13–24. Gentile believers who had been taught that they were now God's people could be easily misled into thinking that this was cause for boasting against the Jews. In these verses, Paul warns against such arrogance.[116] Verses 13–14 are a parenthetical statement in the argument of verses 11–32. Paul writes, "Now I am speaking to you Gentiles. Inasmuch then as I am an apostle to the

113. Bruce 1985, 203.
114. Wright 2002, 681.
115. Robertson 2000, 173.
116. Moo 1996a, 685.

Gentiles, I magnify my ministry in order somehow to make my fellow Jews jealous, and thus save some of them." Moo explains, "As God uses Paul's preaching to bring more and more Gentiles to salvation, Paul hopes that Jews, his own 'flesh and blood,' will become jealous and seek for themselves the blessings of this salvation."[117]

Robertson argues that verses 13 and 14 contradict the idea that there is to be a future conversion of Israel as a whole. Since these verses do provide the weightiest argument for the interpretation Robertson advances, his objection must be considered seriously. Robertson states the argument as follows:

> This reference to the present saving of some in Israel by the provoking of them to jealousy (vv. 13–14) is immediately connected with the "receiving" of the Jews in the following verses (vv. 15–16). The "for if" (*ei gar*) of verse 15 connects the "receiving" of the Jews with the present ministry of the apostle Paul in the gospel era. By his present ministry among the Gentiles the apostle hopes to move the Jews to jealousy and thereby to save some of them. Their "saving" as described in verse 14 corresponds to their "receiving" in verse 15. In each case, Paul describes what he hopes will be the consequence of his current ministry.[118]

In response, several observations are in order. First, if these verses are understood in the way Robertson suggests, it appears to conflict with what Paul writes elsewhere in the chapter. Israel's "rejection" would have to be understood as being simultaneous with her "acceptance" (v. 15). Her hardening (vv. 7–10) would be simultaneous with her salvation (v. 26). When we consider the status of various individuals among the nation of Israel, this is not a problematic concept, but Paul is speaking in this chapter of the nation as a whole in the course of redemptive history. In that context, it makes little sense to say that the rejection of Israel is concurrent with the acceptance of Israel. Although the contextual consideration is decisive, we must also remember that Paul did not know exactly when the last day was to come. It appears that Paul is expressing hope here that his own preaching will result in the eschatological restoration of Israel in his own day.

In verse 15, Paul writes, "For if their rejection means the reconciliation of the world, what will their acceptance mean but life from the dead?"

117. Moo 1996a, 692.
118. Robertson 2000, 169.

Israel's rebellion has providentially resulted in the extension of the gospel to the Gentile nations. But what is Paul saying when he claims that Israel's "acceptance" will mean "life from the dead"? Many argue, and I concur, that what Paul is speaking of is the general resurrection at the time of the second coming of Christ.[119] If Paul is referring here to the general resurrection, then he is saying that the restoration of Israel will be closely associated with the final consummation of all things.[120]

Wright disagrees with the interpretation suggested above. He argues that in verses 13–16, Paul is saying that what he "does not want Gentile Christians to think is that God cannot and will not save any more Jews."[121] While it is true that Paul would not want the Gentiles to think anything like that, the point he is making in this text concerns more than the ongoing salvation of a remnant of Jews. He is making a point about the nation of Israel within redemptive history. Concerning Paul's reference in verse 15 to the Jews' "acceptance" meaning "life from the dead," Wright denies that it is a reference to the future general resurrection. He says, "If, after all that has happened, Jews come back into the family, hearing and believing the gospel as in 10:6–13, then, says Paul, the significance of this will be like a kind of resurrection."[122] The problem with this interpretation is that at the time Paul wrote Romans some Jews had already been hearing and believing the gospel (11:1–10). Why then would the ongoing existence of a remnant of believing Jews be any different than the present existence of such a remnant? Why would the present time, in which there is already a remnant, be portrayed as a time of Israel's failure and casting off while the continuing existence of a remnant throughout the present age is described as Israel's acceptance and as something far greater than "the reconciliation of the world" (v. 15)?

In 11:16–24, Paul explains the development of redemptive history and the place of Israel within it by using the analogy of an olive tree. The tree itself represents the people of God. Paul compares unbelieving Israel to branches that have been broken off from the tree (v. 17a). Believing Gentiles are compared to branches from a wild olive tree that have been grafted

119. As Moo (1996a, 695) explains, "the phrase 'from the dead' is found 47 times in the NT; and every occurrence except one comes in a phrase referring to the resurrection."

120. Cranfield 2004b, 563; Schreiner 1998, 591.

121. Wright 2002, 681.

122. Wright 2002, 683.

into the cultivated tree (vv. 17b–19). Paul warns the Gentiles not to boast about this new state of affairs because their inclusion in the olive tree has been based solely upon God's grace (vv. 20–22).

Paul concludes this paragraph by saying, "And even they, if they do not continue in their unbelief, will be grafted in, for God has the power to graft them in again. For if you were cut from what is by nature a wild olive tree, and grafted, contrary to nature, into a cultivated olive tree, how much more will these, the natural branches, be grafted back into their own olive tree" (11:23–24). Here again, Paul points to specific stages in redemptive history. At the present time, the natural branches (unbelieving Israel) are broken off while wild branches (Gentile believers) are grafted in (v. 17). God is able, however, to regraft the natural branches back into the olive tree (vv. 23–24). That he will do so has already been indicated in previous verses (vv. 12, 15) and will be indicated again in the following verses.

Paul's teaching in verses 25–27 has been at the center of the debate concerning the proper interpretation of chapter 11. Paul writes in verse 25, "Lest you be wise in your own conceits, I want you to understand this mystery, brothers: a partial hardening has come upon Israel, until the fullness of the Gentiles has come in." Here Paul is still speaking directly to the Gentiles (see v. 13). He wants them to understand a "mystery." In this context, "mystery" refers to a previously unrevealed end-time event.[123] The mystery involves the reversal of Jewish expectations concerning the sequence of end-time events. Rather than Israel being restored first followed by the salvation of the Gentiles, the Gentiles are being brought in while Israel is presently hardened. The mystery is that the restoration of Israel *follows* the salvation of the Gentiles.[124]

Robertson argues that the phrase translated "until" (*achris hou*) "brings matters 'up to' a certain point or 'until' a certain goal is reached," but it "does not itself determine the state of affairs after the termination."[125] As Moo explains, however, the phrase *achris hou* "more naturally suggests a

123. Moo 1996a, 714.

124. Robertson (2000, 187) argues that the mystery involves "the fact that some Jews are lost and others are saved." But how is this a mystery? God has never saved, nor promised to save, every individual within the nation of Israel.

125. Robertson 2000, 179.

reversal of the present situation."[126] As he explains, the word *achri* occurs 48 times in the New Testament. It is used in a temporal context 37 times, and of those 37 uses, 25 refer to a period of time and state of affairs that will come to an end.[127] The usage of the word elsewhere in the New Testament, then, indicates that our interpretation is possible. The immediate context, however, is what is determinative. Paul has repeatedly indicated in verses 11–24 that God is not only able to restore Israel, but that he will in fact do so. What Paul is saying in verse 25 is that Israel's hardening will continue until the full number of Gentiles has come in to the people of God, and then it will cease.[128]

In verses 26–27, Paul continues the sentence begun in verse 25, "And in this way all Israel will be saved, as it is written, 'The Deliverer will come from Zion, he will banish ungodliness from Jacob; and this will be my covenant with them when I take away their sins.'"[129] This text raises a number of questions that must be resolved: (1) what is the meaning of "in this way" (*houtōs*); (2) who is "all Israel" (*pas Israēl*); (3) what is the time of this Israel's "salvation" (*sōthēsetai*); and (4) what is the manner of this Israel's salvation? Our answers to these questions will significantly affect our understanding of biblical eschatology.

Regarding the meaning of the word *houtōs*, there are essentially four options: (1) some suggest that it has a temporal meaning (i.e., "and then . . ."), but the word is never used in this way in Greek; (2) some suggest that Paul is using the word to introduce a consequence (i.e., "In consequence of this process . . ."), but this is an extremely rare use of the word; (3) some understand the word to mean "manner" in the sense of "as it is written," but Paul nowhere uses the word like this; (4) most conclude that the word means "manner" and is connected with what has gone before. Moo explains what this means: "The 'manner' of Israel's salvation is the process that Paul has outlined in vv. 11–24 and summarized in v. 25b: God imposes a hardening on most of Israel while Gentiles come into the messianic salvation, with the Gentiles' salvation leading in turn to Israel's jealousy and her own salvation."[130]

126. Moo 1996a, 717.

127. Moo 1996a, 717 n. 30.

128. Dunn 1988b, 680–82; Holwerda 1995, 170; Moo 1996a, 718; Schreiner 1998, 618.

129. The ESV translation separates verses 25 and 26 into two sentences. The Greek, however, is one continuous sentence.

130. Moo 1996a, 720.

Several commentators observe that although *houtōs* does not have a temporal meaning, it does have a temporal reference.[131] In other words, the "manner" in which Israel is saved involves a temporal process with several stages.[132] Others object to this interpretation. Robertson, for example, argues that the "manner" in which Israel is saved is the repentance and faith of individual Jews throughout the present age.[133] While it is certainly true that individual Jews are saved (whether now or in the future) only by faith in Jesus Christ, this is not Paul's point in this specific text. In this text, Paul is speaking of the nation of Israel as a whole in salvation history.

What, then, does Paul mean when he speaks of "all Israel"? Cranfield lists the four main views that have been suggested: (1) all the elect, both Jews and Gentiles; (2) all the elect of the nation Israel; (3) the whole nation Israel, including every individual member; and (4) the nation of Israel as a whole, but not necessarily including every individual member.[134] The least likely interpretation is that Paul is speaking of the whole nation of Israel, including every individual member.[135] There is no indication in this text or elsewhere in Scripture that Paul believed every individual Israelite would be saved.

Another view, popularized by John Calvin, is that "all Israel" refers to the church, gathered from both Jews and Gentiles.[136] This view is also held by Robertson, who summarizes Paul's thought in this passage: "According to Paul, 'hardness has happened to part of Israel until the full number of the Gentiles has come in[to Israel], and in this manner all Israel shall be saved.'"[137] The theological point that Robertson is making is absolutely true. As Paul himself teaches in verses 16–24, there is only one olive tree, only one people of God, and it is composed of believing Jews and Gentiles. The problem is that this theological point about one people of God is not what Paul is talking about when he refers to "all Israel" in verse 26.

131. E.g., Dunn 1988b, 681; Witherington 2004, 274.

132. Moo 1996a, 720.

133. Robertson 2000, 182.

134. Cranfield 2004b, 576.

135. This view is defended by Bell 2005.

136. See Calvin 2003, 19:437. It should be noted that although Calvin interpreted the "all Israel" of verse 26 as the church composed of Jews and Gentiles, this doesn't seem to have caused him to reject the idea of a future conversion of the nation of Israel. In his comments on Romans 11:11, he appears to affirm such a future restoration.

137. Robertson 2000, 188.

Throughout verses 11–25, Paul has not denied that there is only one people of God, but he has consistently distinguished between the Jews and the Gentiles who are part of that one people of God. We have to remember that Paul's concern in these chapters is for his kinsmen according to the flesh (9:1–5). His prayer is for the salvation of the nation of Israel (10:1). In Romans 11:26, Paul is revealing that the prayer of 10:1 will be answered once the fullness of the Gentiles has come in. The restoration of the nation of Israel will not mean the existence of a second people of God. The restoration of the nation of Israel will involve their regrafting into the olive tree, the one people of God. The restoration of the nation of Israel will mean their becoming part of the true Israel.

A third interpretation of "all Israel" is that it refers to all the elect of the nation of Israel throughout the present age. Joseph Fitzmyer is representative of this interpretation. He observes: "The phrase *pas Israēl*, a Hebraism for *kol-Yiśrā'ēl*, occurs 148 times in the OT and always designates historic, ethnic Israel, usually in the synchronic sense of the generations of Israel contemporary with the author; but in Mal. 3:22 it has a diachronic sense, 'all Israel' of every generation."[138] Fitzmyer then states that Paul is using the phrase in the same sense as Malachi. "For Paul *pas Israēl* means Israel in the ethnic sense and diachronically, because of the eschatological sense of the future *sōthēsetai*: the Jewish people as a whole, both 'the remnant' (11:5) or the 'chosen ones' (11:7) and 'the others' (11:7), will be saved."[139]

As with the view that understands "all Israel" to be the church, there is truth in this interpretation. The Jews who are being saved in the present age are not any different than the Jews who are to be saved in the future. The problem with this interpretation, as with the others already examined, is that it conflicts with the immediate context. As John Murray observes, "While it is true that all the elect of Israel, the true Israel, will be saved, this is so necessary and patent a truth that to assert the same here would have no particular relevance to what is the apostle's governing interest in this section of the epistle."[140] In Thomas Schreiner's words, such an interpretation is "stunningly anticlimactic."[141] Again, Paul is not in anguish over the salvation of the remnant because they are already saved. He is in anguish

138. Fitzmyer 1993, 623.
139. Fitzmyer 1993, 623.
140. Murray 1968, 97.
141. Schreiner 1998, 617.

over the nation that has stumbled (Rom. 11:11). He is concerned about the corporate body that has "trespassed" (v. 11), that has "failed" (v. 12), that has been "broken off" due to "unbelief" (v. 20), that has been "partially hardened" (v. 25). He is concerned about the corporate body that is presently considered the enemy of God (v. 28) and "disobedient" (v. 31). It is this Israel for whose salvation he prays (10:1), and it is this Israel that he says will be saved in 11:26.

The interpretation of "all Israel" that best fits the immediate context is that which understands "all Israel" as the nation of Israel as a whole, but not necessarily including every individual member. Paul consistently contrasts Gentiles and Israel throughout this chapter, and continues to do so in the first half of the sentence we are examining (v. 25). There is no contextual reason to assume that Paul changes the meaning of the term "Israel" in mid-sentence here.[142] The "Israel" that will be saved (v. 26) is the "Israel" that has been partially hardened (v. 25). This partially hardened Israel is distinct from the Gentiles (v. 25) and is also distinct from the present remnant of believing Jews, who are not hardened (v. 7).[143]

Robertson objects that our interpretation would require the salvation of every individual Jew. "If a day is coming when the principle of reprobation is lifted from Israel, then every single Israelite living at that time will be saved."[144] This, however, does not follow. Israel's hardening is said to have begun at a specific time in history (vv. 7–10). Prior to Israel's hardening, not every living Israelite was saved. Why would the removal of the hardening require that every living Israelite be saved? Furthermore, the hardening of Israel did not result in the unbelief of every living Israelite, so again, we must ask why the removal of that hardening would necessarily result in the salvation of every living Israelite.

Robertson finds other problems with the idea that "all Israel" refers specifically to ethnic Jews. He writes, "This concept overlooks many aspects of the biblical definition of Israel and contradicts the truth that God does

142. Bruce (1985, 209) says, "It is impossible to entertain an exegesis which understands 'Israel' here in a different sense from 'Israel' in verse 25."

143. Although the remnant comes from within the nation of Israel as a whole, Paul can still distinguish between the two when necessary. When he speaks of Israel as a whole, he looks at her overall condition, and that condition is one that can be characterized at the present time as rejection. Such language echoes that of the prophets who could speak of the sin and rebellion of the corporate body of Israel even though they knew not every individual Israelite was guilty.

144. Robertson 2000, 183.

not guarantee that a person will be saved if he possesses certain external qualifications."[145] This objection is based on a misunderstanding of the position presented here. There is no guarantee that any individual will be saved on the basis of external qualifications, including ethnic descent. Paul has made that point clear elsewhere in this epistle. Nor does the argument presented here overlook the biblical definition of Israel. It is clear, for example, that Paul sometimes uses the term "Israel" in different ways. In Romans 9:6, Paul says that "not all who are descended from Israel belong to Israel." However, if the inclusion of Gentiles in the people of God, the true Israel, means that it is now improper to speak of ethnic Israel in distinction from Gentiles, then Paul himself is guilty throughout chapter 11. Even when speaking of the one people of God in his analogy of the olive tree, Paul distinguishes between Gentile branches and Jewish branches.

Wright raises similar objections to the idea that "all Israel" refers to the nation of Israel as a whole. He insists, for example, that Paul did change the meaning of "Israel" in mid-sentence in verses 11:25–26: "In particular, 9:6 gives the lie to the constantly repeated assertion that one cannot make 'Israel' in 11:26 mean something different from what it means in 11:25. 'Not all who are of Israel are in fact Israel'; Paul opened his great argument with a clear signal that he was redefining 'Israel,' and here the argument comes full circle."[146] The issue here, however, is context. Paul is not talking about precisely the same thing in 9:6 as he is in 11:26. Wright continues:

> The dramatic theological redefinition in 10:13, whereby "the Lord," which in the original clearly referred to YHWH, now refers to Jesus, undergirds the dramatic redefinition of God's people, whereby "Israel," as in 9:6 and Gal. 6:16, now refers to the whole people of God, Gentile and Jew together. When, therefore, at the height of one of his most careful and long, drawn-out arguments, Paul declares with dramatic irony that "all Israel shall be saved," we must stand firm against the irresponsibility that would take the phrase out of its context and insist it must mean something he has carefully ruled out over and over again. However much we might want Paul to have said something else, exegesis will not sustain it.[147]

145. Robertson 2000, 185–86.

146. Wright 2002, 690.

147. Wright 2002, 690. Wright has written elsewhere (1992, xvii): "I frequently tell my students that quite a high proportion of what I say is probably wrong, or at least flawed or skewed in some way which I do not at the moment realize. The only problem is that I do not know which bits are

Is this objection valid? Not entirely. Wright argues that Paul has "redefined" the people of God, and that "Israel" now "refers to the whole people of God, Gentile and Jew together." Paul has, in fact, redefined the people of God, and the people of God does now consist of Jews and Gentiles. However, Paul does not use "Israel" to refer to "the whole people of God, Gentile and Jew together" in every case. Throughout Romans 9–11, Paul continues to use the word "Israel" to refer to the nation of Israel as distinguished from the Gentiles (e.g., 9:30–31; 10:21; 11:1, 2, 7, 11, 25). In none of these instances, does Paul use the word "Israel" to refer to the whole people of God, Gentile and Jew together.

If Wright's objection is valid, Paul himself was irresponsible for continuing to distinguish between the nation of Israel and Gentiles after redefining the people of God. It is true that the people of God now includes both Jews and Gentiles, and both are saved by faith alone in Jesus Christ alone. However, the fact that Paul has redefined the people of God does not mean that God has ruled out the possibility of restoring the nation of Israel back into this redefined people of God, which now consists of both Jews and Gentiles. If it is not inconsistent for Paul to speak of the present salvation of a remnant of Israel (as distinguished from believing Gentiles) even in light of his redefinition of the people of God, it is certainly not inconsistent to speak of the future restoration of Israel as a whole. Israel's future restoration is simply the regrafting of the natural branches back into their own olive tree, a tree that now contains wild (i.e., Gentile) branches as well.

Concerning the time and manner of "all Israel's" salvation, only a few brief comments are necessary, since our answers to these questions have already been indicated in our discussion of the other questions. Regarding the time of Israel's salvation, Wright mentions three possibilities: (1) during the course of present history; (2) immediately before the second coming; and (3) at the second coming.[148] The idea that the salvation of "all Israel" occurs during the course of present history is closely connected to the interpretation of "all Israel" as all the elect of the nation of Israel. P. W. L. Walker clearly states this position: "Paul is not predicting a 'large-scale, last-minute salvation of Jews' but speaking of an ongoing process which

---

wrong; if I did I might do something about it." I would suggest that Wright's interpretation of these verses is clearly one of the wrong bits.

148. Wright 2002, 689.

has now begun through the gospel."[149] As we have already seen, however, such an interpretation does not do justice to the full context of Romans 11. It requires that the salvation of Israel be simultaneous with the rejection of Israel. It requires that the breaking off of the unbelieving branches is simultaneous with the regrafting of these same branches.

Paul indicates that the salvation of "all Israel" is an end-time event. The rejection of Israel results in the salvation of the Gentiles. The salvation of the Gentiles results in the jealousy of Israel. The jealousy of Israel leads ultimately to the salvation of Israel. What Paul foresees is a turning of the nation of Israel as a whole to her God at the time of the end.[150] Since Paul appears to connect the final restoration of the nation of Israel to the general resurrection (v. 15), it appears that this restoration will occur not long before the second coming of Christ.

Wright has two objections to the idea of a future mass-conversion of Jews. He says, "It is not clear why saving only the final generation of Jews would get God off the hook."[151] This objection fails to take into account the corporate nature of Israel that allows one generation to represent the whole. We see something similar when God's promise of the land to Abraham is fulfilled when the land is given to Israel many generations later. Wright also suggests that a future conversion of Israel would undermine God's impartiality: "What would Gentiles alive at the time say about God's impartiality, one of the major underlying themes of the whole letter?" I would suggest that if God's impartiality is not inconsistent with his hardening of Israel at the present time, then it is not in any way inconsistent with his removing that hardening at some point in the future. If the latter is an example of partiality, so is the former. Furthermore, God is not saving "only the final generation of Jews." As we have already observed, God is also saving a remnant during the present age.

Regarding the manner of Israel's salvation, Wright mentions three options: (1) through the people concerned coming to (Christian) faith; (2) through their own faith, whatever that might be; (3) through some direct divine intervention, perhaps through the agency of Christ at his second coming,

149. Walker 1996, 141.

150. Dunn 1988b, 682; Wagner 1988, 103; Moo 1996a, 723–24; Witherington 2004, 275; Cranfield 2004b, 577.

151. Wright 2002, 689.

which may or may not involve some kind of Christian faith.[152] The significant question here is whether Jews will be saved in the same manner that Gentiles are saved, or will God make a different way of salvation for Jews? It is clear from the earlier chapters of Romans that only one answer is possible. Like Gentiles, Jews can be saved only by coming to faith in Jesus Christ. The future restoration of Israel will involve precisely this. When God opens the eyes of the nation of Israel, the nation as a whole (not every individual) will come to faith in Christ. This will come as a result of the proclamation of the gospel to Israel.

In 11:28–29, Paul provides a reason for the restoration of Israel. Although Israel can presently be considered an enemy, she is beloved for the sake of her forefathers. But why does Israel remain beloved in spite of her present rejection of Jesus? Because "the gifts and the calling of God are irrevocable" (v. 29). God has made promises to Israel, and those promises cannot be revoked. Paul sums up his argument in verses 30–32, saying, "Just as you were at one time disobedient to God but now have received mercy because of their disobedience, so they too have now been disobedient in order that by the mercy shown to you they also may now receive mercy. For God has consigned all to disobedience, that he may have mercy on all."

According to some, Paul's use of the word "now" in verse 31b indicates that Paul is speaking of the present response of Israel, not a future restoration.[153] Two observations are in order, however. First, there is some textual uncertainty regarding the word. It is omitted in some important manuscripts. If it was not part of the original letter, there is no conflict at all with the interpretation offered above. If it was included in the original manuscript, the conflict is only apparent, not real. Verses 30–32 sum up the entire argument of chapter 11, not only verses 11–29. If the "now" was part of the original, then Paul is summarizing both answers he has given to the problem of Israel's rejection: it is not total and it is not final. There is now a remnant, and at some point in the future there will be a full restoration.

Praising God

Paul concludes chapter 11 with an expression of praise to God (vv. 33–36), and what else could he do after looking at God's providential plan

152. Wright 2002, 689.
153. E.g., Robertson 2000, 170.

for Israel and the nations? Paul has made it clear that the promise of Jeremiah 31:35–37 is true, and in Romans 11:11–32, he has revealed the amazing grace of God. For thousands of years, the nation of Israel has stubbornly resisted God. In spite of numerous blessings and privileges given to no other nation, Israel turned from God to idols. As a punishment, God sent the nation into exile, but he did not cast her away forever. He brought many of the people back to the land and promised fuller restoration to come. Finally, he sent the promised Messiah, but Israel continued her rebellious ways, rejecting the proffered salvation. What was to become of the Old Testament promises of restoration? Would God now finally give up on this stubborn nation? One might have thought so. But Paul reveals that even in the face of the ultimate rebellion, God does not reject Israel and that his plans for her ultimate restoration remain. Not only that, but Israel's stubborn rejection of Jesus has been used by God as the occasion for the salvation of the Gentiles! And in the ultimate ironic twist, the salvation of the Gentiles will ultimately result in the restoration of Israel!

The Transforming Power of the Gospel (Rom. 12:1–15:13)

The necessity of our extended discussion of Romans 9–11 entails only a cursory look at chapters 12–16. These latter chapters deal with a number of practical matters. Paul's instruction in these chapters is grounded in what he has already taught in the first eleven chapters. Because what he has taught the Romans is true, they are to present their bodies as a living sacrifice to God (12:1). Paul then tells them, "Do not be conformed to this world, but be transformed by the renewal of your mind" (v. 2a). As Cranfield observes, this verse indicates the eschatological basis for the Christian life.[154] With the coming of Christ, believers are no longer governed by "this world" because this world is no longer their true home.

In 12:3–8, Paul calls upon believers to humbly serve one another, using whatever specific gifts God has given them. Paul then urges the Roman Christians to live lives that demonstrate genuine love, joy, and hope (vv. 9–17). They are to live peaceably with all and not attempt to seek vengeance (vv. 18–21). Paul calls upon the Romans to submit to governing authorities because they are appointed by God (13:1–7). Christians are to love one another because love fulfills the law (vv. 8–10). Paul's appeal to love is then

154. Cranfield 2004b, 608.

given an eschatological basis. He tells the Romans that "salvation is nearer to us now than when we first believed" (v. 11). He then says, "The night is far gone; the day is at hand. So then let us cast off the works of darkness and put on the armor of light" (v. 12). Do these statements indicate that Paul believed the end of the world was imminent? Was Paul in error here? The answer is no. We have to always keep in mind that with the resurrection and ascension of Christ, the last days were inaugurated (Acts 2:16–17). Paul is writing under the conviction that Jesus had inaugurated the end time. He did not know, however, exactly when the final consummation of the last days would come.

Moo explains that Romans 14:1–15:13 is a plea for Christian unity among the Romans.[155] Paul urges the Roman believers not to judge one another over secondary matters such as food or the observance of certain days (14:1–12). Rather than passing judgment on one another, believers should go out of their way to avoid placing stumbling blocks in the path of their brothers in Christ (vv. 13–23). Following the example of Jesus Christ, believers should seek to build up their neighbor rather than pleasing themselves (15:1–13). In all things, Christians are to put others before themselves.

The Letter Closing (Rom. 15:14–16:27)

Paul's epistle to the Romans contains a closing section that is longer than the closing found in most of his other letters. First, Paul informs the Romans of his ministry and of his plans to visit Rome (15:14–33). He then includes a lengthy list of personal greetings (16:1–23). He tells those whom he is greeting that God "will soon crush Satan under your feet" (v. 20). The destruction of Satan has begun, but it will not be completed until the final judgment. The author of Hebrews speaks of Christ's death destroying the devil (Heb. 2:14), but the devil is not completely defeated until the last day (Rev. 20:10). Appropriately, considering the glorious nature of the subject of his letter, Paul closes with a doxology of praise to God (Rom. 16:25–27).

Summary

Paul's letters to the church at Corinth and the church at Rome were written near the end of his third missionary journey several years after his earlier

155. Moo 1996a, 826.

letters to the Galatians and Thessalonians, but like his earlier letters they are written with a basic underlying eschatological framework in mind. In addition, each of Paul's letters to the Corinthians and Romans includes sections devoted specifically to significant eschatological issues.

In 1 Corinthians, Paul makes a special point of emphasizing the "yet to come" aspect of the kingdom. The Corinthians are acting as if the final war is over and Paul must remind them that it is not. Paul's eschatology underlies the way he addresses everything in this letter from marriage, to the Lord's Supper, to spiritual gifts. But eschatological themes do not remain in the background in this letter. In one of the most important chapters in all of Scripture, Paul expounds on the doctrine of the resurrection—Christ's and ours, explaining its necessity and bodily character (1 Cor. 15).

In 2 Corinthians, Paul is focused on the defense of his apostolic ministry, but even here, eschatology comes into play as Paul insists that he is a minister of the prophesied new covenant. In addition the suffering he endures in his ministry leads him to reflect on the present transformation of the inner nature and the future transformation of the body. Paul expresses his hope that he will live to see the second coming, but he also knows he may die before it happens. If he does die first, he knows he will have to wait for his resurrection body, but he also knows he will still be present with the Lord.

The epistle to the Romans is Paul's most systematic letter, and in it Paul expounds on the gospel of Jesus Christ. He proclaims that the gospel is not anything unexpected in the plan of God, but was foreseen by the prophets. Jesus Christ is the one who is reversing the effects of Adam's fall. Through him, life and righteousness are now available to all through faith. But what of Israel? Since they have rejected Jesus, has God set them aside? In another highly significant section of Scripture, Paul explains the way Israel fits into God's redemptive historical plan (Rom. 9–11). Their rejection is not total because even at the present time there is a remnant, and their rejection is not permanent because after the fullness of the Gentiles has come in, they will come to faith in the Messiah Jesus.

16

The Pauline Epistles (3)

The Prison Epistles and the Pastoral Epistles

As the book of Acts indicates, Paul was arrested in Jerusalem after returning from his third missionary journey in A.D. 57 (Acts 21:27–36). Not long after his arrest, Paul was sent to the governor Felix in Caesarea (Acts 23:23–35). Paul spent two years imprisoned in Caesarea before his appeal to Caesar and his journey to Rome (Acts 24:27; 25:10–12). After a long and difficult journey, Paul arrived in Rome in A.D. 60. His two-year house arrest in Rome (A.D. 60–62) is recounted in Acts 28:17–31. Paul's Roman imprisonment is important because traditionally four of his letters have been dated from this time period: Colossians, Philemon, Ephesians, and Philippians.[1] These four letters are often referred to as Paul's Prison Epistles. The letters to the Colossians and to Philemon were almost certainly sent at the same time by the same courier (ca. A.D. 60–61). It

1. In each of these four letters, Paul makes at least one reference to being in prison (Col. 4:3; Philem. 1; Eph. 6:20; Phil. 1:14).

is possible, but not as certain, that the letter to the Ephesians was sent along with Colossians and Philemon. The letter to the Philippians, on the other hand, was sent at a later time during Paul's imprisonment (ca. A.D. 61–62).

Colossians and Philemon

Because of their close relationship, we will look at the epistle to the church at Colossae and the epistle to Philemon together. It should be noted first that although the authenticity of Philemon is almost universally granted, there are a large number of scholars who reject the Pauline authorship of Colossians. Because of perceived stylistic and theological differences, it is suggested that someone other than Paul wrote the letter. James Dunn, for example, suggests that Timothy wrote the letter under Paul's supervision and with his approval.[2] Others, however, have pointed out that the perceived differences are not as dramatic as suggested. The suggestion made by some, for example, that Colossians destroys the eschatological tension between the "already" and the "not yet" is overstated since Colossians includes references to both eschatological realities.[3] When all of the evidence is examined, it is clear that there is no sufficient reason to reject Pauline authorship.[4]

It is evident from the content of Colossians that Paul wrote the epistle while imprisoned (Col. 4:3, 10, 18). What is not immediately evident from the content of the letter is the place of his imprisonment. Traditionally, it has been understood that the imprisonment in question is Paul's Roman imprisonment. Some, however, reject Rome and suggest either Ephesus or Caesarea as options. Of the three, Rome and Ephesus are more likely than Caesarea.[5] It is significant, however, that there is no explicit mention of an Ephesian imprisonment of Paul in the book of Acts. Of the three options, then, Rome remains the most likely.[6] If the letter was written during the Roman imprisonment (A.D. 60–62), it was likely written early in this period of time because the city of Colossae was destroyed by an earthquake in A.D. 61, and Paul says nothing about any such disaster.

2. Dunn 1996, 38.
3. Carson and Moo 2005, 519.
4. See O'Brien 1982, xli–xlix, for an overview of the case for Pauline authorship.
5. O'Brien 1982, liii.
6. Carson and Moo 2005, 521.

The city of Colossae was situated in the Lycus Valley in the ancient province of Phrygia (in Asia Minor) approximately one hundred miles east of Ephesus. It was only a few miles southeast of the larger and more significant cities of Laodicea and Hierapolis. The churches in these three inland cities were not founded by Paul (Col. 2:1). Instead, they appear to have been planted by Epaphras (1:7; 4:12–13). It also appears that the majority of the Colossian Christians were Gentile converts (1:12, 21, 27; 3:5–7). Paul apparently wrote to the Colossians because he had heard that false teachers had come to the city and were spreading erroneous doctrine in the young church. He writes to them in order to refute these errors and to encourage them to stand fast in the truth. The nature of the false doctrine is a matter of some controversy, but it seems most likely to have been a syncretistic blend of certain Jewish and Hellenistic beliefs.[7]

Paul opens the letter to the Colossians in his usual manner, with a salutation (1:1–2) and thanksgivings (vv. 3–8). He then prays that God might fill the Colossians with the knowledge of his will that they might walk in God's ways (vv. 9–14). In his prayer, Paul sets the letter within an eschatological framework, declaring that God "has delivered us from the domain of darkness and transferred us to the kingdom of his beloved Son, in whom we have redemption, the forgiveness of sins" (vv. 13–14). Because God "has delivered us" (past), we now "have redemption" (present). The fact that we have already been transferred to the kingdom of God's Son, Jesus Christ, clearly indicates that the kingdom is not wholly future. It has already been inaugurated.

Colossians 1:15–20 is commonly considered to be an early Christian hymn that was inserted by Paul into his letter at this point to establish what he wants to say concerning the preeminence of Christ.[8] Paul states that Jesus Christ is "the image of the invisible God, the firstborn of all creation" and "the beginning, the firstborn from the dead" (vv. 15, 18). Paul's declaration that Jesus is the "firstborn from the dead" is similar to his statement in 1 Corinthians to the effect that Jesus is the "firstfruits of those who have fallen asleep" (1 Cor. 15:20). In both cases, Paul teaches that Christ's resurrection inaugurates the prophesied eschatological resurrection that will be consummated at the general resurrection of the dead.

7. Guthrie 1990a, 568–69.
8. O'Brien 1982, 32.

That which the Jews had expected to occur on the last day had already begun within history.

In Colossians 1:24–2:7, Paul describes his ministry to the church and his concern for the church at Colossae. He then turns his attention to the sufficiency of Christ (2:8–23). He urges the Colossians not to be taken captive by empty deceit because in Christ "the whole fullness of deity dwells bodily" (v. 9). By using the word *theotētos* here, Paul is saying that "Jesus possesses all the divine essence and attributes."[9] Because Jesus is "the head of all rule and authority" (v. 10), the Colossians do not need to follow the false teachers in their submission to the principalities and powers. The One in whom they have life is over all such principalities.

Paul expounds further on the theme of union with Christ in Colossians 2:11–15. Paul describes what has already happened to the Colossians in Christ. They "were circumcised with a circumcision made without hands" (v. 11). They were "buried with him in baptism" (v. 12a). They were "raised with him through faith" (v. 12b). They were "made alive together with him" (v. 13). The central theme of this text is the believer's dying and rising with Christ.[10] The old life is past, and we now share in the new life of Jesus Christ.[11] Our trespasses have been forgiven and our debt canceled, and at the cross the principalities and powers were stripped of their power over believers by Jesus Christ (vv. 14–15).

Because of what Jesus Christ has accomplished and because of believers' union with him, Paul proclaims that they are free from legalistic ascetic observances (2:16–23). Paul writes, "Therefore let no one pass judgment on you in questions of food and drink, or with regard to a festival or a new moon or a Sabbath. These are a shadow of the things to come, but the substance belongs to Christ" (vv. 16–17). The situation in the church at Colossae differs somewhat from the situation in the churches at Corinth and Rome. Peter O'Brien explains:

> In writing to Corinth and Rome, where Christians had scruples about food and drink as well as the observance of holy days, Paul introduces the further principle which might impose a voluntary limitation on one's Christian liberty, i.e., "the strong" should go out of their way to avoid offending the

9. Harris 1992, 288.
10. O'Brien 1982, 119.
11. Bruce 1984, 108.

> tender consciences of "the weak" or scrupulous (Rom 14:1–15:13; 1 Cor 8–10). But at Colossae the scrupulous were threatening to impose their rigid principles on the rest of the congregation. Christian liberty needed to be asserted in the light of false attempts to undermine it.[12]

Believers are not to be judged on these matters because all of these things are but "shadows." The reality, or "substance," belongs to Christ. The contrast here is not a metaphysical Platonic contrast between the earthly copies and the ideal realities. It is a contrast between two ages, the former age of shadows and the present age of the substance in Christ.

Paul draws together all of the threads of what he has been saying in Colossians 3:1–4, which serves as a transition to the exhortations that follow. In the previous text, Paul had begun the conclusion of his argument against asceticism with the words "If with Christ you died . . ." (2:20). He begins his positive exhortations with the words, "If then you have been raised with Christ . . ." (3:1a). Paul urges the Colossians to "seek the things that are above, where Christ is, seated at the right hand of God" (3:1b). Paul is alluding here to Psalm 110:1. Since believers already participate in the resurrection life of Christ, they are to orient the whole of their lives toward Christ.[13] They are to set their minds "on things that are above, not on things that are on earth" (Col. 3:2).

Paul elaborates further on why they are to set their minds on the things above: "For you have died, and your life is hidden with Christ in God. When Christ who is your life appears, then you also will appear with him in glory" (3:3–4). The present and future aspects of the believer's new life are linked here in these verses. Verse 3 describes the believer's life as a present possession tied to Christ, but hidden. Verse 4 looks to the future, describing Christ himself as our very life, and asserting that when he appears, we too will appear with him in glory (Phil. 3:20–21; 1 John 3:2). Our life will be fully revealed when Christ, who is our life, is revealed at the second coming. "The day of the revelation of the *Son* of God will be the day of the revelation of the *sons* of God."[14]

Paul urges the Colossians to put to death that which is earthly because these are the things for which mankind will be judged by God (3:5–11).

12. O'Brien 1982, 139.
13. Bruce 1984, 134.
14. O'Brien 1982, 167.

Having put to death that which is earthly within themselves, they are to "put on . . . compassion, kindness, humility, meekness, and patience . . . and above all these put on love, which binds everything together in perfect harmony" (vv. 12–14). All of these things are to be manifested in the believer's interaction with others, believers and nonbelievers alike. In verse 17, Paul concludes this section, saying, "And whatever you do, in word or deed, do everything in the name of the Lord Jesus, giving thanks to God the Father through him." In Colossians 3:18–4:1, Paul provides some practical examples of that which he wrote about in verses 12–17, giving instructions for the various members of Christian households. He gives some further general instructions to the Colossian church in 4:2–6, and then turns to the closing of his letter in verses 7–18. His closing follows his usual procedure, including both personal greetings and final instructions.

According to Colossians 4:7–9, Paul had the epistle delivered by Tychicus and Onesimus. Furthermore, one of the people in Colossae to whom Paul sends a greeting is Archippus (4:17). Since Onesimus, a resident of Colossae (4:9), also delivered the epistle to Philemon, and since one of the other people greeted in the epistle to Philemon is Archippus, it is almost certain that Philemon was a Christian living in Colossae and that the two letters were delivered together.[15]

The epistle to Philemon is the shortest and most personal of Paul's epistles. Onesimus was a slave who belonged to Philemon. He had left Colossae and at some point had become a Christian and had encountered Paul. The epistle contains a brief greeting (vv. 1–3), thanksgiving and prayer for Philemon (vv. 4–7), a plea on behalf of Onesimus (vv. 8–20), and Paul's final remarks and greetings (vv. 21–25). Although the letter is addressed primarily to Philemon, it is not a completely private letter.[16] It is also addressed to the church in Philemon's house (v. 2). In other words, it was to be heard by all of the Christians in Colossae. According to many commentators, Paul does not ask Philemon to receive Onesimus as a free man or to free him from slavery immediately.[17] Others, however, insist that Paul was implicitly asking Philemon to do exactly that.[18]

15. Carson and Moo 2005, 592.
16. Contra Bruce 1977b, 405.
17. E.g., O'Brien 1982, 269.
18. E.g., Robbins 2007, 26–27.

Ephesians

The epistle to the Ephesians shares a number of similarities with the epistle to the Colossians. There are, for example, a number of verbal parallels.[19] More significant perhaps are the thematic parallels. Both epistles speak similarly of the Gentiles' move from alienation to reconciliation (Col. 1:21–23; Eph. 2:11–22), of Paul's suffering and ministry in relation to the "mystery" (Col. 1:24–2:3; Eph. 3:1–13), of Christ as "head" of his "body" (Col. 2:19; Eph. 4:15–16), and of rejection of the old life and acceptance of the new (Col. 3:5–11; Eph. 4:17–32). Both contain similar exhortations to love (Col. 3:12–15; Eph. 5:1–6), to walk wisely (Col. 3:16–17; Eph. 5:15–21), and to prayer and proclamation of the mystery (Col. 4:2–4; Eph. 6:18–20). Finally, both contain instructions for Christian households (Col. 3:18–4:1; Eph. 5:22–6:9), and a personal commendation of Tychicus (Col. 4:7–9; Eph. 6:21–22). For some, these similarities raise insurmountable problems for the Pauline authorship of the epistle.[20] However, if the two letters were written at approximately the same time to people in a similar geographical and cultural context, such similarities do not present an overwhelming problem. The authorship of Ephesians is disputed, but a good case can be made for the traditional view that ascribes the letter to the apostle Paul.[21]

The epistle to the Ephesians may have been sent from Rome by Paul at the same time he sent the epistles to the Colossians and to Philemon (ca. A.D. 60–61). Both Colossians and Ephesians appear to have been sent along with Tychicus, and considering the distance between Rome and Asia Minor, it would have made sense to send them at the same time rather than having Tychicus make two trips. A more serious problem arises regarding the destination of the letter. Some very reliable ancient manuscripts do not contain the words *en Ephesō* ("in Ephesus") in 1:1.[22] Furthermore, when we consider the fact that Paul had spent a considerable amount of time with the

19. Andrew T. Lincoln (1990, xlviii) observes that of the 1,570 words in Colossians, 34 percent reappear in Ephesians, while of the 2,411 words in Ephesians, 26.5 percent are also in Colossians.

20. E.g., Lincoln 1990, lxvi.

21. For a defense of Pauline authorship and a response to the objections, see O'Brien 1999, 4–47, and Hoehner 2002, 2–61. Although Lincoln rejects Pauline authorship, he grants that a "sizable minority continues to uphold Pauline authorship" (1990, lxii). Hoehner (2002, 6–20), however, has evaluated 390 works by 279 authors (with an emphasis on scholars from the last two centuries), and the results of his study indicate that opinion is more evenly divided than the words "sizable minority" would imply.

22. For details of the manuscript evidence, see Metzger, *TCGNT*, 532.

church in Ephesus (Acts 19:8–10; 20:31), it seems strange that the tone of the letter is so impersonal in comparison with his other letters.[23] Paul also makes several comments in Ephesians that seem to imply that he did not know the intended recipients personally (e.g., Eph. 1:15; 3:2; 4:21). Some have concluded on the basis of the evidence that the letter was possibly intended to be a circular letter.[24] In other words, Paul may have intended it to be taken from city to city.[25]

The epistle to the Ephesians consists essentially of two major sections introduced by a prescript (1:1–2) and concluded with a standard epistolary closing (6:21–24). Following F. F. Bruce, we may describe the contents of the first major section of the epistle in terms of the new humanity as a divine creation (1:3–3:21). The contents of the second major section may then be described in terms of the new humanity in its earthly life (4:1–6:20).[26]

Following his opening greeting, Paul praises God in a single, lengthy Greek sentence (1:3–14).[27] Paul normally follows the greetings in his epistles with a thanksgiving to God for the recipients, but in Ephesians, the thanksgiving follows his paean of praise for what God has done in the salvation of believers. The emphasis of these verses can be seen in the phrase "in Christ" (vv. 3, 9, 12) and its variants "in him" (vv. 4, 7, 10, 11, 13 [2x]), and "in the Beloved" (v. 6). Paul praises God because God "has blessed us *in Christ* with every spiritual blessing in the heavenly places" (v. 3). These blessings involve the work of the Father, the Son, and the Holy Spirit. We were chosen by the Father (vv. 4–6), redeemed through the sacrifice of the Son (v. 7), and sealed with the Holy Spirit (v. 13).

23. Paul had not even been to the church in Rome when he wrote Romans, but the greetings in that epistle are of a far more personal nature than the general greetings found in Ephesians. The same is true of the epistle to the Colossians, another church Paul had not personally visited.

24. Carson and Moo 2005, 488.

25. Ephesus seems to have functioned as a missionary base for Paul, from which he sent out laborers into the larger province of Asia (Acts 19:10). If the words "in Ephesus" were part of the original (as Hoehner argues; 2002, 144–48), the indications in the letter that Paul did not personally know the recipients may be explainable in part if the letter was sent to these scattered churches of Asia Minor via Ephesus. The epistle to the Galatians, which was sent to a group of churches within a region, does not contain personal greetings to specific individuals either. Perhaps Paul considered such greetings inappropriate in letters written to a group of churches in a region.

26. Bruce 1984, 247–48.

27. In Greek, the sentence contains 202 words. It is usually broken up into smaller sentences in translations.

Paul indicates in these verses that God's saving work was part of his eternal plan. He says that God has done these things "according to his purpose, which he set forth in Christ as a plan for the fullness of time, to unite all things in him, things in heaven and things on earth" (1:9–10). If this saving work was part of God's plan from all eternity, then it was not unexpected on his part. God's work of salvation was not an ad hoc plan thrown together after the fall. Instead, Paul tells the Ephesians and us that what God is doing now was always part of his plan. It is part of the same plan that included the promises to the patriarchs and the establishing of Israel. Paul says that we are sealed with the Holy Spirit (vv. 13–14). The giving of the Spirit is not merely a promise of our full redemption, it is a foretaste of it (2 Cor. 1:22).[28]

Following Paul's lengthy blessing is his thanksgiving and prayer for the Ephesians (1:15–23). Like the previous section, these verses too are a single long sentence in the Greek original. Paul prays that the Ephesians will grow in grace and mature in their knowledge. He wants them to appreciate how great their salvation is.[29] In verses 20–23, Paul praises God for the power demonstrated in raising Jesus the Messiah from the dead and exalting him to a place of authority over all things. The power with which God works in the believer is the same power by which he raised Christ from the dead (v. 20).[30]

Paul's emphasis on God's past act of raising Christ from the dead and exalting him at his right hand in the heavenly places reveals the emphasis in Ephesians on the eschatological "already." This is another similarity with Colossians. In both letters, Paul emphasizes what God has already accomplished in the outworking of his eschatological plan. However, as in the case with Colossians, Paul does not in Ephesians reject all future aspects of this plan (1:14; 2:7; 4:30; 5:27). All has not already been accomplished.

In chapter 2, Paul begins by reminding the Ephesians of the change that God had effected in them by bringing them from a state of spiritual death to life in Christ (vv. 1–10; Col. 2:13). When Paul says that God "made us alive together with Christ" (Eph. 2:5), he is referring to our spiritual resurrection, our regeneration. The fact that he raised us "with Christ" is evident when we compare 2:6 with 1:20. In 1:20, Paul says of Christ that

28. O'Brien 1999, 121.

29. Lincoln 1990, 78.

30. O'Brien 1999, 141.

God "raised him from the dead and seated him at his right hand in the heavenly places." In 2:6, Paul says of believers that God "raised us up with him and seated us with him in the heavenly places in Christ Jesus." Our new life is a sharing in Christ's resurrection life.

In verse 7, Paul continues, saying that God raised us with Christ "so that in the coming ages he might show the immeasurable riches of his grace in kindness toward us in Christ Jesus." A. T. Lincoln explains the significance of this statement:

> First, the new order which has begun has a future. The writer knows himself to be in the decisive period of God's redemptive activity, which was inaugurated by Christ's resurrection and exaltation, but which is yet to reach its consummation in the coming ages. Second, the divine activity on behalf of believers was of such finality that it will continue as the display of his grace into those coming ages. Third, what God has done is now a reality for believers, but only in the coming ages will it be fully shown for what it is. Only then will it become evident to all what an abundance of grace and kindness God has bestowed on his people through Christ.[31]

The preceding verses have spoken of what God has already accomplished, and here Paul indicates that there is more to come.

In Ephesians 2:11–22, Paul explains the difference between the readers' past and present in terms of their relation to Israel. In verse 12, Paul lists five ways in which the Gentile Ephesians were outside of God's people. In the past, the believing Gentiles: (1) were separated from Christ; (2) were alienated from the commonwealth of Israel; (3) were strangers to the covenants of promise; (4) had no hope; and (5) were without God in the world. In verse 13, Paul reveals that for believing Gentiles, none of these things are true any longer: "But now in Christ Jesus you who once were far off have been brought near by the blood of Christ."

In 2:14–16, Paul explains how Christ accomplished this change for Gentiles: "For he himself is our peace, who has made us both one and has broken down in his flesh the dividing wall of hostility by abolishing the law of commandments and ordinances, that he might create in himself one new man in place of the two, so making peace, and might reconcile us both to God in one body through the cross, thereby killing the hostil-

31. Lincoln 1990, 111.

ity." According to Paul, Christ tore down the wall "by abolishing the law of commandments and ordinances." Gentiles are no longer required to submit to circumcision and submit to the Mosaic covenant in order to be included in the people of God (Acts 15). In fulfillment of the Old Testament prophecies, the Gentiles have been called to join God's people (e.g., Isa. 19:25). Now Jews and Gentiles both have access to the one God, and they are being built up together in one body (Eph. 2:17–22).

In chapter 3, Paul begins a prayer for the Ephesians (v. 1) before digressing to give an account of his ministry and to explain the mystery that had been revealed to him (vv. 2–13). He does not resume his prayer until verse 14. In verse 6 Paul states the nature of the mystery that has been revealed: "This mystery is that the Gentiles are fellow heirs, members of the same body, and partakers of the promise in Christ Jesus through the gospel." The Gentiles, in other words, will not be saved as a separate body of believers. Because there is one Lord Jesus Christ, there is one body in him, and all who will be saved, Jew and Gentile, are saved in this one body of Christ. All of this was part of God's eternal plan (v. 11). Having completed his digression, Paul returns to his prayer, asking God to grant the Ephesians strength, love, and a full knowledge of Jesus Christ (vv. 14–21).

The second major section of Paul's letter to the Ephesians begins in chapter 4. In fact, all of Ephesians 4:1–6:20 is a lengthy admonition to walk according to the truth that has been revealed. Paul begins by exhorting the Ephesians to walk in unity (4:1–16).[32] The fact that there is one body does not mean that there is not a diversity of gifts (v. 7), but the diversity of gifts is intended for the building up of the whole (vv. 8–16). In verse 8, Paul describes Jesus' exaltation in terms of Psalm 68:18, part of a psalm depicting the victorious divine King ascending Mount Zion in triumph after his defeat of his enemies. Here Paul portrays Jesus as the victorious divine King.

Paul exhorts the Ephesians to walk in holiness in 4:17–32. They are no longer to walk according to the standards of the world, but according to the standards of the new era inaugurated by Christ. They are to put away the works of darkness (vv. 22–29). They are not to grieve the Holy Spirit because by him they are "sealed for the day of redemption" (v. 30). According to 1:7, we already "have redemption through his blood, the forgiveness

32. I have followed Hoehner's description of the various exhortations (2002, 64–69).

of our trespasses." Yet, as Romans 8:23 indicates, our full redemption will involve more, specifically the redemption of our bodies. Here in Ephesians, Paul appeals to this future hope as a reason that believers should not grieve the Holy Spirit.

In Ephesians 5:1–6, Paul urges the Ephesians to walk in love. In this, they are to follow the example of Christ who loved us and gave himself for us (v. 2). To walk in love entails renouncing all sexual immorality and impurity (vv. 3–6). The end result of such things is the wrath of God (v. 6). The Ephesians are exhorted to walk in the light in verses 7–14. They are not to participate in any of the shameful works of darkness. Paul concludes this section with a quotation: "Awake, O sleeper, and arise from the dead, and Christ will shine on you" (v. 14). The phrase is not a direct quotation of any specific Old Testament text, although it shares similarities with some (Isa. 26:19; 60:1–2). It has been suggested by some that the words are addressed to unbelievers and would remind the Ephesians of their conversion (see 2:1–6). Others suggest that these words might have been part of an early baptismal liturgy and reflect what the congregation would have said to the one coming out of the baptismal waters.[33] In either case, it is a call to come out of darkness into the light.

Paul calls upon believers to walk in wisdom in 5:15–6:9. This exhortation can be subdivided into four smaller sections. Paul first addresses general Christian living (5:15–21). He then addresses husbands and wives (vv. 22–33), parents and children (6:1–4), and masters and slaves (6:5–9). In 5:16, Paul says of the present, "the days are evil." Here he indicates that although Christ has been exalted to the right hand of God and placed in authority over all things, the war is not over. As Lincoln explains, "believers still have to live out the life of the age to come, which they already enjoy, in a surrounding moral climate which is predominantly evil."[34] During this time, the church is to live as befits followers of Christ because a day is coming when he will "present the church to himself in splendor, without spot or wrinkle or any such thing" (v. 27; 2 Cor. 11:2; Rev. 21:9–11).

Since we live in an age that requires ongoing warfare against the defeated forces of darkness, Paul urges us to stand fast in the strength of God and prepare for spiritual battle (Eph. 6:10–20). There is speculation regarding

33. See Lincoln 1990, 332.
34. Lincoln 1990, 342.

whether the "evil day" spoken of in verse 13 refers to the entire present age or to some end-time event. The phrase echoes Old Testament prophetic passages that speak of a coming time of judgment (Jer. 17:17–18; Obad. 13), so it may refer to a similar coming judgment. However, the similarities between "the days are evil" in Ephesians 5:16 and "the evil day" in 6:13 indicates that the latter may be referring to individual times of intensified trouble throughout the present age.

Philippians

The epistle to the Philippians is the last of the four Prison Epistles of Paul. That it is a genuine Pauline epistle is generally conceded.[35] There is less agreement concerning the place of writing. Traditionally, Philippians has been understood to have been written during Paul's Roman imprisonment. Some scholars, however, have argued that the geographical distance between Rome and Philippi precludes a Roman provenance because it does not allow enough time for all the journeys between the two cities that had to have occurred. By the time Paul wrote Philippians, the following four events had occurred:

1. The Philippians had learned of Paul's imprisonment.
2. Epaphroditus had journeyed from Philippi to the place of Paul's imprisonment with a gift (Phil. 4:18).
3. News of Epaphroditus's sickness had reached the Philippians (2:26).
4. Epaphroditus had learned of the Philippians' concern for him (2:26).

According to some, the distance between Rome and Philippi would not have allowed all of these events to have occurred while Paul was imprisoned in Rome. The argument, however, is overstated. A trip between Rome and Philippi would have taken between four and seven weeks (i.e., 28–49 days).[36] At most, four trips between the two cities were necessary.[37] Even if we grant four trips and allow eight weeks for each journey, only 224

35. Carson and Moo 2005, 499. Although Pauline authorship is generally agreed upon, there is some dispute regarding the literary unity of the epistle. See O'Brien (1991, 10–18) for a full discussion and defense of the unity of the letter.

36. See Silva 2005, 5.

37. Silva (2005, 6) argues that only three were absolutely necessary.

total days are necessary, far less than the time Paul spent imprisoned in Rome. The bulk of the evidence indicates that Philippians was written from Rome, albeit later than the other prison epistles. In other words, Philippians was likely written sometime between A.D. 61 and 62.

The narrative of Paul's founding of the church in Philippi is found in Acts 16:6–40. Paul first traveled to the city of Philippi during his second missionary journey, and the church at Philippi was the first church to be established by Paul in what is now Europe. The city of Philippi was named after Philip II of Macedon, the father of Alexander the Great. He built the city in 358–57 B.C.[38] By the first century, Philippi was a well-known city. It was the site of the battle in 42 B.C. between Brutus and Cassius on the one hand and Antony and Octavian on the other. Although Antony and Octavian defeated Brutus and Cassius, they too would face each other in the battle of Actium in 31 B.C. Octavian would emerge victorious and soon afterward be named emperor of Rome and given the title Caesar Augustus. After his victories, Augustus made Philippi a Roman colony and gave it the legal standing of a Roman territory within Italy. Not surprisingly, the imperial cult was the dominant, although not exclusive, religion of the city.[39]

The letter to the Philippians was not written for one single purpose. Paul had a number of reasons for writing the letter. He wanted to update the church about his situation. He wanted to thank them for a gift they had sent. He wanted to give them information about Epaphroditus. He wanted to warn them about false teachers (likely Judaizers) and encourage them to remain steadfast in the truth. He wanted to encourage unity in the church, and he wanted to exhort them to rejoice. Most of all, however, he wrote to them because he had a deep care and affection for them. Eschatological issues are not obviously on the surface in most of the epistle, but as with all of Paul's writings, his eschatology provides the basic underlying framework.

Paul opens his letter to the Philippians with his standard salutation (1:1–2). He then proceeds to give thanks to God for them and to pray for them (vv. 3–11). In his expression of thanks, Paul writes, "And I am sure of this, that he who began a good work in you will bring it to completion at the day of Jesus Christ" (v. 6). The "good work" is the work of grace that God begins in the believer's life when he first draws that individual to himself.

38. Hawthorne 1983, xxxiii.
39. O'Brien 1991, 5.

God will bring this work to completion at the day of Christ. Here Paul looks forward to the eschatological completion of the present salvation we have in Christ. This eschatological completion will take place on the "day of Jesus Christ." This phrase has its origin in the Old Testament expression "the day of Yahweh" (or "the day of the Lord"). In this context, Paul uses the phrase to refer to the second coming of Christ. God will complete this work, but Paul urges the Philippians to abound in love that they may be "pure and blameless for the day of Christ" (v. 10).[40]

Paul proceeds in 1:12–26 to explain the priority of the gospel. If the Philippians were concerned that Paul's imprisonment was negatively affecting the spread of the gospel, Paul reassures them that even what has happened to him has served to advance the truth (vv. 12–14). In verses 18–20, Paul turns to his own situation and says, "as it is my eager expectation and hope that I will not be at all ashamed, but that with full courage now as always Christ will be honored in my body, whether by life or by death" (v. 20). Paul's desire is that regardless of what happens to himself Christ will be honored and glorified.

In the light of what he has said in verse 20, Paul looks at these two possibilities of life and death more closely. He writes, "For to me to live is Christ, and to die is gain. If I am to live in the flesh, that means fruitful labor for me. Yet which I shall choose I cannot tell. I am hard pressed between the two. My desire is to depart and be with Christ, for that is far better. But to remain in the flesh is more necessary on your account" (1:21–24). Because Christ is central to Paul, he will benefit regardless of whether he is executed or released.[41] Communion with Christ is sometimes depicted in the letters of Paul as a present experience of the believer (e.g., Rom. 6:5; Gal. 2:20; Col. 2:12). Here, and elsewhere in Paul's writings, it is also depicted as a future experience (e.g., 2 Cor. 4:14; 1 Thess. 4:17). The idea that Paul communicates here is similar to that expressed in 2 Corinthians 5:8. In both letters, Paul indicates that upon death the believer goes to be with the Lord. In this intermediate state the believer awaits the final resurrection of the body.

Paul turns to exhortation in 1:27–2:18, calling upon the Philippians to live lives "worthy of the gospel of Christ." Paul wants to hear that the Philippians are continuing to stand firm, striving for the gospel, and not

40. See 1 Cor. 1:7–8; Col. 1:12; 1 Thess. 3:13; 2 Thess. 1:11–12.

41. Fee 1995, 140.

frightened by their opponents. Paul says, "This is a clear sign to them of their destruction, but of your salvation, and that from God" (1:28). What is this sign of which Paul speaks? It is the Philippians' steadfastness in the face of opposition and persecution.[42] The Philippians are to be engaged in the same conflict that Paul has been fighting (vv. 29–30).

In 2:1–4, Paul calls the Philippians to unity, to be of the same mind, and to look out for the interests of each other. Steadfastness requires unity, and unity requires humility. Therefore, in verses 5–11, Paul emphasizes the necessity of humility by reminding the Philippians of the humble attitude of Jesus:[43]

> Have this mind among yourselves, which is yours in Christ Jesus, who, though he was in the form of God, did not count equality with God a thing to be grasped, but made himself nothing, taking the form of a servant, being born in the likeness of men. And being found in human form, he humbled himself by becoming obedient to the point of death, even death on a cross. Therefore God has highly exalted him and bestowed on him the name that is above every name, so that at the name of Jesus every knee should bow, in heaven and on earth and under the earth, and every tongue confess that Jesus Christ is Lord, to the glory of God the Father.

Most commentators agree that verses 6–11 are an example of an early Christian hymn.[44] This, however, is one of the few aspects of this passage on which scholars agree.[45] The debates on other issues have resulted in

42. O'Brien 1991, 154.

43. Silva 2005, 92.

44. Hawthorne 1983, 76.

45. One issue of debate involves the overarching conceptual framework. Many scholars understand the passage to be describing the movement of Jesus from the preexistent state in heaven downward to the cross and death, then upward again to his exaltation (e.g., O'Brien 1991, 187). Robert Reymond (1990, 251–66) argues, on the other hand, that this presupposition is what has led to so many difficulties with the text. He argues that the key to understanding the text is to perceive that the subject in verses 6–8 is not God the Son in his preincarnate state. Instead, the subject is "God the Son *already incarnately present* with men as Himself the God-man" (p. 262). As the incarnate God-man, he refused to follow a path other than the one his Father set for him. If this is true, according to Reymond, then the statement "he did not count equality with God a thing to be grasped" should be understood against the background of Jesus' wilderness temptation. Unlike Adam, who did count equality with God a thing to be grasped (Gen. 3:5), Jesus did not take matters into his own hands (Matt. 4:1–11). The words "made himself nothing" (v. 7, translated in other versions as "emptied himself") would then be understood against the background of the Servant Song in Isaiah 52:13–53:12 (esp. 53:12, "he poured out his soul").

a vast amount of literature.[46] Here we shall only touch upon the points of major relevance for our study.

Paul says that Jesus "was in the form [*morphē*] of God" (v. 6). There has been much debate regarding the meaning of the word *morphē* in this context, but Gordon Fee is correct when he says that here it means "that which truly characterizes a given reality."[47] It is a strong affirmation of the deity of Jesus the Messiah. After describing Jesus' humiliation in verses 6–8, his exaltation is described in verses 9–11 (cf. Isa. 45:22–25). The one whom people abused and killed, God has exalted as Lord (Acts 2:36). Every knee will ultimately bow to him. The one who was obedient to the point of death will now be obeyed to all eternity.[48]

In 2:19–30, Paul tells the Philippians of his intentions to send Timothy and Epaphroditus to them. He then turns in chapter 3 to an extended warning against the teaching of the Judaizers. After explaining to the Philippians that his Jewish credentials are as high as or higher than any of the Judaizers, Paul makes a significant statement in verses 7–11.

> But whatever gain I had, I counted as loss for the sake of Christ. Indeed, I count everything as loss because of the surpassing worth of knowing Christ Jesus my Lord. For his sake I have suffered the loss of all things and count them as rubbish, in order that I may gain Christ and be found in him, not having a righteousness of my own that comes from the law, but that which comes through faith in Christ, the righteousness from God that depends on faith—that I may know him and the power of his resurrection, and may share his sufferings, becoming like him in his death, that by any means possible I may attain the resurrection from the dead.

As Moisés Silva observes, "A striking feature of this passage is the way it reflects a distinction among the three basic categories present in the application of salvation: justification (righteousness through faith, v. 9), sanctification (experiencing the power of Christ's resurrection as well as participating in his sufferings, v. 10), and glorification (bodily resurrection, v. 11)."[49]

46. See the bibliographies on the passage in Hawthorne 1983, 71–75, and O'Brien 1991, 186–88.

47. Fee 1995, 204.

48. Hawthorne 1983, 92.

49. Silva 2005, 159.

The power of Christ's resurrection is available to believers in the present time (v. 10). But this does not mean that Paul is teaching a fully realized eschatology. We have already been raised with Christ (Col. 3:1), but our bodily resurrection is still to come (Phil. 3:11). The phrase "the resurrection from the dead" in verse 11 is a translation of the Greek *tēn exanastasin tēn ek nekrōn*. The word *exanastasin* ("resurrection") is a word that occurs only here in the New Testament. The usual form of the word for resurrection is *anastasis*. As Peter O'Brien notes, the addition of the preposition *ex-* to the noun *anastasis* reinforces the significance of the preposition *ek* ("out of," or "from") that is found in the phrase before the word *nekrōn* ("dead ones").[50] The entire phrase expresses vividly the concept of physical resurrection. It is therefore describing the bodily resurrection of the dead that is to occur in conjunction with the second advent of Christ.

Paul indicates that he continues to strive for the goal (3:12–16). He calls upon the Philippians to become imitators of himself and to keep an eye out for those who are enemies of the cross (vv. 17–18). Their end is destruction (v. 19). Paul then contrasts the fate of the wicked with that of the believer. "But our citizenship is in heaven, and from it we await a Savior, the Lord Jesus Christ, who will transform our lowly body to be like his glorious body, by the power that enables him even to subject all things to himself" (vv. 20–21). The word translated "citizenship" is the Greek word *politeuma*, which was often used to refer to a colony of foreigners or war veterans. As Gerald Hawthorne explains, Paul's use of this word indicates that "each local church is a colony of heaven, its members enjoying full citizenship of the heavenly city (cf. Gal 4:26; Eph 2:19), but charged with the responsibility of bringing the world to acknowledge the sovereignty of Christ."[51]

Christians await the coming again of Jesus the Messiah from heaven (Phil. 3:20; Acts 1:11). In Philippians 3:21, Paul focuses on the redemptive work Christ will accomplish at his second coming. He will "transform" the bodies of believers (1 Cor. 15:52). The resurrection bodies of believers will "be like his glorious body" (see also 1 Cor. 15:49). As O'Brien explains, "His resurrection is the guarantee of their resurrection, and his resurrected body is the prototype and paradigm of theirs."[52] Paul's assertion that our resurrection body is to be "like his glorious body" stands against those who

50. O'Brien 1991, 415.
51. Hawthorne 1983, 170–71.
52. O'Brien 1991, 465.

affirm nothing more than a spiritual resurrection for believers. It stands against those who affirm that the believer's present body will remain forever in the grave.

Paul's final exhortations to the Philippians are found in 4:1–9. In the midst of this exhortation, Paul makes the statement, "The Lord is at hand" (v. 5). The word translated "at hand" is the Greek word *engys*, which some versions translate as "near" (e.g., NASB, NIV). It may be that Paul means something similar to what the psalmist meant in Psalm 145:18, when he said, "Yahweh is near to all who call on him, to all who call on him in truth." In the Septuagint version of the psalm, the same word *engys* is used, so this possibility cannot be ruled out. However, Paul may also have eschatological considerations in mind (cf. James 5:8). In other words, he may be speaking here of the coming eschatological vindication.[53]

The Pastoral Epistles

The three letters commonly referred to as the Pastoral Epistles (1 Timothy, 2 Timothy, and Titus) are labeled as such because they are the only letters Paul addressed to fellow workers with pastoral responsibilities.[54] All but one of Paul's other letters were explicitly addressed to churches, and that one letter (to Philemon) was addressed to an individual and the church that met in his home. On the contrary, the letters to Timothy and Titus are addressed specifically to individuals. They deal with issues related to the leadership of the church.

The epistles of Paul that we have examined thus far were all written by Paul during the period of time narrated in Acts 14–28. But what about these Pastoral Epistles? Where do they fit? The book of Acts concludes with Paul imprisoned in Rome in A.D. 62. Luke does not tell his readers what happened to Paul, whether he was condemned to death, or released to continue his missionary labors. According to early Christian tradition, Paul was released from his imprisonment to continue his ministry, and he was later imprisoned again in Rome and executed under the reign of Nero.[55] Many have accepted the veracity of this tradition and have argued that the Pastoral Epistles were written by Paul after the imprisonment narrated in Acts 28.

53. Fee 1995, 408.
54. Knight 1992, 3.
55. See Bruce 1977b, 441–55.

Pauline authorship of the Pastoral Epistles was accepted throughout the church until the nineteenth century, when critical scholars began to raise questions about their authenticity. Today, critical biblical scholarship is almost completely united in its denial of the Pauline authorship of these epistles. Critical scholars insist that these letters were composed many years later by someone other than Paul. They point out the difficulty of placing the events described in the Pastorals within the narrative of Acts. They also cite alleged theological, linguistic, and stylistic differences between the Pastorals and the other Pauline epistles.[56]

A significant minority of scholars, however, continue to argue for the Pauline authorship of these epistles.[57] They point out that many of the critical arguments based on alleged theological, linguistic, and stylistic issues are overstated or simply wrong. Two possibilities have been suggested to explain the historical difficulties. As mentioned above, many argue that Paul was released from his first Roman imprisonment and then later reimprisoned and executed. They place the writing of the Pastorals in these years following A.D. 62.[58] Others point out the fact that there are known gaps in the narrative of Acts. The second epistle to the Corinthians, for example, mentions visits to Corinth by Paul that are not recorded in Acts (2 Cor. 1:23–2:1). This means that the journeys mentioned in the Pastorals may be journeys that occurred before A.D. 62 but were not recorded in Acts.[59] Ultimately, I am persuaded that there is more reason to believe Paul was released and later reimprisoned and that he wrote the Pastorals in the years between his release and his execution.

Titus

The epistle to Titus and the first epistle to Timothy were probably written within a short period of time of each other. A slight preponderance of evidence favors the priority of Titus. This, the earliest of the Pastorals, was likely written not very long after Paul's release from his imprisonment in Rome (i.e., some time between A.D. 62 and 64).[60] There is little informa-

56. For a helpful discussion, see Carson and Moo 2005, 554–68.
57. E.g., Carson and Moo 2005; Knight 1992; Guthrie 1990a.
58. E.g., Knight 1992, 17–20.
59. Carson and Moo (2005, 562) explain the hypothesis more fully.
60. Witherington 2006b, 86.

tion in the New Testament about Titus.[61] Since Paul refused to have him circumcised when he took him to Jerusalem, it would appear that he was a Gentile Christian (Gal. 2:1–3). He was a close associate of Paul who helped him in particular with the Corinthian situation (2 Cor. 2:13; 7:6, 13–14; 8:6, 16, 23; 12:18). According to the epistle to Titus, he served Paul on the island of Crete. Paul wrote this letter to Titus from Macedonia to encourage Titus to complete his work in Crete.

Following a brief salutation (Titus 1:1–4), Paul instructs Titus on the task of organizing the church at Crete (v. 5). He explains the necessary qualifications for elders (vv. 6–9) and warns him about false teachers (vv. 10–16). Paul then instructs Titus to teach sound doctrine (2:1) and gives guidance to the various groups within the church (vv. 2–10). In verses 11–14, Paul explains why the Christians in Crete must live in this way:

> For the grace of God has appeared, bringing salvation for all people, training us to renounce ungodliness and worldly passions, and to live self-controlled, upright, and godly lives in the present age, waiting for our blessed hope, the appearing of the glory of our great God and Savior Jesus Christ, who gave himself for us to redeem us from all lawlessness and to purify for himself a people for his own possession who are zealous for good works.

The grace of God appeared with the coming of Christ (3:4). In bringing salvation to all people, a blessing to the nations, Jesus the Messiah fulfills the promise to Abraham (Gen. 12:3). In the present age, Christians are to live holy lives as they await the second coming of Jesus, the "blessed hope."

In the concluding section of the letter, Paul charges Titus to teach all of these things (2:15) and to remind the Christians of Crete to live holy lives (3:1–2). He reminds Titus that without Christ, we were all slaves to sin (v. 3). But now we have experienced the overwhelming grace of God (vv. 4–7). The pouring out of the Holy Spirit (v. 6) is an indicator that the last days have been inaugurated. Paul concludes the letter with a final charge to Titus to avoid unnecessary controversies and quarrels (vv. 8–11) and final personal instructions (vv. 12–15).

61. Titus is referred to by name thirteen times in the New Testament (2 Cor. 2:13; 7:6, 13, 14; 8:6, 16, 23; 12:18 (2x); Gal. 2:1, 3; 2 Tim. 4:10; Titus 1:4).

1 Timothy

The first epistle to Timothy was likely written a few weeks after the epistle to Titus, and both were likely written in the years immediately following Paul's release from his Roman imprisonment.[62] Timothy himself is first mentioned in Acts 16:1–2.[63] He was apparently an inhabitant of Lystra in Asia Minor. His father was a pagan Gentile, and his mother was a devout Jew named Eunice (2 Tim. 1:5). Timothy joined Paul and Silas on their second missionary journey and remained one of Paul's colaborers in the gospel for the remainder of Paul's life. Paul frequently mentions Timothy in his writings, and from his comments we can gather that although Timothy was somewhat timid, he was reliable. By the time Paul wrote this first epistle to his young coworker, Timothy was overseeing the church in Ephesus. The Ephesian church was faced with a number of problems including, most significantly, infiltration by false teachers. Paul writes this first letter in order to assist Timothy with the challenges he is facing.

The first chapter of 1 Timothy addresses the danger of false doctrine. Paul opens by reminding Timothy of his charge to oppose those who teach false doctrine (1:3–7). The false doctrine concerns "the law" (v. 7), indicating that the promoters of this false doctrine may have been Judaizers.[64] In the second chapter, Paul urges the church to pray and intercede for all people (2:1–8) and urges women to live lives in accordance with their Christian faith (vv. 10–15).

Paul turns his attention next to the qualifications for overseers (3:1–7) and deacons (vv. 8–13). He concludes the chapter with a statement that appears to be a confession from the early church: "Great indeed, we confess, is the mystery of godliness: He was manifested in the flesh, vindicated by the Spirit, seen by angels, proclaimed among the nations, believed on in the world, taken up in glory" (v. 16). As Philip Towner explains, this confession forces us to look at all of salvation history through a christological lens.[65] Jesus is the focal point of redemptive history, the hinge on which everything turns.

In chapter 4, Paul writes:

62. Witherington 2006b, 177; Carson and Moo 2005, 571.

63. He is mentioned by name twenty-five times in the New Testament.

64. See Carson and Moo (2005, 563) and Marshall (1999, 51), who detect a strong Jewish element in the opposition.

65. Towner 2006, 278.

> Now the Spirit expressly says that in later times some will depart from the faith by devoting themselves to deceitful spirits and teachings of demons, through the insincerity of liars whose consciences are seared, who forbid marriage and require abstinence from foods that God created to be received with thanksgiving by those who believe and know the truth. (4:1–3)

According to some, these verses refer to an apostasy to occur in the time immediately preceding the second coming of Jesus.[66] There are at least three reasons, however, to doubt this conclusion. In the first place, the New Testament elsewhere characterizes the time inaugurated by the first advent of Christ as "the last days" (Acts 2:16–17; Heb. 1:2).[67] Second, the things described by Paul were already occurring at the time he wrote.[68] People were already departing from the faith (e.g., 1 Tim. 1:19; 1 John 2:19). Third, in the parallel passage in 2 Timothy 3:1–5, Timothy himself is told to avoid the kind of people who will arise "in the last days" (esp. v. 5).[69] As Ben Witherington explains, Paul's words are intended to help Timothy put the problem of heresy and apostasy in its proper perspective.[70]

Paul gives some personal instructions to Timothy (1 Tim. 4:6–16) before providing some specific instructions for specific groups within the church including widows, elders, and slaves (5:1–6:2). Timothy is instructed by Paul to rebuke those who persist in sin (5:20). Paul then tells him that the "sins of some men are conspicuous, going before them to judgment, but the sins of others appear later" (v. 24). Towner helpfully explains the meaning of this statement: "God's eschatological decision is thus the framework within which Timothy's own act of discernment takes place. The blatant sin of obvious sinners forges the path to the ineluctable eschatological judgment, and one in a role such as Timothy's becomes a participant in the judicial process (cf. Matt 16:19)."[71] In short, Timothy's own work of rebuking those who persist in sin plays a part in God's work of judgment.

Paul continues his letter with further instructions to Timothy regarding false teachers (1 Tim. 6:3–5) and contentment (vv. 6–10). He then urges

66. E.g., Chafer 1948, 2:106, 117–18.
67. Knight 1992, 188–89.
68. Marshall 1999, 531.
69. Towner 2006, 289.
70. Witherington 2006b, 248–49.
71. Towner 2006, 377.

Timothy to remain steadfast in his ministry, to "fight the good fight" (vv. 11–16). Paul charges Timothy "to keep the commandment unstained and free from reproach until the appearing of our Lord Jesus Christ, which he will display at the proper time—he who is the blessed and only Sovereign, the King of kings and Lord of lords" (vv. 14–15). The word translated "appearing" is *epiphaneia*. In this context, it refers to the second coming of Christ. In other contexts, it can refer to the first advent of Christ (e.g., 2 Tim. 1:10).[72] God will display Christ's coming appearance "at the proper time." The timing of the second coming cannot be calculated by men. It is in God's hands.[73]

2 Timothy

The historical context of Paul's second epistle to Timothy is different from that of the first epistle. Paul is in prison (2 Tim. 1:16–17; 2:9; 4:16–17), and he expects to die (4:6, 18). This is not the Roman imprisonment narrated in the last chapters of Acts. In that imprisonment, Mark and Timothy were with Paul. In this imprisonment, Luke alone is with Paul, while Mark and Timothy are not (4:11). This epistle was the last of Paul's epistles to be written, but to date it more precisely is difficult. Depending on the date of Paul's martyrdom, it could have been written anytime between A.D. 64 and 68.

After a brief salutation and thanksgiving (1:1–5), Paul urges Timothy not to be ashamed of the gospel or of Paul's imprisonment (vv. 6–14). The power of God "has been manifested through the appearing of our Savior Christ Jesus, who abolished death and brought life and immortality to light through the gospel" (v. 10). In 1 Corinthians 15:26, Paul spoke of death as the "last enemy" to be destroyed. Here Paul speaks of Jesus having already abolished death (cf. Heb. 2:14). It is a perfect example of the "already/not yet" nature of Paul's eschatology. The fatal blow against death was struck when Jesus was raised from the dead. But even though death has been dealt a mortal blow, the final and complete destruction of death awaits the resurrection of God's people and the last judgment (Rev. 20:14).

72. Paul may have used this term as a subtle critique of the Roman Empire. In the first century, the term *epiphaneia* was used to speak of the victories of Augustus Caesar, who had brought about the *pax Romana*.

73. Marshall 1999, 666.

Paul continues, telling Timothy, "I am not ashamed, for I know whom I have believed, and I am convinced that he is able to guard until that Day what has been entrusted to me" (2 Tim. 1:12). This is the first of several instances in this epistle where Paul uses the phrase "that Day" (see also 1:18; 4:8). A comparison of all three verses makes it clear that when Paul speaks of "that Day" in this epistle, he is speaking of the second advent. The phrase seems to be an adaptation of the Old Testament phrase "the day of Yahweh." As we have seen in our study of the Old Testament, the day of Yahweh (or "day of the Lord") was a coming day of judgment for the enemies of God and salvation for the people of God.

In the second chapter of 2 Timothy, Paul encourages Timothy to be strengthened by God's grace and to serve faithfully (2:1–13). He then urges Timothy to stand fast in the face of false teaching (vv. 14–26). Among the false teachers are Hymenaeus and Philetus "who have swerved from the truth, saying that the resurrection has already happened" (vv. 17–18). Their doctrine is spreading like gangrene (v. 17). There is some difficulty identifying exactly what Hymenaeus and Philetus were teaching. It seems unlikely that they would be saying that the general bodily resurrection of Christians had already happened unless they were claiming that believers received their resurrection bodies at the point of conversion.[74]

It may be that Hymenaeus and Philetus were saying that Jesus' past resurrection was the *only* resurrection and that believers should look for no other.[75] Or it may be that they were saying that the believers' past spiritual resurrection was the only resurrection they would experience, and there would be no bodily resurrection for believers. This may have been based on a misunderstanding of Paul's teaching as represented in such passages as Romans 6:3–8; Ephesians 2:1–6; and Colossians 2:12.[76] This last possibility seems to be the most likely in the context. The false doctrine that was spreading like gangrene was the idea that there is no future bodily resurrection of believers.

74. This would entail a drastically different view of the nature of the resurrection body than the view Paul taught, but we know that even in the first century there were misunderstandings about the nature of the resurrection body (see 1 Cor. 15).

75. Quinn and Wacker 2000, 678–83.

76. Towner (2006, 527) notes that there are later references to a Gnostic teaching that understood the resurrection to be a reception of divine knowledge. However, if 2 Timothy is a genuine Pauline epistle written prior to A.D. 68, it probably predates the rise of the first Gnostic sects.

In 2 Timothy 3:1–5, Paul repeats something he taught in 1 Timothy 4:1–3. He writes:

> But understand this, that in the last days there will come times of difficulty. For people will be lovers of self, lovers of money, proud, arrogant, abusive, disobedient to their parents, ungrateful, unholy, heartless, unappeasable, slanderous, without self-control, brutal, not loving good, treacherous, reckless, swollen with conceit, lovers of pleasure rather than lovers of God, having the appearance of godliness, but denying its power. Avoid such people.

As we have already seen, there are some who understand these words to be a prophecy concerning the times immediately before the second coming. However, the fact that Paul tells Timothy to avoid the kind of people who will come in the "last days" indicates that Paul and Timothy were themselves living in the last days.

Paul encourages Timothy to continue as a faithful servant of Christ (2 Tim. 3:10–17). Paul urges Timothy in the name of Jesus, who will judge the living and the dead, to preach the word of God because a time is coming when people will reject sound doctrine (4:1–5). Here Paul uses eschatology as motivation to faithfulness.[77] Paul tells Timothy that he has finished his work and that "there is laid up for me the crown of righteousness, which the Lord, the righteous judge, will award to me on that Day, and not only to me but also to all who have loved his appearing" (v. 8). In the ancient Greek athletic games, the winner was awarded a crown of leaves as an emblem of victory.[78] Paul uses this imagery to depict the reward he will receive for his work.

Summary

The Prison Epistles and Pastoral Epistles of Paul were written in the last years of his ministry. Four were written during his first Roman imprisonment, two were written after his release, and one was written during his final Roman imprisonment. Although eschatology is not at the forefront of any of these letters, it underlies all that Paul writes. In the epistles to the Colossians and Ephesians, Paul emphasizes the eschatological "already," that which Christ has accomplished. Christians have already been transferred

77. Towner 2006, 598.

78. If we were to use contemporary imagery, we would speak of a gold medal.

into the kingdom of God. They already share in the eschatological life by virtue of their union with the risen Christ. Although Paul's emphasis in these letters is on the already, he does not lose sight of that which is not yet. There is more to come.

In his epistle to the Philippians, Paul reveals by his own example the kind of joy Christians are to exhibit even when suffering unjustly. Paul reveals glimpses of the intermediate state when he tells us that death means to be present with Christ. He also reveals more about the nature of the resurrection body, telling us that our resurrection bodies will be like Christ's. The Pastoral Epistles contain Paul's final instructions to two of his colaborers in God's vineyard. He warns them about the danger of false doctrine and tells them not to be surprised when it comes because such false teaching is to be expected in these last days between Christ's first and second appearing. However, the fact that false doctrine is to be expected does not mean that it is to be tolerated. False doctrine, such as the denial of the bodily resurrection of believers at the second coming, is to be rebuked and resisted in order that it does not spread like a disease through the church.

For Paul, as we have seen, the turning point of redemptive history was the death and resurrection of Jesus the Messiah. The long story of Israel culminated with his coming. The death and resurrection of Jesus shape Paul's eschatology. Jesus has inaugurated the last days. In other words, the events that the Jews had expected to occur at the end of history have already begun within history. Christ's death has inaugurated the eschatological salvation of God's people. Christ's resurrection is the firstfruits of the eschatological resurrection. Christ's ascension has inaugurated the eschatological kingdom. Christ's gift of the Holy Spirit at Pentecost has inaugurated the eschatological age of the Spirit. The inauguration of these events, however, does not mean that there is nothing left to come. The eschatological age has begun, but it awaits the final consummation.

17

The Book of Hebrews and the General Epistles

Thirteen of the twenty-one New Testament epistles were written by the apostle Paul. The remaining eight were written by James, Peter, John, Jude, and the anonymous author of Hebrews. These eight books were written over a lengthy period of time and include what is probably the earliest New Testament writing (James) as well as some that may be among the latest (1–3 John). These General Epistles differ in some ways from the epistles of Paul.[1] They do not follow the formal epistolary conventions as closely as Paul does. Hebrews and 1 John, for example, do not contain a typical greeting at the beginning. James and 1 John lack the typical closing of first-century Hellenistic letters. With these letters, it is also sometimes difficult to discern the specific circumstances being addressed by the author. That said, several of these epistles do contribute to a proper understanding of biblical eschatology.

1. As Carson and Moo (2005, 619) note, the General Epistles (the seven books following Hebrews) were given this name because unlike the epistles of Paul, they appeared to be written not to a specific congregation, but to the church in general.

Hebrews

Although the book of Hebrews is traditionally referred to as an epistle, only its closing resembles an epistle. It lacks an epistolary opening, and the main body of the text often resembles a sermon more than a letter. The book does not name its author, and there has been no end of discussion regarding who the author might be. In the first centuries of the church, Christians in the East claimed Paul as the author. This idea was resisted in the West, and other suggestions were made. Tertullian, for example, argued that Hebrews was written by Barnabas. At the time of the Protestant Reformation, John Calvin argued that the author was either Clement of Rome or Luke, while Luther argued that the author was Apollos. In his extensive commentary, Paul Ellingworth examines the evidence that has been presented for thirteen different authors.[2] In the end, we must simply admit our ignorance because the fact of the matter is that we do not know with any certainty who wrote the book.[3] As Origen stated long ago, "Who wrote the epistle is known to God alone."[4]

Because of our lack of information regarding the author, it is difficult to determine with absolute certainty the date of the writing of the epistle. However, the evidence that exists indicates that the book was likely written sometime in the early 60s.[5] It appears from the internal evidence of the book that the Jewish temple was still standing at the time of writing and that the Christian recipients had not yet experienced serious persecution to the point of death. If the recipients of this epistle lived in Rome, as seems likely, such persecution would have begun in A.D. 64 during the reign of Nero.[6] The Jewish temple would be destroyed in A.D. 70. If the epistle was written before these things occurred, it would have to have been written in the early 60s. Although there is some uncertainty regarding when the author of Hebrews wrote the epistle, there is little uncertainty regarding why he wrote it. The author has written this book to warn the recipients about the peril of apostasy.[7]

2. Ellingworth 1993, 3–21. Ellingworth ultimately concludes that Apollos is the least unlikely possibility.

3. Carson and Moo 2005, 604; Blomberg 2006, 411.

4. Quoted in Eusebius, *The History of the Church* 6.25.

5. Hughes 1977, 30–31; Bruce 1990, 21; Lane 1991a, lxvi; Ellingworth 1993, 33; Marshall 2004, 606; Blomberg 2006, 413.

6. Ellingworth 1993, 27–29.

7. Ladd 1993, 618.

In order to guard the hearts of his readers against apostasy, the author of Hebrews makes an effort throughout the epistle to demonstrate the absolute supremacy of Jesus Christ. This recurring theme is closely connected with the author's understanding of the eschatological ramifications of Christ's incarnation and redemptive work. A major emphasis of the book, for example, is the inauguration of the eschatological new covenant through the work of Christ.[8] Because of who Jesus is and because of what he has done, the last days have come and the new covenant has been inaugurated. The inauguration of the new covenant, however, does not mean that everything has been completely fulfilled. Believers presently partake of the new covenant, but there is more to come and believers must remain steadfast in their faith looking forward to the consummation.[9]

The Revelation of God through His Son (Heb. 1:1–2:18)

The opening paragraph of Hebrews (1:1–4) functions as an exordium to that which follows.[10] It introduces the theme of the superiority of Jesus Christ and sets all that follows within an eschatological context. As A. T. Lincoln explains, "God's speaking in the Son is said to have taken place 'in the last days' (literally, 'at the end of these days'), thereby decisively inaugurating the final stage of history and ushering in the age to come."[11] Like Paul, the author of Hebrews understands that with the coming of Christ, the prophesied last days have come.

The author of Hebrews reveals that long ago "God spoke . . . by the prophets" (1:1), but in these last days, "he has spoken to us by his Son" (v. 2). What this statement implies is that in order to understand what God has spoken by his Son, we must understand its context, namely, that which God spoke by the prophets.[12] There is continuity with the old ("God spoke") and discontinuity ("by the prophets" and "by his Son"). The distinction in vv. 1–2 between "long ago" and "in these last days" indicates that something decisive has happened with the coming of Christ. The heir of the promises has now come, and in fulfillment of Psalm 110:1 he has been exalted to the

8. Dumbrell 1984, 183.

9. Lincoln 2006, 95.

10. The outline follows that of William Lane (1991a, viii–ix).

11. Lincoln 2006, 92–93; see also Lane 1991a, 9–10.

12. Lane 1991a, 11.

right hand of God (Heb. 1:3–4). His exaltation to the place of authority at God's right hand demonstrates his superiority.

The collection of Old Testament quotations in Hebrews 1:5–14 provides further confirmation of the Son's superiority over the angels. William Lane observes that there are seven citations divided by topic into three groups.[13] Hebrews 1:5–6 cites three Old Testament texts (Ps. 2:7; 2 Sam. 7:14; Deut. 32:43) as evidence that Jesus is the divine Son of God. Hebrews 1:7–12 cites three Old Testament texts (Pss. 104:4; 45:6–7; 102:25–27) as arguments for the superiority of the Son over the angels. They are ministers and thus subservient, but his royal authority endures forever. Finally, Hebrews 1:13–14 cites Psalm 110:1, which was also cited in 1:3, as a concluding remark on the superiority of the Son. The citation of Psalm 110:1, as Ellingworth explains, "announces the author's concern with the period from Christ's enthronement to his final triumph, the 'until' of this text anticipating the 'not yet' of Heb. 2:8."[14]

Hebrews 2:1–4 follows logically from what has been said in chapter 1. If the Son is greater than even the angels, then believers must pay close attention to the revelation that has been revealed by and through him. In verses 5–9, the author of Hebrews teaches us that "the transcendent Son of God made the human condition, and especially its liability to death, his own in order to achieve for them the glorious destiny designed by God."[15] In Hebrews 2:5, we read, "Now it was not to angels that God subjected the world to come, of which we are speaking." The "world to come" is the messianic age inaugurated by the coming of Christ. This age witnesses the fulfillment of the Old Testament promises and prophecies. This age has been inaugurated, but it has not yet been consummated.[16] Because it has been inaugurated, it is something in which believers can presently participate.

In verses 6–8, the author of Hebrews quotes Psalm 8:4–6. This psalm describes one who completely fulfills the original mandate given to man by God in Genesis 1:26–28. Jesus is the one who finally fulfills the Genesis mandate. Although everything has been put in subjection to Christ, the author of Hebrews writes in 2:8b, "At present, we do not yet see everything in subjection to him." In other words, the readers of Hebrews are not to be

13. Lane 1991a, 24.
14. Ellingworth 1993, 131.
15. Lane 1991a, 49.
16. Hughes 1977, 82.

dismayed that the powers of evil remain in evidence in the world. Christ has won the decisive battle and has been placed in the position of final authority, but he sits at God's right hand until all of these enemies are fully and finally defeated (1:13; 10:13). The present age is here characterized as an age of battle.

The author of Hebrews concludes this paragraph by reminding his readers that Christ was made lower than the angels temporarily in order that he might taste death on behalf of everyone (2:9). Hebrews 2:10–18 then develops the thought at the conclusion of the previous paragraph by explaining that the divine Son of God was incarnated in order that he might die in order to redeem a fallen humanity. The atoning death of Christ was God's solution to the problem of sin. The cross thus became the turning point of the ages.

The High-Priestly Character of the Son (Heb. 3:1–5:10)

The second major section of Hebrews is devoted to an exposition of the Son's high-priestly character. The author has already demonstrated that Jesus is superior to the angels. The author begins this second section by demonstrating that Jesus is superior to Moses. He argues that both Moses and Jesus were "faithful," but Moses was inferior because he was a "servant" whereas Jesus, on the other hand, is the "Son" (3:1–6). Moses testified "to the things that were to be spoken later" (v. 5). His ministry was anticipatory. Jesus' ministry, on the other hand, was and is one of fulfillment. His is the final word.

In Hebrews 3:7–4:13, the author turns to the practical implications of what he has said thus far. He has explained that Jesus is superior to Moses and to angels. Now he exhorts his readers to grasp the promise of eschatological salvation. A quotation from Psalm 95 serves as the basis for his exhortation as the author of Hebrews urges his readers not to imitate the faithlessness demonstrated by the exodus generation at Kadesh (3:7–19). We recall the story recounted by Moses in Numbers 14. On the border of the Promised Land, the people succumbed to fear, failed to trust God, and were not allowed to enter the land. Because of their lack of faith, they were not allowed to enter God's "rest" (Heb. 3:11, 19; Ps. 95:11).

The author of Hebrews views his readers as standing in a position similar to that of the exodus generation, between the Red Sea and the Promised Land. He does not view their present experience as parallel to that of the period of wilderness wandering.[17] At Kadesh, the Israelites were a people who were very near the end of their pilgrimage from Egypt. They stood on the edge of the Promised Land. The author of Hebrews compares his readers to this generation and exhorts them to do what Israel did not do, namely, to remain steadfast in their faith and enter God's rest. They are to persevere in their faith.

In 4:1, the author of Hebrews continues his thoughts, saying, "Therefore, while the promise of entering his rest still stands, let us fear lest any of you should seem to have failed to reach it." God's promise of rest remains open, but how? The key to understanding this, as Harold Attridge explains, is to understand that the promised rest is not the land of Canaan, but a heavenly reality that God entered upon the completion of his work of creation.[18] Lincoln explains this more fully:

> The creation rest that God intended for humanity to share is still available. Joshua's entry into Canaan was only a type of this divine rest (cf. 4.7–9), which has been with God in heaven since the foundation of the world. In the same way that the heavenly city to which Abraham looked forward (11.10) is still to come (13.14) and yet believers already have access to it (12.22), the heavenly rest is both still to be realized and yet already accessible. Those who believe are in the process of entering the rest (4.3) but at the same time, in the tension Hebrews shares with other strands of early Christian eschatology, the consummation of the rest remains future and believers can be exhorted to "make every effort to enter that rest" (4.11).[19]

In this sense, the concept of God's rest is similar to the concept of God's kingdom. The tension between the "already" and the "not yet" is as applicable to the one as it is to the other.

The author of Hebrews continues in 4:3–5, saying:

> For we who have believed enter that rest, as he has said,
>
> > "As I swore in my wrath,
> > 'They shall not enter my rest,'"

17. Lane 1991a, 90; Lincoln 1982b, 211.
18. Attridge 1989, 123; see also Bruce 1990, 105.
19. Lincoln 2006, 95.

although his works were finished from the foundation of the world. For he has somewhere spoken of the seventh day in this way: "And God rested on the seventh day from all his works." And again in this passage he said,

"They shall not enter my rest."

As F. F. Bruce explains, "the 'rest' which God promises to his people is a share in that rest which he himself enjoys."[20] The author of Hebrews associates this rest to which God's people are called with the rest God entered at the completion of his creative work. God's rest continues still, and those who respond in faith to his word enter into it. The Promised Land foreshadowed this rest. Because of the work of Christ, entrance into the ultimate rest is now available, and when those who trust in Jesus enter this rest, God's creation purposes and redemptive purposes are together fulfilled.[21]

The exodus generation failed to enter Canaan, the symbol of God's rest, because of disobedience (Heb. 4:6), but the promise of God's rest remained available in David's generation long afterward (v. 7). This is evident because Psalm 95, written long after the exodus generation, urges God's people to enter God's rest "today" rather than hardening their hearts like the exodus generation. Even the conquest of Canaan under Joshua did not completely fulfill the promise of rest because Canaan foreshadowed something better to come (Heb. 4:8). Had the conquest fulfilled the promise completely, there would have been no need to renew the promise in Psalm 95.[22] The promise of ultimate Sabbath rest therefore still remains for the people of God, and they enter it when they rest from their works as God rested from his (Heb. 9–10; 4:3; Matt. 11:28). The author of Hebrews, therefore, urges his readers to enter God's rest, in other words, to trust the promise of God. They are to stand fast in faith because Jesus is their great high priest (Heb. 4:15–5:10).

The High-Priestly Office of the Son (Heb. 5:11–10:39)

The author of Hebrews indicates that he has much to say about the high-priestly office of the Son (5:11), but he is forced to digress briefly

20. Bruce 1990, 106.
21. Lincoln 1982b, 209.
22. Lane 1991a, 101.

because the believers to whom he is writing "have become dull of hearing." It is possible that the beginnings of persecution had already begun to be felt among them and that this had led to their present condition. The author warns them against the consequences of departing from the faith (6:4–8). He is confident, however, that they are partakers in God's work of salvation (v. 9). In their lives he sees abundant evidence of true salvation and blessing. Because of this he urges them to be "imitators of those who through faith and patience inherit the promises" (v. 12).

After exhorting the readers to faith and patience, the author appeals to Abraham, the prime example of such faithful endurance (6:13–15). He rests his exhortation on the complete reliability of God (vv. 17–18). William Lane explains how the reference to Abraham is relevant to the readers of Hebrews: "The emphasis in 6:13–20 falls on the continuity of the new people of God with Abraham as heirs to the divine promise. The writer's optimism concerning the congregation is shown to be established upon the word of God as promise and oath."[23] God's faithfulness provides the basis for the strong encouragement the author of Hebrews is able to give to his readers, saying, "We have this as a sure and steadfast anchor of the soul, a hope that enters into the inner place behind the curtain, where Jesus has gone as a forerunner on our behalf, having become a high priest forever after the order of Melchizedek" (vv. 19–20).

Hebrews 7 describes the nature of Jesus' high-priestly office and demonstrates that it is superior to the Levitical priesthood. Verses 1–10 demonstrate the superiority of Melchizedek to the Levitical priesthood, while verses 11–28 demonstrate the superiority of the one like Melchizedek to the Levitical priesthood. Genesis 14 narrates the encounter between Abraham and Melchizedek, and the author of Hebrews draws several important points from this biblical text. He observes that Melchizedek received tithes from Abraham and blessed Abraham (Heb. 7:6), both indicating a position of superiority to Abraham. Since the Levites were descendants of Abraham, Melchizedek is in a position of superiority to them as well (v. 9).

In 7:11–28, the author of Hebrews turns his attention to a demonstration of the superiority of the priest like Melchizedek. In verses 11–19, the insufficiency of the Levitical priesthood is argued. Had the Levitical priesthood been sufficient, there would have been no need for another priest to arise

23. Lane 1991a, 155.

after the order of Melchizedek, but this is precisely what Psalm 110 anticipated (Heb. 7:17). The change in the priesthood means a change in the Mosaic law (v. 12) because the Mosaic law said nothing about priests descended from Judah (vv. 13–14). In verses 20–28, the author of Hebrews builds on what he has said, explaining the permanence and efficacy of the new priesthood inaugurated by Christ.

In chapter 8, the author of Hebrews explains that under the old covenant, the earthly priests serve as a copy and a shadow of the heavenly things (v. 5; Col. 2:17). Christ, on the other hand, is a minister and mediator of a better covenant (Heb. 8:6). The author of Hebrews explains that the old covenant was not faultless; had it been faultless, there would have been no need for a new covenant (v. 7). He indicates that the very existence of Jeremiah's prophecy of a coming new covenant is evidence that the old covenant was faulty (v. 8). After quoting Jeremiah's prophecy of the new covenant, he writes, "In speaking of a new covenant, he makes the first one obsolete. And what is becoming obsolete and growing old is ready to vanish away" (v. 13).[24] The main point here is that Jesus Christ fulfills the old covenant. He is the reality to which it looked.

In preparation for a discussion of the redemption obtained by Christ, the author of Hebrews looks to the worship institutions under the old covenant (9:1–10). He describes the tabernacle, the Holy Place, the Most Holy Place, and the furnishings found within it (vv. 1–5). He explains that only once a year does anyone go into the Most Holy Place (v. 7). This indicates that the way into the Most Holy Place is not opened as long as the "first section" remains (v. 8). This "first section" is "symbolic for the present age" (v. 9). As Lane explains, "So long as the cultic ordinances of the Sinaitic covenant were a valid expression of God's redemptive purpose and the front compartment . . . 'had cultic status' . . . , entrance into the Most Holy Place was not yet (μήπω) accessible."[25] All of these cultic ordinances were imposed "until the time of reformation" (v. 10).

24. It is not entirely clear whether the author intends to say that the old covenant is presently (at the time of the writing of Hebrews) becoming obsolete and getting ready to vanish away or to say that at the time Jeremiah spoke of the new covenant, the old was made obsolete and began to grow old and ready to vanish away. If we compare what the author of Hebrews says in verses 4 and 13, the second option seems more likely. The very act of speaking of a new covenant is said to make the first one obsolete. This speaking was done by Jeremiah.

25. Lane 1991b, 223; see also Attridge 1989, 241.

With the coming of Christ, the old gives way to the new, the shadow to the reality.[26]

When Christ our high priest did come, he secured an eternal redemption by means of his own blood, which he himself offered to God (9:11–14). Unlike the earthly priests, Christ entered into the heavenly sanctuary to offer his own blood as a sacrifice (vv. 11–12). The reference to his blood signifies his death on the cross. His sacrificial death stands in contrast to the animal sacrifices of the old covenant. His death "consummated the old order and inaugurated the new."[27] Verses 16–17 then explain why Christ had to die in order to become the mediator of the new covenant. His death provided the blood necessary to ratify a covenant (vv. 18–21). The benefits of Christ's death are summarized in the concluding paragraph of the chapter (vv. 23–28). He has entered the heavenly places to put away sin once and for all (v. 26).

Our author concludes with the statement, "so Christ, having been offered once to bear the sins of many, will appear a second time, not to deal with sin but to save those who are eagerly waiting for him" (v. 28). This is a clear reference to the second coming of Christ.[28] As Bruce explains, "All of the blessings which he won for his people at his first appearing will be theirs to enjoy in perpetual fullness at his second appearing."[29] This should provide incentive for them to persevere in steadfast faith.

In chapter 10, the author of Hebrews delves further into the difference between the insufficient Levitical sacrifices and the perfect sacrifice of Christ (10:1–18). Since the Levitical sacrifices are but a shadow and not the reality, they are never able to make perfect those who draw near (vv. 1–4). As shadows these sacrifices pointed forward to the eschatological reality, the perfect sacrifice of Christ. The insufficient sacrifices of the Mosaic covenant have been superseded by the once-for-all sacrifice of Jesus Christ (vv. 5–10). The difference between the sacrifices of the old covenant and the sacrifice of the new is highlighted by a comparison between the repeated offerings of the old age and the single offering of Christ (vv. 11–12). The repeated Levitical sacrifices could never take away sins, but by a single offering, Christ "perfected for all time those who are being sanctified" (v. 14). Finally, since

26. Bruce 1990, 211.
27. Lane 1991b, 242.
28. Ellingworth 1993, 487.
29. Bruce 1990, 233.

forgiveness has been obtained under the new covenant, there is no longer any offering for sin (vv. 15–18).

The author of Hebrews closes this major section of the book with an appeal for faith (10:19–39). As Lane explains, "In a climactic parenetic passage he summarizes his thematic expositions of Christ as priest and sacrifice and earnestly appeals for the community to apply the blessings of Christ's high priestly ministry to its own daily life."[30] In light of what Christ has done, the only rational and godly response is faith, and that is what the author expects of his readers (vv. 19–22). He also appeals to his readers to maintain their hope (v. 23) and to persevere in love (vv. 24–25). If they reject Christ, the consequence will be terrible judgment (vv. 26–31). The author of Hebrews, however, expects better things. He expects his readers to have persevering faith (vv. 32–39).

Loyalty to God through Persevering Faith (Heb. 11:1–12:13)

In the fourth major section of Hebrews, the author discusses faithfulness and endurance, the two qualities he is most concerned to encourage in his readers. In 11:1–40, he lists a number of Old Testament believers whose lives were characterized by faith.[31] Faith is a trusting response to God's word. It clings to the reality of promises that are not yet seen. Faith, then, is often forward-looking. As Lane observes, "The eschatological, forward-looking character of faith invests the realm of objective hopes and promises with solidity."[32] Significantly, many of those listed in chapter 11 are men and women who persevered in their faith in the face of suffering and death. This is significant as an example to a community that was faced with the same prospect of persecution. In light of the faithfulness of these past witnesses, the readers are urged to remain steadfast in faith (12:1–13), with Christ himself being the supreme example of such persevering faith (vv. 2–3).

Orientation for Life as a Christian in a Hostile World (Heb. 12:14–13:25)

In the final section of Hebrews, the author turns his attention again to the threat of apostasy (12:14–29). He first demonstrates the differ-

30. Lane 1991b, 281.
31. Bruce 1990, 276.
32. Lane 1991b, 394.

ence between the Israelites' experience at Sinai and the experience of Christians (vv. 18–24). Unlike the Israelites who came to Mount Sinai, Christians have come to Mount Zion, the heavenly Jerusalem (vv. 22–24). In other words, Christians are now experiencing the fulfillment of the eschatological hopes of ancient Israel. The emphasis here is upon that which is already the experience of believers. The author will emphasize that which is "not yet" below (13:14). The author also contrasts the shaking of Mount Sinai with the eschatological shaking of the heavens and earth (12:26). This shaking symbolizes the judgment of God against the godless nations (Isa. 13:13; Joel 2:10). In the aftermath of this eschatological shaking of heaven and earth, only the kingdom of God will remain standing (Heb. 12:28).

In the concluding chapter, the author of Hebrews gives his readers some final exhortations to godly living (13:1–19). His exhortations cover a wide variety of actions, from hospitality, to marriage, to contentment. He encourages them not to be led astray, but to bear the same reproach Jesus bore (vv. 9–13). He tells them that they have no lasting city here and are to seek the city that is to come (v. 14). As Lincoln explains, that which is present in heaven (12:22) is at the same time still to come (13:14).[33] The author closes the book with a standard epistolary benediction (13:20–21) and final greetings (vv. 22–25).

James

The book of James is possibly the earliest writing found in the New Testament canon. It was likely written after Paul began to bring the gospel to the Gentiles but before he and James met at the Jerusalem Council (Acts 15). In short, the book of James was likely written sometime in the early to mid-40s. Traditionally, the epistle has been attributed to James the brother of Jesus, and a strong case can be made for this traditional view.[34] The letter was likely written in Jerusalem by James and sent to Jewish Christians who had been scattered because of the persecution that arose over Stephen (Acts 11:19). Aside from a few comments, eschatology is not at the forefront of the message of James. Instead, as in the case of Galatians and some of the

33. Lincoln 2006, 95.

34. Carson and Moo 2005, 622.

other epistles, eschatology provides the context for everything that is said in the book.[35]

The book of James opens with a typical epistolary greeting, "James, a servant of God and of the Lord Jesus Christ, to the twelve tribes in the Dispersion: Greetings" (1:1).[36] The word translated "Dispersion" is *diaspora.* The term was typically used to describe the Jewish community that lived outside of Palestine. Here it appears to be used in a related sense to refer to Jewish believers in Christ who have been scattered outside of Palestine due to persecution.[37]

Following the greeting, James touches on a number of subjects. As Douglas Moo observes, James "encourages his readers to respond positively to their trials (1:2–4)"; "exhorts them to ask in faith for wisdom (1:5–8)"; "comforts the poor and warns the rich (1:9–11)"; "pronounces a blessing on Christians who endure trials (1:12)"; "warns believers not to blame God for temptations (1:13–15)"; "reminds his readers that all good gifts, including the new birth, come from God (1:16–18)"; "warns his readers about sins of speech (1:19–20)"; "exhorts believers to be obedient to the word they have received (1:21–25)"; and "reminds them of the essence of 'true religion' (1:26–27)."[38]

The Jewish believers to whom James writes are encouraged not to look at suffering and trials from a worldly perspective, but to look at them from an eschatological perspective (1:2–4). Suffering and trials have an eschatological goal in the lives of believers. Such trials contribute to the sanctification of the believer. Believers who understand the end goal of suffering can view it with joy. Those who stand fast in trials receive the "crown of life" (v. 12). This crown will be received at the time of final judgment.[39] Between the present and the last day, believers are to both hear and do the word regardless of the suffering such obedience might entail (vv. 19–27).

In chapter 2, James applies many of the principles of chapter 1 to a social situation in the church. In 2:1–13, James warns against showing partiality to the rich. The world looks at the poor one way, but God looks at poor believers

35. Davids 1982, 39.

36. The English name James is a derivative of the French Gemmes, which itself is a derivative of the late Latin Jacomus. The name Jacomus is a softening of the older Latin Jacobus, which is a transliteration of the Greek *Iakōbos.* The Greek name itself is a transliteration of the Hebrew name Jacob (*ya'aqōb*). See Johnson (1995, 92–93) for more on the name James.

37. Davids 1982, 64; Martin 1988, 9.

38. Moo 2000, 50.

39. Davids 1982, 80.

differently. They are "rich in faith and heirs of the kingdom" (v. 5). Christians are to view the poor among them from God's perspective, looking forward to eschatological exaltation. The following passage, James 2:14–26, is the most controversial paragraph in the entire book. While some accuse James of directly contradicting Paul on the subject of justification here, careful exegesis has shown that the alleged contradiction is only apparent, not real. The simple fact of the matter is that James and Paul are dealing with two distinct issues.[40]

In chapters 3 and 4, James addresses a number of practical issues. First, he warns his readers about the danger of godless speech (3:1–12). He then explains the difference between earthly and heavenly wisdom (vv. 13–18). In chapter 4, he tells his readers that the source of quarrels and fights is evil desires (4:1–6). He then calls upon them to humble themselves and submit to God (vv. 7–10). James warns his readers against the sin of slander (vv. 11–12), and then urges them again to submit to the will of God (vv. 13–17).

In chapter 5, James proclaims a warning to the rich that is reminiscent of the prophetic oracles of Amos (5:1–6; Amos 6:1–6, 8–14). The most direct eschatological passage in James follows in 5:7–11. James writes, "Be patient, therefore, brothers, until the coming [*parousias*] of the Lord" (v. 7). If the "coming" in question here is the same as that referred to by Jesus in the Olivet Discourse, then James is looking at that series of first-century events that culminated in the destruction of Jerusalem in A.D. 70. If not, then the reference is to the second advent of Jesus. In either case, believers are called to the patient endurance of suffering. James tells his readers, "You also, be patient. Establish your hearts, for the coming of the Lord is at hand" (v. 8). The inclusion of the words "at hand" lends weight to the idea that the coming in question here is the coming of the Son of Man spoken of by Jesus rather than the second coming. James 5:9 also supports this interpretation since the words "the Judge is standing at the door" echo Jesus' words from the Olivet Discourse (Matt. 24:32–33; Mark 13:28–29).

The Epistles of Peter and Jude

Although the authorship of 2 Peter is debated, I have chosen to consider it in conjunction with 1 Peter because both epistles claim Petrine authorship.

40. An examination of all of the issues involved in the debates over this text would take us far afield and is beyond the scope of this present work. For a helpful discussion of the issue, see Morris 1986, 313–14.

The epistle of Jude is examined here, rather than in its canonical order, because of its similarity with the second chapter of 2 Peter.[41] It appears that the first epistle of Peter was written by the apostle from Rome sometime around A.D. 62–63, immediately before severe persecution began under Nero.[42] The letter was written to Christians in Asia Minor (1 Peter 1:1) who were already suffering for their Christian faith. Peter writes to encourage these embattled believers.

The first epistle of Peter opens with a standard epistolary greeting. Peter describes himself as "an apostle of Jesus Christ," and he addresses the "elect exiles of the dispersion" in "Pontus, Galatia, Cappadocia, Asia, and Bithynia" (1:1). These regions were Roman provinces that covered most of Asia Minor. The fact that Peter addresses these believers as the "elect exiles of the dispersion" indicates that many if not most of them may have been Jewish Christians who fled from Jerusalem when persecution arose there after the death of Stephen (Acts 11:19). There are other passages in 1 Peter that seem to point to a Jewish-Christian audience (e.g., 2:9, 12), but this conclusion is not certain because at the same time there are also texts that appear to be more readily applicable to an audience consisting primarily of Gentile believers (e.g., 1:14, 18; 2:10). John Calvin argues that the letter is written to a primarily Jewish-Christian audience, and despite the difficulties, this is probable.[43]

Peter follows his greeting with an extended thanksgiving (1:3–12). He begins with a blessing:

> Blessed be the God and Father of our Lord Jesus Christ! According to his great mercy, he has caused us to be born again to a living hope through the resurrection of Jesus Christ from the dead, to an inheritance that is imperishable, undefiled, and unfading, kept in heaven for you, who by God's power are being guarded through faith for a salvation ready to be revealed in the last time. (vv. 3–5)

41. I am looking at Jude after 2 Peter because I believe the evidence slightly favors the priority of Peter's epistle. As Moo (1996b, 18) explains, the situation seems to have been something like this: "Peter, having written a letter castigating false teachers in a specific community, shared its contents with Jude. Jude then borrowed freely those portions of 2 Peter that were relevant to a similar false teaching that he was dealing with in his community."

42. Hillyer 1992, 3.

43. Calvin 2003, 22:25.

Peter here praises God for raising Jesus from the dead and through this causing us to be born again.[44] As Edmund Clowney explains, "By the resurrection of Christ, God has given life, not only to him, but to us."[45] Our inheritance is "kept in heaven" for us, and nothing can destroy it.[46] Furthermore, we are "being guarded" through faith for our salvation. In short, our inheritance is kept for us, and we are kept for it.[47] Although the specific nature of our inheritance is not described here, it will be revealed in the last time. It is an eschatological reality.[48]

In verses 6–9, Peter contrasts the present time of suffering with the future time of rejoicing. The consolation and encouragement Peter offers his readers are grounded in eschatological hope. Peter tells his readers in verses 10–12 that the prophets searched carefully inquiring what the Holy Spirit was referring to "when he predicted the sufferings of Christ and the subsequent glories" (v. 11). This text points to the fact of continuity between God's purposes under the old and new covenants. Peter's main point is that his readers have received the full revelation of Christ. The things the prophets desired to know "have now been announced to you through those who preached the good news" (v. 12).

Peter follows his thanksgiving with exhortations to consistent Christian living (1:13–2:10). He begins, "Therefore, preparing your minds for action, and being sober-minded, set your hope fully on the grace that will be brought to you at the revelation of Jesus Christ" (1:13). Clowney makes an important point, observing that the mind of the Christian should be fixed not simply on the coming of Christ, but on the one who will come, Jesus Christ.[49] Christians are now to live in the hope they have been given. They have been redeemed by the precious blood of Christ (vv. 18–19) and now live in the last times inaugurated by the resurrection of Christ, the one who was foreknown before the foundation of the world (v. 20). "God has revealed Christ now, at the end of time, to accomplish the purpose that was his before creation."[50]

44. Michaels 1988, 23.
45. Clowney 1988, 45.
46. In contrast with the Old Testament inheritance of the land (Isa. 24:3–4).
47. Clowney 1988, 49.
48. Achtemeier 1996, 95.
49. Clowney 1988, 63.
50. Clowney 1988, 72.

Peter continues by urging his readers, those who now live in the inaugurated last days, to love one another (1:22–2:3). They are not to stand still waiting for the second advent. Instead, they are to live in light of the first. In 2:4–10, Peter describes Christians as God's people, his temple, his kingdom, and his priests. Christians are "a chosen race, a royal priesthood, a holy nation, a people for his own possession" (v. 9). Peter contrasts God's people with unbelievers. Those who reject Christ are walking a path toward shame and destruction. Believers, on the other hand, are walking a path toward vindication and honor.[51]

In 2:11–3:12, Peter turns his attention to the social conduct he expects of his readers. He writes, "Beloved, I urge you as sojourners and exiles to abstain from the passions of the flesh, which wage war against your soul" (2:11). Peter describes believers here much in the same way that Paul describes believers in Philippians 3:20 ("But our citizenship is in heaven"). The world is not our home. Believers are sojourners and as such, they should not adopt the customs of the land in which they temporarily abide.[52] Peter instructs his readers, "Keep your conduct among the Gentiles honorable, so that when they speak against you as evil-doers, they may see your good deeds and glorify God on the day of visitation" (1 Peter 2:12). It appears that what Peter is describing is the day of judgment on which unbelievers will be compelled to acknowledge those who lived lives of faithfulness to Christ.[53]

In 2:13–17, Peter urges his readers to be subject to those who rule over them, whether emperors or governors. He then advises similar submission on the part of servants to their masters, even if those masters are cruel (2:18–25). In doing so they are imitating Christ (vv. 21–25). Wives are to be subject to their own husbands with the purpose of winning their husbands over by their example (3:1–7). Peter concludes this section by calling all Christians to like-mindedness, sympathy, brotherly love, compassion, and humility (vv. 8–12). Although the kingdom has not yet been consummated, the ethics of the kingdom are to be put into practice by the people of the King today.

The final main section of 1 Peter concerns the Christian's attitude toward suffering and persecution (3:13–5:11). Peter assures his readers that God will

51. Michaels 1988, 113.

52. Clowney 1988, 101. As Jobes (2005, 44) explains, this is a major theme in 1 Peter.

53. Jobes 2005, 172.

vindicate his own no matter what kind of suffering they endure (3:13–17).[54] In 3:18–22, Peter points to Jesus as an example of how to handle suffering. Peter turns first to the cross. As Clowney explains, "Our willingness to suffer for the sake of Christ is grounded in the wonder of Christ's willingness to suffer death for our sake."[55] He is our example. In the midst of this, Peter tells his readers that Christ "went and proclaimed to the spirits in prison, because they formerly did not obey, when God's patience waited in the days of Noah" (3:19–20). To what does this text refer?

Some argue that this text is referring to the preincarnate Christ preaching through Noah to the world of his day. Others suggest that the text refers to Christ preaching during his descent into hell between his death and resurrection. Still others suggest that the text refers to Christ's announcement of victory to the angels described as "sons of God" in Genesis 6. Finally, some argue that this text refers to Christ's proclamation of victory to fallen angels at the time of his ascension. Each of these views has been defended by able expositors, but the fourth interpretation involves the least amount of difficulties.

In 4:1–6, Peter exhorts his readers to think in the same way Christ thought, willing to suffer death for the sake of God. In verse 6, Peter makes a concluding statement that has raised some questions. After speaking of the judgment of the godless, Peter writes, "For this is why the gospel was preached even to those who are dead, that though judged in the flesh the way people are, they might live in the spirit the way God does." Who are the "dead" spoken of here? Several suggestions have been made, but the evidence supports the idea that Peter is speaking of some who heard the gospel in their lifetime but who are now dead.[56]

In the next paragraph (4:7–11), Peter calls upon his readers to live lives of service to one another in light of the fact that Jesus has inaugurated the last days. He writes, "The end of all things is at hand; therefore be self-controlled and sober-minded for the sake of your prayers" (4:7). What does Peter mean when he says that the "end of all things is at hand"? On the one hand, it is possible that he is merely speaking of the fact that since the coming of Christ, the church lives in the last days.[57] However, consid-

54. Michaels 1988, 193.
55. Clowney 1988, 154.
56. See Michaels 1988, 236.
57. Jobes 2005, 275.

ering that Peter wrote this letter in A.D. 62 or 63, it is also possible that he had in mind the words he heard Jesus speak thirty years earlier about the judgment that was to be expected within a generation. If that is the case, then the end Peter has in mind is not the end associated with the second coming of Christ and the final judgment. It is the end associated with the destruction of Jerusalem.

Peter continues, reminding his readers that suffering is to be expected for Christians and that they should not be surprised, but rejoice instead (4:12–16). They should suffer, however, only for righteousness, not for doing evil. In the following verses, Peter compares the suffering endured by believers to the judgment that is to come upon those who reject God (vv. 17–19). The one is nothing compared to the other. Christians, therefore, are to entrust their souls to their faithful Creator and continue to do good (v. 19).

In 5:1–5, Peter exhorts the elders in the churches to shepherd the flock of God, not as domineering types, but as examples of service. Elders have a unique responsibility for building up believers under their care. Those who are younger are to be subject to their elders (v. 5a). Peter urges the elders and the younger members of the church alike, "Clothe yourselves, all of you, with humility toward one another, for God opposes the proud but gives grace to the humble" (v. 5b). Humility and resistance to evil are both required for those who live in the last days inaugurated by the coming of the Messiah. The people of God who are suffering for righteousness' sake will be vindicated by God (vv. 6–11).

When we turn to Peter's second epistle, we encounter more difficulties than we find in connection with his first letter. Most contemporary scholars, for example, reject Petrine authorship of his second epistle. They do so, however, on insufficient grounds. A thorough examination of this complicated debate is beyond the scope of this work. Suffice it to say that there is not enough evidence to reject the claim of authorship made in the first verse of the epistle.[58] The suggestion that the work is pseudepigraphal causes more problems than it solves.

The content of Peter's second epistle clearly indicates the occasion for its writing. Peter is sending this letter because false teachers have infiltrated the Christian community (2 Peter 2:1–3). Peter addresses his second epistle

58. See Carson and Moo 2005, 659–63.

to "those who have obtained a faith of equal standing with ours by the righteousness of our God and Savior Jesus Christ" (1:1). This statement is significant, first, because it refers to Jesus Christ not only as Savior but also as God.[59] Jesus the Messiah is God incarnate. Peter also tells his readers that their faith is not a subordinate faith. It is of equal standing with the faith of the apostles. Peter writes, "May grace and peace be multiplied to you in the knowledge of God and of Jesus our Lord" (v. 2). It is the abandonment of this knowledge and faith that Peter will warn against in the remainder of his letter.

The theme of Peter's second epistle is summarized in 1:3–11. Here Peter sets forth the foundation for the Christian life, namely, that which Christ has already done for believers and that which he has already promised them (vv. 3–4). He urges his readers to live godly lives and to maintain their faith and hope (vv. 5–10). His closing comment in this summary emphasizes the eschatological framework of the Christian life: "For in this way there will be richly provided for you an entrance into the eternal kingdom of our Lord and Savior Jesus Christ" (v. 11). Verses 12–15, then, are transitional. In these verses, Peter commends his readers and indicates that he is nearing death.

The main body of Peter's second epistle begins with Peter's replies to several objections to his eschatological doctrine (1:16–21). The first objection apparently raised by the false teachers is that Peter's eschatological teaching concerning the coming of Christ and of judgment is merely a myth (vv. 16–18). Peter assures his readers that the apostles did not follow cleverly devised myths, but were eyewitnesses of Christ's majesty. At the transfiguration of Jesus, they were even witnesses to a foretaste of the glory to be revealed at the second advent (vv. 17–18). Peter also argues that the eschatological doctrine of the apostles is based on the writings of the Old Testament prophets (v. 19), men who spoke the very word of God (vv. 20–21).

Peter introduces the main topic of his letter in 2:1–3a, explaining, "But false prophets also arose among the people, just as there will be false teachers among you, who will secretly bring in destructive heresies, even denying the Master who bought them, bringing upon themselves swift destruction." Just as false prophets arose during the Old Testament era to obscure

59. For the evidence, see Reymond 1990, 288–91; Harris 1992, 232–35.

the eschatological message of the true prophets, so too will false prophets obscure and debate the eschatological teaching of the apostles. That these false prophets would arise had been predicted by the apostles.[60] In verses 3b–10a, Peter explains that God reserves these false prophets for judgment, but he rescues godly men.

The false prophets, according to Peter, are characterized particularly by their arrogance (2:10b–13a) and by their sensuality (vv. 13b–16). Peter strongly denounces this godless behavior. Richard Bauckham explains the meaning of the following verses (17–22): "The two metaphors with which this section begins condemn the author's opponents as people who purport to be religious teachers. Like dry wells which disappoint the thirsty, and hazy mists which are blown away without relieving the heat of the atmosphere, these people have in reality nothing to offer those who look to them for spiritual sustenance."[61] The arrogance and godlessness of these false prophets combined with the uselessness of their teaching render them fit for judgment on the last day.

In chapter 3, Peter tells his readers that they need to remember the predictions of the Old Testament prophets and know "that scoffers will come in the last days with scoffing, following their own sinful desires. They will say, 'Where is the promise of his coming? For ever since the fathers fell asleep, all things are continuing as they were from the beginning of creation'" (vv. 3–4). Peter responds to such statements by noting that the scoffers fail to take into account the judgment that occurred at the time of the flood (vv. 5–6). He assures his readers that the world will be judged again (v. 7). It is being preserved by God until that time.

Peter continues, saying:

> But do not overlook this one fact, beloved, that with the Lord one day is as a thousand years, and a thousand years as one day. The Lord is not slow to fulfill his promise as some count slowness, but is patient toward you, not wishing that any should perish, but that all should reach repentance. But the day of the Lord will come like a thief, and then the heavens will pass away with a roar, and the heavenly bodies will be burned up and dissolved, and the earth and the works that are done on it will be exposed. (3:8–10)

60. Bauckham 1983, 243.
61. Bauckham 1983, 280.

These verses have been used in the past to support numerological interpretations such as those that view all of world history in terms of a six- or seven-day period of time with each "day" lasting one thousand years. Such interpretations are based more on reader imagination than authorial intent. In the context, Peter is responding to those who are saying that God is slow to fulfill his promises. His response is threefold. First, Peter asserts that God's perspective on time is not the same as man's perspective (v. 8).[62] Second, he explains that what the scoffers count as slowness is really God's patience on display (v. 9). He is providing the opportunity for repentance. Finally, Peter warns his readers that God will not delay his judgment forever (v. 10). Judgment will come. The language Peter uses to describe the coming judgment in verse 10 is the kind of highly figurative language the Old Testament prophets used to describe coming judgments (Isa. 34:4; Joel 2:31).

Peter concludes this section saying:

> Since all these things are thus to be dissolved, what sort of people ought you to be in lives of holiness and godliness, waiting for and hastening the coming of the day of God, because of which the heavens will be set on fire and dissolved, and the heavenly bodies will melt as they burn! But according to his promise we are waiting for new heavens and a new earth in which righteousness dwells. (2 Peter 3:11–13)

The judgment that is coming is to provide grounds for holy living now. But Peter also explains that the judgment will also be accompanied by renewal. There will be new heavens and a new earth, a re-creation as it were (Gen. 1:1).

When we turn to the epistle of Jude, the first thing we notice is its similarity with the second chapter of 2 Peter. Because of the similarity, this brief letter will not occupy as much of our time.[63] Regarding authorship, the epistle of Jude was likely written by Jude the brother of Jesus.[64] His letter resembles part of Peter's letter because both are dealing with the same

62. As Green (1987, 146) and Bauckham (1983, 309) demonstrate, this interpretation has parallels in the Jewish literature of the first century.

63. Debates surround the relationship between Jude and 2 Peter. It is difficult to determine whether Jude based his work on 2 Peter, 2 Peter on Jude, or both on a third writing. My own tentative conclusion is that Jude used 2 Peter.

64. Bauckham 1983, 14.

problem. Like Peter, Jude is writing to combat the rise of false teachers in the Christian churches. From the content of his epistle, we can infer that the primary doctrinal and practical error of these false teachers is an extreme libertinism. Richard Bauckham explains Jude's basic message: "To help his readers resist the influence of the false teachers, Jude reminds them that their initial instruction by the apostles at their conversion and baptism included teaching about God's judgment on disbelief and disobedience, and specific warnings of false teachers who would incur this judgment."[65]

The Epistles of John

The three epistles of John were likely written from Ephesus between A.D. 80 and 85.[66] This would make them among the last New Testament books to be written.[67] The recipients of these letters were likely members of regional churches associated with the church in Ephesus, which itself was under the leadership of the apostle John.[68] The recipients of the first epistle of John were apparently dealing with a situation caused by a group of people who had separated from the Ephesian church and who were now teaching false doctrine.[69] Their continued contact with the members of the churches was causing problems, and John writes to address these problems. Eschatology is not at the forefront of his teaching, but where it is evident, his emphasis is on that which is already realized in the present.[70]

The first epistle of John lacks a typical epistolary opening. Instead, the letter leaps immediately into the body of the message. John begins by claiming that he was an eyewitness of the Word and that he has proclaimed the Word to his readers. He writes:

> That which was from the beginning, which we have heard, which we have seen with our eyes, which we looked upon and have touched with our hands, concerning the word of life—the life was made manifest, and we have seen it, and testify to it and proclaim to you the eternal life, which was with the

65. Bauckham 1983, 63.

66. Carson and Moo 2005, 676.

67. Many argue that the book of Revelation was the last New Testament book to be written, but a strong case can be made that it was the earliest of John's canonical writings. See chapter 18 for a full discussion of the date of Revelation.

68. It may be that these churches are the same churches addressed by John in Revelation 2–3.

69. Kruse 2000, 15.

70. Lieu 1991, 88.

> Father and was made manifest to us—that which we have seen and heard we proclaim also to you, so that you too may have fellowship with us; and indeed our fellowship is with the Father and with his Son Jesus Christ. And we are writing these things so that our joy may be complete. (1 John 1:1–4)

There are clear echoes of the opening of John's gospel in these verses. Both speak of the Word and the beginning (John 1:1). Both invite the reader to reflect on Genesis 1:1. By using this language, John forces the reader to view Jesus as the one who inaugurates a new beginning. The emphasis in these opening verses is upon Jesus as the object of John's proclamation. Jesus and his message are described as one.[71] John describes that which he had seen and touched as that which he also proclaims. John also makes it very clear that the eternal life God has made available is manifest only in Jesus Christ (1 John 1:2).

In 1 John 1:6–2:11, the apostle elaborates on the basic message he summarizes in 1:5, "This is the message we have heard from him and proclaim to you, that God is light, and in him is no darkness at all." Because God's character is holy, those who would have fellowship with him must also be holy. Those who were troubling the church were apparently making several claims. They were claiming to have fellowship with God (1:6), but they were also claiming that they were without sin (v. 8) and that they had not sinned (v. 10). According to John, these men are self-deceived (v. 8). Even worse, they make God a liar by denying his verdict on mankind, namely, that all have sinned (Rom. 3:23).[72] Rather than denying their sin, they should be confessing it (1 John 1:9).

Lest anyone interpret his words as a license to sin, John makes it clear that he is writing in order that his readers not fall into sin (2:1). When Christians do sin, however, they have an advocate in Jesus Christ. He is not only the advocate but also "the propitiation for our sins" (v. 2). In other words, Christ is the advocate as well as the sacrifice that provides the grounds for the advocate's intercession. In verses 3–11, John continues to contrast the claims of the opponents with the Christian life. In verses 12–17, he poetically describes the present status of Christians as those whose sins are forgiven and as those who have overcome the evil one. Here the emphasis is

71. Marshall 1978b, 101–2.
72. Marshall 1978b, 115.

on the eschatological already. Even now Christians are already experiencing a foretaste of the eschatological blessings of the coming age.

In 2:18–27, John turns from exhortation to warning. He writes, "Children, it is the last hour, and as you have heard that antichrist is coming, so now many antichrists have come. Therefore we know that it is the last hour" (2:18). The phrase "the last hour" (*eschatē hōra*) occurs only here in the New Testament. Elsewhere, the similar phrases "the last days" or "the last times" occur (e.g., Acts 2:17; Heb. 1:2; 1 Peter 1:20). The New Testament authors understood the last days to have begun with the death and resurrection of Jesus. Here John describes his time as "the last hour." Does this mean John believed the second coming would certainly happen within a few short years of his writing?[73] No, as we have seen, the New Testament writers understood the present age as one that continually runs along the brink of the final end. The final end, therefore, always remains imminent and could occur at any time.

John also mentions a figure he refers to as "antichrist" (1 John 2:18). It is possible, although not certain, that John is referring here to the same entity described by Paul as "the man of lawlessness" (2 Thess. 2:3). If so, the same difficulty exists in identifying this antichrist with any precision.[74] It is possible that both John and Paul are speaking of an individual person who is to arise sometime near the time of the second coming. In light of 1 John 4:3, however, it is also possible that John is speaking of something that has already come. John refers to "many antichrists" who have already come. These antichrists are the false teachers who separated from the churches and who are denying that Jesus is the Christ (2:19–25). The "spirit" of antichrist, then, is already alive and well in John's day (4:3).

John encourages his readers to abide in Christ that they might not be ashamed at his coming (2:28). When Christ comes, Christians will be conformed to his image. They will be made like him (3:2). Christians are to understand that Jesus came to take away sin (3:5) and to destroy the works of the devil (3:8). In doing these things, Christ fulfills the purpose God set forth to accomplish from the time of the fall. Those who belong to Christ have passed from death to life (3:14). They now participate in

73. If these books are to be dated in the 80s or 90s of the first century as seems likely, then John's statement rules out any type of full preterism that places the second advent and the final end of all things at or near A.D. 70, since John still speaks of it as a future event after A.D. 70.

74. For a helpful, and nonsensationalistic, recent discussion, see Riddlebarger 2006.

the life of the eschatological age, and their lives should manifest this fact in love toward one another (3:11–15).

Believers are to test the spirits to see whether they are from God (4:1). This is necessary because there are many false prophets in the world. Those who do not confess Christ are not from God. Those who do not confess Christ manifest the spirit of antichrist, which is in the world already (4:3). John assures his readers that they have overcome these antichrists because the Spirit in them is greater than the one who is in the world (4:4). John concludes by giving his readers evidence that they may know they belong to God (5:13–21).

The second and third epistles of John are letters to individuals. The second epistle is addressed to "the elect lady and her children" (v. 1). John commends them for walking in the truth and encourages them to love one another (v. 5). He warns them against deceivers (vv. 7–8) and against showing hospitality to such people (vv. 9–11). The third epistle expands on the theme of hospitality. John addresses this letter to Gaius, a member of one of the local churches (v. 1). He commends Gaius for showing hospitality (vv. 5–8) and condemns Diotrephes for failing to show hospitality to believers and for opposing Gaius and John himself (vv. 9–10).

Summary

The book of Hebrews and the General Epistles, like the Pauline Epistles, were written to real churches during the first century. Most were written during the same general period of time that Paul wrote, but some (1–3 John) were written much later. The book of Hebrews was written to warn its readers against apostasy. The author of Hebrews argues continually for the absolute supremacy of Christ. Jesus has inaugurated the eschatological new covenant, but there is more to come. Believers, therefore, must remain steadfast in the faith as they await his second coming.

Eschatology is not emphasized in the epistle of James. Instead, eschatology forms the contextual background for the letter. James encourages his readers to endure suffering, and he instructs them to view their suffering from an eschatological perspective. Like James, Peter encourages his readers to understand their suffering in an eschatological light and to live in the light of their future hope. In his second epistle, Peter specifically combats those who scoff at the eschatological teaching of the apostles. Finally, although he does not emphasize eschatology, John in his epistles also assumes it as a contextual background. He describes that which is already true of the Christian and warns of the spirit of antichrist.

A common theme in all of these epistles is the exhortation to remain steadfast in the faith even in the face of suffering. The apostles know that the kingdom has been inaugurated. Jesus Christ has been given all authority. But they also know that the kingdom has not yet been consummated. The enemy is not going down without a fight. The kingdom will grow, but its growth will be in the context of a spiritual war. The entire interadvent age, then, is an age of intense conflict. Such conflict will result in suffering for believers. Believers, therefore, must be prepared for the ongoing battle as they await the second coming of their Lord.

18

The Book of Revelation

The book of Revelation is the capstone of Scripture. Here all of the threads of redemptive history come together in a final glorious vision of victory. Here all of the promises of God find their ultimate fulfillment. The promise given to Adam in the garden is fulfilled as we witness the climax of the long battle between good and evil and the final destruction of sin, the serpent, and death through the redemptive work of Christ. The promise given to Abraham is fulfilled as we witness an innumerable multitude from every tribe, and tongue, and nation worshiping God. The promise given to David is fulfilled as we witness the consummation of God's plan to establish his kingdom on earth under Jesus Christ, the one who is both Son of David and Son of God.

Introduction to Revelation

The book of Revelation is significant, but it is also difficult. Like many of the prophetic books, it is filled with unusual symbolism and imagery. Like the other New Testament books, but on a much larger scale, it frequently alludes to or echoes Old Testament texts. Its author, date, genre, and even its basic structure are disputed. In fact, the interpretation of almost every paragraph in the book is disputed. Despite these difficulties, however, the basic theme of the book shines through clearly. Revelation is about the victory of Jesus Christ. The book concerns the transfer of authority over this world from Satan and his followers to Jesus and his. It concerns the full establishment of the kingdom of God. As Richard Bauckham observes, "The whole of Revelation could be regarded as a vision of the fulfillment of the first three petitions of the Lord's Prayer: 'Your name be hallowed, your kingdom come, your will be done, on earth as it is in heaven' (Matt. 6:9–10)."[1]

The author of Revelation describes himself merely as John (Rev. 1:1). Various men named John have been suggested as the author, including an unknown elder named John, an unknown prophet named John, John Mark, and even John the Baptist, but there is still strong evidence for the early tradition that the John in question is John the apostle.[2] The genre of John's book is somewhat unique in Scripture. It shares many features of Old Testament apocalyptic literature. However, John specifically identifies the book as a prophecy (1:3; 19:10; 22:7, 10, 18, 19). Lastly, the book has many features in common with epistles, including a standard epistolary greeting (1:4) and closing (22:21).

Generally speaking, then, the book of Revelation is an apocalyptic prophecy, much like Ezekiel, Daniel, and Zechariah, but this prophecy is set within the form of a letter to seven churches.[3] This latter feature of the book is particularly important when we consider our basic approach to the visions within it. As George Beasley-Murray explains, "An important corollary of this feature of the work [i.e., its epistolary nature] is the relation which the book was intended to have to a group of Christian people in a known area of the world at a particular time in history."[4] In other words, the situation of these real historical churches was in John's mind as he wrote.

One of the most difficult problems faced by interpreters of the book of Revelation involves its structure. This remains one of the most intractable problems related to any study of the book, and there is still no consensus.[5] Some see a threefold structure based on Revelation 1:19 (1:1–20; 2:1–3:22;

1. Bauckham 1993b, 40; see also Ford 1975, 76.
2. For the various arguments, see Guthrie 1990a, 932–48; Carson and Moo 2005, 700–707.
3. See Witherington 2003, 48; Beale 1999, 37.
4. Beasley-Murray 1978, 13.
5. Aune 1997, xci.

4:1–22:21).[6] Others see a fourfold structure based on John's experiences "in the Spirit" (1:1–19; 1:20–3:22; 4:1–22:5; 22:6–21).[7] A few see a "dramatic" structure (1:1–8; 1:9–3:22; 4:1–8:1; 8:2–11:18; 11:19–15:4; 15:5–16:21; 17:1–19:10; 19:11–21:8; 21:9–22:19; 22:20–21).[8] Numerous other suggestions have also been made. Because of the complexity of the issues involved, it is beyond the scope of this work to address the problem of the structure of the book in any great detail.[9] We will, however, address some of the more basic questions as we proceed.

As mentioned above, the book of Revelation alludes to or echoes the Old Testament more than does any other New Testament book. Because allusions and echoes are more difficult to identify than direct quotations, there is no agreement on the exact number, but the estimate of one author that there are over five hundred Old Testament allusions in the book of Revelation is not unusual.[10] A little more than half of these Old Testament references are taken from the books of Psalms, Isaiah, Ezekiel, and Daniel.[11] These intertextual echoes must be recognized in order to comprehend what John is saying to the churches. It is simply not possible to fully comprehend the meaning of the book of Revelation in isolation from God's earlier revelation to his people. John not only alludes to previous biblical revelation, however; he also reveals its ultimate fulfillment. The book of Revelation is truly "the climax of prophetic revelation."[12]

It is important to realize that our understanding of the book of Revelation depends not only upon a grasp of the biblical texts that precede it, but it also depends on a grasp of the historical context of the book. It is important to understand, for example, that the seven churches to whom John writes were all situated in the western region of Asia Minor, a crucial part of the Roman Empire, and that one of the problems faced by Christians in the Roman Empire during the first century was the imperial cult, the official worship of the Roman emperor. As Grant Osborne explains, "Emperor worship was linked to civic loyalty and patriotism."[13] It was the

6. E.g., Walvoord 1966, 48.
7. E.g., Beale 1999, 115.
8. E.g., Wilcock 1975, 20; Smalley 1994, 103–10.
9. For a good discussion of the issues involved, see Aune 1997, xc–cv; Beale 1999, 108–51.
10. Witherington 2003, 72; see also Beale 1998, 60.
11. Beale 1998, 60–61.
12. Bauckham 1993a, xi.
13. Osborne 2002, 139.

social glue that held the cities, and even the region, together.[14] Refusal to participate was considered subversive and even treasonous. Part of John's purpose, then, is to strengthen the resolve of the churches in the region to resist this blatant form of pagan idolatry. We will look at more specific aspects of the historical context as we proceed.

One aspect of the historical context that has been the source of much debate is the date of the book's composition. When did John write the book of Revelation? We know that it was written sometime in the second half of the first century, but is it possible to be more precise? Two main options have been suggested by scholars: a date between A.D. 64 and 70, during or just after the reign of Nero, and a date around A.D. 95–96, during the latter part of the reign of Domitian. The general consensus among contemporary scholars is that the latter view is correct. In other words, the majority of scholars today believe that the book was written sometime around A.D. 95 or 96, during the last years of the reign of Domitian.[15]

Although numerous arguments have been made in support of a Domitianic date, most of them can be summarized under six headings.[16] First, there is the evidence from Irenaeus (A.D. 130–202), who says that the Apocalypse was seen near the end of the reign of Domitian. Second, it is said that the situation of the churches addressed in chapters 2–3 reflects changes that could not have occurred before A.D. 70. Third, it is argued that the persecution described in Revelation points to a situation more likely to have existed under Domitian than Nero. Fourth, it is said that Revelation reflects a stage in the development of the imperial cult that was not reached until Domitian. Fifth, it is argued that Revelation makes use of the *Nero redivivus* myth and that this demands a date long after the death of Nero. Finally, it is argued that the internal evidence of Revelation 13 and 17 points to a Domitianic date. These arguments have persuaded many,

14. Witherington 2003, 25.

15. E.g., Sweet 1979, 21; Thompson 1990, 15; Mounce 1998, 316; Beale 1999, 4; Kistemaker 2001, 28; Osborne 2002, 9. Some (e.g., Sweet, Osborne) grant that the evidence is inconclusive but still argue that the later date is more likely. David Aune, on the other hand, believes that both views are partially correct because he believes that the book went through stages of composition. He argues (1997, cxx) that a large part of the book (1:7–12a; 4:1–22:5) was probably composed around A.D. 70. The final edition of the book, he claims (1997, cxxxii), was written during the reign of Trajan (A.D. 98–117).

16. Smalley (1994, 40–42) provides a helpful summary of these pieces of evidence.

but there is a significant minority of scholars who argue that the book of Revelation was written during or soon after the reign of Nero.[17]

Before looking at the arguments presented by advocates of an early date, we must examine the arguments set forth in support of a late date. The strongest piece of external evidence for a Domitianic date is the statement of Irenaeus to the effect that John's vision was seen near the end of Domitian's reign (*Against Heresies* 5.30.3).[18] The strength of this evidence, however, is not as great as is often assumed. It is telling, for example, that Irenaeus also taught that Jesus' ministry lasted more than ten years and that Jesus lived to be almost fifty years old (*Against Heresies* 2.22.5). On both counts, Irenaeus got his facts wrong. Of course, his errors regarding these facts do not necessarily mean that he was wrong about the date of Revelation, but it does mean that his testimony cannot be accepted uncritically. Obviously, at least some of his sources were wrong, and they were wrong on some fairly basic details concerning the life of Jesus. At best, the evidence from Irenaeus should be considered inconclusive.

What about the situation of the churches addressed by John? Could some of these churches have strayed so far before A.D. 70? Advocates of a late date say no, but considering how quickly the Thessalonian church, the Corinthian church, and the Galatian churches experienced both spiritual and practical problems, it seems that this piece of evidence for a late date is also overstated. Paul's epistles indicate that these first Christian churches could quickly go astray (e.g., Gal. 1:6). There is no reason, then, that the same could not have occurred in the churches addressed in Revelation.

But what about the evidence based on the persecution described in Revelation? Does it lend support to a Domitianic date? While there is a great deal of evidence for severe persecution of Christians under Nero, no clear evidence has yet been found indicating that Christians were systematically

17. E.g., Robinson 1976, 221–53; Bell 1979; Gentry 1989a; Wilson 1993; Smalley 1994, 40–49.

18. The statement reads: "We will not, however, incur the risk of pronouncing positively as to the name of Antichrist; for if it were necessary that his name should be distinctly revealed in this present time, it would have been announced by him who beheld the apocalyptic vision. For that was seen no very long time since, but almost in our day, towards the end of Domitian's reign." It has been noted (e.g., Gentry 1989a, 48–57) that the word translated "that was seen" (Gk. *heōrathē*) could also be translated "he was seen," thus referring to John rather than to John's vision, but the context points to the translation "that was seen." The clause immediately preceding the words "was seen" speaks of the apocalyptic vision. That would be the most likely antecedent.

persecuted under Domitian.[19] Gregory Beale attempts to lessen the weight of this observation. He writes, "There is no evidence that Nero's persecution of Christians in Rome extended also to Asia Minor, where the churches addressed in the Apocalypse are located."[20]

Two brief observations are in order. First, it seems a bit odd to discount a date around the reign of Nero because the evidence points to a localized persecution while at the same time accepting a date during the reign of Domitian where there is no clear evidence of systematic persecution at all. Second, even if Nero's persecution was largely localized in Rome, its effects would have been felt throughout all the Christian churches. Nero's persecution of Christians was a massacre.[21] It is also significant that Nero's persecution resulted in the deaths of two of the church's most important leaders, Peter and Paul. It was an extraordinarily traumatic event for the young church.

The evidence for a late date based on the development of the imperial cult and the *Nero redivivus* myth is also inconclusive.[22] The seeds of the imperial cult were sown as early as the time of Julius Caesar, and by the time of Augustus (27 B.C.–A.D. 14), emperor worship was already strong in Asia Minor. It is impossible, therefore, to use any allusions to the imperial cult in Revelation to date the book specifically to the reign of any one emperor. Evidence based on the alleged use of the *Nero redivivus* myth in Revelation is likewise inconclusive. Rumors of Nero's return were already spreading soon after his death.[23] Imposters also appeared quite early. As Albert Bell points out, "False Neros appeared in 79 and 88, but neither had the impact of the one who, according to Tacitus, threw Asia and Achaea into an uproar early in 69."[24] In other words, even if the author of Revelation used elements of this myth in his book, its use does not point automatically to a late date.

We will look more closely at the arguments based on Revelation 13 and 17 in our examination of the text of the book itself. Suffice it to say for now that this evidence is also contested. As we have seen, the arguments

19. Wright 1992, 355; Wilson 1993, 589.
20. Beale 1999, 12; see also Witherington 2003, 4.
21. See Tacitus, *Annals* 15.44; cf. *1 Clement* 6:1.
22. Smalley 1994, 44–45.
23. Smalley 1994, 44.
24. Bell 1979, 98.

used in support of a late date are, at best, inconclusive. Is there, however, any positive evidence for an earlier date? There are actually several lines of evidence that seem to point toward a date during or very soon after the reign of Nero.[25] In the first place, as we will see, a number of the judgment oracles in the book of Revelation echo Jesus' pronouncement of coming judgment upon Jerusalem and the temple (Matt. 24; Mark 13; Luke 21). We have already argued that in those texts, Jesus was speaking of a judgment to come within the first century. The similarity between John's prophecies and Jesus' pronouncements indicates that John is speaking of this same judgment.

A second line of evidence for an early date is based on the number of times John indicates that his prophecy will be fulfilled very soon (e.g., Rev. 1:1, 3, 19; 2:16; 3:10–11; 22:6–7, 10, 12, 20). If John speaks of the same judgment spoken of by Jesus, and if he continues to refer to it as a future event, this would lend weight to the claim that he wrote before the final destruction of Jerusalem in A.D. 70. Had the book been written during the last years of Domitian's reign, the language of imminence would become much more difficult to explain. Nothing on the scale of the destruction of Jerusalem occurred anytime soon after the reign of Domitian.

A third piece of evidence for an early date is the fact that the book of Revelation appears to have been written at a time when there remained a strong Jewish or even Judaizing element in the church (2:9; 3:9; 7:4–8; 14:1; 21:12). The book of Acts indicates that this was a problem in the first decades of the church. This was not as much the case after A.D. 70. A fourth line of evidence is the internal evidence based upon the interpretation of Revelation 13 and 17. As noted above, this evidence is contested, so we will have to examine it in our study of the text. Suffice it to say at this point that Revelation 17 in particular seems to provide a strong clue to the precise time of the writing of the book.[26] As we will see below, a strong case can be made that it points rather clearly to a time during or just after the reign of Nero.

25. There is disagreement on some specifics among those who argue for an early date. Some argue that the book was written during Nero's reign. Gentry (1989a, 336), for example, argues that the book was written sometime in A.D. 65 or 66. Others suggest that the book was written soon after Nero's death. Bell (1979, 100) argues that the book was written during the brief reign of Galba (June, A.D. 68–January, A.D. 69). Smalley (1994, 40–49), on the other hand, believes the book was written in the early part of the reign of Vespasian, just before the fall of Jerusalem in A.D. 70.

26. Wilson 1993, 599.

A final issue that must be addressed before proceeding to an examination of the text is our basic hermeneutical approach to the book. Over the course of the church's history there have been four main approaches: the futurist, historicist, preterist, and idealist approaches.[27] The futurist approach understands everything from Revelation 4:1 forward to be a prophecy of things that are to occur just before the second coming of Christ. In other words, all of these prophesied events are still in the future from the perspective of the twenty-first century. According to proponents, this conclusion grows out of a belief that there is no correspondence between these prophesied events and anything that has yet occurred in history.[28]

The historicist approach understands Revelation to be a prophecy of church history from the first advent until the second coming of Christ. This approach appears to have had its roots in the writings of Joachim of Fiore.[29] It was later adopted by most of the Protestant Reformers, but it is held by very few today.[30] The preterist approach to Revelation is most clearly contrasted with the futurist approach. According to the preterist approach, most of the prophecies in the book of Revelation were fulfilled not long after John wrote.[31] In other words, their fulfillment is past from the perspective of the twenty-first century.[32] The fourth major approach to the book is the idealist or symbolic approach. According to this view, Revelation does not contain prophecies of specific historical events. Instead, it uses symbols to express timeless principles concerning the conflict between good and evil.

Until recently these various approaches have been considered by many to be mutually exclusive. A number of scholars, however, have begun to propose a fifth approach, which may be termed the eclectic approach. As one proponent of this view explains, "The solution is to allow the preterist, idealist, and futurist methods to interact in such a way that the strengths

27. For a good summary overview of the history of interpretation, see Wainwright 1993, 21–103.

28. Walvoord 1966, 101.

29. Wainwright 1993, 49.

30. The most able contemporary proponent of the historicist interpretation of Revelation is Francis Nigel Lee (2000).

31. The most well known contemporary proponent of the preterist interpretation of Revelation is Kenneth L. Gentry Jr. (1998). Gentry is currently completing a full-length commentary on Revelation.

32. Of course, their fulfillment was future from the perspective of John at the time he wrote the book.

are maximized and the weaknesses minimized."[33] One of the first to espouse such an approach was George Ladd. He concluded that the correct method of interpreting the book of Revelation was to blend the futurist and preterist methods.[34] He has been followed in this basic eclectic approach, although with different emphases, by a number of scholars including Gregory Beale, Grant Osborne, and Vern Poythress.[35]

Because the approach one takes to the book of Revelation dramatically affects one's exegetical conclusions, it is necessary that I explain the reasons I take the approach I do. I believe that the book itself demands a basically preterist approach. This does not mean that all of the prophecies in the book have already been fulfilled. Some of the prophecies in Revelation (e.g., 20:7–22:21) have yet to be fulfilled, but many, if not most, of the prophecies in the book have been fulfilled. My approach then may be considered basically preterist.[36]

Before explaining why I believe this approach to be correct, I must explain why I do not believe the other approaches to be fully adequate. Proponents of the futurist view say that their approach is necessary because there is no correspondence between the events prophesied in the book and anything that has happened in history. As we shall see, this conclusion is reached because of an overly literalistic approach to the symbolism of the book and a lack of appreciation for how such language was used in the Old Testament prophetic books. This, however, is not the most serious problem with the futurist approach.

The most fundamental problem with the futurist approach is that it requires a very artificial reading of the many texts within the book itself that point to the imminent fulfillment of its prophecies. The book opens and closes with declarations indicating that the things revealed in the book "must soon take place" (1:1; 22:6). It opens and closes with declarations indicating that "the time is near" (1:3; 22:10). The book of Revelation

33. Osborne 2002, 21.

34. Ladd 1972, 14.

35. See Beale 1999; Osborne 2002; Poythress 2000b. Beale takes an eclectic approach with an emphasis on the idealist approach. Osborne, on the other hand, emphasizes futurism in his eclecticism.

36. Since I believe that some prophecies in the book have not yet been fulfilled (i.e., I take a futurist approach to some specific prophecies), and since I believe some of the individual observations made by idealist interpreters are valuable, there may be those who would refer to my view as eclectic with an emphasis on the preterist aspect. The particular label is of little concern to me.

does not begin in the way the pseudepigraphal *Book of Enoch* begins, with a statement to the effect that the content is not for the present generation, but for a remote generation that is still to come. The book of Revelation has direct relevance to the real historical first-century churches to whom it was addressed, and the text of the book itself points to the imminent fulfillment of most of its prophecies.

The historicist approach faces more serious difficulties than the futurist approach. As Poythress observes, "Of the four schools of interpretation, historicism is undoubtedly the weakest, though it was popular centuries ago."[37] The most serious problem with the historicist approach is its subjectivity and arbitrariness.[38] Historicist interpreters through the ages invariably identify their own age as the final age.[39] They then fit the prophecies of the book with whatever important events have transpired between the first century and their own day. The result is that the basic historicist interpretation of the book changes from one generation to the next.

The idealist approach is held by many in the present day, but it is fundamentally flawed as a method of interpreting the book of Revelation. Its most serious problem is that it brushes over the specificity found within the text. Bauckham explains why such an approach is problematic:

> Thus it would be a serious mistake to understand the images of Revelation as timeless symbols. Their character conforms to the contextuality of Revelation as a letter to the seven churches of Asia. Their resonances in the specific social, political, cultural and religious world of their first readers need to be understood if their meaning is to be appropriated today.[40]

Not only does the idealist approach tend to ignore the historic specificity demanded by its character as a letter, it also tends to ignore the hermeneutical implications of its character as a prophecy. The Old Testament prophets used highly figurative and symbolic language, but they used this language

37. Poythress 2000b, 36.

38. Mounce 1998, 27.

39. This includes many of the classic Reformation, post-Reformation, and Puritan commentaries on Revelation. Contemporary Reformed historicists cannot follow those classic Reformed historicists completely because those classic Reformed historicists were wrong about their own age being the final age.

40. Bauckham 1993b, 19.

to speak of real historical nations and specific impending historical judgments. Writing his own prophetic book, John does the same.[41]

Proponents of the futurist, historicist, and idealist approaches offer several criticisms of the preterist approach to the book. Probably the most serious criticism is that this approach robs the book of any contemporary significance. John Walvoord, for example, writes, "The preterist view, in general, tends to destroy any future significance of the book, which becomes a literary curiosity with little prophetic meaning."[42] Leon Morris echoes this sentiment, claiming that the preterist approach "has the demerit of making it [the book of Revelation] meaningless for all subsequent readers (except for the information it gives about that early generation)."[43]

It is actually rather surprising that this criticism is repeated so often by conservative evangelical scholars. It implies that any biblical prophecies that have already been fulfilled are meaningless for readers in later generations. But are the Old Testament prophecies that were fulfilled in the birth, life, death, and resurrection of Jesus meaningless for later generations? Are the multitudes of Old Testament prophecies concerning the destruction of Israel and Judah and the subsequent exile meaningless for later generations? Obviously not, and neither would the prophecies in Revelation be any less meaningful or significant if it were shown that many or most of them have already been fulfilled. All Scripture is profitable (2 Tim. 3:16), even those parts of Scripture containing already fulfilled prophecies.

When misguided criticisms, such as the one above, are set aside and the case for a basically preterist approach is objectively considered on its own merits, it is seen to be quite strong. In the first place, our basic hermeneutical approach to the book should be determined by the nature and content of the book itself. As we have already seen, the book itself indicates when at least most of its prophecies are to be fulfilled. In both the first and last chapters, John tells his first-century readers that the things revealed in the book "must soon take place" (Rev. 1:1; 22:6) and that "the time is near" (1:3; 22:10). These statements are generalizations, so they do not require that every event prophesied in the book must be fulfilled in the first century, but the generalizations do provide us with a "general" idea of how

41. The idealist approach to the text of Revelation often appears to be more akin to an application of the text than an interpretation of the author's original intended meaning.

42. Walvoord 1966, 18.

43. Morris 1987, 18–19.

we should understand the book.[44] The bulk of John's prophecy concerns something that was impending in his own day.

Secondly, when the genre of the book is taken into consideration, it provides strong evidence for a basically preterist approach to the book. The book is a prophecy (1:3; 19:10; 22:7, 10, 18, 19). It is an apocalyptic prophecy set within the form of an epistle, but it is a prophecy nonetheless. Why is this important? It is important because it means that our approach to the other prophetic books of the Bible should provide us with some guidance in how we approach this last prophetic book of the Bible. We should approach it and read it in the same basic way. We do not read any of the Old Testament prophetic books as a whole in an idealist or historicist manner. We recognize that these prophecies were given to specific people in specific historical contexts. Many of the Old Testament prophecies deal with impending judgments upon either Israel or Judah or the nations that oppressed Israel. They also contain glimpses of ultimate future restoration. In short, we take a basically preterist approach to the Old Testament prophetic books, recognizing that they speak largely of impending events, yet also deal at times with the distant future.[45] Given that this is the way in which the Old Testament prophetic books are approached, it seems that our presumption should be in favor of the same basic approach to the prophetic book of Revelation.

It is also easy to forget when reading the book of Revelation that it is the capstone of the entire narrative of Scripture. The bulk of the biblical narrative has concerned the story of Israel, leading up to the coming of the promised Messiah. We recall that most of the content of the Old Testament prophetic books concerned the coming exile of Israel and Judah on account of their rejection of God. The prophecies continued right up to the time of the destruction of Jerusalem and the temple by the Babylonians in 586 B.C. (see Jeremiah and Ezekiel). In the first century, Jesus foretold another coming judgment of Israel on account of her rejection of himself, and he connected this coming judgment with his accession to the throne of the kingdom of God. In light of the history of prophecy in Israel, and in light of the redemptive-historical significance Jesus himself places on

44. John himself included a prophecy of a "thousand year" period that would be followed by the final judgment (Rev. 20:1–10). At the very least, it seems reasonable to suppose that John did not believe the events that would follow the thousand-year period would also be fulfilled in the very near future.

45. Stuart 1987, xxxii.

this first-century judgment of Israel, would it be terribly surprising if at the conclusion of the biblical narrative God once again sent a prophet to declare the impending judgment of Israel as well as the ultimate future restoration? When the genre, the statements of the book itself, and the larger biblical context are taken into consideration, a basically preterist approach to the book emerges as the most appropriate approach to take.[46]

Revelation

Despite the numerous debates concerning the structure of the book of Revelation, the outline of its surface narrative is somewhat straightforward.[47] The book begins with a prologue (1:1–8). The first major section contains John's opening vision of Christ and the messages to the seven churches (1:9–3:22). The book continues with John's opening vision of heaven (4:1–5:14), which itself leads to the three series of sevenfold judgments. The judgments associated with the seven seals come first (6:1–8:5). The judgments associated with the seven trumpets follow (8:6–11:19). Before the final series of judgments, John reveals the story of the conflict of God's people with evil (12:1–15:4). This is followed by the judgments associated with the seven bowls (15:5–16:21). John continues by describing the judgment of the great harlot Babylon (17:1–19:10) and the transition from Babylon to the new Jerusalem (19:11–21:8). Finally, in the last major section, the new Jerusalem is described (21:9–22:9). The book concludes with a brief epilogue (22:10–21).

The Prologue (Rev. 1:1–8)

The book of Revelation opens with the words "The revelation of Jesus Christ, which God gave him to show to his servants the things that must

46. One of the most well known recent commentaries on Revelation written from a preterist perspective is David Chilton's *The Days of Vengeance* (Fort Worth: Dominion, 1987). The reader will observe that I have not cited this commentary in this chapter. It is not that there are not helpful observations here and there in the book. The problem with Chilton's commentary is that he uses a hermeneutical method sometimes described as "interpretive maximalism." This method of hermeneutics does more to obscure the meaning of Scripture than it does to explain it. One is able to learn a lot about the imagination of a commentator who uses this method, but very little about the intention of the author of the book being interpreted. For a very helpful critique of Chilton's commentary and his use of interpretive maximalism, see Bahnsen 1988 (also available online).

47. I have followed Bauckham's general outline throughout this chapter (1993a, 21–22).

soon take place. He made it known by sending his angel to his servant John" (1:1). This opening pronouncement is similar to those found in the books of some of the prophets (e.g., Hosea 1:1; Joel 1:1). The pronouncement establishes the divine authority of the book by describing it as a revelation, the source of which is Jesus. The word translated "revelation" is the Greek word *apokalypsis.*

Through the mediation of an angel, Jesus reveals to John "the things that must soon take place" (see also Rev. 22:6). Some have attempted to reduce the force of these words by arguing that they do not mean the events in question are to occur soon, but that whenever they do occur, they will occur suddenly.[48] Others suggest that from the prophetic perspective, the end is always imminent.[49] Neither suggestion does justice to John's words. Like the Old Testament prophets writing in the years leading up to the exile, John is speaking of a specific imminent judgment, a judgment that Jesus himself had said would occur within a generation (Matt. 24:34). If, as we have argued, John was writing during or soon after the reign of Nero, the judgment upon Jerusalem about which Jesus spoke would have been imminent.[50]

John continues, "Blessed is the one who reads aloud the words of this prophecy, and blessed are those who hear, and who keep what is written in it, for the time is near" (1:3). Here John identifies the book as a "prophecy" (see also 10:11; 22:7, 10, 18, 19). It is in fact the culmination of all biblical prophecy. In this text John pronounces a blessing upon those who read, hear, and keep what is written in the prophecy. This is the first of seven beatitudes in the book of Revelation (1:3; 14:13; 16:15; 19:9; 20:6; 22:7, 22:14).[51] Echoing what he has already said in verse 1, John tells his readers that "the time is near" (see also Rev. 22:10). Again, he is emphasizing the fact that he is prophesying about something that is imminent at the time he is writing.

48. E.g., Walvoord 1966, 35.

49. Mounce 1998, 41.

50. Beale (1999, 181–82) argues that John's words here are deliberately contrasted with Daniel 2:28–30, 45–47. There Daniel was shown what was to come "in the latter days." John is saying that the things which Daniel expected "in the latter days" would begin in his own time or in fact had already begun.

51. Interestingly, the seven beatitude sayings correspond to sayings in the seven letters to the churches (compare 1:3 and 3:3; 14:13 and 2:10; 16:15 and 3:2–3; 19:9 and 3:20; 20:6 and 2:11; 22:7 and 3:10; 22:14 and 2:7).

John's prophecy is set within the form of a letter. Revelation 1:4–6 is a standard epistolary prescript, identifying the writer and addressees and containing a salutation and blessing. It is similar to the openings of the Pauline letters.[52] The book is addressed to the "seven churches that are in Asia" (v. 4a).[53] John then proclaims a blessing from God, "the one who is and who was and who is to come" (v. 4b). The first part of this title echoes the Septuagint version of Exodus 3:14 (see also Isa. 41:4). This text teaches that God is the sovereign Lord. John then refers to the "seven spirits who are before his throne" (Rev. 1:4c). Some have identified the seven spirits as a title of the Holy Spirit. While this is possible, John himself identifies the seven spirits with angels elsewhere in the first chapters of the book.[54] In 5:6, for example, John identifies the seven spirits with the seven eyes of the Lamb that are "sent out into all the earth" (cf. Heb. 1:14). In Revelation 8:2, he specifically refers to the seven angels who stand before God.

John describes Jesus Christ as "the faithful witness, the firstborn of the dead, and the ruler of kings on earth" (1:5a). John's description echoes the language of Psalm 89:27. This psalm is a hymnic reflection on the promises of the Davidic covenant, specifically the promise of an everlasting throne. The psalm looks forward to a messianic King. By using the language of this psalm, John is identifying Jesus as the messianic King. John also alludes to Christ's resurrection, calling him "the firstborn of the dead." His resurrection indicates that the last days have arrived. His authority over the kings on earth indicates that he is the one who fulfills the prophecy of Daniel 7:14.[55] It is significant that John refers to Jesus as the ruler of kings on earth in the present tense. Jesus does not have to await the second coming to receive this authority. It is already his (Matt. 28:18).

Jesus is the one who "loves us and has freed us from our sins by his blood and made us a kingdom, priests to his God and Father" (Rev. 1:5b–6; 5:10).

52. Bauckham 2001, 1290.

53. The number seven is used repeatedly throughout the book, indicating its symbolic significance. There are references to seven churches (1:4, 11, 20), seven spirits (1:4; 3:1; 4:5; 5:6), seven lampstands (1:12, 20; 2:1), seven stars (1:16, 20; 2:1; 3:1), seven lamps (4:5), seven seals (5:1, 5; 6:1), seven horns (5:6), seven eyes (5:6), seven angels (8:2, 6; 15:1, 6, 7, 8; 16:1; 17:1; 21:9), seven trumpets (8:2, 6), seven thunders (10:3, 4), seven heads (12:3; 13:1; 17:3, 7, 9), seven crowns (12:3), seven plagues (15:1, 6, 8; 21:9), seven bowls (15:7; 16:1; 17:1; 21:9), seven mountains (17:9), and seven kings (17:10).

54. Aune 1997, 40; Witherington 2003, 75.

55. Beale 1999, 221.

John here refers to the redemption accomplished by Christ through his atoning death on the cross. The description of Christ's people as "a kingdom, priests to his God" is an allusion to Exodus 19:6 where God tells the people he has just redeemed from Egypt that they shall be a kingdom of priests. We have seen that the Old Testament prophets often spoke of the coming restoration in terms of a new exodus. By using the language of Exodus 19, John picks up on this theme, describing the redemption of Christ's people within such a context.[56] The church, therefore, is the reconstitution of the people of God, a new Israel as it were.[57]

In Revelation 1:7, John writes, "Behold, he is coming with the clouds, and every eye will see him, even those who pierced him, and all tribes of the earth will wail on account of him. Even so. Amen." This verse is in the form of a prophetic oracle. It combines allusions to Daniel 7:13 and Zechariah 12:10.[58] As we have seen in our examination of the Gospels, Jesus frequently alluded to the prophecy of Daniel 7:13–14, indicating that it would be fulfilled imminently (e.g., Matt. 10:23; 16:28; 24:30, 44). It is important to remember that in its context, Daniel 7:13–14 is not a prophecy of the second coming of Jesus from heaven to earth. It is a prophecy of his coming to the Ancient of Days in heaven to receive his kingdom. In Daniel 7, Christ's reception of his kingdom is closely associated with the judgment of the fourth beast Daniel saw arise from the sea. This is the first prophecy to which John alludes in Revelation 1:7.

The second prophecy to which John alludes in this verse is Zechariah 12:10. This verse occurs in the context of an oracle that prophesies the coming of Israel's Messiah (Zech. 12:1–14:21). We recall that this oracle is somewhat unusual. In the first part of the oracle, Zechariah describes a siege of Jerusalem from which Israel is rescued by the divine warrior (Zech. 12:8–9). In the second part of the oracle, Zechariah describes a siege in which the city is taken (14:1–2). In connection with the first siege, the people of Israel mourn because they have killed someone and are overcome by grief (Zech. 12:10–13:1). This death, however, leads to salvation for the people. This prophecy was fulfilled with the crucifixion of Jesus. It is possible, as we have seen, that Zechariah spoke of two separate events. One

56. Beasley-Murray 1978, 57; Bauckham 2001, 1290.

57. Beale 1999, 193–94.

58. Bauckham (2001, 1290) also sees an allusion to Genesis 12:3 in the phrase "all tribes of the earth."

definitely had to do with events associated with Christ's death. It is possible that the other has to do with events associated with either the first-century judgment on Jerusalem or events associated with Christ's second coming. Texts such as Zechariah 14:8 point toward the latter interpretation. If this is correct, then John's oracle in Revelation 1:7 encompasses everything from the crucifixion to the new heavens and new earth.

John's prologue concludes with a declaration by God, "'I am the Alpha and the Omega,' says the Lord God, 'who is and who was and who is to come, the Almighty'" (1:8). This is one of only two places in the book of Revelation where God himself speaks (see also 21:5–8). The words are an echo of Isaiah 44:6 and 48:12, texts which speak of God's uniqueness as the Creator who is before all things and who will bring all things to their planned end.[59] It is significant also that the same language is used by John elsewhere in Revelation to describe Jesus. He too is said to be the Alpha and the Omega in 22:13.[60]

Opening Vision of Christ and Messages to Seven Churches (Rev. 1:9–3:22)

The main body of the book of Revelation begins with John's vision of the exalted Christ and his commission to write what he has seen and send it to the seven churches (1:9–20). John's commission is very similar to Old Testament descriptions of the calling of several of the prophets, indicating that like them, he too is a prophet of God (Isa. 6; Jer. 1; Ezek. 1–3).[61] John received his vision while on the island of Patmos (Rev. 1:9b), which was off the west coast of Asia Minor. He describes himself as already participating with his readers in "the tribulation and the kingdom" (v. 9a). As we have seen, the two are not mutually exclusive during the present age.

John says, "I was in the Spirit on the Lord's day" (v. 10a). This language is reminiscent of the language Ezekiel uses a number of times to describe his experiences with God (Ezek. 2:2; 3:12, 14, 24; 11:1; 43:5). John then hears a voice commanding him to "Write" (v. 11). This too is comparable to what happened to Old Testament prophets (Ex. 17:14; Isa. 30:8; Jer. 36:28). By writing down what he sees, the book is preserved as a witness

59. Bauckham 2001, 1290.

60. Compare Rev. 1:8 (describing God), 1:17 (describing Jesus), 21:6 (describing God), and 22:13 (describing Jesus).

61. Osborne 2002, 78.

to the truth of God's word. The voice also commands John to send that which he writes to the Asian churches of Ephesus, Smyrna, Pergamum, Thyatira, Sardis, Philadelphia, and Laodicea (Rev. 1:11).

When John turns to see who is speaking to him, he sees one like a Son of Man standing in the midst of seven lampstands (1:12–13). The description of Christ found in verses 13–16 is mostly indebted to Daniel's description of the Ancient of Days (Dan. 7:9), but John borrows other Old Testament images as well. The long robe and the golden sash (Rev. 1:13) remind the reader of the robe and sash worn by the high priest (Ex. 28:4; 39:29). His white hair and blazing eyes (Rev. 1:14) remind the reader of Daniel's vision of God (Dan. 7:9) and of the mighty angel (Dan. 10:6). The remaining descriptions in Revelation 1:15–16 contain other Old Testament allusions and echoes: bronze feet (Ezek. 1:7; Dan. 10:6), a powerful voice (Ezek. 1:24; 43:2), and a sword coming from his mouth (Isa. 11:4; 49:2). Through the use of this Old Testament imagery "Christ is portrayed as the eschatological heavenly priest, end-time ruler, and judge."[62]

Upon seeing the exalted Christ in his glory, John falls at his feet as though dead (Rev. 1:17). This is a common reaction to such encounters (Josh. 5:14; Ezek. 1:28; Dan. 8:17–18; 10:7–9; Matt. 17:6; John 18:6). Jesus declares to John that he is "the first and the last" (Rev. 1:17). He is also "alive forevermore" and has "the keys of Death and Hades" (v. 18). Beasley-Murray observes that "this is an assertion of authority such as God alone possesses."[63] Jesus then commands John in verse 19: "Write therefore the things that you have seen, those that are and those that are to take place after this" (Gk. *genesthai meta tauta*). Some argue that this verse provides a clue to the outline of the book, with chapter 1 corresponding to the things John has seen, chapters 2 and 3 corresponding to the things that are, and chapters 4 through 22 corresponding with the things that are to take place after this.[64] In Revelation 4:1, Christ tells John that he will show him what must "take place after this" (Gk. *genesthai meta tauta*), lending weight to this view.[65] However, even if chapters 4–22 are largely concerned with events that were still to come when John wrote, the argument should not be pressed too far. There are things referred

62. Beale 1999, 206.

63. Beasley-Murray 1978, 68.

64. E.g., Walvoord 1966, 48.

65. The words are the same as those used in Rev. 1:19.

to in chapters 4–22 that were already past at the time John wrote (e.g., Rev. 12:5).

After explaining the meaning of the seven stars and the seven lampstands (1:20), Jesus gives John seven messages, each addressed to one of the seven churches mentioned in 1:11. The inclusion of such specific messages, or letters, within the context of a prophecy is not without precedent in Scripture. The prophetic book of Jeremiah, for example, contains a lengthy letter to the exiles (Jer. 29:1–23). John's seven messages, however, share more similarities with Old Testament oracles than with first-century epistles. They are similar in some ways to the seven oracles in Amos 1–2.[66] It is important that these messages or oracles are addressed to seven real historical churches in Asia Minor. This indicates that John's prophecy had specific relevance to their situation.[67] This prophecy is intended to prepare these churches for the things that must soon take place (Rev. 1:1).

Each of the seven messages follows a basic pattern with minimal variation. Each contains (1) a greeting, (2) a description of Christ, (3) a section beginning with the words "I know" that praises what the church has done well (missing in the letter to Laodicea), (4) a criticism of the church (missing in the letters to Smyrna and Philadelphia), (5) a warning, (6) an exhortation beginning with the words "He who has an ear," (7) and a promise. As Leon Morris observes, the order of (6) and (7) is reversed in the final four letters.[68]

The first message is addressed to the church in Ephesus (Rev. 2:1–7). This city was the most powerful city in the region of Asia Minor at the time. It was probably most well known for its enormous temple to Artemis, one of the seven wonders of the ancient world.[69] Ephesus was also a strong supporter of the imperial cult.[70] S. R. F. Price lists a number of imperial temples that were built in the city in the first century, including one honoring both Roma and Julius Caesar and two honoring Augustus.[71] Such paganism surrounded the Christians in the city. The church at Ephesus is praised for its patience and endurance and for its testing of those who claim

66. Bauckham 2001, 1291; Beasley-Murray 1978, 22.
67. Beasley-Murray 1978, 13.
68. Morris 1987, 58.
69. Witherington 2003, 95.
70. Osborne 2002, 109.
71. Price 1984, 254–56; see also Friesen 2001, 26–28, 95–101.

to be apostles, but it is criticized for abandoning its first love. Jesus exhorts the church to repent and do the things they did in the beginning.

Christ's second message is addressed to the church in Smyrna (2:8–11). Smyrna appears to have been the first city in Asia to have built a temple to the goddess Roma, and as Grant Osborne notes, "in A.D. 26, because of its long loyalty to Rome, it beat out ten other cities for the privilege of building a temple to the emperor Tiberius."[72] To the church in Smyrna, Christ declares, "I know your tribulation and your poverty (but you are rich) and the slander of those who say that they are Jews and are not, but are a synagogue of Satan" (v. 9). This description of the slanderers, which is very similar to something Paul writes in Romans 2:28–29, is almost certainly a reference to unbelieving Jews who are persecuting the church.[73] Jesus does not find anything to criticize in the church at Smyrna. Instead he warns them of coming persecution and encourages them to remain steadfast in the faith even unto death.

The third church addressed by Jesus is the church at Pergamum (Rev. 2:12–17). Like Ephesus and Smyrna, Pergamum was filled with representatives of pagan religion. In addition to temples honoring Rome and the emperor, there were temples to Zeus, Athena, Dionysus, and Asklepios.[74] Jesus refers to Pergamum as the place "where Satan's throne is" (v. 13). This may be a reference to the large altar to Zeus at the top of the city's acropolis, an altar that was visible for miles.[75] On the other hand, it may be a reference to the imperial cult and the worship of the emperor of Rome, since the city was the location of the first temple to the deified Augustus.[76] The church is praised for persevering under the threat of persecution, but the church is also criticized for tolerating false teachers who promote compromise with paganism. Jesus exhorts the church to repent.

The fourth message of Jesus is addressed to the church in Thyatira (2:18–29). This small commercial town was the least significant of the seven cities mentioned in Revelation 2–3.[77] Robert Mounce helpfully summarizes the message to this small church: "Christ commends the church at Thyatira for

72. Osborne 2002, 127.

73. As we have seen, the existence of strong Jewish persecution of the church points toward a date before the destruction of Jerusalem and the temple in A.D. 70.

74. Osborne 2002, 139.

75. Witherington 2003, 102.

76. Aune 1997, 194; Ladd 1972, 46.

77. Osborne 2002, 151.

their life of active service but holds against them the fact that they tolerate the prophetess Jezebel whose influence has led them into an unholy alliance with the doctrine and practice of their pagan neighbors."[78]

The church at Sardis is the fifth church to whom Jesus addresses a message in these first chapters of Revelation (3:1–6). Like the other cities we have looked at, Sardis promoted the imperial cult. As an example, the city, "in commemoration of the coming of age of Gaius Caesar, Augustus' son, decreed a festival and the consecration of a cult statue to Gaius Caesar in Augustus' temple."[79] The church at Sardis is criticized by Christ for being at the point of death. He exhorts the church to wake up and repent.

Christ's sixth message is addressed to the church at Philadelphia (3:7–13). As with the message to the church in Smyrna, this message contains no criticism. The church is praised for keeping God's word and not denying the name of Christ. Within this message, there is also another reference to those who say they are Jews and who are not (v. 9). The church, then, was experiencing pressure not only from its pagan surroundings, but persecution from unbelieving Jews as well. Jesus promises to keep these believers from a coming hour of trial (v. 10). This is probably in reference to the specific judgment described in Revelation as opposed to the general tribulation that is characteristic of the entire present age of conflict between the reigning messianic King and the serpent.

The final message is addressed to the church at Laodicea (3:14–22). This church is in precisely the opposite spiritual condition of the church at Philadelphia. Christ had no criticism for the Philadelphian church. He has nothing but criticism for the Laodicean church. This church is neither cold nor hot, but is instead lukewarm (vv. 15–16). This church thinks it is rich, but it is instead "wretched, pitiable, poor, blind, and naked" (v. 17). The self-confidence of the Laodiceans has deluded them. Christ calls upon this endangered church to be zealous and repent lest they should experience God's wrath.

Opening Vision of Heaven (Rev. 4:1–5:14)

John states, after hearing Christ's messages to the seven churches, "I looked, and behold, a door standing open in heaven! And the first voice,

78. Mounce 1998, 84.
79. Price 1984, 66.

which I had heard speaking to me like a trumpet, said, 'Come up here, and I will show you what must take place after this'" (4:1). John is then taken up in the Spirit and sees God seated on his throne in heaven (v. 2). This vision, as Osborne explains, "dominates the next two chapters, indeed the rest of the book."[80] The vision of heaven in Revelation 4–5 depicts the fulfillment of the prophecy of Daniel 7. It depicts the reign of the Messiah and his people. That Revelation 4–5 fulfills Daniel 7 is evident from the many parallels between the two texts:[81]

1. Introductory vision phraseology (Rev. 4:1; Dan. 7:9).
2. A throne(s) set in heaven (Rev. 4:2, 4; Dan. 7:9).
3. God sitting on a throne (Rev. 4:2; Dan. 7:9).
4. God's appearance on the throne (Rev. 4:3; Dan. 7:9).
5. Fire before the throne (Rev. 4:5; Dan. 7:9–10).
6. Heavenly servants surrounding the throne (Rev. 4:4; Dan. 7:10).
7. Book(s) before the throne (Rev. 5:1–5; Dan. 7:10).
8. The seer's emotional distress (Rev. 5:4; Dan. 7:15).
9. Messianic figure approaching the throne (Rev. 5:6–7; Dan. 7:13–14).
10. The book(s) opened (Rev. 5:9; Dan. 7:10).
11. The kingdom's scope is all peoples, nations, and tongues (Rev. 5:9; Dan. 7:14).
12. The saints given divine authority to reign (Rev. 5:10; Dan. 7:18, 22).
13. Concluding mention of God's eternal reign (Rev. 5:13–14; Dan. 7:27).

Daniel 7 is a vision of Christ's reception of the kingdom, and this has been fulfilled. Christ's reign has already been inaugurated (Rev. 5:9–10; 1:5). His death and resurrection has already made his people into a kingdom of priests.[82] Daniel 7 is also a vision of the judgment of earthly kingdoms. Revelation 4–5, then, sets the stage for the judgments that are prophesied in the following chapters.

80. Osborne 2002, 220.
81. See Wilson 2007, 71; Beale 1999, 314–15.
82. Beale 1999, 312.

The vision of God's throne in chapter 4 depicts the absolute sovereignty of God. His authority is already acknowledged in heaven, and in the end it will be acknowledged on earth as well.[83] In the context of the first-century Roman Empire, the statement that true authority rests with the throne of God in heaven and not with the throne of the emperor in Rome was a distinctly political statement.[84] What John is clearly affirming is that Jesus is the true Lord and Caesar is not. Christ's description of what he is about to do as things that "must" take place demonstrates that God is the true authority. Everything that happens is according to his sovereign plan.

John's vision of the throne shares much in common with Daniel 7, but there are also allusions to Ezekiel 1 and Isaiah 6. Around the throne, John sees twenty-four thrones, and on the thrones, twenty-four elders (Rev. 4:4). The identity of these twenty-four elders has been much disputed. According to some, they represent Old Testament saints, corresponding to the "elders" of Hebrews 11:2.[85] According to others, they are the sum of the twelve tribes of Israel and the twelve apostles and represent the redeemed saints, the new people of God.[86] The most common interpretation, however, is that these elders are some kind of angelic heavenly beings (Isa. 24:23).[87] As Osborne explains, there is a clear differentiation between the function of the elders and the function of the saints in the book of Revelation (5:8; 7:13–14; 11:18; 14:3; 19:4).[88] This last interpretation, then, appears to have the most contextual support.

In addition to the elders, John sees around the throne "four living creatures" (4:6). One is like a lion, one like an ox, one with the face of a man, and one like an eagle (v. 7). They each have six wings and are full of eyes all around and within (v. 8). The description of these creatures is very similar to the description of the cherubim in Ezekiel 1:10 and 10:14 and the seraphim in Isaiah 6:2.[89] The description indicates that the creatures

83. Bauckham 2001, 1292–93.

84. Harrington 1993, 81.

85. Sweet 1979, 118.

86. Clark 1989, 46; Kistemaker 2001, 188.

87. Ladd 1972, 75; Morris 1987, 86; Mounce 1998, 121–22; Beale 1999, 322; Johnson 2001, 100; Osborne 2002, 228–29.

88. Osborne 2002, 229.

89. Aune 1997, 314.

John sees here are the highest order of heavenly beings.[90] They ceaselessly praise God (Rev. 4:8).

John's heavenly vision continues with a vision of the Lamb and the scroll (5:1–14). In the right hand of God, John sees a scroll with writing on the front and back and sealed with seven seals (v. 1). The identification of John's scroll is disputed. Osborne notes that there are at least six suggestions concerning its identity: (1) the Lamb's book of life; (2) the Old Testament Torah; (3) a last will and testament; (4) a divorce bill; (5) a contract deed; and (6) a heavenly book containing God's redemptive plan.[91] The features of the scroll itself, with seals and with writing on the front and back, are very similar to the features of ancient Jewish and Roman contract deeds, but this in itself does not identify the content of the scroll. The scroll contains God's redemptive plan for the establishment of his kingdom on earth.[92] The correspondences between this vision and Ezekiel 2:9–10 indicate that part of that plan includes the imminent judgment of Jerusalem.[93]

When no one in heaven is found worthy to open the scroll, John weeps loudly (Rev. 5:2–4). Then one of the elders says, "Weep no more; behold, the Lion of the tribe of Judah, the Root of David, has conquered, so that he can open the scroll and its seven seals" (v. 5). These descriptions are allusions to prophecies in Genesis 49:9 and Isaiah 11:10, prophecies of a Messiah who would conquer Israel's enemies.[94] When John looks to see this conquering Lion, he sees "a Lamb standing, as though it had been slain" (Rev. 5:6b). The description of this figure as a Lamb is likely an allusion to both the Passover lamb (Ex. 12:1–6) and to Isaiah's Suffering Servant (Isa. 53:7). Bauckham explains the fundamental idea revealed in these verses:

> The key point to be noticed is that, in the contrast between what is said to John (5:5) and what he sees (5:6), he first evokes the idea of the Messiah as the Jewish nationalistic military conqueror and then reinterprets it by means of the notion of sacrificial death for the redemption of people from all nations (cf. 5:9–10). The juxtaposition of the contrasting images of the Lion

90. Osborne 2002, 235.
91. Osborne 2002, 248–49.
92. Bauckham 1993a, 249; Aune 1997, 374; Osborne 2002, 249.
93. Ezekiel's prophecy concerned the judgment of Jerusalem as well as future restoration.
94. Beale 1999, 349.

> and the Lamb expresses John's Jewish Christian reinterpretation of current Jewish eschatological hopes.[95]

When John looks at the Lion, what he sees is a slain Lamb. This reveals that it is through his death on the cross that Christ won the decisive victory over the enemies of God and his people.[96]

The Lamb approaches the throne of God and takes the seven-sealed scroll (Rev. 5:7). When he does this, the four living creatures and the twenty-four elders fall down before the Lamb and worship him (v. 8).[97] They declare that the Lamb is worthy for he was slain and by his blood he ransomed people for God "from every tribe and language and people and nation" (v. 9). This is the first of seven instances in Revelation where John uses a fourfold formula to describe the nations (7:9; 10:11; 11:9; 13:7; 14:6; 17:15). In this case, we see the ultimate fulfillment of God's promise to bless all the nations (Gen. 12:3). In the song of praise, these nations are said to have been made into "a kingdom and priests to our God" (Rev. 5:10; Ex. 19:6). Here again, John is indicating that the prophesied new exodus has been and is being fulfilled through Jesus Christ.

The Seven Seals (Rev. 6:1–8:5)

Beginning in chapter 6, the book of Revelation describes a series of progressively intensifying judgments associated with the breaking of the seals on the scroll and the opening of the scroll itself. There are a series of judgments associated with the seven seals, with seven trumpets, and with seven bowls. This series of intensifying sevenfold judgments appears to be in fulfillment of the warnings found in Leviticus 26. In this chapter of Leviticus, God is describing the blessings that will come to Israel if she remains faithful to the covenant and the curses that will come if she is unfaithful. After describing some of the judgments that will be the result of unfaithfulness, God declares, "And if in spite of this you will not listen to me, then I will discipline you again sevenfold for your sins" (Lev. 26:18). If Israel remains unfaithful in spite of these chastisements, God warns that he will strike them sevenfold again and again (vv. 21, 24, 28). In the series

95. Bauckham 1993a, 214.

96. Ladd 1972, 84; Bauckham 1993b, 73; Beale 1999, 351.

97. In verse 9, it is said that they sing a "new song." This phrase is common in the Psalms (Pss. 33:3; 40:3; 96:1; 98:1; 144:9; 149:1).

of sevenfold judgments associated with the seals, trumpets, and bowls, we appear to be witnessing that which is threatened in Leviticus.

One of the most difficult structural problems in the book of Revelation concerns the relationship among the seal, trumpet, and bowl judgments of chapters 6–16. Although somewhat oversimplified, there are basically four main views.[98] Some see the three series of judgments as completely parallel, with each series covering the exact same period of time. Others see the judgments as chronologically sequential, each judgment following the last. Some see partial recapitulation in the three series, with each series beginning closer to the end. Finally, some see the judgments telescoping, with the seventh seal containing all of the trumpet judgments, and the seventh trumpet containing all of the bowl judgments.[99]

There are several lines of evidence in support of the idea that these chapters picture a chronological sequence of judgments. In Revelation 8:1–2, for example, there is a clear impression that the judgments associated with the trumpets follow the completion of the judgments associated with the seals. The scroll cannot even be opened until all of the seals are removed.[100] In 15:1, the seven bowl judgments are distinguished from the seal and trumpet judgments in that they are described as the "last" judgments, for with them the wrath of God "is finished." If these series of sevenfold judgments are a fulfillment of what God threatened in Leviticus 26, this also lends weight to a sequential interpretation since Leviticus 26 describes God as repeatedly sending one sevenfold judgment followed by another if the preceding one does not result in repentance.

There is also strong evidence, however, in favor of some kind of recapitulation. One of the strongest pieces of evidence is the fact that each series of judgments ends with a similar description of thunder, lightning, and an earthquake (Rev. 8:5; 11:19; 16:18–21). There are also parallels between the objects of God's judgment in the first four trumpet judgments and the first four bowl judgments (8:7–12; 16:2–9). Furthermore, the fact that John sees the visions in a certain sequence does not necessarily mean that the judgments represented by the visions must occur in the same sequence. Following his vision of the seventh trumpet (11:15–19), for example, John

98. It is important to realize that there are variations among adherents of each of the four basic views. The number of variations complicates the discussion tremendously.

99. See Beale 1999, 116–51, for a good discussion of the various views.

100. Osborne 2002, 269.

sees a vision symbolizing the birth of Christ (12:5), but the event or events symbolized by the seventh trumpet did not precede the birth of Christ. As we shall see in our examination of the text itself, there appears to be chronological sequence in some places, but not in all.

The judgments associated with the opening of the first four seals in Revelation 6 appear to be the same judgments described by Jesus in the first part of his Olivet Discourse (Matt. 24:4–10).[101] In both cases, there is a description of wars, international strife, famine, persecution, and death. As we have seen, this section of the Olivet Discourse deals with judgments that would characterize the entire time between the first advent and the end of history in broad general terms. The judgments associated with the first four seals appear to describe the same judgments.

With the breaking of each of the first four seals, John witnesses the appearance of riders on various colored horses who bring judgments of war, famine, and death (Rev. 6:1–8; Jer. 14:12; Ezek. 5:12, 17; 14:21). The basic imagery of the vision is derived from Zechariah's prophecy involving riders (Zech. 1:7–11; 6:1–8). The first horse John sees is a white horse, and its rider wears a crown and comes out conquering (Rev. 6:1–2). Some see this horse and rider as a symbol of Christ sending forth his gospel throughout the world.[102] If this is the meaning of the first rider, then this vision corresponds with Matthew 24:14, which foresees the proclamation of the gospel throughout the whole world. Others argue that the association of the first rider with the following three indicates that he symbolizes the destructive forces of conquest.[103] In the first century, this was manifested through the power of Rome's armies, but the suffering associated with conquest has continued beyond the first century.

The second rider (Rev. 6:3–4) symbolizes war and corresponds with Matthew 24:6. J. Massyngberde Ford observes that during the reign of Claudius (A.D. 41–54) wars broke out in Britain, Germany, Armenia, and Parthia. She adds: "In the year 66 the Jewish War occurred. The period following Nero's death, A.D. 69 saw three emperors, Otho, Galba, and Vitellius, quickly succeeding each other and civil upheavals shaking the empire to its foundations."[104] Wars have continued almost without end to

101. Keener 2000, 200; Beasley-Murray 1978, 130.

102. Ladd 1972, 99; Kistemaker 2001, 224.

103. Poythress 2000b; Johnson 2001, 119–20; Osborne 2002, 277.

104. Ford 1975, 106.

the present. The point is simply that the fulfillment of this prophecy cannot be relegated wholly to some unspecified future time. Wars are a feature of the entire present age prior to the return of Christ.

The third and fourth riders (Rev. 6:5–8) symbolize famine and death respectively. Like war, famine has existed throughout human history, including the first century. Ford notes, "During Claudius' reign famine occurred in Rome in A.D. 42, and food shortage was reported in Judea in 45–46, in Greece in 49, and in Rome in 51."[105] Josephus reports terrible famine associated with the siege of Jerusalem by the Roman armies.[106] So famine as well cannot be relegated completely to the future. The rider of the fourth horse is death, and Hades follows him (6:8). This is the first appearance in the book of these enemies of God. Ultimately they will be destroyed along with all of God's enemies (20:14).[107]

With the opening of the fifth seal, John sees "under the altar the souls of those who had been slain for the word of God and for the witness they had borne" (6:9). If Revelation was written during or just after the persecution initiated by Nero in A.D. 64, then it is very possible that John is speaking here of those believers martyred under this tyrant. They cry out to God, asking how long it will be before they are avenged (v. 10; cf. Deut. 32:43; Ps. 79:10). They are told to wait until the number of those who would be killed as they had been killed is complete (Rev. 6:11).

When the sixth seal is opened, John sees "a great earthquake, and the sun became black as sackcloth, the full moon became like blood, and the stars of the sky fell to the earth as the fig tree sheds its winter fruit when shaken by a gale. The sky vanished like a scroll that is being rolled up, and every mountain and island was removed from its place" (6:12–14). Many argue that the cosmic events described in these verses are events associated with the second coming and final judgment.[108] But as we have seen, in the Old Testament such language does not necessarily, or even usually, refer

105. Ford 1975, 107.

106. Josephus, *J.W.* 5.10.3 §§429–30; 5.12.3 §§512–13.

107. Bauckham (1993a, 20) observes that the enemies of God are destroyed in the reverse order of their appearance in the book of Revelation. They appear in the following order: Death and Hades (6:8); the dragon (12:3); the beast and the false prophet (13:1, 11); and Babylon (17:5). They are destroyed in reverse order: Babylon (18); the beast and the false prophet (19:20); the dragon (20:2, 10); Death and Hades (20:14).

108. E.g., Poythress 2000b, 117; Beale 1999, 395–96.

to the end of the space-time universe.[109] The prophets regularly use such metaphorical language to describe judgments that have already occurred without involving the literal end of the world. Such language was used to describe the judgments of Babylon (Isa. 13:1, 10, 19), Egypt (Ezek. 32:2, 7–8, 16, 18), Idumea (Isa. 34:3–5), and Judah (Jer. 4:14, 23–24).

John says that when these things occurred, men everywhere "hid themselves in the caves and among the rocks of the mountains, calling to the mountains and rocks, 'Fall on us and hide us from the face of him who is seated on the throne, and from the wrath of the Lamb, for the great day of their wrath has come, and who can stand?'" (Rev. 6:15b–17). This language is also common in the Old Testament prophetic books. In Isaiah 2:6–4:1, for example, the prophet describes the judgment of God that is coming upon Judah. In this prophecy, Isaiah describes the reaction of the people of Judah to the coming judgment in the same way that John describes human reaction to God's judgment in Revelation 6:15–17 (Isa. 2:18–22).[110] The point is simply that John could very easily be describing a judgment or judgments other than the final judgment.

The opening of the seven seals is interrupted briefly in chapter 7. John sees four angels holding back the four winds of the earth (7:1). The four winds probably refer to the four horsemen of 6:1–8 (Zech. 6:5).[111] John then sees another angel with the seal of God who calls out to the four angels who had been given power to harm the earth and the sea (Rev. 7:2). He tells the four angels not to harm the earth or the sea until the servants of God have been sealed on their forehead (v. 3). The Old Testament background for this imagery is Ezekiel 9:4–6 where faithful Israelites are protected from the Lord's judgment. John hears a voice indicating that the number of those sealed is 144,000, and that 12,000 are sealed from each of the twelve tribes of Israel (Rev. 7:4–8).

The description of the number sealed from each tribe is in the form of a census. As Bauckham observes, "In the Old Testament a census is always a counting up of the *military* strength of the nation."[112] Revelation 7:1–8, then, depicts these 144,000 as a messianic army. But who are these 144,000,

109. Caird 1980, 256; Sweet 1979, 58.

110. The statement of the wicked in Rev. 6:17 is also paralleled in other prophetic books dealing with past historical judgments (Joel 2:11; Nah. 1:6).

111. Morris 1987, 110; Beale 1999, 406.

112. Bauckham 1993a, 217; see also Osborne 2002, 313.

and are they the same as the group described in 7:9–17?[113] Some argue that the 144,000 represent the church as the new Israel.[114] Others argue that the 144,000 are Jewish believers in Christ, who are protected by God from the judgment that is about to fall on Israel.[115] The distinction John makes between those "from every tribe of the sons of Israel" (v. 4) and those "from every nation, from all tribes and peoples and languages" (v. 9) as well as the distinction he makes between the number 144,000 (v. 4) and "a great multitude that no one could number" (v. 9) indicates that the first group is smaller and more specific than the second group. This lends weight to the idea that the 144,000 represent believing Jews.

After his vision of the 144,000, John sees a great, innumerable multitude from every tribe and tongue and nation (7:9). This multitude stands before the throne of God and along with the angels worship him (vv. 9–12). The major interpretive difficulty here concerns the relationship between this multitude and the 144,000 of verses 1–8. Are they the same? Those who argue that the 144,000 represent the church as the true Israel tend to suggest that the two groups are the same.[116] If the 144,000 are believing Jews, as I have suggested, then the innumerable multitude is representative of the entire church from every nation. There is also a chronological difference between the two groups. The 144,000 are seen just before the onset of judgment. The innumerable multitude is seen in a situation following all judgment.[117] The descriptions of this multitude in verses 15–17 are similar to John's descriptions of conditions in the new heavens and new earth in chapters 21–22, indicating that John is seeing here a glimpse of something beyond the final judgment.[118]

Revelation 8:1–5 describes John's vision of the opening of the seventh seal of the scroll. When the Lamb opens the seventh seal, there is silence in heaven for about half an hour (v. 1). In the Old Testament, such silence is sometimes associated with coming divine judgment (Hab. 2:20; Zech. 2:13).[119]

113. See Aune 1998a, 440–45, for a full discussion of the different interpretations.

114. E.g., Morris 1987, 112; Mounce 1998, 158.

115. E.g., Adams 1966, 65; Clark 1989, 60; Gentry 1998, 56–57.

116. E.g., Ladd 1972, 116; Beale 1999, 424; Osborne 2002, 316.

117. See Osborne 2002, 303; Beale 1999, 405–6.

118. This alone does not prove that the two groups are different, since John could see a vision of the saints at different points of time within redemptive history and even beyond it, but combined with the other differences, it may lend some weight to the idea that the two are different groups.

119. Beale 1999, 445–46.

It certainly has that connotation here. John then sees seven angels who are given seven trumpets (Rev. 8:2).[120] George Caird suggests that John borrows the trumpet imagery from Joshua's account of the fall of Jericho (Josh. 6). In that account, after marching around the city seven times, seven priests blow seven trumpets and the wall of Jericho falls (Josh. 6:4–5). In Revelation, the trumpets are associated primarily with the judgment of Jerusalem.

John sees the angel take a censer filled with incense and the prayers of the saints and throw it to earth (Rev. 8:5a). The point seems to be that God uses the prayers of the saints in the outworking of his redemptive plan. When the prayers are thrown to earth, there are "peals of thunder, rumblings, flashes of lightning, and an earthquake" (v. 5b). Some argue that because each series of seven judgments ends with a description of thunder, lightning, and an earthquake, the three series must therefore end at the same time—the final judgment.[121] The clue to the actual meaning of the thunder, lightning, and earthquake, however, can be found in Revelation 4:5. These phenomena are associated with theophanies. They trace their origin to the description of God's coming to Mount Sinai (Ex. 19:16). The descriptions of the phenomena are the same because God is the same. The phenomena described in Revelation 8:5; 11:19; and 16:18–21 do not imply the end of history any more than the phenomena described in Exodus 19:16 implied the end of history.[122]

The Seven Trumpets (Rev. 8:6–11:19)

The judgments associated with the first four trumpets are similar in nature to the judgments associated with the Egyptian plagues (Ex. 7–10).

120. In the Jewish apocalyptic tradition, there were seven angels who presented the prayers of the saints before God's throne (Tobit 12:15). Their names are given in *1 Enoch* 20:2–8 as Uriel, Raphael, Raguel, Michael, Saraqa'el, Gabriel, and Remiel (see Osborne 2002, 342).

121. E.g., Witherington 2003, 130; Beale 1999, 459.

122. Josephus's description of the siege of Jerusalem contains the following noteworthy remarks: "For there broke out a prodigious storm in the night, with the utmost violence, and very strong winds, with the largest showers of rain, with continual lightnings, terrible thunderings, and amazing concussions and bellowing of the earth, that was in an earthquake. These things were a manifest indication that some destruction was coming upon men, when the system of the world was put into this disorder, and anyone would guess that these wonders foreshowed some grand calamities that were coming" (*J.W.* 4.4.5 §§286–87). I should make it clear that I am not suggesting that what Josephus describes was *the* fulfillment of Revelation 8:5. I note his description to point out that such language could be understood not only in a metaphorical sense, but also in a more literal sense, and it could be associated with events that were not connected to the end of the world.

This again reflects the theme of the new exodus found in the book of Revelation. Just as the first exodus was associated with plagues, so too is the eschatological exodus.[123] Israel now stands in the position of Egypt, a nation that was once one of her enemies, and like that ancient enemy nation, Israel will be judged. When the first angel sounds his trumpet, there follow "hail and fire, mixed with blood, and these were thrown upon the earth" (Rev. 8:7a). This judgment unleashed by the first trumpet is similar to the Egyptian plague described in Exodus 9:22–25 (see also Joel 2:30–31). As a result of the first trumpet judgment, "a third of the earth was burned up, and a third of the trees were burned up, and all green grass was burned up" (Rev. 8:7b). This description of the destruction wrought echoes the language of Ezekiel 5:2 and 12 where the prophet speaks of the first destruction of Jerusalem. John here uses similar language to describe the second destruction of Jerusalem.[124]

The judgments associated with the second and third trumpets (Rev. 8:8–11) are similar to the plague described in Exodus 7:20–25. In both cases, the waters are affected.[125] When the fourth angel sounds his trumpet, "a third of the sun was struck, and a third of the moon, and a third of the stars, so that a third of their light might be darkened" (Rev. 8:12). This judgment is similar in some ways to the plague of darkness described in Exodus 10:21–23. The language is closer, however, to Old Testament prophetic descriptions of the day of the Lord (Amos 5:20; 8:9; Joel 2:2; Zeph. 1:15). After the fourth trumpet, John sees an eagle crying out "Woe" to those who dwell on earth (Rev. 8:13). In doing so the eagle identifies the final three trumpets as "woe oracles" (Isa. 5:8–9; Amos 6:1–2; Hab. 2:9–10).[126]

Revelation 9:1–11 describes the judgment associated with the fifth trumpet. John sees "a star fallen from heaven to earth, and he is given the key to the shaft of the bottomless pit" (9:1). When he opens the pit, smoke ascends followed by monstrous locusts (vv. 2–3, 7–10). The locusts tor-

123. Caird 1966, 115.

124. It may also be worth noting that in Josephus's description of the destruction wrought by the Roman armies as they laid siege to Jerusalem, he says that they "cut down all the trees . . . for ninety furlongs round about" Jerusalem (*J.W.* 6.1.1 §5).

125. Josephus describes the result of one of the sea battles between the Romans and the Jews in his account of the Jewish War. He describes the scene of a lake filled with blood and swollen dead bodies (*J.W.* 3.10.9 §§529–30).

126. In the Old Testament, eagles are sometimes connected with judgment oracles (Deut. 28:49; Jer. 4:13; 48:40; 49:22; Lam. 4:19; Ezek. 17:3; Hos. 8:1; Hab. 1:8).

ment those without the seal of God on their forehead (7:3) for five months (9:4–6). These locusts have as their king the angel of the bottomless pit, the one whose name is Abaddon, or Apollyon (v. 11). The angel whom John sees fall to earth is likely Satan (cf. Luke 10:18). He looses a demonic army that is compared to locusts. In the Old Testament, human armies are sometimes compared to locusts, and it would appear that John is using the same analogy, in this case to describe the Roman armies of Vespasian and Titus (Judg. 6:5; 7:12; Joel 1:2–12). It is worth noting that the Roman siege of Jerusalem lasted about five months.[127]

The description of the judgment associated with the sounding of the fifth trumpet is followed by the judgment of the sixth trumpet (Rev. 9:13–21). When the sixth angel sounds his trumpet, John hears a voice telling the sixth angel to release the four angels who are bound at the Euphrates River (vv. 13–14). When they are released, John sees an enormous army of "twice ten thousand times ten thousand" (v. 16). As David Clark observes, it is not certain whether the army described in this vision is another general description of the Roman armies or whether it represents confederate armies who assisted Rome.[128] Ford notes the argument of Giet that this force represents "the four sections of the army of the legate Cestius, which was particularly strong in cavalry and did come from regions near the Euphrates to invade Palestine."[129] In any case, these judgments do not result in repentance (vv. 20–21).

Just as chapter 7 served as an interlude between the opening of the sixth and seventh seals, so too does Revelation 10:1–11:14 serve as an interlude between the sounding of the sixth and seventh trumpets. In chapter 10, John sees an angel coming down from heaven with a little scroll in his hand (vv. 1–2).[130] The angel calls out, and seven thunders sound, but John is not allowed to write what he hears (vv. 3–4). Then the angel raises his right hand to heaven and swears that there will be no more delay, but the mystery of God will be fulfilled just as God had announced to his prophets (vv. 5–7). This passage clearly echoes Daniel 12:7. The implication is that the final period of history predicted in Daniel has now arrived.[131] John is

127. Bruce 1971b, 382.
128. Clark 1989, 68.
129. Ford 1975, 154.
130. As Bauckham (1993a, 243) explains, this is likely the same scroll that is described in 5:1.
131. Bauckham 1993a, 261.

commanded to eat the little scroll that is in the hand of the angel (vv. 8–9). This command echoes the one given to Ezekiel when he was commissioned as a prophet (Ezek. 2:8–3:3). After John eats the scroll, he is told that he must prophesy "about many peoples and nations and languages and kings" (Rev. 10:11).

After being given the scroll, which he is told to eat, John is given a measuring rod and is told to measure the temple of God and the altar and those who worship there (11:1). He is told not to measure the court outside, but to leave it, since it has been given over to the nations. These nations, he is told, will trample the holy city for forty-two months (v. 2). The meaning of every part of this prophecy is disputed. There is disagreement about the significance of the measurement, the identity of the temple, and the meaning of the forty-two months.

In some places in the Old Testament, the measurement of something symbolizes God's ownership and protection (e.g., Ezek. 40:3; Zech. 2:1–5). In other places, however, such measurements symbolize judgment and destruction (e.g., 2 Kings 21:13; Lam. 2:8; Amos 7:7–9).[132] Determining what is symbolized by the measuring is complicated by disagreements concerning the identity of the temple that is measured. R. H. Charles argues that 11:1–2 is a fragment of a Zealot (false) prophecy written before A.D. 70 that predicted the temple would be preserved from destruction by the Roman armies.[133] Dispensationalists tend to argue that this temple is a temple that will be rebuilt prior to the second coming of Christ.[134] Many argue that the temple here symbolizes the true church.[135] Some believe the temple represents the Jewish people, with the inner portion representing believing Jews and the outer court representing unbelieving Jews.[136]

A combination of the last two suggestions appears to be the most likely interpretation. The temple and court that John sees represent the covenant people of God. The inner court represents the church in Jerusalem, which was composed predominantly of Jewish believers. The outer court represents unbelieving Jews and their city. This interpretation is plausible considering

132. Robinson 1976, 241.

133. Charles 1920, 1:274.

134. E.g., Walvoord 1966, 176.

135. E.g., Osborne 2002, 409; Buis 1960, 61; Poythress 2000b, 127; Morris 1987, 140.

136. E.g., Beckwith 1919, 584–90; Pieters 1943, 146; Ladd 1972, 152–53.

that the Bible uses temple imagery elsewhere to symbolize God's people (e.g., 2 Cor. 6:16; Eph. 2:21; Rev. 3:12).

John is told that the nations will trample the city for forty-two months (Rev. 11:2). This apparently symbolic period of time is found several times in the book of Revelation. It is described as "forty-two months" (11:2; 13:5), "1,260 days" (11:3; 12:6), and "a time, and times, and half a time" (12:14). In Daniel, the last phrase was used to speak of an indefinite but limited period of suffering (Dan. 7:25; 12:7). If the three time designations in Revelation are interchangeable, then the forty-two months likely refers to an indefinite but limited period of suffering as well.

Revelation 11:3–16 describes John's vision of two witnesses who are given authority to prophesy for 1,260 days. With imagery borrowed from Zechariah, the witnesses are described as "the two olive trees and the two lampstands that stand before the Lord" (Rev. 11:4; Zech. 4:3, 11–14). Fire pours from their mouth, they have the power to stop the rain, turn the water to blood, and strike the earth with every kind of plague (Rev. 11:5–6). Their power is clearly modeled after Moses and Elijah (Ex. 7:17–20; 1 Kings 17:1; 2 Kings 1:10; see also Jer. 5:14). When the two prophets finish their testimony, they are killed by the beast (Rev. 11:7), and their bodies lie in the streets of "the great city that symbolically is called Sodom and Egypt, where their Lord was crucified" (v. 8). After three and a half days, they are raised from death and ascend into heaven (vv. 9–12). John then sees a great earthquake in which a tenth of the city falls and seven thousand people are killed (v. 13).

As George Eldon Ladd notes, it is difficult to determine whether the two witnesses are intended to be understood as two literal historic persons or as a symbol of the church and its witness.[137] The majority of evangelical commentators understand the two witnesses to be symbolic of the church.[138] Some, on the other hand, think it more likely that they are to be understood as two actual historical persons.[139] The specific description of the location of their death as Jerusalem (11:8) lends weight to the latter interpretation.

137. Ladd 1972, 154.

138. E.g., Swete 1977, 134; Beasley-Murray 1978, 184; Bauckham 1993a, 273; Mounce 1998, 217; Beale 1999, 573; Kistemaker 2001, 329; Johnson 2001, 171.

139. E.g., Ladd 1972, 154.

Although it appears that the two witnesses are two historic persons, there is not enough evidence to identify them with certainty.[140]

Following the interlude of Revelation 10:1–11:14, John sees the result of the seventh trumpet (11:15–19). He hears loud voices in heaven saying, "The kingdom of the world has become the kingdom of our Lord and of his Christ, and he shall reign forever and ever" (v. 15). Then the twenty-four elders fall on their faces and worship God, thanking him for beginning his reign (vv. 16–18). John then sees the temple in heaven opened, accompanied by lightning, thunder, and an earthquake (v. 19). Gregory Beale argues that these verses are a clear description of the final consummation of all things.[141] These kinds of statements, however, are used elsewhere in Scripture to describe events associated with the first advent. In fulfillment of the prophecy of Daniel 7, the events from the resurrection and ascension of Christ to the destruction of Jerusalem mark the inauguration of the kingdom of Jesus Christ (Matt. 28:18; Acts 2:36).

The Conflict of God's People with the Dragon and the Beast (Rev. 12:1–15:4)

Beginning in Revelation 12, John's attention begins to turn from Jerusalem to Rome, the fourth beast of Daniel 7. This is in keeping with the form of many Old Testament prophetic books, which declare judgment upon apostate Israel but also pronounce judgment against the nations. In chapter 12, John sees a vision that depicts in prophetic language the ages-long conflict between Satan and the seed of the woman.[142] John sees an image of a woman in verse 1 that is quite similar to the image Joseph saw in a dream (Gen. 37:9). If John is alluding to this Genesis text, then the woman represents the old covenant people of God, Israel.

John also sees a vision of a great dragon, which symbolizes Satan (Rev. 12:3, 9). The dragon sweeps away "a third of the stars of heaven" (v. 4). This is possibly an allusion to the primordial rebellion of Satan and his angelic

140. Ford (1975, 180) notes the theory of Giet, who believes that John's reference to the two witnesses may be a historical allusion to the two high priests Ananus and Joshua (Jesus), who were murdered in Jerusalem and left unburied (Josephus, *J. W.* 4.4.3–4; 4.5.2 §§236–70; 314–25). Josephus refers to the murder of Ananus as the beginning of the destruction of the city (*J. W.* 4.5.2 §318).

141. Beale 1999, 122.

142. Ladd 1972, 166.

followers.[143] But in light of verses 7–12, it is more likely a description of the defeat of Satan associated with the first advent of the Messiah. John sees the woman give birth to a male child who is caught up to the throne of God (v. 5). Although only his birth and ascension are mentioned, it is clear that the child is the Messiah, the one "who is to rule all the nations with a rod of iron" (v. 5). After the child is caught up, the woman flees into the wilderness and is nourished by God for 1,260 days (v. 6). If 1,260 days (i.e., 42 months of 30 days each) has the same meaning as the "time, times, and half a time," then it too refers to an indefinite but limited period.

In verses 7–9, John backtracks and elaborates further on the content of verse 4, describing in more detail the war in heaven. He sees Satan thrown down to earth, having been defeated by the Messiah and his people (vv. 10–12; Luke 10:18; John 12:31).[144] After being cast down, Satan attempts to destroy the woman, but is unable (Rev. 12:13–16). God protects his people now, just as he did at the time of the exodus (v. 14; Ex. 19:4). When Satan realizes that he cannot defeat the woman, he goes off "to make war on the rest of her offspring" (Rev. 12:17). This is a likely reference to the followers of Christ.

In chapter 13, Satan summons assistance in his war against Christ's people.[145] At the end of chapter 12, John had seen Satan standing on the shore of the sea (v. 17).[146] John now sees "a beast rising out of the sea, with ten horns and seven heads, with ten diadems on its horns and blasphemous names on its heads" (13:1). The beast looks like a leopard, but with the feet of a bear and the mouth of a lion (v. 2a). The dragon gives this beast his power (v. 2b). The imagery here is reminiscent of Daniel's visions of the four beasts from the sea (Dan. 7:1–7). In Daniel, the beasts represented successive world empires. John uses similar imagery to the same effect. The beast he describes symbolizes the Roman Empire.[147]

143. Osborne 2002, 461.

144. Harrington 1993, 133.

145. Beasley-Murray 1978, 206.

146. Some manuscripts read "I stood," indicating that the one on the shore is John, but the context lends support to those manuscripts that read "he stood," referring to the dragon.

147. Charles 1920, 1:345; Swete 1977, 161; Beasley-Murray 1978, 209; Clark 1989, 86; Aune 1998a, 735; Mounce 1998, 246; Friesen 2001, 146. Ford (1975, 220) suggests that the ten horns of the beast may represent the ten Roman provinces of Italy, Achaea, Asia, Syria, Egypt, Africa, Spain, Gaul, Britain, and Germany.

John writes regarding the beast, "One of its heads seemed to have a mortal wound, but its mortal wound was healed" (Rev. 13:3a). This difficult text has been the source of much discussion. Albertus Pieters, in fact, lists ten different interpretations that have been suggested.[148] Part of the difficulty involves the translation of the Greek word *mian*. It can be translated either as a cardinal number ("one") or as an ordinal number ("the first").[149] If it is translated as a cardinal number, then the verse may refer to the survival of the Roman Empire following the death of Nero.[150] If it is translated as an ordinal number, then it more likely refers to the survival of the Roman Empire after the assassination of Julius Caesar in 44 B.C.[151] As David Aune explains, the second occurrence of the pronoun *autou* ("its") refers not to the head, but to the beast. One of the heads is mortally wounded, but it is the beast that is healed.[152]

John says that the beast was worshiped (13:4). This appears to be a clear allusion to the imperial cult, the worship of Rome and its emperors.[153] The beast is given authority for "forty-two months" (v. 5). As we have already seen, this time reference that appears in various forms in Revelation refers to an indefinite but limited period.[154] It describes a limited period of persecution of the church by Rome. The beast is given authority over "every tribe and people and language and nation" (v. 7). This verse emphasizes the extent of the Roman Empire, which stretched from the Atlantic Ocean to the Euphrates River.

Following his vision of the beast rising from the sea, John witnesses another beast rising out of the earth (13:11). This beast "makes the earth and its inhabitants worship the first beast" (v. 12). Some suggest that this second beast is the "asiarch," the high priest of the imperial cult.[155] It is more likely, however, that the second beast represents the imperial priest-

148. Pieters 1943, 219.

149. Wilson 1993, 599–600; Aune 1998a, 736.

150. The suicide of Nero plunged the empire into a year and a half of civil war that almost destroyed it (Sweet 1979, 207; Bauckham 1993a, 442; Harrington 1993, 138).

151. The assassination of Julius Caesar had led to crisis and civil war that was not resolved until the accession of Augustus Caesar (Octavian).

152. Aune 1998a, 736.

153. Aune 1998a, 741; Osborne 2002, 497.

154. If, in this case, it does refer to something more literal, then it is possible that it refers to Nero's persecution of Christians which lasted almost exactly forty-two months (Gentry 1998, 69–70).

155. E.g., Witherington 2003, 184.

hood collectively considered.[156] The imperial priesthood was composed of elite members of each city, and its duty was to promote the imperial cult, the worship of Rome and its emperor.

The second beast causes all people to be marked on the right hand or forehead with the name of the beast or the number of his name (13:16–17). Just as God had sealed his servants (7:3), so Satan seals his. Verse 18, which describes the number of his name, is one of the most discussed and disputed texts in all of Revelation. Here John writes, "This calls for wisdom: let the one who has understanding calculate the number of the beast, for it is the number of a man, and his number is 666." Most contemporary commentators believe that John is making use of *gematria*, adding the numerical value of a word's individual letters.[157] Most believe the number 666 likely represents the name Nero Caesar.[158] When the Greek form of the name (*Nerōn Kaisar*) is transliterated into Hebrew (*qsr nron*), the sum of the numerical value of the letters equals 666.[159]

Some have objected that this solution depends upon a defective spelling of the name in Hebrew.[160] This "defective" spelling of the name is attested, however, in documents dating from this time period.[161] It may also be objected that John's readers would not have been able to understand a *gematria* that was done in Hebrew. It should be recalled, however, that most early Christians were Jewish believers. Paul evangelized Jews and God-fearing Gentiles in the synagogues throughout the empire. John, therefore, likely had those in his audience who had the necessary background to

156. Bauckham 1993a, 446; Beasley-Murray 1978, 216; Aune 1998a, 756; Mounce 1998, 254–55.

157. Keener 2000, 355. For a chart showing the numerical values of the letters of the Hebrew and Greek alphabets, see Wilson 2007, 85.

158. E.g., Charles 1920, 1:367; Robinson 1976, 235–36; Beasley-Murray 1978, 219–20; Giblin 1991, 135; Bauckham 1993a, 387–88; Metzger 1993, 76–77; Wilson 1993, 598; Aune 1998a, 770; Osborne 2002, 521. If the number does represent Nero, this text lends weight to the argument that Revelation was written during or soon after the reign of Nero. There would be little reason for such an emphasis on Nero if the book were written thirty years after his death.

159. There is a textual variant in some manuscripts of Rev. 13:18 in which the number of the beast is said to be 616. Interestingly, if the Latin form of the name ("Nero" rather than the Greek "*Nerōn*") is transliterated into Hebrew, the numerical value of the name Nero Caesar is 616 (Bauckham 1993a, 387).

160. E.g., Kistemaker 2001, 39.

161. Aune 1998a, 770; Bauckham 1993a, 388; Beasley-Murray 1978, 220.

understand what he was doing.[162] When all of these factors are taken into consideration, it seems clear that the number of the beast, 666, represents the Roman emperor Nero.[163]

Revelation 14:1–5 contains a description of John's vision of the Lamb and the 144,000 standing on Mount Zion. These 144,000 sing a new song to the Lord. They are described as those "who have not defiled themselves with women, for they are virgins" (v. 4). Bauckham explains the meaning: "The reference is to the ancient demand for ritual purity in the Lord's army (cf. Deut 23:9–14), which required David's troops to abstain from all sexual relations while on campaign (1 Sam 21:5; 2 Sam 11:9–13)."[164] What John sees here, then, is a vision of the Lord's army, readied for spiritual battle with the forces of the dragon.

After seeing the army of the Lord, John sees three angels who each proclaim a message to those on earth. The first angel calls upon all men everywhere to fear God and worship him (Rev. 14:6–7). The second angel proclaims judgment on Babylon the great (v. 8; Isa. 21:9). As we will see, the term "Babylon the great" is a reference to Rome (1 Peter 5:13; Rev. 18:1–3). The third angel proclaims judgment on all who worship the beast and receive his mark (Rev. 14:9–11). John then states one of the basic themes of Revelation, exhorting his readers to endure in their faith (v. 12). In verses 14–20, we see the results of two possible responses to the proclamation of the angels: salvation (vv. 14–16) or judgment (vv. 17–20). In 15:1–4, John sees a vision of those who conquer the beast and his image. They are described as singing the song of Moses and the song of the Lamb, thereby connecting the redemption accomplished by the Lamb with the new exodus promised by the Old Testament prophets.[165]

The Seven Bowls (Rev. 15:5–16:21)

John has already seen the seven angels with the seven last plagues (15:1). In the next section of the book, John witnesses a vision of the judgments associated with these seven last angels. The judgments associated with the

162. Bauckham (1993a, 388) notes that this way of practicing gematria (Greek → Hebrew) is found in the *Greek Apocalypse of Baruch* (*3 Baruch* 4:3–7; 4:10).

163. It may also be worth noting that a number of ancient writers referred to Nero as a *thērion*, the Greek word meaning "beast" (Aune 1998a, 771).

164. Bauckham 1993a, 231.

165. Bauckham 1993a, 296.

first four bowls are similar in many ways to the judgments associated with the first four trumpets (16:2–8; 8:7–12). The bowl and trumpet judgments, however, are not different perspectives on the same exact judgments. They have the same targets, but the bowl judgments are much more intense than the trumpet judgments. The trumpet judgments affect "one third" of their target. The bowl judgments affect all. In spite of all these judgments, however, the wicked do not repent (16:9).

The fifth bowl is poured out on the throne of the beast, Rome (v. 10), and the kingdom of the beast is plunged into darkness (see also Isa. 8:22). The people, however, refuse to repent of their deeds (Rev. 16:11). The sixth angel pours out his bowl on the river Euphrates and its water is dried up to prepare the way for the kings from the east (v. 12). John may be referring here to the Parthians, who had been in conflict with the Roman Empire off and on since 53 B.C. and had recently defeated the Romans in A.D. 63.[166] John then sees three demonic spirits gather the kings of the whole world together for battle at the place called Armageddon (vv. 13–16).

There have been numerous interpretations of this place called Armageddon. The most natural meaning, as Osborne points out, would be "mountain (*har*) of Megiddo," but there is no mountain of Megiddo—only a city and a plain.[167] Since there is no literal mountain of Megiddo, it appears that John does not intend this reference to be taken absolutely literally. It may simply be a general reference building on the Old Testament associations of Megiddo with warfare (Judg. 4–5, 7; 1 Sam. 31).[168] John is using a variety of Old Testament images to depict the coming judgment of Rome. He does the same with the pouring out of the seventh bowl, which also depicts the judgment of Rome (Rev. 16:17–21).

The Judgment of Babylon the Great (Rev. 17:1–19:10)

In Revelation 17:1–19:10, John elaborates on the seventh bowl judgment against Babylon the great (Rome).[169] As we will see below, there are a large number of linguistic and thematic parallels between this section of the book and 21:9–22:9.[170] The present section deals with the city of Bab-

166. For more on the Parthians and their relationship with Rome, see Aune 1998a, 891–94.

167. Osborne 2002, 594.

168. Osborne 2002, 596.

169. Beasley-Murray 1978, 248; Beale 1999, 847; Osborne 2002, 607.

170. See Wilson (2007, 93–94) for a chart listing the many parallels.

ylon the great, while 21:9–22:9 deals with another city, the new Jerusalem. These chapters portray the destruction of one city and its replacement by the other.[171] Some argue that the Babylon depicted in 17:1–19:10 is Jerusalem.[172] While this interpretation is possible, it is more likely that Babylon symbolizes Rome.[173] John has dealt with the judgment of Jerusalem, but in this latter part of the book, he has turned his attention to the other great persecutor of the church, the pagan empire of Rome.

One of the seven angels who had the seven bowls comes to John telling him that he will be shown the judgment of the great prostitute who is seated on many waters and with whom the kings of the earth have committed sexual immorality (17:1–2). The Old Testament uses the imagery of a prostitute or harlot in several ways. Sometimes, the imagery is applied to Israel in reference to her apostasy (e.g., Isa. 1:21; Jer. 3:1; Ezek. 16:15–22; 23:1–21). At other times, it is applied to pagan cities in reference to their wickedness. Both Tyre (Isa. 23:16–17) and Nineveh (Nahum 3:4), for example, are described as prostitutes. John is using the imagery in this second sense to describe the pagan city of Rome.

The description of the woman and the beast upon which she sits in 17:7–14 is one of the most difficult passages in the book of Revelation. As John marvels at the vision, an angel says, "I will tell you the mystery of the woman, and of the beast with seven heads and ten horns that carries her" (v. 7). The angel tells John that the beast he saw "was, and is not, and is about to rise from the bottomless pit and go to destruction" (v. 8a). The angel then says to John, "This calls for a mind with wisdom: the seven heads are seven mountains on which the woman is seated; they are also seven kings, five of whom have fallen, one is, the other has not yet come, and when he does come he must remain only a little while. As for the beast that was and is not, it is an eighth but it belongs to the seven, and it goes to destruction" (vv. 9–11).

This text is important not only in the context of John's vision, but also because it is potentially relevant to the question of the date of the book.[174]

171. Bauckham 1993a, 4.

172. Ford 1975, 285; Provan 1996, 94; Gentry 1998, 74–79. I was persuaded of this interpretation at one point (Mathison 1999, 153–54), but in light of further study, I am no longer convinced that this is the best interpretation of this passage.

173. Bauckham 1993a, 343; Mounce 1998, 306; Bahnsen 1999, 15; Osborne 2002, 605.

174. Wilson 1993, 599. It is relevant to the date of the book's composition because if the kings can be identified, John's reference to the one who "is" would place the writing of the book within the

In verse 9, the angel says that the seven heads "are seven mountains on which the woman is seated." The reference to Rome as the city built on seven hills was widely used during the first century.[175] It would have been familiar to John's audience. There is no reason, then, to suppose that John meant anything other than Rome by the use of this description.[176]

In verse 10, the angel tells John that the seven heads also symbolize seven kings, "five of whom have fallen, one is, the other has not yet come, and when he does come he must remain only a little while." The identity of these kings has been the source of endless debate. Part of the difficulty is due to the unwillingness of some commentators to even consider the possibility that the book was written prior to A.D. 70. Some grant that the solution would be much simpler had John written the book earlier, but they do not consider an early date to be plausible.[177] If an early date for the book is not ruled out automatically, it is possible to make much more sense out of this obscure text.

The "seven heads" of the beast are seven kings. If the beast is the Roman Empire, then it would seem clear that the seven kings are seven emperors of Rome. The difficulty arises when we attempt to figure out which seven emperors John has in mind. Part of the problem concerns the starting point. The Roman author Suetonius began his list of emperors with Julius Caesar. Tacitus, on the other hand, appears to have considered Augustus the first Roman emperor.[178] If we begin with Julius and count consecutively, then the five kings who have fallen would be Julius, Augustus, Tiberius, Gaius Caligula, and Claudius. The sixth king, the one who is, would then be Nero. This interpretation is quite possible, and it would place the date of the writing of Revelation sometime in the latter part of Nero's reign (i.e., A.D. 64–68).[179]

---

reign of a specific king. Since the dates of the reigns of the Roman emperors are known, we could establish the date of Revelation within a few years.

175. Aune 1998b, 944. Mounce (1998, 315) notes uses of the description in Virgil, Martial, and Cicero. A coin minted in A.D. 71 depicts the goddess Roma sitting on the seven hills of Rome (17:9) with a sword (Osborne 2002, 608).

176. Contra Smalley (2005, 435–36) it is not a general description of "oppressive, secular government in its totality and at any period of world history." This may be an application of the text, but it is not an interpretation of the author's intended meaning. The reference to Rome is simply too specific and too clear.

177. E.g., Bauckham 1993a, 406; Osborne 2002, 618.

178. See Wilson 1993, 599.

179. Gentry 1989a.

The difficulty with this interpretation arises when we attempt to identify the seventh and eighth king. The emperor who followed Nero was Galba, and he did reign a very little while (June 68 to January 69). But he was followed by Otho (January to April 69), and it is difficult to see how Otho could fit the description in 17:11—"the beast that was and is not, it is an eighth but it belongs to the seven, and it goes to destruction." J. Christian Wilson has suggested the possibility of beginning the count of emperors with Augustus.[180] This would make the sixth king Galba, and the seventh would then be Otho. Unfortunately, the same problem arises in connection with the eighth king because it is very difficult to see how Vitellius (April to December 69) would fit the description of the eighth king.

Because of the difficulties involved with identifying the kings as emperors, some have suggested that the seven kings should be understood as seven kingdoms. The five that have fallen are Egypt, Assyria, Neo-Babylonia, Persia, and Greece. The one that is, the sixth kingdom, is Rome. Dispensationalists who take this approach tend to see the seventh kingdom as a revived Roman Empire and see the eighth kingdom as the kingdom of the antichrist.[181] Nondispensationalists take a different approach. Simon Kistemaker, for example, says that the seventh kingdom is a "collective title for all antichristian governments between the fall of Rome and the final empire of antichrist."[182] The text of Revelation, however, appears to identify the beast itself, rather than one of its seven heads, as the Roman Empire. The heads, then, are more likely the emperors.

A final suggestion that must be considered understands the seven kings as seven emperors, but it omits the brief reigns of Galba, Otho, and Vitellius. Is there any justification for such a move? Suetonius includes all three in his *Lives of the Caesars*, but he does refer to these three as rebels.[183] There is then some warrant for excluding these three from our reckoning. If we follow Tacitus and begin the count with Augustus, and if we exclude the three rebel emperors, the five kings who have fallen would be Augustus,

180. Wilson 1993, 599.

181. E.g., Hitchcock 2007, 480.

182. Kistemaker 2001, 472. Kistemaker also interprets the first five kingdoms differently. He identifies them as ancient Babylonia, Assyria, Neo-Babylonia, Medo-Persia, and Greco-Macedonia. But why move from literal historical referents (the first six kingdoms) to abstract referents (the seventh kingdom)? There does not seem to be a consistent reason for the hermeneutical change of direction in the middle of the prophecy.

183. Beasley-Murray 1978, 257.

Tiberius, Gaius Caligula, Claudius, and Nero. The sixth king, the one who is, would be Vespasian (A.D. 69–79).[184] The seventh king, the one who "has not yet come, and when he does come he must remain only a little while" would be Vespasian's son Titus, who reigned briefly from A.D. 79 to 81.

As we have seen, the other attempts to understand the seven kings as seven emperors faced their biggest challenge in identifying the eighth king in a way that made sense. If Vespasian is identified as the sixth king, and Titus as the seventh, the eighth would be Domitian, who reigned from A.D. 81 to 96. Can the description of the eighth king in 17:11 be legitimately understood as a reference to Domitian? It is possible. Of the eighth king, John writes, "As for the beast that was and is not, it is an eighth but it belongs to the seven, and it goes to destruction." This is where the history of the Roman emperors is informative. When Vespasian was named the emperor in December 69, he was preoccupied in Egypt for approximately six months before he was able to come to Rome. During the first six months of his reign, his son Domitian ruled in his place, accepting the title of Caesar and all the authority of the throne.[185]

Supposing John wrote during Vespasian's reign in the summer of A.D. 70, just after Domitian's temporary time on the throne ended and several months before the final destruction of Jerusalem, then the five kings who have fallen would be Augustus, Tiberius, Gaius Caligula, Claudius, and Nero. The one who is would be Vespasian. The other who has not yet come and must remain only a little while would be Titus. The eighth would be Domitian. Domitian, then, could be described as one who "was," in the sense that he had already reigned as Caesar in his father's stead for a short time. He could be described as one who "is not," in the sense that he has now vacated the throne upon the arrival of his father Vespasian. He could be described as "an eighth," in the sense that he will be the eighth emperor. He could be described as one who "belongs to the seven," in the sense that he ruled in the place of the sixth emperor and is also the son of the same emperor. The strongest objection to this interpretation is that it requires excluding Galba, Otho, and Vitellius. But all of the suggested interpretations face difficulties. Of the possible interpretations, the two most plausible appear to be the one that sees Vespasian as the sixth king or the one that understands Nero to

184. Charles 1920, 2:69; Beasley-Murray 1978, 257; Giblin 1991, 165.

185. Robinson 1976, 249 (Josephus, *J.W.* 4.11.4 §654).

be the sixth king.[186] The case for Vespasian as the sixth king is somewhat stronger than the case for Nero. In either case, the text points to an early date of composition before the destruction of Jerusalem.

The angel goes on to explain that the ten horns are "ten kings who have not yet received royal power" (Rev. 17:12a). They are to receive authority "for one hour" (v. 12b). This may be a reference to the ten senatorial provinces of Rome, or it may be an indication that there will be more emperors after Domitian and that the empire will not go on indefinitely. These ten kings will make war on the Lamb, but the Lamb will conquer them (v. 14). This appears to be a proclamation foreseeing the judgment of the Roman Empire by the Lord Jesus Christ. The ten kings and the beast (the Roman Empire) will hate the prostitute (the city of Rome), indicating that the conquered lands making up the empire will hate the seat of authority in Rome (vv. 15–18).

The vision John sees in Revelation 18 is a lament for Babylon/Rome. It echoes several prophetic laments in the Old Testament, including laments for Tyre (Isa. 23; Ezek. 27) and laments for Babylon (Isa. 13:1–14:23; 21:1–10; Jer. 25:12–38; 50–51).[187] Revelation 18:1–3 depicts the lament of "another angel" over Babylon/Rome. Verses 4–20 are a summons to come out of this city. This summons echoes similar calls in the Old Testament (Gen. 19:15, 17; Isa. 48:20; 52:11; Jer. 50:8; 51:45, 50; Ezek. 20:41). In Revelation 18:21–24, the angel symbolically enacts the judgment of Babylon/Rome, casting a giant stone into the sea (cf. Jer. 51:63–64). It may be objected that Revelation 18 pictures a sudden and complete fall and that this did not occur in the case of Rome. However, as Jay Adams points out, even though Jeremiah prophesied a similar sudden destruction of the literal city of Babylon (Jer. 51:8), it was centuries before Babylon fell utterly into ruin.[188]

In Revelation 19:1–4, the scene shifts, and John hears a multitude in heaven crying out with a loud voice, praising God for judging the prostitute. In verse 3, the heavenly multitude praises God for the eternal punishment

186. There does not appear to be any plausible reading that results in Domitian being the sixth king, the one who "is" at the time John writes. All such readings require arbitrary selections of emperors with no historical or exegetical warrant. As Bell (1979, 97) argues, all such attempts to read Revelation 17:9–11 in a way that results in Domitian being the sixth king "make nonsense of the seer's list and are merely examples of special pleading in an effort to arrive at a predetermined date for the composition of the Apocalypse, i.e. A.D. 95–6."

187. Bauckham 1993a, 345; Osborne 2002, 638.

188. Adams 1966, 79.

of the church's great persecutor.[189] John then hears a great multitude praising God and crying out:

> Hallelujah!
> For the Lord our God
> the Almighty reigns.
> Let us rejoice and exult
> and give him the glory,
> for the marriage of the Lamb has come,
> and his Bride has made herself ready. (vv. 6–7)

The angel then says to John, "Blessed are those who are invited to the marriage supper of the Lamb" (v. 9).

Transition from Babylon to the New Jerusalem (Rev. 19:11–21:8)

Between the visions of the two cities of Babylon/Rome (17:1–19:10) and the new Jerusalem (21:9–22:9) is a section that describes the transition between the two.[190] In Revelation 19:11–21, John sees heaven opened and a rider on a white horse coming as the divine warrior.[191] Most evangelical commentators understand this passage to be speaking of the second coming of Christ.[192] Some, on the other hand, understand the text to be speaking of Christ's coming in judgment upon Jerusalem in A.D. 70.[193] The context, however, indicates that both of these interpretations miss the basic thrust of the passage. In verse 20, John explicitly connects this coming of the divine warrior to the judgment of the beast and the false prophet (i.e., Rome and the priesthood of the Roman imperial cult). In other words, the vision in Revelation 19:11–21 is a vision that graphically depicts the judgment of Rome that began in heaven when Christ was seated at the right hand of God (see Dan. 7:11–14).[194] It draws heavily on imagery from Old Testament texts that depict God the divine warrior coming in judgment on the nations (e.g., Ex. 15; Deut. 33; Judg. 5; Hab. 3; Isa. 59:15–20).

189. This should give pause to those who think that such punishment is inconsistent with the goodness of God.

190. Bauckham 1993a, 5.

191. Aune 1998b, 1048.

192. E.g., Walvoord 1966, 274; Aune 1998b, 1053; Beale 1999, 948; Osborne 2002, 679.

193. E.g., Gentry 1998, 81.

194. Adams 1966, 80.

Like Ezekiel, John sees heaven opened, and he sees a rider on a white horse (Rev. 19:11; Ezek. 1:1). The description of the rider's eyes in Revelation 19:12 indicates that this figure is the same figure described in 1:14, namely the exalted Jesus. The description of his robe as "dipped in blood" echoes Old Testament prophetic texts that describe the divine warrior (e.g., Isa. 63:1–6). He is followed by the armies of heaven and comes to judge his enemies (Rev. 19:14). From his mouth comes a sharp sword, and he will rule with a rod of iron (v. 15). The imagery echoes Old Testament texts such as Psalm 2:9 and Isaiah 11:4. The divine warrior will tread the winepress of the fury of the wrath of God (Rev. 19:15). This is an Old Testament metaphor for divine judgment (Isa. 63:2–3).

Following his vision of the divine warrior, John sees an angel standing in the sun crying out to the birds and calling them to gather together for the great supper of God (Rev. 19:17). Echoing the language of Ezekiel 39:17–20, the angel calls upon the birds to eat the flesh of the wicked who opposed God (Rev. 19:18). The beast gathers his armies against the Lord, but he and the false prophet are captured and cast into the lake of fire (v. 20). As Osborne observes, this is the first of four instances in which something or someone is cast into the lake of fire: (1) the beast and the false prophet (19:20); (2) the devil (20:10); (3) Death and Hades (20:14a); and (4) unbelievers (20:15).[195]

Revelation 20:1–10 is another text in the book that has been the source of much disagreement. This text describes a period of a "thousand years," or a millennium, and is at the center of the ongoing debate between premillennialists, amillennialists, and postmillennialists.[196] Because of its significance in contemporary debates, we must examine this text carefully. It is important to keep in mind, however, that verses 1–3 refer to events preceding or at the beginning of the thousand years. Verses 4–6 refer to the millennium itself, and verses 7–10 refer to events occurring at the end of the thousand years.[197]

The first question that we must ask is whether the events described in Revelation 20:1–10 follow the events described in Revelation 19:11–21 chronologically. Some argue that if the events are chronologically successive, then the millennium of Revelation 20 must follow the second coming of

195. Osborne 2002, 689–90.

196. For a good discussion of the various views, see Grenz 1992.

197. Osborne 2002, 697.

Christ described in Revelation 19.[198] Because this entails premillennialism, and because many believe premillennialism is ruled out in other parts of Scripture, some conclude that the events described in Revelation 20:1–10 are a recapitulation of events described in Revelation 19.[199] The problem with this view is that there does appear to be chronological succession between the events described in Revelation 19:11–21; 20:1–10; and 20:11–15. The source of the difficulty, however, is the assumption that Revelation 19:11–21 is a vision of the second coming of Christ. Once we realize that it is a prophecy concerning the judgment of Rome, which began in the first century, then we see that granting chronological succession does not demand premillennialism.[200] In fact, it precludes it.

In his vision, John first sees an event that occurs at some point prior to the beginning of the millennium, namely the binding of Satan (20:1–3). Some argue that this cannot have already occurred.[201] There is, however, evidence in the Gospels that the binding of Satan had begun already during the earthly ministry of Christ (Matt. 12:26–29; Mark 3:26–27; Luke 10:18). Hebrews, in fact, uses language that is stronger than that found in Revelation. The author of Hebrews says that through death, Jesus "destroyed" the devil (Heb. 2:14). If such language is appropriate for what Christ accomplished on the cross in the first century, it is not inappropriate to speak of the binding of Satan as having already occurred. This binding is the penultimate judgment of God's ancient enemy (Gen. 3).

The angel binds Satan "for a thousand years" (Rev. 20:2). Is this intended by John to be understood as a literal thousand-year period of time? Were the binding of Satan still future, this would be a plausible interpretation. However, since the binding of Satan is associated with the first advent of Christ, the thousand years represents a period of time that began then. And since the events associated with the end of the thousand years (i.e., the resurrection of the dead and the final judgment) have not occurred yet, then it would appear that the thousand years is intended to be understood as a symbolic number representing a long but indefinite period of time.[202]

198. E.g., Hoekema 1979, 226.

199. E.g., Hendriksen 1939, 221.

200. The coming of the Son of Man (closely associated with the ascension of Christ) is connected in Daniel 7 with the judgment of the fourth beast (Rome). This judgment began in the first century and continued over the next several hundred years.

201. Walvoord 1966, 292.

202. Kistemaker 2001, 536; Beale 1999, 972.

The next section of John's vision, 20:4–6, is somewhat more difficult than the first section. Here John sees thrones and those to whom authority to judge was committed (v. 4a). He also sees the souls of those who had been beheaded for the testimony of Jesus, those who had not worshiped the beast and had not received its mark (v. 4b). John says, "They came to life and reigned with Christ for a thousand years" (v. 4c). Those "to whom the authority to judge was given" would appear to be representative of all the saints (1 Cor. 6:2). The phrase "those who had been beheaded for the testimony of Jesus" would appear to be referring specifically to those who were martyred by the Romans. They are specifically identified as those who "had not worshiped the beast or its image and had not received its mark." In the context of the book, this refers to something specific to the Roman Empire. The theological point of this verse that is most relevant to its first readers is that those martyred by the beast/Rome will triumph and reign with Christ.[203]

John tells us that all of the saints, the martyrs included, "came to life and reigned with Christ for a thousand years" (Rev. 20:4c). He then continues, "The rest of the dead did not come to life until the thousand years were ended. This is the first resurrection. Blessed and holy is the one who shares in the first resurrection! Over such the second death has no power, but they will be priests of God and of Christ, and they will reign with him for a thousand years" (vv. 5–6). We know from elsewhere in Scripture, and from Revelation itself, that all Christians now reign with Christ (Rom. 5:17; Eph. 2:6; Rev. 1:6). But what is the "first resurrection"? The first resurrection is the resurrection of Jesus (1 Cor. 15:20–23), and all Christians partake of this resurrection.[204]

Our participation in this first resurrection is spoken of in the past tense in terms of our regeneration or spiritual resurrection (Eph. 2:5–6; Col. 2:12), and in the future tense in terms of our bodily resurrection (Rom. 6:5; 1 Cor. 15:23, 52–56; 1 Thess 4:16). In short, all who participate in the resurrection of Christ have been spiritually resurrected and will be raised bodily as well. Some argue that the first and second resurrections mentioned in Revelation 20:4 and 5 have to refer to the same kind of resurrection, because John wouldn't speak of two kinds of resurrection in such a brief space.[205] In response, we must make two brief comments. In the first place,

203. Bauckham 1993b, 107.
204. Beale 1999, 1014.
205. E.g., Ladd 1972, 266.

John does precisely this in another of his writings. In John 5:28–29, he speaks of spiritual resurrection and physical resurrection in the same brief context. Furthermore, if the two deaths (Rev. 20:6) can refer to two different kinds of death, there is no reason that the two resurrections cannot also refer to two different kinds of resurrection.

In Revelation 20:7–10, John sees a vision of what is to transpire at the end of the thousand years. Satan will be released and will come out to deceive the nations and gather them together for battle (vv. 7–8). John sees them surround the saints, but before they can do any damage, God destroys them with fire (v. 9). Then Satan himself, God's ancient enemy, is finally cast into the lake of fire (v. 10). The imagery of this final rebellion borrows heavily from Ezekiel's vision of Gog and Magog (Ezek. 38–39). Here John uses this imagery to depict a final satanically inspired rebellion that is to occur just prior to the final judgment.[206]

Following his vision of the events associated with the thousand years, John sees a vision of the final judgment (Rev. 20:11–15). Here there is little controversy among Christian interpreters. All agree that this is a vision of the judgment that is to occur at the end of the present age after the second advent of Christ.[207] John sees a great white throne, and he sees all of the dead standing before the throne (vv. 11–12a). The dead are judged according to what they have done (vv. 12b–13). After giving up their dead, Death and Hades are thrown into the lake of fire, which is the second death (v. 14). Anyone whose name is not found in the book of life is cast into the lake of fire (v. 15). Verse 15 is likely an elaboration on the meaning of verse 14 since Death and Hades are not literal persons who can be cast into hell.[208]

This section of Revelation concludes with a vision that provides a glimpse of the new heaven and new earth (21:1–8). In 21:9–22:5, John will provide more details about this coming reality.[209] He will describe the new heavens, the new earth, and the new Jerusalem. In short, these final two chapters of Revelation describe the ultimate fulfillment of all of the

206. If the man of lawlessness in 2 Thessalonians 2 refers to a future figure, this is likely the point in time when he makes his appearance.

207. Osborne 2002, 719.

208. Aune 1998b, 1103.

209. Beasley-Murray 1978, 314.

prophetic themes of the Old and New Testament.[210] In 21:1, John sees a "new heaven and a new earth, for the first heaven and the first earth had passed away." This is the fulfillment of the prophecies expressed so beautifully in Isaiah 65:17–25 and 66:22. It is the restoration of the original creation (Gen. 1:1).

John sees the new Jerusalem coming down out of heaven as a bride adorned for her husband (Rev. 21:2). All of the Old Testament hopes for Jerusalem are now fulfilled in the new Jerusalem from above (Gal. 4:26; Heb. 12:22; Isa. 2:1–5; 18:7; 52:1; 65:18). John then hears a voice saying, "Behold, the dwelling place of God is with man. He will dwell with them, and they will be his people, and God himself will be with them as their God" (Rev. 21:3). Here the fulfillment of all that the tabernacle and temple symbolized comes to fruition, as the heart of the covenant is fulfilled with all men and not just Israel: He will be our God, and we will be his people.[211] The curse and its results will be removed as God wipes away all tears. There will be no more death or mourning or pain, "for the former things have passed away" (v. 4).

In verses 5–8, God speaks directly again for the first time since 1:8. He declares, "Behold, I am making all things new" (v. 5). He then commands John to write down these words:

> It is done! I am the Alpha and the Omega, the beginning and the end. To the thirsty I will give from the spring of the water of life without payment. The one who conquers will have this heritage, and I will be his God and he will be my son. But as for the cowardly, the faithless, the detestable, as for murderers, the sexually immoral, sorcerers, idolaters, and all liars, their portion will be in the lake that burns with fire and sulfur, which is the second death. (vv. 6–8)

The fact that this is only the second place in the prophecy where God himself speaks indicates the importance of these words. They help us understand one of the basic purposes of the book for its first readers, and for all subsequent readers. God is exhorting the readers of this book to conquer the forces of the serpent by remaining faithful unto death. All of God's people in every age are exhorted to the same kind of enduring faithfulness.

210. Beale 1999, 1119; Osborne 2002, 726.
211. Bauckham 1993a, 311.

The New Jerusalem (Rev. 21:9–22:9)

Following John's introductory vision of the new heaven and new earth, an angel gives him a detailed look at the new Jerusalem. As mentioned above, this section contains numerous linguistic and thematic parallels with Revelation 17:1–19:10. Both begin with one of the seven angels who had the seven bowls speaking with John and saying, "Come, I will show you . . ." (21:9; 17:1). Both conclude with an angel saying, "You must not do that! I am a fellow servant with you and your brothers. . . . Worship God" (22:9; 19:10). Similar parallels exist throughout the two texts.[212] Since the first text deals with a city portrayed as a woman (Babylon the prostitute), and the second text also deals with a city portrayed as a woman (new Jerusalem the bride), it is clear that these sections are deliberately contrasting antithetical realities.[213]

The angel carries John to a high mountain where he sees the new Jerusalem coming down out of heaven (21:10–11). Here John sees the fulfillment of God's original goal for creation, the establishment of his kingdom on earth.[214] The city has a wall with twelve gates, and on the gates are written the names of the twelve tribes of Israel (vv. 12–13; Ezek. 48:30–35). The wall also has twelve foundations, and on the foundations are written the names of the twelve apostles of the Lamb (Rev. 21:14). The Old Testament people of God and the New Testament people of God are here depicted as one. The promises to both find their ultimate fulfillment in the new Jerusalem.[215]

Echoing Ezekiel's vision (Ezek. 40–48), John is given a measuring rod and told to measure the city that he sees (Rev. 21:15). The length and width and height of the city all measure 12,000 stadia—between 1,416 and 1,566 miles (v. 16).[216] The city is pictured as cubical in shape, like the Holy of Holies in the temple (1 Kings 6:20).[217] The dimensions of the city make it clear that the vision is not to be understood literally.[218] The dimensions

212. See Wilson 2007, 93–94.

213. Aune 1998b, 1187; Bauckham 1993a, 4.

214. Dumbrell 1985, 31.

215. Bauckham 1993a, 312.

216. The length of a stadium in the first-century Hellenistic world was not uniform. The size of the city in miles depends on which stadium John had in mind (Aune 1998b, 1161).

217. Beasley-Murray 1978, 322.

218. Considering the fact that the diameter of the earth is approximately 8,000 miles, a city 1,500 miles high and wide would be about one-fifth the size of the earth. The diameter of the earth's moon

of the wall make this fact even more obvious since it is described as being 144 cubits, or approximately 216 feet (Rev. 21:17). John does not indicate clearly whether the wall is 216 feet high or 216 feet thick. In either case, the wall is out of proportion to the 1,500-mile-high city if the images are taken literally.[219]

After revealing the measurements of the city, John describes the precious materials out of which it is made (21:18–21). As Bauckham explains, "the city is built out of the jewels and metals of Paradise: cf. Gen 2:11–12; Ezek 28:13."[220] John reveals the inner purity of the city in Revelation 21:22–27. He reveals that the city has no temple, for the Lord himself is its temple (v. 22; Jer. 3:16–17). The city has no need of the sun or moon for the glory of the Lord gives it light, and by its light the nations will walk (Rev. 21:23–24; Isa. 60:19). Nothing unclean will ever enter the city, but only those who are written in the Lamb's book of life (Rev. 21:27; 20:15).

In Revelation 22:1–6, John is shown more details of the new Jerusalem. He sees the river of the water of life flowing from the throne of God (v. 1; Gen. 2:10; Ezek. 47:1–2; Zech. 14:8), indicating that the life source of the new creation is God himself. On either side of the river, John sees the tree of life with twelve kinds of fruit, and the leaves of the tree are said to be for the healing of the nations (Rev. 22:2; Gen. 3:22; Ezek. 47:12). John writes, "No longer will there be anything accursed, but the throne of God and of the Lamb will be in it, and his servants will worship him" (Rev. 22:3). Here John describes the reversal of the Adamic curse (Gen. 3:14–19). In the new Jerusalem, sin and its accompanying curse are no more.

God's people will see him, and his name will be on their foreheads, and night will be no more, and they will reign forever (Rev. 22:4–5). What John describes here is the fulfillment of the ultimate hopes of the people of God throughout the ages (Pss. 11:7; 27:4; Isa. 52:8; 60:2; Zech. 9:14). Creation is renewed with the throne of God, the river of the water of life, and the tree of life in its midst.[221] Every hope of the people of God reaches its consummate fulfillment in the new Jerusalem and the new creation.

---

is approximately 2,160 miles, meaning that such a city would be approximately two-thirds the size of the moon.

219. Why would a city two-thirds the size of the moon need a 216-foot-high wall? The existence of a wall also weighs heavily against the views of some who suggest that the new Jerusalem is a literal 1,500-mile-high cube orbiting the earth. A literal orbiting city has no need of a wall.

220. Bauckham 2001, 1304.

221. Aune 1998b, 1187.

The kingdom of God is now established on earth. The curse is removed. The Edenic river of life flows from God's throne. Nothing unclean or sinful will ever harm God's creation or his people again. People from every tongue, tribe, and nation now receive the restored blessing of God and worship him forever.[222]

The vision of the new Jerusalem concludes with the words of the angel to John (Rev. 22:6–9). The angel tells John that his words are trustworthy and true, and he says the Lord "has sent his angel to show his servants what must soon take place" (v. 6). Just as the opening of the prophecy indicated that it concerned things that must soon take place (1:1), so too does the conclusion. Again, the significance of these framing words must be stressed. John's prophecy primarily concerns events that are impending at the time John is writing. In 22:7, we hear the words of the Lord saying, "Behold, I am coming soon. Blessed is the one who keeps the words of the prophecy of this book" (cf. 1:3). This is not a reference to the second coming, but to the coming of the divine warrior to judge Israel and later Rome. Jesus here also stresses the importance of doing what is commanded in this book, namely remaining faithful in the face of suffering and persecution. The words of this book are not a mere puzzle for the amusement of prophecy buffs. They are words to be heeded and obeyed.

The Epilogue (Rev. 22:10–21)

The book of Revelation closes with a brief epilogue (22:10–21). The structure of this concluding section is difficult to discern. There are statements by the angels, by Jesus, and by John himself. The epilogue begins with the angel telling John, "Do not seal up the words of the prophecy of this book, for the time is near" (v. 10). The words here are in direct contrast to the words spoken by an angel to Daniel: "But you, Daniel, shut up the words and seal the book, until the time of the end" (Dan. 12:4). At the time John writes, the time of the end has drawn near. The Messiah has come. By his atoning death on the cross he has secured the redemption of his people. He has received his kingdom. Now the judgment of the nations associated with his accession to the throne is about to begin (Dan. 7).

Jesus declares again, "I am coming soon," and he says, "I am the Alpha and the Omega, the first and the last, the beginning and the end" (Rev.

222. Dumbrell 1985, 31–32.

22:12–13). Here Jesus closely identifies himself with God the Father (21:6). In 21:8, the fate of the wicked had been described as the lake of fire. In 22:15, it is described as outside of the city.[223] Since there will be no wicked people living anywhere in the new creation, the second description is synonymous with the first. To be outside of the city means to be in the lake of fire. In verse 16, Jesus draws on two Old Testament messianic titles as a self-description. He says, "I am the root and the descendant of David, the bright morning star" (Isa. 11:10; Num. 24:17). Both of these Old Testament titles are found in prophecies which portray the Messiah as the one to whom the nations will come for salvation.[224] John is likely alluding to those contexts in this passage indicating that they find their ultimate fulfillment in the new heavens and new earth.

Echoing Isaiah 55:1, John continues, "The Spirit and the Bride say, 'Come.' And let the one who hears say, 'Come.' And let the one who is thirsty come: let the one who desires take the water of life without price" (Rev. 22:17). These are invitations to John's readers then and now. John concludes the epilogue and the book with a warning against adding to the words of the prophecy or taking away from the words of the prophecy (vv. 18–19; Deut. 4:2). To those who add to the words of the prophecy, God will add to him the plagues described in the book. To those who take away from the words of the prophecy, God will take away his share in the tree of life and in the holy city. Finally, one last time, Jesus reminds the readers of the prophecy that he is coming soon (Rev. 22:20). The book closes with an epistolary benediction: "The grace of the Lord Jesus be with all. Amen" (v. 21).

Summary

For many, Revelation is a closed book, but it was not intended to be so. Our Lord intended this book to be read, understood, and obeyed (1:3; 22:7). Much of our difficulty with the book stems from our lack of familiarity with the biblical narratives that precede it, the Old Testament prophets in particular. Too many Christians are familiar only with the New Testament. When those who are familiar only with the New Testament come to the book of Revelation, they are not equipped to understand its language

223. Beasley-Murray 1978, 341.
224. Bauckham 1993a, 325.

and its imagery. More than any other New Testament book, Revelation draws on the images and language of the Old Testament. Eschatological themes that are developed at length throughout the Old Testament find their fulfillment in the book of Revelation. If one is not familiar with the development of these themes, one will not be able to fully grasp the way John depicts their fulfillment.

The book of Revelation is an apocalyptic prophecy in the form of a letter to seven churches. As a prophecy, it follows the conventions of Old Testament prophetic books. It uses the same kind of highly stylized and figurative language that they use. Like Old Testament apocalyptic prophecies, it is filled with heavenly visions and unusual symbols. It is not intended to be read in the same manner as a prose narrative. Like many of the Old Testament prophetic books, the book of Revelation deals with an impending judgment upon Israel and upon an enemy Gentile nation. In the case of Revelation, that enemy Gentile nation is Rome.

Jesus had warned of the judgment of Israel that was to come within a generation of his death. Now, as the time of Jerusalem's destruction is imminent, John becomes a New Testament version of Ezekiel and Jeremiah, warning of the destruction that is at the door. Like the Old Testament prophets, John does not stop with his prophecy of the destruction of Jerusalem by the Romans; he also prophesies the judgment of Rome itself. The Roman Empire is the kingdom of the beast. Its rulers blaspheme by taking divine honors and titles to themselves and by accepting and encouraging worship directed to them. For such arrogance, Rome too will be judged.

John writes to encourage the seven churches to remain faithful in the face of suffering and persecution. At the time of his writing, Christians were still being persecuted by Jews, and they had just begun to be persecuted by the Roman state under Nero. Nero, in fact, had unleashed a ferocious persecution of Christians not long before the book was written. Such persecution presented a great temptation to believers. They were tempted to compromise or even to renounce their faith. John informs his readers that just as Christ conquered his enemies and gained victory through suffering and death, so too will they conquer through suffering and death. The true conquerors, according to John, are not the persecutors. The true conquerors are those who remain faithful to Christ, even unto death.

Those who remain faithful will reign with Christ even if they are martyred, for they are seated in the heavenly places with Christ who is at the right hand of God. Those who belong to Jesus will inherit a new heavens and a new earth, free from the taint of sin and the curse. They will be citizens of the new Jerusalem. As the bride of Christ, they will participate in the wedding supper of the Lamb. They will partake of the water of the river of life that flows from God's throne. They will partake of the fruit of the tree of life that is for the healing of the nations. They will sing a new song and worship the Lord who redeemed them by his precious blood. For them, there will be no more death, nor crying, nor mourning, nor pain, for these former things will have passed away. Therefore, with the saints of the ages, we pray, Come, Lord Jesus!

Conclusion

As we have seen, the eschatology of the Bible is far more than a particular view of the "last things." Eschatology certainly involves the last things, but it also involves everything God has done to prepare for those last things. Biblical eschatology involves the first advent of Jesus Christ as much as his second advent. Biblical eschatology involves God's entire redemptive plan, determined by the Father, Son, and Spirit before the foundation of the world. All of redemptive history is, in fact, the outworking of God's eschatological plan, involving the establishment of his kingdom on earth.

Contemporary evangelical Christians tend to equate eschatology with particular millennial views, but to do so means that we miss the bigger picture. It is as if we were to equate the biblical doctrine of the church with particular views of baptism. It is certainly part of the picture, but it is not the whole. Likewise, the biblical doctrine concerning the millennium is only one small part of biblical eschatology. The big picture involves much, much more. We simply cannot discern what the Bible teaches on this subject by turning to a handful of Old Testament prophetic texts and the New Testament book of Revelation.

Biblical eschatology is good news. It is "gospel." Unlike the scenarios presented by many other religions and by modern secularists, biblical eschatology is an eschatology of hope. Some religions tell us we will be endlessly reincarnated after we die, and that how we will be reincarnated will depend on how we live our lives today. This is a counterfeit hope. Modern secularists tell us that our death is the end of our personal existence, that our life and death is ultimately no more significant than the life and death of a common housefly. The modern secularist adopts the famous line from *Macbeth* as his motto: Life, he assures us, is a "tale told by an idiot, full of sound and fury, signifying nothing." This is hopelessness.

Left to our own devices, we might be forced to choose from among the world's various false eschatologies. But God has not left us to our own devices. He has revealed himself and his plan in the books of Holy Scripture. It is here that we learn who God is, and what he is doing. God reveals in his Word that the world is not the way it is ultimately intended to be. God's original creation was good, but because of the first man's sin, the creation is now under a curse, and man is doomed to die. The biblical eschatology of hope is first revealed when Adam is not immediately cast into hell for his act of cosmic treason but is instead given a redemptive promise.

The gradual outworking of God's eschatological plan of redemption initially involves the making of a covenant with one man, Abraham, to whom God gives a number of promises. He will become a great nation, he will be given a land, and through him all the nations of the earth will be blessed. Somehow, in some way, God will use this one man and his descendants as the means by which he will bless all of mankind. Over the next several centuries, the descendants of Abraham's grandson Jacob multiply in the land of Egypt and are ultimately enslaved. God, however, has not forgotten his promises or his plan. When the time is right, he calls Moses to lead his people out of Egypt. In the exodus, the nation of Israel is born.

The remainder of the Old Testament narrates the story of Israel, and one wonders throughout: How is God going to use this small nation to deal with the problem of sin, to establish his kingdom on earth, to bless all the nations? God makes a covenant with the nation, calling them to be a kingdom of priests, and giving them a law that will define them as a holy nation. From the beginning, however, Israel fails to obey the law. The people of Israel ask for a king in order to be like the other nations, when being like the other nations is precisely what they are not to do. But God grants their request, and gives them a king. Israel's first king is very much a king like the kings of other nations, and because of this he fails to obey God.

Israel's next king is David, a man after God's own heart. With David, God makes a covenant, promising to establish his throne forever. David's offspring, however, do not follow in the footsteps of their godly father. They divide the nation and lead it on a downward spiral of apostasy. God sends prophets to the northern kingdom of Israel and to the southern kingdom of Judah. These prophets remind the people of the covenant they had made with God, and they call the people to repentance. They warn that if repentance is not forthcoming, the curses of the covenant will come. The ultimate curse will involve exile. Still, the people refuse to repent, and exile does come. The northern kingdom falls first, going into exile in Assyria. Because of a few godly kings, the southern kingdom lasts a century and a half longer, but eventually Judah goes into exile in Babylon.

Although the preexilic prophets had focused primarily on warning Israel and Judah of coming judgment, they did promise future restoration as well. God's promises to Abraham would not fail. When the judgment of exile finally did come, the prophets turned their focus more and more to future restoration. The promises to David formed the basis for many of their prophecies, as they looked forward to a coming King, a Messiah, who would restore Israel and establish the kingdom of God on earth. The prophets also indicated that this Messiah would suffer and die for his people's sins. Could such prophecies be fulfilled by the same person? Eventually, many of those in exile were permitted to return to the land and rebuild the temple. But was this the time of promised restoration? Would God now establish his kingdom? It was a partial fulfillment, but according to the postexilic prophets, there was much more to come.

After four hundred years of prophetic silence, a voice is heard in Israel—the voice of one crying in the wilderness: "Prepare the way of the Lord; make his paths straight," and "Repent, for the kingdom of heaven is at hand." According to John the Baptist, the long-awaited promises were now about to be fulfilled. He announces the arrival of the Messiah. The one to whom he points is Jesus. This Jesus is the Son of Abraham and the Son of David. He is the one in whom and through whom all of the Old Testament promises will find their ultimate fulfillment. He is the one who will save his people from their sins. How will Israel receive her long-awaited Messiah? This is the story told in the Gospels.

Jesus goes throughout the land of Israel, proclaiming the kingdom of God, healing all manner of diseases, indicating that he is the promised Messiah, but in spite of everything, most of the people reject him. As they have done throughout their history, Israel again rejects her God. Jesus calls to himself a number of disciples and prepares them for what is to come, knowing that his rejection by the people of Israel will lead to his death. Eventually, Jesus is betrayed and handed over to the Romans. At the instigation of the crowds, he is scourged and crucified. After his death, he is placed in a tomb, but this tomb is not the end of his story.

On the third day after his crucifixion, Jesus' disciples learn that he has risen from the dead. On the cross, his heel had been bruised, but by rolling away the stone from the grave, he has now crushed the head of the serpent. Through his death, he has paid the price for our sins. Now he is alive, and death has no more hold over him. Soon, it becomes clear to the disciples that God has used the long-standing rebelliousness of his people Israel to accomplish his redemptive plans. By rejecting Jesus, they have unwittingly brought their Messiah, the Lamb of God, to the cross, where he has died as an atonement for the sins of his people.

The resurrection and ascension of Jesus mark the turning point in redemptive history. The eschatological age has begun. Jesus has been given all authority and has been seated at the right hand of God as King of kings and Lord of lords. The usurper, however, will not go quietly. The decisive battle has been won, but the war is not over. The kingdom has been inaugurated, but it has not yet been consummated. The present age, therefore, is characterized by the spread of the gospel and the growth of the kingdom, but this growth is accompanied by intense conflict and suffering as the church wages war with the very gates of hell. This is illustrated throughout the book of Acts. Although the kingdom has not come in its fullness, Christians are called to live by the eschatological ethics of the kingdom even now. They are also called, in the midst of such intense spiritual warfare, to remain steadfast in the faith to the point of death. It was through Christ's suffering and death that his decisive victory was won, and it is through the suffering and death of his followers that victory continues to be won.

What then of Israel? What of the nation to whom God made so many promises? What of the nation whose story has formed so large a part of the biblical narrative? Has Israel fallen completely? According to the apostle Paul, the answer is no! Through Israel's sin, salvation came to the Gentiles. But Israel will not remain hardened in her heart forever. Her hardening is partial, and will last until the fullness of the Gentiles has come in. This is the mystery. The Gentiles came into the kingdom of the Messiah first. When Israel repents, Israel herself will be regrafted into the people of God as well. Gentile believers, therefore, are not to be arrogant toward Israel. Instead, the prayer of Gentiles everywhere should be the same as the prayer of Paul—for the salvation of Israel.

At Christ's ascension, the disciples were promised that he would come again. Believers today live in the light of that hope, for at his coming the kingdom will be established in its fullness. At his coming, the dead in Christ will rise, and those who are alive will be changed. Our resurrection bodies will be like his, glorious and free from the taint of sin. At that time, God will judge all men. Those who have placed their faith in Jesus Christ, and in him alone, will inherit eternal life. The wicked who have rejected Christ will inherit eternal punishment. God will create a new heavens and earth in which the curse is no more. There will be no more pain, or suffering, or crying, or death. All of those things will pass away. Sin and death will be no more. In the ultimate fulfillment of the covenant promises, God will be our God and we will be his people. And we will sing a new song of praise to the Father, Son, and Holy Spirit forever.

References

Achtemeier, Paul J. 1996. *1 Peter*. Edited by Eldon Jay Epp. Hermeneia. Minneapolis: Fortress.

Ackroyd, Peter R. 1968. *Exile and Restoration: A Study of Hebrew Thought of the Sixth Century BC*. London: SCM.

Adams, Edward. 2005. "Where Is the Promise of His Coming? The Complaint of the Scoffers in 2 Peter 3.4." *NTS* 51, no. 1:106–22.

Adams, Jay. 1966. *The Time Is at Hand*. Greenville, SC: A Press.

Ahlström, G. W. 1971. *Joel and the Temple Cult of Jerusalem*. VTSup 21. Leiden: Brill.

Alexander, J. A. 1846. *Commentary on the Prophecies of Isaiah*. New York: Scribner's.

Alexander, T. D. 1988. "Jonah: An Introduction and Commentary." In David W. Baker, T. Desmond Alexander, and Bruce Waltke, *Obadiah, Jonah, Micah*, 45–131. Downers Grove, IL: InterVarsity.

———. 2002. *From Paradise to the Promised Land: An Introduction to the Pentateuch*. 2d ed. Grand Rapids: Baker Academic.

Allen, Leslie C. 1976. *The Books of Joel, Obadiah, Jonah and Micah*. NICOT. London: Hodder and Stoughton.

———. 1983. *Psalms 101–150*. WBC 21. Waco: Word.

———. 1990. *Ezekiel 20–48*. WBC 29. Dallas: Word.

Allen, Lindsay. 2005. *The Persian Empire*. Chicago: University of Chicago Press.

Allis, Oswald T. 1947. *Prophecy and the Church*. Phillipsburg, NJ: P&R.

———. 1949. *The Five Books of Moses*. Philadelphia: P&R.

———. 1950. *The Unity of Isaiah*. Philadelphia: P&R.

———. 1951. *God Spake by Moses: An Exposition of the Pentateuch*. Phillipsburg, NJ: P&R.

Allison, Dale C., Jr. 1985. *The End of the Ages Has Come: An Early Interpretation of the Passion and Resurrection of Jesus*. Philadelphia: Fortress.

———. 1993. *The New Moses: A Matthean Typology*. Minneapolis: Fortress.

———. 2005. *Studies in Matthew: Interpretation Past and Present*. Grand Rapids: Baker Academic.

Alter, Robert. 1985. *The Art of Biblical Poetry*. New York: Basic Books.

Andersen, Francis I. 1976. *Job: An Introduction and Commentary*. TOTC 13. Downers Grove, IL: InterVarsity.

Andersen, Francis I., and David Noel Freedman. 1980. *Hosea*. AB 24. New York: Doubleday.

———. 1989. *Amos*. AB 24A. New York: Doubleday.

———. 2000. *Micah*. AB 24E. New York: Doubleday.

Anderson, A. A. 1989. *2 Samuel*. WBC 11. Waco: Word Books.

Anderson, Bernhard W. 2000. *Out of the Depths: The Psalms Speak for Us Today*. 3d. ed. Louisville: Westminster.

Anderson, Bernhard, and Walter Harrelson, eds. 1962. *Israel's Prophetic Heritage*. New York: Harper and Brothers.

Ashton, John, ed. 1986. *The Interpretation of John*. IRT 9. Philadelphia: Fortress; London: SPCK.

Attridge, Harold W. 1989. *The Epistle to the Hebrews*. Edited by Helmut Koester. Hermeneia. Minneapolis: Fortress.

Aune, David E., ed. 1972. *Studies in New Testament and Early Christian Literature: Essays in Honor of Allen P. Wikgren*. NovTSup 33. Leiden: Brill.

———. 1987. *The New Testament in Its Literary Environment*. LEC 8. Philadelphia: Westminster.

———. 1997. *Revelation 1–5*. WBC 52A. Dallas: Word Books.

———. 1998a. *Revelation 6–16*. WBC 52B. Dallas: Word Books.

———. 1998b. *Revelation 17–22*. WBC 52C. Dallas: Word Books.

Austin, J. L. 1962. *How to Do Things with Words*. Edited by J. O. Urmson. New York: Oxford University Press.

Ayer, A. J. 1952. *Language, Truth and Logic*. New York: Dover.

Bahnsen, Greg L. 1988. "Another Look at Chilton's *Days of Vengeance*." *Journey* 3, no. 2:11–14.

———. 1999. *Victory in Jesus: The Bright Hope of Postmillennialism*. Edited by Robert R. Booth. Texarkana, AR: Covenant Media.

Baker, David L. 1994. "Typology and the Christian Use of the Old Testament." In *The Right Doctrine from the Wrong Texts*, edited by G. K. Beale, 313–30. Grand Rapids: Baker.

———. 2005. "Covenant: An Old Testament Study." In *The God of Covenant: Biblical, Theological and Contemporary Perspectives*, edited by Jamie A. Grant and Alistair I. Wilson, 21–53. Leicester: Apollos.

Baker, David W. 1988a. *Nahum, Habakkuk, Zephaniah: An Introduction and Commentary*. TOTC 23b. Downers Grove, IL: InterVarsity.

———. 1988b. "Obadiah: An Introduction and Commentary." In David W. Baker, T. Desmond Alexander, and Bruce Waltke, *Obadiah, Jonah, Micah*, 17–44. Downers Grove, IL: InterVarsity.

Balabanski, Vicky. 1997. *Eschatology in the Making: Mark, Matthew and the Didache*. SNTSMS 97. Cambridge: Cambridge University Press.

Baldwin, Joyce G. 1972. *Haggai, Zechariah, Malachi: An Introduction and Commentary*. TOTC 24. Downers Grove, IL: InterVarsity.

———. 1978. *Daniel: An Introduction and Commentary*. TOTC 21. Downers Grove, IL: InterVarsity.

———. 1984. *Esther: An Introduction and Commentary*. TOTC 12. Downers Grove, IL: InterVarsity.

———. 1988. *1 and 2 Samuel: An Introduction and Commentary*. TOTC 8. Downers Grove, IL: InterVarsity.

———. 1993. "Jonah." In *The Minor Prophets*, edited by Thomas McComiskey, 2:543–90. Grand Rapids: Baker.

Banks, Robert, ed. 1974. *Reconciliation and Hope: New Testament Essays on Atonement and Eschatology Presented to L. L. Morris on his 60th Birthday*. Grand Rapids: Eerdmans.

Barker, Kenneth L. 1997. "Evidence from Daniel." In *The Coming Millennial Kingdom: A Case for Premillennial Interpretation*, edited by Donald K. Campbell and Jeffrey L. Townsend, 135–46. Grand Rapids: Kregel.

Barnett, Paul. 1997. *The Second Epistle to the Corinthians*. NICNT. Grand Rapids: Eerdmans.

Barr, James. 1961. *The Semantics of Biblical Language*. London: Oxford.

———. 1977. "Some Semantic Notes on the Covenant." In *Beiträge zur alttestamentlichen Theologie: Festschrift für Walther Zimmerli zum 70 Geburtstag*, edited by H. Donner, R. Hanhart, and R. Smend, 23–38. Göttingen: Vandenhoeck and Ruprecht.

Barrett, C. K. 1960. *The Gospel according to St John*. London: SPCK.

———. 1962. *From First Adam to Last: A Study in Pauline Theology*. New York: Charles Scribner's Sons.

———. 1964. "The Eschatology of the Epistle to the Hebrews." In *The Background of the New Testament and Its Eschatology: Studies in Honor of C. H. Dodd*, edited by W. D. Davies and D. Daube, 363–93. Cambridge: Cambridge University Press.

———. 1968. *A Commentary on the First Epistle to the Corinthians*. HNTC. New York: Harper & Row.
———. 1973. *A Commentary on the Second Epistle to the Corinthians*. HNTC. Peabody, MA: Hendrickson.
———. 1994. *Acts 1–14*. ICC. London: T&T Clark.
———. 1998. *Acts 15–28*. ICC. London: T&T Clark.
———. 2002. *The Acts of the Apostles: A Shorter Commentary*. London: T&T Clark.
Barth, Karl. 1933. *The Resurrection of the Dead*. Translated by H. J. Stenning. London: Hodder and Stoughton Limited.
———. 1986. *Witness to the Word: A Commentary on John 1*. Edited by Walther Fürst. Translated by Geoffrey W. Bromiley. Grand Rapids: Eerdmans.
Bartholomew, Craig, Colin Greene, and Karl Möller, eds. 2001. *After Pentecost: Language and Biblical Interpretation*. SHS 2. Grand Rapids: Zondervan.
Bartholomew, Craig, C. Stephen Evans, Mary Healy, and Murray Rae, eds. 2003. *Behind the Text: History and Biblical Interpretation*. SHS 4. Grand Rapids: Zondervan.
Bartholomew, Craig, Mary Healy, Karl Möller, and Robin Parry, eds. 2004. *Out of Egypt: Biblical Theology and Biblical Interpretation*. SHS 5. Grand Rapids: Zondervan.
Bartholomew, Craig, and Michael W. Goheen. 2004. *The Drama of Scripture: Finding Our Place in the Biblical Story*. Grand Rapids: Baker Academic.
Bartlett, David L. 1983. *The Shape of Scriptural Authority*. Philadelphia: Fortress.
Barton, John. 1986. *Oracles of God: Perceptions of Ancient Prophecy in Israel after the Exile*. London: Darton, Longman, and Todd.
Bauckham, Richard. 1982. "Sabbath and Sunday in the Post-Apostolic Church." In *From Sabbath to Lord's Day*, edited by D. A. Carson, 251–98. Grand Rapids: Zondervan.
———. 1983. *Jude, 2 Peter*. WBC 50. Nashville: Thomas Nelson.
———. 1993a. *The Climax of Prophecy: Studies on the Book of Revelation*. Edinburgh: T&T Clark.
———. 1993b. *The Theology of the Book of Revelation*. Cambridge: Cambridge University Press.
———, ed. 1998. *The Gospels for All Christians: Rethinking the Gospel Audiences*. Grand Rapids: Eerdmans.
———. 2001. "Revelation." In *The Oxford Bible Commentary*, edited by John Barton and John Muddiman, 1287–1306. Oxford: Oxford University Press.
———. 2006. *Jesus and the Eyewitnesses: The Gospels as Eyewitness Testimony*. Grand Rapids: Eerdmans.
Beale, Gregory K., ed. 1994. *The Right Doctrine from the Wrong Texts? Essays on the Use of the Old Testament in the New*. Grand Rapids: Baker.

———. 1998. *John's Use of the Old Testament in Revelation*. JSNTSup 166. Sheffield: Sheffield Academic Press.
———. 1999. *The Book of Revelation*. NIGTC. Grand Rapids: Eerdmans.
———. 2003. *1–2 Thessalonians*. IVPNTC 13. Downers Grove, IL: InterVarsity.
———. 2004. *The Temple and the Church's Mission: A Biblical Theology of the Dwelling Place of God*. NSBT 17. Nottingham: Apollos; Downers Grove, IL: InterVarsity.
———. 2005. "Eden, the Temple, and the Church's Mission in the New Creation." *JETS* 48, no. 1:5–31.
Beasley-Murray, George R. 1978. *The Book of Revelation*. Rev. ed. NCB. London: Marshall, Morgan and Scott.
———. 1986. *Jesus and the Kingdom of God*. Grand Rapids: Eerdmans.
———. 1992. "The Kingdom of God in the Teaching of Jesus." *JETS* 35, no. 1:19–30.
———. 1993. *Jesus and the Last Days: The Interpretation of the Olivet Discourse*. Peabody, MA: Hendrickson.
———. 1999. *John*. 2d ed. WBC 36. Nashville: Thomas Nelson.
Beasley-Murray, Paul. 2000. *The Message of the Resurrection*. Downers Grove, IL: InterVarsity, 2000.
Beckwith, Isbon T. 1919. *The Apocalypse of John*. New York: Macmillan.
Bell, Albert A., Jr. 1979. "The Date of John's Apocalypse: The Evidence of Some Roman Historians Reconsidered." *NTS* 25:553–70.
Bell, Richard H. 2005. *The Irrevocable Call of God: An Inquiry into Paul's Theology of Israel*. WUNT 184. Tübingen: Mohr Siebeck.
Ben Zvi, Ehud. 2000. *Micah*. FOTL 21B. Grand Rapids: Eerdmans.
Bergen, Robert D. 1996. *1, 2 Samuel*. NAC. Nashville: Broadman.
Berkhof, Louis. 1939. *Systematic Theology*. Grand Rapids: Eerdmans.
———. 1979. *Introduction to Systematic Theology*. Grand Rapids: Baker.
Berkouwer, G. C. 1952. *The Providence of God*. Grand Rapids: Eerdmans.
Best, Ernest. 1986. *A Commentary on the First and Second Epistles to the Thessalonians*. HNTC. Peabody, MA: Hendrickson.
Betz, Hans Dieter. 1979. *Galatians*. Hermeneia. Philadelphia: Fortress.
Blaising, Craig A. 2001. "The Future of Israel as a Theological Question." *JETS* 44, no. 3:435–50.
Blaising, Craig A., and Darrell L. Bock, eds. 1992. *Dispensationalism, Israel and the Church*. Grand Rapids: Zondervan.
———. 1993. *Progressive Dispensationalism*. Wheaton, IL: Victor Books.
Blenkinsopp, Joseph. 1988. *Ezra-Nehemiah*. OTL. Philadelphia: Westminster.
———. 1996. *A History of Prophecy in Israel*. Rev. and enl. ed. Louisville: Westminster.

Blocher, Henri. 1984. *In the Beginning: The Opening Chapters of Genesis.* Translated by David G. Preston. Downers Grove, IL: InterVarsity.

———. 1994. *Evil and the Cross: An Analytical Look at the Problem of Pain.* Translated by David G. Preston. Grand Rapids: Kregel Academic.

Block, Daniel I. 1988. "The Period of the Judges: Religious Disintegration under Tribal Rule." In *Israel's Apostasy and Restoration*, edited by Avraham Gileadi, 39–58. Grand Rapids: Baker.

———. 1997. *The Book of Ezekiel: Chapters 1–24.* NICOT. Grand Rapids: Eerdmans.

———. 1998. *The Book of Ezekiel: Chapters 25–48.* NICOT. Grand Rapids: Eerdmans.

———. 1999. *Judges, Ruth.* NAC 6. Nashville: Broadman.

———. 2003. "My Servant David: Ancient Israel's Vision of the Messiah." In *Israel's Messiah in the Bible and the Dead Sea Scrolls*, edited by Richard S. Hess and M. Daniel Carroll R., 17–56. Grand Rapids: Baker Academic.

Blomberg, Craig L. 1987. *The Historical Reliability of the Gospels.* Downers Grove, IL: InterVarsity.

———. 1992. *Matthew.* NAC 22. Nashville: Broadman.

———. 1994. *1 Corinthians.* NIVAC. Grand Rapids: Zondervan.

———. 1997. *Jesus and the Gospels: An Introduction and Survey.* Nashville: Broadman.

———. 1998. "The Christian and the Law of Moses." In *Witness to the Gospel: The Theology of Acts*, edited by I. Howard Marshall and David Peterson, 397–416. Grand Rapids: Eerdmans.

———. 2001. *The Historical Reliability of John's Gospel.* Downers Grove, IL: InterVarsity.

———. 2002. "Interpreting Old Testament Prophetic Literature in Matthew: Double Fulfillment." *TrinJ* 23, no. 1:17–33.

———. 2006. *From Pentecost to Patmos: An Introduction to Acts through Revelation.* Nashville: Broadman and Holman Academic.

———. 2007. "Matthew." In *Commentary on the New Testament Use of the Old Testament*, edited by G. K. Beale and D. A. Carson, 1–109. Grand Rapids: Baker Academic.

Bock, Darrell L. 1994a. *Luke 1:1–9:50.* BECNT. Grand Rapids: Baker.

———. 1994b. "Current Messianic Activity and OT Davidic Promise: Dispensationalism, Hermeneutics, and NT Fulfillment." *TrinJ* 15, no. 1:55–87.

———. 1996. *Luke 9:51–24:53.* BECNT. Grand Rapids: Baker.

———, ed. 1999. *Three Views of the Millennium and Beyond.* Grand Rapids: Zondervan.

———. 2007. *Acts.* BECNT. Grand Rapids: Baker.

Bock, Darrell L., and Buist M. Fanning, eds. 2006. *Interpreting the New Testament Text: Introduction to the Art and Science of Exegesis*. Wheaton, IL: Crossway.

Bockmuehl, Markus. 2000. *Jewish Law in Gentile Churches: Halakhah and the Beginning of Christian Public Ethics*. Grand Rapids: Baker Academic.

Bolin, Thomas M. 1997. *Freedom beyond Forgiveness: The Book of Jonah Re-Examined*. JSOTSup 236. Sheffield: Sheffield Academic Press.

Bolt, Peter G. 1998. "Life, Death, and the Afterlife in the Greco-Roman World." In *Life in the Face of Death: The Resurrection Message of the New Testament*, edited by Richard N. Longenecker, 51–79. Grand Rapids: Eerdmans.

Borgen, Peder. 1965. *Bread from Heaven: An Exegetical Study of the Concept of Manna in the Gospel of John and the Writings of Philo*. NovTSup 10. Leiden: Brill.

Botterweck, G. Johannes, and Helmer Ringgren, eds. 1974–2006. *Theological Dictionary of the Old Testament*. 15 vols. Grand Rapids: Eerdmans.

Braaten, Carl E., and Robert W. Jenson, eds. 2002. *The Last Things: Biblical and Theological Perspectives on Eschatology*. Grand Rapids: Eerdmans.

Braun, Roddy. 1986. *1 Chronicles*. WBC 14. Waco: Word Books.

Briggs, Richard S. 2001. *Words in Action: Speech Act Theory and Biblical Interpretation*. Edinburgh: T&T Clark.

Bright, John. 1965. *Jeremiah*. AB 21. New York: Doubleday.

———. 1976. *Covenant and Promise: The Prophetic Understanding of the Future in Pre-Exilic Israel*. Philadelphia: Westminster.

Brooks, James A. 1991. *Mark*. NAC 23. Nashville: Broadman.

Brooks, J. A., and C. L. Winbury. 1979. *Syntax of New Testament Greek*. Washington, DC: University Press of America.

Brower, Kent E., and Mark W. Elliott, eds. 1997. *Eschatology in Bible and Theology: Evangelical Essays at the Dawn of a New Millennium*. Downers Grove, IL: InterVarsity.

Brown, Colin, ed. 1986. *New International Dictionary of New Testament Theology*. 4 vols. Grand Rapids: Zondervan.

———. 1990. *Christianity and Western Thought*, vol. 1. Downers Grove, IL: InterVarsity.

Brown, Raymond E. 1966. *The Gospel according to John I–XII*. AB 29. New York: Doubleday.

———. 1970. *The Gospel according to John XIII–XXI*. AB 29A. New York: Doubleday.

———. 1977. *The Birth of the Messiah: A Commentary on the Infancy Narratives in Matthew and Luke*. London: Geoffrey Chapman.

Brownlee, William H. 1986. *Ezekiel 1–19*. WBC 28. Waco: Word.

Bruce, F. F. 1963. *Israel and the Nations: From the Exodus to the Fall of the Second Temple*. Grand Rapids: Eerdmans.

———. 1968. *New Testament Development of Old Testament Themes*. Grand Rapids: Eerdmans.

———. 1970. *Tradition Old and New*. Grand Rapids: Zondervan.

———. 1971a. "Inter-testamental Literature." In *What Theologians Do*, edited by F. G. Healey, 83–104. Grand Rapids: Eerdmans.

———. 1971b. *New Testament History*. Garden City, NY: Doubleday.

———. 1977a. *The Defense of the Gospel in the New Testament*. Grand Rapids: Eerdmans.

———. 1977b. *Paul: Apostle of the Heart Set Free*. Grand Rapids: Eerdmans.

———. 1978. *The Time Is Fulfilled*. Grand Rapids: Eerdmans.

———. 1981. *The New Testament Documents: Are They Reliable?* 6th ed. Grand Rapids: Eerdmans.

———. 1982a. *1 and 2 Thessalonians*. WBC 45. Waco: Word Books.

———. 1982b. *The Epistle to the Galatians*. NIGTC. Grand Rapids: Eerdmans.

———. 1983. *The Gospel of John*. Grand Rapids: Eerdmans.

———. 1984. *The Epistles to the Colossians, to Philemon, and to the Ephesians*. NICNT. Grand Rapids: Eerdmans.

———. 1985. *Romans: An Introduction and Commentary*. TNTC 6. Downers Grove, IL: InterVarsity Academic.

———. 1988a. *The Book of Acts*. Rev. ed. NICNT. Grand Rapids: Eerdmans.

———. 1988b. *The Canon of Scripture*. Downers Grove, IL: InterVarsity.

———. 1990. *The Epistle to the Hebrews*. Rev. ed. NICNT. Grand Rapids: Eerdmans.

———. 1993. "Habakkuk." In *The Minor Prophets*, edited by Thomas McComiskey, 2:831–96. Grand Rapids: Baker.

Brueggemann, Walter. 1977. *The Land: Place as Gift, Promise, and Challenge in Biblical Faith*. Philadelphia: Fortress.

———. 1978. *The Prophetic Imagination*. Minneapolis: Fortress.

———. 1982. *Genesis*. Interpretation. Louisville: Westminster.

———. 1986. *Hopeful Imagination*. Philadelphia: Fortress.

———. 1988. *Israel's Praise: Doxology against Idolatry and Ideology*. Philadelphia: Fortress.

———. 1990. *First and Second Samuel*. Interpretation. Louisville: Westminster.

———. 1997. *Theology of the Old Testament: Testimony, Dispute, Advocacy*. Minneapolis: Fortress.

———. 1998. *A Commentary on Jeremiah: Exile and Homecoming*. Grand Rapids: Eerdmans.

Brunner, Emil. 1946. *Revelation and Reason*. Translated by Olive Wyon. Philadelphia: Westminster.

Buchanan, George W. 1961. "Eschatology and the 'End of Days.'" *JNES* 20:188–93.

Budd, Philip J. 1984. *Numbers*. WBC 5. Waco: Word Books.

Buis, Harry. 1960. *The Book of Revelation*. Philadelphia: P&R.

Bullock, C. Hassell. 1986. *An Introduction to the Old Testament Prophetic Books*. Chicago: Moody.

———. 1988. *An Introduction to the Old Testament Poetic Books*. Revised and expanded. Chicago: Moody.

———. 2001. *Encountering the Book of Psalms*. Grand Rapids: Baker.

Bulman, James M. 1973. "The Identification of Darius the Mede." *WTJ* 35:247–67.

Bultmann, Rudolf. 1961. "New Testament and Mythology." In *Kerygma and Myth: A Theological Debate*, edited by Hans Werner Bartsch, translated by Reginald H. Fuller, 1–44. New York: Harper & Brothers.

Burge, Gary M. 1987. *The Anointed Community: The Holy Spirit in the Johannine Tradition*. Grand Rapids: Eerdmans.

———. 1994. "Territorial Religion, Johannine Christology, and the Vineyard of John 15." In *Jesus of Nazareth: Lord and Christ*, edited by Joel B. Green and Max Turner, 384–96. Grand Rapids: Eerdmans.

Burridge, Richard A. 2004. *What Are the Gospels? A Comparison with Graeco-Roman Biography*. 2d ed. Grand Rapids: Eerdmans.

Burton, Ernest De Witt. 1921. *The Epistle to the Galatians*. ICC. Edinburgh: T&T Clark.

Butler, Trent C. 1983. *Joshua*. WBC 7. Waco: Word Books.

Caird, G. B. 1965. *Jesus and the Jewish Nation*. The Ethel M. Wood Lecture delivered before the University of London on 9 March 1965. London: Athlone.

———. 1966. *The Revelation of Saint John*. BNTC 19. Peabody, MA: Hendrickson.

———. 1980. *The Language and Imagery of the Bible*. Philadelphia: Westminster.

———. 1994. *New Testament Theology*. Edited by L. D. Hurst. Oxford: Oxford University Press.

Calvin, John. 1960. *Institutes of the Christian Religion*. Edited by John T. McNeill. Translated by Ford Lewis Battles. LCC 20–21. Philadelphia: Westminster.

———. 2003. *Calvin's Commentaries*. 22 vols. Reprint, Grand Rapids: Baker.

Campbell, Antony F., 2004. *Joshua to Chronicles: An Introduction*. Louisville: Westminster.

Campbell, Antony F., and Mark A. O'Brien. 2000. *Unfolding the Deuteronomistic History*. Minneapolis: Fortress.

Campbell, Donald K., and Jeffrey L. Townsend, eds. 1997. *The Coming Millennial Kingdom: A Case for Premillennial Interpretation*. Grand Rapids: Kregel.

Carr, G. Lloyd. 1984. *The Song of Solomon: An Introduction and Commentary*. TOTC 17. Downers Grove, IL: InterVarsity.

Carroll, John T. 1988. *Response to the End of History: Eschatology and Situation in Luke-Acts*. SBLDS 92. Atlanta: Scholars.

Carroll, Robert P. 1979. *When Prophecy Failed: Cognitive Dissonance in the Prophetic Traditions of the Old Testament*. New York: Seabury.

Carson, D. A., ed. 1982. *From Sabbath to Lord's Day*. Grand Rapids: Zondervan.

———. 1984. "Matthew." In *The Expositor's Bible Commentary*, edited by Frank E. Gaebelein, 8:3–599. Grand Rapids: Zondervan.

———. 1987. *Showing the Spirit: A Theological Exposition of 1 Corinthians 12–14*. Grand Rapids: Baker.

———. 1991. *The Gospel according to John*. PNTC. Grand Rapids: Eerdmans.

———. 1996. *Exegetical Fallacies*. 2d ed. Grand Rapids: Baker Academic.

Carson, D. A., and Douglas J. Moo. 2005. *An Introduction to the New Testament*. 2d ed. Grand Rapids: Zondervan.

Carson, D. A., Peter T. O'Brien, and Mark A. Seifrid, eds. 2001. *Justification and Variegated Nomism*, vol. 1, *The Complexities of Second Temple Judaism*. Grand Rapids: Baker Academic.

———, eds. 2004. *Justification and Variegated Nomism*, vol. 2, *The Paradoxes of Paul*. Grand Rapids: Baker Academic.

Carson, D. A., and John D. Woodbridge, eds. 1986. *Hermeneutics, Authority and Canon*. Leicester: Inter-Varsity.

———, eds. 1992. *Scripture and Truth*. Grand Rapids: Baker.

Carter, Warren. 2003. "Are There Imperial Texts in the Class? Intertextual Eagles and Matthean Eschatology as 'Lights Out' Time for Imperial Rome (Matthew 24:27–31)." *JBL* 122, no. 3:467–87.

———. 2006. *John: Storyteller, Interpreter, Evangelist*. Peabody, MA: Hendrickson.

Casselli, Stephen J. 1997. "Jesus as Eschatological Torah." *TrinJ* 18, no. 1:15–41.

Cassuto, Umberto. 1961. *The Documentary Hypothesis*. Jerusalem: Magnes.

Chafer, Lewis Sperry. 1948. *Systematic Theology*. 8 vols. Dallas: Dallas Seminary Press.

Chamblin, Knox. 1988. "The Law of Moses and the Law of Christ." In *Continuity and Discontinuity: Perspectives on the Relationship between the Old and New Testaments*, edited by John S. Feinberg, 181–202. Wheaton, IL: Crossway.

Chance, J. Bradley. 1988. *Jerusalem, the Temple, and the New Age in Luke-Acts*. Macon: Mercer University Press.

Charles, R. H. 1920. *The Revelation of St. John*. 2 vols. ICC. Edinburgh: T&T Clark.

Charlesworth, James H., ed. 1983. *The Old Testament Pseudepigrapha*, vol. 1. Garden City, NY: Doubleday.

———, ed. 1985. *The Old Testament Pseudepigrapha*, vol. 2. Garden City, NY: Doubleday.

Chester, Andrew, and Ralph P. Martin. 1994. *The Theology of the Letters of James, Peter, and Jude*. Cambridge: Cambridge University Press.

Childs, Brevard S. 1974. *The Book of Exodus*. OTL. Louisville: Westminster.

———. 1985. *Old Testament Theology in a Canonical Context*. Philadelphia: Fortress.

———. 1992. *Biblical Theology of the Old and New Testaments: Theological Reflection on the Christian Bible*. Minneapolis: Fortress.

———. 2001. *Isaiah*. OTL. Louisville: Westminster.

Chilton, David. 1987. *The Days of Vengeance: An Exposition of the Book of Revelation*. Fort Worth: Dominion.

Chisholm, Robert B., Jr. 2006. *Interpreting the Historical Books: An Exegetical Handbook*. Grand Rapids: Kregel Academic.

Ciampa, Roy E. 2007. "The History of Redemption." In *Central Themes in Biblical Theology*, edited by Scott J. Hafemann and Paul R. House, 254–308. Grand Rapids: Baker Academic.

Clark, David S. 1989. *The Message from Patmos: A Postmillennial Commentary on the Book of Revelation*. Grand Rapids: Baker.

Clements, Ronald E. 1965. *Prophecy and Covenant*. SBT 43. London: SCM Press.

———. 1992. *Wisdom in Theology*. Grand Rapids: Eerdmans.

———. 1996. *Old Testament Prophecy: From Oracles to Canon*. Louisville: Westminster.

Clines, D. J. A. 1984. *Ezra, Nehemiah, Esther*. NCB. London: Marshall, Morgan & Scott.

———. 1989. *Job 1–20*. WBC 17. Dallas: Word Books.

Clowney, Edmund. 1988. *The Message of 1 Peter*. BST. Downers Grove, IL: InterVarsity.

Coady, C. A. J. 1992. *Testimony: A Philosophical Study*. Oxford: Clarendon.

Cochrane, Arthur C., ed. 2003. *Reformed Confessions of the Sixteenth Century*. Louisville: Westminster.

Cohen, Shaye J. D. 1987. *From the Maccabees to the Mishnah*. Philadelphia: Westminster.

Cole, R. Alan. 1973. *Exodus: An Introduction and Commentary*. TOTC 2. Downers Grove, IL: InterVarsity.

———. 1989a. *The Gospel according to Mark*. TNTC 2. Grand Rapids: Eerdmans.

———. 1989b. *The Epistle of Paul to the Galatians: An Introduction and Commentary*. TNTC 9. Grand Rapids: Eerdmans.

Colless, Brian E. 1992. "Cyrus the Persian as Darius the Mede in the Book of Daniel." *JSOT* 56:113–26.

Collins, Adela Yarbro. 1984. *Crisis and Catharsis: The Power of the Apocalypse*. Philadelphia: Westminster.

Collins, C. John. 2006. *Genesis 1–4: A Linguistic, Literary, and Theological Commentary*. Phillipsburg, NJ: P&R.

Collins, John J. 1993. *Daniel*. Edited by Frank Moore Cross. Hermeneia. Minneapolis: Fortress.

———. 1998. *The Apocalyptic Imagination: An Introduction to Jewish Apocalyptic Literature*. 2d ed. Grand Rapids: Eerdmans.

———. 2000. *Between Athens and Jerusalem: Jewish Identity in the Hellenistic Diaspora*. 2d ed. Grand Rapids: Eerdmans.

Collins, John J., and Peter W. Flint, eds. 2001. *The Book of Daniel: Composition and Reception*. 2 vols. VTSup 83. Leiden: Brill.

Collins, Raymond F. 1999. *First Corinthians*. SacPag 7. Collegeville, MN: Liturgical.

Collins, Roger G. 1986. "Eschatology within the Prophetic Speeches of Micah." Th.M. thesis, Reformed Theological Seminary.

Conn, Harvie M., ed. 1988. *Inerrancy and Hermeneutic: A Tradition, A Challenge, A Debate*. Grand Rapids: Baker.

Conzelmann, Hans. 1987. *Acts of the Apostles*. Edited by Eldon Jay Epp and Christopher R. Matthews. Translated by James Limburg, A. Thomas Kraabel, and Donald H. Juel. Hermeneia. Philadelphia: Fortress.

Copan, Paul, and William Lane Craig. 2004. *Creation out of Nothing*. Grand Rapids: Baker Academic.

Cotterell, Peter, and Max Turner. 1989. *Linguistics and Biblical Interpretation*. Downers Grove, IL: InterVarsity.

Cowles, C. S., Eugene H. Merrill, Daniel L. Gard, and Tremper Longman III. 2003. *Show Them No Mercy: 4 Views on God and Canaanite Genocide*. Grand Rapids: Zondervan.

Cox, William E. 1963. *The New Covenant Israel*. Philadelphia: P&R.

Coxhead, Steven R. 2006. "Deuteronomy 30:11–14 as a Prophecy of the New Covenant in Christ." *WTJ* 68:305–20.

Cragg, Gerald R. 1970. *The Church and the Age of Reason 1648–1789*. New York: Penguin.

Craigie, Peter C. 1976. *The Book of Deuteronomy*. NICOT. Grand Rapids: Eerdmans.

———. 1983. *Psalms 1–50*. WBC 19. Waco: Word Books.

———. 1984–85. *Twelve Prophets*. 2 vols. DSB. Louisville: Westminster.

Cranfield, C. E. B. 1977. *The Gospel according to St. Mark*. CGTC. Cambridge: Cambridge University Press.

———. 2004a. *Romans 1–8*. ICC. London: T&T Clark.

———. 2004b. *Romans 9–16*. ICC. London: T&T Clark.

Crenshaw, James L. 1971. *Prophetic Conflict*. BZAW 124. Berlin: Walter de Gruyter.

———. 1981. *Old Testament Wisdom: An Introduction*. Atlanta: John Knox.

Cullmann, Oscar. 1956. *The State in the New Testament*. New York: Charles Scribner's Sons.

Cundall, Arthur E., and Leon Morris. 1968. *Judges and Ruth: An Introduction and Commentary*. TOTC 7. Downers Grove, IL: InterVarsity.

Dahood, Mitchell. 1966. *Psalms I:1–50*. AB 16. New York: Doubleday.

———. 1968. *Psalms II:51–100*. AB 17. New York: Doubleday.

———. 1970. *Psalms III:101–150*. AB 17a. New York: Doubleday.

Dana, H. E., and J. R. Mantey. 1927. *A Manual Grammar of the Greek New Testament*. Toronto: Macmillan.

Das, A. Andrew. 2001. *Paul, the Law, and the Covenant*. Peabody, MA: Hendrickson.

———. 2003. *Paul and the Jews*. Peabody, MA: Hendrickson.

Davids, Peter H. 1982. *The Epistle of James*. NIGTC. Grand Rapids: Eerdmans.

———. 1989. *James*. NIBC 15. Peabody, MA: Hendrickson.

Davidson, Richard M. 1981. *Typology in Scripture: A Study of Hermeneutical* τύπος *Structures*. AUSDDS 2. Berrien Springs, MI: Andrews University Press.

Davies, W. D. 1967. *Paul and Rabbinic Judaism: Some Rabbinic Elements in Pauline Theology*. New York: Harper & Row.

———. 1974. *The Gospel and the Land: Early Christianity and Jewish Territorial Doctrine*. Berkeley: University of California Press.

Davies, W. D., and D. C. Allison. 1988. *Matthew 1–7*. ICC. London: T&T Clark.

———. 1991. *Matthew 8–18*. ICC. London: T&T Clark.

———. 1997. *Matthew 19–28*. ICC. London: T&T Clark.

Davis, Stephen T. 1993. *Risen Indeed: Making Sense of the Resurrection*. Grand Rapids: Eerdmans.

Dawson, Gerrit Scott. 2004. *Jesus Ascended: The Meaning of Christ's Continuing Incarnation*. Phillipsburg, NJ: P&R.

Dearman, J. Andrew. 2002. *Jeremiah and Lamentations*. NIVAC. Grand Rapids: Zondervan.

Dempster, Stephen G. 2003. *Dominion and Dynasty: A Theology of the Hebrew Bible*. NSBT 15. Nottingham: Apollos; Downers Grove, IL: InterVarsity.

deSilva, David A. 1992. "The Social Setting of the Revelation to John: Conflicts Within, Fears Without." *WTJ* 54, no. 2:273–302.

———. 2000. "Entering God's Rest: Eschatology and the Socio-Rhetorical Strategy of Hebrews." *TrinJ* 21, no. 1:25–43.

———. 2002. *Introducing the Apocrypha: Message, Context, and Significance.* Grand Rapids: Baker Academic.

DeVries, Simon J. 1985. *1 Kings.* WBC 12. Waco: Word Books.

Dillard, Raymond B. 1987. *2 Chronicles.* WBC 15. Waco: Word Books.

———. 1992. "Joel." In *The Minor Prophets,* edited by Thomas McComiskey, 1:239–313. Grand Rapids: Baker.

Dillard, Raymond B., and Tremper Longman III. 1994. *An Introduction to the Old Testament.* Grand Rapids: Zondervan.

Dobbs-Allsopp, F. W. 2002. *Lamentations.* Interpretation. Louisville: John Knox.

Dockery, David S., ed. 2001. *The Challenge of Postmodernism.* 2d ed. Grand Rapids: Baker Academic.

Dodd, C. H. 1961. *The Parables of the Kingdom.* Revised edition. New York: Charles Scribner's Sons.

———. 1962. *The Apostolic Preaching and Its Developments.* New York: Harper & Brothers.

———. 1965. *The Interpretation of the Fourth Gospel.* Cambridge: Cambridge University Press.

Duguid, Iain M. 1999. *Ezekiel.* NIVAC. Grand Rapids: Zondervan.

———. 2006. "But Did They Live Happily Ever After? The Eschatology of the Book of Esther." *WTJ* 68:85–98.

Dumbrell, William J. 1984. *Covenant and Creation: A Theology of Old Testament Covenants.* Nashville: Thomas Nelson.

———. 1985. *The End of the Beginning: Revelation 21–22 and the Old Testament.* Grand Rapids: Baker.

———. 1994. *The Search for Order: Biblical Eschatology in Focus.* Grand Rapids: Baker.

———. 2002. *The Faith of Israel: A Theological Survey of the Old Testament.* 2d ed. Grand Rapids: Baker Academic.

Dunn, James D. G. 1988a. *Romans 1–8.* WBC 38A. Dallas: Word Books.

———. 1988b. *Romans 9–16.* WBC 38B. Dallas: Word Books.

———. 1990. *Jesus, Paul and the Law: Studies in Mark and Galatians.* Louisville: Westminster.

———. 1993. *The Epistle to the Galatians.* BNTC 9. Peabody, MA: Hendrickson.

———. 1996. *The Epistles to the Colossians and to Philemon.* NIGTC. Grand Rapids: Eerdmans.

———. 1998. *The Theology of Paul the Apostle*. Grand Rapids: Eerdmans.

———, ed. 2001a. *Paul and the Mosaic Law*. Grand Rapids: Eerdmans.

———. 2001b. "The Danielic Son of Man in the New Testament." In *The Book of Daniel: Composition and Reception*, edited by John J. Collins and Peter W. Flint, 2:528–49. VTSup 83. Leiden: Brill.

Durham, John I. 1987. *Exodus*. WBC 3. Waco: Word Books.

Eaton, John H. 1976. *Kingship and the Psalms*. SBT, Second Series 32. Naperville, IL: Alec R. Allenson Inc.

Eaton, Michael A. 1983. *Ecclesiastes: An Introduction and Commentary*. TOTC 16. Downers Grove, IL: InterVarsity.

Edwards, James R. 2002. *The Gospel according to Mark*. PNTC. Grand Rapids: Eerdmans.

Edwards, Jonathan. 2005. *Unless You Repent*. Grand Rapids: Soli Deo Gloria.

Edwards, O. 1992. "The Year of Jerusalem's Destruction." *ZAW* 104:101–6.

Ellingworth, Paul. 1993. *The Epistle to the Hebrews*. NIGTC. Grand Rapids: Eerdmans.

Elliott, Neil. 2000. "Paul and the Politics of Empire: Problems and Prospects." In *Paul and Politics: Ekklesia, Israel, Imperium, Interpretation*, edited by Richard A. Horsley, 17–39. Harrisburg, PA: Trinity Press International.

Ellis, E. Earle. 1972. *Eschatology in Luke*. Philadelphia: Fortress.

———. 1977. "How the New Testament Uses the Old." In *New Testament Interpretation: Essays on Principles and Methods*, edited by I. Howard Marshall, 199–219. Grand Rapids: Eerdmans.

Ellison, H. L. 1979. *From Babylon to Bethlehem: The People of God from the Exile to the Messiah*. Atlanta: John Knox.

Enns, Peter. 2000. *Exodus*. NIVAC. Grand Rapids: Zondervan.

———. 2001. "Expansions of Scripture." In *Justification and Variegated Nomism*, vol. 1, *The Complexities of Second Temple Judaism*, edited by D. A. Carson, Peter T. O'Brien, and Mark A. Seifrid, 73–98. Grand Rapids: Baker Academic.

Eskenasi, Tamara C. 1988. *In an Age of Prose: A Literary Approach to Ezra-Nehemiah*. SBLMS 36. Atlanta: Scholars.

Estes, Daniel J. 2005. *Handbook on the Wisdom Books and Psalms*. Grand Rapids: Baker Academic.

Evans, C. Stephen. 1982. *Philosophy of Religion*. Downers Grove, IL: InterVarsity.

———. 1996. *The Historical Christ and the Jesus of Faith*. Oxford: Oxford University Press.

Evans, Craig A. 2001. "Daniel in the New Testament: Visions of God's Kingdom." In *The Book of Daniel: Composition and Reception*, edited by John J. Collins and Peter W. Flint, 2:490–527. VTSup 83. Leiden: Brill.

Fairbairn, Patrick. 2000. *The Typology of Scripture*. Grand Rapids: Kregel.
Fee, Gordon D. 1987. *The First Epistle to the Corinthians*. NICNT. Grand Rapids: Eerdmans.
———. 1994. *God's Empowering Presence: The Holy Spirit in the Letters of Paul*. Peabody, MA: Hendrickson.
———. 1995. *Paul's Letter to the Philippians*. NICNT. Grand Rapids: Eerdmans.
———. 2002. *New Testament Exegesis*. 3d ed. Louisville: Westminster.
Fee, Gordon D., and Douglas Stuart. 1993. *How to Read the Bible for All Its Worth*. 2d ed. Grand Rapids: Zondervan.
Feinberg, Charles Lee. 1969. *The Prophecy of Ezekiel*. Chicago: Moody.
Feinberg, John S. 1986. "1 Peter 3:18–20, Ancient Mythology, and the Intermediate State." *WTJ* 48, no. 2:303–36.
———, ed. 1988. *Continuity and Discontinuity: Perspectives on the Relationship between the Old and New Testaments*. Wheaton, IL: Crossway.
Fensham, F. Charles. 1982. *The Books of Ezra and Nehemiah*. NICOT. Grand Rapids: Eerdmans.
Ferguson, Everett. 2003. *Backgrounds of Early Christianity*. 3d ed. Grand Rapids: Eerdmans.
Ferguson, Sinclair B. 1988. *Daniel*. CCom. Waco: Word.
———. 1996. *The Holy Spirit*. Downers Grove, IL: InterVarsity.
Finley, Thomas J. 1990. *Joel, Amos, Obadiah*. WEC. Chicago: Moody.
Fiorenza, Elisabeth Schüssler. 1985. *The Book of Revelation: Justice and Judgment*. Philadelphia: Fortress.
Firth, David, and Philip S. Johnston, eds. 2005. *Interpreting the Psalms: Issues and Approaches*. Downers Grove, IL: InterVarsity Academic.
Fish, Stanley. 1980. *Is There a Text in This Class?* Cambridge: Harvard University Press.
Fitzmyer, Joseph A. 1981. *The Gospel according to Luke (I–IX)*. AB 28. New York: Doubleday.
———. 1985. *The Gospel according to Luke (X–XXIV)*. AB 28A. New York: Doubleday.
———. 1993. *Romans*. AB 33. New York: Doubleday.
———. 1998. *The Acts of the Apostles*. AB 31. New York: Doubleday.
Fletcher-Louis, Crispin H. T. 1997. "The Destruction of the Temple and the Relativization of the Old Covenant: Mark 13:31 and Matthew 5:18." In *Eschatology in Bible and Theology: Evangelical Essays at the Dawn of a New Millennium*, edited by Kent E. Brower and Mark W. Elliott, 145–69. Downers Grove, IL: InterVarsity.
Floyd, Michael H. 2000. *Minor Prophets, Part 2*. FOTL 22. Grand Rapids: Eerdmans.

Foerster, Werner. 1964. *From the Exile to Christ: A Historical Introduction to Palestinian Judaism*. Translated by Gordon E. Harris. Philadelphia: Fortress.

Ford, J. Massyngberde. 1975. *Revelation*. AB 38. New York: Doubleday.

Foulkes, Francis. 1958. *The Acts of God: A Study of the Basis of Typology in the Old Testament*. London: Tyndale.

Frame, James Everett. 1912. *The Epistles of St. Paul to the Thessalonians*. ICC. Edinburgh: T&T Clark.

France, R. T. 1982. *Jesus and the Old Testament*. Grand Rapids: Baker.

———. 1985. *The Gospel according to Matthew*. TNTC 1. Grand Rapids: Eerdmans.

———. 1989. *Matthew: Evangelist and Teacher*. New Testament Profiles. Downers Grove, IL: InterVarsity.

———. 2002. *The Gospel of Mark*. NIGTC. Grand Rapids: Eerdmans.

———. 2007. *The Gospel of Matthew*. NICNT. Grand Rapids: Eerdmans.

Freedman, David Noel. 1997. *Divine Commitment and Human Obligation: Selected Writings of David Noel Freedman*. Edited by John R. Huddlestun. 2 vols. Grand Rapids: Eerdmans.

Fretheim, Terence E. 1977. *The Message of Jonah: A Theological Commentary*. Minneapolis: Augsburg.

———. 1983. *Deuteronomic History*. Nashville: Abingdon.

———. 1990. *Exodus*. Interpretation. Louisville: Westminster.

Friesen, Steven J. 2001. *Imperial Cults and the Apocalypse of John: Reading Revelation in the Ruins*. New York: Oxford University Press.

———. 2005. "Satan's Throne, Imperial Cults and the Social Settings of Revelation." *JSNT* 27, no. 3:351–73.

Fuller, George C. 1966. "The Olivet Discourse: An Apocalyptic Timetable." *WTJ* 28, no. 2:157–63.

———. 1994. "The Life of Jesus, after the Ascension (Luke 24:50–53; Acts 1:9–11)." *WTJ* 56, no. 2:391–98.

Fung, Ronald Y. K. 1988. *The Epistle to the Galatians*. NICNT. Grand Rapids: Eerdmans.

Funk, Robert W., and the Jesus Seminar. 1998. *The Acts of Jesus: The Search for the Authentic Deeds of Jesus*. San Francisco: Harper San Francisco.

Funk, Robert W., Roy W. Hoover, and the Jesus Seminar. 1993. *The Five Gospels: The Search for the Authentic Words of Jesus*. New York: Macmillan.

Furnish, Victor Paul. 1984. *II Corinthians*. AB 32A. New York: Doubleday.

Fyall, Robert S. 2002. *Now My Eyes Have Seen You: Images of Creation and Evil in the Book of Job*. NSBT 12. Nottingham: Apollos; Downers Grove, IL: InterVarsity.

Gaffin, Richard B., Jr. 1979. *Perspectives on Pentecost: New Testament Teaching on the Gifts of the Holy Spirit*. Phillipsburg, NJ: P&R.
———. 1987. *Resurrection and Redemption: A Study in Paul's Soteriology*. 2d ed. Phillipsburg, NJ: P&R.
García Martínez, Florentino. 1996. *The Dead Sea Scrolls Translated: The Qumran Texts in English*. 2d ed. Grand Rapids: Eerdmans.
Gardner, Paul. *2 Peter and Jude*. Fearn, Ross-shire: Christian Focus.
Garland, David E. 1999. *2 Corinthians*. NAC. Nashville: Broadman.
———. 2003. *1 Corinthians*. BECNT. Grand Rapids: Baker.
Garrett, Duane. 1991. *Rethinking Genesis*. Grand Rapids: Baker.
Gaston, Lloyd. 1970. *No Stone on Another: Studies in the Significance of the Fall of Jerusalem in the Synoptic Gospels*. NovTSup 23. Leiden: Brill.
Gathercole, Simon J. 2002. *Where Is Boasting? Early Jewish Soteriology and Paul's Response in Romans 1–5*. Grand Rapids: Eerdmans.
Geisler, Norman L., ed. 1980. *Inerrancy*. Grand Rapids: Zondervan.
Geldenhuys, Norval. 1952. *Commentary on the Gospel of Luke*. NICNT. Grand Rapids: Eerdmans.
Gentry, Kenneth L., Jr. 1989a. *Before Jerusalem Fell: Dating the Book of Revelation*. Tyler, TX: Institute for Christian Economics.
———. 1989b. *The Beast of Revelation*. Tyler, TX: Institute for Christian Economics.
———. 1992. *He Shall Have Dominion: A Postmillennial Eschatology*. Tyler, TX: Institute for Christian Economics.
———. 1998. "A Preterist View of Revelation." In *Four Views on the Book of Revelation*, edited by C. Marvin Pate, 35–92. Grand Rapids: Zondervan.
———. 1999. *Perilous Times: A Study in Eschatological Evil*. Texarkana, AR: Covenant Media.
———, ed. 2003. *Thine Is the Kingdom: Studies in the Postmillennial Hope*. Vallecito, CA: Chalcedon Foundation.
George, Timothy. 1994. *Galatians*. NAC. Nashville: Broadman.
Georgi, Dieter. 1997. "God Turned Upside Down." In *Paul and Empire: Religion and Power in Roman Imperial Society*, edited by Richard A. Horsley, 148–57. Harrisburg, PA: Trinity Press International.
Gerstenberger, Erhard S. 1988. *Psalms, Part 1*. FOTL 14. Grand Rapids: Eerdmans.
———. 2001. *Psalms, Part 2, and Lamentations*. FOTL 15. Grand Rapids: Eerdmans.
Giblin, Charles H. 1967. *The Threat to Faith: An Exegetical and Theological Reexamination of 2 Thessalonians 2*. AnBib 31. Rome: Pontifical Biblical Institute.
———. 1991. *The Book of Revelation*. GNS 34. Collegeville, MN: Liturgical.

———. 1999. "The Millennium (Rev 20:4–6) as Heaven." *NTS* 45, no. 4:553–70.

Gileadi, Avraham, ed. 1988. *Israel's Apostasy and Restoration: Essays in Honor of Roland K. Harrison*. Grand Rapids: Baker.

Glasson, T. Francis. 1963. *Moses in the Fourth Gospel*. SBT 40. London: SCM Press.

Glenny, W. Edward. 1997. "Typology: A Summary of the Present Evangelical Discussion." *JETS* 40, no. 4:627–38.

Gloer, W. Hulitt, ed. 1988. *Eschatology and the New Testament: Essays in Honor of George Raymond Beasley-Murray*. Peabody, MA: Hendrickson.

Golding, Peter. 2004. *Covenant Theology*. Fearn, Ross-shire: Mentor.

Goldingay, John E. 1989. *Daniel*. WBC 30. Dallas: Word Books.

———. 2001a. "Daniel in the Context of Old Testament Theology." In *The Book of Daniel: Composition and Reception*, edited by John J. Collins and Peter W. Flint, 2:639–60. VTSup 83. Leiden: Brill.

———. 2001b. *Isaiah*. NIBC 13. Peabody, MA: Hendrickson.

———. 2003. *Old Testament Theology*. Vol. 1. Downers Grove, IL: InterVarsity.

Good, Edwin M. 1981. *Irony in the Old Testament*. 2d ed. BLS 3. Sheffield: Almond.

Goodman, Martin. 1997. *The Roman World: 44 BC–AD 180*. New York: Routledge.

Goppelt, Leonhard. 1982. *Typos: The Typological Interpretation of the Old Testament in the New*. Grand Rapids: Eerdmans.

Gordon, Robert P., ed. 1995. *The Place Is Too Small for Us: The Israelite Prophets in Recent Scholarship*. Edited by David W. Baker. SBTS 5. Winona Lake, IN: Eisenbrauns.

Gottwald, Norman K. 1954. *Studies in the Book of Lamentations*. SBT 14. London: SCM.

Gowan, Donald E. 1994. *Theology in Exodus*. Louisville: Westminster.

———. 1998. *Theology of the Prophetic Books: The Death and Resurrection of Israel*. Louisville: Westminster.

———. 2000. *Eschatology in the Old Testament*. 2d ed. Edinburgh: T&T Clark.

Grabbe, Lester L. 1988. "Another Look at the *Gestalt* of 'Darius the Mede.'" *CBQ* 50:198–213.

———. 1995. *Priests, Prophets, Diviners, and Sages: A Socio-Historical Study of Religious Specialists in Ancient Israel*. Valley Forge, PA: Trinity Press International.

Gradel, Ittai. 2002. *Emperor Worship and Roman Religion*. Oxford: Oxford University Press.

Grant, Jamie. 2005. "The Psalms and the King." In *Interpreting the Psalms: Issues and Approaches*, edited by David Firth and Philip S. Johnston, 101–18. Downers Grove, IL: InterVarsity Academic.

Grant, Jamie A., and Alistair I. Wilson, eds. 2005. *The God of Covenant: Biblical, Theological and Contemporary Perspectives*. Leicester: Apollos.

Green, Gene L. 2002. *The Letters to the Thessalonians*. PNTC. Grand Rapids: Eerdmans.

Green, Joel B. 1995a. *The Theology of the Gospel of Luke*. Cambridge: Cambridge University Press.

———, ed. 1995b. *Hearing the New Testament: Strategies for Interpretation*. Grand Rapids: Eerdmans.

———. 1997. *The Gospel of Luke*. NICNT. Grand Rapids: Eerdmans.

Green, Joel B., and Max Turner, eds. 1994. *Jesus of Nazareth: Lord and Christ*. Grand Rapids: Eerdmans.

———. 2000. *Between Two Horizons: Spanning New Testament Studies and Systematic Theology*. Grand Rapids: Eerdmans.

Green, Michael. 1987. *The Second Epistle of Peter and the Epistle of Jude*. TNTC 18. Grand Rapids: Eerdmans.

———. 2000. *The Message of Matthew*. BST. Downers Grove, IL: InterVarsity.

Greenberg, Moshe. 1983. *Ezekiel 1–20*. AB 22. New York: Doubleday.

———. 1987. "The Design and Themes of Ezekiel's Program of Restoration." In *Interpreting the Prophets*, edited by James Luther Mays and Paul J. Achtemeier, 215–36. Philadelphia: Fortress.

Grenz, Stanley J. 1992. *The Millennial Maze: Sorting Out Evangelical Options*. Downers Grove, IL: InterVarsity.

Grogan, Geoffrey. 2001. *Prayer, Praise and Prophecy: A Theology of the Psalms*. Fearn, Ross-shire: Mentor.

Grudem, Wayne. 1988. *The First Epistle of Peter*. TNTC 17. Grand Rapids: Eerdmans.

Gundry, Robert H. 1973. *The Church and the Tribulation*. Grand Rapids: Zondervan.

———. 1982. *Matthew: A Commentary on His Literary and Theological Art*. Grand Rapids: Eerdmans.

———. 1987. Sōma *in Biblical Theology: With Emphasis on Pauline Anthropology*. Grand Rapids: Zondervan.

———. 1993. *Mark: A Commentary on His Apology for the Cross*. Grand Rapids: Eerdmans.

Gunkel, Hermann. 1967. *The Psalms: A Form-Critical Introduction*. Translated by Thomas M. Horner. Philadelphia: Fortress.

Gunkel, Hermann, and Joachim Begrich. 1998. *Introduction to Psalms: The Genres of the Religious Lyric of Israel.* Translated by James D. Nogalski. MLBS. Macon, GA: Mercer University Press.

Gurney, Robert. 1977. "The Four Kingdoms of Daniel 2 and 7." *Them* 2:39–45.

Guthrie, Donald. 1990a. *New Testament Introduction.* 4th ed. Downers Grove, IL: InterVarsity.

———. 1990b. *The Pastoral Epistles.* TNTC 14. Grand Rapids: Eerdmans.

Habel, Norman C. 1985. *The Book of Job.* OTL. Louisville: Westminster.

Haenchen, Ernst. 1971. *The Acts of the Apostles: A Commentary.* Translated by Bernard Noble and Gerald Shinn. Revised by R. McL. Wilson. Philadelphia: Westminster.

Hafemann, Scott J. 2000. *2 Corinthians.* NIVAC. Grand Rapids: Zondervan.

———, ed. 2002. *Biblical Theology: Retrospect and Prospect.* Downers Grove, IL: InterVarsity.

———. 2007. "The Covenant Relationship." In *Central Themes in Biblical Theology,* edited by Scott J. Hafemann and Paul R. House, 20–65. Grand Rapids: Baker Academic.

Hafeman, Scott, and Paul R. House, eds. 2007. *Central Themes in Biblical Theology: Mapping Unity in Diversity.* Grand Rapids: Baker Academic.

Hagner, Donald A. 1993. *Matthew 1–13.* WBC 33A. Dallas: Word Books.

———. 1994. "Matthew's Eschatology." In *To Tell the Mystery: Essays on New Testament Eschatology in Honor of Robert H. Gundry,* edited by Thomas E. Schmidt and Moisés Silva, 49–71. JSNTSup 100. Sheffield: Sheffield Academic.

———. 1995. *Matthew 14–28.* WBC 33B. Dallas: Word Books.

———. 1998. "Gospel, Kingdom, and Resurrection in the Synoptic Gospels." In *Life in the Face of Death,* edited by Richard N. Longenecker, 99–121. Grand Rapids: Eerdmans.

Hagopian, David G., ed. 2001. *The Genesis Debate: Three Views on the Days of Creation.* Mission Viejo, CA: Crux.

Ham, Clay Alan. 2005. *The Coming King and the Rejected Shepherd: Matthew's Reading of Zechariah's Messianic Hope.* NTM 4. Sheffield: Sheffield Phoenix.

Hamilton, Victor P. 1990. *The Book of Genesis: Chapters 1–17.* NICOT. Grand Rapids: Eerdmans.

———. 1995. *The Book of Genesis: Chapters 18–50.* NICOT. Grand Rapids: Eerdmans.

———. 2004. *Handbook on the Historical Books.* Grand Rapids: Baker Academic.

Harnack, Adolf von. 1909. *The Acts of the Apostles.* Translated by J. R. Wilkinson. *NTS* 3. London: Williams & Norgate.

Harrington, Wilfrid J. 1993. *Revelation.* SacPag 16. Collegeville, MN: Liturgical.

Harris, Murray J. 1992. *Jesus as God: The New Testament Use of* Theos *in Reference to Jesus*. Grand Rapids: Baker.
Harris, R. Laird, Gleason L. Archer Jr., and Bruce K. Waltke, eds. 1980. *Theological Wordbook of the Old Testament*. Chicago: Moody.
Harrison, R. K. 1969. *Introduction to the Old Testament*. Grand Rapids: Eerdmans.
———. 1973. *Jeremiah and Lamentations: An Introduction and Commentary*. TOTC. Downers Grove, IL: InterVarsity.
———. 1980. *Leviticus: An Introduction and Commentary*. TOTC. Downers Grove, IL: InterVarsity.
Hasel, Gerhard F. 1974. *The Remnant: The History and Theology of the Remnant Idea from Genesis to Isaiah*. AUMSR 5. Berrien Springs, MI: Andrews University Press.
———. 1978. *New Testament Theology: Basic Issues in the Current Debate*. Grand Rapids: Eerdmans.
———. 1982. *Old Testament Theology: Basic Issues in the Current Debate*. Rev. ed. Grand Rapids: Eerdmans.
Hawthorne, Gerald F. 1983. *Philippians*. WBC 43. Waco: Word Books.
Hayes, John H., and Sara R. Mandell. 1998. *The Jewish People in Classical Antiquity: From Alexander to Bar Kochba*. Louisville: Westminster.
Hays, Richard B. 1989. *Echoes of Scripture in the Letters of Paul*. New Haven: Yale University Press.
———. 1997. *First Corinthians*. Interpretation. Louisville: John Knox.
———. 1999. "The Conversion of the Imagination: Scripture and Eschatology in 1 Corinthians." *NTS* 45, no. 3:391–412.
———. 2005. *The Conversion of the Imagination: Paul as Interpreter of Israel's Scripture*. Grand Rapids: Eerdmans.
Heater, Homer, Jr. 1997. "Evidence from Joel and Amos." In *The Coming Millennial Kingdom: A Case for Premillennial Interpretation*, edited by Donald K. Campbell and Jeffrey L. Townsend, 135–46. Grand Rapids: Kregel.
Heide, Gale Z. 1997. "What Is New about the New Heaven and the New Earth? A Theology of Creation from Revelation 21 and 2 Peter 3." *JETS* 40, no. 1:37–56.
Helm, Paul. 1983. "Universalism and the Threat of Hell." *TrinJ* 4, no. 1:35–43.
———. 1989. *The Last Things: Death, Judgment, Heaven and Hell*. Carlisle, PA: Banner of Truth.
———. 1994. *The Providence of God*. Downers Grove, IL: InterVarsity.
Helyer, Larry R. 1993. "Luke and the Restoration of Israel." *JETS* 36, no. 3:317–29.
———. 2002. *Exploring Jewish Literature of the Second Temple Period*. Downers Grove, IL: InterVarsity.

———. 2004. *Yesterday, Today, and Forever: The Continuing Relevance of the Old Testament*. 2d ed. Salem, WI: Sheffield.

Hemer, Colin J. 1986. *The Letters to the Seven Churches of Asia in Their Local Setting*. JSNTSup 11. Sheffield: JSOT Press.

———. 1989. *The Book of Acts in the Setting of Hellenistic History*. Edited by Conrad H. Gempf. WUNT 49. Tübingen: Mohr Siebeck.

Hendriksen, William. 1939. *More than Conquerors: An Interpretation of the Book of Revelation*. Grand Rapids: Baker.

———. 1959. *The Bible on the Life Hereafter*. Grand Rapids: Baker.

Hengel, Martin. 1977. *Crucifixion in the Ancient World and the Folly of the Message of the Cross*. Translated by John Bowden. Philadelphia: Fortress.

Hess, Richard S. 1996. *Joshua: An Introduction and Commentary*. TOTC. Downers Grove, IL: InterVarsity.

Hess, Richard S., and M. Daniel Carroll R., eds. 2003. *Israel's Messiah in the Bible and the Dead Sea Scrolls*. Grand Rapids: Baker Academic.

Hiebert, D. Edmond. 1997. "Evidence from 1 Corinthians 15." In *The Coming Millennial Kingdom: A Case for Premillennial Interpretation*, edited by Donald K. Campbell and Jeffrey L. Townsend, 225–34. Grand Rapids: Kregel.

Hill, Andrew E., and John H. Walton. 1991. *A Survey of the Old Testament*. Grand Rapids: Zondervan.

Hill, Craig C. 2002. *In God's Time: The Bible and the Future*. Grand Rapids: Eerdmans.

Hill, John. 1999. *Friend or Foe? The Figure of Babylon in the Book of Jeremiah MT*. BIS 40. Leiden: Brill.

Hillyer, Norman. 1992. *1 and 2 Peter, Jude*. NIBC. Peabody, MA: Hendrickson.

Hindson, Edward E. 1978. *Isaiah's Immanuel*. Edited by Robert L. Reymond. ILPT. Phillipsburg, NJ: P&R.

Hirsch, E. D., Jr. 1967. *Validity in Interpretation*. New Haven: Yale University Press.

Hitchcock, Mark L. 2007. "A Critique of the Preterist View of Revelation 17:9–11 and Nero." *BSac* 164, no. 4:472–85.

Hobbs, T. R. 1985. *2 Kings*. WBC 13. Waco: Word Books.

Hoehner, Harold W. 1997. "Evidence from Revelation 20." In *The Coming Millennial Kingdom: A Case for Premillennial Interpretation*, edited by Donald K. Campbell and Jeffrey L. Townsend, 235–62. Grand Rapids: Kregel.

———. 2002. *Ephesians: An Exegetical Commentary*. Grand Rapids: Baker Academic.

Hoekema, Anthony. 1979. *The Bible and the Future*. Grand Rapids: Eerdmans.

———. 1986. *Created in God's Image*. Grand Rapids: Eerdmans.

Holladay, William L. 1986. *Jeremiah 1*. Edited by Paul D. Hanson. Hermeneia. Minneapolis: Fortress.

———. 1989. *Jeremiah 2*. Edited by Paul D. Hanson. Hermeneia. Minneapolis: Fortress.

Holland, Tom. 2004. *Contours of Pauline Theology*. Fearn, Ross-shire: Mentor.

Holleman, Joost. 1996. *Resurrection and Parousia: A Traditio-Historical Study of Paul's Eschatology in 1 Corinthians 15*. NovTSup 84. Leiden: Brill.

Holt, Else Kragelund. 1995. *Prophesying the Past: The Use of Israel's History in the Book of Hosea*. JSOTSup 194. Sheffield: Sheffield Academic.

Holwerda, David E. 1995. *Jesus and Israel: One Covenant or Two?* Grand Rapids: Eerdmans.

Hooker, Morna D. 1967. *The Son of Man in Mark*. London: SPCK.

———. 1991. *The Gospel according to St Mark*. BNTC 2. Peabody, MA: Hendrickson.

Hopkins, Martin. 1965. "The Historical Perspective of Apocalypse 1–11." *CBQ* 27:42–47.

Horrell, David G. 2003. "Who Are 'The Dead' and When Was the Gospel Preached to Them? The Interpretation of 1 Peter 4.6." *NTS* 49, no. 1:70–89.

Horsley, Richard A., ed. 1997. *Paul and Empire: Religion and Power in Roman Imperial Society*. Harrisburg, PA: Trinity Press International.

———. 2000. *Paul and Politics: Ekklesia, Israel, Imperium, Interpretation*. Harrisburg, PA: Trinity Press International.

———. 2003. *Jesus and Empire: The Kingdom of God and the New World Disorder*. Minneapolis: Fortress.

———, ed. 2004. *Paul and the Roman Imperial Order*. Harrisburg, PA: Trinity Press International.

Horsley, Richard A., and Neil Asher Silberman. 1997. *The Message and the Kingdom: How Jesus and Paul Ignited a Revolution and Transformed the Ancient World*. Minneapolis: Fortress.

Horton, Michael S. 1993. *The Law of Perfect Freedom*. Chicago: Moody.

———. 2002. *Covenant and Eschatology: The Divine Drama*. Louisville: Westminster.

———. 2006. *God of Promise: Introducing Covenant Theology*. Grand Rapids: Baker.

House, Paul R. 1995. *1, 2 Kings*. NAC. Nashville: Broadman.

———. 1998. *Old Testament Theology*. Downers Grove, IL: InterVarsity.

Houston, Walter. 1995. "What Did the Prophets Think They Were Doing? Speech Acts and Prophetic Discourse in the Old Testament." In *The Place Is Too Small for Us: The Israelite Prophets in Recent Scholarship*, edited by Robert P. Gordon, 133–53. SBTS 5. Winona Lake, IN: Eisenbrauns.

Howard, David M., Jr. 1993. *An Introduction to the Old Testament Historical Books*. Chicago: Moody.
Hubbard, David A. 1983. "Hope in the Old Testament." *TynBul* 34:33–59.
———. 1989a. *Hosea: An Introduction and Commentary*. TOTC 22a. Downers Grove, IL: InterVarsity.
———. 1989b. *Joel and Amos: An Introduction and Commentary*. TOTC 22b. Downers Grove, IL: InterVarsity.
Huffmon, Herbert B. 1959. "The Covenant Lawsuit in the Prophets." *JBL* 78:285–95.
Hugenberger, G. P. 1994. "Introductory Notes on Typology." In *The Right Doctrine from the Wrong Texts*, edited by G. K. Beale, 331–41. Grand Rapids: Baker.
Hughes, James A. 1973. "Revelation 20:4–6 and the Question of the Millennium." *WTJ* 35, no. 3:281–302.
Hughes, Philip Edgcumbe. 1962. *Paul's Second Epistle to the Corinthians*. NICNT. Grand Rapids: Eerdmans.
———. 1977. *A Commentary on the Epistle to the Hebrews*. Grand Rapids: Eerdmans.
———. 1990. *The Book of Revelation: A Commentary*. Grand Rapids: Eerdmans.
Jauhiainen, Marko. 2003. "Recapitulation and Chronological Progression in John's Apocalypse: Towards a New Perspective." *NTS* 49, no. 4:543–59.
Jeffers, James S. 1999. *The Greco-Roman World of the New Testament Era*. Downers Grove, IL: InterVarsity.
Jensen, Peter. 2002. *The Revelation of God*. Downers Grove, IL: InterVarsity.
Jeremias, Joachim. 1969. *Jerusalem in the Time of Jesus*. Translated by F. H. Cave and C. H. Cave. Philadelphia: Fortress.
———. 1972. *The Parables of Jesus*. 2d ed. Translated by S. H. Hooke. New York: Charles Scribner's Sons.
Jewett, Robert. 1986. *The Thessalonian Correspondence: Pauline Rhetoric and Millenarian Piety*. Philadelphia: Fortress.
Jobes, Karen H. 1999. *Esther*. NIVAC. Grand Rapids: Zondervan.
———. 2005. *1 Peter*. BECNT. Grand Rapids: Baker.
Johnson, Dennis E. 1997. *The Message of Acts in the History of Redemption*. Phillipsburg, NJ: P&R.
———. 2001. *Triumph of the Lamb: A Commentary on Revelation*. Phillipsburg, NJ: P&R.
Johnson, Luke Timothy. 1991. *The Gospel of Luke*. SacPag 3. Collegeville, MN: Liturgical.
———. 1992. *The Acts of the Apostles*. SacPag 5. Collegeville, MN: Liturgical.
———. 1995. *James*. AB 37A. New York: Doubleday.
Johnson, Thomas F. 1993. *1, 2, and 3 John*. NIBC 17. Peabody, MA: Hendrickson.

Johnston, Philip S. 1997. "Psalm 49: A Personal Eschatology." In *Eschatology in Bible and Theology: Evangelical Essays at the Dawn of a New Millennium*, edited by Kent E. Brower and Mark W. Elliott, 73–84. Downers Grove, IL: InterVarsity.

———. 2002. *Shades of Sheol: Death and Afterlife in the Old Testament*. Downers Grove, IL: InterVarsity.

———. 2005. "The Psalms and Distress." In *Interpreting the Psalms: Issues and Approaches*, edited by David Firth and Philip S. Johnston, 63–84. Downers Grove, IL: InterVarsity Academic.

Johnston, Philip, and Peter Walker, eds. 2000. *The Land of Promise*. Downers Grove, IL: InterVarsity.

Johnston, Robert K., ed. 1985. *The Use of the Bible in Theology: Evangelical Options*. Atlanta: John Knox.

Jones, A. H. M. 1938. *The Herods of Judaea*. Oxford: Clarendon.

Joüon, Paul. 1993. *A Grammar of Biblical Hebrew*. 2 vols. Translated and revised by T. Muraoka. SubBi 14/I–II. Rome: Pontifical Biblical Institute.

Kaiser, Walter C., Jr. 1995. *The Messiah in the Old Testament*. Grand Rapids: Zondervan.

Kalluveettil, Paul. 1982. *Declaration and Covenant: A Comprehensive Review of Covenant Formulae from the Old Testament and the Ancient Near East*. AnBib 88. Rome: Biblical Institute Press.

Kapelrud, Arvid S. 1961. "Eschatology in the Book of Micah." *VT* 11:392–405.

Käsemann, Ernst. 1980. *Commentary on Romans*. Translated and edited by Geoffrey W. Bromiley. Grand Rapids: Eerdmans.

Keener, Craig S. 1999. *A Commentary on the Gospel of Matthew*. Grand Rapids: Eerdmans.

———. 2000. *Revelation*. NIVAC. Grand Rapids: Zondervan.

———. 2003. *The Gospel of John: A Commentary*. 2 vols. Peabody, MA: Hendrickson.

———. 2005. *1–2 Corinthians*. NCBC. Cambridge: Cambridge University Press.

Kelly, Brian E. 1996. *Retribution and Eschatology in Chronicles*. JSOTSup 211. Sheffield: Sheffield Academic.

Kelly, Douglas F. 1999. *Creation and Change*. Fearn, Ross-shire: Mentor.

Kelly, J. N. D. 1969. *A Commentary on the Epistles of Peter and of Jude*. HNTC. Peabody, MA: Hendrickson.

Khoo, Jeffrey. 2001. "Dispensational Premillennialism in Reformed Theology: The Contribution of J. O. Buswell to the Millennial Debate." *JETS* 44, no. 4:697–717.

Kidner, Derek. 1964. *Proverbs: An Introduction and Commentary*. TOTC 15. Downers Grove, IL: InterVarsity.

———. 1967. *Genesis: An Introduction and Commentary.* TOTC 1. Downers Grove, IL: InterVarsity.

———. 1973a. *Psalms 1–72: An Introduction and Commentary.* TOTC 14a. Downers Grove, IL: InterVarsity.

———. 1973b. *Psalms 73–150: An Introduction and Commentary.* TOTC 14b. Downers Grove, IL: InterVarsity.

———. 1976. *A Time to Mourn, and a Time to Dance: Ecclesiastes and the Way of the World.* BST. Downers Grove, IL: InterVarsity.

———. 1979. *Ezra and Nehemiah: An Introduction and Commentary.* TOTC 11. Downers Grove, IL: InterVarsity.

———. 1981. *The Message of Hosea.* BST. Downers Grove, IL: InterVarsity.

———. 1985. *The Wisdom of Proverbs, Job and Ecclesiastes: An Introduction to Wisdom Literature.* Downers Grove, IL: InterVarsity.

Kierkegaard, Søren. 1983. *Fear and Trembling.* Translated and edited by H. V. Hong and E. H. Hong. Princeton: Princeton University Press.

Kikawada, Isaac M., and Arthur Quinn. 1985. *Before Abraham Was: The Unity of Genesis 1–11.* Nashville: Abingdon.

Kim, Seyoon. 2002. *Paul and the New Perspective: Second Thoughts on the Origin of Paul's Gospel.* Grand Rapids: Eerdmans.

Kistemaker, Simon J. 1990. *Acts.* NTC. Grand Rapids: Baker.

———. 2000. "The Temple in the Apocalypse." *JETS* 43, no. 3:433–41.

———. 2001. *Revelation.* NTC. Grand Rapids: Baker.

Kitchen, K. A. 2003. *On the Reliability of the Old Testament.* Grand Rapids: Eerdmans.

Kittel, G., and G. Friedrich, eds. 1964–76. *Theological Dictionary of the New Testament.* 10 vols. Grand Rapids: Eerdmans.

Klauck, Hans-Josef. 2003. *The Religious Context of Early Christianity: A Guide to Graeco-Roman Religions.* Minneapolis: Fortress.

Klein, Ralph W. 1979. *Israel in Exile: A Theological Interpretation.* Philadelphia: Fortress.

———. 1983. *1 Samuel.* WBC 10. Waco: Word Books.

Klein, William W., Craig L. Blomberg, and Robert L. Hubbard Jr. 1993. *Introduction to Biblical Interpretation.* Edited by Kermit A. Ecklebarger. Dallas: Word Books.

Kline, Meredith G. 1963. *Treaty of the Great King.* Grand Rapids: Eerdmans.

———. 1975. "The First Resurrection." *WTJ* 37, no. 3:366–75.

———. 1978. "Primal Parousia." *WTJ* 40, no. 2:245–80.

———. 1996. "Har Magedon: The End of the Millennium." *JETS* 39, no. 2:207–22.

———. 2000. *Kingdom Prologue: Genesis Foundations for a Covenantal Worldview*. Overland Park, KS: Two Age.

———. 2001. *Glory in Our Midst: A Biblical-Theological Reading of Zechariah's Night Visions*. Overland Park, KS: Two Age.

Klooster, Fred H. 1962. "Karl Barth's Doctrine of the Resurrection of Jesus Christ." *WTJ* 24, no. 2:137–72.

Knight, George W., III. 1992. *The Pastoral Epistles*. NIGTC. Grand Rapids: Eerdmans.

Knowles, Louis E. 1945. "The Interpretation of the Seventy Weeks of Daniel in the Early Fathers." *WTJ* 7, no. 2:136–60.

Knowles, Melody D. 2004. "Pilgrimage Imagery in the Returns in Ezra." *JBL* 123, no. 1:57–74.

Koch, Klaus. 1983–84. *The Prophets*. Translated by Margaret Kohl. 2 vols. Philadelphia: Fortress.

Koester, Helmut. 1997. "Imperial Ideology and Paul's Eschatology in 1 Thessalonians." In *Paul and Empire: Religion and Power in Roman Imperial Society*, edited by Richard A. Horsley, 158–66. Harrisburg, PA: Trinity Press International.

Köstenberger, Andreas J. 2004. *John*. BECNT. Grand Rapids: Baker.

Kraus, Hans-Joachim. 1993a. *Psalms 1–59*. Translated by Hilton C. Oswald. CC. Minneapolis: Fortress.

———. 1993b. *Psalms 60–150*. Translated by Hilton C. Oswald. CC. Minneapolis: Fortress.

Kruse, Colin G. 1987. *The Second Epistle of Paul to the Corinthians*. TNTC 8. Grand Rapids: Eerdmans.

———. 2000. *The Letters of John*. PNTC. Grand Rapids: Eerdmans.

———. 2003. *The Gospel according to John*. TNTC 4. Grand Rapids: Eerdmans.

Kugel, James L. 1981. *The Idea of Biblical Poetry: Parallelism and Its History*. New Haven: Yale University Press.

Kuhl, Curt. 1960. *The Prophets of Israel*. Translated by Rudolf J. Ehrlich and J. P. Smith. Richmond: John Knox.

Kümmel, Werner G. 1957. *Promise and Fulfilment: The Eschatological Message of Jesus*. Translated by Dorothea M. Barton. London: SCM.

Kynes, William L. 1991. *A Christology of Solidarity: Jesus as the Representative of His People in Matthew*. Lanham, MD: University Press of America.

Kysar, Robert. 1986. *John*. ACNT. Minneapolis: Augsburg.

Laato, Antti. 1997. *A Star Is Rising: The Historical Development of the Old Testament Royal Ideology and the Rise of the Jewish Messianic Expectations*. ISFCJ 5. Atlanta: Scholars.

Ladd, George Eldon. 1956. *The Blessed Hope*. Grand Rapids: Eerdmans.

———. 1972. *A Commentary on the Revelation of John*. Grand Rapids: Eerdmans.

———. 1974a. *The Presence of the Future*. Rev. ed. Grand Rapids: Eerdmans.

———. 1974b. "Apocalyptic and New Testament Theology." In *Reconciliation and Hope: New Testament Essays on Atonement and Eschatology Presented to L. L. Morris on his 60th Birthday*, edited by Robert Banks, 285–96. Grand Rapids: Eerdmans.

———. 1993. *A Theology of the New Testament*. Rev. ed. Edited by Donald A. Hagner. Grand Rapids: Eerdmans.

Lampe, Peter. 2003. *From Paul to Valentinus: Christians at Rome in the First Two Centuries*. Edited by Marshall D. Johnson. Translated by Michael Steinhauser. Minneapolis: Fortress.

Landes, George M. 1967a. "The Kerygma of the Book of Jonah: The Contextual Interpretation of the Jonah Psalm." *Int* 21:3–31.

———. 1967b. "The 'Three Days and Three Nights' Motif in Jonah 2:1." *JBL* 86:446–50.

Lane, William L. 1974. *The Gospel according to Mark*. NICNT. Grand Rapids: Eerdmans.

———. 1991a. *Hebrews 1–8*. WBC 47A. Dallas: Word Books.

———. 1991b. *Hebrews 9–13*. WBC 47B. Dallas: Word Books.

Larkin, Clarence. 1921. *The Spirit World*. Glenside, PA: Rev. Clarence Larkin Estate.

LaRondelle, Hans K. 1983. *The Israel of God in Prophecy: Principles of Prophetic Interpretation*. Berrien Springs, MI: Andrews University Press.

Lea, Thomas D. 1986. "A Survey of the Doctrine of the Return of Christ in the Ante-Nicene Fathers." *JETS* 29, no. 2:163–77.

Lee, Francis Nigel. 2000. *John's Revelation Unveiled*. Brisbane: Queensland Presbyterian Theological College.

Leithart, Peter J. 2003. *A Son to Me: An Exposition of 1 and 2 Samuel*. Moscow, ID: Canon.

Letham, Robert. 1993. *The Work of Christ*. Downers Grove, IL: InterVarsity.

Levenson, Jon Douglas. 1976. *Theology of the Program of Restoration of Ezekiel 40–48*. HSM 10. Missoula, MO: Scholars.

Lieu, Judith M. 1991. *The Theology of the Johannine Epistles*. Cambridge: Cambridge University Press.

Lincoln, A. T. 1981. *Paradise Now and Not Yet: Studies in the Role of the Heavenly Dimension in Paul's Thought with Special Reference to His Eschatology*. Grand Rapids: Baker.

———. 1982a. "From Sabbath to Lord's Day: A Biblical and Theological Perspective." In *From Sabbath to Lord's Day*, edited by D. A. Carson, 343–412. Grand Rapids: Zondervan.

———. 1982b. "Sabbath, Rest, and Eschatology in the New Testament." In *From Sabbath to Lord's Day*, edited by D. A. Carson, 197–220. Grand Rapids: Zondervan.

———. 1990. *Ephesians*. WBC 42. Dallas: Word Books.

———. 1998. "'I Am the Resurrection and the Life': The Resurrection Message of the Fourth Gospel." In *Life in the Face of Death: The Resurrection Message of the New Testament*, edited by Richard N. Longenecker, 122–44. Grand Rapids: Eerdmans.

———. 2005. *The Gospel according to Saint John*. BNTC 4. Peabody, MA: Hendrickson.

———. 2006. *Hebrews: A Guide*. London: T&T Clark.

Lindars, Barnabas, ed. 1972. *The Gospel of John*. NCB. London: Marshall, Morgan & Scott.

Lindblom, Johannes. 1962. *Prophecy in Ancient Israel*. Philadelphia: Fortress.

Livingston, G. Herbert. 1974. *The Pentateuch in Its Cultural Environment*. Grand Rapids: Baker.

Longacre, Robert E., and Wilber B. Wallis. 1998. "Soteriology and Eschatology in Romans." *JETS* 41, no. 3:367–82.

Longenecker, Richard N. 1990. *Galatians*. WBC 41. Nashville: Thomas Nelson.

———, ed. 1997. *The Road from Damascus: The Impact of Paul's Conversion on His Life, Thought, and Ministry*. Grand Rapids: Eerdmans.

———, ed. 1998. *Life in the Face of Death: The Resurrection Message of the New Testament*. Grand Rapids: Eerdmans.

Longman, Tremper, III. 1988. *How to Read the Psalms*. Downers Grove, IL: InterVarsity.

———. 1993. "Nahum." In *The Minor Prophets*, edited by Thomas McComiskey, 2:765–829. Grand Rapids: Baker.

———. 1998. *The Book of Ecclesiastes*. NICOT. Grand Rapids: Eerdmans.

———. 1999. *Daniel*. NIVAC. Grand Rapids: Zondervan.

———. 2001. *Song of Songs*. NICOT. Grand Rapids: Eerdmans.

———. 2002. *How to Read Proverbs*. Downers Grove, IL: InterVarsity.

———. 2003. "The Case for Spiritual Continuity." In C. S. Cowles et al., *Show Them No Mercy: 4 Views on God and Canaanite Genocide*, 159–87. Grand Rapids: Zondervan.

———. 2005. *How to Read Genesis*. Downers Grove, IL: InterVarsity.

———. 2006. *Proverbs*. BCOTWP. Grand Rapids: Baker Academic.

Longman, Tremper, III, and Daniel G. Reid. 1995. *God Is a Warrior*. Grand Rapids: Zondervan.

Lucas, Ernest. 2002. *Daniel*. AOTC 20. Downers Grove, IL: InterVarsity.

Lundbom, Jack R. 1999. *Jeremiah 1–20*. AB 21A. New York: Doubleday.

———. 2004a. *Jeremiah 21–36.* AB 21B. New York: Doubleday.
———. 2004b. *Jeremiah 37–52.* AB 21C. New York: Doubleday.
Lundin, Roger. 1993. *The Culture of Interpretation: Christian Faith and the Postmodern World.* Grand Rapids: Eerdmans.
Lundin, Roger, Clarence Walhout, and Anthony C. Thiselton. 1999. *The Promise of Hermeneutics.* Grand Rapids: Eerdmans.
Luz, Ulrich. 1995. *The Theology of the Gospel of Matthew.* Translated by J. Bradford Robinson. Cambridge: Cambridge University Press.
Mackay, John L. 2001. *Exodus.* Fearn, Ross-shire: Mentor.
Macleod, Donald. 1998. *The Person of Christ.* Downers Grove, IL: InterVarsity.
Magonet, Jonathan. 1983. *Form and Meaning: Studies in Literary Techniques in the Book of Jonah.* 2d ed. BLS 8. Sheffield: Almond.
Maier, Gerhard. 1994. *Biblical Hermeneutics.* Translated by Robert W. Yarbrough. Wheaton, IL: Crossway.
Mann, Thomas W. 1988. *The Book of Torah: The Narrative Integrity of the Pentateuch.* Atlanta: John Knox.
Margalioth, Rachel. 1964. *The Indivisible Isaiah: Evidence for the Single Authorship of the Prophetic Book.* Rev. ed. New York: Yeshiva University.
Marshall, I. Howard, ed. 1977. *New Testament Interpretation: Essays on Principles and Methods.* Grand Rapids: Eerdmans.
———. 1978a. *The Gospel of Luke.* NIGTC. Grand Rapids: Eerdmans.
———. 1978b. *The Epistles of John.* NICNT. Grand Rapids: Eerdmans.
———. 1980. *The Book of Acts: An Introduction and Commentary.* TNTC 5. Grand Rapids: Eerdmans.
———. 1983. *1 and 2 Thessalonians.* NCB. Grand Rapids: Eerdmans.
———. 1988. *Luke: Historian and Theologian.* 3d ed. NTP. Downers Grove, IL: InterVarsity.
———. 1991. *1 Peter.* IVPNTC 17. Downers Grove, IL: InterVarsity.
———. 1997. "A New Understanding of the Present and the Future: Paul and Eschatology." In *The Road from Damascus: The Impact of Paul's Conversion on His Life, Thought, and Ministry,* edited by Richard N. Longenecker, 43–61. Grand Rapids: Eerdmans.
———. 1999. *The Pastoral Epistles.* ICC. London: T&T Clark.
———. 2004. *New Testament Theology: Many Witnesses, One Gospel.* Downers Grove, IL: InterVarsity.
Marshall, I. Howard, and David Peterson, eds. 1998. *Witness to the Gospel: The Theology of Acts.* Grand Rapids: Eerdmans.
Martens, Elmer A. 1998. *God's Design: A Focus on Old Testament Theology.* 3d ed. Richland Hills, TX: Bibal.
Martin, Ralph P. 1986. *2 Corinthians.* WBC 40. Waco: Word Books.

———. 1987. *Philippians: An Introduction and Commentary*. TNTC 11. Downers Grove, IL: InterVarsity.

———. 1988. *James*. WBC 48. Waco: Word Books.

Martin, Thomas R. 2000. *Ancient Greece: From Prehistoric to Hellenistic Times*. New Haven: Yale University Press.

Martyn, J. Louis. 1997. *Galatians*. AB 33A. New York: Doubleday.

Matera, Frank J. 2003. *II Corinthians*. Louisville: Westminster.

Mathewson, Dave. 2001. "A Re-examination of the Millennium in Rev. 20:1–6: Consummation and Recapitulation." *JETS* 44, no. 2:237–51.

Mathison, Keith A. 1999. *Postmillennialism: An Eschatology of Hope*. Phillipsburg, NJ: P&R.

———, ed. 2004. *When Shall These Things Be? A Reformed Response to Hyper-Preterism*. Phillipsburg, NJ: P&R.

Matthews, Victor H. 2002. *A Brief History of Ancient Israel*. Louisville: Westminster.

Matthews, Victor H., and James C. Moyer. 1997. *The Old Testament: Text and Context*. Peabody, MA: Hendrickson.

Mattill, A. J., Jr. 1979. *Luke and the Last Things: A Perspective for the Understanding of Lukan Thought*. Dillsboro, NC: Western North Carolina Press.

Mauro, Philip. 1965. *The Seventy Weeks and the Great Tribulation*. Swengel, PA: Reiner.

Mayhue, Richard L., and Robert L. Thomas, eds. 2002. *The Master's Perspective on Biblical Prophecy*. MPS 4. Grand Rapids: Kregel.

Mays, James Luther. 1969a. *Amos: A Commentary*. OTL. Philadelphia: Westminster.

———. 1969b. *Hosea: A Commentary*. OTL. Philadelphia: Westminster.

———. 1976. *Micah: A Commentary*. OTL. Philadelphia: Westminster.

Mays, James Luther, and Paul J. Achtemeier, eds. 1987. *Interpreting the Prophets*. Philadelphia: Fortress.

McCarthy, Dennis J. 1963. *Treaty and Covenant: A Study in Form in the Ancient Oriental Documents and in the Old Testament*. AnBib 21. Rome: Pontifical Biblical Institute.

McCartncy, Dan G. 1994. "*Ecce Homo*: The Coming of the Kingdom as the Restoration of Human Vicegerency." *WTJ* 56, no. 1:1–21.

McCartney, Dan, and Charles Clayton. 1994. *Let the Reader Understand: A Guide to Interpreting and Applying the Bible*. Wheaton, IL: Victor.

McComiskey, Thomas E. 1985a. *The Covenants of Promise: A Theology of the Old Testament Covenants*. Grand Rapids: Baker.

———. 1985b. "The Seventy Weeks of Daniel against the Background of Ancient Near Eastern Literature." *WTJ* 47:18–45.

———. 1992. "Hosea." In *The Minor Prophets*, edited by Thomas McComiskey, 1:1–237. Grand Rapids: Baker.

———. 1993. "Alteration of OT Imagery in the Book of Revelation: Its Hermeneutical and Theological Significance." *JETS* 36, no. 3:307–16.

———. 1998. "Zechariah." In *The Minor Prophets*, edited by Thomas McComiskey, 3:1003–1244. Grand Rapids: Baker.

McConville, J. Gordon. 1985. *Ezra, Nehemiah, and Esther*. DSB. Philadelphia: Westminster.

———. 1986. "Ezra-Nehemiah and the Fulfillment of Prophecy." *VT* 36:203–24.

———. 1993. *Grace in the End: A Study in Deuteronomic Theology*. Grand Rapids: Zondervan.

———. 2002. *Deuteronomy*. AOTC 5. Downers Grove, IL: InterVarsity.

McLaren, James S. 2005. "Jews and the Imperial Cult: From Augustus to Domitian." *JSNT* 27, no. 3:257–78.

Meier, John P. 1976. *Law and History in Matthew's Gospel: A Redactional Study of Mt. 5:17–48*. AnBib 71. Rome: Biblical Institute Press.

Mendenhall, George E. 1955. *Law and Covenant in Israel and the Ancient Near East*. Pittsburgh: Biblical Colloquium.

Merkle, Ben L. 2000. "Romans 11 and the Future of Ethnic Israel." *JETS* 43, no. 4:709–21.

Merricks, Trenton. 1999. "The Resurrection of the Body and the Life Everlasting." In *Reason for the Hope Within*, edited by Michael J. Murray, 261–86. Grand Rapids: Eerdmans.

Merrill, Eugene H. 1996. *Kingdom of Priests: A History of Old Testament Israel*. Grand Rapids: Baker Academic.

Metzger, Bruce M. 1957. *An Introduction to the Apocrypha*. New York: Oxford University Press.

———. 1968. *Historical and Literary Studies: Pagan, Jewish, and Christian*. NTTS 8. Leiden: Brill.

———. 1972. "Literary Forgeries and Canonical Pseudepigrapha." *JBL* 91:3–24.

———. 1993. *Breaking the Code: Understanding the Book of Revelation*. Nashville: Abingdon.

Meyer, Ben F. 1994. *Reality and Illusion in New Testament Scholarship: A Primer in Critical Realist Hermeneutics*. Collegeville, MN: Liturgical.

———. 2002. *The Aims of Jesus*. PTMS 48. San Jose: Pickwick.

Meyers, Carol L., and Eric M. Meyers. 1987. *Haggai, Zechariah 1–8*. AB 25B. New York: Doubleday.

Michaels, J. Ramsey. 1988. *1 Peter*. WBC 49. Waco: Word.

———. 1992. *Interpreting the Book of Revelation*. Grand Rapids: Baker.

Mickelsen, A. Berkeley. 1984. *Daniel and Revelation: Riddles or Realities?* Nashville: Nelson.

Millard, A. R., and D. J. Wiseman, eds. 1983. *Essays on the Patriarchal Narratives*. Winona Lake, IN: Eisenbrauns.

Miller, Patrick D., Jr. 1986. *Interpreting the Psalms*. Philadelphia: Fortress.

Mitchell, Christopher Wright. 1987. *The Meaning of* BRK *"To Bless" in the Old Testament*. SBLDS 95. Atlanta: Scholars.

Mitchell, David C. 1997. *The Message of the Psalter: An Eschatological Programme in the Book of Psalms*. JSOTSup 252. Sheffield: Sheffield Academic.

Moessner, David P., ed. 1999. *Jesus and the Heritage of Israel: Luke's Narrative Claim upon Israel's Legacy*. Harrisburg, PA: Trinity Press International.

Moloney, Francis J. 2004. *Mark: Storyteller, Interpreter, Evangelist*. Peabody, MA: Hendrickson.

Montgomery, John Warwick, ed. 1974. *God's Inerrant Word*. Minneapolis: Bethany House.

Moo, Douglas J. 1985. *The Epistle of James*. TNTC 16. Grand Rapids: Eerdmans.

———. 1996a. *The Epistle to the Romans*. NICNT. Grand Rapids: Eerdmans.

———. 1996b. *2 Peter, Jude*. NIVAC. Grand Rapids: Zondervan.

———. 2000. *The Letter of James*. PNTC. Grand Rapids: Eerdmans.

Moore, A. L. 1966. *The Parousia in the New Testament*. NovTSup 13. Leiden: Brill.

Morgan, Christopher W., and Robert A. Peterson, eds. 2004. *Hell under Fire: Modern Scholarship Reinvents Eternal Punishment*. Grand Rapids: Zondervan.

Morris, Gerald. 1996. *Prophecy, Poetry and Hosea*. JSOTSup 219. Sheffield: Sheffield Academic.

Morris, Leon. 1959. *The First and Second Epistles to the Thessalonians*. NICNT. Grand Rapids: Eerdmans.

———. 1971. *The Gospel according to John*. NICNT. Grand Rapids: Eerdmans.

———. 1984. *The Epistles of Paul to the Thessalonians: An Introduction and Commentary*. TNTC 13. Grand Rapids: Eerdmans.

———. 1985. *The First Epistle of Paul to the Corinthians: An Introduction and Commentary*. TNTC 7. Grand Rapids: Eerdmans.

———. 1986. *New Testament Theology*. Grand Rapids: Zondervan.

———. 1987. *The Book of Revelation*. TNTC 20. Grand Rapids: Eerdmans.

———. 1988. *The Gospel according to Luke*. TNTC 3. Grand Rapids: Eerdmans.

———. 1989. *Jesus Is the Christ: Studies in the Theology of John*. Grand Rapids: Eerdmans.

———. 1992. *The Gospel according to Matthew*. PNTC. Grand Rapids: Eerdmans.

Motyer, J. Alec. 1974. *The Message of Amos*. BST. Downers Grove, IL: InterVarsity.

———. 1993. *The Prophecy of Isaiah: An Introduction and Commentary*. Downers Grove, IL: InterVarsity.

———. 1996. *Look to the Rock*. Leicester: Inter-Varsity.

———. 1998a. "Haggai." In *The Minor Prophets*, edited by Thomas McComiskey, 3:963–1002. Grand Rapids: Baker.

———. 1998b. "Zephaniah." In *The Minor Prophets*, edited by Thomas McComiskey, 3:897–962. Grand Rapids: Baker.

———. 1999. *Isaiah: An Introduction and Commentary*. TOTC 18. Downers Grove, IL: InterVarsity.

———. 2005. *The Message of Exodus*. BST. Downers Grove, IL: InterVarsity.

Mounce, Robert H. 1998. *The Book of Revelation*. Rev. ed. NICNT. Grand Rapids: Eerdmans.

Murphy, Roland E. 1998. *Proverbs*. WBC 22. Nashville: Nelson.

Murray, John. 1968. *The Epistle to the Romans*. NICNT. Grand Rapids: Eerdmans.

Murray, Michael J. 1999. "Heaven and Hell." In *Reason for the Hope Within*, edited by Michael J. Murray, 287–317. Grand Rapids: Eerdmans.

Nash, Ronald H. 1982. *The Word of God and the Mind of Man*. Phillipsburg, NJ: P&R.

———. 1998. *The Meaning of History*. Nashville: Broadman.

Nebeker, Gary L. 2000. "Christ as Somatic Transformer (Phil 3:20–21): Christology in an Eschatological Perspective." *TrinJ* 21, no. 2:165–87.

Neill, Stephen, and Tom Wright. 1988. *The Interpretation of the New Testament*. New ed. Oxford: Oxford University Press.

Nelson, Neil D., Jr. 1995. "'This Generation' in Matt 24:34: A Literary Critical Perspective." *JETS* 38, no. 3:369–85.

Nelson, Richard D. 1987. *First and Second Kings*. Interpretation. Atlanta: John Knox.

Newman, Carey C., ed. 1999. *Jesus and the Restoration of Israel: A Critical Assessment of N. T. Wright's* Jesus and the Victory of God. Downers Grove, IL: InterVarsity.

Nichols, Stephen J. 2001. "Prophecy Makes Strange Bedfellows: On the History of Identifying the Antichrist." *JETS* 44, no. 1:75–85.

Nicholson, Ernest W. 1986. *God and His People: Covenant and Theology in the Old Testament*. Oxford: Oxford University Press.

Nickelsburg, George W. E. 1981. *Jewish Literature between the Bible and the Mishnah: A Historical and Literary Introduction*. Philadelphia: Fortress.

Niehaus, Jeffrey J. 1992. "Amos." In *The Minor Prophets*, edited by Thomas McComiskey, 1:315–494. Grand Rapids: Baker.

———. 1993. "Obadiah." In *The Minor Prophets*, edited by Thomas McComiskey, 2:495–541. Grand Rapids: Baker.

———. 1995. *God at Sinai: Covenant and Theophany in the Bible and Ancient Near East.* Grand Rapids: Zondervan.

Nolland, John. 1989. *Luke 1–9:20.* WBC 35A. Dallas: Word Books.

———. 1993a. *Luke 9:21–18:34.* WBC 35B. Dallas: Word Books.

———. 1993b. *Luke 18:35–24:53.* WBC 35C. Dallas: Word Books.

———. 1998. "Salvation-History and Eschatology." In *Witness to the Gospel: The Theology of Acts,* edited by I. Howard Marshall and David Peterson, 63–81. Grand Rapids: Eerdmans.

———. 2005. *The Gospel of Matthew.* NIGTC. Grand Rapids: Eerdmans.

Noth, Martin. 1967. *The Laws in the Pentateuch and Other Studies.* Translated by D. R. Ap-Thomas. Philadelphia: Fortress.

———. 1981. *The Deuteronomistic History.* Translated by D. Orton. JSOTSup 15. Sheffield: Sheffield Academic.

O'Brien, Peter T. 1982. *Colossians, Philemon.* WBC 44. Waco: Word Books.

———. 1991. *The Epistle to the Philippians.* NIGTC. Grand Rapids: Eerdmans.

———. 1999. *The Letter to the Ephesians.* PNTC. Grand Rapids: Eerdmans.

Odendaal, Dirk H. 1970. *The Eschatological Expectation of Isaiah 40–66 with Special Reference to Israel and the Nations.* ILPT. Edited by Robert L. Reymond. Phillipsburg, NJ: P&R.

Oegema, Gerbern S. 1998. *The Anointed and His People: Messianic Expectations from the Maccabees to Bar Kochba.* JSPSup 27. Sheffield: Sheffield Academic.

Olmstead, A. T. 1948. *History of the Persian Empire.* Chicago: University of Chicago Press.

Oropeza, B. J. 2007. "Paul and Theodicy: Intertextual Thoughts on God's Justice and Faithfulness to Israel in Romans 9–11." *NTS* 53, no. 1:57–80.

Osborne, Grant R. 1991. *The Hermeneutical Spiral.* Downers Grove, IL: InterVarsity.

———. 2002. *Revelation.* BECNT. Grand Rapids: Baker Academic.

———. 2006. *The Hermeneutical Spiral.* Revised ed. Downers Grove, IL: InterVarsity.

Oswalt, John N. 1986. *The Book of Isaiah: Chapters 1–39.* NICOT. Grand Rapids: Eerdmans.

———. 1998. *The Book of Isaiah: Chapters 40–66.* NICOT. Grand Rapids: Eerdmans.

Packer, J. I. 1980. "The Adequacy of Human Language." In *Inerrancy,* edited by Norman L. Geisler, 197–226. Grand Rapids: Zondervan.

Pao, David W. 2002. *Acts and the Isaianic New Exodus.* Grand Rapids: Baker Academic.

Park, Aaron Pyungchoon. 1971. "The Christian Hope according to Bultmann, Pannenberg, and Moltmann." *WTJ* 33, no. 3:153–74.

Pate, C. Marvin. 1995. *The End of the Age Has Come: The Theology of Paul.* Grand Rapids: Zondervan.

———, ed. 1998. *Four Views on the Book of Revelation.* Grand Rapids: Zondervan.

Pate, C. Marvin, et al. 2004. *The Story of Israel: A Biblical Theology.* Downers Grove, IL: InterVarsity.

Patterson, Richard D. 1991. *Nahum, Habakkuk, Zephaniah.* WEC. Chicago: Moody.

———. 2000. "Wonders in the Heavens and on the Earth: Apocalyptic Imagery in the Old Testament." *JETS* 43, no. 3:385–403.

Paul, Shalom M. 1991. *Amos.* Edited by Frank Moore Cross. Hermeneia. Minneapolis: Fortress.

Pentecost, J. Dwight. 1958. *Things to Come: A Study in Biblical Eschatology.* Grand Rapids: Zondervan.

Perriman, A. C. 1989. "Paul and the Parousia: 1 Corinthians 15.50–57 and 2 Corinthians 5.1–5." *NTS* 35:512–21.

Peters, F. E. 1970. *The Harvest of Hellenism: A History of the Near East from Alexander the Great to the Triumph of Christianity.* New York: Simon and Schuster.

Petersen, David L., and Kent Harold Richards. 1992. *Interpreting Hebrew Poetry.* Minneapolis: Fortress.

Peterson, Robert A. 1995. *Hell on Trial: The Case for Eternal Punishment.* Phillipsburg, NJ: P&R.

Pfeiffer, Charles F. 1959. *Between the Testaments.* Grand Rapids: Baker.

Pieters, Albertus. 1943. *Studies in the Revelation of St. John.* Grand Rapids: Eerdmans.

Pitre, Brant. 2005. *Jesus, the Tribulation, and the End of the Exile: Restoration Eschatology and the Origin of the Atonement.* Grand Rapids: Baker Academic.

Plantinga, Alvin. 2003. "Two (or More) Kinds of Scripture Scholarship." In *Behind the Text,* edited by Craig Bartholomew et al., 19–57. Grand Rapids: Zondervan.

Plöger, Otto. 1968. *Theocracy and Eschatology.* Translated by S. Rudman. Richmond: John Knox.

Pope, Marvin H. 1973. *Job.* 3d ed. AB 15. New York: Doubleday.

———. 1977. *Song of Songs.* AB 7C. New York: Doubleday.

Poythress, Vern S. 1976. "The Holy Ones of the Most High in Daniel VII." *VT* 26:208–13.

———. 1994a. "2 Thessalonians 1 Supports Amillennialism." *JETS* 37, no. 4:529–38.

———. 1994b. *Understanding Dispensationalists.* 2d ed. Phillipsburg, NJ: P&R.

———. 1995. *The Shadow of Christ in the Law of Moses.* Phillipsburg, NJ: P&R.

———. 2000a. "Currents within Amillennialism." *Presbyterion* 26, no. 1:21–25.

———. 2000b. *The Returning King: A Guide to the Book of Revelation*. Phillipsburg, NJ: P&R.

Pratt, Richard L., Jr. 1990. *He Gave Us Stories*. Phillipsburg, NJ: P&R.

———. 1998. *1 and 2 Chronicles*. Mentor Commentary. Fearn, Ross-shire: Christian Focus.

Price, J. Randall. 1994. "Prophetic Postponement in Daniel 9 and Other Texts." In *Issues in Dispensationalism*, edited by Wesley R. Willis and John R. Master, 133–65. Chicago: Moody.

Price, S. R. F. 1984. *Rituals and Power: The Roman Imperial Cult in Asia Minor*. Cambridge: Cambridge University Press.

Prior, David. 1985. *The Message of 1 Corinthians*. BST. Downers Grove, IL: InterVarsity.

Provan, Iain W. 1991. *Lamentations*. NCB. Grand Rapids: Eerdmans.

———. 1995. *1 and 2 Kings*. NIBC. Peabody, MA: Hendrickson.

———. 1996. "Foul Spirits, Fornication and Finance: Revelation 18 from an Old Testament Perspective." *JSNT* 64, no. 1:81–100.

Provan, Iain, V. Philips Long, and Tremper Longman III. 2003. *A Biblical History of Israel*. Louisville: Westminster.

Pryor, John W. 1992. *John: Evangelist of the Covenant People: The Narrative and Themes of the Fourth Gospel*. Downers Grove, IL: InterVarsity.

Quinn, Jerome D., and William C. Wacker. 2000. *The First and Second Letters to Timothy*. ECC. Grand Rapids: Eerdmans.

Rad, Gerhard von. 1967. *The Message of the Prophets*. Translated by D. M. G. Stalker. New York: Harper & Row.

Rainbow, Paul A. 1996. "Millennium as Metaphor in John's Apocalypse." *WTJ* 58, no. 2:209–21.

Ramm, Bernard. 1959. *The Witness of the Spirit*. Grand Rapids: Eerdmans.

Ravens, David. 1995. *Luke and the Restoration of Israel*. JSNTSup 119. Sheffield: Sheffield Academic.

Reicke, Bo. 1972. "Synoptic Prophecies on the Destruction of Jerusalem." In *Studies in New Testament and Early Christian Literature: Essays in Honor of Allen P. Wikgren*, edited by David E. Aune, 121–34. NovTSup 33. Leiden: Brill.

Reymond, Robert L. 1990. *Jesus, Divine Messiah: The New Testament Witness*. Phillipsburg, NJ: P&R.

Richard, Earl J. 1995. *First and Second Thessalonians*. SacPag 11. Collegeville, MN: Liturgical.

Richardson, Peter. 1996. *Herod: King of the Jews and Friend of the Romans*. Columbia: University of South Carolina Press.

Riches, John, and David C. Sim, eds. 2005. *The Gospel of Matthew in Its Roman Imperial Context*. JSNTSup 276. London: T&T Clark International.

Ricoeur, Paul. 1980. *Essays on Biblical Interpretation*. Edited by Lewis S. Mudge. Philadelphia: Fortress.

Ridderbos, Herman. 1962. *The Coming of the Kingdom*. Edited by Raymond O. Zorn. Translated by H. de Jongste. Phillipsburg, NJ: P&R.

———. 1975. *Paul: An Outline of His Theology*. Translated by John Richard De Witt. Grand Rapids: Eerdmans.

———. 1997. *The Gospel of John: A Theological Commentary*. Translated by John Vriend. Grand Rapids: Eerdmans.

Ridderbos, Jan. 1985. *Isaiah*. Translated by John Vriend. BSC. Grand Rapids: Zondervan.

Riddlebarger, Kim. 2003. *A Case for Amillennialism: Understanding the End Times*. Grand Rapids: Baker.

———. 2006. *The Man of Sin: Uncovering the Truth about the Antichrist*. Grand Rapids: Baker.

Robbins, John W. 2007. *Slavery and Christianity: Paul's Letter to Philemon*. Unicoi, TN: Trinity Foundation.

Robertson, A. T. 1923. *A Grammar of the Greek New Testament in the Light of Historical Research*. 4th ed. New York: Hodder & Stoughton.

Robertson, O. Palmer. 1980. *The Christ of the Covenants*. Phillipsburg, NJ: P&R.

———. 1990. *The Books of Nahum, Habakkuk, and Zephaniah*. NICOT. Grand Rapids: Eerdmans.

———. 1995. *Prophet of the Coming Day of the Lord: The Message of Joel*. WCS. Darlington: Evangelical.

———. 1996. *Understanding the Land of the Bible: A Biblical-Theological Guide*. Phillipsburg, NJ: P&R.

———. 2000. *The Israel of God: Yesterday, Today, and Tomorrow*. Phillipsburg, NJ: P&R.

———. 2004. *The Christ of the Prophets*. Phillipsburg, NJ: P&R.

Robinson, John A. T. 1976. *Redating the New Testament*. Philadelphia: Westminster.

Rojas-Flores, Gonzalo. 2004. "The Book of Revelation and the First Years of Nero's Reign." *Bib* 85:375–92.

Rooker, Mark F. 1997. "Evidence from Ezekiel." In *The Coming Millennial Kingdom: A Case for Premillennial Interpretation*, edited by Donald K. Campbell and Jeffrey L. Townsend, 119–34. Grand Rapids: Kregel.

Rosner, Brian S. 1998. "The Progress of the Word." In *Witness to the Gospel: The Theology of Acts*, edited by I. Howard Marshall and David Peterson, 215–33. Grand Rapids: Eerdmans.

Ross, Allen P. 1988. *Creation and Blessing: A Guide to the Study and Exposition of Genesis*. Grand Rapids: Baker Academic.

———. 1991. "Proverbs." In *The Expositor's Bible Commentary*, edited by Frank E. Gaebelein, 5:883–1134. Grand Rapids: Zondervan.

———. 2002. *Holiness to the Lord: A Guide to the Exposition of the Book of Leviticus*. Grand Rapids: Baker Academic.

———. 2006. *Recalling the Hope of Glory: Biblical Worship from the Garden to the New Creation*. Grand Rapids: Kregel.

Russell, D. S. 1960. *Between the Testaments*. Philadelphia: Fortress.

Russell, James Stuart. 2003. *The Parousia*. Bradford, PA: International Preterist Association.

Ryken, Leland, James C. Wilhoit, and Tremper Longman III, eds. 1998. *Dictionary of Biblical Imagery*. Downers Grove, IL: InterVarsity.

Ryrie, Charles. 1953. *The Basis of the Premillennial Faith*. Neptune, NJ: Loizeaux Brothers.

———. 1986. *Basic Theology*. Wheaton, IL: Victor Books.

———. 1995. *Dispensationalism*. Rev. ed. Chicago: Moody.

Sacchi, Paolo. 2000. *The History of the Second Temple Period*. JSOTSup 285. Sheffield: Sheffield Academic.

Sailhamer, John H. 1992. *The Pentateuch as Narrative: A Biblical-Theological Commentary*. Grand Rapids: Zondervan.

Sanday, William, and Arthur C. Headlam. 1902. *The Epistle to the Romans*. ICC. Edinburgh: T&T Clark.

Sanders, E. P. 1977. *Paul and Palestinian Judaism: A Comparison of Patterns of Religion*. Minneapolis: Fortress.

———. 1983. *Paul, the Law, and the Jewish People*. Philadelphia: Fortress.

Sandy, D. Brent. 2002. *Plowshares and Pruning Hooks: Rethinking the Language of Biblical Prophecy and Apocalyptic*. Downers Grove, IL: InterVarsity.

Sarna, Nahum M. 1996. *Exploring Exodus: The Origins of Biblical Israel*. New York: Schocken.

Sawyer, John F. A. 1993. *Prophecy and the Biblical Prophets*. Rev. ed. OBS. New York: Oxford University Press.

Schmidt, Thomas E., and Moisés Silva, eds. 1994. *To Tell the Mystery: Essays on New Testament Eschatology in Honor of Robert H. Gundry*. JSNTSup 100. Sheffield: Sheffield Academic.

Schmitz, Philip C. 2003. "The Grammar of Resurrection in Isaiah 26:19a–c." *JBL* 122, no. 1:145–55.

Schreiner, Thomas R. 1993. *The Law and Its Fulfillment: A Pauline Theology of Law*. Grand Rapids: Baker.

———. 1998. *Romans*. BECNT. Grand Rapids: Baker Academic.

———. 2001. *Paul, Apostle of God's Glory in Christ: A Pauline Theology*. Downers Grove, IL: InterVarsity.

Schweitzer, Albert. 1953. *The Mysticism of Paul the Apostle*. 2d ed. Translated by William Montgomery. London: Adam and Charles Black.

Scobie, Charles H. H. 2003. *The Ways of Our God: An Approach to Biblical Theology*. Grand Rapids: Eerdmans.

Scott, J. Julius, Jr. 1972. "Paul and Late-Jewish Eschatology—A Case Study, I Thessalonians 4:13–18 and II Thessalonians 2:1–12." *JETS* 15, no. 3:133–43.

———. 1995. *Jewish Backgrounds of the New Testament*. Grand Rapids: Baker.

Searle, John R. 1969. *Speech Acts: An Essay in the Philosophy of Language*. Cambridge: Cambridge University Press.

———. 1979. *Expression and Meaning: Studies in the Theory of Speech Acts*. Cambridge: Cambridge University Press.

Selman, Martin J. 1994a. *1 Chronicles*. TOTC 10a. Downers Grove, IL: InterVarsity.

———. 1994b. *2 Chronicles*. TOTC 10b. Downers Grove, IL: InterVarsity.

Shea, William H. 1982. "Darius the Mede: An Update." *AUSS* 20:237–40.

———. 1991. "Darius the Mede in His Persian-Babylonian Setting." *AUSS* 29:235–57.

Shepherd, Michael. 2006. "Daniel 7:13 and the New Testament Son of Man." *WTJ* 68:99–111.

Silva, Moisés. 1976. "Perfection and Eschatology in Hebrews." *WTJ* 39, no. 1:60–71.

———. 1994a. *Biblical Words and Their Meaning: An Introduction to Lexical Semantics*. Rev. ed. Grand Rapids: Zondervan.

———. 1994b. "Eschatological Structures in Galatians." In *To Tell the Mystery: Essays on New Testament Eschatology in Honor of Robert H. Gundry*, edited by Thomas E. Schmidt and Moisés Silva, 140–62. JSNTSup 100. Sheffield: Sheffield Academic.

———. 1996a. *Explorations in Exegetical Method: Galatians as a Test Case*. Grand Rapids: Baker.

———. 1996b. "Has the Church Misread the Bible?" In *Foundations of Contemporary Interpretation*, edited by Moisés Silva, 11–90. Grand Rapids: Zondervan.

———. 2005. *Philippians*. 2d ed. BECNT. Grand Rapids: Baker.

Slater, Thomas B. 1998. "On the Social Setting of the Revelation to John." *NTS* 44, no. 2:232–56.

Smalley, Stephen S. 1994. *Thunder and Love: John's Revelation and John's Community*. Milton Keynes, Eng.: Word Books.

———. 1998. *John: Evangelist and Interpreter*. 2d ed. NTP. Downers Grove, IL: InterVarsity.

———. 2005. *The Revelation to John: A Commentary on the Greek Text of the Apocalypse*. Downers Grove, IL: InterVarsity.

Smick, Elmer. 1968. "The Bearing of New Philological Data on the Subjects of Resurrection and Immortality in the Old Testament." *WTJ* 31, no. 1:12–21.

Smith, D. Moody. 1986. *John*. 2d ed. Proclamation Commentaries. Philadelphia: Fortress.

———. 1995. *The Theology of the Gospel of John*. Cambridge: Cambridge University Press.

Smith, Ralph L. 1984. *Micah–Malachi*. WBC 32. Nashville: Nelson.

Spong, John Shelby. 1993. *This Hebrew Lord: A Bishop's Search for the Authentic Jesus*. New ed. New York: HarperCollins.

Sproul, R. C. 1998. *The Last Days according to Jesus*. Grand Rapids: Baker.

———. 1999. *The Gospel of God: An Exposition of Romans*. Fearn, Ross-shire: Christian Focus.

Stanton, Graham N. 1993. *A Gospel for a New People: Studies in Matthew*. Louisville: Westminster.

Stauffer, Ethelbert. 1955. *Christ and the Caesars: Historical Sketches*. Translated by K. and R. Gregor Smith. London: SCM Press LTD.

Stein, Robert. 1987. *The Synoptic Problem: An Introduction*. Grand Rapids: Baker.

Stevenson, Kalinda Rose. 1996. *The Vision of Transformation: The Territorial Rhetoric of Ezekiel 40–48*. SBLDS 154. Atlanta: Scholars.

Storkey, Alan. 2005. *Jesus and Politics: Confronting the Powers*. Grand Rapids: Baker Academic.

Stott, John R. W. 1988. *The Letters of John*. TNTC 19. Grand Rapids: Eerdmans.

Strauss, David Friedrich. 1972. *The Life of Jesus: Critically Examined*. Edited by Peter C. Hodgson. Translated by George Eliot. London: SCM.

Strauss, Mark L. 1995. *The Davidic Messiah in Luke-Acts*. JSNTSup 110. Sheffield: Sheffield Academic.

Strimple, Robert B. 2004. "Hyper-Preterism on the Resurrection of the Body." In *When Shall These Things Be? A Reformed Response to Hyper-Preterism*, edited by Keith A. Mathison, 287–352. Phillipsburg, NJ: P&R.

Strom, Mark. 2000. *Reframing Paul: Conversations in Grace and Community*. Downers Grove, IL: InterVarsity.

———. 2001. *The Symphony of Scripture*. Phillipsburg, NJ: P&R.

Stuart, Douglas. 1987. *Hosea–Jonah*. WBC 31. Nashville: Nelson.

———. 1998. "Malachi." In *The Minor Prophets*, edited by Thomas McComiskey, 3:1245–1396. Grand Rapids: Baker.

———. 2001. *Old Testament Exegesis*. 3d ed. Louisville: Westminster.

———. 2006. *Exodus*. NAC 2. Nashville: Broadman.

Stuart, Moses. 1845. *Commentary on the Apocalypse*. 2 vols. Andover, MA: Allen, Morrill and Wardwell.

Stuhlmacher, Peter. 1979. *Historical Criticism and Theological Interpretation of Scripture: Toward a Hermeneutics of Consent*. London: SPCK.

———. 1994. *Paul's Letter to the Romans: A Commentary*. Translated by Scott J. Hafemann. Louisville: Westminster.

———. 1995. *How to Do Biblical Theology*. PTMS 38. Allison Park, PA: Pickwick Publications.

Surburg, Raymond F. 1975. *Introduction to the Intertestamental Period*. St. Louis: Concordia.

Svigel, Michael J. 2001. "The Apocalypse of John and the Rapture of the Church: A Reevaluation." *TrinJ* 22, no. 1:23–74.

Sweeney, Marvin A. 1996. *Isaiah 1–39 with an Introduction to Prophetic Literature*. FOTL 16. Grand Rapids: Eerdmans.

———. 2000. *The Twelve Prophets*. 2 vols. Berit Olam. Collegeville, MN: Liturgical.

Sweet, J. P. M. 1979. *Revelation*. WPC. Philadelphia: Westminster.

Swete, Henry Barclay. 1977. *Commentary on Revelation*. Grand Rapids: Kregel.

Tanner, J. Paul. 2005. "The 'Marriage Supper of the Lamb' in Rev 19:6–10. Implications for the Judgment Seat of Christ." *TrinJ* 26, no. 1:47–68.

Tasker, R. V. G. 1960. *The Gospel according to St. John*. TNTC 4. Grand Rapids: Eerdmans.

Tate, Marvin E. 1990. *Psalms 51–100*. WBC 20. Dallas: Word Books.

Taylor, John B. 1969. *Ezekiel: An Introduction and Commentary*. TOTC 20. Downers Grove, IL: InterVarsity.

Temple, William. 1961. *Readings in St John's Gospel*. London: Macmillan.

Tetley, M. Christine. 2005. *The Reconstructed Chronology of the Divided Kingdom*. Winona Lake, IN: Eisenbrauns.

Thiele, Edwin R. 1983. *The Mysterious Numbers of the Hebrew Kings*. Rev. ed. Grand Rapids: Kregel.

Thielman, Frank. 1989. *From Plight to Solution: A Jewish Framework for Understanding Paul's View of the Law in Galatians and Romans*. NovTSup 61. Leiden: Brill.

———. 1994. *Paul and the Law: A Contextual Approach*. Downers Grove, IL: InterVarsity.

———. 1999. *The Law and the New Testament: The Question of Continuity*. New York: Herder & Herder.

———. 2005. *Theology of the New Testament*. Grand Rapids: Zondervan.

Thiselton, Anthony C. 1977. "Semantics and New Testament Interpretation." In *New Testament Interpretation: Essays on Principles and Methods*, edited by I. Howard Marshall, 75–104. Grand Rapids: Eerdmans.

———. 1980. *The Two Horizons: New Testament Hermeneutics and Philosophical Description*. Grand Rapids: Eerdmans.

———. 1992. *New Horizons in Hermeneutics*. Grand Rapids: Zondervan.

———. 2000. *The First Epistle to the Corinthians*. NIGTC. Grand Rapids: Eerdmans.

Thomas, Robert. 1992. *Revelation 1–7: An Exegetical Commentary*. Chicago: Moody.

———. 1995. *Revelation 8–22: An Exegetical Commentary*. Chicago: Moody.

Thompson, J. A. 1974. *Deuteronomy: An Introduction and Commentary*. TOTC 5. Downers Grove, IL: InterVarsity.

———. 1980. *The Book of Jeremiah*. NICOT. Grand Rapids: Eerdmans.

Thompson, Leonard L. 1990. *The Book of Revelation: Apocalypse and Empire*. New York: Oxford University Press.

Thorsell, Paul R. 1998. "The Spirit in the Present Age: Preliminary Fulfillment of the Predicted New Covenant according to Paul." *JETS* 41, no. 3:397–413.

Throntveit, Mark A. 1992. *Ezra-Nehemiah*. Interpretation. Louisville: John Knox.

Tomasino, Anthony J. 2003. *Judaism before Jesus: The Events and Ideas That Shaped the New Testament World*. Downers Grove, IL: InterVarsity.

Torrance, Thomas F. 1956. *Kingdom and Church*. Edinburgh: Oliver and Boyd.

———. 1976. *Space, Time, and Resurrection*. Grand Rapids: Eerdmans.

Towner, Philip H. 2006. *The Letters to Timothy and Titus*. NICNT. Grand Rapids: Eerdmans.

Treier, Daniel J. 1997. "The Fulfillment of Joel 2:28–32: A Multiple-Lens Approach." *JETS* 40, no. 1:13–26.

Tripolitis, Antonía. 2002. *Religions of the Hellenistic-Roman Age*. Grand Rapids: Eerdmans.

Tuell, Steven Shawn. 1992. *The Law of the Temple in Ezekiel 40–48*. HSM 49. Atlanta: Scholars.

Turner, Geoffrey. 1975. "Pre-Understanding and New Testament Interpretation." *SJT* 28:227–42.

VanderKam, James C. 1994. *The Dead Sea Scrolls Today*. Grand Rapids: Eerdmans.

———. 2001. *An Introduction to Early Judaism*. Grand Rapids: Eerdmans.

VanGemeren, Willem A. 1983. "Israel as the Hermeneutical Crux in the Interpretation of Prophecy." *WTJ* 45, no. 1:132–44.

———. 1984. "Israel as the Hermeneutical Crux in the Interpretation of Prophecy (II)." *WTJ* 46, no. 2:254–97.

———. 1988a. *The Progress of Redemption*. Grand Rapids: Zondervan.

———. 1988b. "The Spirit of Restoration." *WTJ* 50, no. 1:81–102.

———. 1990. *Interpreting the Prophetic Word: An Introduction to the Prophetic Literature of the Old Testament.* Grand Rapids: Zondervan.

———. 1991. "Psalms." In *The Expositor's Bible Commentary*, edited by Frank E. Gaebelein, 5:3–880. Grand Rapids: Zondervan.

———. 1993. "The Law Is the Perfection of Righteousness in Jesus Christ: A Reformed Perspective." In *The Law, the Gospel, and the Modern Christian: Five Views*, edited by Wayne G. Strickland, 13–58. Grand Rapids: Zondervan.

———, ed. 1997. *New International Dictionary of Old Testament Theology and Exegesis.* 5 vols. Grand Rapids: Zondervan.

Van Groningen, Gerard. 1990. *Messianic Revelation in the Old Testament.* Grand Rapids: Baker.

Vanhoozer, Kevin J. 1986. "The Semantics of Biblical Literature: Truth and Scripture's Diverse Literary Forms." In *Hermeneutics, Authority and Canon*, edited by D. A. Carson and John D. Woodbridge, 49–104. Leicester: Inter-Varsity.

———. 1998. *Is There a Meaning in This Text?* Grand Rapids: Zondervan.

———. 2002. *First Theology: God, Scripture and Hermeneutics.* Downers Grove, IL: InterVarsity.

———, ed. 2005a. *Dictionary for Theological Interpretation of the Bible.* Grand Rapids: Baker Academic.

———. 2005b. *The Drama of Doctrine: A Canonical Linguistic Approach to Christian Theology.* Louisville: Westminster.

Van Leeuwen, Raymond C. 1997. "The Book of Proverbs." In *The New Interpreter's Bible*, edited by Leander E. Keck, 5:17–264. Nashville: Abingdon.

Vasholz, Robert. 2004. "The Character of Israel's Future in Light of the Abrahamic and Mosaic Covenants." *TrinJ* 25, no. 1:39–59.

Vaux, Roland de. 1997. *Ancient Israel: Its Life and Institutions.* Translated by John McHugh. Grand Rapids: Eerdmans.

Venema, Cornelis P. 2000. *The Promise of the Future.* Carlisle, PA: Banner of Truth.

———. 2006. *The Gospel of Free Acceptance in Christ: An Assessment of the Reformation and "New Perspectives" on Paul.* Carlisle, PA: Banner of Truth.

Verhoef, Pieter A. 1987. *The Books of Haggai and Malachi.* NICOT. Grand Rapids: Eerdmans.

Vos, Geerhardus. 1948. *Biblical Theology: Old and New Testaments.* Grand Rapids: Eerdmans.

———. 1954. *The Self-Disclosure of Jesus.* Edited by Johannes G. Vos. Grand Rapids: Eerdmans.

———. 1972. *The Teaching of Jesus concerning the Kingdom of God and the Church.* Nutley, NJ: P&R.

———. 1977. *The Teaching of the Epistle to the Hebrews.* Nutley, NJ: P&R.

———. 1991. *The Pauline Eschatology*. Phillipsburg, NJ: P&R.

———. 2001. *Redemptive History and Biblical Interpretation: The Shorter Writings of Geerhardus Vos*. Edited by Richard B. Gaffin Jr. Phillipsburg, NJ: P&R.

Wagner, Günter. 1988. "The Future of Israel: Reflections on Romans 9–11." In *Eschatology and the New Testament*, edited by W. Hulitt Gloer, 77–112. Peabody, MA: Hendrickson.

Wainwright, Arthur W. 1993. *Mysterious Apocalypse: Interpreting the Book of Revelation*. Nashville: Abingdon.

Walker, P. W. L. 1996. *Jesus and the Holy City: New Testament Perspectives on Jerusalem*. Grand Rapids: Eerdmans.

Wallace, Daniel B. 1996. *Greek Grammar beyond the Basics: An Exegetical Syntax of the New Testament*. Grand Rapids: Zondervan.

Wallace, Ronald S. 1984. *The Message of Daniel*. BST. Downers Grove, IL: InterVarsity.

Wallis, Wilber B. 1981. "Eschatology and Social Concern." *JETS* 24, no. 1:3–9.

Waltke, Bruce K. 1988a. "Micah: An Introduction and Commentary." In David W. Baker, T. Desmond Alexander, and Bruce Waltke, *Obadiah, Jonah, Micah*, 133–207. Downers Grove, IL: InterVarsity.

———. 1988b. "The Phenomenon of Conditionality within Unconditional Covenants." In *Israel's Apostasy and Restoration*, edited by Avraham Gileadi, 123–39. Grand Rapids: Baker.

———. 1993. "Micah." In *The Minor Prophets*, edited by Thomas McComiskey, 2:591–764. Grand Rapids: Baker.

———. 2001. *Genesis: A Commentary*. Grand Rapids: Zondervan.

———. 2004. *The Book of Proverbs: Chapters 1–15*. NICOT. Grand Rapids: Eerdmans.

———. 2005. *The Book of Proverbs: Chapters 15–31*. NICOT. Grand Rapids: Eerdmans.

———. 2007. *An Old Testament Theology*. Grand Rapids: Zondervan.

Walton, John H. 1986. "The Four Kingdoms of Daniel." *JETS* 29, no. 1:25–36.

———. 2006. *Ancient Near Eastern Thought and the Old Testament*. Grand Rapids: Baker Academic.

Walvoord, John F. 1955. *The Thessalonian Epistles*. Findlay, OH: Dunham.

———. 1959. *The Millennial Kingdom*. Grand Rapids: Zondervan.

———. 1966. *The Revelation of Jesus Christ*. Chicago: Moody.

———. 1971. *Daniel: The Key to Prophetic Revelation*. Chicago: Moody.

———. 1990. *The Prophecy Knowledge Handbook*. Wheaton, IL: Victor Books.

Wanamaker, Charles A. 1990. *The Epistles to the Thessalonians*. NIGTC. Grand Rapids: Eerdmans.

Ward, Rowland S. 2003. *God and Adam: Reformed Theology and the Creation Covenant*. Wantirna: New Melbourne Press.

Waters, Guy Prentiss. 2004. *Justification and the New Perspectives on Paul: A Review and Response*. Phillipsburg, NJ: P&R.

Watson, Francis. 1994. *Text, Church and World: Biblical Interpretation in Theological Perspective*. Grand Rapids: Eerdmans.

———. 1997. *Text and Truth: Redefining Biblical Theology*. Grand Rapids: Eerdmans.

Watts, John D. W. 1985. *Isaiah 1–33*. WBC 24. Dallas: Word Books.

———. 1987. *Isaiah 34–66*. WBC 25. Dallas: Word Books.

Watts, Rikki E. 1997. *Isaiah's New Exodus in Mark*. Grand Rapids: Baker.

Webb, Barry G. 2000. *Five Festal Garments: Christian Reflections on the Song of Songs, Ruth, Lamentations, Ecclesiastes, and Esther*. NSBT 10. Nottingham: Apollos; Downers Grove, IL: InterVarsity.

Webb, William J. 1993. *Returning Home: New Covenant and Second Exodus as the Context for 2 Corinthians 6.14–7.1*. JSNTSup 85. Sheffield: Sheffield Academic.

Weinfeld, M. 1970. "The Covenant of Grant in the Old Testament and in the Ancient Near East." *JAOS* 90:184–203.

Wenham, David. 1982. " 'This Generation Will Not Pass . . . ': A Study of Jesus' Future Expectation in Mark 13." In *Christ the Lord: Studies in Christology Presented to Donald Guthrie*, edited by Harold H. Rowdon, 127–50. Leicester: Inter-Varsity.

———. 1984. *The Rediscovery of Jesus' Eschatological Discourse*. Gospel Perspectives 4. Sheffield: JSOT Press.

———. 1987. "The Kingdom of God and Daniel." *ExpTim* 98:132–34.

Wenham, Gordon J. 1979. *The Book of Leviticus*. NICOT. Grand Rapids: Eerdmans.

———. 1981. *Numbers: An Introduction and Commentary*. TOTC 4. Downers Grove, IL: InterVarsity.

———. 1987. *Genesis 1–15*. WBC 1. Waco: Word Books.

———. 1988. "Genesis: An Authorship Study and Current Pentateuchal Criticism." *JSOT* 42:3–18.

———. 1994. *Genesis 16–50*. WBC 2. Dallas: Word Books.

Wenham, John. 1992. *Redating Matthew, Mark and Luke: A Fresh Assault on the Synoptic Problem*. Downers Grove, IL: InterVarsity.

Westerholm, Stephen. 2004. *Perspectives Old and New on Paul: The "Lutheran" Paul and His Critics*. Grand Rapids: Eerdmans.

———. 2006. *Understanding Matthew: The Early Christian Worldview of the First Gospel*. Grand Rapids: Baker Academic.

Westermann, Claus. 1962. *A Thousand Years and a Day*. Translated by Stanley Rudman. Philadelphia: Fortress.

———. 1967. *Basic Forms of Prophetic Speech*. Translated by Hugh Clayton White. Philadelphia: Fortress.

———. 1980. *The Psalms: Structure, Content and Message*. Translated by Ralph D. Gehrke. Minneapolis: Augsburg.

———. 1982. *Elements of Old Testament Theology*. Translated by Douglas W. Stott. Atlanta: John Knox.

Whitcomb, John. 1959. *Darius the Mede*. Grand Rapids: Eerdmans.

White, R. Fowler. 1989. "Reexamining the Evidence for Recapitulation in Rev 20:1–10." *WTJ* 51, no. 2:319–44.

———. 1999. "On the Hermeneutics and Interpretation of Revelation 20:1–3: A Preconsummationist Perspective." *JETS* 42, no. 1:53–66.

Whybray, R. Norman. 1994. *The Making of the Pentateuch*. Sheffield: JSOT Press.

———. 1995. *Introduction to the Pentateuch*. Grand Rapids: Eerdmans.

———. 1996. *Reading the Psalms as a Book*. JSOTSup 222. Sheffield: Sheffield Academic.

Wilcock, Michael. 1975. *The Message of Revelation: I Saw Heaven Opened*. BST. Downers Grove, IL: InterVarsity.

Wilkins, Michael J., and J. P. Moreland. 1996. *Jesus under Fire*. Grand Rapids: Zondervan.

Williams, James G. 1981. *Those Who Ponder Proverbs: Aphoristic Thinking and Biblical Literature*. Sheffield: Almond.

Williams, Michael D. 1998. "Rapture or Resurrection?" *Presbyterion* 24, no. 1:9–37.

———. 1999. "On Eschatological Discontinuity: The Confession of an Eschatological Reactionary." *Presbyterion* 25, no. 1:13–20.

———. 2002. "A New and More Glorious Covenant." *Presbyterion* 28, no. 2:77–103.

———. 2005. *Far as the Curse Is Found: The Covenant Story of Redemption*. Phillipsburg, NJ: P&R.

Williams, Michael J. 2003. *The Prophet and His Message: Reading Old Testament Prophecy Today*. Phillipsburg, NJ: P&R.

Williamson, H. G. M. 1977. "Eschatology in Chronicles." *TynBul* 28:115–54.

———. 1982. *1 and 2 Chronicles*. NCB. London: Marshall, Morgan & Scott.

———. 1985. *Ezra, Nehemiah*. WBC 16. Waco: Word Books.

Williamson, Paul R. 2000. "Promise and Fulfillment: The Territorial Inheritance." In *The Land of Promise*, edited by Philip Johnston and Peter Walker, 15–34. Downers Grove, IL: InterVarsity.

———. 2007. *Sealed with an Oath: Covenant in God's Unfolding Purpose*. NSBT 23. Nottingham: Apollos; Downers Grove, IL: InterVarsity.

Willis, Wesley R., and John R. Master, eds. 1994. *Issues in Dispensationalism*. Chicago: Moody.

Wilson, Gerald H. 1985. *The Editing of the Hebrew Psalter*. SBLDS 76. Chico: Scholars.

———. 2005. "The Structure of the Psalter." In *Interpreting the Psalms: Issues and Approaches*, edited by David Firth and Philip S. Johnston, 229–46. Downers Grove, IL: InterVarsity Academic.

Wilson, J. Christian. 1993. "The Problem of the Domitianic Date of Revelation." *NTS* 39:587–605.

Wilson, Mark. 2007. *Charts on the Book of Revelation: Literary, Historical, and Theological Perspectives*. Grand Rapids: Kregel.

Wilson, Robert R. 1980. *Prophecy and Society in Ancient Israel*. Philadelphia: Fortress.

Wiseman, Donald J. 1965. "Some Historical Problems in the Book of Daniel." In *Notes on Some Problems in the Book of Daniel*, edited by Donald J. Wiseman et al., 9–19. London: Tyndale.

———. 1979. "Jonah's Nineveh." *TynBul* 30:29–51.

———. 1985. *Nebuchadrezzar and Babylon*. Oxford: Oxford University Press.

———. 1993. *1 and 2 Kings*. TOTC 9. Downers Grove, IL: InterVarsity.

Witherington, Ben, III. 1990. *The Christology of Jesus*. Minneapolis: Fortress.

———. 1992. *Jesus, Paul and the End of the World: A Comparative Study in New Testament Eschatology*. Downers Grove, IL: InterVarsity.

———. 1994. *Paul's Narrative Thought World: The Tapestry of Tragedy and Triumph*. Louisville: Westminster.

———. 1995a. *John's Wisdom: A Commentary on the Fourth Gospel*. Louisville: Westminster.

———. 1995b. *The Jesus Quest: The Third Search for the Jew of Nazareth*. Downers Grove, IL: InterVarsity.

———. 1998. *The Acts of the Apostles: A Socio-Rhetorical Commentary*. Grand Rapids: Eerdmans.

———. 2001a. *The Gospel of Mark: A Socio-Rhetorical Commentary*. Grand Rapids: Eerdmans.

———. 2001b. *New Testament History: A Narrative Account*. Grand Rapids: Baker Academic.

———. 2003. *Revelation*. NCBC. Cambridge: Cambridge University Press.

———. 2004. *Romans: A Socio-Rhetorical Commentary*. Grand Rapids: Eerdmans.

———. 2006a. *1 and 2 Thessalonians: A Socio-Rhetorical Commentary*. Grand Rapids: Eerdmans.

———. 2006b. *Letters and Homilies for Hellenized Christians.* Vol. 1. *A Socio-Rhetorical Commentary on Titus, 1–2 Timothy, and 1–3 John.* Downers Grove, IL: InterVarsity Academic.

Wolff, Hans Walter. 1974. *Hosea.* Edited by Paul D. Hanson. Translated by Gary Stansell. Hermeneia. Philadelphia: Fortress.

———. 1977. *Joel and Amos.* Edited by S. Dean McBride Jr. Translated by Waldemar Janzen, S. Dean McBride Jr., and Charles A. Muenchow. Hermeneia. Philadelphia: Fortress.

———. 1986. *Obadiah and Jonah: A Commentary.* Translated by Margaret Kohl. Minneapolis: Augsburg.

———. 1987. "Prophecy from the Eighth through the Fifth Century." In *Interpreting the Prophets,* edited by James Luther Mays and Paul J. Achtemeier, 14–26. Philadelphia: Fortress.

———. 1990. *Micah: A Commentary.* Translated by Gary Stansell. Minneapolis: Augsburg.

Wolters, Al. 2004. "Zechariah 14 and Biblical Theology." In *Out of Egypt: Biblical Theology and Biblical Interpretation,* edited by Craig Bartholomew, Mary Healy, Karl Möller, and Robin Parry, 261–85. Grand Rapids: Zondervan.

Woudstra, Marten H. 1981. *The Book of Joshua.* NICOT. Grand Rapids: Eerdmans.

Wright, Christopher J. H. 2005. "Covenant: God's Mission through God's People." In *The God of Covenant: Biblical, Theological and Contemporary Perspectives,* edited by Jamie A. Grant and Alistair I. Wilson, 54–78. Leicester: Apollos.

———. 2006. *The Mission of God: Unlocking the Bible's Grand Narrative.* Downers Grove, IL: InterVarsity.

Wright, N. T. 1991. *The Climax of the Covenant: Christ and the Law in Pauline Theology.* Minneapolis: Fortress.

———. 1992. *The New Testament and the People of God.* Christian Origins and the Question of God, vol. 1. Minneapolis: Fortress.

———. 1996. *Jesus and the Victory of God.* Christian Origins and the Question of God, vol. 2. Minneapolis: Fortress.

———. 1997. *What Saint Paul Really Said.* Grand Rapids: Eerdmans.

———. 1999a. "In Grateful Dialogue: A Response." In *Jesus and the Restoration of Israel: A Critical Assessment of N. T. Wright's* Jesus and the Victory of God, edited by Carey C. Newman, 244–77. Downers Grove, IL: InterVarsity.

———. 1999b. "Five Gospels but No Gospel: Jesus and the Seminar." In *Authenticating the Activities of Jesus,* edited by Bruce Chilton and Craig A. Evans, 83–120. Leiden: Brill.

———. 2000. "Paul's Gospel and Caesar's Empire." In *Paul and Politics: Ekklesia, Israel, Imperium, Interpretation,* edited by Richard A. Horsley, 160–83. Harrisburg, PA: Trinity Press International.

———. 2002. "The Letter to the Romans." In *The New Interpreter's Bible*, edited by Leander E. Keck, 10:393–770. Nashville: Abingdon.

———. 2003. *The Resurrection of the Son of God*. Christian Origins and the Question of God, vol. 3. Minneapolis: Fortress.

Wuest, Kenneth S. 1957. "The Rapture—Precisely When?" *BSac* 114, no.1:60–69.

Yamauchi, Edwin A. 1980. "Hermeneutical Issues in the Book of Daniel." *JETS* 23, no. 1:13–21.

———. 1997. *Persia and the Bible*. Grand Rapids: Baker Academic.

———. 2004. *Africa and the Bible*. Grand Rapids: Baker Academic.

Young, Edward J. 1949. *Daniel*. Grand Rapids: Eerdmans.

———. 1952. *My Servants the Prophets*. Grand Rapids: Eerdmans.

———. 1953a. "The Immanuel Prophecy—Isaiah 7:14–16." *WTJ* 15, no. 2:97–124.

———. 1953b. "The Immanuel Prophecy—Isaiah 7:14–16—II." *WTJ* 16, no. 1:23–50.

———. 1957. *Thy Word Is Truth*. Grand Rapids: Eerdmans.

———. 1958. *Who Wrote Isaiah?* Grand Rapids: Eerdmans.

———. 1964. *An Introduction to the Old Testament*. Grand Rapids: Eerdmans.

Young, Rodger C. 2005. "Tables of Reign Lengths from the Hebrew Court Recorders." *JETS* 48, no. 2:225–48.

Zerhusen, Bob. 1995. "An Overlooked Judean *Diglossia* in Acts 2?" *BTB* 25, no. 3:118–30.

———. 1997. "The Problem of Tongues in 1 Corinthians: A Reexamination." *BTB* 27, no. 4:139–52.

Zimmerli, Walther. 1979. *Ezekiel 1*. Edited by Frank Moore Cross and Klaus Baltzer. Translated by Ronald E. Clements. Hermeneia. Minneapolis: Fortress.

———. 1983. *Ezekiel 2*. Edited by Paul D. Hanson. Translated by James D. Martin. Hermeneia. Minneapolis: Fortress.

Index of Scripture and Extrabiblical References

John

APOCRYPHA

2 Esdras

1 Maccabees

Index of Subjects and Names

Keith A. Mathison (M.A., Reformed Theological Seminary; Ph.D., Whitefield Theological Seminary) is dean of the Ligonier Academy of Biblical and Theological Studies and an associate editor of *Tabletalk* magazine at Ligonier Ministries. He is the author of *Dispensationalism: Rightly Dividing the People of God? Postmillennialism: An Eschatology of Hope; The Shape of Sola Scriptura; and Given for You: Reclaiming Calvin's Doctrine of the Lord's Supper*. He is editor of *When Shall These Things Be: A Reformed Response to Hyper-Preterism* and associate editor of *The Reformation Study Bible*. He lives in Lake Mary, Florida, with his wife and children.